REVIEWS OF BOOKS ABOUT HISTORY & HAUNTINGS BY TROY TAYLOR

How does Troy Taylor continue to produce one quality book after another? Perhaps only the spirits know for sure! HAUNTED ILLINOIS is truly another top-notch, in-depth look at the Land of Lincoln. I highly recommend this book to anyone interested in Illinois ghost stories, as it goes to show that ghosts can be found anywhere throughout the state!
DALE KACZMAREK, author of WINDY CITY GHOSTS

Troy Taylor has done it yet again. In HAUNTED ILLINOIS, the author has hit that rare (and delightful) middle ground between fascinating paranormal research and compelling storytelling. His stories will put you on the edge of your seat and his insights into the supernatural will keep you there. A rare and delightful find and a must-read from one of the best ghost authors writing today.
MARK MARIMEN, author of HAUNTED INDIANA and SCHOOL SPIRITS

Troy Taylor's books are a sure-fire hit for tourists, regional historians and investigators of the unexplained.. they have filled a significant gap in my reference library on Illinois' local phenomena and folklore. I highly recommend them for the serious and casual reader.
LOREN COLEMAN, author of MYSTERIOUS AMERICA

HAUNTED ILLINOIS is a generous introduction to the resident wraiths of one of the nation's most haunted states, from its most prolific ghost writer. This book is a must for natives, ghost hunters and aficionados of Americana and holds captive anyone with an interest in the wonderful experiences so often omitted from the "proper" historical record.
URSULA BIELSKI, author of CHICAGO HAUNTS

Troy Taylor works hard to unearth new hauntings and to keep the old lore alive. In spite of this, many of the stories which shaded our cemeteries and lingered over our abandoned buildings are lost. So while some of us wonder about the light burning in the old warehouse, or quicken our step in the dusky graveyard, or pause to make sure those are our own footsteps echoing off the attic wall, most of us won't. Yesterday's stories, like yesterday's spirits, draw their power from being remembered. In the absence of memory, legends die, and like forgotten ghosts are left to fade away.
JOE RICHARDSON in ILLINOIS COUNTRY LIVING Magazine

GHOST BOOKS BY TROY TAYLOR

Haunted Illinois (1999 / 2001)
Spirits of the Civil War (1999)
The Ghost Hunter's Guidebook (1999)
Season of the Witch (1999)
Haunted Alton (2000)
Haunted New Orleans (2000)
Beyond the Grave (2001)

The Haunted Decatur Series
Haunted Decatur (1995)
More Haunted Decatur (1996)
Ghosts of Millikin (1996)
Where the Dead Walk (1997)
Dark Harvest (1997)
Haunted Decatur Revisited (2000)

Ghosts of Springfield (1997)
The Ghost Hunter's Handbook (1997)
Ghost Hunter's Handbook (Second Edition - 1998)
Ghosts of Little Egypt (1998)

- Ghost Tours -
Haunted Decatur Tours (1994-1998)
Haunted Decatur Tours (Guest Host - 2000)
History & Hauntings Tours of St. Charles (1999)
History & Hauntings Tours of Alton (1999 - 2001)

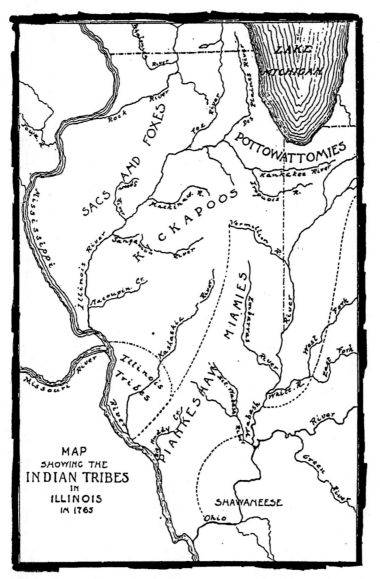

MAP
SHOWING THE
INDIAN TRIBES
IN
ILLINOIS
IN 1765

HAUNTED ILLINOIS
HISTORY & HAUNTINGS FROM LITTLE EGYPT TO THE WINDY CITY

- a Whitechapel Productions Press Publication -

This Second Edition of "Haunted Illinois" is dedicated again (with much thanks) to my friends in the ghostly field, without whom this book could not have been written.. especially the members of the "American Ghost Society", Dale Kaczmarek, Ursula Bielski, Loren Coleman and many others.

And this book, like all the others, is also dedicated with much love and admiration to my wife, Amy, who continues to have my support, respect, admiration and love. Without her, this book, and nothing else would be possible.

Original Cover Artwork Designed by

Michael Schwab, M & S Graphics & Troy Taylor
Visit M & S Graphics at www.manyhorses.com

This Book is Published by

~ Whitechapel Productions Press ~
A Division of the History & Hauntings Book Co.
515 East Third Street ~ Alton, Illinois ~62002
(618) 465~1086 / 1~888~GHOSTLY
Visit us on the Internet at www.prairieghosts.com

First Printing (Second Edition) ~ March 2001
ISBN: 1~892523~01~9

Printed in the United States of America

One of the things that has always fascinated me about the Midwest is its ability to hide its secrets. Out there, across blowing fields of grain, lurking in the shadows of the forest, perhaps even lingering in the frame farmhouse... is a dark secret that no man knows.
And only a few are unlucky enough to find...
FROM THE HAUNTING OF AMERICA

Nearly every community in the United States can claim at least one haunted house. Some have more than one.... In most places, the citizenry, except for a few knowledgeable individuals, is totally unaware of the fact that macabre dwellings are standing in their midst.
RICHARD WINER IN "HAUNTED HOUSES"

From the most ancient days, men have not merely believed in ghosts; they claim to have seen them, heard them and even to have touched them... and the mystery remains unsolved. As far as science goes, there has never been a satisfactory answer... none of the natural sciences has ever determined whether or not there are any rips of gaps in the impalpable curtain that divides the natural world or our experience from all the tremendous mystery that lies beyond.
Many attempts, however, have been made.
FROM GREAT TALES OF TERROR & THE SUPERNATURAL

Haunted Houses are separated from other, more ordinary abodes in being effective containers of the past. The clutch tight at old events; they refuse to forget; they carefully shelter the hopes and obsessions and miseries of the humans who died in their bedrooms, or fatally fell down the stairs or expired, all forgotten, from lack of air in their hidden chambers. Perhaps the creepiest thing about haunted houses is that they not only shelter ghosts, but that they confine you with them...
GAHAN WILSON

The oldest and strongest emotion known to mankind is fear.
The oldest and strongest kind of fear is fear of the unknown.
HP LOVECRAFT

I have never believed in ghosts.... but I've been afraid of them all my life!

HAUNTED ILLINOIS
- TABLE OF CONTENTS -

- HAUNTED ILLINOIS -

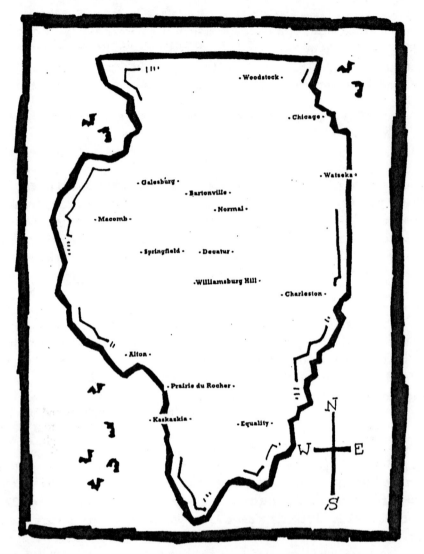

NOTE: In the writing of this book, some of those who have chosen to tell their stories have requested that their names be changed to protect their privacy. In these cases, an asterisk (*) follows the name the first time it is mentioned.

INTRODUCTION

WELCOME TO HAUNTED ILLINOIS

Illinois is a very haunted place.

I'm certainly glad that's out of the way, now we can go on about the business of this book. Why did "Haunted Illinois" require a second edition? That's a fair question and one that many of you, especially those who bought the original edition of the book, must be asking. The answer to that question goes back to the very first statement that I made in this introduction... it's because Illinois is a very haunted place!

Since the publication of the original "Haunted Illinois" (two years ago as of this writing), there have been a number of new haunted places that have been brought to my attention. More dark history has been unearthed and more strangeness has seen the light of day. In all honesty, these new tales were simply too good to pass up and I felt the need to include them in this book. I declined to do a sequel because in many cases, a sequel is often inferior to the original. In the case of "Haunted Illinois", I decided to give the reader a bigger and better edition of the original book. There are many things that you will find here that we never dreamed of putting into the old edition. There are more ghosts here, more personal accounts, more spine-chilling encounters, more dark history and more general weirdness. Illinois is an "oddball" state and the pages that follow are bound to prove that to you!

So, why write a book like "Haunted Illinois" in the first place?

For one thing, I have always been fascinated with ghosts, hauntings and legends. Growing up in the state of Illinois, and as I turned out to be a writer, it seemed a natural progression for me to write about spirits in the so-called Land of Lincoln. But this book is not only about ghosts, it also encompasses my love of history as well. Now, I know what you must be thinking but this is not some dry textbook of Illinois dates and facts. I am fascinated with the history of the state, but I am no historical expert or collegiate scholar. I did not spend hours going through obscure manuals searching for data to put this book together and there will be no serious discussions of which Native American's lived where or if Abraham Lincoln really slept in all of the places where people claim he did.

On the other hand, if you are looking for nothing more than breathless first-person accounts of waking up in the middle of the night to see Aunt Tilly standing at the foot of the bed, then this may not be the book for you! It has always been my belief that no great ghost story can exist without a basis in history. One of the best ways to discover why a location might be haunted is to look back and see what happened there in the past. As you will discover in the pages that follow, almost every important event in Illinois history, from the War of 1812 to the first state capital, boasts at least one ghost story. Some of them, like the Civil War, even have more than one!

And while this book contains more history, and many more hauntings, than the original volume of "Haunted Illinois", it still falls short when it come to collecting every single story to ever "haunt" this state. However, I believe that I have collected stories that are both familiar and strange. Many of them, you will have undoubtedly never heard before. Some of them may be old favorites, but regardless, every single one of them comes from the landscape of Illinois. They are tales of haunted houses, old cemeteries, terrifying locations, unusual people, bizarre legends and more. In some cases they are not even ghost stories at all. These latter tales are so unusual however, and such a part of Illinois lore, that they had to be included here anyway.

Even with that said, I am sure there are tales of Illinois that have still managed to elude me. There are haunted places here that have remained unknown since the first settlers came to the prairie and these spots remain hidden, or forgotten, today. I do not claim to have uncovered every ghost story in the state of Illinois, but I do feel that this book will reveal the history and the hauntings of Illinois in a way that no book has ever done before.

But can I tell you that every one of the stories in this book is true? Can I vouch for their complete authenticity? No, I cannot do that. What I can tell you though is that each of them was told to me, or was documented, as being the truth. The stories that are included in this book are presented as "real" stories that have been told by "real" people. The truth of each story is up to the reader to decide.

I have already mentioned my interest in history, but I am often asked how I got interested in hauntings and spirits? It began quite simply with ghost stories. You see, I have been collecting stories and legends for more than a decade now but my interest goes back even further than that. I can't really remember when I first started to be fascinated with ghosts, but I must have been a very small child.

What first caught my interest? I have no idea! That's one of the questions I am always asked, just after I tell people what I do for a living. Usually, they are disappointed when I tell them the truth. I have always suspected they want me to say that my mother died when I was 12 and came back to visit me from beyond the grave (but my mom is alive and well, thanks) or that I receive flashes of psychic insight from the spirit world (although I am about as psychic as a fence post). They are usually disappointed when they hear the truth!

Regardless, of how or why I got started collecting and investigating tales of ghosts and haunted places, I don't plan to stop doing gathering them any time soon. Over the past number of years, I have found there is just nothing like the thrill of finding a really good story, taking a trip to visit an alleged haunted house or even taking the first steps into a dark and forgotten graveyard. So, growing up in Central Illinois, I was delighted to find a treasure trove of not only strange and ghostly tales but many haunted places as well. I was later able to channel my fascination with these stories and tales into an ongoing number of books, some of them about Illinois and some of them not, but all of them concerned with ghosts!

In nearly every book I write, I always like to take the reader along on another short trip before beginning the journey into the heart of the book. That small trip always involves the "lore" of the ghosts themselves. What sort of hauntings can the reader expect to find in the lonely places ahead?

There are many theories and ideas out there as to what, or who, ghosts actually are and why they choose to haunt the places they do. I can't tell you that I know everything about ghosts because I don't believe there are any "experts" when it comes to the supernatural. I usually prefer the term "knowledgeable", because no one can say what ghosts really are, they can only describe their own experiences with these elusive creatures. As mentioned before, I have been tracking down ghosts for some time now and really don't know much more about them than I did when I started. Still, in that time, I have visited several hundred allegedly haunted locations.

People often ask me if I have seen a ghost? (That's the other question that people always ask when I tell them what I do for a living!). I would still have to say that I'm not for sure. I have certainly seen and experienced a lot of things that I cannot explain, but seeing a ghost isn't the only way to experience them. I have had some strange encounters over the years, all over the country, which I don't have easy explanations for!

But what are ghosts? And what is a haunting? And how do these things relate to the ghostly locations in this book?

First of all, what exactly is a haunting?

It is defined as being the repeated manifestation of strange and inexplicable sensory phenomena at a certain location. There are no general patterns to hauntings, which is what makes them so hard to define. Some phenomena may manifest on occasion or even continually for periods which last from several days to centuries; others may only occur on certain anniversaries; and others may make no sense whatsoever.

The general public assumes that hauntings involve apparitions, or ghosts, of the dead, but in fact, apparitions are connected to only a minority of cases. Most hauntings involve noises like phantom footsteps; strange, unexplainable sounds; tapping; knocking sounds; strange smells; and sensations like the cold prickling of the skin, chilling breezes and even the feeling of being touched by an invisible hand. Other hauntings involve poltergeist-like activity such as furniture and solid objects being moved about; broken glass; doors which open and close by themselves; and the paranormal manipulation of lights and electrical devices.

While attempts have been made to try and categorize certain types of hauntings (as you'll soon see) many locations seem to defy this labeling and manifest a variety and a combination of different types. In fact, it has been my experience that some locations seem to act as catalyst for activity, causing visitors to manifest their own unconscious phenomena and giving rise to accounts which don't fit into any categories at all. The two different types of hauntings that seem to be most commonly reported are what we call the "intelligent haunting" and the "residual haunting", but they aren't alone.

The intelligent spirit is everyone's traditional idea of a ghost. It is a lost personality, or spirit, that for some reason did not pass over to the other side at the moment of death. It shows an intelligence and a consciousness and often interacts with people. It is the most widely accepted kind of paranormal activity because it is the easiest to understand. It "haunts" a place because of a connection to the site or to the people at the location. This ghost is the personality of a once living person who stayed behind in our world. This sometimes happens in the case of a murder, a traumatic event, or because of some unfinished business which was left undone in a person's life. At the time of death, this spirit refused to cross over to the other side because of these events. There is also a good chance that this spirit does not even realize that it has died, which could happen if the death was sudden or unexpected. Many of the greatest Illinois ghost stories involve these chilling and interactive spirits.

Another type of haunting that is often reported has nothing to do with intelligent, or conscious, spirits at all. It is more common than people think and you might be surprised as to how many ghost stories that you have heard over the years just may fit into this category. This haunting is both unexplainable and fascinating..... and can be downright spooky too!

This type of haunting is called a "residual haunting" and the easiest way to explain it is to compare it to an old film loop, meaning that it is a scene which is replayed over and over again through the years. These hauntings are really just a piece of time that is stuck in place. Many haunted places experience events that may imprint themselves on the atmosphere of a place in a way that we don't yet understand. This event suddenly discharges and plays itself at various times, thus resulting in a place being labeled as haunted. These "phantom" events are not necessarily just visual either. They are often replayed as sounds and noises that cannot be explained, like footsteps that go up and down the stairs when no one is there. They can also sometimes appear as smells or other sensory events.

Often the sounds and images "recorded" are related to traumatic events that took place at the location and caused what might be called a "psychic disturbance". In other situations, they have been events or actions repeated over and over again to cause the impression. The locations where these hauntings exist act like storage batteries, saving up the impressions of sights and sounds from the past. Eventually, many of these hauntings wear down and fade away, while others continue for eternity.

There is another type of haunting that you are bound to discover within the pages of this book as well. It's one that I have started to think deserves a category all its own and that's the "graveyard ghost". Let me first say that it is a common belief among students of the occult that cemeteries are not the best places to find ghosts. While most would fancy a misty, abandoned graveyard to be the perfect setting for a ghost story, such stories are not as common as you might believe. However, nearly every ghost enthusiast will concede that a place becomes haunted after a traumatic event occurs at that location, whether that event actually occurred to a person or to the place itself.

But what of a haunted cemetery? Do such places really exist? Most assuredly they do, but ghosts who haunt cemeteries seem to be a different sort than those you might find lingering in a haunted house. Most of these ghosts seem to be connected to the cemetery in some way that excludes events that occurred during their lifetime. As most spirits reportedly remain in this world because of some sort of unfinished business in life, this seems to leave out a cemetery as a place where such business might remain undone.

Graveyard ghosts seem to have a few things in common. These spirits seems to be connected to the burial ground because of events that occurred after their deaths, rather than before. In other cases, the ghosts seem to be seeking eternal rest that eludes them at the spot where their physical bodies are currently found. Cemeteries gain a reputation for being haunted for reasons that include the desecration of the dead and grave robbery, unmarked or forgotten burials, natural disasters that disturb resting places, or sometimes even because the deceased was not properly buried at all!

Some of the best-known, and the most frightening, ghost stories of Illinois center around our graveyards. In fact, Illinois has even become famous for the inordinate number of haunted cemeteries that can be found within its borders, as you will discover later on in this book.

So, what do you think? Do you find this all hard to believe?

Or are ghosts real? Is Illinois really a haunted and mysterious place?

Those readers who do not believe in ghosts say that spirits are merely the figments of our imagination. Such stories, these readers insist, are the creations of fools, drunkards and folklorists. Such a reader will most likely finish this book and still be unable to consider the idea that ghosts might exist. In that case, I can only hope to entertain this person with the history and horrific tales of Illinois.

If you are this person, then I ask that you not be too sure that you have all the answers.

Can you really say for sure that ghosts aren't real? Are you totally convinced that spirits do not wander the open fields and the lonely forests of Illinois? Those are questions that you should ask yourself, but before you immediately reply, try answering them while standing in some fog-shrouded Illinois cemetery at midnight.

Is the moaning sound that you hear really just the wind whispering in your ear, or could it be the voices of the dead, crying for eternal peace?

Is that merely a patch of fog on the hill, or could it be the ethereal form of a girl in a wedding gown, still searching for the spirit of her murdered lover?

Are those lights in the distance simply the reflections of passing headlights, or are they the souls of the forgotten searching for the graves in which their bodies are buried?

Is that rustling in the leaves really just the passing breeze, or is it the ominous sound of footsteps coming up behind you?

If you suddenly turn to look, then you just might realize that, despite the fact there is no living person around you, you just might not be alone! Perhaps you are not as sure as you thought you were about the existence of ghosts. Perhaps they are not simply a part of fanciful fiction after all? Perhaps no one person among us has all of the answers....

The unknown still beckons to us today and in spite of the hurried world around us and the hard reality of modern life, the unknown remains difficult for us to ignore. There are stranger things, to paraphrase the poet, than are dreamt of in our philosophies. Some of these strange things are lurking just around the corner, in the dark shadows of Illinois!

Happy Hauntings!
Troy Taylor
Winter 2001

CHAPTER ONE

HISTORY & HAUNTINGS OF EARLY ILLINOIS

I believe that perhaps the most haunted state in the Midwest is Illinois. There are probably more ghosts per capita there than anywhere else. I have traveled all over the state and have seen some pretty spooky things. I am not sure that I can explain this feeling that I have, but look at it this way... even the origins of the state are shrouded in mystery....

FROM THE HAUNTING OF AMERICA

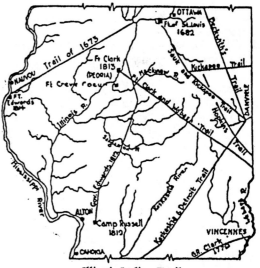

Illinois Indian Trails

If there is one solitary thing that causes the state of Illinois to be ripe for hauntings, then it is the history of the state itself. As even the most hesitant of readers and enthusiasts can attest, ghosts and hauntings are born from violence, murder and bloodshed. The tragedies of yesterday so often become the ghost stories of today. Even from its very beginning, Illinois was a place where death was commonplace and unsolved mysteries thrived.

The land that would someday become known as "Illinois" was steeped in the legend and lore that surrounded the "Louisiana Purchase" and the rolling "prairie seas of grass". This was a rich land and one that would be coveted by the streams of settlers and frontiersmen who traveled west from the original American colonies.

The recorded history of Illinois actually began in 1673 when the first French explorers came to the region but man first walked here centuries before that. The Frenchmen found Native Americans here who roamed the land, with no written language and no real communities or culture, however, scattered across the region, they discovered strange mounds, altars, burial sites and what appeared to be the ruins where towns and villages once stood. It seemed that a civilization, far advanced of the current natives, had once prospered in the Mississippi River Valley. Who these mysterious dwellers were remains a mystery. They have been called the "Mound Builders", thanks to the monuments of earth they left behind, but the people have so utterly disappeared that their true identity will never be known. They left only silent graves and magnificent mounds in their wake, located in places like Fulton County and Cahokia.

At Cahokia, near present-day Collinsville, are the remains of Illinois' most ancient city. The site boasts a number of mounds but one main centerpiece. It is sometimes called "Monk's Mound" after Trappist monks who farmed the terraces of the structure in the early 1800's. It is a stepped pyramid that covers about 16 acres and one that was apparently rebuilt several times in the distant past. At the summit of the mound, are the buried remains of some sort of temple, further adding to the mystery of the site. The settlers who later came to this area were intrigued by the mounds and they believed them to be evidence of some long vanished and forgotten culture. As they dug into the mounds, they found extraordinary artifacts like pottery, carved pipes and stone trinkets, effigies of birds and serpents made from copper and mica and vast numbers of human bones.

During the Middle Ages, Cahokia was a larger city than London and yet today, is an abandoned place about which we know almost nothing. Centuries ago, there were more than 120 mounds at the Cahokia site, though the locations of only 106 have been recorded. Many of them have been destroyed or altered because of modern farming and construction, although 68 have been preserved inside of the state historic area boundaries.

A Sacrificial Symbol thought to have come from the "Death Cult" period.

It is generally believed that about 20,000 people once occupied Cahokia, living inside of a wooden stockade that surrounded various pyramids. The site is named after a tribe of Illiniwek Indians, the Cahokia, who lived in the area when the French arrived in the late 1600's. What the actual name of the city may have been in ancient times is unknown. The site is believed to have existed from 700 A.D. until its decline in 1300. By 1500, it is thought to have been completely abandoned.

So, what happened to the Mound Builders of Cahokia? Some archaeologists believe the last survivors of the Mound Builders were the Natchez Indians of the Lower Mississippi Valley. These Indians were known for being devout worshippers of the sun, which may explain the uses of the mounds at Cahokia and the so-called "Woodhenge" of the site. These 48 wooden posts make up a 410-foot diameter circle and by lining up the central observation posts with specific perimeter posts at sunrise, the exact date of all four equinoxes can be determined.

It has been suggested that perhaps the Mound Builders abandoned the area because of overcrowding or contamination of the local water supply, while others have theorized that it may have been a breakdown of the civilization itself. Around 1500, the Mississippi Valley was seized by a religious movement that has been dubbed the "Death Cult". A new type of grotesque artwork became prevalent, portraying winged beasts, skulls and weird faces. The rituals practiced during this period of decline are unknown, but scholars have imagined them to be quite dark. Some have even hinted at human sacrifice and cannibalism. Regardless, this proved to be the death knell for the civilization.

According to legend, a bearded and robed god had originally visited the Mound Builders and inspired them to love one another, live in harmony with the land and built the great earthen works. But later, they degenerated to human sacrifice and warfare during the Death Cult period. The possible survivors of the Mound Builders, The Natchez, were described by the French as being the "most civilized of the native tribes" but their tribal traditions sometimes had dark elements to them. It was reported that in 1725, the death of a chieftain touched off a sacrificial orgy when several aides and two of the man's wives agreed to be strangled so they could escort him into the next world.

Could the degeneration of the Mound Builder's society have brought the civilization to ruin? Perhaps, although many people still consider the Cahokia site to be a sacred place. In August 1987, the Monk's Mound was the meeting place of more than 1000 people who took part in a worldwide "harmonic convergence" that was designed to bring peace to the planet. Many Native Americans and metaphysical groups believe Cahokia is a source of powerful psychic energy even today.

The Mound Builders, who seem to have disappeared shortly after Columbus landed in the West Indies, were followed by the Native American hunters and wanderers. They were the sole occupants of the land when the explorers arrived, their small villages scattered across the prairie and nestled close to the rivers and water sources. They hunted the deer and the buffalo, which were once prevalent here, and were descended from the Algonquin tribes who had once hunted much further to the east.

When these Indians were encountered by the French at the mouth of the Des Moines River, they referred to themselves as the "Illiniwek". This was actually interpreted to mean "the men", which was how these Native Americans referred to their tribe. This designation was designed to separate them from the Iroquois Indians, who were their mortal enemies and who they referred to as "animals". From that time on, this branch of the Algonquin tribe was known as the "Illinois" confederation and it would be from this band that the state would later take its name. The confederation was made up of several tribes who had banded together for the purpose of defense. They held a large portion of the state, which they shared with several other tribes, including the powerful Kickapoo Indians.

THE EXPLORERS

No one will ever know who the first white man to set foot in Illinois actually was. It is possible that some French adventurer arrived here first, but recorded history of the state begins with the arrival of Louis Jolliet and Father Jacques Marquette in June of 1673.

Jolliet was a young Canadian from France who was an explorer and map-maker, while Marquette was a Jesuit priest who longed to bring his religion to the native people of the wilderness. These two men, along with several Indians and nineteen white men, began a treacherous journey that would take them down the Mississippi River and along the western border of Illinois. They traveled as far south as the Arkansas River and then crossed the land on their return journey, paddling northward on the Illinois and Des Plaines rivers to Lake Michigan. After they arrived safely at the lake, Marquette vowed to return to Illinois and establish a mission.

Marquette and Jolliet parted at the Des Peres mission at the mouth of Green Bay. The priest was sick and stayed behind while his friend continued on to Montreal. When he was almost home, Jolliet's canoe capsized in a river and his maps and journals from the Illinois trip were lost. Because of this, only Marquette's notes remain about the discovery of Illinois. He would return to Illinois in the latter part of 1674 to keep his promise of returning to set up a mission. By the time he arrived at the Chicago portage, he was seriously ill. He spent the winter in a small hut and in the spring built his mission. He never recovered though and by May of 1675, he passed away on the east shore of Lake Michigan, where a river was later named in his honor.

Marquette would open the way for other priests, many of whom would meet danger and death in the wilderness. They were some of the earliest residents of the state and perhaps met with greater hardships than any of those who followed. Sadly however, most of their names cannot be recalled today.

Perhaps the greatest explorer to roam Illinois was Robert Cavalier, who was better known as the flamboyant promoter, sieur de LaSalle. He was the first of the early arrivals to comprehend the economic importance of the territory and also became the first to explore many of the waterways and forests of the region. In spite of his courage and his brilliance, LaSalle was regarded by most as haughty, arrogant and rude. He was often referred to as a "man of magnificent failures" as he brutalized the Indian tribes, borrowed huge sums of money and squandered fortunes. Somehow though, he managed to gain the respect and loyalty of a true adventurer, Henri de Tonti. He was an Italian soldier of fortune who became a character in his own right. He was admired and feared by the Indians, thanks to the wicked metal hook that replaced a hand that he had once lost in battle. Tonti would become LaSalle's boon companion and perhaps his anchor of sanity as well.

LaSalle had been born into a noble French family in 1643. He came to America two decades later and took up exploration as a means of creating his fortune. On his first trip, seeking the Ohio River, he encountered the explorer Louis Jolliet, who was returning from Illinois. Jolliet's fortunes would never be made, LaSalle believed, because he was unable to get land grants from the French government. Because of his friendship with Marquette, the explorer would always be linked to the Jesuit order of the Catholic Church. LaSalle did not have such a problem, he despised the Jesuits, and thanks to this he was able to gain a grant that gave him control of the fur trade south of the Great Lakes. In return for it, he agreed to explore the lower Mississippi Valley and try to discover a water passage to the Pacific Ocean.

LaSalle, based in the north, began building a ship called the "Griffon", which became the first sailing ship on the Great Lakes. He planned to use it to take his cargoes of furs to the east and then on to Europe. The vessel set sail with a full crew and a hold filled with cargo, then disappeared without a trace. It has since become known as one of the greatest mysteries of the lakes. The lore of the vanished vessel has spawned tales of murder and of course, of ghosts. One such tale is connected to Lake Solitude, a small body of water located along the eastern shore of Lake Michigan. The lake was once connected to the larger body of water, but now only a narrow stream passes between them. The stories say that the passage was closed by the sinking of the Griffon. The ship is believed to be hidden beneath the dark surface of the lake and the ghosts of the ship's crew are said to be haunting the shoreline.

Meanwhile, LaSalle made his first trip into Illinois during the dead of winter. He pioneered the St. Joseph - Kankakee River route and built a shelter called Fort Crevecoeur at present-day Peoria in 1680. It was a crude, wooden structure, but was the first building erected by the French in the west. It did not last long. While LaSalle was in Canada, preparing supplies for a journey down the Mississippi, the men who remained at the fort mutinied and destroyed the building. It was never rebuilt.

In the spring of 1682, LaSalle and Tonti made the first journey down to the mouth of the Mississippi River. When they arrived, LaSalle claimed all of the land for France and dubbed the region "Louisiana". In so doing, he created a vast territory that stretched from the Appalachians to the Rocky Mountains.

After that, they returned to Illinois and LaSalle built another fort, this one called Fort St. Louis, on Starved Rock in northern Illinois. It had been at this site where fighting had occurred two years before between the Illiniwek confederation and the Iroquois. Tonti had been wounded during the battle. On this site, the men erected a blockhouse, a storehouse and a dwelling on the summit of the rock. It was impassable on three sides and had only a narrow trail to defend on the fourth. While it seemed the perfect defensive position, it would prove to be a deathtrap for the remaining Illiniwek a few years later.

LaSalle left Illinois after only five years. He returned home to France, where he was considered a hero. He was asked again to serve his country, as France was now at war with Spain, and LaSalle promised to set up a base of operations at the mouth of the Mississippi River. He departed with two hundred colonists but somehow managed to miss Louisiana and land in Texas instead. He conducted several expeditions in search of the Mississippi but he never found it again. While on the fourth mission, he was shot and killed by one of his own men. It was a rather strange, but somehow fitting, end for the "man of magnificent failures".

In the years that followed LaSalle's departure, Tonti became a well-known figure on his own. Being less adversarial than LaSalle, he made many friends and allies and spent more than fifteen years guiding French settlers to Illinois. Despite LaSalle's many faults, Tonti remained loyal to him and after his expedition vanished (no one knew yet that he had been killed), Tonti led a search party to find him. He eventually gave up and returned to Illinois. Tonti died in Mobile, Alabama from yellow fever in 1704, leaving a legacy of adventure and heroism behind.

THE GHOSTS OF STARVED ROCK

In the latter years of the 1600's, the Illiniwek were nearly wiped out by the rampaging Iroquois and Fox Indians and their numbers grew smaller. They were constantly beaten and harassed by their more powerful enemies and their numbers dwindled. Later, the arrival of the white settlers would bring about the ruin of their hunting grounds and the Illiniwek occupation would be officially at an end.

Prior to that, the Illinwek battled courageously against the attacks from the other tribes. The Fox in particular had staged a series of bloody skirmishes against the Illiniwek and had also been killing French trappers who were taking furs in the region. By the last months of 1722, the fighting between them had grown so intense that the Fox had allied other tribes into their numbers and they pursued the struggling Illiniwek to a point along the Illinois River. They sought safety atop a steep bluff, where LaSalle and Tonti had constructed Fort St. Louis years before. At first, the fortress seemed a safe refuge from the Fox, Macaoutin, Winnebago and Sauk tribes below, but they soon realized they were trapped.

The Illiniwek quickly discovered they had no way to escape from the bluff. Below them, the enemy waited and at their backs was a steep drop to the rocky banks and swirling waters of the Illinois River. The Illiniwek numbers began to slowly dwindle from sickness, cold and most of all, from hunger. Most of those who tried to escape were killed after jumping from the edge of the cliff. A few of the more daring warriors attempted to flee through the forest, only to be struck down and slaughtered by those who laid siege below. Others who were captured were horrifically burned at the stake.

No one really knows how long the Illinwek were trapped on Starved Rock. A number of accounts say that at least a dozen of them escaped through the woods or by the river. They took shelter with friendly tribes or with the French trappers. Others told stories of miraculous escapes and of a mysterious snow that fell one night and covered the tracks of the desperate Illiniwek, giving them just enough time to escape. When they were gone, they left nothing behind at the old fort save for items they could not carry and the bodies of the dead. Or did they leave something else as well?

As the years have passed, a number of eerie tales have been told about Starved Rock State Park and the fearsome rock itself. The legends say that strange cries and screams have often been heard in the forests and around the precipice of stone. Enthusiasts who are canoeing on the nearby river also maintain that they have experienced bloodcurdling screams that seem to come from nowhere. The stories say that these screams, moans and terrifying voices are the death cries of the Illinwek Indians who did not survive their attempted escape from Starved Rock. It seems that the terrible ordeal of three centuries ago has left an indelible mark on this otherwise peaceful place.

By the end of the ordeal, the once great Illinwek confederation had collapsed to less than one hundred persons. Eventually, they were all sent to a reservation in Kansas. It is believed that not a single descendant of the Illiniwek nation still lives today.

THE CURSE OF KASKASKIA

The French began to move southward and westward into the Illinois territory and they began colonizing the fertile plain along the Mississippi River. A new settlement was started near along the western edge of the region in 1703 and it was called Kaskaskia. For more than a century, it was the commercial and cultural capital of Illinois. Little of the city remains today, although it was once a prosperous and thriving settlement. Strangely, many believe that the city was destroyed because of an old curse, leaving nothing but a scattering of houses, and ghosts, behind.

Many years ago, Kaskaskia was a part of the mainland of Illinois, a small peninsula that jutted out just north of the present-day location of Chester. There still remains a portion of what was once Kaskaskia, which is accessible from Illinois today, but the peninsula is now an island, cut off from the state by a channel change in the Mississippi River that took place decades ago. Much of the area was flooded at that time and it is now largely a ghost town, consisting of a few scattered homes and a handful of residents. The remains of the town, while still considered part of Illinois, can now only be reached from Missouri. There is an ancient bridge between St. Genevieve and St. Mary's which crosses the Mississippi to the island. It is the only physical link this desolate spot has to either state. There are only a few scattered buildings left here, including the Kaskaskia Bell Memorial site, which indicate that the city ever existed.

The French settlers founded the vanished town and it was once considered the "metropolis" of the Mississippi Valley and the main rendezvous point for the whole territory. It also served as a springboard for explorations to the west and in time, became the state and territorial capital of Illinois. The area grew and in 1804, Kaskaskia became a land-office town and the territorial capital in 1809. The town was made up of stone mansions and homes of typical French architecture, which according to contemporary sources, were inclined to be "shabby".

Half of the inhabitants were French or French-Indian mixtures who raised cattle, horses and hogs and worked small farms. The city also boasted a post office and a number of general stores, a hat shop and three tailor shops. There was only one tavern in town and it was said to be constantly overcrowded by state officials, soldiers, adventurers and land speculators.

The First State Capitol at Kaskaskia

In 1818, the state capital was moved to the new city of Vandalia, in the central part of the state. Illinois had just gained its statehood and legislators began searching for a place that was more centrally located than Kaskaskia. The move was made with some regret, but of course no one knew that the river city would be destroyed in just a few more years.

About 25 years later, the waters of the Mississippi began to shift in their channel and flooding attacked the edges of Kaskaskia, destroying homes and farms. By 1881, the peninsula was completely cut off by the river and the city nearly ceased to exist.

But what happened to change the fates of this once marvelous city? Was it simply nature taking its course.... or were more dire circumstances behind the demise of Kaskaskia?

According to some, there was a terrible curse placed on the town many years before which predicted the city and the land around it would be destroyed and that the dead would rise from the graveyard in eternal torment. Believe it or not, these events actually came to pass!

The legend of the curse dates back to 1735, when Kaskaskia was a thriving community of French settlers. There was a wealthy fur trader who lived there and who is remembered only by the name of Bernard. He lived in a luxurious stone home in the company of his daughter, Maria, a beautiful young girl who was the pride of his life. Bernard owned a trading post on the edge of the city and he frequently hired local men, both French and Indian, to work for him. Most of the Indians were hired to do the menial work, as Bernard cared little for them and considered them a "necessary evil" at best. At some point, he hired a young Indian to work for him who had been educated by French missionaries. As the two spent time together, Bernard actually began to become fond of the young man, at least until he realized that his daughter had also become fond of him. In fact, Maria and the Indian had fallen in love.

When Bernard learned this, he became enraged. He immediately fired the young man and spoke to friends and other merchants, who then refused to put him to work. Eventually, the young man left town. Before he left, he promised Maria that he would return for her.

Needless to say, Maria was heartbroken by her father's actions. She pretended that nothing was wrong, so as to not arouse her father's curiosity, but deep down, she secretly hoped, waited and watched for the return of her lover. Several local men attempted to court her, but while she feigned interest in their attentions, she secretly pined away for the young Indian.

A year passed and one day, a group of unknown Indians visited Kaskaskia from the west. Among them was Maria's lover, wearing a disguise so that he would not be recognized by Bernard. Maria and the Indian arranged to meet in secret and then quickly fled Kaskaskia to the north.

When Bernard learned what had happened, he vowed to seek vengeance on the young man. He gathered several of his friends and began hunting his daughter and her lover. They found them and captured them near Cahokia. Maria begged her father to understand but he refused to hear her cries. He decided to kill the young man by drowning him. The Indian was silent as the rough trappers tied him to a log and then set him adrift on the Mississippi. Just as they placed him in the water, he swore a terrible curse. He swore that Bernard would be dead within the year and soon he and Maria would be reunited forever. Kaskaskia was damned and would be destroyed, along with all of the land around it. The altars of the churches would be destroyed and the homes along with them. Even the dead of Kaskaskia would be disturbed from their graves!

Some of the Ruins of Kaskaskia, Photo Circa 1903

The river then swallowed the Indian beneath the muddy water. He was silenced, but the curse eventually came to pass. Within the year, the prophecy began to come true. Maria became distraught over her lover's fate and refused to leave the house or eat. She soon died and rejoined her lover on the other side. Bernard became involved in a bad business deal and challenged the man that he believed to have cheated him to a duel. Bernard was killed by the other man.

And the river began to seek the Indian's revenge on Kaskaskia. The river channels shifted and flooded the peninsula over and over again until, by 1881, Kaskaskia was completely cut off from the mainland. The homes and farms were abandoned and people began to slowly leave the island. The church was moved over and over again, but it did no good. The altar was eventually destroyed in the 1973 flood. By this time, Kaskaskia had become a desolate ghost town, but not before the Kaskaskia cemetery was washed away and the bodies of those buried there erupted to the surface and then vanished beneath the river. The dead of Kaskaskia had risen from their graves!

INDIAN MASSACRES & THE WAR OF 1812

The years that followed the American Revolution were part of a period of lawlessness and lack of order for Illinois. The British overthrew the French occupation and then the British were kicked out of the territory by the new American rule in what were once the eastern colonies. Under the control of the United States, the region would go from being a part of Virginia, to being included in the Indiana territory to becoming the Illinois Territory in 1809. By this time, government had come to the region and with it came the settlers.

In 1812, war broke out once again with the British and Illinois became an integral part of the fighting. Along the east coast and along the Canadian border, the American forces fought against British invasion. Illinois, being the far western frontier, was left out of this part of the war but the state was torn apart by terrible massacres and battles with Indian allies of the British, who created more havoc and committed more horrific murder than the English could ever dream of. Shortly after the outbreak of the war, the infamous Fort Dearborn Massacre took place at the site of present-day Chicago. This terrifying incident took the lives of numerous settlers, including many women and children.

While the beginning of the war in the Illinois Territory was certainly dark, the years that followed certainly grew no brighter. Immediately after the massacre, British representatives started down the Mississippi River as far as Rock Island, spreading discontent, gifts and alcohol among the Indians. In retaliation for this, the Territorial Governor, Ninian Edwards, collected a group of three hundred fifty Illinois frontiersman at Camp Russell, which is the site of present-day Edwardsville. The men were organized as mounted riflemen and were reinforced by three companies of United States Rangers under the command of Colonel Russell. The troops advanced north on the Illinois River, destroying Indian towns and slaying many of the inhabitants. When the men returned to Camp Russell, only one of their own men had been wounded.

By 1813, Illinois was prepared for a strong defense. Blockhouses and forts had appeared along the frontier and settlers in remote locations were moved to safety. New companies of rangers were formed and scattered across the state, but this was not enough to stop the marauding Indians. Along the western Mississippi, from present-day Alton to Kaskaskia, twenty-two forts had been built for defense, but Indians broke through and attacked the Lively family, who lived four miles southeast of Covington. The family was discovered later in shocking condition. Mr. Lively had been mutilated, while the two women present had been raped, savaged and killed. One of the sons, a boy of only seven, had been dragged out of the house and his head severed from his body. Luckily, one of the Lively sons and a stranger who had been passing by escaped the massacre and summoned help. A company of Rangers under Captain Bond pursued the Indians, but they vanished into the wilderness.

Shortly after, near the present-day town of Carlyle, two other men were murdered, followed by several other attacks on the Cache River, the Wabash River and near the present-day town of Albion, in Edwards County.

Another expedition was sent north toward the area of Peoria Lake, where a large number of natives had gathered and were launching attacks across the state. Nine hundred men were sent under the command of General Howard of the United States Army and they were to rendezvous with troops from Missouri under Colonel McNair, who would go on to become governor of that state. The Missouri men marched one hundred miles on the west side of the Mississippi to Fort Madison, where they swam the river naked and mounted on their horses while their clothing and weapons were rafted across. The troops, now banded together, continued their northward march.

Near the site of Quincy, they turned east and headed toward the mouth of the Spoon River, then followed the Illinois to Peoria. Here, they found a small stockade under the command of Captain Nicholas. He explained that Indians had attacked the fort two days before, but he and his men had repulsed it. The men continued on but found only deserted Indian villages as they marched. Apparently, the raiders had moved on to another location. The entire expedition turned out to be bloodless, but it did succeed in temporarily halting the attacks on the Illinois settlers.

Despite the efforts of the rangers and frontier defenders, the year 1814 opened with several horrible atrocities. A number of changes had taken place in the war, including American naval victories on Lake Erie, Detroit being recovered, the British being defeated at the Battle of Thames, and the driving out of the Indians along the Canadian border. While this looked good for overall victory in the war, it would have dire results for Illinois settlers. The Indians began to gather along the upper Mississippi and started to attack the small Illinois settlements.

In July, a band of Indians attacked the Wood River settlement, near present-day Alton, and massacred a woman named Reagan and her six children. Her husband, who had been absent at the time, was the first to discover the slaughter. Captain Samuel Whiteside, with a company of Rangers, took up pursuit and followed the marauders as far as the Sangamon River. All but one of the Indians escaped and when this attacker was killed, the scalp of Mrs. Reagan was found dangling from his belt.

More attacks took place and dozens of settlers were killed. In August, however, a band of Rangers attacked a war party near the site of the previously mentioned Lively family massacre and killed all of them. Only one of the Rangers did not return to camp.

That same year brought a close to the War of 1812.

After the war, a strong movement began to bring settlers to the region and to move the Native Americans out. Not surprisingly, after the hostilities that had taken place during the war, the white men were rarely honest when it came to business dealings with the Indians and large portions of land were purchased for small amounts of money. In many cases, the Indians were just driven out altogether. Although the last treaty relocating the Indians would not be signed until the 1830's, the federal government already controlled most of Illinois by 1818, when it was decided to make the territory into a state.

From the first days of statehood, passion and tragedy ruled the state of Illinois. In the years to come, the prairie would create legends like Abraham and tangle with the cruelty of slavery. It would turn ordinary men like Ulysses S. Grant into heroes and men like Elijah P. Lovejoy into martyrs. Illinois would build one of the greatest cities in America and send men to die in the Civil War. The state would riot, burn, become famous for violence and excess and continue to grow and thrive in more ways than the early settlers could have ever imagined.

In the chapters to come, we will continue to explore the history of this haunted state and uncover the people and places around which the ghostlore of the prairie has been created. The history and the hauntings of Illinois have only just begun in this book. You see, the spirits of today were born in the events of yesterday.....

Especially in Haunted Illinois.

·CHAPTER TWO·

GHOSTS OF LITTLE EGYPT

HISTORY & HAUNTINGS OF SOUTHERN ILLINOIS

There is little doubt that horrifying and terrible events from the past can leave an impression on a location... dooming that place to relive those events over and over again over the course of centuries.

FROM THE HAUNTING OF AMERICA

There is a fatality, a feeling so irresistible and inevitable that it has the force of doom, which almost invariably compels human beings to linger around and haunt, ghost-like, the spot where some great and marked event has given color to their lifetime... and still more irresistibly, the darker the tinge that saddens it.

NATHANIEL HAWTHORNE

Southern Illinois, or "Little Egypt" as it is often called, is a place like no other. Once you leave the central part of Illinois and drive south, it's as though you have entered another state altogether, or perhaps even another world. The scenery and the landscape becomes as varied as the people, with vast acres of forest, caves, swamps, and even the edge of the Ozark Mountains. The people here embody the culture of the region with strange tales, a rich folklore and southern drawls that you can rarely find outside of the deep south.

But below the surface, another place lurks, hidden in the dark forests and forgotten among the bluffs and secret hollows. It is here where the memory of the region's violent history still lingers... and where ghosts and "boogers" dwell.

The history of southern Illinois is as rich, colorful and turbulent as the landscape. Not surprisingly, it lends itself to ghost stories and haunts, many of which have become quite well known over the years. Nearly all of them take shape from the bloody history of the region. But where did a nickname like "Little Egypt" come from?

The section of Illinois located in the southern tip of the state has long been known as "Little Egypt" and several of the towns here bear names associated with the Egypt of the ancient world. These include Boaz, Karnak, Carmi, Thebes, Herod and of course, Cairo (although in southern Illinois, it is pronounced "CAY - ROE"). Some say this is how the region gained the nickname, but the real roots are thought to be found further back in Illinois history.

According to tradition, the people of the prairie region in central Illinois gave southern Illinois its nickname when they were forced to travel there for grain, following a series of droughts and the terrible winter of 1830, which destroyed their own supplies. The settlers in the wagon trains were compared to the ancient Israelites in the Bible, traveling to Egypt to buy their grain. The name may have come into use before that, but nevertheless, this anecdote probably helped it to become a permanent name for the region.

The area known as Egypt lies just south of a line that extends from the Alton / East St. Louis area to Vincennes, Indiana on the eastern side of the state. At this point, the prairie of the north begins to give way to rolling hills that eventually become the foothills of the Ozarks. Agriculture has long been the chief industry here, thanks to the mild weather, but rich coal deposits once made it one of the chief mining regions in America.

The first people in southern Illinois were the ancient Americans, who came before the Indians and built mysterious mounds and stone forts. Many of these structures have disappeared over the years, but many remain, some known and some unknown, to puzzle curiosity-seekers today. Even stranger than the mounds that exist in places like Cahokia, the stone forts have provided a puzzle all their own. They have been studied many times over the years, but so far, no one can comprehend their purpose. According to Loren Coleman's book, "Curious Encounters", there are at least 10 pre-Columbian forts in southern Illinois and others may exist in the remote areas of the Shawnee Forest, a vast and mysterious wilderness that engulfs a large portion of Little Egypt. These walled structures form a rough alignment between the Ohio and Mississippi Rivers and are located on high bluffs, facing outward. The walls may be approached from behind but face steep cliffs on both sides. While only one of them, near Stonefort in Saline County, has a water source inside of it, all of them have stone-lined pits where water could be stored.

The question remains as to what these forts were used for? Who built them, and why? The puzzle may never be solved, but one has to wonder... If the forts truly are scattered in a rough line between the two rivers, what enemy were the inhabitants trying to keep out? Or stranger yet, were they trying to keep something else within?

The French were the first white settlers in southern Illinois. They came in the early 1700's and established settlements at Kaskaskia and Cahokia, along the Mississippi River. After the War of 1812, the region was opened to American settlers and most came from the southern states of North Carolina, Kentucky, Tennessee and Virginia. They brought with them their southern ideas and traditions and these traditions would long hold reign over the thoughts and politics of the region. For a number of years, slavery was even allowed here, as the owners of the salt mines in the southeastern corner of the state were allowed to lease slaves from Kentucky to work their holdings.

So strong was the southern influence that shortly after the outbreak of the Civil War, Williamson County attempted to secede from the Union. Many in Little Egypt even went south to fight for the Confederacy. Discontent and strife were common throughout the war, aggravated by the activities of southern sympathizers like the Knights of the Golden Circle.

The early southern settlers also brought with them the feuds and violence of the Appalachians. One feud in Johnson County, at a place called Hell's Neck, flared into a bitter conflict that cost several lives. But none could compare to the "Bloody Vendetta" that took place in Williamson County.

BLOODY WILLIAMSON

Williamson County in southern Illinois is well-known by historians and crime enthusiasts as "Bloody Williamson", a dark (and most likely not appreciated) nickname that came about in the 1920's after being the scene of a bloody massacre, brutal battles with the Klan, and a fantastic Prohibition war between battling bootleggers. Regardless of how you look at it, the moniker of "Bloody" is something that Williamson County has earned!

An Illinois Map showing the Location (highlighted) of infamous "Bloody" Williamson County

Long before Prohibition and labor problems plagued the region, death came calling in Williamson County. Like most of southern Illinois, this region was settled by immigrants from the south, most especially the mountain regions of Kentucky, Tennessee and North Carolina. They brought with them their tradition, superstitions, hot-blooded pride and family honor. In his book, "Bloody Williamson", Paul M. Angle points out that many of these settlers were quick to resent an insult and given what they considered provocation, they would kill with little compunction. He wrote that Milo Erwin, the first historian of the county, counted 495 assaults with a deadly weapon and 285 murderous assaults between 1839 and 1876. He also listed 50 murders that had taken place but out of all of those, only six people had ever been convicted or served prison time. Williamson County was a rough, and sometimes lawless, place.

It would not be until the "Bloody Vendetta" though that murder would become an art form. It began as merely a tavern brawl on July 4, 1868. Several members of the Bulliner family were playing cards in a saloon with a man named Henderson. He made the mistake of calling one of the Bulliners a "damn lying son of a bitch" and in the fight that followed, Henderson was badly beaten.

After that, the two families became bitter enemies and soon involved other families in the feud, including the Sisneys, the Russells and the Crains. Between 1868 and 1876, the families fought out the Vendetta in the barnyards, bars and streets of Williamson County.

The Sisneys entered the Vendetta a year after the first troubles began between the Bulliners and the Hendersons. Sisney won a lawsuit against a Bulliner man over a crop of oats. Later, during a meeting to settle the affair Bulliner accused Sisney of lying. A fight started and soon other Bulliners were attacking the Sisney house with weapons. Sisney ran into a nearby field and although hit four times by bullets, managing to hold off the Bulliners from the cover of a large tree. The Sisneys were now involved in the feud on the side of the Hendersons. The way they saw it, there was no way to stay out of it.

Two years later, the Crains came into the Vendetta after a fight with several of the Sisneys at the general store in Carterville and Tom Russell also got involved. The battles continued for years and a dozen men were either killed or wounded in the fighting. The most unlucky of the fighters was George Sisney. After the unsuccessful attack on his home, he moved to Carbondale to get clear of the battle. However, a short time later, he was badly hurt by a shotgun blast through his living room window. He managed to recover, then less than a year later, was killed by another shotgun blast.

Finally, in 1876, Marshall Crain was tried and hanged for murder and the feud died out. After seven years of reluctance on the part of the authorities to do anything about the violence, Crain was hanged and three others, John Bulliner, Allen Baker and Samuel Music were imprisoned.

THE HERRIN MASSACRE

On a hot June day in 1922, the event that would give Williamson County its permanent nickname would take place. What became known as the "Herrin Massacre" would gain national attention and outrage and would forever leave a scar on the region.

The small town of Herrin is located in the heart of what was once considered "coal country". Here, rich veins of coal were discovered in the late 1800's and for a time, became the chief source of wealth and industry in southern Illinois, overshadowing the farms that once dominated the economy.

However, conditions for the workers were less than adequate. In "Bloody Williamson", Paul M. Angle states that the life and health of the employees were of little concern to the mine owners. Men worked in water up to their knees, in gas filled rooms, and in unventilated mines where the air was filthy and filled with toxins. There was no compensation for accidents (which frequently occurred) and the average daily wage was from $1.25 to $2.

Then, around 1900, the mine workers began to organize and they formed unions to combat the low pay and horrible conditions. New laws were implemented and wages grew to $7 and $15 for a day's work. Standards of living finally began to rise and small towns like Herrin began to prosper.

However, none of this came easy and there were many struggles between the miner's unions and the mine companies, who were only interested in profits. Many of the struggles resulted in strikes, violence and even death before the mine unions were recognized. The area around Herrin was not immune to these troubles either. In 1910, an attempt by a mine owner in Zeigler to maintain a non-union mine was met with bloodshed and he failed.

By the 1920's, the miner's unions were secure in southern Illinois and at this same time, the method of "strip mining" also came into practice. Here, large shovels and drag lines were used to strip the earth above coal beds that were close to the surface. In September 1921, William Lester (of the Southern Illinois Coal Company) opened a new strip mine about halfway between Herrin and Marion. The mine employed fifty workers, all members of the United Mine Workers of America.

Then came trouble.....

On April 1, 1922, the United Mine Workers went on a strike across the country, ceasing all coal mining operations. Lester, who was deeply in debt with his new operation, was in fear of losing his company, so he negotiated with the local union and they agreed to let him continue taking coal from the ground, as long as he did not try to ship it out. With this stockpile in place, Lester could ship the coal as soon as the strike ended.

By June, the union workers had dredged almost 60,000 tons of coal. The price for the product had risen considerably, thanks to the strike, and the chance for high profit was a temptation too great for Lester to withstand. At that point, he fired all of his union miners and hired fifty strike breakers and mine guards from Chicago. On June 16, he shipped out sixteen railroad cars of coal, effectively breaking the arrangement he had made at the start of the strike.

Word got out about what Lester was doing and soon officials from the United Mine Workers Union, from the National Guard and from the Illinois State government tried to convince him to stop.

Local miners were angry and began to rally. They knew that if Lester got away with what he was attempting to do, other mine owners would follow his lead. If this happen, everything the union had fought for would be lost.

In the days that followed, many tried to reason with Lester, but he refused to listen. He was contacted repeatedly by Colonel Samuel Hunter of the Illinois National Guard, who warned him that the situation he was causing could be very dangerous. Lester ignored him, as did the local sheriff. Hunter advised the lawman to deputize additional men in case of problems, but the sheriff ignored the warnings. Rumbling also continued among the local miners. On June 21, a truck carrying eleven armed guards and strike breakers was ambushed east of Carbondale. The driver was killed and a number of others were wounded.

Later that same day, several hundred miners gathered at the Herrin Cemetery, followed by looting in the local hardware stores. The mob took all of the firearms and ammunition they could find and then moved out to the mine site. There were no law enforcement officials present at the time!

That same afternoon, Colonel Hunter received a call from the mine superintendent. He explained that the mine had been surrounded and shots were being fired. The sheriff could not be located and he begged that Hunter send troops. Soon, National Guardsmen were dispatched with orders to stop the attack and to try and disperse the miners. The National Guard never arrived, having been called off by Hunter after the miners and the operators reached a tentative truce... a truce that would soon be broken.

By evening, more union supporters arrived at the mine. Colonel Hunter, worried over the situation, tried to call the mine but he found the phone lines were dead. Strangely, in spite of the fact that the local sheriff could not be reached, the troops were still not sent out.

The terms of the truce called for the strike breakers to be safely escorted out of the county and late that evening (June 21) the local sheriff reluctantly agreed to see if the truce was still holding. Then, he decided that he was tired and that it could wait until morning. He agreed to meet Colonel Hunter and Major Davis of the Carbondale Guard unit the following day.

Meanwhile, Hugh Willis, the spokesman for the United Mine Workers union in the area, arrived in Herrin and addressed the local supporters. His take on the situation was that the strike breakers should have never come to Herrin and whatever happened to them.... well, they had it coming. Needless to say, things were not going well.

Throughout the night, miners began destroying the equipment and machinery around the mine itself, using dynamite, shovels and hammers. Finally, after being begged by the strike breakers inside, the superintendent agreed to surrender. He told the assembled miners that they would all come out, as long as they could leave the county unharmed. The miners agreed and the men inside cautiously emerged from the mine. They lined up and the union miners began marching them toward Herrin. They began walking, stopping once when they were approached by an armed procession who threatened to kill the strike breakers. Cooler heads apparently prevailed and the procession continued on. A short distance later, at Moake Crossing, the procession stopped again and a car drove up. A man got out who the surviving strike breakers later recalled was referred to as "Hugh Willis". According to accounts from the survivors, he told the miners not to kill the captives on the public road, instead, he said "take them over to the woods and give it to them. Kill all you can."

The prisoners were then marched to the woods, near a barbed wire fence. Shots began to ring out and the strike breakers ran. Some of them never even made it to the fence. Others scrambled up and over it, or became terrifyingly trapped in the wire, then blasted apart with bullets. The strike breakers, unfamiliar with the area, plunged into the woods or ran towards Herrin. The miners tracked them through the woods and continued to slay them, one by one. One group that was captured was marched to Herrin Cemetery, only to be slaughtered there in front of a crowd that contained both women and children. One miner ended the massacre by going from one wounded man to another and cutting the throats of those who remained alive. It was a scene of unbelievable horror.

During all of it, the sheriff was noticeably absent. When he failed to meet Colonel Hunter and Major Davis, they went looking for him. The three men soon arrived at the mine to find the operation was in flames. They were able to follow the footsteps of the mob and found a trail of bodies left behind. Those who had not died were taken to Herrin Hospital but at least twenty of the strike breakers died in the slaughter. Three union miners were shot and killed while attacking the mine. The strike breakers who died were buried in a common grave in Herrin Cemetery. Their identities remain unknown to this day.

Not surprisingly, word quickly spread across the country about the terrible events. Newspapers and officials cried for justice to be done in the case. A coroner's reports ruled that the strike breakers were killed by "unknown individuals" and declared that the deaths had been caused by the actions of the Southern Illinois Coal Company and not the striking miners. These findings further outraged the public and several months later, pressure forced a grand jury to hand down indictments against six men for the murder of one of the strike breakers. The prosecutor used eyewitness testimony from surviving workers to present his case, but the defense managed to try and justify the mob's actions. The jury acquitted all six of the defendants.

The press and public officials outside of the area were again infuriated and called for a new trial, which took place in 1923. By this time, public interest in the case had waned but the prosecutor again tried the same six defendants, although this time for the murder of another strikebreaker. Reliable testimony was once again presented, but once more, the defense attorney justified the mob's actions. The jury was convinced and the defendants were again set free.

This was the last trial held and none of the killers were ever punished for their part in the massacre. "Bloody" Williamson gained a notoriety that lingers to this day.

THE KU KLUX KLAN IN WILLIAMSON COUNTY

Prohibition turned many from southern Illinois into bootleggers during the 1920's. With the liquor stills and illegal booze shipments came lawlessness, violence and bloodshed. Many in the region believed that they needed more help than local law enforcement could provide and welcomed the arrival of the Ku Klux Klan in 1923. The Klan saw the discontent of the people as an opportunity to step in and provide relief, as well as their version of law and order. As most of the bootleggers were "Catholics and foreigners" anyway, this provided the Klan with the perfect opportunity.

The Klan began its movement into the county by appearing at local churches with gifts of money and speeches on law and order and "walking the line of Americanism", wrote Paul Angle in "Bloody Williamson". Such sentiment was greeted warmly by the mostly Protestant and largely uneducated residents of the county. They were also embraced by the local Law and Order League, which had formed in 1923 to stamp out bootlegging and gambling. The local officials did little to curb the lawless elements in the region and Williamson County was ready for a "cleaning up" after the shameful events of the Herrin Massacre. The Klan was now offering them a chance to put the bootleggers and the gamblers out of business and make Williamson County "more like home and less like hell."

Concerned by the growing number of Klansmen in the county, the local sheriff also made an effort to curb the violence and the liquor, going out on ineffectual raids and making token arrests. The Klan was not happy and were impatient to see something done. The county would be cleaned up, they said, "if we have to do it ourselves."

The first move was to appeal to the Illinois governor for control. They were rebuffed, but didn't stop there. A committee then went to Washington, where they met with Roy Haynes, the Commissioner of Prohibition. He sympathized but could do little to help, although someone (and it is unknown who it was) put the committee in touch with a former Prohibition agent named S. Glenn Young. The committee retained him to conduct the clean-up in Williamson County.

Young arrived in Illinois in November 1923 in the company of his father-in-law, George Simcox, who had once been a US Marshal. The two men began visiting speakeasys in the county and compiling evidence against the owners. By the end of the month, they had bought illegal liquor in one hundred different establishments. With such evidence in hand, Young appealed to Roy Haynes in Washington and Haynes deputized him once again as a Prohibition agent. Shortly after, Young began recruiting men from the Klan into his private army. He would go on to become essentially an "enforcer", operating far outside of the reach of Haynes and the government.

Young and his 500 recruits began a series of raids that would fill the jails in Herrin and Benton. Young decked himself out in a military uniform, with two .45's strapped to his legs and carrying a submachine gun. He was at once both a comical figure on a reckless quest for power... and a terrifying one. After three raids, which resulted in 256 arrests, Williamson County was in an uproar.

The raiders did not limit themselves to speakeasys either. Many of the attacks fell on private homes and it was probably not a coincidence that most of these homes belonged to Italians and Catholics. There were stories of brutality, robbery and even planted evidence. The Klan scoffed at the charges leveled against them by the "foreigners" but many concerned citizens (outside the ranks of the Klan of course) found them convincing.

Chaos reigned in Williamson County. Most of the charges of brutality had been directed toward Young. After a fight, Young was arraigned on assault charges. During the hearing, several Klansmen stalked into the courtroom. They were heavily armed and carrying the machine guns used in their raids. The jury retired and immediately returned with a verdict of not guilty. This was only the beginning though. Shortly after, Young was also able to get the local sheriff to dismiss his deputies and hire all Klan supporters. Essentially, he was continuing the organization of his personal army.

But all was not well for Young in the county. One night in Herrin, a meeting of an anti-Klan group, which included bootleggers Carl and Earl Shelton, erupted into violence when the meeting was breached by two Klan officers, John Ford and Harold Crain. A scuffle followed and an anti-Klan supporter named John Layman was shot. In the confusion that followed, other Klansmen were disarmed and as prisoners, were taken away.

Shortly after, word of the fighting reached Ceasar Cagle, a bootlegger turned Klan supporter, who rounded up a group of men and went after the Sheltons and their friends. Cagle was killed shortly after and when word spread, the Klan converged on Herrin. Hundreds of them began patrolling the city streets and stopping cars, looking for Cagle's killers. Warrants were sworn out against several of the men and even CE Anderson, the mayor of Herrin. The Klansmen headed for the hospital and demanded entrance from Dr. JT Black, the administrator. When he refused, the Klan opened fire on the hospital, endangering the lives of the doctors, nurses and innocent patients. Within hours, the National Guard had arrived and they quickly dispersed the mob. The hospital itself was terribly damaged as broken glass covered the floors and bullet marks pitted the walls facing every outside window. Amazingly, not a single person in the building was injured.

Young ignored the presence of the troops and his men continued to patrol the streets wearing crude tin stars. He arrested the mayor and pretty much anyone who opposed him. He even arrested the sheriff, who he blamed for Cagle's murder. Young then appointed himself the sheriff and no one dared to oppose him. So, in a little more than three months, S. Glenn Young had made himself the dictator of an American county... but it would not last. Soon, officials were starting to complain about the Klan's "Reign of Terror".

In a short time, Young was charged with trying to overthrow the civil authorities of Williamson County and he later moved to East St. Louis. Regardless, the charges against Young were overshadowed by a number of liquor-related trials and the fact that the Klan managed to sweep the November elections, remaining in control of Williamson County. And the last had not yet been heard from Young.

On May 23, 1924, Young and his wife were driving to East St. Louis when a Dodge pulled up alongside them and fired a volley of bullets into the Young's car. Young was wounded and his wife was blinded by the fire. Word of the attack quickly reached Klan supporters, who swore revenge. A large number of them organized and began searching for the car. At 10:00 AM, the Dodge was spotted in Carterville and Klansmen opened fire. The Dodge ran off the road and two men emerged from the wreckage and tried to flee. One was wounded and the other killed. The dead man was named Jack Skelcher, a bootlegger. His companion, Charles Briggs had earlier been indicted with Bernie Shelton for highway robbery. A coroner's jury would rule that Skelcher's death had been at the hands of "unknown persons".

Now, Young was back in the spotlight again and he pushed for indictments in his attack. In June, he swore out warrants for attempted murder against Briggs and also against Carl and Earl Shelton, who he claimed were in the Dodge with the other two men. He was probably right, but it's unlikely that he saw them. Regardless, the case would never go to trial, in spite of a preliminary hearing where Young showed up with 30 carloads of armed Klansmen to identify the assailants. After this, Young continued to be involved in several altercations and in political and legal blunders that would get him indicted and force him to finally lose his position as a Prohibition agent.

A short time later, the case against the Shelton Brothers for the murder of Caesar Cagle came to trial. The only witness for the prosecution, Tim Cagle, the victim's father, stated that he did not believe the Sheltons were involved and they were freed. A half-hour later, anti-Klan men, George Galligan, Bud Allison, Ora Thomas, the Sheltons, and others drove to Smith's garage in Herrin to demand the return of the Dodge driven by Jack Skelcher. The incident resulted in a shoot-out, leaving six men dead. Three of them were Klansmen. Fearing more trouble, the National Guard was again dispatched.

In the meantime, Young had his own problems. On September 13, he was officially expunged from the Klan, although this had little effect on the Klan supporters in Williamson County. He was also "slapped in the face" by George Galligan, the local anti-Klan sheriff who had gotten rid of Young's men on the force and now replaced his special deputy with Ora Thomas, a man Young hated. Thomas was reportedly connected to the "Egan's Rats" mobsters in St. Louis and was a violent Klan hater. The two men would clash often, but it would all come to a head in January 1925 in a Herrin cigar store.

Thomas walked into the store, located in the European Hotel, with his hand on a pistol that he carried in his coat pocket. In the corner of the room, Young was arguing with a man as several onlookers watched, absorbed in what was taking place. One of the onlookers glanced toward Thomas and then quickly went out the back door. At that, Young turned around. In an instant, both men had drawn guns and began firing.

When the smoke cleared, four bodies were on the floor, including two of Young's guards. Both Young and Thomas were dying, having shot each other.

In time, the hold of the Klan over Williamson County was broken, but this would not mark the end of the violence and lawlessness. With the Klan gone, the county was now at the mercy of two warring factions of bootleggers, the Shelton Brothers and Charlie Birger. Death had not yet departed from Bloody Williamson.

WAR IN ILLINOIS

Located in the Chesed Shel Emeth Cemetery in the St. Louis neighborhood of University City stands a small, gray tombstone that is marked with the name "Shachnai Itzik Birger". Although few people know it, this unassuming stone stands over the body of a legend and an almost mythical character whose memory still lingers in southern Illinois. His name was Charlie Birger, a swashbuckling bootlegger, gambler, saloon-keeper and self-styled "do-gooder", who left an indelible mark on the bloody history of Little Egypt. He lived hard, died early and became the last man to hang on the gallows in the state of Illinois.

Charlie Birger was born of Jewish Russian immigrants sometime between 1880 and 1883. He was raised in St. Louis and in the coal town of Glen Carbon, Illinois.

Charlie Birger, from a sketch made by Harvey Dungey, a member of his gang.

In 1901, he joined the 13th US Cavalry and served in the Spanish-American War. Afterward, he worked as a cowboy in the west and then drifted back to East St. Louis. Here, he would make friends who would eventually go on to become his bitter enemies and deadly foes in the prohibition gang wars. These friends were the Shelton brothers, Carl, Earl and Bernie, and with Birger, they would battle the powerful Ku Klux Klan during the troubles in "Bloody" Williamson County.

In the early 1920's, Birger moved to Harrisburg and by this time, was married to his second wife, had two children and was a successful "businessman". He had started a number of profitable speakeasys and brothels that offered not only liquor and prostitutes, but gambling as well. Most of the establishments could be found in and around Harrisburg, including a notorious one on West Poplar Street, but he also had others. The most famous of the time was "Halfway House", located between Marion and Johnston City.

Birger also earned a reputation to go along with his business, both good and bad. On one hand, he called himself the "protector of Harrisburg" and helped many people who were in need. On the other hand, in 1923, he was said to have killed two men in a span of three days, one of them at Halfway House. Birger claimed self-defense for the first killing and was cleared of all charges. He was wounded himself in the second and spent time in the Herrin Hospital after a stray bullet struck his lung. Needless to say, these were only two of the murders linked to Birger in his career. Before his death he readily admitted that he had killed men... "but never a good one", he stated.

In December 1923, Birger got caught up in one of the early bootlegging raids organized by S. Glenn Young and his Klan supporters. It would not be the last time these two powerful forces would clash. Once Birger got out of jail, he began building what would become his most prominent establishment, Shady Rest. It was located about halfway between Marion and Harrisburg on Route 13 and the roadhouse drew disreputable characters and customers from all over the region. It would become the base of Birger's illegal operations.

At about this same time, Birger joined forced with the Shelton brothers, who were essentially, as Paul Angle described them in "Bloody Williamson", wild and reckless young men who had been driven bad by the persecution of Young and his Klansmen in Williamson County. The Shelton "gang" mostly consisted of friends and relatives from all over Little Egypt. At the time they joined up with Birger, the Sheltons were running bootleg liquor from the south for distribution in southern Illinois and in the East St. Louis area. Birger allowed the Sheltons to use Harrisburg as a layover and shipping point and they also worked together to establish slot machines and gambling across the region.

Shady Rest opened for business in 1924 and offered bootleg liquor, gambling, cockfights and dog fights. During the day, things stayed pretty quiet, catering mostly to liquor runners who would make the last leg of their trip to St. Louis after dark. Although notorious all over southern Illinois, no police officials ever raided or bothered the place. It was no secret what it was being used for or that it had been built to withstand a siege if necessary. The building had been constructed with foot-thick log walls and a deep basement. Rifles, sub-machine guns and boxes of ammunition lined the walls, alongside canned food and water. Floodlights, supplied with electricity that was generated on the grounds, prevented anyone from sneaking up on Shady Rest in the night.

The place became very popular with the locals until early 1926, when the relationship between Birger and the Sheltons fell apart. After that, the bloody climate of the location kept many customers away. Regardless, a number of people in the area still chose to see Charlie Birger as a public benefactor rather than as a killer and bootlegger. My friend Bernie Bernard, who grew up in the area, told me that his grandfather fondly recalled buying barbeque from the stand at Shady Rest and often selling milk and eggs to Birger, who he remarked was a "kind and very polite man". In addition, accounts have it that Birger once gave coal to all of the destitute families in Harrisburg during one bitterly cold winter. He also allegedly provided school books for children and vowed that he would not let Harrisburg residents play at his gambling tables. He had no desire, he claimed, to take their money.

Why the bloody rift developed between Birger and the Sheltons is unclear. Most likely, it was simply business that became personal. The two groups had originally united to fight back against Young and the Klan's encroachment on their business. Once the Klan was wiped out, there was no one left to fight but each other. Regardless of why it started though, it plunged southern Illinois once more into chaos. The war began in 1926 and small towns, farms and roadhouses in the region were terrorized as both sides built armed vehicles to carry out deadly reprisals against one another. Machine guns blasted, speakeasys were torn apart with gunfire and many died during the fighting.

In November 1926, a Birger associate named Milroy was gunned down as he left a roadhouse in the town of Colp. The mayor and the chief of police, called in from another roadhouse nearby, were shot at from the darkness as they got out of their car. The mayor was fatally wounded but the police chief managed to escape with a shattered hand. Both men, it was said, were enemies of the Sheltons.

A few days later, a homemade bomb was tossed from a speeding car toward Shady Rest. The bomb had been intended for the barbeque stand, but it had missed and Birger's hideout was unharmed. Two days later, machine gunner's (allegedly sent by Birger) shot up the home of Joe Adams, the mayor of West City. He was a friend of the Sheltons and a mechanic who often did work on the armored vehicle they had built.

Then, hours later, the only bombs ever dropped during aerial warfare in America fell on Shady Rest. In full daylight, an airplane flew low over Birger's hideout as his men watched. A few bundles were thrown from the cockpit, which turned out to be dynamite bound around bottle of nitroglycerine. The "bombs" were so poorly constructed that they never exploded. The following week, a more effective bomb was thrown in response, this time by the Birger gang. It exploded in front of Adams' house, damaging the front porch, blowing the door off its hinges, and shattering the windows. No one was injured, but it would not stay that way for long.

On December 12, two men came to the door of Mayor Joe Adams' house and told his wife they had a letter from Carl Shelton. When he answered his wife's call, one of the men handed Adams a note. While he read it, both of them pulled guns from their coats and shot the man in the chest. He lived just long enough to tell his wife that he hadn't recognized the killers. She blamed the killing on Charlie Birger.

The gang war soon reached its climax. Around midnight on January 9, 1927, a farmer who lived a short distance from Shady Rest was awakened by five or six gunshots. They were followed a short time later by a massive explosion that destroyed Shady Rest and shook his own home. The fire burned so hot that no one dared approach the ruined structure until morning. By then, it was merely ashes and burned embers. However, among the remains were four bodies, charred beyond recognition. One of the bodies later turned out to be Elmo Thomasson, a member of the Birger gang.

From all appearances, Birger was finished but he still managed to beat the Sheltons in the end. Although he had failed to best his rivals with guns and dynamite, he did manage to beat them by using the US government against them instead. Back in 1925, a post office messenger in Collinsville had been robbed of a mine payroll adding up to around $21,000. The crime had remained unsolved. Birger contacted the postal inspector and managed to convince him that the Sheltons had pulled the job. A federal grand jury indicted the brothers and the courts convicted them. The Sheltons were each given 25 years in federal prison but were later awarded new trials.

After the gang war, the Sheltons never returned to Williamson County. They moved their operations to East St. Louis, continuing with bootlegging, prostitution and gambling until they were driven out of the area. They re-established themselves in the Peoria area, where they continued their activities for many years. Carl was killed there in 1947. Bernie was fatally shot outside a tavern he owed in the summer of 1948 and Earl died peacefully after surviving a murderous attack near Fairfield in 1949. Eerily, Bernie Shelton will return again later on in this book.

As for Charlie Birger, he had won the gang war and had put his rivals out of business, but his victory wouldn't last. Things started to break bad when the police arrested Harry Thomasson on a robbery charge. Franklin County State's Attorney Roy Martin suspected the man also was involved in the murder of West City's Mayor, Joe Adams. Thomasson was associated with Charlie Birger, but their relationship had been rocky since the burning of Shady Rest. Harry had begun to suspect that Birger himself had been responsible for the bombing of the roadhouse, which had killed his brother, Elmo. Looking for a deal, he confessed to the murder of Joe Adams and he implicated Birger in the crime. He explained that Charlie had paid him $150 per shot.

This was the beginning of the end. Another Birger gang member, Art Newman, who had once owned the Arlington Hotel in East St. Louis, had fled to California but was captured there and brought back to Illinois on a murder charge. On the trip back, he confessed to taking part in the murder of Lory Price, a state patrol officer who had been a friend of Birger. Witnesses had indicated that Price had been at Shady Rest on the night of the explosion and he and his wife had disappeared mysteriously a short time later. Newman was indicted for the murder, along with Birger and four other gang members. The details of the murder have never been clear, but Price's body was found in a field by a farmer, while his wife's corpse was later discovered in an old mine shaft near Johnston City.

Birger was arrested for the murder of Joe Adams on April 29, 1927 and he was that summer in Franklin County. In late July, after 24 hours of deliberation, the jury returned with its verdict, finding Birger guilty. He was sentenced to death, although was granted a stay of execution as he appealed the verdict. In late February 1928, the Illinois Supreme Court denied his appeal and sentenced him to die on April 13. Birger claimed to be relieved and said that he would "rather die than spend another ten months in jail".

Another appeal was attempted but turned down on April 12 by the State Board of Pardons and Paroles. After this failure, Birger's lawyer rushed to Benton and filed another petition. This one was in the name of Charlie's nephew, Nathan Birger, and it asked for a sanity hearing. The execution was postponed again and on April 16, the hearing began. Birger made a desperate attempt to escape death, making a fool of himself by cursing at reporters, cowering and rolling his head from side to side. Spectators in the crowd actually laughed at him and the jury took just twelve minutes to find him totally sane. He was now scheduled to die on April 19. He would be the last man to die on the gallows in the state of Illinois. During that same month, the Illinois legislature abolished hanging and substituted the electric chair as a humane method of execution in the state.

Thanks to Charlie's notoriety, a "county fair atmosphere" was used to characterize the town of Benton on the day of the hanging. Thousands of people jammed the streets, although only a few hundred of them actually had tickets to the execution. Birger climbed the steps of the scaffold with a bright smile on his face, laughing and joking with the officials. "It's a beautiful world," he grinned and those became the last words of the man who had become a larger-than-life part of Little Egypt. Six minutes later, Charlie Birger was dead.

As time has gone by, Little Egypt has greatly changed and gone are many of the old ways of the past. In some places, however, little has changed. Deep in some of the woods and hills, the customs, traditions and tales of the past are not yet forgotten. And of the region's entire myriad of tales, stories of the supernatural seem to be more common than any other. While many of the stories fall firmly into the realm of the folk legend, there are plenty of stories to give the reader a good case of the goosebumps.... all from a weird and mysterious place called "Little Egypt".

THE OLD SLAVE HOUSE

High on a windswept rise in Little Egypt is one of the region's most haunted spots. It is a place called Hickory Hill and over the years, it has been many things from plantation house to tourist attraction to chamber of horrors for the men and women once brought here in chains. Thanks to this dark blight on its history, Hickory Hill has long been known by its more familiar name, the "Old Slave House".

For decades, travelers have come from all over Illinois and beyond to see this mysterious and forbidding place. The secrets of slavery that were hidden here were given up many years ago, but there are other dark whispers about the place. These stories claim that the dead of Hickory Hill do not rest in peace.

Hickory Hill was built by a man named John Hart Crenshaw, a descendant of old American family with ties to the founding of our country. His grandfather, John Hart, was one of the signers of the Declaration of Independence and a tree that once shaded the lawn of Hickory Hill was carried as a seed from the gravesite of George Washington. Crenshaw himself has a notable spot in the history of Illinois, thanks to both his public and private deeds.

He was born in November 1797 in a house on the borders of North and South Carolina. His family moved west and settled in New Madrid, Missouri, only to have their home destroyed by the great earthquake of 1811. A short time later, they moved to Saline County, Illinois and started a farm on the east side of Eagle Mountain. There was a salt well on the farm called Half Moon Lick.

Not long after settling in Illinois, William Crenshaw died and left his eldest son, John, to provide for his mother and six brothers and sisters. By the time he was 18, he was already toiling in the crude salt refinery at Half Moon Lick.

Today, it is hard for us to understand the demand that existed for salt in times past. In those days, salt was often used as money or as barter material when purchasing goods and supplies. In the early 1800's, there was great need for salt, thanks to the westward movement into the frontier. It could be used for both flavoring and as a preservative for meat.

Hickory Hill in Southern Illinois

Early on, a large salt reservation was discovered in southern Illinois and the land began to be leased out by the government in 1812. Individual operators rented tracts of land and hired laborers to work them. The work in these salt mines was brutal and in many cases, black men who would work cheaply were hired in from the region. Many of them had escaped from slavery in the south, limiting them in the job market, but even free blacks from Illinois had a hard time finding other work. As these men made little money, and few had homes of their own, the mine operators constructed a small village called "US Salines", where the blacks could live. In 1827, the town became Equality, Illinois.

In 1829, the government decided to sell off the salt lands to raise money for a new prison and other state improvements in Illinois. The individual operators were given the opportunity to purchase their holdings and one man who did so was John Hart Crenshaw. He made a number of such purchases over the years and eventually owned several thousand acres of land. At that time, he also owned a sawmill and three salt furnaces for processing.

Eventually, Crenshaw would become an important man in southern Illinois. In 1817, he had married Sinia Taylor and began developing wide-reaching business interests that would allow him to amass quite a fortune. In fact, at one point he made so much money that he paid one-seventh of all of the taxes collected in the state. He would become known as not only a salt operator but also as a toll bridge owner, farmer, land speculator, railroad builder, state bank director for a bank in Shawneetown, a supporter for the Methodist Church and as an important figure in the Gallatin County Democratic party.

Despite all of these accomplishments, Crenshaw is best remembered today for Hickory Hill and his ties to Illinois slavery, kidnapping and illegal trafficking in slaves. But how is this possible in Illinois, a state where slavery was not allowed?

In the early years of the state's history, Illinois was far from a "northern" state. Cairo, Illinois lies geographically further south than Richmond, Virginia and many of the settlers, especially in Little Egypt, came from southern states. They brought with them their customs and traditions, including slavery.

Illinois was technically a free state, although it did recognize three types of slavery. The slaves, and their descendants, of the French settlers along the Mississippi were protected under the Treaty of 1783. The state also allowed indentured servitude for a contracted length of time and it also allowed slaves to be leased for one-year terms in the salt lands of Gallatin, Hardin and Saline counties.

Workers were always needed for the salt mines. They worked the salt wells and cut trees and hauled wood for the fires that boiled the salt water in thirty or more cast-iron kettles. After boiling, the salt was loaded into wooden barrels, which were also made at the site. A fifty-pound bushel of salt was made from as much as three hundred gallons of spring water and a daily yield ran from eighty to one hundred bushels each day. The salt was then hauled by oxen to Shawneetown, where it was loaded onto keelboats. The work was backbreaking, hot and brutal and attracted only the most desperate workers. Because of this, slavery became essential to the success of the salt operations. A provision for it to continue here was written into the 1818 Illinois Constitution, allowing the mine owners to lease slaves from Kentucky and Tennessee.

As imagined, the slaves had no protection under the law and free blacks had very little. There were a number of laws concerning slavery in Illinois. In the early days, it was discouraged but actually stopped short of being illegal. The 1819 Illinois Slave Code gave only minimum protection to free blacks. A certificate of freedom and a description of every member of the family had to be placed on file at the county clerk's office to keep them from being harassed as slaves. Regardless, the word of a black man could not be taken as testimony in court and if a man was deemed as "lazy" or "disobedient" he could be publicly whipped. The Slave Code also regulated whites in that a fine could be levied against any white man who hired a black person without a certificate of freedom. Whites could also be fined and whipped if they provided any sort of assistance to a runaway slave, or brought a slave into Illinois for the purpose of allowing them freedom.

While the law did provide some small protection for free blacks living in Illinois, it did nothing to discourage the common practice of kidnapping them and selling them into slavery. Only civil prosecution was used to punish this practice and few officials ever interfered with the gangs of men who seized blacks in river towns and carried them down south for sale at auction.

Perhaps the most guilty of this practice were the "night riders" of the 1830's and 1840's. Originally, groups like this were formed when local residents felt that organized law had failed them. A case in point would be the formation of a vigilante gang called the "Regulators" around 1831. This group of citizens banded together in Pope and Massac Counties to fight back against the illegal activities of the "Flatheads", a loose-knit criminal organization that lived in the river bottoms and engaged in cattle stealing and murder. The local folks could find no officials to stand up to them, so they organized and went to war. After heated battles, they lynched several of the leaders, but then the counties were plunged into anarchy and the militia had to be called in to restore order. The Regulators themselves were not always on the right side of the law either and many blamed them for thievery, violence and corruption. In the 1840's, some of these bands were connected to the kidnapping of free blacks.

The night riders were alleged to always be on the lookout for escaped slaves and they posted men along the Ohio River at night. The slaves were then captured and could be ransomed back to their masters or returned for a reward. They also kidnapped free men, and their children, and sold them in the south. The night riders created a "reverse underground railroad", where slaves were spirited away to the southern plantations instead of to the northern cities and freedom.

Egyptian tradition has it that John Hart Crenshaw, who leased slaves to work the salt mines, kept a number of night riders in his employ to watch for escaped slaves. He used this as a profitable sideline to his legitimate businesses. By law, Crenshaw's men could capture the runaway slaves and turn them into a local law officer for a reward. If no reward had been offered for the runaway, the county paid a flat $10 fee. In addition to the fee, Crenshaw could then lease the slave from the county at a lower rate. However, many believe that Crenshaw had little interest in rewards and leases. He learned that he could make much more money by simply working the captured slaves himself or by selling them directly back into the southern market. While there exists no written evidence that Crenshaw was involved in illegally holding slaves, it has long been believed that he was.

Crenshaw was seen as a respected businessman and a pillar of the church and community. No one had any idea that he was holding illegal slaves or that he was suspected of kidnapping black families and selling them into slavery. They would have been even more surprised to learn that the slaves were being held captive in his home. In the third floor attic of Hickory Hill, barred chambers kept the men and women captive. The men were often subjected to cruelty and the women to the "breeding chamber". It was here, the stories say, the women and girls met a slave called "Uncle Bob". He was a giant of a man who had been chosen as a stud slave because of his intelligence and physical size. He had been selected to breed better and stronger slaves and make more money for Crenshaw at auction. A pregnant slave on the southern market was worth nearly twice as much as a female with no child. Crenshaw was believed to have sold as slaves any workers that were in excess of what he needed on his farms and in the salt mines. The practice turned a handsome profit and kept him supplied with workers.

According to "Uncle Bob", or Robert Wilson as he came to be called, he sired no less than three hundred children in a span of ten years at Hickory Hill. Historians have more than forty affidavits from people who met and talked with Wilson about his life in service to Crenshaw. After leaving southern Illinois, Wilson served in the Confederate Army during the Civil War. He lived to be 112 years old and died in the Elgin Veteran's Hospital in 1949.

Hickory Hill, the classic Greek plantation house, still stands today. It is located near the town of Equality, a short distance from Harrisburg. The border of Kentucky, where Crenshaw stationed his "slave catchers" on the river at night, is just a short horseback ride away.

Crenshaw contracted an architect to begin on the house in 1833, but thanks to his lengthy attempt to get a spur line of the Shawneetown and Alton Railroad run into Equality, he had little time to spend on the new project. Hickory Hill did not end up getting completed until 1842. It stands on a high hill, overlooking the Saline River. The structure was built in the Classic Greek style of the time period and rises three stories. Huge columns, cut from the hearts of individual pine trees, span the front of the house and support wide verandahs. On the porch is a main entrance door and above it, on the upper verandah, is another door that opens onto the balcony. Here, Crenshaw could look out over his vast holdings. He furnished the interior of the house with original artwork and designs that had been imported from Europe. Each of the rooms, and there were thirteen on the first and second floors, were heated with separate fireplaces.

The house was certainly grand, but the most unusual additions to the place were not easily seen. Legend had it that there was once a tunnel that connected the basement to the Saline River, where slaves could be loaded and unloaded at night. In addition, another passageway, which was large enough to contain a wagon, was built into the rear of the house. It allowed the vehicles to actually enter into the house and, according to the stories, allowed slaves to be unloaded where they could not be seen from the outside. The back of the house is still marked by this carriage entrance today.

Located on the third floor of Hickory Hill are the infamous confines of the attic and proof that Crenshaw had something unusual in mind when he contracted the house to be built. The attic can still be reached today by a flight of narrow, well-worn stairs. They exit into a wide hallway and there are about a dozen cell-like rooms with barred windows and flat, wooden bunks facing the corridor. Originally, the cells were even smaller, and there were more of them, but some were removed in the past. One can only imagine how small and cramped they must have been because even an average-sized visitor to the attic can scarcely turn around in the ones that remain. The only cell that is really bigger than the rest is one that is designated as "Uncle Bob's Room", but even this chamber only measures nine by twelve feet. The corridor between the cells extends from one end of the room to the other. Windows at the ends provided the only ventilation and during the summer months, the heat in the attic was unbearable. The windows also provided the only source of light.

The slaves spent their time secured in their cells, chained to heavy metal rings. There are still scars on the wooden walls and floors today and chains and heavy balls are still kept on display. There are also two frames that are said to have been "whipping posts" located in the attic. It was said that the slaves were often flogged for disobeying orders are failing to complete their work. It was written that the whipping posts were "built of heavy timber pegged together. A man of average height could be strung up by his wrists and his toes would barely touch the lower cross-piece."

The infamous confines of the Hickory Hill Attic

Stories have long been told about the cruelties that Crenshaw inflicted on the slaves, from beatings to disfigurement. Owners of the house have told many of the stories but even worse are the stories passed on by descendants of the Crenshaw family. One relative recalled stories told by her grandmother about the family being forced to watch when the slaves were whipped. Other descendants swear that Crenshaw was unjustly accused of such crimes, while others in the family say that his actions went beyond inhumane and beyond the mere mistreatment of the slaves.

Earlier, it was mentioned that most local residents were unaware of Crenshaw's activities, but this was not the case with everyone. In the late 1820's, Crenshaw was actually indicted by a Gallatin County grand jury for kidnapping a free black family. A jury acquitted him of the charges and although it was later learned that the family had been sold to a plantation in Texas, Crenshaw could not be tried again for the same crime. He continued to maintain his standing in the community.

Ironically, in September 1840, Hickory Hill played host to a guest who would someday achieve fame not only as an American president, but also as the man who emancipated the southern slaves. His name was Abraham Lincoln and according to tradition, he spent the night in the southeast bedroom of the house. At that time, Lincoln was in Gallatin County for a series of debates held in Equality and Shawneetown. Lincoln then attended a party at Hickory Hill in honor of the politicians. Following the customs of the time, Lincoln spent the night at the house along with several other guests. Whether or not he ever learned the secrets of the house's attic is unknown.

In 1842, Crenshaw was once again indicted on criminal charges. It was reported that he had engineered the kidnapping of a free black woman named Maria Adams and her children. According to the "Illinois Republican" newspaper in Shawneetown, Crenshaw had the family abducted from their home and kept them hidden for several days. They were then tied up in a wagon and were driven out of state. Unfortunately though, the prosecutor in the case knew more than he could prove and Crenshaw was again set free.

Soon, rumors began to spread about Crenshaw's business activities. Around the same time, a newspaper account publicly declared that a nephew of Crenshaw was accusing him of cheating him out of his father's estate. These rumors and rumblings, combined with the Adams indictment, started to upset a lot of people in the area. On March 25, 1842, a steam mill that Crenshaw owned in Cypressville was burned to the ground. According to the "Sangamo Journal" newspaper, the burning of the mill touched off several events in the region:

"The steam mill of Mr. John Crenshaw, in Gallatin County, was burnt. It appears... that a short time previous, he sold a family of Negroes, on whose services he had claims, to a trader, and that these Negroes were shipped to the lower country, probably to be sold into perpetual slavery. By some it was believed that the mill was burnt by Negroes in revenge for this act... Great excitement followed and a band of "Regulators" had been raised with the design of driving all free Negroes out of Gallatin County..."

The mill was burned just two days before Crenshaw's trial began in the Adams case and although no one was killed in the blaze, two of the workers were injured and badly burned. The fire was believed to have been started by a group of free black men, angry over Crenshaw's actions.

On April 2, after Crenshaw's acquittal, a group of night riders rode into Equality and began firing their guns into the air. They announced that they planned to return and lynch all of the blacks who had attacked John Crenshaw. After that, they declared that they would remove every black person from Gallatin County. All of the law enforcement officials, including attorneys, were warned not to interfere or they would be killed. The riders promised to return the following week as they rode out of town. True to their word, they returned the next Saturday, again brandishing weapons. They made more threats but the promises of death and violence were left unfulfilled. The incidents ended with no one harmed.

In 1846, Crenshaw's business holdings began to decline. In addition to several civil court actions against him, salt deposits were discovered in both Virginia and Ohio that proved to be more profitable than those in southern Illinois were. To make matters worse, Crenshaw was also attacked by one of his slaves, resulting in the loss of one leg. The stories maintain that he was beating a woman in his fields one day when an angry slave picked up an ax and severed Crenshaw's leg with it. After that, most of the slaves were sold off and his operations dwindled with the end of the salt mining.

During the Civil War, Crenshaw sold Hickory Hill and moved to a new farmhouse closer to Equality. He continued farming but also diversified into lumber, railroads and banks. He died on December 4, 1871 and was buried in Hickory Hill Cemetery, a lonely piece of ground just northeast of his former home.

Whether John Crenshaw rests in peace is unknown, but according to the tales of Little Egypt, many of his former captives most certainly do not. According to the accounts, "mysterious voices can be heard in that attic, sometimes moaning, sometimes singing the spirituals that comfort heavy hearts".

And those accounts, as the reader will soon learn, are just the beginning.

I have visited the Old Slave House more than a dozen times. The attic of the house, I believe, is still quite disturbing today. There has never been a time when I have climbed that old staircase to the third floor that I have not felt my heart clench a little. The remains of the slave quarters are often hot and cramped and at other times, are filled with mysterious chills that no one seems quite able to explain. I have yet to encounter one of the ghosts of Hickory Hill, but others have not been so lucky, leading me to believe that something lingers there. Could the tormented souls of the slaves still linger in the attic?

I have spoken with George Sisk, the last private owner of the house, on many occasions. I once asked him if he believed in ghosts and whether he thought there were any at Hickory Hill. "The house is haunted," he insisted, " I don't believe in ghosts but I respect them." This curious statement of non-belief was followed by the fact that he never goes into the attic of the place unless he has to. On those occasions, he never stays for long and, if no one else is in the house, the door to the attic is always kept locked.

Is the house haunted? Based on the stories, most likely it is, but despite what some people have claimed, the Sisk family did not create the ghost stories of Hickory Hill. That distinction belongs to the scores of visitors who have come to the house over the years and who have encountered something there that is beyond the ordinary. The house has been in the Sisk family since 1906, when George's grandfather purchased it from a descendant of John Hart Crenshaw. It was already a notorious place in the local area, but it would soon become even more widely known.

To locals, the house was known more as the "Old Slave House" than as Hickory Hill, thanks to the stories surrounding the place. In the 1920's, the Sisk's began to have visitors from outside the area. They would come to the door at just about any hour and request a tour of the place, having heard about it from a local waitress or gas station attendant as they were passing through. This time period marked the early era of automobile vacations in America. As motor cars began to be more affordable to families, they began to travel, especially in the summer months. The Old Slave House, thanks to a savvy advertising campaign, became a destination point for many travelers and tourists were so numerous that the owners began charging an admission in 1930. For just a dime, or a nickel if you were a child, you could tour the place where "Slavery Existed in Illinois", as the road signs put it.

Soon, Hickory Hill was one of the most frequently visited places in Little Egypt. And soon, it would gain a reputation for being the most haunted one!

Shortly after the house became a tourist attraction, visitors began reporting that strange things were happening in the place. They complained of odd noises in the attic especially, noises that sounds like cries, whimpers and even the rattling of chains. A number of people told of uncomfortable feelings in the slave quarters like sensations of intense fear, sadness and of being watched. Cold chills filled a number of the tales, along with being touched by invisible hands and feeling unseen figures brush by them. Soon, the stories spread that the Old Slave House was haunted!

Some have argued that the house could not be haunted because no records exist to say that anyone ever died there. Perhaps slaves did die in the house and it was not recorded but regardless, most experts believe that death may not be the only thing that causes ghosts to stay behind. Some feel the great trauma and horrific events that took place in the attic may have caused the spirits of the slaves to return to the house after death. Or perhaps the gruesome past replays itself in the place, causing impressions of days gone by to remain in the atmosphere.

The rumored hauntings had little effect on tourist traffic and if anything, the stories brought more people to the house. Other legends soon began to attach themselves to Hickory Hill. The most famous is the story that "no one could spend the entire night in the attic". The story got started because of an incident involving a "ghost chaser" from Benton, Illinois named Hickman Whittington. The Benton newspaper, the "Post-Dispatch", noted in a late 1920's edition that "whether ghost chaser Hickman Whittington expects to see a white or black ghost remains to be seen. He said he recently learned that cries have been heard coming from the post where slaves were whipped for disobedience, and he intended to do something about it."

George Sisk told authors Richard Winer and Nancy Osborn Ishmael that whatever happened to Whittington after coming to the house that night scared the life right out of him. He told them that "when he visited the place he was in fine health but just after he left here, he took sick and he died just hours after his visit... you might say that something scared him to death."

Winer asked him what he thought that "something" might have been, but Sisk had no answer. "I wouldn't want to be the one to say," he told them, "but it could have been the same thing that scared those two Marines that tried to stay in the attic overnight in 1966. They had the good sense to leave before anything disastrous happened... they came flying down the stairs at about one-thirty in the morning. Said they saw forms coming at them. They were in a state of shock. I really didn't get to talk to them very long. They tore out of here in a hurry... didn't even bother to go back upstairs to get their belongings."

What had they seen? The two Marines, who had both seen action in Vietnam, volunteered to spend the night in the attic. They were certainly not the first to attempt such a thing either. After the incident involving Hickman Whittington and the story that no one could make it through the night, literally dozens had tried. None of them had been successful, but the two veterans were sure they would be the first. Each of them scoffed when they were told that others had fled the house in terror and after several hours in the attic, they began to get bored. Finally, just as they were about to go to sleep, their kerosene lantern began to flicker. There were no drafts but the light began to get dimmer and dimmer. Then, an agonized moan filled the air, seeming to come from all around them. The moaning was followed by other voices and then, just before the lantern blew itself out, the Marines claimed to see "swirling forms" coming out of the shadows. Terrified, they fled the attic and never returned.

Other would-be thrill seekers followed the Marines, but for one reason or another, no one managed to make it until daybreak in the attic of Hickory Hill. Eventually, the practice was ended because, as Mr. Sisk informed me later, a small fire got started one night by an overturned lantern. After that, he turned down requests for late night ghost hunting.

He only relented on one other occasion. In 1978, he allowed a reporter from Harrisburg named David Rodgers to spend the night in the attic as a Halloween stunt for a local television station. The reporter managed to beat out nearly 150 previous challengers and became the first person to spend the night in the slave quarters in more than a century. Sisk never believed that he would make it through the night and in fact announced that he would flee the house before one in the morning. "Other reporters before Rodgers had tried to stay the night, but none of them made it. They all said they heard shuffling feet and whimpering cries in the slave quarters at night," he told newspapers.

Rodgers later admitted that he was "queasy" going into the house and also said that his experience in the attic was anything but mundane. "I heard a lot of strange noises," he said the next morning. " I was actually shaking. The place is so spooky. The tape recorder was picking up sounds that I wasn't hearing." He felt pretty good about himself afterward, but confessed that he "didn't want to make the venture an annual event".

Stories from visitors and curiosity seekers have continued to be told over the years. One incident was even witnessed by George Sisk. A woman came down from the attic one day and asked about the peculiar things going on up there. He and his wife followed the woman back to the attic and she showed them how, in certain locations, all of the hair on her arms would stand on end. She demanded to know why it was happening, but of course, no one could tell her.

I have since spoken with others who have had similar experiences and with other witnesses who claim to have been touched and poked by fingers and who have heard the now famous voices and mumbling snatches of song that have long been reported on the third floor. The whispers and sounds are certainly unsettling, but more so are the encounters reported by those who have seen the ghosts here face to face!

One such person was a college professor named David Anderson*, who visited Hickory Hill around 1977. He was passing through the area on his way to Chicago, where he still teaches at a well-known university, and decided to see the place. There were no other visitors at the house that day, so he took his time wandering through it. The only place where he did not spend much time was the attic because "I was sure that someone was there," he told me. "I was constantly turning around to see who was behind me, but there was never anyone there."

Finally, unnerved, he left the house and walked out to his car. It was parked in the gravel drive out front and when he reached it, he glanced back towards the high window of the attic. His previous feelings of discomfort became cold needles of fear. There was a face looking out the window at him, even though no one else had been in the house! "I returned back inside and asked the owner if anyone else had come inside while I was there. He said that no one had."

Anderson laughed uneasily as he related the story to me, more than twenty years later. "I have no explanation for what happened. I never believed in ghosts before that, and while I'm still not sure that I do, I just have no explanation for what I saw in that window."

For most visitors though, a visit to Hickory Hill is not so bizarre. Many experience nothing, while others say they feel unsettled or frightened in the attic. Often, emotions become very overwrought here and grown men have often been reduced to tears. Proof of the supernatural? Perhaps not, but the attic is certainly an odd place with a lot of odd energy.

The Sisk's have also had their share of weird experiences at Hickory Hill over the years. Mr. Sisk has always maintained that he has never encountered any of the ghosts, but his wife can't say the same. She has talked about her experiences in the past. "The sounds here bother me a lot. I can make excuses for some of them... I tell myself that it's the wind but one night when we were lying in bed, I heard a loud crashing like glass breaking. Thinking that a window had broken, we got up to investigate. There was nothing broken... Another sound that shook me up tremendously happened one night when I was lying in bed. There was a sound like something, or someone, banging from under the floor with a hammer. I clearly heard it three times, but what it was, I don't know."

She also said that she never takes baths in the evenings anymore, but only in the morning or when her husband is home. The bathroom in the residence area of the house was located in the rear part of the building. She often heard the sound of someone calling her name when she took baths in the house alone. Mrs. Sisk eventually stopped trying to discover a source for the strange sounds and simply states that "I know now that there is something here."

Ever since the days of Hickman Whittington, the Old Slave House has been a frequent stopping place for ghost hunters, psychic investigators and supernatural enthusiasts. Sisk keeps a number of books and clippings related to some of these visits and has been interviewed (by myself and others) many times about the ghostly happenings here. Most of the ghost hunters, many of who are historians at heart, come to the house looking for ghosts and hoping to soak up some of the rich history of the place. Others however show up with offers of "exorcisms". One couple even claimed that if they were not allowed to perform their ceremony, a negative energy would enter the bodies of the Sisk family and possess them.

The Sisk's declined the offer. "We decided that whatever's upstairs can stay there... I believe in leaving things like that alone."

In 1996, the Old Slave House was closed down, due to the declining health of Mr. and Mrs. Sisk. Although it looked as though the house might never re-open, it was finally purchased by the state of Illinois just over three years later. Plans are in the works (as of this writing) to open the house again in the future as a state historic site. What will become of the ghosts, or at least the ghost stories, is unknown. As many readers know, legends and lore don't often fare well at official state locations.

Regardless, if should get the chance, mark Hickory Hill as a historical and haunted place to visit. If you climb those stairs to the attic, you will feel your stomach drop just a little and you might even be overwhelmed by sadness.

Is it your imagination or does the tragedy of the house still make itself felt here? I can't say for sure, but I can guarantee that you will find yourself speaking softly in the gloomy, third floor corridor as your voice lowers in deference to the nameless people who once suffered here. We must remember this part of the past, no matter how difficult this may be, because he who does not remember the past is doomed to repeat it.

THE GHOST OF LAKEY'S CREEK

Located in southern Illinois is the small town of McLeansboro. For nearly 150 years, a headless rider has been seen haunting a concrete bridge that spans the murky waters of Lakey's Creek. While the identity of this spectral rider has long been known in the area, only a few people are aware of why this phantom still rides.

The creek that is spanned by the bridge was named after an early settler to this community and his name was "Lakey". After settling here, he began building a small cabin near the creek, just off of a main road that connected Mt. Vernon to Carmi. Perhaps he also planned to open a small business to cater to the needs of travelers along what was then a busy roadway, but we will never know. Lakey made quick work of the cabin, although he often could be found stopping his work and chatting with travelers and neighbors who passed by. This was what he was reported doing on the last evening that he was seen alive. A few neighbors later recalled riding by and stopping to talk with Lakey, who had completed the walls of his home and was now cutting clapboards for the roof.

The next morning, a neighbor from the settlement stopped to drop off some extra eggs for Lakey. He knew that his friend planned to purchase some laying hens soon, but with the cabin nearly completed, there had simply not been time. He called out to Lakey but receiving no answer, he looked around the back of the house. He found a gruesome sight! Rounding the back of the house, he discovered Lakey's bloody and headless body beside a tree stump. His head had rolled a few feet away and now lay propped against the murder weapon, Lakey's own ax!

The news of the horror quickly spread and settlers came to examine the scene. The local sheriff was dispatched but he was as befuddled as everyone else was. Lakey had been a friendly man, with no known enemies and no hidden wealth to speak of. There was also nothing to suggest that Lakey had struggled with anyone. Why someone might kill him, and in such a terrible manner, was a mystery. The killer (or killers), whoever it might have been, was never found. Lakey was buried next to his unfinished cabin, but he would not stay in his grave for long!

One night, a short time after Lakey's somber funeral, two men who lived on the west side of McLeansboro were walking near the cabin. Suddenly, they spotted a headless figure on a large, black horse. The specter appeared alongside the creek and followed along with them as they walked. Neither of them men spoke, as they were too afraid to say anything, and the rider was also silent. The only sound came from the muffled hooves and the occasional snort of the black horse. The rider seemed to be aware of them though and kept pace with them as they passed. As the men headed down into the shallow crossing of the stream, the rider turned also. They waded out into the middle of the creek and as they did, the horseman turned left, passed downstream and then inexplicably vanished into a deep pool near the river crossing.

The two men hurried home, happy to see that the ghostly rider had disappeared. They hesitated to tell anyone what they had seen, but it didn't matter. Soon, other locals were seeing the rider too. Two nights later, a small group of travelers from the western side of the state also spotted the rider and told others about it. The horseman began to be seen on a regular basis, giving birth to an eerie legend. The story was told over and over again as traveler after traveler encountered the spirit. Locals believed the ghost was that of Lakey himself, searching for the man who killed him. They said that his ghost followed the travelers until he could be sure that they were not the people he was looking for.

The rider, always reportedly headless and always riding the black horse, would join travelers as they approached the river crossing from the east, always on the downstream side. Each time, as they reached the center of the creek, the rider would turn and then vanish. As time passed, the river crossing was replaced with a bridge and the story changed to say that the rider now appeared on the river bank, would cross the bridge to the center of the river and then vanish.

Many years have passed since then and the legend of Lakey's ghost is largely forgotten. Perhaps the pace of modern life has rendered the ghost and his phantom steed somewhat obsolete? Despite the fact that it is seldom told, the story has never been completely lost, leading some to speculate that perhaps Lakey is still out there. Perhaps he still seeks the justice, or the vengeance, that he never found.

Do travelers still encounter the ghost as they cross the old bridge over Lakey's Creek? Perhaps not in the way that they used to, but many area residents will assure you that both Lakey and his legend live on. Some still say that it is not uncommon for people walking near the bridge to hear odd sounds coming from the roadway. They claim these sounds are the clip-clop of horse's hooves on the pavement but that the horse that walks there is never seen. Could it be Lakey out on a midnight ride?

MYSTERY MONSTERS OF LITTLE EGYPT

The vast reaches of forest and open fields of southern Illinois, combined with the sparse population in some areas, seem to invite weirdness that might not occur in cities and more crowded locales. In the most southern portions of the region, the Shawnee National Forest covers miles and miles of territory. The acres of forest seem almost untouched by man and some believe that strange things occasionally pass through here, unseen by human eyes.

A friend of mine, who grew up in southern Illinois, had an uncle who worked for the forestry department of the Shawnee National Forest. The uncle had the peculiar habit of driving his work truck along the unpaved back roads of the forest in the very early hours of the morning. One day, my friend asked him why he did this and his reply was nearly as mysterious as the habit itself was. "You wouldn't believe the things that you see on those roads at night," he told his nephew and that was the last time that he would ever speak of his late-night forays.

This southern portion of the state is sometimes referred to as the "Devil's Kitchen", a designation that is very telling when it comes to the question of strange phenomena in Little Egypt. Many believe that the early explorers and the Native Americans left behind evidence of their beliefs in the unknown by the names that they gave to certain places. What we might refer to as "mystery" sites, became the first "haunted" places in America. They were spots where the explorers, settlers and the Indians witnessed strange sights and sounds like unexplained balls of light, apparitions, screams in the night and various other unsettling types of phenomena. The Native Americans often considered such sites as "sacred" but the settlers usually believed them to be "cursed", or at least well avoided.

The idea that such locations were linked to the "Devil" was the first thought that crossed the minds of the bible-reading, god-fearing folks and they promptly set about to do two things. They learned to avoid these strange and haunted places and secondly, they gave names to the spots to alert other visitors and settlers of the dangers of the area. Such places, they believed, were best shunned or at least entered with caution. Over the years, there have been many locations that bear a link between supernatural phenomena and a "Devil" name. In many of these places, strange things are prone to happen and spirits are sometimes seen. In the case of the Devil's Kitchen, just about anything is possible, from ghosts reports to mystery animals and weird monster sightings.

Perhaps strangest monster reports to ever take place in Illinois began in April 1973 in the small town of Enfield. This tiny community in southeastern Illinois became the scene of bizarre happenings for a short period of time and while the case has largely been forgotten today, it remains a part of the high strangeness of the region.

Henry McDaniel of Enfield almost became the first man to be arrested because of the Enfield Horror. White County Sheriff Roy Poshard Jr. threatened to lock McDaniel for telling folks about the weird events that took place at his home in April 1973, but McDaniel stuck by his story and his initial report would begin what became a nightmare for the small town. According to McDaniel, he was at home on the evening of April 25 when he heard a scratching on his door. When he opened it, he couldn't believe his eyes! "It had three legs on it," McDaniel swore, " as short body, two little short arms coming out of its breast area and two pink eyes as big as flashlights. It stood four and a half to five feet tall and was grayish-colored. It was trying to get into the house."

Needless to say, McDaniel was not letting it in and he quickly retrieved a pistol. He kicked open the door and opened fire. After his first shot, McDaniel knew that he had hit it. The creature "hissed like a wildcat" and scampered away, covering 75 feet in three jumps. It disappeared into the brush along a railroad embankment near the house.

McDaniel quickly called the police and Illinois state troopers who responded to the call found tracks "like those of a dog, except they had six toe pads." The tracks were measured and two of them were four inches across and the third was slightly smaller.

Investigators soon learned that a young boy, Greg Garrett, who lived just behind McDaniel, had been playing in his yard about a half-hour before. Suddenly, the creature had appeared and attacked him. Apparently though, it just stepped on his feet, but this was enough to tear the boy's tennis shoes to shreds. Greg had run into the house, crying hysterically.

On May 6, Henry McDaniel was awakened in the middle of the night by howling neighborhood dogs. He looked out his front door and saw the monster again. It was standing out near the railroad tracks. "I didn't shoot at it or anything," McDaniel reported. "It started on down the railroad track. It wasn't in a hurry or anything."

McDaniel's reports soon brought publicity to Enfield and prompted the threats from the county sheriff, but it was too late. Soon, hordes of curiosity-seekers, reporters and researchers descended on the town. Among the "monster hunters" were five young men who were arrested by Deputy Sheriff Jim Clark as "threats to public safety" and for hunting violations. This was after they had opened fire on a gray, hairy thing that they had seen in some underbrush on May 8. Two of the men thought they had hit it, but it sped off, moving faster than a man could.

One more credible witness to the monster was Rick Rainbow, who was then the news director of radio station WWKI in Kokomo, Indiana. He and three other persons spotted the monster near an abandoned house, just a short distance from McDaniel's place. They didn't get much of a look at it as it was running away from them, but they later described it as about five feet tall, gray and stooped over. Rainbow did manage to tape record its cry. The wailing was also heard by eminent researcher Loren Coleman, who also came to try and track down the creature. He also heard the sound while searching an area near the McDaniel home.

A short time later, the sightings ended as abruptly as they began. No explanation was ever given as to what this bizarre monster may have been, where it may have come from, or where it disappeared to. Some had surmised that perhaps it was connected to UFO activity that was also reported in the general area at the time... but we will never really know for sure!

In the summer of 1973, the town of Murphysboro in southwestern Illinois was the site of another bizarre series of monster sightings. The enigmatic creature, now recalled as the "Murphysboro Mud Monster" appeared without warning and then suddenly disappeared just two weeks later, seemingly without a trace. In its wake, the monster left a number of confused and frightened witnesses, baffled law enforcement officials and of course, an enduring legend.

The monster was first seen around midnight on June 25, 1973. A young couple, Randy Needham and Judy Johnson, were parked near a boat ramp into the Big Muddy River near Murphysboro when they heard a strange, roaring cry that shattered the stillness of the night. It came from the nearby woods and both of them looked up to see a huge shape lumbering toward them. Whatever it was, it continue to make the horrible sound and they later described the noise as "something not human".

According to their account, the monster was about seven feet tall and covered with a matted, whitish hair. The "fur" was streaked liberally with mud from the river. By the time the creature approached to within 20 feet of them, they quickly left the scene. They went directly to the Murphysboro police station.

A short time later, Officers Meryl Lindsay and Jimmie Nash returned to the area and surveyed the scene. Although skeptical, they were surprised to find that a number of footprints had been left in the mud. The footprints were "approximately 10-12 inches long and approximately three inches wide". At 2:00 AM, Nash, Lindsay, another officer named Bob Scott, and Randy Needham returned to the scene again. This time, they discovered more tracks and Lindsay left to go and get a camera. The others followed the new footprints, tracing their path along the river.

Suddenly, from the woods about 100 yards away, came the creature's terrifying scream. They didn't wait to see if they could spot the monster and instead, made a quick retreat for the patrol car. After waiting in the darkness for a little while, they got back out again and spent the rest of the night trying to track down a splashing sound they heard in the distance. Things quieted down after daylight, but the next night, the creature was back!

The first to see the monster this time was a four-year old boy named Christian Baril, who told his parents that he saw a "big white ghost in the yard". They didn't believe him, but when Randy Creath and Cheryl Ray saw an identical monster in a neighboring yard just ten minutes later, Christian's parents, and the police, quickly reconsidered the little boy's statement.

Randy and Cheryl spotted the monster at about 10:30 PM, while sitting on the back porch of the Ray house. They heard the sound of something moving in the woods near the river and then spotted the muddy, white creature staring at them with glowing pink eyes. Cheryl would insist that the eyes were actually glowing and were not reflecting light from some other source. They estimated that it weighed at least 350 pounds, stood seven feet tall, had a roundish head and long, ape-like arms. Cheryl turned on the porch light and Randy went for a closer look. The creature seemed unconcerned and finally ambled off into the woods. Investigators would later find a trail of broken tree branches and crushed undergrowth, along with a number of large footprints. They also noticed a strong odor left in the monster's wake, but it didn't last for very long.

The officers who arrived on the scene, Jimmie Nash and Ronald Manwaring, quickly summoned a local man named Jerry Nellis, who had a trained German Shepherd that was often used by the police department as an attack dog and to search buildings and track suspects. The dog immediately was sent in pursuit of the monster. He managed to track the creature through the woods and down a hill to a small pond. Eventually, the trees and undergrowth became too thick for the dog to continue and it was pulled off the track just moments after almost pulling its handler down a steep embankment. The officers began searching the area with flashlights and the dog began sniffing near the trees, hoping to pick up the scent again. He then set off toward an abandoned barn, but refused to go inside. In fact, the animal began shaking with fear and barking.

Nellis called the two officers over and they opened the barn and went inside. After a few moments, they realized that it was empty. The three men were puzzled. The dog had been trained to search buildings and Nellis could not explain why it had refused to enter the barn. A short time later, the search was called off for the night.

The Mud Monster was reported two more times that summer. On the night of July 4, traveling carnival workers stated that they spotted the creature looking at some Shetland ponies that were being used for the holiday celebration. Then, on July 7, Mrs. Nedra Green heard a screaming sound coming from a shed on her rural farm. She did not go out to investigate.

So what was the Murphysboro Mud Monster? Local authorities admitted that they didn't know. "A lot of things in life are unexplained," Police Chief Toby Berger admitted at the time, "and this is another one. We don't know what the creature is, but we do believe what these people saw was real."

According to the St. Louis "Post-Dispatch" newspaper, the Mud Monster emerged again as a possible culprit to an attack that allegedly occurred at the Rend Lake campground near Benton in August 1989. During the attack, gaping holes were left in a tent and animal blood was left behind at the scene. The attack was later determined to have been from dogs, but that didn't stop local residents from speculating about the Murphysboro Mud Monster again!

In the 1989 newspaper reports, Jerry Nellis, the dog handler in the original case stated his own theories on the famous case, which left he and the other witnesses to the events as "hunted" as the Mud Monster itself. Reporters and "monster hunters" came from everywhere asking questions about the case but Nellis maintained that "in my opinion ... we were tracking a bear."

But for the rest of Southern Illinois (the news story continued) and for every outdoorsman who has, as Nellis suggests, "seen something we can't make out just beyond the headlights," that original vision reported to police on June 25, 1973, is all we need to imagine.

THE THREE-MILE HOUSE

Even though it burned to the ground on a cold March morning in 1985, the historic Three Mile House has long been considered to have been one of the most haunted places in the Edwardsville, Illinois region. This historically haunted building was once located on Illinois 159 in the far northwestern corner of Little Egypt. Even though it has been gone for years, the stories about the place continue to be recalled today as new generations of ghost enthusiasts still get chills from retellings of the ghostly events that took place here.

The history of the Three Mile House began in 1858, when it was built by a St. Louis barber named Frederick Gaertner. It opened its doors along the St. Louis-Springfield stage road, at a time when this would have been main road through the region. The inn and tavern proved to be a popular roadside establishment. The first brick section of the Three Mile House was ready for business by 1860. The place had been built to primarily serve as a tavern or inn where travelers could eat, rest and spend the night. Those to whom the inn offered hospitality were mostly individuals traveling by horseback or buggy and most importantly, farmers and cattle drivers taking their stock to the markets in St. Louis.

The Three Mile House (Circa 1900)

Gaertner's business increased enough to justify enlarging the original building to include a dining room, kitchen, tavern, grocery store and post office on the first floor and between 10 and 15 sleeping rooms on the second. A large attic may have also served as to house guests.

Thanks to the thriving trade from travelers and the stagecoach line, a blacksmith shop was opened next door to the tavern in 1863. The two buildings served as a social and business center for the surrounding area for many years. Frederick Gaertner was well-known and liked throughout the area and became famous for his generous hospitality. He became friends with many of the upscale citizens of Edwardsville and threw lavish parties and receptions at the Three Mile House, drawing visitors from around the area. In addition to the friendships that he cultivated with members of local society and politicians, he also made many friends among the common people, farmers and cattlemen, who made up the largest part of his business. Because of this, the Three Mile House was known all over the region and became a destination point for travelers.

The inn remained prosperous for more than two decades, although things began to decline by the 1880's. By this time, the railroads had begun to make stagecoach travel, at least in the east, obsolete. The rail lines were also able to provide a more economical way to take cattle to market thereby eliminating the need to take the herds by an overland route to St. Louis. After a few seasons of declining trade, Gaertner decided to close the inn and he returned to his birthplace in Pittsburgh, Pennsylvania. When he passed away, the land, and the now abandoned tavern, was left to his son, Tony.

The Three Mile House stood empty for the next 25 years, slowly deteriorating, until Tony Gaertner sold it to an Illinois road contractor named Orrie Dunlap. Dunlap was in possession of some very lucrative contracts with the state to build and pave Route 112 (now Route 159). In order to more easily service the contracts, he wanted to find a building along the highway line that could be used as a headquarters for his construction crew. He discovered the empty Three Mile House and decided to buy and renovate the building for this purpose. Here, offices could be set up and his men could be fed and even quartered during the many months it would take for the road to be built.

After the highway was completed, several others leased the inn until Roy Mohrman of Collinsville bought the land outright. In the year priors to this, and during a period in which a succession of different owners claimed the property, the house was allegedly used for a variety of notorious purposes. The Three Mile House was said to have been used as a gambling house, a bordello, and a bootlegging operation during Prohibition. As all of these activities were obviously illegal, no records remain to say exactly who ran these operations and only rumor and legend exist to tell us what went on there during these lost years. The decades of the 1920's and 30's are lost but we do know that in the 1940's, the house operated as a roadside tavern.

In 1970, the Three Mile House was purchased by a real estate developer named Merrill Ottwein, who hoped to renovate the place and open it again for business. Rumor had it that Ottwein planned to turn the place into a nightclub, which upset local residents, but the developer consistently denied the story. According to Ottwein, he merely wanted to restore the historic site and open the place as a restaurant. Some time later, he did begin some of the work on the building, which had fallen into a state of disrepair. Much of the old plaster was stripped and two attic dormers were added. Some old photographs showed that the dormers had been present on the original structure. He also replaced many of the windows with modern glass.

Unfortunately though, Ottwein never had the time to devote to the project and the house was placed on the back-burner, where it remained for five years until it caught the attention of Doug and Beverly Elliot. They had noticed the building some time before and always expressed in interest in renovating the place and opening a restaurant.

As luck would have it, they were in the market for a new home and discovered the Three Mile House was for sale. At that time, it was still in pretty bad shape and it had been more than 12 years since anyone had lived in it. Still, the Elliot's felt drawn to the place and decided to buy it, having no idea how the house would change their lives.

The Elliot's oldest daughter, Lori, was the first to encounter anything unusual about the house. It happened on the day they were moving in. She was carrying a large box into the basement and was suddenly hit on the leg by a brick which, seemed to fly through the air by itself. She decided right then and there that whatever inhabited the house was going to have to put up with the new arrivals! She became the first member of the family to accept, and to literally make contact with, the spirits in the house. It would be some time later before the rest of the Elliot family came to the realization that they were not alone in the Three Mile House. By that time, there would be no way to deny it!

The family spent the next year carefully renovating the house. It was back-breaking work that would eventually pay off by getting the house listed in the National Register of Historic Places. They reinforced floors, put in first floor rest rooms, a scullery was added to the kitchen for dish washing, they installed modern plumbing and cleaned and repaired the place from top to bottom. During the work, they discovered the mysterious tunnels extending out from the basement. Apparently, other excavation work had been done in the tunnels in the past because the Elliot's discovered that some of the brick walls in the basement were hollow, leading to secret rooms. They also found names and dates carved into the old wooden beams. Doug Elliot later heard a story that a previous owner had found a skeleton between the walls in the 1930's. Stories had long circulated that the Three Mile House had once been a stop on the Underground Railroad. These new discoveries were believed to confirm this.

While the discoveries in the basement were strange, they weren't nearly as strange at the small balls and sparks of light which flickered about in the building each night or the fact the Elliot's younger daughter, Lynn, swore that dark shadows were chasing her about her room. There had to be a logical explanation for what was going on, but what was it?

At this point, only Lori suspected that the house might be haunted. So, one night she and some of her friends decided to conduct a seance in the attic. Believing that spirits were present, they planned to use a Ouija board to find out for sure. Not long after their impromptu seance began, eerie things began to occur. Loud banging sounds began to be heard on the third floor, along with tapping and rappings on the walls. The unexplainable noises continued for a long time and wouldn't stop, confirming for Lori that the place was inhabited, and possibly infested, by ghosts.

The weird events continued and soon, the balls of energy, strange sounds and weird tapping and knocking noises became everyday events to the Elliot's and they got used to them. Slowly, they were beginning to accept the idea that the Three Mile House might be haunted after all. They could learn to live with the inexplicable little events, they thought, it was just a part of life in the old house. However, as opening day for the new restaurant approached, they started to wonder if the customers would be so forgiving? Would they scare the business away? Would the new restaurant fail before it even got a chance to get started?

On opening night, in the spring of 1976, Bev Elliot's worst fears seemed to be coming true! The first evening, a little while before the customers arrived, the heavy dining room chairs began sliding away from the tables and rocking back and forth. Each time a chair was replaced and the staff member turned her back, the same chair (or another one) would mysteriously rumble away from the table again! Then, dishes began rattling in the china cabinet, vibrating as if they were about to fly across the room. But, as soon as the first guests arrived, the activity suddenly stopped and the house remained quiet for the rest of the evening.

At first, the spirits only seemed to perform for the Elliot family, but then odd things started to happen around the restaurant workers as well. One of the cooks claimed to see a misty-looking man in an Irish derby, who appeared at the top of the stairs. Another waitress saw a face in a mirror (that wasn't hers) and others saw candles lifted off tables under their own power. Another cook reported seeing a tray filled with coffee mugs hovering about a foot above a table. Water taps were also turned on and off, stove knobs were twisted, and even the piano played by itself.

A former employee who I spoke with told me of many nights when she would feel the tug of an invisible hand on the back of her shirt. Each time she turned around, she would find no one there. Apparently, this was a regular occurrence, along with dishes which would move about from place to place; water glasses that would suddenly empty their contents onto the floor; and napkins which would somehow fold and unfold with no one around to assist them.

After about the year, the ghosts began to perform other tricks and started entertaining the customers as well. While many of them were fascinated and intrigued by the bizarre events, others were not amused. Tables jumped and hopped across the floor, dishes were reported to levitate and on occasion, customers had to keep scooting their chairs forward just to keep up with their food!

One past customer of the restaurant explained to me that he was having dinner one night and the table kept sliding away from him as he tried to eat. He kept moving his chair forward, thinking that he must have inadvertently moved backward on the wooden floor. Then he finally realized that his table was almost directly on top of the table next to him! Needless to say, the nearby diners were almost as surprised as he was!

In October 1977, Doug Elliot got his first really good scare in the house. The Elliot's had an apartment on the second floor of the building and he woke up one night and realized that something was not right in the bedroom. He looked down to the end of the bed and saw the hulking figure of a massive, black man, well over six feet tall, who was wearing rough gray work clothes. He was terrified to think that a burglar had broken into the house, so terrified that he was unable to even call out! Elliot waited for the man to do something and then he did, he turned and walked out of the room. Still shaken, he found his gun and searched the entire house. He found no one there and discovered that nothing had been disturbed. The whole house was dark, silent and empty and all of the doors and windows were locked and secured. Doug fell asleep with his gun in his lap.

When his wife awakened him the next morning, he was still shaking and unnerved. He told her about the prowler and when they told their daughters, they were in for quite a surprise. Lori explained to them that the man her father had seen was "Herman", a ghost that she was very familiar with and who inhabited the house. He was completely harmless and may have simply been checking in our parents or trying to communicate with them. She also explained that after Doug's reaction to him, Herman was now frightened of her father!

After the restaurant had been open awhile, newspapers in the area began giving them good reviews and they later won several awards. However, with every article written also came mention of the ghosts. The stories helped business and put the Elliot's into contact with psychics and ghost hunters from around the country, many of who traveled to the Three Mile House. Among them were Chris Mitchum, the son of actor Robert Mitchum and Cyril Clemens, the cousin of author Mark Twain.

In 1977, several members of the cast of the movie "Stingray", which was filmed in the area, decided to hold a seance in the house. They wanted to try and get in touch with Herman, the ghost of the black man who had so frightened Doug Elliot. According to psychics, Herman was the unofficial leader of the ghosts in the house.

What they learned was that the spirit's name was actually Tom and that he had been an escaped slave who had come to the Three Mile House along the Underground Railroad line. In fleeing from the south, he had accidentally killed a white woman. A group of men somehow managed to track him down and had brutally murdered him. He was buried in one of the tunnels beneath the house but his spirit was not at rest. Tom had been a deeply religious man in life and as he had not received a proper Christian burial, his spirit was disturbed.

Doug Elliot was moved by this story and spent quite a bit of time looking for Tom's grave. There were just too many tunnels though and sadly, the grave was never found.

Psychics who came to the house told stories about the other ghosts too. One of the resident spirits was said to be a lady in black who had caught her fiancée with another woman. She had killed them both and then hanged herself in the attic. In the basement was said to be the ghost of a Civil War deserter who had also hanged himself, this time on one of the beams in the cellar. Interestingly, the beam was inscribed with markings which read... "died here..18.." The tunnels were also said to be haunted by the ghosts of slaves who had not survived their flight to freedom. Many of them were reportedly buried in the basement and their spirits had remained close by.

As time passed the ghosts remained a constant part of the business. Tom was perhaps the most active and playful of the spirits, leaving faucets running and flooding the kitchen and the bathrooms and generally being a nuisance. One day, an upset waitress informed Bev that she would not be able to work in the afternoons any more. When asked why, she stated that Tom had found a new toy, an antique coffee grinder. He had been amusing himself by turning it all day and the clanking noise that it made was driving the waitress crazy.

One Saturday afternoon, the Elliot's were in town on errands but Bev's mother was upstairs reading a book. There was no one else in the house with her... but she was certainly not alone! At some point that afternoon, a skillet in the kitchen caught fire. Her mother reported that a ribbon of white mist floated between her face and the book. She put the book down and watched as the mist floated past and then slide under the door. She blinked her eyes and imagined that she was seeing things, but the mist soon came again, this time fuller. She watched it disappear under the door, but this time, she followed it to the kitchen. She found the room was filled from smoke from the burning fry pan! If she had not found the pan, the house may have burned down.

But the ghosts were not always so helpful. They provided the restaurant with a lot of good press but the Elliot's had never been sure the haunting was well-received by the new and potential customers. It also seemed that problems with the restaurant had started to multiply. Despite a reputation for fine food, the restaurant began to see a slow-down, thanks to its rural location. It also seemed as though power bills had become astronomical, thanks to the fact that the large, old home was so hard to heat. Plus, operations costs for the restaurant continued to increase monthly.

To make matters worse, a frightening incident took place in 1980 when radio personality Jim White of KMOX in St. Louis asked to broadcast his popular Halloween show from the Three Mile House. The Elliot's agreed, with the condition that no Ouija boards were to be used and no seances take place for the show. Unfortunately, one of the guests either forgot about this stipulation, or ignored it, and brought a Ouija board along anyway.

According to the Elliot's, the result was chaos. A loud scream frightened everyone in the restaurant as a cook ran from the kitchen, claiming to be terrified by a green-faced, red-eyed monster that had appeared in their midst. Soon after, psychics worked to try and clear the house of this spirit. Eventually, they announced the malevolent ghost had been expelled and order was restored to the place. Even so, the incident left the Elliot's wondering if the continued cost and stress of running the restaurant was worth it.

Soon, they decided to put the place up for sale. Some believed the spirits had drained them of their energy, but the Elliot's dismissed this. The tension, pressure and exhaustion of running the business had just become too much for them, they said. Regardless, they were heartbroken when they left the house for the final time.

In 1982, the Three Mile House was sold to John Henkhaus, who also operated the house as a restaurant. He continued the renovation of the building and added a new kitchen and some additional plumbing. In an article dated from around the time he opened the place again, Henkhaus admitted that many people came to the house because of the hauntings. "People swear by it," he said. "Ninety percent of the people that come in here have stories of it being haunted. A lot of this is not documented, but it could very well be true. There's a lot of fact mixed with fiction."

Henkhaus, who also lived in the second-floor apartment, stated that he had not had any contact with the spirits but added that things seemed to disappear quite often. Many times they were from places people would not be able to steal from. He also said that the restaurant staff reported some pretty bizarre encounters, like the feeling of being tripped just before taking a fall. He also acknowledged the stories of Tom and his lack of a proper burial. He said that a number of clergymen and curiosity-seekers had come to the house, hoping to find where Tom was buried. Many holes were dug in and around the basement, but the burial site was never found.

A short time later, Henkhaus was also added to the list of previous owners of the Three Mile House. The building was then bought by Steve and Mitzi Ottwell, who owned the house at the time of the fire in 1985.

Today, all that remains of the Three Mile House is a large, grassy mound, a few scattered bricks and of course, an enduring reputation as the most haunted place in the area, a title that it will most likely hold for many, many years to come.

GHOSTS OF DUG HILL

There are a number of places in southern Illinois that have gained their ghostly reputations in years past, in times when the land was more primitive and untamed. These were times when modern conveniences and paved roads had not yet intruded on the landscape of Little Egypt. Such a place is Dug Hill. Many years ago, the road that cut through this hill was constructed so that settlers could pass from the Mississippi River to the interior regions. While it saw the frequent passing of many travelers, it was a still a secluded spot and one that was considered to be both dark and dangerous for those who used it.

Today, Dug Hill is located about five miles west of Jonesboro, Illinois on State Highway 126. Unfortunately, the more sinister aspects of the passage have vanished and the road is unrecognizable from the way that it once was. Because of this, the ghost stories of Dug Hill have been largely forgotten and few remember a time when it was one of the most haunted places in southern Illinois.

The stories vary as to how this area became so haunted. Most agree however, that it involved an incident that took place near the closing days of the Civil War. The murder that occurred is believed to have given birth to the accounts of later years. Although accounts of violence and robbery were common here, it was not until the bloody ambush of a provost marshal named Welch in April 1865 that ghosts appeared in the lore.

According to the legend, Welch arrested three deserters from the Union Army one day and turned them over to the authorities in Jonesboro. A day or so later, word reached Illinois that the war had ended with General Lee's surrender in Virginia, so the deserters were released. They remained angry over their treatment by Welch and were determined not to let things pass by easily with him.

Late that night, Welch was riding home and he passed through the cut alongside Dug Hill. He had no idea that the deserters were waiting for him there. They shot and killed him as he rode by and left his body lying in the road. Although Welch's body was found a short time later, no one was ever arrested for the crime and the mystery remained unsolved.

Soon after, travelers and local farmers began to report Welch's ghost on the old road. While some accounts stated that he was seen walking along the roadway in bloody clothing, imploring people to help him, his phantom was most commonly seen lying in the center of the dusty trail.

According to one account, a wagon driver was passing along Dug Hill road one evening when he saw the body of a man lying facedown in the center of the road. He stopped his horses and climbed down to see if he could help. When he leaned down to try and turn the man over, his hands passed right through him. The teamster tried again to lift the body and again, he only touched the dirt beneath it. Terrified, he ran back to his wagon. Cracking the whip, he drove the wagon forward and felt the distinct thump of the wheels passing over the spectral corpse! He looked back once and the body had vanished.

Apparently, Welch's ghost was not the only haunt of Dug Hill. Another legend involves a spectral wagon that was often seen passing along the roadway. In one account, a farmer was passing along the road one night, shortly after darkness had fallen. He was driving his team of horses, heading west, when the neck-yoke came off one of the animals, forcing him to stop and replace it.

He was off the wagon when he heard a terrible sound approaching from behind him. It was late December and the road had been frozen hard, leaving ruts and grooves that caused wooden wagons to rattle and shake as they passed over them. The sound that he heard coming was that of an old wagon, being driven hard and fast on the nearly impassable road. A chill ran down the farmer's spine. The wagon was coming toward him much too fast on the darkened road. There was little room to pass on the narrow trail and if the farmer could not warn the other driver, or get out of the way, they would both be killed! He looked back up the road and yelled as loudly as he could into the darkness. He hoped the other driver could hear him over the racket, but if he did, there was no sign of it. The wagon kept coming toward him, growing louder as it came closer.

The noise finally crested the hill and the farmer looked up as he realized that the sound was no longer coming from the road, but from right above his head! There, coming over the hill, was a large pair of black horses, pulling a heavy wagon with sideboards. There was a man driving them, cracking the reins, but the farmer couldn't make out his features. The hooves of the horses seemed to pound the air and the wheels of the wagon spun as if they were on the ground. The wagon rattled and rumbled as though passing over the uneven earth.

The eerie apparition soared over the farmer's head, struck the crest of the next hill and then kept going. The horrible sounds the wagon made echoed into the blackness until they finally faded away.

There is another tale from Dug Hill that is as strange as any in the region. It involves what most of us would consider a mythical creature that has its roots in the nightmares of children. Many refer to this monster as the "boogeyman" but to early residents of Little Egypt, it was simply the "booger". Some readers might wonder why this obviously legendary creature would appear in a book that purports to contain "real" ghost stories? Surely, such a monster has no place here. Or does it?

According to an account from many years ago, a man named Frank Corzine encountered a booger one night when he was riding over Dug Hill. The sun had just set on Corzine's journey but he was in a great rush to make it to the local doctor's house. Corzine's wife had been taken ill with cholera and he needed to doctor to come and see what he could do for her.

He turned his horse down a narrow trail and saw the figure of a man appear at the edge of the woods. Corzine described the figure as being between eight and ten feet tall and wearing a white shirt, black pants and a scarf that hung over his shoulders with both ends dangling in the front. When Corzine first spotted the man-like creature, it was about thirty feet away, but in an instant, it came to within inches of the rider.

Needless to say, Corzine was terrified by the mysterious figure and his heels dug sharply into the sides of his horse. The animal bolted and broke into a run, snapping a strap on the saddle in the process. Corzine later claimed that no matter how fast the horse ran though, the booger managed to keep pace with them.

They crossed the hill and Corzine rode straight to the doctor's house. By the time that Dr. Russell had appeared on the porch, the booger from the woods was gone. The doctor quickly realized that both the man and the horse were very frightened. Corzine was pale and trembling and the horse was shaking, snorting and stamping his feet on the dusty road. He also realized that he knew what the visitor had seen!

The doctor had also encountered the booger a few nights before, also at the same spot on the road. He questioned Corzine and found that his description of the creature matched Russell's exactly. Fearful, he refused to go to Corzine's house that night and insisted that he would only cross the hill in the daylight. He knew that the sick woman could not be left alone though, so he woke up eight men who lived nearby and told them to fetch their shotguns. The armed party escorted Corzine back over Dug Hill and to his house.

The monster didn't show itself again that night and as far as I know, that was the last time that anyone ever heard of the booger of Dug Hill. What could this strange creature have been? Was he real or merely folklore? I have no idea but he certainly made a lasting impression on the strange tales of Little Egypt.

THE PHANTOM FUNERAL PROCESSION

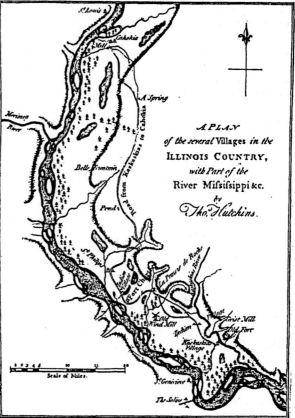

The first settlers in southern Illinois were the French. They established trading posts and settlements in places like Kaskaskia and Cahokia, near the Mississippi River. Not far from the present-day town of Prairie du Rocher, is the site of Illinois' earliest military post, Fort de Chartres.

There were several different forts that stood at this site, but the first was built around 1720. The area was beginning to be settled by this time and the French were laying claim to as much land as possible. The fort became an outfitting location for further colonization. It would also play several roles in regional history, including a part in a tragic event of 1736. In that year, the commander of the fort, Pierre d'Artaugette, received orders to attack the Chickasaw Indians. He led thirty regular soldiers, one hundred volunteers and a number of Indian allies downriver from Fort de Chartres. At the mouth of the Ohio River, the expedition was met by Chevalier Vincennes from the French post on the Wabash. He came with an additional twenty soldiers and a small contingent of Indians. The combined forces then marched into Chickasaw territory, only to face disaster.

Vincennes, d'Artaugette and a priest named Senat were all captured by the Chickasaw and held for ransom. When none came, all of the captives were slowly roasted at the stake.

In 1751, an Irish soldier of fortune named Richard MacCarty became commander of the French fort. The original fort had fallen into ruin by this time and it was his responsibility to construct a new one using slave labor and local limestone. The new fort took three years to build and cost over $1 million, an enormous expense at that time. When completed, the fort could house over four hundred soldiers and it enclosed an area of more than four acres. It also boasted a powder magazine, a storehouse, a prison with four dungeons, barracks, and quarters for officers. During the construction of the fort, the men stationed here would become involved in a series of incidents that would become the French and Indian War.

In 1753, a group of French explorers in Pennsylvania were attacked by a company of Virginia militia under the command of George Washington. In the fighting, the commander was killed, touching off what historians believe led to the war. Neyon de Villiers, the second in command at Fort de Chartres asked for and received permission from MacCarty to lead an expedition against the British in retaliation for the deaths of the French explorers. He took more than one hundred hand-picked men, and several hundred Indians, and started the long journey toward Pennsylvania. The troops were joined by other French forces at Fort Duquesne and they marched on Washington at Great Meadow in Pennsylvania. The American troops surrendered the battle but eventually, with the British, would win the war.

France was defeated and ceded the Illinois territory to Britain in 1763. The Indians, led by Chief Pontiac, were hostile to the new British rulers however and two years would pass before the English could take possession of Fort De Chartres.

Under British command, the fort would decline and fall into ruin. Many of the French farmers and merchants migrated west across the Mississippi during the British years, abandoning the area. To make matters worse, a river flood in 1772 damaged the fort and left seven feet of water standing inside of the walls. Finally, the river channel shifted and the west wall of the structure collapsed. After this, the military garrison was transferred to Kaskaskia and Fort de Chartres was never occupied again.

As time wore on, the ruins fell apart and birds began nesting in the crumbling stone. The site was largely forgotten until the middle 1900's, when historic restoration efforts began. Today, the original foundations have been exposed and a few of the old buildings have been restored. Living history groups frequent the place and visitors are invited to this isolated place to learn about the earliest settlements in Illinois.

But time never completely forgot about Fort de Chartres. The events of the past never died here completely and it is said that at least one of them replays itself over and over again in the form of a phantom funeral procession that has become one of the most famous haunts in southern Illinois. According to the legend, three people along the road from Fort de Chartres to a small cemetery in Prairie du Rocher will be able to witness the funeral procession between the hours of eleven and midnight, but only when July 4 falls on a Friday.

The modern version of this intriguing story begins in July 1889. A woman named Mrs. Chris and her neighbor were sitting on the front porch of the Chris house near Prairie du Rocher one night. It was near midnight and the two women had escaped the heat of the house by going out into the cooler air of the porch.

They talked quietly for a short time and then one of the women noticed a large group of people coming toward them on the road. She caught the attention of her friend and they both puzzled over why such a procession of people and wagons would be on the road from the old fort at such an hour. As they spoke, the wagons rolled into view, looking strange and eerie in the pale light of the moon. Behind the wagons came carriages and men and women walking along the dusty road. There was no clue as to their purpose on this night until a low wagon holding a casket came into view. It was apparently a funeral procession, Mrs. Chris thought, by why so late at night?

The two women continued to watch and they counted nearly forty wagons, followed by horsemen and mourners on foot. Then, they noticed something very peculiar about the grim parade. Even though the wagon wheels seemed to pound the earth and the feet of the men and women stirred up clouds of dust, none of them made any sound at all! The entire procession was impossibly silent!

The only sounds came from the rustling of the trees in the breeze and the incessant barking of the Chris family dog, which also sensed that something was not quite right with the spectral and silent procession. The barking of the dog awakened the neighbor woman's husband, who also looked out and witnessed the strange entourage on the road. He verified the women's account early the next morning and other than those three people, no one else saw the phantom funeral march.

Eventually, the procession passed by and faded away into the darkness. The two women waited the entire night for the funeral to return, but they saw nothing more. What was it that they had seen, and whose funeral was being conducted? The answers would come some years later and they would learn that the procession had apparently also been seen in the past. In fact, it was a replaying of an actual event that occurred many years before.

During the French occupation of Fort de Chartres, a prominent local man had gotten into a violent disagreement with one of the officers of the garrison. The two men exchanged heated words and the local merchant was accidentally killed. Unsure of how to handle the affair, the fort's commander sent a delegation to the government offices in Kaskaskia. They advised keeping the incident very quiet and ordered the local man be buried at midnight in the small cemetery that is now outside of Prairie du Rocher.

There is also another story to explain the phantom funeral procession. In this version, a quarrel took place between two young officers, one British and one French, at the fort in 1765. They fought for the affections of a local girl and dueled one morning with swords. The British officer was killed and the Frenchman fled downriver to escape the authorities. The British officer was allegedly buried in secret to prevent hostilities between the two European factions in the region.

While the truth behind the story has been lost, it is believed that Mrs. Chris and her neighbors were witnesses to an inexplicable event that was replayed more than a century after it first occurred. Since 1889, accounts have been sketchy as to when, or even if, the phantom procession has been seen. It is known that July 4 fell on a Friday as recently as 1986, but there is nothing to say if the procession walked or not.

In 1997, July 4 once again fell on the designated day and while no one actually saw the procession (thanks to a lot of foolishness and people driving back and forth along the four mile stretch of road between the fort and the cemetery all evening), there was one odd event that took place. A staff member at the fort reported to me later that summer that on the stroke of midnight, all of the coyotes in the area began to howl in unison. It only lasted for a minute or two, but I couldn't help but think what a strange coincidence it was. Or was it? Perhaps they sensed something in the air that no animals of the two-legged variety could discern?

Coincidence or not, you'll have the chance to search for the phantom funeral on your own in the future. July 4 will fall on a Friday in the years 2003, 2014 and 2025. If you are feeling brave, take along two friends and stake out the old road that leads to Fort de Chartres. You might just be in the right place at the right time when the dead decide to walk once more!

-CHAPTER THREE-

GHOSTS ALONG THE RIVER

HISTORY & HAUNTINGS ON THE MISSISSIPPI RIVER

Incidents relating to nautical manifestations have taken place hundreds of miles inland. There is a stretch of the Mississippi River... where strange things have happened, and still are happening. The region abounds with Indian lore of the spirits and the supernatural.

RICHARD WINER FROM MORE HAUNTED HOUSES

The early days of exploration in the Midwest, or what was the Northwest Territory at that time, always involved the rivers as a source of transportation. Because of this rich history, we have a plethora of haunts. In fact, one town on the Illinois side of the Mississippi River has been named as one of the most haunted small towns in America today!

FROM THE HAUNTING OF AMERICA

There is no other river in America with a history like the Mississippi, nor a body of water of such scale and magnitude. Nebraska author John Neihardt called the Mississippi the "river of an unwritten epic" and called it a place that has given birth to both heroes and villains and to the greatest legends of America. This may be true, for one thing is sure, the region is certainly rich in history.

The first of the Europeans to see the Mississippi River were De Soto and his men in 1541. We have no idea what he may have called the river, for the adventurer was not one who cared for naming places, but he was most likely content with the old name "Espiritu Santo". His scribes, on the other hand, inquired of the natives as to what the great river was called and learned that it had many names. The records of the expedition recorded names like Chucagua, Tamalisieu, Nilco, Mico and others, although the most common title was simply, "The River".

Among the Indians to the north, in the land of Marquette and Jolliet, they called the river the

Kitchi-zibi or the Mis-sipi, words that were roughly translated to mean "big River". However, even after this name became known, it did not establish itself for some time. Even Marquette and Jolliet used different terms for the Mississippi. Jolliet called it Buade, while Marquette referred to it as Conception. Eventually, the Indian name stuck and it has been the Mississippi River ever since.

The Mississippi has long been a breeding ground for ghosts and legends. There are scores of haunted places located along, and connected to, the river, including many in Illinois. In addition to ghostly tales that "haunt" the land along the Mississippi, there are the stories of the river itself.

Many are strange superstitions and odd events that cannot be explained, like the tales of ghost lights and phantom riverboats.

One story tells of a steamship and a boiler that exploded one night and took the life of a young steersman. The captain of the ship was especially fond of the young man and spent days and nights searching for him in the river and along the banks. After the captain's own death, a ghostly light was said to appear near where the accident took place. The stories say that it is the light of the captain's lantern as he still searches for the body of the crew member.

Other stories tell of a phantom riverboat that has been known to appear all along the Mississippi River. They say that when the boat appears, and its whistle is heard, a river worker will be injured in an accident. ·

The Spoon River region has another story that is similar to this one of the "phantom riverboat". This tale has been a part of Fulton County lore for generations. It seems that in the late 1840's, the Spoon River rose dramatically one spring after a particularly wet season. The experienced river pilots avoided the swollen and muddy waterway, but one morning, a crew of adventurous and unseasoned men launched a small steamboat onto the river. They took with them a group of passengers, boarded the boat and set off downriver. According to the St. Louis "Republican" newspaper, the last thing that was heard from the boat was the sharp sound of its whistle and the passengers on deck singing the old hymn "Sweet By and By". The vessel steamed off around a bend in the river... and disappeared without a trace.

The passengers from the steamboat were never seen again and despite several searches, the boat was never recovered. It was thought that perhaps the vessel had run aground somewhere, but if it had, there was no sign of it.

Several years passed and in the spring of 1853, the waters of the Spoon River once again swelled and rushed over the banks. According to reports from people who lived along the river, they heard the distinctive sound of a steamboat whistle piercing the air one night around midnight. Several of them, curious to see what fool would be trying to navigate the river after dark, hurried to the banks to see the boat. A heavy mist lay over the river but they watched as the fog bank parted and a steamboat appeared. It was the same vessel that had disappeared several years before!

The craft moved silently on the water, giving off a strange and eerie glow. As the people on the shore watched, white apparitions appeared on the deck and the faint snatch of a song could be heard echoing on the river. The song was the old hymn... "Sweet By and By"! The steamboat drifted past and floated down the river and out of sight. It was never seen again.

LEGENDS OF CAVE-IN-ROCK

The rivers and waterways of southern Illinois have always played a dominant role in its history and folklore. The early settlers, like the French, established themselves along the rivers and later, farmers would come to realize how much more simple it was to use the river to transport grain to market. The era of the steamboat created towns like Chester, Elizabethtown, Cairo, Metropolis, Golconda and

Shawneetown. These towns became shipping ports with flour and lumber mills and even an iron foundry in Grand Tower. Travelers came to the towns by boat and hotels and establishments on the riverfront flourished.

Many stories have emerged from the rivers and the towns surrounding them, of wrecks, lawlessness, pirates and even ghosts. Perhaps the most famous pirate location on the river was an outlaw hideout called Cave-in-Rock, which is located along the Ohio River at the southeastern edge of the state. The cave became the stronghold of pirates who plundered flatboats on the river and who murdered and robbed travelers. It was also here, around 1800, that a robber named Samuel Mason began operating a tavern and gambling parlor in the cave. He used whiskery, cards and prostitutes to lure travelers in off the river and many of these customers found themselves beaten, robbed and sometimes dead, after tying up at the crude wharf.

Cave-in-Rock, located close to the town of the same name, was a perfect place for criminal enterprises along the river. At that time, it boasted a partially concealed entrance and a wide view up and down the river. The cave is about one hundred feet deep, with a level floor and a vertical chimney that ascends to the bluff above.

Samuel Mason operated here for several years. He was said to be a man of gigantic size and possessing no conscience, he killed for both pleasure and profit. He also operated along the Mississippi River and on the fabled Natchez Trace, a series of trails in the south that became known as a haven for thieves and pirates. Eventually a reward was offered for Mason, $1000 dead or alive, and a hatchet was put into his back by one of his own men. This traitorous wretch never collected the reward though as he was in turn killed by other members of the gang. Mason's cronies eventually scattered to the wind and other outlaws took their place at Cave-In-Rock.

The pirates were also said to have preyed upon ferryboat passengers at Ford's Ferry, a few miles upriver. The ferryman himself, James Ford, was said to have been in league with the pirates. He was also said to be one of the "slave catchers" in the employ of John Hart Crenshaw. Ford eventually came under attack by the vigilante "Regulators" and this would lead to his demise. One night, in 1834, he was having dinner at the home of a Mrs. Vincent Simpson, the widow of one of Ford's men. He was eating his food at the table and someone brought him a candle and asked that he read a letter aloud for him. Using the candle as a signal, the "Regulators" outside opened fire, aiming between the logs of the cabin. Ford died with 17 bullets in his body!

For years after his death, the slaves told stories about how Jim Ford had died and "landed in Hell head first". At his funeral, attended only by his widow, a few family members, neighbors and some slaves, a terrible thunderstorm came up. Just as Ford's coffin was being lowered into the ground, lightning flashed and a deafening clap of thunder filled the air, causing one of the slaves to loose his grip on the rope holding the coffin. The box dropped into the grave head first and wedged there at a strange angle. The heavy rain that began to fall made it impossible to move the casket, so it was covered over the way that it had fallen. This left Ford to spend eternity standing on his head.

Ford's death would not bring an end to the thievery at Cave-in-Rock. Many of the remaining pirates continued to prey on travelers from the sanctuary of the cave, while others joined with villains like John Murrell and his "Mystic Band". Murrell was a "slave catcher", thief and murderer, who killed his first man when he was only sixteen. He later died after serving time in prison.

By the late 1830's, most of the outlaws, pirates and counterfeiters were driven away from Cave-in-Rock and the bloody past of the place began to fade with time. As years passed, the cave became more of a recreation area than a den of thieves and remains a natural attraction in southern Illinois today. The legends have never died completely though and many still remember the area's blood-soaked past... and the stories of ghosts. In years gone by, travelers passing on the river often claimed to hear the keening moans of the dead echoing out from the mouth of the cave. These same cries are still sometimes reported today. Do these eerie voices belong to the crime victims of long ago, who were lured to their death at Cave-in-Rock? That answer remains as mysterious as the history of the cave itself.

THE LEGEND OF THE DEVIL'S BAKE OVEN

The small town of Grand Tower slumbers peacefully along the muddy banks of the Mississippi River. Once a booming ironworks town, there is little remaining of the city that was in these modern times. Regardless, Grand Tower has been a southern Illinois landmark for years, thanks to the vast array of tales that have been told about the area, including one of the most famous ghost stories in the region.

When Jolliet and Marquette journeyed down the Mississippi River in 1673, they recorded in their journals a large rock that is known as Tower Rock today. At one time, it was also known as Le Cap de Croix, meaning "the Rock of the Cross" to the French settlers and explorers. The name was given to the landmark after three French missionaries erected a large wooden cross on the rock's crest in 1678.

During the heyday of river travel and exploration, a number of people were killed in the rapids that sometimes run at the base of the rock. Thanks to this, the Native Americans were convinced that evil spirits lurked here, waiting to claim the lives of unwitting victims. The white men who settled the area would later acknowledge these beliefs by giving the towering rocks a suitable name. There is one landmark called the Devil's Backbone, which is a rocky ridge about one-half mile long. It begins on the northern edge of Grand Tower's city limits. If you look closely, you can see that a large piece of the knobby "spine" is missing. A railway spur once passed through here and connected to the ironworks. At the north edge of the Backbone, there is steep gap and then the Devil's Bake Oven, a larger rock that stands on the edge of the river and rises to heights of nearly one hundred feet.

The area has had a long and strange past, beginning with the days of the early settlers. One day, many years ago, a band of immigrants were ascending the Mississippi River after coming down the Ohio from the east. They were on their way to Kaskaskia when they were attacked and killed by Indians at the south edge of the Devil's Backbone. The only survivor was a boy named John Moredock. He was able to hide in the rocks until the killers had departed. He buried his family and then made his way upstream to Kaskaskia. According to legend, he swore revenge on the Indians who had murdered his family and the story says that, one by one, he claimed the lives of the attackers.

In the years that followed, river navigation came to the Mississippi and keelboats and flatboats passed the area in great numbers. According to early records, the rapids along the Backbone caused many problems for pilots when the river was in its low stages. Crews often had to disembark and walk along the shore, using ropes to pull their boats through the rapids. When going downstream, it was often necessary to reverse the process and use the long ropes to ease the boats carefully along.

During the steamboat days, the Backbone served as a landmark for river pilots. It also afforded an excellent lookout point from which boats could be seen coming for miles away. The two outcroppings of rocks also made excellent hiding places for Indians and river pirates to hide and wait for their victims to come along. In fact, the raids by river pirates became so bad that in 1803, a detachment of US Cavalrymen were dispatched to drive the outlaws from the area. They set up camp at the Devil's Bake Oven from May to September of that year. While the soldiers waited, the river pirates simply moved their camp to a rock overhang on the Big Muddy River. The place is still known as "Sinner's Harbor" today. Once the military left, they returned to attacking boats on the river. Later on, as settlers and a semblance of civilization arrived, the pirates moved on and the rapids beneath the Devil's Backbone became a much safer place.

The years passed and the town of Grand Tower began to grow. It was first known as "Jenkin's Landing", but the name was later changed to correspond with the recognizable river landmark. The town became a busy river port where goods were shipped and received daily. On the west side of the Devil's Backbone, between the rock formation and the river, is the site of two vanished iron furnaces that operated there until around 1870. Iron ore was brought to these furnaces from Missouri and they were fired with coal from Murphysboro. It is said that Andrew Carnegie once considered making Grand Tower the "Pittsburgh of the West".

The population soon expanded and a lime kiln was started in Grand Tower, along with a box factory and a shipyard. A number of river barges and one steamer, the "Mab", were constructed here. New businesses came to the area and even an amusement park was opened on Walker's Hill, just east of town. Time marched on however and the population dwindled. A cholera epidemic many years ago wiped out a number of the residents and the decline of river transportation succeeded in driving away the rest. Grand Tower was once a town of more than 4000 souls, but only a fraction of those still remain. One local even said to me that the graveyards hold more bodies than the town can boast as residents these days.

A Rare Photo of the Superintendent's House on the Devil's Bake Oven (photo courtesy of Vicky Cripps)

It was the expansion of the iron industry in Grand Tower that brought about the ghost story that still haunts the town today. The Devil's Bake Oven also played a major part in the story because besides serving as a river landmark for years, it became the site of Grand Tower's first iron works. When the new industry came, several attractive homes were built for the officials of the company, including the house built for the superintendent. This house was built on top of the Devil's Bake Oven. The foundation of the old house can still be seen on the eastern side of the hill today and it is here where the ghost is said to walk. It has been said that she is heard among the ruins of the old house, where tragedy and despair in the past have led to a modern-day haunting.

According to the old story, the ghost is that of the superintendent's young daughter. The girl was said to be very beautiful but was also sheltered and naive about life. Her doting father kept her away from the rough men of the foundry and although she had a number of suitors seeking her hand in marriage, he accepted none of them. Finally, one day, the girl fell in love with one of the young men who came to court her. As is often the case, the young man was a handsome, roguish and irresponsible fellow of whom her father strongly disapproved. He forbid her to see him and after she slipped away to meet the young man a few times in the night, he father confined her to the house for a long period of time.

The young man was convinced to move on from Grand Tower, possibly from money offered by the superintendent, and the young girl wept over him for days and weeks. At last, either because of grief or because of some illness brought on by her despair, the young woman died.

But she did not leave the Devil's Bake Oven.

The spirit of the young girl was said to have lingered at the site of the house. For many years after her death, visitors to the area reported seeing a strange, mist-like shape, which resembled the dead girl, walking along the pathway and vanishing among the rocks near the old house. Her disappearance was often followed by the sounds of moans and wails. It was also believed that when thunderstorms swept across the region, those moans and wails would become blood-curdling screams.

How long the girl haunted the place, and whether she still does or not, is unknown. It was said that the ghost appeared long after her father's house was razed and the timbers used to build a railway station. But does the ghost still haunt the Devil's Bake Oven today? If she does, she probably finds the area unfamiliar to her now. The stone landmarks still remain but the land around it is greatly changed. The town of Grand Tower has also faded into a scattering of houses and there is little to remind us of the history that once enriched this small area.

And little to remind us of the young girl who once died here of a broken heart and whose spirit refuses to rest in peace.

HAUNTED ALTON

Ghost stories are found everywhere, but Alton is one of those places that seems to attract more than their fair share of stories.

JIM LONGO IN GHOSTS ALONG THE MISSISSIPPI

In all honesty, I don't believe there is any other town along the Mississippi River that is as haunted as Alton, Illinois. Mark Twain once called the place as "dismal little river town", but it has since earned a more distinguished reputation as "one of the most haunted small towns in America"! The history of the place is filled with all of the makings of ghosts and ghost stories... death, murder, disease, tragedy, the Civil War, the Underground Railroad and much more. With that in mind, is it any wonder that there are so many allegedly haunted houses, businesses and sites here?

The city of Alton was platted by Colonel Rufus Easton (who had a son named "Alton") in 1821, but the first settlers arrived a few years prior to that. Recognizing the importance of the river, ferryboats soon went into operation and eventually the Alton docks became a major steamboat landing on the Mississippi River. Settlers continued to arrive and the town prospered, until a tragic event took place in 1837 that almost destroyed Alton altogether.

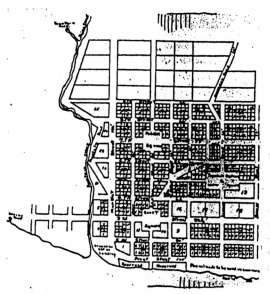

An Original Plat Map of Alton from 1821.

This event would start a panic in the city and cause the banks and railroads to collapse. Property values shrank and newspapers all over the country began to attack the city for allowing this horrible event to occur. The more discerning residents packed up and left town, realizing that Alton would never recover. The city had become a "lawless" place and soon it was nearly a ghost town. What had once been a thriving river port was now reduced to a "doomed" city.

What was this tragic event? It was the murder of abolitionist publisher Elijah P. Lovejoy. It would be this event that would inspire later abolitionists like John Brown, and an event that some believe may have been the initial spark that started the Civil War.

THE "CURSE" OF ELIJAH LOVEJOY

On November 7, 1837, a mob of nearly two hundred men carrying torches surrounded a brick warehouse on the edge of the Mississippi River. The warehouse held the offices of an abolitionist newspaper called the Observer and the editor's name was Reverend Elijah P. Lovejoy. The outspoken denouncer of slavery had already been driven out of St. Charles, Missouri for his abolitionist views. In August, Lovejoy had been warned to stop publishing his anti-slavery newspaper, but he refused. On three different occasions, angry mobs had hurled the newspaper's printing presses into the river.

On the afternoon of November 7, a boat arrived in Alton carrying Lovejoy's fourth printing press and it was taken to a warehouse on the river, belonging to Godfrey, Gilman and Co.. Lovejoy and a number of his friends gathered at the warehouse with guns to defend it but the day passed without incident. It would not be until that evening that trouble would come.

The events that followed that night would blacken the reputation of Alton for many years to come, all over the issue of slavery. The actions of the mob would not settle the issue of slavery, they would merely fan the flames. The news spread quickly among abolitionist circles... Elijah P. Lovejoy was dead on the streets of Alton. The first white man had been killed in the fight over slavery.

Elijah P. Lovejoy was born in the town of Albion, Maine on November 8, 1802. He graduated from Waterville College in 1823 and then moved west to St. Louis four years later. In 1832, he was licensed to preach but instead, began a religious newspaper called the St. Louis "Observer". Articles with an anti-slavery bent began appearing in the newspaper in 1834 and, despite warnings from a number of prominent citizens, continued to appear into 1835.

Hard feelings against the abolitionist movement were strong in St. Louis. Rumors spread through the city like wildfire as many citizens were convinced the abolitionists were plotting to encourage a slave rebellion in the city. Free blacks were watched closely with both suspicion and fear. Then, in October 1835, things took a turn for the worse for Lovejoy. Reports surfaced which claimed that two Illinois men had helped several slaves from St. Louis escape across the Mississippi River. This was followed by the first threat against Lovejoy's printing press. Only a mass show of force discouraged the mob from destroying his business. In early 1836, Lovejoy and his family traveled to Pittsburgh for a meeting of the assembly of the Presbyterian Church. When the Lovejoy's returned to St. Louis, they found the city in the midst of a racially inspired panic, thanks to the murder of a police officer and the lynching of a black riverboat cook.

Lovejoy was outraged and quickly returned to his office and wrote a fiery editorial about the incident. Not long after, Lovejoy and his family returned to Pittsburgh. The editor was consumed with guilt over the fact that his abolitionist stand may have caused the violence to erupt. While he was away from St. Louis, vandals broke into the offices of the newspaper several times and heavily damaged his printing press.

Lovejoy realized that he was finished in St. Louis. The city would no longer tolerate him and he could not subject his family to the violence that seemed to be coming. He sent his wife and son to her mother's home in St. Charles and made plans to move his newspaper to Alton. His last editorial in St. Louis was aimed at the city leaders and produced a mob of over 200 people at his office. A smaller group of 20 men broke down the doors to the print shop and wrecked the place. Somehow, the printing press itself was not harmed.

He arrived in Alton in late July 1836. He sent for his family with the hopes that the free state of Illinois would provide a better environment for his abolitionist work, but he couldn't have been more wrong.

On Sunday, July 23, a steamboat called the Palmyra delivered Lovejoy's printing press to the Alton docks, even through it was contrary to Lovejoy's explicit instructions. He was unwilling to have the press moved on the Sabbath, so it was left on the Alton wharf until morning. Shortly before dawn, a group of men who were reportedly from Missouri, wrecked the press and dumped it into the river. And this would not be the last. Lovejoy would have other presses while in Alton, but it is the story surrounding the arrival of the fourth printing press which is still told, and some say re-lived, today.

On the night of November 7, 1837, Lovejoy and his friends gathered at the riverfront warehouse, standing guard over the new printing press. Some time that night, a mob gathered outside of the warehouse. Most of them were intoxicated and they called loudly for the press to be surrendered to them. Once that demand was refused, they tried a different approach and used rocks to shatter the windows of the warehouse. Several members of the mob waved guns and Lovejoy, or someone inside the building, fired his own weapon through a broken window. One of the men outside crumpled to the ground and the mob became enraged. They stormed the warehouse, intent on revenge.

Someone placed a ladder against the building and climbed to the roof, a burning torch in his hands. Lovejoy ran outside with a pistol and ordered the man to come down. Before he could fire his own weapon though, several men in the crowd opened fire on the editor and he was hit five times. He fell to the ground, crying out, "My God, I am shot!", and died in just moments. After he fell, the defenders inside of the warehouse surrendered. The mob pushed their way into the place and broke the printing press into pieces, then flung them into the Mississippi River.

Lovejoy's body was left in the warehouse overnight. The next day, on what would have been his 35th birthday, a grave was hastily dug on a high bluff and the body, without a proper ceremony, was thrown into it and haphazardly covered up. Some years later, this spot was chosen as a place for a cemetery and in 1852, when a road was set to cross over Lovejoy's grave, his body was exhumed and moved to another location. Today,

A period illustration showing the 1837 attack on Lovejoy and the Godfrey, Gilman & Co. Warehouse in Alton.

a fine monument stands in tribute to fallen abolitionist and while he is highly regarded in these less troubled times, his death was never avenged.

The tragedy of the Lovejoy murder spawned what seemed like a curse to many of Alton's citizens. Property values in the city shrank and when the tales of the riots spread across America, the press attacked from all directions. The abolitionist newspapers loudly condemned the city, as did the free press, which saw the rights of the First Amendment in jeopardy.

The court proceedings surrounding the affair made the city look even more corrupt. At a January 1838 session of the Alton municipal court, the grand jury brought indictments against both Lovejoy's defenders and some of the rioters. The cases later came to trial and Lovejoy's friends were acquitted of charges.... but so were the members of the mob. This was seen by outsiders and national newspapers, who had watched the entire affair very closely, as an official endorsement of Lovejoy's assassination. Alton was branded a lawless place and shunned by many. Thanks to all this, new settlers avoided the area and many current residents packed up and moved out, believing that Alton had little future. It would be years later before the vacancies created would be filled.

While no one was ever legally punished for the Lovejoy murder, legend had it that a "curse" followed many of the ringleaders of the riot to their graves. One of the leaders of the mob was later killed in a brawl in New Orleans, another died in an Ohio prison, another was killed in a freak steamboat explosion, while another was stabbed to death in St. Louis. Many of the others ended their lives in violence and disgrace.

Along the banks of the Mississippi River is the place where the old warehouse once stood that held the printing presses of Lovejoy's abolitionist newspaper. It's hard to recognize the spot these days, as it is little more than a space between two large grain mills at the base of William Street. As the years passed, grain mills replaced the warehouse and all trace of it has vanished.... or has it?

According to those who live on the nearby bluffs and those who are natives of the area, the martyred Lovejoy may not rest in peace. The legends say that his spirit may still roam the waterfront in despair. Others claim that the spirits of that night in November do not walk, but the terror experienced here has left an impression on the area that still reverberates today. Many who have visited the location claim to be able to feel the madness of the crowd, the desperation of Lovejoy and his friends and the energy pulsing through the entire incident.

Alton did not rally from the death of its early prosperity until about 1844, just in time for the beginning of the Golden Age of Steamboats on the Mississippi. The city's prime location would make it attractive to not only the steamship companies, but the railroads as well. They discovered that Alton was the perfect place to bring goods to be shipped on the river and would also make an excellent railroad crossing to St. Louis and points further west.

Alton also became the site for the last of the great debates between Abraham Lincoln and Stephen Douglas in 1858. While staying in the city, Lincoln slept at a hotel called the Franklin House. Although unconnected to the president, the building today is believed to be haunted by the ghost of a little girl who was killed in the street in front of the establishment in the early 1900's. She has been encountered many times over the years and is still lingering in the building today.

In 1833, Alton became the site of the first state prison in Illinois. Prisons in those days were grim and almost barbaric places. They were usually plagued with rats and disease and the Alton prison was no exception. In fact, in 1847, social reformer Dorothea Dix would visit the prison and declare the place unfit for habitation, even by criminals. In spite of this, it would later be used as housing for Confederate prisoners during the Civil War. The events that took place during this period would create perhaps the greatest historical haunting that Alton would ever know.

SPIRITS OF THE CIVIL WAR

The Alton penitentiary was completed in 1833 and originally held 24 cells. The prison was operated under the "lease" system. It would be rented from the state by an individual, who was then supposed to feed, house and guard the prisoners, also paying for their medical care. This person would receive about $5000 from the state and would take on the role of a warden. This man was then responsible for the conditions of the prison, as money allowed. As more prisoners were incarcerated, additional cells and buildings were added to the prison, along with a warden's residence, which was located at the southwest corner of the site. In 1846, 96 new cells were added and by 1857 they numbered 257, with an average of 2 convicts per cell.

One has to wonder just how the leasing system worked and how much money the wardens managed to pocket during the years the prison was in operation as a state facility. Conditions deteriorated badly here, as mentioned earlier, and the prison would be replaced by a new penitentiary in Joliet by 1859. In May of that year, the prisoners were transferred to Joliet in batches of 40 or 50 and by June of 1860, the Alton prison was abandoned.

Early in the years of the Civil War, Alton was made a military post, thanks to its location on the Missouri border and its access to the river. It had become apparent by 1862 that the war was not going to come to a swift end and more space was needed for the growing numbers of prisoners of war. In February 1862, the old Alton penitentiary was turned a military prison. The first prisoners arrived on February 9 by way of a river steamer. They were marched from the river landing to the prison. Not all of the prisoners were soldiers. They included spies, bridge burners, train wreckers, guerilla fighters and southern sympathizers. Even a few women were incarcerated there and two of them died in Alton.

As the war continued on, new prisoners arrived in Alton on a regular basis. The prison sometimes contained as many as 2,000 inmates from all over the south. Plots to escape were constantly hatched and while most failed, there was an escape attempt worth noting in July of 1864. There were 46 prisoners at labor in a nearby stone quarry who made a desperate effort against their guards. Acting at a given signal, the prisoners nearly overpowered the soldiers and seized a number of rifles before the guards could act. The escape was not to be however and the guards quickly recovered and killed seven and wounded five of the prisoners. All but two of the Confederates were quickly recaptured.

Many of the escape attempts failed because of the health of the prisoners themselves. Living conditions in the prison were sometimes unbearable and most of the men were badly clothed, food was often withheld or not edible, bathing facilities were not available, gnats and lice were common, as were rats, and diseases like dysentery, scurvy and anemia felled many of the men.

Then, in 1863, several isolated cases of smallpox broke out among the prisoners and then spread, quickly turning into an epidemic. The prisoners, at the time of the outbreak, probably numbered several thousand in quarters that were designed for 1,300 or less. They slept three in a bed, ate standing up and used a common latrine. Nothing was clean in the prison and the men were often unshaved and filthy. As mentioned before, they could not bathe, their sleeping mattresses were never changed or washed and the prison yard was filled with pools of stagnant water and urine.

The smallpox virus could live for hours on contaminated clothing and blankets and had an incubation period of two weeks. It was spread to others long before the carrier ever realized he was sick. And there was little that could be done for the disease, other than to let it run its course. Those with smallpox would be completely dehydrated and as it progressed, victims would develop oozing pustules on their legs, arms and faces. Survivors were often badly scarred.

During the war, smallpox inoculations were given at many prisons with mixed results. According to one source, prisoners given an "impure" smallpox vaccine at Andersonville, the notorious southern prison camp, ended up with such severe gangrene that "some arms almost rotted in two". Despite mandatory vaccinations for smallpox at the Alton prison, men began to get sick and soon, both prisoners and guards began to die.

The prison death toll quickly began to climb but Alton's mayor, Edward T. Drummond, refused to have any of the prisoners treated away from the prison. There were no hospitals in the city of Alton in those days. The patients were quartered in hallways, storage rooms and stables, as the prison hospital was woefully inadequate with only five beds. Before the outbreak, there had been about a half dozen deaths per week in the prison but soon, they were counting more than five a day. Once the disease started to spread, there was no way to stop it. The men were weakened by poor diets and filthy living conditions and were helpless against the disease.

By the second week, prison guards also began to be infected with smallpox. It was said that those soldiers who were not sick had to be threatened with court-martial to get them to continue with their duties.

Soon, there were other problems... namely, where to bury the bodies of the prisoners who died? At first, the dead were buried in Alton and two hundred Union soldiers were interred at the Alton Cemetery on Fifth Street. Confederate soldiers were buried at the old prison graveyard on Rozier Street in North Alton. When space began to run out, legend has it that some of the prisoners were also buried along Hopp Hollow Road, a rough track that led from the riverfront to the cemetery on Rozier Street. The stories say the bodies of these luckless prisoners were often simply dumped into the woods here and the corpses were then left to the elements. Over the years, accounts of sprung up about the ghost sightings along this roadway. Some believe that the men who were left here have returned as specters, hoping to catch a ride in a passing vehicle. These "hitchhiking ghosts" are trying in vain to reach the Rozier Street burying ground!

When news of the epidemic spread throughout the city, the residents of Alton quite naturally began to panic and they demanded the bodies be taken elsewhere. The corpses of the smallpox victims were then taken to a small island in the middle of the Mississippi River, called "Sunflower Island", or "Smallpox Island" in some chronicles. Guards transported the wrapped bodies to the island in the darkness, where they were placed in shallow holes. The island was located about 200 yards away from the prison and a temporary, isolation hospital was also set up there. The healthy prisoners were ordered to act as hospital attendants and stretcher-bearers although few of them were well enough to work. Prisoners, guards and doctors feared going to the island, afraid they would never return. By the end of the third week of the epidemic, about seventy prisoners had died and more than 600 were infected.

The epidemic lasted throughout the winter of 1863 and into the following spring. Prison officials were said to have given up trying to keep an accurate account of the dead. Estimates made after the war ranged from 1,000 to over 5,000 deaths. Official numbers listed anywhere from 1,354 to 1,434.

Finally, by the summer of 1864, a group of nuns from an order called the Daughters of Charity arrived at the prison from St. Louis. They demanded better medical supplies and permission to conduct burial services for the men. Later that summer, the epidemic started to subside and by September, the hospital on the island was closed down. Those who were buried there remain unknown today and their graves, and the island itself, have vanished. In 1874, a wing dike built downstream on Ellis Island caused the shore of Smallpox Island to erode, washing some of the bodies away. The island was later dredged during the construction of the Locks and Dam. Much of the island's sandy soil was used as fill around the southern leg of the dam and for a levee. Finally, in 1938 the Locks and Dam were completed and as the water level behind the dam was raised, the remainder of the island was obliterated. Over the years, the site of the island has been lost, vanished beneath the waters of the Mississippi River.

The burying ground on Rozier Street however, does remain. Several years after the war, wooden markers were placed on the graves of the Confederates buried there, but soon, the burial ground was allowed to deteriorate badly and the markers either rotted or were carried away. The identities of those buried there were lost and by 1893, the small plot was surrounded by barbed wire and used for pastureland. Since that time, a large monument has been placed in memory of the men who died at Alton prison, thanks to the efforts of the Sam Davis Chapter of the Daughters of the Confederacy. They petitioned the government to erect a monument to the dead and it was completed in 1909.

The prison itself was closed down after the war and abandoned, despite a brief effort to once again have it used as a state facility. The walls were torn down between 1870 and 1875 and most of the stone was hauled off for other projects around Alton and the vicinity. The area where the prison was located was turned into a public park and playground called "Uncle Remus Park", in honor of the character created by southern author Joel Chandler Harris.

A Confederate veteran returns to the Alton prison in 1936.

Even then, the entire wall was not demolished and whenever Alton residents needed stone for any sort of construction, they would bring a wagon to the old prison wall and take what they wanted. Sadly, even a number of Confederate veterans, who once were incarcerated at the prison, returned to Alton after the war and took away stones to use for their own grave markers.

The last remaining section of the wall was moved in 1973 and reconstructed along nearby Williams Street as a monument to the past. The area where the prison was once located is now a public parking lot. Today, only this small portion of the wall still remains on the site of the penitentiary, where visitors can find historical information and displays about the prison and the Civil War.

From the preceding pages, you have no doubt realized that death came with many faces during the Civil War. Horrible diseases claimed many lives during the war, especially in the prison camps, and most of us conjure up some pretty terrifying images of what life must have been like in those prisons.

In many of the camps, prisoners died from disease, hunger and exposure to the elements. Why did commanders and citizens of the respective sides tolerate such terrible conditions? Bitterness and revenge? Lack of food and a poor economy? Or simply the darker side of human nature? These questions will never be answered and even though the war has been over for well over a century, the devastating effects of the prison camps are still reverberating today as ghosts from the past.

And the site in Alton is no exception. The area surrounding the old prison is now a parking lot but was once filled with prison buildings and the yard. Over the years, it has claimed its share of ghostly reports. On certain nights, residents and passersby claim to have seen apparitions of men and soldiers still lingering on the ground where the prison once stood. These ragged-looking men have been generally accepted to be either the ghosts of the former prisoners, or at least the residual impressions they have left behind. And some of these encounters have been more than a little unsettling!

One Alton man I spoke with, Bob Richards*, was walking near the old prison site one evening. He was cutting across the parking lot, which is located next to the historical marker, and stopped for a moment to tie his shoe. He bent down quickly and when he looked up again, he saw a man standing not more than three feet away from him. The man appeared to be solid and was wearing a pair of heavy pants that ended near his shins. He was barefoot and was wearing a filthy shirt. He had cropped hair but a long, scraggly beard. "To be honest, I thought he was like a homeless man or something," Bob would later recall. "He was absolutely filthy... but I never thought for a moment that he wasn't real."

At least until the man vanished! The sighting lasted for not more than forty-five seconds or so before the man simply disappeared. Not surprisingly, Bob was more than a little shaken by the event and hurried home to tell his wife about it. It had been she who suggested that the ragged man might have been the ghost of a Confederate prisoner. "I'm still not convinced about that," he told me. "But then I don't have any other explanation for it either."

Another strange event took place in the late 1960's, when the area was still a public park and the last of the prison wall had not yet been moved to its current location. A man I spoke with told me of playing near there as a child. "My grandma would do some shopping on Third Street and I would come over here to play," he recalled. "My sister and I used to climb all over what was left of the wall."

He remembered that he used to hear stories from other kids sometimes, about strange noises around the wall, but never thought anything of it... until it happened to he and his sister one afternoon.

"It was a bright, sunny day," he told me, "and not spooky at all. Then we heard the sound of someone crying from over by the wall. I thought maybe someone had gotten hurt... you know, climbing around on the rocks, so I went over there. Only thing was, there was nobody there... but me and my sister could still hear the crying.

"We got out of there," he stated," and honestly, I don't think we ever played in that park again after that. At least I know I didn't!"

As you can plainly see, ghosts and hauntings abound in Alton. A visitor to this place will often be mystified by the sheer wealth of reported and anecdotal supernatural happenings. These stories help to make Alton one of the most fascinating and historically rich towns on the Mississippi River. Another intriguing aspect of the town is the willingness of the people here to share their stories of haunts and restless ghosts. Never before have I encountered a place where people speak so nonchalantly of the ghost who walks in their attic, or has been seen on the basement stairs. Ghosts are simply a part of life here, which of course, provides a wealth of information for someone like me. I was so fascinated with the ghostly lore of the place that the town spawned an entire book of its own!

If you have never visited this small Mississippi River town, I encourage you to do so. There is much to see here for the history buff and ghost enthusiast alike. If you do make it to town, look me up. I just might have a new story or two to tell you that will chill your blood... or at least give you a few goosebumps!

THE GHOST OF THE MONTICELLO SEMINARY

The front gates to the Monticello Seminary for Women as they were restored after a terrible fire in 1888.

Monticello College was founded in 1838 by Captain Benjamin Godfrey, a pioneer financier of the Alton area and a former sea captain. Captain Godfrey was a well-liked, adventurous man and in light of his earlier career, it is somewhat surprising that he would found a college for "females", especially at a time when it was almost unheard of for a woman to attend school at all. Godfrey was an uneducated Cape Cod shipmaster who had sailed the seven seas and had never seen the inside of a college building before coming to Alton.

He did, however, have nine children, and one morning, overheard one of his daughters imitating her mother. As he then put it, "Educate a man and you educate an individual, educate a woman and you educate a family."

Godfrey had been born in Chatham, Massachusetts in 1794 and went to sea as a boy, where he gained a practical education and a knowledge of navigation. In addition to learning about the sea, he also gained a knowledge of business. After a merchant vessel under his command was shipwrecked, Godfrey was stranded in Mexico. He took advantage of the opportunity and opened a mercantile business in Matamoros. He accumulated more than $200,000 and was transporting it by mule when he was attacked and robbed. He lost all of his money but traveled on to New Orleans anyway, and then upriver to Alton in 1832.

Prior to opening the school, Godfrey had amassed a considerable fortune through business dealings in the Alton area, mostly in connection with Mississippi River steamboat traffic. He and an associate were the heads of the newly chartered Alton State Bank and his business dealings had put him into partnership with a close friend named Winthrop S. Gilman. The firm prospered and was known up and down the river. It was in the Godfrey, Gilman & Co. warehouse, on the Alton riverfront, where Elijah P. Lovejoy hid his printing press and was murdered in 1837. After leaving the banking business, Captain Godfrey became a railroad promoter and built the line between Alton and Springfield. During the construction, he lived in a railway coach and followed the work as it progressed.

When the railroad was completed, Godfrey returned to his stone mansion on the outskirts of Alton and once more devoted himself to the Monticello Female Seminary. He contributed over $110,000 to the founding of the college and would remain a trustee of the school until his death.

Godfrey chose Reverend Theron Baldwin, a Yale-educated minister, to be the first principal of Monticello, which was now being called the first "female seminary in the west". Baldwin had also been instrumental in founding several other Midwestern colleges, including Illinois College at Jacksonville.

In 1838, most girls' schools were merely finishing schools that emphasized music, needlework and other "womanly arts". The goal was a good marriage. However, at Monticello, the ladies were actually given a higher education. They studied difficult courses in mathematics, English, history, religion, philosophy, foreign language and music. The goal was still a good marriage, but the faculty at Monticello was determined the ladies would learn something as well.

For 50 years, the plan had flourished, right up until a terrible fire in 1888 that threatened to close the school for good. Two weeks later though, re-building was already under way. The camaraderie between the students and the staff, created by the fire, intensified the school spirit and the feeling of family at Monticello. This was a feeling that would last until the school closed down in 1971.

After Theron Baldwin retired, he was replaced by Miss Philomena Fobes, who continued the original plan for the school through the Civil War. As the college grew, it began to gain national notoriety and attracted students from all over the country. During the Civil War years, the campus became bitterly divided as girls from both Union and Confederate families attended Monticello.

However, in 1867, Harriet Newell Haskell arrived as the new principal at Monticello and quickly mended the rift. She devoted the next 40 years to making the school one of the most respected female institutions in the country, battling everything from a shortage of funds to the tragic fire of 1888.

Harriet Haskell had been born in Waldoboro, Maine in 1835. Always regarded as a tomboy, she was a favorite companion of both the boys and the girls of her neighborhood. She had a fertile imagination and was educated at Castleton Academy and Mount Holyoke, then went on to become the first female headmaster of the Franklin School in Boston. She would also be named as president of Castleton and when she was first asked to come to Monticello, she refused. Strangely, as the school would later inspire so much devotion from her, she made her decision after visiting the college and found that it wasn't to her liking. The Monticello board elected her to the job, despite her refusal, and this time Miss Haskell accepted, perhaps seeing the school as a challenge that she could meet head-on.

The students at Monticello took to Miss Haskell right away, perhaps because of her wit and her sharp sense of humor. She was also an early advocate of sports for women, believing that if they were well off physically, they would be fit emotionally and morally as well. After the fire, Miss Haskell began a spectacular fund-raising campaign for the school, collecting thousands of dollars and launching a new building called Caldwell Hall, which was designed by the architect of Union Station in St. Louis, Theodore Link. By 1902, Miss Haskell announced that the college was officially out of debt.

Although she never married, Miss Haskell raised two nieces and purchased a Federal Style home on campus, called the "Evergreens", in the 1890's. Although she may have never raised daughters, many students at Monticello left with the feeling that Miss Haskell had loved them as much as she would have her own children. She was often described as "an educator who had no superior among ladies in similar positions throughout the land. She was not only an educator, but also a vital, uplifting force to the students, and also their tender, sympathetic friend".

Miss Haskell began a reign at Monticello Seminary that would endure for 40 years... and some believe that it has never ended. Her tenure as the head of the college was the school's highest point, both by educational standards and financially. She had a real knack for securing donations for the school and was respected by parents and board members alike. She was also adored by the students and when she died, the "Haskell Girls", as they called themselves, were deeply grieved. Former students from across the country sent flowers and cards and came from great distances to attend her funeral.

Miss Haskell's tenure was followed by that of Miss Catherine Burrowes, but things were never the same again for many of the girls. The school would never again achieve the fame that it had when Harriet Haskell was alive. It did continue to grow and prosper for some time although eventually, time and co-educational colleges caught up with the school. The last class graduated from Monticello in 1971 and the campus became the home of Lewis and Clark Community College. Much of the campus has since been renovated and what used to be dorm rooms are now offices and the old school chapel is now a library.

While many things have changed at the college, others have remained the same. One of those things is the presence of Harriet Haskell. Her days at Monticello may have ended in 1907... but some people insist that she is still present, at least in spirit.

In 1971, on the day Monticello Seminary officially became Lewis and Clark, one of the largest and oldest trees on campus crashed to the ground. There was no storm, high wind or act of nature that day, and some say that it was Harriet Haskell, upset over what had become of her beloved Monticello, who knocked down the tree.

Others are not so sure. "There are believers, non-believers and those who are neutral about the existence of ghosts," said Lars Hoffman, a Lewis and Clark professor and former Godfrey mayor, in a 1988 newspaper interview. Hoffman is considered an open-minded skeptic about the haunting of the college, but he does collect stories about the ghost of Harriet Haskell and alleged encounters with her spirit.

Whether or not the ghost is real, the legend is a huge part of the tapestry of the college. Believers are said to speak in quiet voices about the ghost and the non-believers, well, they refuse to acknowledge the stories at all. The college has no official stand on the haunting but consider it simply a part of the school. "The Haskell legend is as much a part of the school as the books and buildings," said Hoffman.

The stories about Harriet Haskell's ghost actually began long ago, shortly after her death in 1907. At the time, Monticello girls were scaring the new students with tales of Miss Haskell's ghost, wandering up and down the hallways at night. Others told of seeing her face reflecting back at them from mirrors and of seeing apparitions in darkened corridors.

Were the ghostly tales of Harriet Haskell merely legends to frighten new arrivals at the school? Perhaps... or perhaps not. Along with these chilling stories were events not so easy to explain away, like the fact that the oldest house on campus had lights and fountains that would periodically turn on and off by themselves. There was also the steam-operated elevator in the old administration building that would suddenly start up and run by itself. The security guards would discover that no one was in it, however it would mysteriously travel between floors at night.

As time passed, more and more people were encountering odd occurrences and even apparitions of Miss Haskell herself. Others were reporting the fact that lights were turning on in empty rooms at night and that water would sometimes run in the bathrooms for no reason.

One of the most haunted places on campus is the library, which was once the Monticello chapel. It was said this was Miss Haskell's favorite room. It is an incredibly beautiful place and it is not surprising that compulsory chapel was held each day. It is in this room where the spirit of Harriet Haskell is encountered the most.

A librarian who was working alone in the room one night claimed to feel someone touch her on the shoulder. When she turned around to see who it was, she found that no one was there. She turned back to her work and again, felt a hand tap her arm once again. This time, after finding no one was there, she closed up and went home. The woman later stated that while she does not believe in ghosts, there was something in the library with her that night. She was positive that someone tapped her on the shoulder!

One Halloween night, a student, who was very skeptical about ghosts and the supernatural, decided to do a radio broadcast from the library. He set up his equipment to air a reading of some of Harriet Haskell's writings, read aloud by a speech professor. The radio crew was set up at one of end of the room and the professor was at the other. The lights had been turned down very low making the library quite eerie, even to those who were non-believers.

Around midnight, the student signed off the air and was shutting down the transmitter. He had just flipped off the switch when he felt a cool hand touch him on the shoulder. He turned quickly and when he found no one was there, he figured that one of his buddies was playing a trick on him. He pulled off his earphones and grabbed a flashlight. Quickly, he searched the library, guessing that he would find someone sneaking out. Strangely, no one was there. He came back and sat down again and put the headphones back on. He didn't want to admit, even to himself, that he was rattled, but he was. His hands shook a little as he turned the dial for some music and little by little, he began to relax.

At least until he felt that familiar hand on his shoulder again! This time, he tore the headphones from his head and leaving all of his equipment behind, he ran full-speed out of the library!

Another haunting attributed to Miss Haskell, which also occurs in the library, is the overwhelming smell of lilac perfume. It seems that that Miss Haskell's trademark scent signals the fact that her presence is near. Many people have encountered this scent over the years, including many who either disbelieve or have no interest in ghosts at all. Is this simply their imagination at work? "I don't believe in ghosts at all," one former student told me, "but I can't explain that smell. I didn't find out until later that lilacs were supposed to mean that Harriet was around... and I didn't like it much when I found out either."

So, is Lewis and Clark College really haunted? I will leave that up to the reader to decide, but before making that judgment, let me leave you with one more tale from the school.

Over the years, I have heard literally hundreds of stories of ghosts, hauntings and strange encounters that have been experienced by ordinary people. Of all the stories I hear, the most convincing ones remain those which are told to me by people who profess to not believe in ghosts, who are skeptical of anything which reeks of the supernatural, or who have no more interest in the paranormal than most of us have in the feeding habits of saltwater fish. These are the most chilling tales because those who tell them simply have no earthly explanation for what has happened to them!

This was the case one afternoon in the early 1990's when the maintenance staff at the college received a call from a campus security guard. One of the new elevators had gotten stuck between floors with a female student inside of it. Could they please come over right away and get it working again? The young lady inside of it was becoming very agitated and was crying for help. Two maintenance workers came over and set to work on the elevator. The woman inside constantly called out to them, very upset, asking them to hurry. After several minutes, she began to cry. The maintenance man who was working with the electrical panel worked as fast as he could and finally, he had it fixed.

They brought the elevator down to free the trapped woman. The doors opened and they waited for her to step off. When no one came out, they looked inside... the elevator was empty! There was no young woman inside of it, even though the car had made no stops before opening up. The maintenance men, and the security guards who made the call, swear to this day they had been talking with the woman inside of the elevator... even though no one was there!

HAUNTED MILTON SCHOOL

Another of the area's haunted schools is the former Milton School building, located on the east side of the city. The strange tales that surround this old building are not like those of Lewis and Clark in that we don't have stories of a beloved administrator who chose to remain behind at the school because she couldn't bear to be away from it. In this location, we have tales of a much darker sort. These stories tell of a murdered student, and the man who took her life, still attached to the place where the tragic events of the past took place.

Milton School was built in 1904 and remained open for 80 years, serving students until it closed down for good in the summer of 1984. After the school closed, it was abandoned for some time and then re-opened in the early 1990's as a factory for Intaglio Design, a company that manufactures items of decorative glass. The company still operates here today and includes a warehouse, a showroom and an antique mall. While some believe that only old memories still haunt the corridors of the school, the legends of the place tell a different story. According to these stories, an event occurred in the late 1930's (possibly 1937 according to one source) that was not reported in the newspapers of the time.

According to the legend, the events began one fall afternoon, a few hours after school had dismissed for the day. The building was deathly silent by this time and the shadows began to grow longer as twilight was now coming earlier with each passing week. The teachers and students had all left for the day, except for one, a young girl (who later generations of students would dub "Mary") who was finishing a seasonal bulletin board for her classroom.

By the time that she had stapled the last construction paper leaf on the board, the sun was beginning to dip low in the sky. Mary knew that she had better get home, before her mother started to worry. She gathered up her school books and hurried down the shadowy corridor to the doors by the gymnasium. She knew that she could push them open and leave the building and they would lock behind her. As she skipped down the last stairway and rounded the corner into the gymnasium, she heard a noise behind her. Curiosity about that noise was the last conscious thought that she ever achieved.

Mary was discovered the next morning in the girl's shower room, in the basement of the school. Her small body was bloody and battered, her clothing torn and scattered about. Most horrific of all was that fact that the young girl had been brutally raped.

The hunt was on for the culprit, but the police had no leads. What sort of animal would commit such a terrible act? During her last moments, Mary had managed to scratch her assailant, as his bloody skin was still under her fingernails. The authorities warned school officials to be on the lookout for anyone with scrapes or scratches on their hands or face.

Several days passed before someone realized that a janitor who worked in the school was missing. He had not shown up for work in several days, so police officers went to his house to ask him a few questions about where he had been on the night of Mary's attack. Not surprisingly, they found scratch marks on both of his hands, although he claimed his cat had left them there. The man lived with his elderly mother, who maintained that he had been sick with the flu and had been at home with her on the afternoon of the murder.

The detectives did not believe his story, but had nothing to arrest him for. He was moved to the top of their list of suspects. Police officers began driving past his house at night and the janitor was kept under surveillance. Rumors began to fly and teachers and staff members at the school began to talk of the janitor's strange habits and of his inappropriate attention to some of the children.

Did the harassment of law enforcement and the gossip of the staff at the school drive an innocent man to take his life? Probably not, but we may never know. A few days later, the body of the janitor was also discovered in the school. He was found hanging, the end of the rope around an exposed beam above an upstairs hallway. Beneath his dangling feet were an overturned chair and a scrawled note which read simply "I DID IT". Was it the confession of a depraved pedophile? The rantings of a man who had been driven to madness by the hounding of the police? Or, as some have hinted, an obvious clue left behind by someone carrying out their own brand of vigilante justice?

As the years have passed, these questions have continued to be asked, although no answers are forthcoming. Rumors, stories and whispered legends floated about the school for years and while many students would never learn that the building had a dark and tainted past, others would not be so lucky.

During the years when the school was still open, many students spoke of strange encounters in the building, odd events, unexplained sounds, and strange shadows that didn't belong. Many of these stories could be dismissed as nothing more than a creepy old building settling on its foundations, or the overactive imaginations of elementary school students.

However years later, when Intaglio Design took over the building, some of the employees of the company began to notice some very peculiar things were going on in the place. Footsteps were heard in the dark hallways at night, when no one else was there, items began to appear and disappear around the offices and soon, one of the staff members even spotted the apparition of a small girl! Was this the ghost of Mary?

This little girl even reportedly became very attached to one particular employee of the business, a young woman named Vickie*. The spirit began to make frequent (and sometimes unnerving) appearances in her office, which was located at the bottom of a stairwell outside of the gymnasium. It was not uncommon to find that things in the room had been moved from place to place. She would also sometimes catch a glimpse of the girl out of the corner of her eye, playing quietly or sitting on the stairs near her office. On other occasions, Vickie would come into the office and find that someone had been tapping on the keys to her computer keyboard, leaving behind patterns of X's and O's. There had been no one in the office at the time!

While the ghost of the little girl was completely benevolent, and was in fact welcomed by Vickie...

the problem was that she did not haunt the school alone! Another presence was also in the building and this one was a threatening spirit! The staff believed that this other ghost was the janitor who had taken the girl's life so many years ago. He was apparently still trapped in the building where he had committed this terrible act.

Vickie, who had grown attached to Mary, now nervously found herself being stalked by the janitor's more malevolent ghost. According to reliable witnesses, Vickie became absolutely terrified by the unseen presence in the building. The majority of her encounters with the ghost took place on the stage area of the gym and down in the hallway behind the girl's shower room. She became so frightened by the things that were going on that she simply refused to work in the building at night. Eventually, she left her job and although this was several years ago, strange things continue to happen at Milton School today.

I met with Doug Wenzel, a Manager for Intaglio Design, at Milton School one early fall afternoon in 1999. He was nice enough to take me on a tour of the building and to point out some of the areas where people have reported strange things in the past. Doug and I were accompanied on our tour by my friend Sonny Irvin, who had also been involved in some strange happenings in the building.

"I was out here in the warehouse one night, after everyone else had gone on to another part of the building," Sonny explained to me as we stood among the jumble of boxes and tall shelves in the warehouse. It had been constructed on what was once the playground of the school. "I turned off my flashlight, just to get a feel for the place and it was pitch dark. I heard a lot of sounds out here and even saw some lights moving around that I don't have an explanation for. It was probably just the ordinary sounds of the building, but it was very strange."

He then led Doug and I up a short flight of stairs and through a doorway into the gym. " I had just come through this doorway and there were several people standing over there across the room," Sonny gestured across the gym floor. "They told me that I was standing in the middle of some sort of mist.... I didn't see anything, but they kept insisting it was all around me."

Doug took me through the school, to the stage and to the former girl's shower room, where Mary's body had been discovered. I noticed that staff members of Intaglio had placed shelving units in front of the shower stalls where the corpse was actually found, as if to blot out the fact that the event had ever taken place.

I also explored the hallways and classrooms, now empty and abandoned or filled with decorative glass items and office furniture. Outside of one of the corridors, I turned to Doug. "Have you ever had anything weird happen to you in the building?", I asked him.

"I haven't ever had anything happen to me," he replied, " but it's the strangest thing... sometimes I bring my dog in here to work with me and when we come down this hallway, he always stops and starts whining and growling outside of one particular door. I can never get him to go inside, but it's like he sees something in there."

Doug paused for a moment and looked down the dark hallway toward the stairs. " Nothing has ever happened to me," he repeated and then looked back at me. "I'm a believer though... this can be a really spooky place."

THE MANSION HOUSE

One of my favorite "historic haunts" of Alton involves a place called the Mansion House. It is perhaps the most legendary site in the city. It is located on State Street in Alton and was built in 1834 by a Captain Botkin, who operated the place for many years as a hotel. He offered lodging to travelers and to those who were living in the area on a temporary basis. For a short period in 1836, it was the only hotel in Alton.

The building was later used as a Catholic boarding school by nuns of the Ursuline Order and the Daughters of Charity. In 1864, during the height of the smallpox epidemic at the Alton Prison, the house was turned into a hospital and in fact, was the very first hospital in the city. Three Daughters of Charity nuns from St. Louis responded to a plea from President Lincoln to come to Alton and try to get the smallpox epidemic under control. They began treating the sick at the hospital and at the isolation camp on Smallpox Island. Gradually, under their watchful care, the epidemic began to subside.

The legends say that many diseased prisoners died in the Mansion House and claim their ghosts still walk there, restless and frightened of the illness that suddenly ended their lives.

And if these ghosts walk here.... they may not walk alone. According to stories, anecdotes and even historical records, this house was haunted long before the Civil War. In fact, the Mansion House has the rather dubious honor of being one of the first documented haunted houses in the city of Alton.

The most famous otherworldly resident of the place is the ghost of a man named Tom Boothby. He was a grizzled, old Indian fighter who came to live in the hotel in 1836. Boothby had seen more than his share of adventure during the Indian battles of the War of 1812. As a result, he had retired to Alton with only one arm and one eye, an arrow having put out the other one. Boothby took an upstairs room in the back, left corner of the house and quickly became known as an eccentric recluse. It is believed that he did not leave his room until his death in 1838 and the stories say that he had a boy who would deliver his meals to him each morning. The following day, Boothby would leave a payment, and the empty tray, for the young man to exchange for a full one.

Boothby soon became well known at the Mansion House. He was obsessed with the idea that the ghosts of the Indians he had killed in the past were coming to kill him and would often wake up screaming in the middle of the night. Needless to say, this would also rouse the other tenants in the house and soon, someone would be pounding on Boothby's door to settle him down. Although he never opened the door, he would normally murmur a few words of apology to the guests in the hallway outside his room and the rest of the night would pass in peace.

How often this late-night screaming would occur is unknown, but apparently it happened often enough that Boothby gained a reputation among the guests. Only the most recent tenants ever bothered to venture out into the dark corridors when Boothby began crying out in the night. Soon, they too learned to ignore the chilling sounds. And so it went for the next two years.

Then, one night, Boothby's screams were different than in the past. Instead of his crying that the Indians were coming to kill him... this time, they had found him! In fact, as Boothby yelled for help, he stated that the savages were strangling him! If his screams roused anyone that night, they did not come to his aid. The other guests had been awakened so many times before that they had trained themselves to simply ignore the ruckus. Perhaps they flinched in their sleep at the urgency of Boothby's call but if they did, they did not come to help him.

The next day passed like all of the others. The young man who came to deliver Boothby's meals picked up the empty tray and left a full one, just as he always did. It would not be until the following morning when he realized something was wrong. The tray from the day before had been untouched, something which had never happened in the previous two years!

Concerned, (probably more for his future salary than for Boothby's welfare) the young man fetched the owner of the hotel, who opened the door to Boothby's room. They found the old man inside, sprawled sideways across the bed. His night shirt was ripped and torn, as if he had been involved in a struggle, and his one good eye stared wide with fright.

The Indians were strangling him, Boothby had screamed... but it was the man's own good hand which was so tightly holding his throat!

As the years have passed, it has been said that Tom Boothby has never rested. His cries and frantic footsteps have often been heard in the house and still continue to echo there today. During the period when the Mansion House was still used as a hotel, it was said that only guests who were unaware of the story of Tom Boothby were given his old room. That way, when they were awakened by the sounds of his spirit screaming in the darkness, they would think that it was coming from some other room!

The house today is leased as private apartments and is not open to the public, however this does not stop new stories about Tom Boothby from being told. In October 2000, I was chatting with some new arrivals in Alton and they were telling me about the strange incidents that were taking place in their new home. They described the sound of a man's footsteps and even the sound of cries that were sometimes heard in the night. I asked them where they lived and to my surprise, they gave the address of the Mansion House. They also stated that their apartment was upstairs... in the back, left corner of the building!

"Have you ever heard the story of Tom Boothby?" I asked them.

They told me that they had not, so I proceeded to scare them right into looking for a new place to live!

THE MINERAL SPRINGS HOTEL

Even though the place hasn't actually been a hotel for quite a few years now, you almost expect to see guests strolling through the lobby of the Mineral Springs Hotel. For a number of years now, the place has been a busy antique mall, owned by Bob Love, who operates a real estate office on the lower floor. When you walk inside though, you will find that traces of the old hotel still exist, including shops now housed in what were once spacious sleeping quarters. You will also find the hotel's original safe, which still boasts the lingering aroma of cigars that were once stored there by the hotel's tobacco shop. In the far reaches of the building, there are even unused rooms that appear just as they did decades ago.

As I mentioned, you can almost expect to see the guests of yesterday walking up and down the corridors or lingering in the hotel bar..... and according to some, they still do.

The Mineral Springs Hotel opened in 1914 and it was a pretty spectacular place. Early advertising boasted that the hotel featured the "largest swimming pool in Illinois", mineral spring "cures", and the biggest table in the city of Alton, said to seat 26 people.

The hotel was constructed by August and Herman Luer, successful meat packers, who intended to open an ice storage plant on the property in 1909. August Luer was a German immigrant who had started a meat packing plant in Alton in 1881. When he had first come to this country, he had lived in St. Louis with his brother, who was a butcher. Concerned about the health of his young wife, Luer set up his own shop in Alton, where he found clean air and the opportunity for new business. Herman joined him here in 1893. The Luers soon began promoting their product around the countryside and posted daily prices for hogs on the corner of their receiving station. That way, farmers could drive by and stop if they liked the price, or go on to East St. Louis if they didn't. The chili, hams and sausages produced by the Luers became Alton favorites. They also went on to found the Alton Banking & Trust.

As excavations began on the site of the new ice storage plant, a natural spring was discovered during the digging. A chemist tested the water and he declared that the water had medicinal qualities. He recommended that the brothers build a spa on the site instead of a building for storing ice.

Construction was started in October 1913 with the excavation of the basement swimming pool and the hotel opened the following June. The building was five stories high and done in a beige stucco in Italian Villa style. The ornate interiors contained terrazzo floors, marble staircases, decorated plaster cornices and designs and art glass throughout. It was elaborate and luxurious and an immediate success, especially after the mineral pool opened on the lower level.

This was the biggest draw for the hotel and was said to have caused "remarkable cures". It became a popular place for swimming lessons, water polo clubs and for those seeking the healing powers of the mineral waters. A man named "Doc" Furlong also organized hydrotherapy baths and while his methods may have been questionable, the guests and customers went away pleased.

Thanks to some savvy advertising, the water was soon being shipped to customers as far away as Memphis and New Orleans. In July 1914, the hotel was bottling and selling more than 100 bottles every day. Consumption of the water increased that year to 350 gallons weekly and the hotel boasted that its curative powers equaled those of water found in Hot Springs, Arkansas. People began pouring into Alton to partake of the healing waters and the hotel held its grand opening in September 1914. It was said that one point, the swimming pool attracted over 3,000 people in a season.

The hotel enjoyed its heyday throughout the late 'teens and the early 1920's. In 1918, Hollywood actress Marie Dressler spoke at the hotel on behalf of the Liberty Loan committee. A number of new rooms were added to the hotel in 1925, the same year that an orchestra was hired to play on Sunday afternoons and for the evening dining.

August Luer sold the hotel in 1926 but it continued to thrive for many years afterward, although it finally began to deteriorate in the 1950's. In 1971, the Mineral Springs closed down for good, despite efforts to restore the place to its former popularity with the addition of a huge ballroom. In 1978, it was restored by Roger Schubert, who developed the building as a mall featuring shops and restaurants. Years later, it would see life again, thanks to further renovations by the Love family.

Once the hotel re-opened again, this time as an antique mall, stories started to be told about the place. Only these tales had nothing to do with "miracle cures" and the golden days of the hotel... these stories had to do with murder and ghosts.

You see, the Mineral Springs Hotel is a very haunted place.

The legends of the place say that three very different ghosts haunt the corridors and rooms of the Mineral Springs. The first is said to be that of an itinerant artist who was unable to pay his hotel bill many years ago. His ghost apparently haunts the former hotel bar. This section of the building is an antique store today but the saloon that once existed here was decorated with fine woods and marble, ornate trim and gargoyle-like figures on the crossbeams. All traces of the bar have since vanished and all that remains behind is an unfinished mural of the city of Alton that has been pained on one wall. The stories say that the artist who lived here was allowed to paint the mural in exchange for his bill. Unfortunately, he died before he was able to finish it and his ghost has remained here ever since. Building tenants and visitors who have encountered him say that he is more of a benign presence than a frightening one. He is usually seen simply standing around, as though he has no idea of exactly where he is. Many have described him as looking slightly drunk and others, not realizing that he is a phantom, have recalled the faint smell of liquor around him.

If any of the ghosts in the old hotel are truly frightening, it might be the phantom that allegedly haunts the hotel swimming pool. It isn't so much because of his tendency to scare the living but more because of his reason for lingering behind. That reason is a thirst for revenge.

During the early days of the business, the swimming pool was one of the big draws to the place. When it was built, it was called "the largest swimming pool in Illinois" and throughout the 1920's, parties and receptions were often held in the pool area and guests used the pool on a daily basis. Today, the pool is located in a basement area of the building that is closed off to visitors.

The story of the ghost began in the 1920's, during the heyday of the hotel. One evening, there was a large reception held at the Mineral Springs and people were gathered in the pool area for the party. One of the couples attending the event had an apparently volatile relationship, probably because the husband had quite an eye for the ladies. Throughout the evening, he flirted and danced with a number of young women until his wife could stand it no longer. In a fit of anger, she came over and started shouting accusations at him. Laughing, he attempted to just brush away her concerns but finally, she took off her shoe and smashed him in the face with the heel of it. Blood spurted out between the fingers of the hand that he pressed to his face and he stumbled over, colliding with one of the columns next to the pool. Stunned, he reeled and tumbled over into the water. Whether he was dazed by the blow to his face, or simply a bad swimmer, we'll never know. Before anyone realized what was going on, the man had slipped beneath the water and had drowned. What became of his wife is unknown.

In the years after the tragic event, and after the hotel closed down, the man began to be seen standing near the side of the pool, or in other lower parts of the building. His ghost has been described as angry and brooding, but impeccably dressed in black tie and tails.

And he has is said to have a reason for staying behind here.... revenge. According to the legend, he is waiting here for the return of his wife's spirit. It is believed that when he finds her, he intends to kill her by pushing her into the swimming pool and allowing her to drown. Will he ever find her? Perhaps someday he will and if that time ever comes, then maybe he will finally rest in peace. If not, well, then he may not be the ghost you would want to encounter on some dark night in the hotel basement!

Undoubtedly, the most famous ghost of the Mineral Springs is the legendary "Jasmine Lady". The accounts say that she has haunted a particular part of the old hotel for years. This area is a staircase that is located a short distance from the former lobby. According to the hotel legend, this lady was once a guest at the hotel who had come here to take in the "healing waters" with her husband. While she was here, she became involved romantically with another guest and started an affair with him. One evening, while her husband was away, she took the other man up to her room, with disastrous results. Her husband returned unexpectedly and caught the adulterous couple "in the act". Needless to say, he was enraged. In the course of the violent encounter, she ran away from him and started down the steps. What happened next remains a mystery....

The stories vary as to whether the woman may have tripped on the stairs or whether her angry spouse pushed her down the staircase. In the end, it didn't matter, because somehow she fell and broke her neck and she was instantly killed. Her despondent husband then returned to their upstairs room and committed suicide.

In the years that have followed, staff members and visitors to the building have caught glimpses of this woman's tragic flight down the stairs as her apparition replays the terrible event over and over again. Stranger still, they have also caught whiffs of her pungent perfume, a jasmine scent, near the staircase and in other nearby places in the building. Even people like Bob Love, who is not a believer in ghosts, have puzzled over the coming and going of this strong odor.

I had contacted him back in 1998, when I first heard about the haunting of the former hotel. He admitted that he was unsure about the existence of ghosts but never could explain one odd happening that had taken place in the building. "I have to say I'm not a believer," Mr. Love had said, "but one morning I walked in the Alton Street entrance and I smelled a strong, almost putrid, jasmine scent. It was strange."

And employees of the place have not been the only ones to have unsettling encounters with the Jasmine Lady. One woman approached me about her own incident at the former hotel. She was shopping one day when she passed the staircase. "I had no idea the place was supposed to be haunted," she said, "I wouldn't find out until later that everybody knew about the ghosts but me."

As she passed the bottom of the stairway, she caught a sickening, flowery scent but as mentioned, she had no idea that it usually signaled the presence of a ghost. What happened next though, shocked her. "Just after I smelled the perfume, I felt this cold chill, almost like a breeze blowing. It didn't just hit me... it, well, I guess sort of brushed past me, but it was real cold, " she said. "Then, I looked up. See, there are these signs that hang out in front of some of the stores down the hallway.... and all of the ones close to me start swinging back and forth."

That was enough shopping for her that day. "I just left after that," she told me. "I have been back there since and nothing else has happened, but I'll never forget that."

While these three spirits may be the most famous haunts of the Mineral Springs Hotel, they may not be alone here. Hotels are notorious for the ghosts the living leave behind. Imagine, if you will, just how many people pass through a hotel in a single year. Then, recall how many guests an old hotel might boast after decades in operation. It isn't a reach to think there might be a ghost, or two, around. If you factor in the deaths, murders and suicides that sometimes take place in hotels.... well, then you may be talking about a regular infestation! And it is unlikely that the Mineral Springs is an exception to this rule.

Besides encounters with the notorious trio of spirits, the building boasts other strange encounters as well. Michael Love, the son of the building's owner, once had an apartment in the building and he collected his own strange reports, including unexplained cold chills that have been reported by customers, items that have been seen to move about, voices and laughter than come from nowhere and more. He also heard distinct footsteps on the back stairs when he was home alone one evening. When he checked to see who had come to visit, he found no one there.

Do guests from the past still walk in the Mineral Springs Hotel? You'll have to be the judge of that. I invite you to go down and do a little shopping some afternoon.... you just might find more than you bargained for!

THUNDERBIRDS OVER ILLINOIS

As many visitors leave the city of Alton and drive north along the Great River Road, they are often surprised to see a rock painting on the side of a bluff that portrays a pretty vicious-looking winged creature. Years ago, this rock painting was actually a petroglyph that showed two such creatures. These monsters, like the modern rendering of the paintings, were called the "Piasa" by the Illinwek Indians. The original painting existed bear this location for hundreds of years and was first described in the journals of Marquette in 1673. The original site of the painting is now long gone, but Marquette described the creatures portrayed there in this manner:

> As we were descending the river we saw high rocks with hideous monsters painted on them and upon which the bravest Indian dare not look. They are as large as a calf, with head and horns like a goat, their eyes are red, beard like a tiger's and face like a man's. Their tails are so long that they pass over their bodies and between their legs, under their bodies, ending like a fish tail. They are painted red, green and black and so well drawn that I could not believe they were drawn by the Indians, for what purpose they were drawn seems to me a mystery.

Father Hennepin, another early explorer of the west, published a book in 1698 called "A New Discovery of a Vast Country in America" and he also wrote about seeing the paintings of the Piasa, which incidentally, were first incised and cut into the bluff and then painted over.

The Piasa Rock (Henry Lewis - 1854)

The petroglyphs were located immediately below where the first state prison was located in Alton. The paintings were partially destroyed in the 1840's when quarrying was done on the bluff by convicts from the prison.

The painting was later described by a Professor William McAdams, an Illinois State Geologist, who created an illustration of the bird in the 1880's. It is from his drawing that all of the modern-day renditions of the Piasa Bird come. McAdams also seems to be the person responsible for creating the mythology of a single bird-like creature, instead of two monsters, as the Indians originally passed along the story. Even in McAdam's day, the original painting no longer existed. A quarry had purchased the property and they had blasted away the wall on which it could be found some time around 1847. The drawing that McAdams created was based on the testimony of five men who recalled seeing the painting before it was destroyed. It was later featured in the "Literary Digest" and it is believed to be the most accurate drawing of the Piasa.

Who created the original painting? No one will ever know for sure, but it must have existed for some time as part of the culture of the local Native Americans. It was said that on a flat ledge below the painting were hundreds of arrow heads and spear points. It is believed that the Indians who passed the Piasa on the river would "attack" the creature by firing an arrow at it. It apparently became a custom when floating past the future site of Alton.

The Piasa Bird is considered one of the most enduring legends of the Riverbend region... a tall tale, an Indian myth that is sufficient to entertain children. But what if it isn't? What if there is more to the "legend" than meets the eye? And what if I told you that strange winged creatures have been seen in the Illinois in times more recent than that of the Native Americans?

The legend of the Piasa Bird dates back to long before the white man came to region. It has been traced to a band of Illiniwek Indians who lived along the Mississippi in the vicinity north of present-day Alton. This tribe, led by a chief named Owatoga, hunted and fished the valley and the river and lived a contented life until the "great beast" came.

One morning, Owatoga's son, Utim, and a friend were fishing when they heard a terrible scream. They looked and saw a huge bird rising from the edge of the river. The legend states that the bird was of such dimensions that it could carry away a full-grown deer in its talons, and that once it obtained a taste for human flesh, it would eat nothing else. The creature the two men saw had a young man gripped in its claws and it carried him away and out of sight. Quickly, the two young men returned to their village and found their people very frightened. They waited all day for the young man to escape from the bird and return, but he did not.

After that, nearly every morning, the great bird would appear in the sky and carry away a member of the tribe, either a man, woman or a child. Those who were carried off were never seen again. The people began to call the bird the "Piasa", which meant "the bird which devours men". Owatoga realized that they were powerless against this beast and he retreated to his lodge to fast and to pray for guidance. He emerged the next day with a plan that had been revealed to him in a vision.

According to his vision, Owatoga was to take six of his finest braves and climb to the top of one of the highest bluffs. The young men were to carry with them only their bows and a quiver of poisoned arrows. They were to hide themselves while Owatoga stood on the edge of the bluff and waited for the Piasa to appear. When the monster came, the chief was to throw himself down on the rocks and hold on while the bird attempted to carry him away. As it did so, the braves would appear with their bows and slay the beast.

Of course, all of the men in the tribe offered to help kill the Piasa, but Owatoga chose only young, unmarried men, his own son among them. The arrows were sharpened and poisoned and the group climbed to the top of the bluff. The six young men hid themselves beneath a rock ledge and Owatoga stepped out to the edge of the cliff. He folded his arms and waited for the creature to appear. Suddenly, the sky darkened overhead and the bird's massive wings were heard. The Piasa swooped down toward Owatoga. Just as the tip of the creature's sharp talon sunk into this shoulder, Owatoga threw himself flat upon the rocks. His hands curled around the roots of a tree and he clung desperately to them. The Piasa roared in frustration and its wings beat furiously, trying to lift the Indian from the rocks.

The wings unfolded once more and as it exposed itself, the young men burst from their hiding place and fired their arrows at the beast. The arrows found their mark but the Piasa continued to fight, trying over and over to lift Owatoga from the rocks. Then, with a howl of agony, the creature released him and collapsed backward, crashing over the edge of the bluff. It spiraled down out of sight and plunged beneath the waters of the Mississippi. The terrible creature was never seen again.

Despite his wounds, Owatoga recovered from his battle and joined in the celebration over the death of the Piasa. They ate, danced and celebrated into the night and the next day, they painted a colorful tribute to the Piasa bird on the stone face of the bluff where it had been destroyed. From that time on, any Indian who went up or down the river fired an arrow at the image of the Piasa Bird in memory of their deliverance from the monster.

There is also another legend of the Piasa and in this case, the legend tells of two creatures. The Miami Indians apparently told this version of the story. This legend of the Piasa states that many centuries before the white men came, there lived two monsters with the wings of eagles in the caves of the bluffs. These creatures were said to have had the claws of alligators and they spent much of their time resting and dozing on the rocks, or flying low above the river and surrounding country. One of the monsters had the roaring voice of a buffalo bull, while the other sounded with the scream of a panther. They swooped down and carried off deer and elk and took them back to their cavern to devour at their leisure.

Although the local Indians feared the creatures, the monsters never bothered them until one morning when the Miami and the Mestchegami met in battle in Piasa Valley. In the midst of the carnage, and just as the Mestchegami were wavering and about to flee, the two creatures appeared overhead, bellowing and shrieking and with their wings flapping with a thundering sound. The monsters, perhaps enraged by the sight of blood, each carried away one of the combatants. Unfortunately, both men were Miami chieftains. The Mestchegami, believing the Great Spirit had sent the monsters to aid them against their enemies, gave a great war whoop and renewed the battle, which became a massacre. The Miami fled across the country, journeying north to the Wabash River.

Years later, after they had vanquished the Mestchegami, the Miami visited the scene of the battle and painted and carved the petroglyphs of the two monsters. For years after, Indians who passed on the river would fire an arrow at the monsters in small revenge for the Miami who were slaughtered that day.

When the white men settled this region and heard the tales of the Piasa, they found no evidence (at first) to suggest that this creature really existed. But the Indians who still lived here at that time certainly believed it had. As mentioned previously, they took great pleasure in loosing arrows at the creature as they passed on the river and later would fire their rifles at it also.

In July 1836, a Professor John Russell discovered something very unusual concerning the legend of the Piasa Bird. Russell was a professor at Shurtleff College in Alton and had interest enough in the local legend to do a little exploring and research into the story of the creature. His adventures were later recounted in a magazine article in 1848 and in "Records of Ancient Races in the Mississippi Valley" by William McAdams in 1887. Here is how his story appears, written in his own words:

"Near the close of March of the present year, I was induced to visit the bluffs below the mouth of the Illinois River, above that of the Piasa. My curiosity was principally directed to the examination of a cave, connected with the above tradition as one of those to which the bird had carried his human victims.

"Preceded by an intelligent guide, who carried a spade, I set out on my excursion. The cave was extremely difficult of access, and at one point in our progress I stood at an elevation of one hundred fifty feet on the perpendicular face of the bluff, with barely room to sustain one foot. The unbroken wall towered above me, while below me was the river.

"After a long and perilous climb, we reached the cave, which was about fifty feet above the surface of the river....The roof of the cavern was vaulted, and the top was hardly less than twenty feet high. The shape of the cavern was irregular; but, so far as I could judge, the bottom would average twenty by thirty feet.

"The floor of the cavern throughout its whole extent was one mass of human bones. Skulls and other bones were mingled in the utmost confusion. To what depth they extended I was unable to decide; but we dug to a depth of 3 or 4 feet in every part of the cavern, and still we found only bones. The remains of thousands must have been deposited here. How, and by whom, and for what purpose, it is impossible to conjecture."

Was this cave really the lair of the Piasa Bird? Did this bird, always thought to be merely a mythological creature, actually exist? Did the monster really carry off and slay a large number of the Native Americans who once lived in this region? Could such a giant bird actually exist? And could it be found near Alton?

American Indian lore is filled with stories of strange, monster birds with enormous wingspans and the propensity to carry away human victims. They called these creatures "Thunderbirds" because the legends claimed that their flapping wings made a sound like rolling thunder. The birds have been described as having wingspans of 20 feet or more; hooked talons; razor-sharp beaks; and sometimes descriptions that seem oddly close to the pterodactyls of prehistoric times. But not all of these stories and accounts date back to the times of the early Americans. Most of them come from times that are not so long ago.... and some of them are disturbingly close to home.

One modern day "flap" of Thunderbird sightings began in April 1948, according to Loren Coleman in his book, "Curious Encounters". On April 4, a former Army Colonel named Walter F. Siegmund revealed that he had seen a gigantic bird in the sky above Alton, Illinois. He had been talking with a local farmer and Colonel Ralph Jackson, the head of the Western Military Academy, at the time. "I thought there was something wrong with my eyesight," he said, "but it was definitely a bird and not a glider or a jet plane. It appeared to be flying northeast... from the movements of the object and its size, I figured it could only be a bird of tremendous size."

A few days later, a farmer named Robert Price from Caledonia would see the same, or a similar, bird. He called it a "monster bird... bigger than an airplane". On April 10, another sighting would take place and this time in Overland. Mr. and Mrs. Clyde Smith and Les Bacon spotted a huge bird. They said they thought the creature was an airplane until it started to flap its wings furiously.

On April 24, the bird was back in Alton. It was sighted by EM Coleman and his son, James. "It was an enormous, incredible thing with a body that looked like a naval torpedo," Coleman recalled later. "It was flying at about 500 feet and cast a shadow the same size as a Piper Cub at that height."

Then, on May 5, the bird was sighted for the last time in Alton. A man named Arthur Davidson called the police that evening to report the bird flying above the city. Later on that same night, Mrs. William Stallings of St. Louis informed the authorities that she had also seen it. "It was bright, about as big as a house," she said. A number of sightings then followed in the St. Louis are, but ironically, just when the public excitement over the bird reached its peak, the sightings came to an end.

Sightings of strange birds have not ended in Illinois and in fact continue today. One of the most exciting, and frightening, Illinois encounters occurred in 1977 in Lawndale, a small town in Logan County. On the evening of July 25, two giant birds appeared in the sky above Lawndale. The birds were reported several times as they circled and swooped in the sky. Finally, they headed straight down. and reportedly attacked three boys who were playing in the backyard of Ruth and Jake Lowe. One of the birds grasped the shirt of ten-year-old Marlon Lowe, snagging its talons into the cloth. The boy tried in vain to fight the bird off then cried loudly for help.

The boy's cries brought Marlon's mother running outside. She later reported that she had seen the bird actually lift the boy from the ground and into the air. She screamed loudly and the bird released the child. It had carried him, at a height of about three feet, for a distance of about forty feet. She was sure that if she had not come outside, the bird had been capable of carrying the boy away. Luckily, although scratched and badly frightened, Marlon was not seriously injured.

Four other adults appeared on the scene within seconds of the attack. They described the birds as being black in color, with bands of white around their necks. They had long, curved beaks and a wingspan of at least 10 feet. The two birds were last seen flying toward some trees near Kickapoo Creek.

Three days later, a McLean County farmer spotted a bird of the same size and description flying over his farm. He, his wife, and several friends were watching radio-controlled airplanes when the bird flew close to the models. He claimed the bird had a wingspan of again, at least 10 feet across. It dwarfed the small planes that buzzed close to it.

The next sighting took place near Bloomington when a mail truck driver named James Majors spotted the two birds. He was driving from Armington to Delevan when she saw them alongside of the highway. One of the birds dropped down into a field and snatched up a small animal. He believed the two birds were probably condors, but with 8 to 10 foot wingspans!

On July 28, Lisa Montgomery of Tremont was washing her car when she looked up and saw a giant bird crossing the sky overhead.

At 2:00 AM on Saturday, July 30, Dennis Turner and several friends from Downs reported a monstrous bird perched on a telephone pole. Turner claimed that the bird dropped something near the base of the pole. When police officers investigated the sighting, they found a huge rat near the spot.

Reports of giant birds continued to come in from Bloomington and the north central Illinois area, then finally further south, from Decatur to Macon and Sullivan. On July 30, the same day the birds were reported near Bloomington, a writer and construction worker named "Texas John Huffer" filmed two large birds while fishing at Lake Shelbyville. Huffer was a resident of Tuscola and was spending the day with his son when they both spotted the birds roosting in a tree. Huffer frightened the birds with his boat horn and when they took flight, he managed to shoot over 100 feet of film. He sold a portion of the footage to a television station in Champaign for a newscast. Huffer said that the largest bird had a wingspan of over 12 feet.

After the footage aired, experts were quick to dismiss Huffer's claims, along with the reports of everyone else who reported the birds. Officials from the Department of Conservation insisted the birds were merely turkey vultures and were nothing out of the ordinary. Not surprisingly, these claims were also refuted by wildlife experts and cryptozoologists (who study mysterious animals) who all stated that no turkey vultures were of the size reported by witnesses. The largest flying bird in North America is the California Condor, which has a wingspread of up to 9 feet. The Condor is also on the endangered species list and is restricted to a few areas in California. There is little chance that a few stray birds traveled to Illinois to attack small children!

Another tale, related by Loren Coleman, involved the killing of a giant bird in December 1977. Strangely, this event also took place near Lawndale. Apparently a woman was on her way to work one morning when she saw something that looked like "a man standing in the road with something over its arms". The woman collapsed and was hospitalized, but later recovered. A group of men, after hearing this report, went to the spot, killed a large bird and then burned the body. The story was kept under wraps for some time for fear of ridicule.

So, what are these creatures? Some cryptozoological researchers like Loren Coleman believe that these thunderbirds may be "Teratorns", a supposedly extinct bird that once roamed North and South America. If these prehistoric survivors are still around today, they could certainly account for the reports of the giant birds.

At this point, such creatures remain a mystery but one thing is sure, the sightings have continued over the years and occasionally an unusual report still trickles in from Central Illinois. So keep that in mind the next time that you are standing in an open field and a large, dark shadow suddenly fills the sky overhead. Was that just a cloud passing in front of the sun... or something else??

SPIRIT OF THE RUEBEL HOTEL

Located along the western edge of Illinois, where the waters of the Mississippi and Illinois Rivers meet, is the town of Grafton. This small village came into existence thanks to one man, James Mason. He was a settler from Grafton, Massachusetts who lived in Edwardsville and worked as a real estate agent. In 1818, he married the sister of one of the most prominent businessmen in St. Louis, Henry Von Phul, and it would be from this union that Grafton would be born.

Around the time of Mason's marriage, he began joining in conferences with the governor of Illinois and a number of St. Louis businessmen. Their concern was the city of Alton, Illinois. At that time, Alton was actually growing faster than its rival city of St. Louis and these men conspired together on ways to stop this. Mason offered a solution. He would purchase the lands along the river where Grafton is now located and would establish ferries across the Mississippi and the Missouri to St. Louis. He would also establish a road from

Grafton to Carrolton, Illinois that would allow easy access from Illinois to St. Louis, bypassing Alton altogether.

Business and the riverboats soon made the small community a thriving one and in 1832, Mason built 4 log cabins, and later a frame house, before passing away in St. Louis in 1834. His widow, who eventually re-married, platted and named the town which was built here, Grafton, in honor of her late husband's birth place. By 1836, Grafton was still growing. New businesses and stores were coming to town; warehouses were constructed for industry; and even a wharf was built to accommodate traffic along the river.

Then, in 1844 came a terrible flood that drove all of the merchants and residents from Grafton's business district. Many of them never returned, but the flood was actually a blessing in disguise because in ushered in the steamboat era in Grafton. Thanks to the overflow of water from the rivers, the Grafton channel was now able to accommodate larger riverboats. These boats brought not only prosperity and commerce to the city, but excitement and violence too.

The steamboat era was the most exciting time in the history of Grafton but it came to an end in the 1930's. The era also took place at the same time the railroad was active in Grafton. The railroad came in the 1880's and at its peak, there were three rail lines that came into town. The last line ended in 1948, bringing an end to commerce and turning the place into a ghost town until the late 1960's, when the Great River Road was extended from Alton.

Although Grafton boasts a handful of ghost stories, the most famous haunted site is the Ruebel Hotel. A man named Michael Ruebel built the establishment in 1884 and when it opened, it was the largest commercial hotel in Jersey County. It had 32 rooms with a bath house in the back and mainly played host to river travelers. Room rates at the time were $1.00 per day, while weekly rooms could be had for a rate of $8.00 and included three meals a day.

The hotel also boasted the finest saloon in town, at a time when 26 saloons operated in Grafton. Needless to say, this was a rowdy place to be but with a population made up of mainly Irish and German quarry workers, who were used to brawling and drinking contests, this number of saloons became a necessity. Because of its reputation on the river, the hotel was also frequently visited by river travelers and steamboat operators, further adding to the colorful atmosphere. The hotel thrived until 1912, when it was damaged by fire. It was quickly rebuilt however, this time adding a restaurant on the first floor and a dance hall on the second. During World War II, the dance hall was turned into quarters for 30 Coast Guard men, who were stationed in Grafton to provide protection for the river traffic.

As time went on, the rest of the world passed Grafton by. After two World Wars, the Great Depression, floods, the end of the steamboat era and the closing of the local rail lines, the town slowly withered. And the Ruebel Hotel died along with it. By the 1980's, the building had become an abandoned derelict, its heyday long forgotten. Then, in 1996, the hotel was purchased by the Jeff Lorton family, who completely restored the place and opened it for business in spring of 1997.

But what of the ghosts?

Yes, according to some staff members and a number of guests who have stayed here, the hotel is haunted. While most of the ghosts here are more than likely just residual images from the past, there does seem to be at least one with a personality, although just who she may be is unknown.

Hotels, especially older ones, are always ripe for a haunting. Literally hundreds of people pass through a hotel in any given year and are bound to leave a little piece of themselves behind. With a hotel like the Ruebel, which dates back more than 100 years, there have been thousands of people who have stayed here.

Shortly after the Ruebel opened again, at least three guests and a hotel housekeeper reported encountering a ghost in the building. In April of 1997, the three overnight guests told the owners the next morning they had spoken to the ghost of a little girl named "Abigail". Since then, a number of other folks who have spent the night in the hotel say they too have seen the young girl in the upstairs hallway and at the top of the stairway to the second floor.

"As many years as this place has been around, I'm sure that someone has died here, but none of us have seen anything," said Jeff Lorton in a 1997 newspaper interview. "I figure if I don't bother them, they won't bother me."

THE HAUNTSTOWN TREASURE

Another Illinois river story tells of an old cabin that was once located near a place with the unlikely name of "Hauntstown". According to the story, the cabin belonged to an old recluse named Jesse Barnes who, years before, had amassed a considerable fortune in the lumber business. It was said that he had owned several steamships and they made regular runs downstream to New Orleans.

Jesse was also said to have been an eccentric, especially after his wife had died in childbirth years before, and he had a distrust for banks and bankers. Because of this, he kept all of his money hidden at his home near Hauntstown. Neighbors in the area often talked about Barnes and his elusive treasure, although none of them knew for sure where he kept the money hidden. The old hermit was not a very friendly man and rarely allowed anyone on his property.

Sometime prior to 1910, Jesse passed away and after the funeral, the rumors once again began to circulate about his hidden fortune. The money had not been with the rest of his personal belongings and most in the area were sure that it was still hidden somewhere on his property. One night, the Barnes cabin mysteriously burned to the ground. Many believe the fire may have been the work of looters, hoping to flush out the location of any gold coins secreted with the structure. Regardless, the blaze did not deter local folks from searching for the hidden loot.

As these things tend to happen, other rumors began to spread. Those who ventured out to the old Barnes cabin to look for the gold began to tell of a ghost who haunted the place. Most believed this spirit was that of Jesse Barnes, still trying to hide his money.

Were these stories true? Or were the merely the creation of treasure-hunters who were trying to keep other people away from the property? That much is unknown but according to one story, told about a particular treasure hunt, it seems that supernatural forces may have been at work after all!

One night, a small group of people came from the local settlement of Batchtown to look for the treasure. One of them, a woman named Elizabeth, had recently been to see a Spiritualist medium. The medium had informed her that she was soon going to come into a large sum of money, which she would find hidden beneath a hearth stone for a fireplace. Excited, Elizabeth convinced three male companions to accompany her out to the site of the old Barnes cabin. She had heard the stories of the missing treasure and was sure this was the money she was due to discover.

They arrived at the wooded cabin site very late in the evening. As the drove back along the winding, dirt road through the forest, they noticed the flicker of lightning in the dark sky. A thunderstorm was quickly approaching, so they knew they had to work fast, or face being trapped in the woods at the end of washed out and muddies road.

Armed with shovels and a large lever, the group quickly got to work. They found the hearth stone amidst the ruins of the cabin and except for the crumbling chimney, it was one of the only remaining structures from the house. After about an hour, they had dug far enough beneath the stone to begin to raise it up from the ground. The stone slowly raised a few inches and as Elizabeth bent down to peer into the dark hole, she heard the sound of a moaning voice that seemed to be coming from beneath the stone! She sprang backwards and as she did so, she collided with the men who were levering the stone. They fell to the ground and the hearthstone pitched sideways, uncovering the hole underneath it!

Suddenly, the sky overhead erupted with thunder and lightning and rain began to fall in sheets! The treasure-hunters reeled back from the uncovered pit and.....

Well, we don't know for sure what they saw....

None of the four members of the group ever spoke about what they saw that night. Whether or not the treasure (or something worse) rested in that hole remains a mystery. What we do know is that they managed to get down the dirt road through the forest before the rain washed it out completely and after arriving home, they were never heard from again. The last trace we have of Elizabeth is a letter that she sent her mother from New Orleans. She never returned to Batchtown again.

The following day, a neighbor who lived along a woods trail not far from the Barnes cabin, decided to walk down to the old place. He was fairly sure that lightning had struck near the ruins of the cabin the night before and wanted to see what damage had been done. He later told, after hearing the story of the treasure hunters, that when he arrived at the remains of the house, he saw nothing out of place. The hearthstone was in the same place it had been the last time he had seen it and as far as he could tell it had never been moved.

The neighbor also firmly stated that he did not believe in ghosts.

So, what had they seen that night? Was the stone really moved out of place? Or was the secret of the missing fortune covered over by supernatural forces?

I can't really say for sure. Of course, if the story is true (or even if it isn't) that means that a fortune in hidden treasure is still lying out there in the woods near the former site of Hauntstown.... just waiting for someone to find it!

THE DIAMOND ISLAND MYSTERY

Another strange tale involves the "fiery phantom" of Diamond Island, which was reported in 1888 on a tiny island near Hardin, a small town between the Illinois and Mississippi Rivers.

The first report of the spook actually came in 1885 when two young men were fishing along the river one night. Shortly after midnight, a bright ball of light suddenly appeared on the small island, which was directly in front of them on the river. The ball of light, which was described as a "fire ball" shot through the trees and then flew up into the air, where it hung suspended over the island. The two boys ran home and awakened their parents to tell them about the eerie event. They insisted that they had actually seen a face within the ball of fire!

Needless to say, their story was dismissed around town until other people, including a number of reputable town citizens, began to also report the strange light. "It was about the size of a barrel and there were definite features in it," said one local businessman. "I could see the shape of something fuzzy inside the fire."

Finally, in September 1888, a group of skeptical locals banded together for an all-night hunt for the island phantom. Armed with guns, knives, clubs and pitchforks, they rowed out to the island in secrecy. They stayed as quiet as possible with the idea that if someone was hoaxing the weird events, they didn't want him to know they were there. The boats were hidden in the weeds along the riverbank and the men quickly took cover at the edge of the trees. They were nervous, tense and alert for any sign of the ghostly manifestation.

Suddenly, the entire end of the island where they were hidden was bathed in a glowing red-orange light! An inexplicable ball of flame rose out of the trees, swooped into the air and then simply hung above the men's heads. Their frightened cries echoed out over the water and they raised their weapons and began to fire at the glowing object.

The shotguns and rifles had no effect on the strange light and instead of fleeing, it moved even closer to the men. Finally, one of them shouted to "run" and all of them scrambled for the boats. What happened next was even more terrifying!

Before the men could get to their boats, the fiery ball of light arced into the sky and landed inside of the closest skiff. The boat plunged backward into the river and moved away from island. As it did so, the glowing light suddenly transformed into the shape of a small old man who was wearing a pair of denim overalls! He simply stood there in the boat for a few moments, as it drifted out into the river, then he was gone. The apparition seemed to catch fire and then, as a ball of light once again, it took off into the sky. It vanished quickly above the trees on the island.

The would-be "ghost hunters" were terrified and trembling. They could not believe what they had seen. Some of them shouted to the shore for help while others fell to their knees and prayed. The cries from the island awakened a local farmer, who managed to rescue them, even though one of their boats still remained moored on the island. "They were just too frightened to move," he later said. "One of the boys had to be carried on and off my rowboat."

The bizarre happenings continued on Diamond Island for several more months, much to the dismay of the local people. Then, like many other mysteries, the weird phenomena suddenly ceased without explanation. And Hardin's fiery phantom was never heard from again.

GHOSTS OF QUINCY

Another haunted Mississippi River town is Quincy, Illinois. Located along the riverbanks, the town was started back in 1822 when a settler named John Wood built a cabin here at what is now the foot of Delaware Street. The city grew rapidly, thanks to both river traffic and the railroads. In later years, it became known as the "Jewel of the West" and later, the "Gem City".

Thanks to its rich history, the city is also known for its many ghostly legends and lore. There are said to be a number of haunted houses and sites here, including one of the most famous buildings in the region. The stories say that Villa Catherine, the only Moorish castle built on the Mississippi, is haunted by the wife of George Metz, who constructed the house in 1900. Her spirit is rumored to still haunt this historic mansion.

There is also said to be a haunted cemetery in the area known as "Ghost Hollow", located south of Quincy. This eerie graveyard is supposedly surrounded by a high stone wall and is filled with crumbling stone crypts. In the center of the burial ground is a black tomb that bears a one-word inscription in Latin. Few are believed to know the exact location of this cemetery and my inquiries into the site were mostly met with silence. The few who did speak about it claimed that "you could hear the sound of whispers and singing" in the place at night.

Also located just outside of the city limits is a housing area known as Harrison Hills, or the "Indian Mounds", as it is sometimes called. According to local legend, the houses here were built directly on some Indian burial sites. Residents still find the occasional arrowhead on the property, not to mention spot the occasional ghost in the surrounding wooded area. Stories say that you can sometimes hear voices chanting in native languages being carried on the wind at night.

Quincy's history during the Civil War has also given birth to several legends. Once such story comes from the fact that the city is located just across the river from Missouri, a state that stayed loyal to the Confederacy during the war. Southern sympathizers and spies often came across the Mississippi and stayed in Quincy. One house that legends say often harbored southerners was the "Old Rebel House", which was located at the corner of Second and Vermont Streets. For many years after the Civil War, locals told of spies and saboteurs who stayed at the house and to add to its reputation, it was also regarded as being haunted.

Beth Scott and Michael Norman's book, "Haunted Heartland", recounts a spooky incident that took place in the house in 1880's. At that time, the Old Rebel House was occupied by a mother and three children who lived on the top floor, while the woman's married daughter and her husband lived downstairs. There was a long balcony on the second floor that stretched from one end of the house to the other and doors opened from this porch into nearly every room. It should also be pointed out that there was no way to gain access to this balcony from outside.

One morning, the mother left for work and placed her daughters in charge of her infant son. Almost as soon as she departed, the two girls began to argue over who got to rock their baby brother's cradle. Suddenly, in the midst of their bickering, a door that led in from the balcony opened up and a sinister-looking man stepped inside. Years later, the two girls would say that the man "looked just like the picture you see of the devil". They simply stared at him as he stumbled across the room and out into the hallway. There was a wooden banister that surrounded the staircase leading down to their sister's apartment and their mother had placed several handmade quilts along the railing. The strange man proceeded to throw the quilts onto the floor, and then he picked them back up again and arranged them differently on the rail. After a moment, he turned and started walking toward the two girls. Before he reached them though, he changed directions and lurched out through the door he had entered through.

The girls didn't waste any time and immediately began screaming, bringing their sister upstairs. They explained to her what had happened and pointed out the door the "devil man" had disappeared through. She walked over but found it locked. Refusing to believe the story, she spanked her sisters, a punishment that was repeated by their mother when she returned from work and heard the odd tale.

In spite of this, the girls maintained that the story was true. Years after the event, when others had encountered their own specters in the Old Rebel House, the doubters were forced to grudgingly admit that there may have been more to the story than they first imagined!

Madison School, which can also be found in Quincy, has a history of connections to the next world. The location was thought to be haunted long before the school was ever constructed and even after the previous structure was torn down, the strange events didn't stop. Some believe that a nearly disastrous fire in 1982 could have been linked to ghosts, as no cause for the blaze was ever discovered.

Many years before the school was built at Twenty-Sixth and Maine Streets, a house stood at that location. According to local stories, a woman was murdered there, although the crime was never solved. The unknown killers broke into the house and attacked the woman at the top of a staircase leading to the upper floor. She was then dragged screaming down the stairs and was stabbed to death at the foot of the steps. A trail of blood was left behind as she was pulled across the floor and then deposited inside of a closet beneath the staircase. Her body was discovered there a few days later.

The owners of the house began to have a hard time keeping the place rented. Families moved out in rapid succession, all claiming that the place was haunted. They were never able to remove the bloodstains from the floor at the bottom of the stairs and took to covering it up with rugs. No one ever used the closet below the stairs either, claiming that the sound of a woman weeping could be heard inside. There were also reports of footsteps going up and down the stairs and a door on the east side of the house that would open by itself, even if it were locked.

Later on, the house was torn down to make room for the Madison School. This brought an end to the supernatural activity at the site, or did it? Just where do the ghosts go when the houses they haunt are torn down? Could this one now be lingering in Madison School?

Perhaps the strangest supernatural legend of Quincy involves Burton Cave, located about four miles east of town. The area remains a popular recreation site and many have visited the cave, not realizing the eerie story connected to it.

At some point in the late 1880's, a group of young people from Quincy came out to the cave to enjoy a Sunday afternoon picnic. After lunch, the group decided to do some exploring in the cave. Using only candlelight, they carefully navigated the entrance and walked a few yards into the gloomy interior. Quite suddenly, the group was startled by the appearance of a figure in the cave. Whoever this person was, he darted out of the shadows and scurried deeper into the cave. They only got a quick glimpse of the person, but he appeared to be a man in a black, hooded robe. Although the teenagers were now a little nervous, they quickly decided to follow the man into the dark cavern.

Within moments, they spotted a dim light coming from further back in the cave. As they rounded a corner, they saw a stone ledge that protruded from the wall. The light seemed to be coming from the ledge. As they got closer, a strange scene appeared before them. Lying on the ledge was the body of a woman, clad all in white and stretched out as though in preparation for burial. She seemed to be completely lifeless. All around her, candles burned, illuminating the bizarre tableau. Now the picnickers were genuinely frightened and they retreated from the cave. They hurriedly returned to Quincy to inform the authorities about what they had seen.

A short time later, the county sheriff, several deputies and two members of the picnic group came back to Burton Cave. The two young men led the officers inside, but there was no trace of the woman, the candles or the figure in the black robe. The cave was untouched and deserted and it did not appear as if anyone, save for the frightened teenagers, had been inside in quite some time. The sheriff admitted that he believed the story however. They were simply too frightened to be pretending or playing a prank.

What actually happened at Burton Cave that day remains a mystery.

HAUNTED GALENA

Located in the far northwest corner of Illinois is the historic town of Galena. Although not actually along the banks of the Mississippi, it is connected to the waterway by the Fever River, which winds its way past the city. Although Galena was founded officially in 1823, there were legions of men in the area several years before that. The region that would become Jo Daviess County was filled with lawless "boom camps" of lead miners. The mining companies had come in 1819 to uncover the vast deposits of lead that could be found in the area and soon, Galena was born.

Although remote, isolated and plagued with Indian problems, Galena quickly turned into one of the most important cities in Illinois. By 1827, there were over one hundred homes and stores in the town and six to seven thousand inhabitants. The city's newspaper, the "Miner's Journal" started five years before Chicago had a newspaper at all. Riverboats and barges frequently loaded in Galena and carried lead ore downriver to Alton and St. Louis, where it was transported east by water, rail and road. The Great Lakes portage was considered very difficult and not worth the effort to make. In this way, Galena stayed out of touch with its near neighbors of Chicago and Peoria. Eventually, this isolation would make Galena a poor commercial outlet and the boom times faded away. Galena remains today as a historic treasure in northern Illinois and is known for its glorious preservation efforts and for being the home of General Ulysses S. Grant before the Civil War.

It is also widely known for its ghosts!

This colorful aspect to the town history is thanks to the work of Daryl Watson, the executive director of the Galena- Jo Daviess County Historical Society and Museum. In 1995, he published a book called "Ghosts of Galena", which chronicled both the current ghost stories of the area and also the older stories that he had gleaned from antique newspaper reports. He soon discovered that Galena was filled with spirited sites, including the 1858 mansion where the Historical Museum is located!

The haunting apparently began in 1989 when staff members started to notice unexplained footsteps pacing the rooms and hallways of the old house. Over the next two years, they recorded accounts of thumping and shuffling noises, repeated footsteps, a chandelier that moved by itself, a piano that played under its own power and furniture being moved without explanation. One night in January 1991, during a reception at the house, two trays of champagne glasses mysteriously upended themselves and crashed to the floor. At first, careless servers were blamed for the problem until Watson himself was standing in the museum gift shop and saw a tray of glasses begin to move. The tray, which rested alone on a counter, suddenly began to shake and vibrate and then pitched forward. Several of the glasses were shattered before anyone could get to them!

The stories of hauntings range the entire history of Galena, from the early days to the present. Many of the older stories come from newspapers and accounts, but other stories are modern and sometimes frighteningly current!

LANTERN LIGHT OF HORSESHOE MOUND

Located just east of Galena is a large, curved hill called Horseshoe Mound. According to the "Galena Weekly Gazette", a ghost began haunting the area around the mound back in 1907. Today,

Highway 20 wraps around the hill just before it stretches into town, but years ago, this was an area called the School Section and folks who lived nearby began reporting a ghost who appeared between Horseshoe Mound and Shot Tower Hill.

These local residents told of seeing a glowing apparition that would appear at the base of the mound and then travel across the ground that separated it from Shot Tower Hill. It would appear each night around eight o'clock or so and seemed to be a man carrying a lantern. Legend had it that this "ghost light" was the specter of a railroad man who was killed as the result of a collision between two trains on the Illinois Central tracks. The crash had occurred near the stockyards sometime around 1900. It was believed that this man's spirit was unable to rest and that every night, with glimmering lantern in hand, he made the melancholy walk between the two hills. Then, he would vanish as mysteriously as he had come.

That was the story told in 1907 at least, but could the ghost still appear today? Most didn't think so, preferring the tale to be nothing more than vintage ghostlore from a by-gone era. But was this really the case? Not according to two men who saw the "railroad man" one night just a few years ago!

One evening, two travelers were driving along Highway 20 and rounded the curve around Horseshoe Mound. It was a pleasant night and they chatted as they journeyed along, glad to be back in Galena. As they talked, they made it around the curve and then were stunned to see something that was completely beyond their comprehension! It was the form of a human face and body that materialized just past the windshield of the car! The driver slammed on the brakes and got a vivid look at the strange apparition. The face was not distinct, but was recognizably human, and the body had a torso, legs and arms that were a smoky-grayish in color. The shape hovered there for a few moments and then disappeared over the roof of the car.

The driver turned to his passenger. He didn't know if the other man had also seen the same thing, but his friend assured him that he had. Shaken, they realized that they had probably just seen a ghost! Neither of the men had ever had an experience like that before and according to Daryl Watson, neither of them has had one since.

So what did the two men see that night near Horseshoe Mound? Was it the ghost of the railroad man, still lingering after all of these years? Or another ghost altogether?

THE GHOST OF TURNER HALL

The historical building called Turner Hall is a landmark to the people of Galena. A German group called the Turner Society built it in 1874. They believed in encouraging a "sound mind in a sound body" and built the hall as a place for gymnastics, theater and literature. The building still stands today and over the years has served musicians, politicians, theater groups and both public and private community organizations. With the hall's rich history, it's not surprising that a haunting is mixed into the building's past.

In the mid-1990's, the Save Turner Hall foundation began working to restore and preserve the building. A number of the volunteers for the group experienced their own weird happenings in the place. One of those who worked to renovate the place, and who had several strange experiences, was a woman named "Ann". One night, she and a fellow worker were standing backstage near a stone wall. All of the sudden, both of them felt an icy chill sweep over them, as if they had just stepped into a freezer. Ann suggested to her friend that they move, wondering if perhaps a draft had been caused by an open door somewhere. The other woman agreed and they stepped aside. At the moment they did, a small stone, which had come loose from high up on the wall, came crashing to the floor where they had just been standing! There was no one else backstage and certainly no one up on the wall. Coincidence? Or the resident ghost trying to tell them something?

On another evening, Ann and three others were standing just inside of the hall's foyer. They were getting ready to leave after spending several hours working on sets for an upcoming production. As they were turning to go, all four of them suddenly noticed the shape of a person walk past one of the dressing room doors at the far end of the hall. As no one else was supposed to be in the building they were alarmed. After a quick search though, they discovered that no one else was there. Who this shadowy figure may have been was anyone's guess.

Over the years, there have been many people, volunteers and visitors alike, who have experienced all sorts of odd and unexplainable things in the hall. Some of these have included the already mentioned cool drafts, things going missing and lights turning on and off by themselves.

One night, a volunteer named "Mike" was in Turner Hall, helping with the restoration work. He was up in the third floor attic of the building and when he came down the stairs to leave, he switched the light off. As he turned to walk away from the steps, he caught the shape of a person behind him in the attic. He realized that he had just turned all of the lights off on someone! He flipped the switch back on and called out an apology. When no one answered, he climbed back up the stairs. A quick search revealed that he was in the attic by himself!

One evening, while getting ready for the "Ground Hog Dance", a fundraiser for the Galena Arts and Recreation Center, a minister had an unusual experience with what seemed to be an angry ghost. He related the story to Daryl Watson and explained that he had been in Turner Hall with his daughter one evening. All of the other volunteers had already left and they were in the place alone... or so they thought. The two of them were in the balcony, putting a projector in place, planning to cast the image of a groundhog onto the curtain behind the stage. They were nearly finished and ready to leave when a loud male voice boomed out from the north side of the balcony. They could not distinguish his words, but he sounded quite angry. The shouting went on for a few moments and then stopped.

Startled, the minister and his daughter both quickly looked to see who was in the balcony with them, but there was no one to see. The theater was empty! With that, they quickly finished what they were doing and prepared to leave. Before they could make it to the stairs though, they heard the voice cry out again. Once more, the angry shouts seemed to come from nowhere! Without a doubt, the sounds quickened their steps as they descended the stairs to the main floor and departed from Turner Hall.

The haunting continued, but who might the ghost of the building be? Research into the history of the hall revealed a man named Charles Scheerer, who was the first manager of the place. He was a furniture dealer and part of a firm called Scheerer, Armbruster & Coleman. In addition to furniture, they also made caskets and Charles was a part-time undertaker, along with his other duties. His office was located right next door to Turner Hall and he was active in the society, as well as the group's treasurer.

For many years, he took care of Turner Hall and faithfully watched over the place. In fact, he even spent his final moments here. On March 14, 1910, his body was discovered in the hall. He had passed away from natural causes. After all of this time though, many believe that he has never left. It's thought that perhaps it's his ghost who lingers in the building, still watching over the place for future generations to enjoy.

- CHAPTER FOUR -

SPIRITS OF THE PRAIRIE

HISTORY & HAUNTINGS OF CENTRAL ILLINOIS

When traveling across America, there are certainly places that are bound to give you a bit of a chill. Some of these places are not the first that you might think of when pondering ghosts and the spirit world, but they are among the most haunted spots that you will probably encounter on your journey. I have always found the prairies of central Illinois to be one of these places.

FROM THE HAUNTING OF AMERICA

For the last several decades or so, the main way of life in Central Illinois has been built around farming, but it wasn't always this way. In fact, when the early settlers came here, they chose to live in the shelter of the forests that grew along the nearby sources of water. The vast prairie land that stretched before them was both inviting and frightening and it would be some years to come before the waves of grass and rich ground would be broken to eke an existence out of the soil. These first settlers were mostly hunters, with a few farmers mixed in, and all of them made their homes on the edge of the timber. They would not realize for some time that there was nothing wrong with the Central Illinois soil. They didn't understand how soil that grew prairie grass, yet no trees, could possibly be fertile. In addition to that, the trees were essential for survival, providing wood for fires, tools and most especially, a home to live in. When most of the populace turned to farming, they found that wooden split rail fences would protect the fields and would keep the livestock from roaming into the forest and being killed by wolves.

The farmers soon found that corn was an ideal crop for the prairie. It was easy to sow and to cultivate and was easily turned into many food products and a marketable whiskey. Many farmers owned stills that converted corn mash into a clear but potent whiskey that could then be transported to market via pack horse or river barge. This corn alcohol became a popular western drink and the jug would circulate freely at social events like dances, barn-raisings and especially at election time.

The secondary crop became wheat, which could be converted to flour, but only at a mill. The mills came a little later, following the small settlements, and bringing rudimentary mechanics to the frontier. The mills were built along rivers for power but where dams could not be built, horses and oxen provided the power for the grinding stones. Soon, the mill became the leading establishment in many of the settlements and other businesses followed closely behind, like blacksmith shops and general stores.

In those days, almost no one on the prairie had money. The settlers made their own clothing by tanning the hides of deer and cattle for shoes while women with spinning wheels and looms produced trousers, shirts and dresses. They grew their own food, or hunted it in the forests, and the small farms provided eggs, milk and butter. In the general stores, the settlers could trade any surplus goods for whiskey, sugar, salt, tools, crockery, or coffee.

But as idyllic as this all sounds, the frontier was not without its dangers and many did not survive. In the early years, much of that danger came from the Native American populace. The Kickapoo, and other Indians, would keep the settlers in a constant state of alarm for many years. Whether laboring in the forest or in the fields, the rifle was always kept handy and families rarely enjoyed a feeling of continual security.

And Indians were not the only problem, as weather and disease were other important obstacles to overcome. Being level and low, the land was hard to drain in the days of the pioneers. Ponds and lakes often formed in areas where drainage was poor and small streams would clog with leaves after a storm and create problems for homes and fields. In the wet places and swampy spots, swarms of mosquitoes would thrive, although no one recognized what a health problem they were for many years.

Disease often ran rampant and Illinois was cursed with a reputation for being an "unhealthy" state. A strange form of malaria was common, but doctors had no idea what caused it and it was referred to as simply a fever, or "ague". They believed the cause was a noxious gas that came from the wet swamps and from damp and rotting vegetation, not realizing that the mosquitoes probably carried it instead. With no quinine available, those with the sickness were forced to allow the fever to run its course. It was rarely fatal, but patients often had relapses. The attacks would start with a series of cold chills that left the victim shaking, their teeth chattering. This would be followed by flushes of burning heat and terrible pains in the head and back. In time, those with the sickness would simply "sweat it out of them" and return to normal, at least until the next time.

More deadly was the disease known as "milk sickness", which took the life of Abraham Lincoln's mother. It was probably caused by thirsty animals eating white snakeroot in the dry season and then becoming sick. This would pass the disease on from cattle to humans through the milk. For many years, no cause could be found and the terrifying illness was often thought to be arsenic poisoning or typhus.

Another problem with the spread of disease may have been the lack of personal cleanliness, which was common on the frontier. In the heat of summer, common flies would seek the shelter of the cabins, which had no screens on the doors or windows. Little soap was available, and what was available was rarely used. There was also an ignorance of sanitation practices too, which made human and animal waste in the drinking supply commonplace. This lack of hygiene made childhood diseases, typhoid, tuberculosis, dysentery and smallpox spread quickly among the pioneers.

In the winter, many settlers died from the extreme cold, having little protection from it. Over the winter of 1830-31, Central Illinois was hit with disaster. This terrible season would be remembered for many years as the "deep snow". Early that winter, snow began to fall and continued to come in intervals, sometimes alternating with sleet and freezing rain. This treacherous mixture would form a layer of snow and ice that was three to four feet thick. The snow drifted so high that loaded wagons could be driven over the top of fence rails. Livestock perished and soon game became scarce. It would be years later before the squirrels and prairie chickens could be found to hunt again. Many settlers died in the bitter cold and snow and that terrible winter gave birth to legends of cannibalism and depravity (see "Legend of Hell Hollow" in the following chapter).

As you can see, life in this region was never easy and the death and tragedy that sometimes triumphed over the hard life of the settlers gave birth to legends and ghost stories. One such tale was actually discovered by researcher Glen Elam in no less a book than the 1880 " History of Macon County, Illinois". According to the story, a man named Thomas Nelms came to Central Illinois in 1829 from Logan County, Kentucky. A year later, in August, he died during a woodcutting accident when a tree that he was working on fell and struck him. The older settlers stated that after the tree was cut down, but before it was split into rails, a number of witnesses reported a curious "tingling" sound that came from the tree. They described these sounds as being like those of an ax striking a particularly tough piece of wood. Apparently, the unexplained sounds continued even after the tree was spilt into rails and turned into a fence. Travelers who passed the fence were often attracted by the strange noise and despite a number of investigations, no one could discover a cause for it. Most came to believe that it was the ghost of Thomas Nelms, still connected to the tree that had taken his life.

And there were other tales from the early settlers as well...

Another tale concerned the spirit of a Mrs. Stewart, whose ghost haunted a stand of trees on the south side of Macon County. According to the records, two brothers named James and Hargus Stewart, settled in the Long Grove area in the South Macon township. It was said that Mrs. Stewart died some time between 1840-1845 and her passing apparently caused a chilling sensation in the immediate neighborhood. She was buried in the southeastern part of the grove and shortly after, a great many of the people who lived nearby came to believe that Mrs. Stewart's spirit was not at rest. In fact, many of them could not be induced to pass that portion of the grove after dark.

Another old story was told in the vicinity of early Decatur and involved a tragedy that occurred to one of the pioneer families. This family consisted of a father and his wife, and their two sons. The boys were playing in the woods near their cabin one day when a storm approached from the west. Somehow, in the darkness and rain that followed, the boys became lost. Hours passed and when they did not return home, their father set out to look for them, calling loudly and wandering about in the forest until nightfall came. The next day, he organized a group of men and they searched the surrounding woods again, but still turned up no sign of the boys.

Later that same afternoon, the boy's mother was waiting for word from the search party when a small, ragged figure emerged from the woods near the cabin. It was her oldest son, sick, weak and exhausted from his ordeal in the woods. He fell down in the clearing in front of the house and never regained consciousness. The doctor was summoned, but the boy died the next morning. He was never able to tell what had happened to his brother.

The search party did not give up until the next day. The youngest boy was lost, and most likely dead, and his older brother was buried on the far edge of the clearing near the family cabin.

Late that night, a tapping sound came from the window near the parent's bed. The mother lifted her head and saw a pale face peering in at her from outside. It was the lifeless face of her dead son! Her screams woke her husband, who went outside to find no one there. He calmed his wife, insisting that it had been her imagination, and they went back to bed. Needless to say, the woman had trouble going back to sleep, but eventually drifted off again. An hour passed and she was awakened once again by a tapping sound. Her son had come back! This time, she did not scream, but got silently out of bed and went outside in her nightdress and bare feet.

She rounded the side of the cabin and saw her oldest son standing there in the darkness. A faint glow seemed to come from his body and he was dressed in his best Sunday meeting clothes, which he had been buried in. He did not speak but simply motioned for his mother to follow him.

The boy led her deep into the dark woods. She stumbled and tripped over underbrush and branches, but managed to follow behind him. The path took her nearly one mile into the forest and then suddenly, the glowing boy stopped near the base of a huge, fallen tree. He looked at his mother one last time... then disappeared. The woman heard a faint sound from close by and realized that it was the sound of someone whimpering softly. She bent down and heard her youngest son's voice. He was trapped in a shallow ditch beneath the fallen tree. The storm had knocked it down, pinning the small boy beneath it.

His older brother had saved him after all.... from beyond the grave.

Growing up in Central Illinois, I have always regarded it as one of the strangest parts of the state. In this chapter, and in the two that follow, you will discover many of the ghosts, hauntings and weird happenings of the region. I wish that I could say that I have collected them all here, but when it comes to the spirits of Central Illinois, these pages can only scratch the surface!

So enjoy these tales from different periods and times and you'll soon agree with me and see for yourself that Central Illinois is a very eerie place!

RAILROAD GHOSTS

The railroads first came to Central Illinois in the 1850's and completely changed the way of life for those who lived in what were once little more than farm communities. With the coming of the railroads, the outside world was now open to these simple folk. All at once, goods from the east could be purchased in local stores and products from the prairie, like grain and cattle, could be shipped to expanding markets all over the country. One of the greatest railroad hubs in Central Illinois was the city of Decatur. All of the major rail lines that came through Illinois had headquarters and rail service through this small midwestern town. The arrival of the railroad in Decatur in 1854 would change the future of the city forever.

The first railroad to establish service in Decatur was the Great Western Line, which eventually became a part of the Norfolk & Western Railroad in later years. There was also a number of other rail services to Decatur but the greatest of these were most likely the Wabash and the Illinois Central.

The first Wabash roundhouse was built in Decatur in 1869 and it had eight stalls. The Wabash shops were moved to Decatur in 1884 and operations here expanded rapidly. Decatur became the hub of all of the railroad's operation and in 1925 had a peak employment of 3500 men, making it the largest employer in the city. Eventually, the railroad died out in the city and the Wabash merged with Norfolk & Western in 1964. A heavy loss in passenger service was cited as the main reason for the merger and most of the service was finally abandoned. At one point, at its peak, the Wabash Railroad operated 25 passenger trains out of Decatur every day.

The second rail service to come to the city was the Illinois Central, which arrived here in October 1854. A Union station was built in 1856 at the southeast corner of the intersection of the Illinois Central and Wabash lines. This building served until 1903, when both companies built their own stations. The old Union Station included the Central House hotel, which offered sleeping quarters, offices and a dining room. Abraham Lincoln stayed the night at the hotel while attending the Republican convention here in 1860.

The new Illinois Central Station was built in 1900 and was the loading point for 27 daily passenger trains. Decatur was once the main stop between Chicago and St. Louis but eventually the passenger service died out and the station was razed in 1951, leaving only memories behind.

The old train stations were once located just north of Eldorado Street in Decatur. Today, this area is a forgotten place, although it was once one of the busiest parts of the city. Now, only the distant rumble of freight cars can be heard here and provide only the remembrance of the things that were.

During the day, this was a stopping place for passengers who were riding the trains and passing through the city. During the heyday of the railroad in Decatur, hundreds of people came here every single day, possibly heading for a city as near as Chicago or possibly on the first link to a final destination on the other side of America. Besides the two train stations, the Wabash and the Illinois Central, there were a number of hotels, restaurants and businesses located here, all hoping for the prosperity delivered with each train that arrived in the city.

But that was in the daylight hours.... After darkness fell, the area became the Levee District, considered to be one of the most dangerous parts of the city and the hub of Decatur's most illicit activities. The Levee District extended from Water Street on the west to Wabash Street on the north, and ending at the Illinois Central tracks. The place became a magnet for crime and criminals over the years and was known for its collection of saloons, gambling houses and brothels. Despite the lurid reputation of the Levee though, it should be noted that there were also a number of fine hotels and restaurants that prospered in this area of the city, both during the height of criminal activity in the district and after. One such place was Sullivan's saloon, which was the first business in the city to have electric lights in 1883. They were a novelty in Decatur for several months before electricity became more widely available.

The old Levee is deserted today though. The saloons, restaurants, hotels and stores have vanished and little remains save for empty buildings, a few remnants of stone and a lot of memories.

It has been many years since passengers have been able to leave Decatur by railroad but freight trains still use the aging tracks everyday. Late at night, in some parts of the city, one can hear the rolling, booming sounds of the cars as they rumble along the tracks or the lonely whistle of the engine as it rides along through the darkness. The railroads are not completely forgotten in Decatur... and neither are the railroad's ghosts.

If you travel down Front Street today and wind up in front of the decaying remains of the old Wabash station, you can't help but feel a little sad. The remaining train station is but a shadow of its former self, the tower long since torn down and the yard overgrown and abandoned. The Illinois Central Station was demolished in 1951. The concrete lines of its foundation still remain, along with a small freight depot that once rested just south of the station itself. No so many years ago, this was one of the most vital areas of the city. Today, the silent Wabash station is allowed to crumble, useless and forgotten, but perhaps not empty.

One of Central Illinois' railroad ghost stories concerns the phantom of a young girl who was reportedly seen inside of the station during the years when it was still in operation, especially in the 1940's. Back in those days, the building was a still a hub of activity and passengers came and went all day long and into the night. It would be during these nighttime shifts that staff members and railroad workers would encounter the eerie woman in white who was seen sitting on a bench in the station.

According to the legends, this young lady had once been married to a man who went off to fight in the Great War in 1918. After many months of fighting, she received a letter from him stating that he was coming home. Eagerly, she went down to the train station on the scheduled date of his arrival to meet the train. She waited all afternoon, watching the passengers disembark from each train, but her husband did not appear. She returned home disappointed, but came back the next day, thinking that perhaps he had been delayed. Another day passed and then another, until finally, an entire week had gone by. Still, there was no sign of him. Then, a telegram arrived the following afternoon. Her husband had been killed in a bus accident in New York, on his way to the train that would have taken him home. Distraught, the young woman swallowed a bottle of pills and committed suicide. She had been unable to cope with the loss of her true love. As the years passed, those who worked, and even passed through, the Wabash station reported the sight of a lovely young woman, still waiting expectantly on a bench in the station.

Was she merely the residual image of a woman who carried so much grief that she left an impression behind in the building? Possibly, although John Turner* never thought so. He worked in the Wabash station for a number of years and had several sightings of the woman in white. He told me that a number of other employees encountered her as well. He believed that she was a conscious spirit, still trapped in a place where her heart had been so badly broken. "You would see her at different times," he explained, "and she always looked like a real person. She would be there one minute and the next, she would be gone. After awhile, you began to realize that she was a ghost."

Another employee who had a brush with the lady was a former cleaning woman for the station. "She was working in the ladies restroom one day, "Turned recalled, "and she was in there by herself. All of the sudden, the door opened and this flowery perfume filled the bathroom. She [the cleaning lady] looked out to see who was in the room with her... but there was nobody there. She knew the door had never opened again either. She was convinced that it was the ghost."

Turner went on to say that the sightings continued for many years but then seemed to peter out in the 1950's. There were no reports of the ghost from the later years of station's operations.

Another of Decatur's popular railroad tales is a folk legend of some endurance. I have heard this story, or at least one similar to it, in various parts of the country. Locally, the story provides an explanation for the strange light that has been reported bobbing along the tangle of tracks beyond the Wabash station. What is this mysterious round light and what causes it? No one really knows for sure but there has been a story told about it for years.

In the old days of the steam trains, each train had a brakeman, who rode in the train's caboose. His job was to remain on watch in tunnels, at crossings or at the station, for any signs of trouble. He always carried a lantern with him so that he could signal the engineer with any problems. When the train was stopped for loading, the brakeman would walk alongside the train and check the couplings that held the cars together.

According to the story, a train was stopped in Decatur one night in the late 1890's. The steam engines had to be filled on a regular basis and on the Wabash line, there was a water tower just east of the train station. The train pulled to a stop and the brakeman climbed down from the rear platform of the caboose to begin his usual system of checking the cars with his lantern. He had only gone a short distance when he spotted trouble. He leaned into the space between two freight cars and looked down. The couplings between the two cars were open and the cars were only connected by the safety chain.

At the front of the train, the engineer was running the locomotive a few feet closer to the pipe off the water tower. As he did this, it caused the train to lurch forward a short distance. The safety chain between the two loose cars snapped upwards and the brakeman was knocked off his feet. He stumbled and fell, and as he did, his head passed between the grips and the couplings slammed closed.

The train's fireman saw the brakeman's lantern fall and he ran to help. A crowd of men quickly gathered around the brakeman's body and they quickly took the fallen man into the train station. In all of the excitement, no one thought to look for what was left of his head.

To this day, the ghost of the brakeman is said to still walk the tracks just past the old railroad station. On certain nights, the bobbing light of a railroad lantern can be seen tracing the line of a long forgotten freight train... as a phantom brakeman searches in vain for his missing head.

Another railroad that passed through Central Illinois, and could boast at least one ghost story, was the Chicago & Alton Railroad. According to the legends, one midnight in January 1935, the engineer of a C&A train who was entering the station in Springfield suddenly applied the brakes. A switchman was standing next to the tracks ahead and was signaling for him to stop. At that moment, the light turned red, indicating that the switch was closed and the right-of-way was not clear.

As the train screeched to a stop just short of the crossover, a switch engine roared past on the opposite tracks. It was running without lights and moving at a high rate of speed. If the Chicago & Alton train had not stopped, there would have been a serious accident. In addition to the many passengers and crew, the men on the other switch engine would have been killed as well. The C&A engineer, cursing to his crew members about the close call, jumped down from the cab. He was followed by his fireman and together, they hurried over to thank the switchman for his last minute signal.

However, before they could speak to him, the switchman, who was wearing a heavy, checkered coat and a stocking cap, turned around, reached for the track lever and switched it back to its original position. He turned back around as the engineer and fireman approached and then, right before their eyes, vanished without a trace!

"What the....?", the fireman stammered.

"Where'd he go?", the engineer cried out.

The two men quickly decided that they would say nothing about that had happened or anything about the apparent ghost who had rescued them from serious injury or possible death. The fireman was due to retire within two years and neither of them wanted to chance his getting laid off the job for seeing things.

The fireman retired two years later and did tell several people the story of what had happened that night. One of the men who heard his story introduced him to another fellow. This man had been a crew member of the switch engine that had narrowly missed the C&A engine that January night.

He explained what had happened. Apparently, some of the men had been drinking and decided to take the switch engine out and see how fast it would go. Somehow, they had gotten onto the wrong track and saw the C&A right-of-way switch. It had been thrown and a train was coming. The man telling the story explained that he had called for his friends to stop the engine, but they hadn't heard him over the noise. Suddenly, they saw the oncoming train as well but they had no way to stop!

Just as suddenly, the oncoming C&A train came to a halt, just short enough of the track the engine was on to avoid a wreck.

"Whoever stopped your train must have been a mind-reader," the other fellow told the fireman. "There wasn't anybody who knew we were on those tracks."

So, who was the mysterious switchman who stopped the Chicago & Alton train? Was he some sort of railroader's "guardian angel"? A slain railroad man from years past? No one ever knew and the story remains an unsolved mystery of the railroad today.

There is another story of a railroad ghost in the Central Illinois and this one caused such a sensation during its first appearance that hundreds of people showed up just to get a glimpse of it. The phantom was known for years as the "Forsyth Ghost". She appeared along a stretch of tracks in Forsyth, Illinois, a small town located north of Decatur.

One January 25, 1871, a young woman, who was walking along the railroad tracks at night, was killed by a speeding Illinois Central train called the "Diamond Special". The train was heading south to Decatur when it struck the woman, pulling her along the tracks and tearing away all of her clothing save for her corset and her underskirt. After striking her, the rain finally screeched to a halt and rescuers managed to free the girl from the tangle of the engine.

She was horribly mangled by the force of the train and covered with blood. She was only a few breaths away from death, but somehow she managed to whisper a dire warning to the engineer of the train. She vowed that she would come for him and take her revenge. She would return from the grave, she told him, in 20 years, which was her exact age on the day he had killed her.

Apparently, the vow proved true. The engineer continued working that same line for the next two decades and as the train thundered along the tracks near Forsyth in 1891, he was the man still driving the locomotive. Suddenly, at the exact spot of the accident, a woman appeared on the side of the tracks. The engineer would later claim in interviews and published reports that she had "long streaming hair and eyes like balls of fire". The mysterious woman was also nearly naked, wearing nothing more than a brief corset and a tattered scrap of an underskirt.

The engineer was so shocked by the sight of this creature that he slammed on the air brakes. Passengers were thrown from their seats and cases were strewn all about the baggage car. The train stopped and several men jumped off and tried to approach the woman. When they got near to her, she inexplicably vanished. Strange screams and cries were heard in the darkness and the passengers hurried back to the train.

For several nights after, the ghost appeared along the route. The story of the weird specter began to spread, especially after it was featured in a small, local newspaper called the Forsyth "World". The following night, townspeople, farmers and even Decatur residents began lining the tracks, hoping to catch a glimpse of the ghost. Even though the creature failed to appear on schedule, the curiosity-seekers refused to leave. They came back each night and the crowd increased in number each evening.

Finally, the railroad tried to nip the story in the bud. They never denied the existence of the ghost but instead criticized the newspaper for publicizing her appearances. They blamed the news stories and claimed the paper was responsible for "immense crowds who broke down fences and nearly trampled the track out of existence."

Needless to say, the "Diamond Special" was re-routed to another line and the ghost of the young woman was never seen again.

SCHOOL SPIRITS · HAUNTED SCHOOLS & COLLEGES

The Midwest is filled with haunted schools and colleges. In the years that I have been collecting ghost stories and strange events, I have discovered that nearly every school seems to have a dark tale or two floating around the campus. Many of them are familiar tales of murdered coeds, whose spirits have returned to their former residences after death.

But how much truth is there to these stories? Are they merely legends that have been told over and over again for the purpose of getting a cute sorority girl to squeeze just a little closer while walking through a particularly spooky spot on campus? Or could there be something more? What is these tales of slain students just happen to be true? Are those tales so easily to dismiss?

Many have surmised that most campus ghost stories are simply the product of overactive imaginations. These same people say they are the result of students who are far too susceptible to the trappings of the supernatural. But what about the stories of ghosts that have been passed on, not only by students, but also by teachers, professors, maintenance workers and in some cases, people who claim to not even believe in ghosts? Are these school spirits simply imaginations working overtime?

Perhaps some of these stories are simply the mixture of fact and fancy. It seems that few of us can deny that we have chuckled a little over yet another report of a ghostly coed who was murdered years before and now haunts her former dorm room. In so many cases, a simple check of the local newspaper files reveals that no coed was ever murdered at the school... so how then do we explain the activity which has been reported there?

In other words, what if these academic ghosts are real? What if the energy produced by hundreds of students in one location attracts spirits who are seeking such energy to exist? Perhaps some of these ghosts really are the spirits of former students, teachers and janitors who left some sort of unfinished business in this world. Or perhaps the proverbial murdered students are sometimes real! What if their traumatic deaths have really caused them to linger behind?

Many would argue and say that these stories couldn't possibly be true but in the coming chapter, I will show you that some of these stories just may be! And some of the readers know, if they have ever had their own brush with the supernatural, that there may be more to the local college campus or school building than first meets the eye! Something just may lurk in the shadows here.... but whether it is the cold image of truth or the stuff of legend is up to you to decide!

GHOSTS OF MILLIKIN

Many colleges have checkered pasts and forgotten incidents that are only whispered of by generations to follow and Millikin University in Decatur is just such a school. There are universities all across the country that claim to have their own resident ghosts, but Millikin seems to have more than its share.

The college began less than a century ago in a grassy field on the west side of Decatur. The land the university now rests on started out as a drilling field for Civil War recruits and later became a recreational park. In those days, it was called Oakland Park and it boasted a lake, an icehouse, a boathouse and a dance hall. It was a popular spot until 1900, when James Millikin purchased the land as a site for his college.

Millikin was an affluent banker and businessman who received a charter to start a university in Decatur in 1901. He supplied the land for the school and offered to match funds for construction with local residents and business owners. Construction began in 1902 with the removal of the small Oakland Park Lake and with the leveling of West Main Street, making the frontage of the campus on level with the street. The four original campus buildings were built over the course of the next year in a modified, Elizabethan design. They were constructed from rough, brown and red brick and ornamented with terra cotta. Each structure was further decorated with round, bay windows and a red tile roof.

Shilling Hall at Millikin University. Inside of this building is the Albert Taylor Theater, home to one of the college's most famous ghosts!

The official opening of the school was a grand event and President Theodore Roosevelt dedicated the campus in June 1903. He arrived in Decatur by way of a Wabash train at the southeastern edge of the Millikin campus. He spoke for some time, praising James Millikin and the new school and then departed, continuing on with his two-month tour of the western states.

The college opened in September 1903 and continues to expand and grow today, a legacy to the generosity and dreams of James Millikin. The banker passed away in 1909 and funeral services were held in the Assembly Hall of his beloved school.

The earliest tales of ghosts in the area that is now Millikin date back to the days when the settlers of Decatur were still living in log cabins. There were stories told about the woods to the west of the struggling village concerning ghosts and Indian spirits. These stories were usually told around the fire at night and were designed to keep children at home after the sun went down. Were they merely folklore? Possibly, although I learned long ago that many folk legends have a basis in truth!

Despite these shadowy tales, most believe the stories of ghosts at Millikin University began in more modern times. However, there is one story that has endured from the early days of the school, although it has been largely forgotten.

His name was "Tommy the Watchman", or at least that was what everyone called him. He was the flagman for the Wabash Railroad crossing near Oakland Avenue. This site was just off the Millikin campus and Tommy was a favorite local character among the students. After years of service, modern times finally caught up with Tommy and he was replaced with an electric signal that alerted passers-by that a train was approaching. The signal was later replaced by an underpass that still exists today.

Even though he was no longer needed, Tommy loitered around the flagman's shanty that had been built at the intersection. He came nearly every day, sitting in a rocker out front, talking and laughing with the passing students. Then, one morning, Tommy didn't return. Students later learned that he had passed away in his sleep the night before.

Soon after, legend on the campus said that on certain nights, you could still see Tommy's light as it moved around the old shanty and lit up the windows from the inside. Those brave enough to approach the small building found no one inside.

They say that every good theater has a ghost and the Albert Taylor Theater on Millikin's campus is no exception. In fact, I would say that perhaps the most famous of the college's ghosts is that of the "Rail Girl", who haunts this theater. She takes her name from the fact that she normally appears, when she chooses to appear at all, along a rail in the upper part of the theater. However, she often makes her presence known in other ways... and nearly every Millikin theater student can tell you at least one story about the spirit's handiwork or the problems she has caused in the theater during one show or another.

The legends say that this little girl haunts the theater and that she will do anything to get the attention of the actors and stage crew here. No one seems to know why this phantom child has chosen to make the theater her home, although one student told me a rather strange tale. According to one rumor, she was a child who was murdered around the time the college was being built. Apparently, the killer had entombed her body within the walls of the theater and her ghost has stalked the place ever since. Regardless of why she remains here, there have been literally dozens of reports of strange sounds and noises in the theater; eerie footsteps; the sound of weeping; and items that disappear and then show up later in different places. And that isn't all....

The most famous tradition of the theater is the long-standing ritual of leaving three pieces of candy for the ghost prior to any performance. This is said to insure the approval of the ghost and to make certain that she does nothing to ruin the show. In the past, those who have scoffed at the tradition have suffered for it with botched performances; lighting problems; sound equipment failures; rigging and prop damage; and even actual injuries. Anything that could possibly disrupt the show can and does happen under these circumstances.

Most of the students who perform here, and who have performed here in the past, can tell you at least one frightening anecdote related to failure to leave candy for the "Rail Girl". Other stories are simply chilling....

One student told me of a night when she was in the theater alone and rehearsing for an upcoming show. It was very late when the back door of the theater swung open and a little girl stuck her head into the auditorium and looked around. Then, as quickly as she had come, she disappeared back outside again. The student, wondering what a little girl was doing inside of the campus building at such a late hour, went to the door and looked out. Only a few seconds had passed, but the mysterious little girl was nowhere to be found.

Does the ghost of the Albert Taylor Theater really exist? The Millikin theater students of the past and the present will tell you most assuredly that she does!

The college's old gymnasium was added to the campus in 1911, about eight years after the school was opened to students. Initially, both James Millikin and Dr. Albert Taylor, the school's first president, were skeptical about the presence of sports on the campus. Later, both men relented and Millikin had its first football team in the fall of 1903. A basketball team was added for the 1911 season, hosting their home games in the old gymnasium, and they managed to win the state championship that year.

As the years passed, the old Gym was replaced by the Griswold Physical Education Center and today, only a weight room and a dance studio are left to remind us that the building was once the sports center for the college. Since the departure of most sports activities, the upstairs portion of the gym, with its high ceilings and elevated running track, has been abandoned. It has been used by the theater department for many years as an area for both prop storage and as space to build sets for upcoming performances.

It is in this part of the building where ghostly sounds from the past echo into the present.

Countless students claim to have had strange encounters in the building and most of these encounters seem to tell of events from the past repeating in the present day. These events, strangely enough, are repeating in the form of sounds. Visitors, staff members and students who come to the upstairs portion of the building tell of hearing voices, laughter, cheers, applause, whistles blowing and even the sound of a basketball bouncing across the floor when no one else is present.

One student told me of coming to the old gym one night and having an encounter of his own. A group of students were putting together a show uptown at the Lincoln Theater and this student had returned to the gym to pick up some props that had been left behind. He walked into the dark, upstairs gymnasium and was surprised to hear the sound of someone loudly bouncing a basketball across the floor. Curious, he quickly reached for a light switch but when the lights came up, he found the room was deserted. A quick search of the building revealed not only that no one else was there, but that no basketballs were there either!

A former Millikin security guard told me of an event he experienced here during the holiday season of 1994. At that time of the year, the campus is mostly deserted and because most of the buildings are empty, the security staff has to make sure that everything is locked up tight. The watchman entered the old gym and from upstairs, he could hear the sound of someone running around the elevated track that circles the gym and overlooks the basketball court from the third floor.

He cautiously climbed the stairs and stepped through a doorway and onto the track. He looked around with his flashlight, peering first from the dizzying heights to the floor below and then around the track itself. The echo of the pounding footsteps circled quickly away from him, rounding the track to the far side of the gymnasium. He quickly discovered that no one was there... and not only that, he realized the track was completely blocked with stored props and set pieces! There was no way that anyone could be running around the track, and yet, he could distinctly hear the sound of the running feet! Unnerved, he flipped on the lights and the sound abruptly stopped. A search of the building revealed that no living person was present.

This type of experience has been repeated many times in the building with inexplicable sounds being heard and then ceasing when the lights are turned on. Could this be the connection to the haunting? There are many places on the Millikin campus where electrical disturbances are common. In many locations, these anomalies cause cameras and stereos to stop working, televisions to shut off and lights to turn on and off at will. Several years ago, I was on campus recording strange events experienced by students and I found my tape recorder refused to work correctly in some places. Strangely, it would work fine everywhere else!

There is a theory that the reason for this strange activity may be the lake that was once located where the campus is today. It was fed by a natural spring and when it was forced underground, the water table remained beneath the campus. This could be why Millikin seems to act like a giant battery, storing up energy to replay over and over again. On the other hand, this water source may also be responsible for the resident ghosts as well. Spirits and supernatural energy are often generated and attracted to water in much the same way that an electrical current is.

But regardless of why the weird happenings take place, the old gym remains a strange and haunted place. It is an odd sort of "mystery spot" where the past is still present in a way that we don't yet understand.

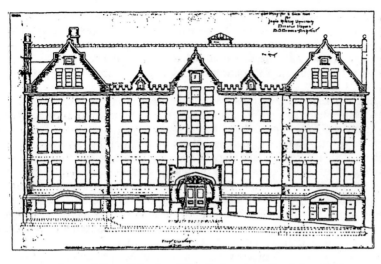

A Copy of the original architect's drawings for Aston Hall

Aston Hall is the oldest building on campus devoted to women's housing. It was originally called simply the "Women's Hall" and that name was later changed in honor of the wife of James Millikin, Anna Aston Millikin. The hall was completed in the fall of 1907 but is barely recognizable from older photographs as two separate halls have been added to the structure in a line running south.

One thing about Aston Hall that has not changed over the years however, is its resident ghost. This building boasts the oldest reported spirit on the Millikin campus. The stories of this phantom have been around for many years.

She is allegedly the spirit of a former resident who committed suicide in the early 1940's. According to the story, she was in love with a young man who was drafted during World War II. He was killed in Europe and she took her life soon after learning of his death. She has haunted Aston Hall ever since.

The legend of the ghost is so widely accepted here that there are stories of the third floor of the hall being closed down at one time because of the ghost. It was said that residents refused to stay in their rooms because of frequent sightings of the specter. Witnesses have reported that the apparition is female and very solid looking. Most frightening is the fact that she is only visible from the waist up. The ghost is famous for her journeys through the Aston Hall dorm rooms on the third floor. The accounts say that she appears out of the wall of one room and crosses the room to the opposite wall. She then vanishes into this wall and enters the next room, passing from one room to the next as if the walls did not even exist.

In addition, residents of this floor also speak of poltergeist-like events where items move about, disappear and appear at will. Most believe that these events and the restless ghost are somehow linked together.

But what causes this spirit to make her frightening journey through the building and to cause personal items in the rooms to vanish and then return? No one knows for sure... perhaps her tragic death has left her forever tied to her former residence. Whatever the reason, she does not seem to be leaving anytime soon.

Located just south of Aston Hall is Blackburn Hall, a women's housing dorm that is a more recent addition to the campus. It was not constructed until 1967 and it was named in honor of Bonnie Blackburn, a popular, former head of Millikin's Foreign Language Department. The ghost of the hall has been nicknamed "Bonnie", after the building's namesake, although she is reportedly not the ghost who haunts here.

The spirit of Blackburn Hall is said to be that of a young student who disappeared from the campus back in the 1950's. While there are stories told about "murdered coeds" at colleges all over the country, this young woman was very real. More than 50 years ago, she vanished without a trace from the campus and was never found. While many feel that she may have left voluntarily, she was regardless, never heard from again... at least in this life. According to campus legend though, it is her spirit who has returned to haunt the corridors of Blackburn Hall.

It has been reported that the ghost sometimes appears here, passing up and down the halls as a wispy shape, or even as a full-blown apparition, which is seen and then which inexplicably vanishes. One former student that I spoke with told me of returning to her room late one evening, after a long night of studying, and seeing the shimmering, half-formed figure of a young woman in the hall. Thinking that perhaps her eyes were playing tricks on her, she rubbed them, then looked again. The specter was still there but suddenly darted away and vanished into the wall!

She usually makes herself known in other ways though. Blackburn Hall has become notorious over the years for its bizarre electrical problems, namely on the third floor, and all said to be caused by the resident ghost. Many of the residents have come to expect unexplained interference when it comes to lights, radios and televisions. The erratic behavior of electronic equipment has become so commonplace here that most generally accept the fact that "Bonnie" must be somewhere in the vicinity.

As mentioned, the spirit seems to want to draw attention to herself through her manipulation of these appliances. She will often turn off radios and televisions that have been left on late at night, as if she believes the residents should be sleeping rather than staying up late. One former resident complained to me that the ghost refused to let her listen to the stereo one night. Every time the student turned it on, "Bonnie" repeatedly snapped it off. Finally, the young woman simply gave up and let the ghost have her way.

The "Kappa Sigma" fraternity house is located just west of the Millikin campus and is home to the ghost of a boy who allegedly committed suicide here in the days when the structure was still being used as a boarding house. It was a pretty run-down place at the time and no records were kept of the occupants, although oral history tells of a young man named "Nathan" who stayed here for a short time. It was said that in a fit of despair, he took his own life in a bathroom on an upper floor of the house. The bathroom has since been removed and is now a dorm room.

Actual sightings of apparitions in the house are rare, but apparently do happen. One summer, two residents claimed to see a shadowy, black figure that appeared around a corner in one of the downstairs rooms and then disappeared. Another person in the house, an alumnus of the fraternity, was doing some carpentry work during some renovations in the mid-1990's. He was on the second floor of the house and cutting wood. In the sawdust that was still hanging in the air, he reported seeing the distinct outline of a person in the cloud. The sawdust floated to the floor and the shape was gone.

This house has also been plagued with electrical problems, especially in the area of the former bathroom where Nathan committed suicide. There have been reports of lights that, while broken, have suddenly flared to life and accounts of radios, clocks and stereo speakers that have suddenly launched themselves across room, seemingly under their own power. One room had an answering machine that would record on its own, with no telephone hooked up to it. On one occasion, there was a strange voice on it that didn't belong to any of the occupants of the house... and the machine had been unplugged at the time the voice was recorded.

Another room has been the site of more problems. An alarm clock once flew off a table and shot straight into the air. It flew so hard that the cord pulled taut behind it and then snapped out of the wall socket. In the same room, a stereo speaker lifted from a shelf and took off across the room, in full view of more than a dozen startled witnesses!

Merely strange energy... or the ghost of a young man who refuses to leave?

The most famous of the Greek houses on campus (at least for its ghosts) is the "Delta Delta Delta" sorority house, which is also located just west of the campus. The ladies who live in this house are used to the fact that they have one of the best known ghosts of Millikin.

I have spoken to scores of former residents of the house who have had encounters with this phantom and the sightings go back through several generations of students. Most of the witnesses, being completely unconnected to each other, had strikingly eerie stories to tell. Besides seeing the ghost, many of them also spoke of hearing her and feeling her presence. It seems that chilling whispers are sometimes heard in the upper dormers and residents tell of walking into small patches of extremely cold air, which defy explanation and then vanish moments later. It is in the same area of the house where these encounters take place where the ghost is normally seen.

The apparition is described as being a young woman who is faded, or very pale in coloring. Her clothing appears to be homespun and like that of the early settlers to the area. Her skin is transparent and she is sometimes hard to see, as if she is a reflection in a pool of murky water. Some have told me that the apparition is off-white or gray in color.

Residents of the house have been encountering this ghost for many years and some students say that she visits the dorm rooms in the night, as if checking in on the sleeping residents. There seems to be little question that the presence is a benevolent one, although some are frightened of her anyway. Of course, this may be because of the way that the ghost makes her infrequent appearances! Several different sorority sisters claim to have been awakened at night to find the ghost standing directly over their beds. In fact, one young woman even recalled waking up at night to see the ghost standing over her roommate. After that, she started sleeping with the covers pulled over her head at night, convinced that she would be the one who was visited next. She took the blankets down on only one other occasion and when she opened her eyes, she saw the face of the ghost, looking down directly above her own! She stopped sleeping in the house for quite some time after that!

So, what of the Ghosts of Millikin? Are they real or simply imaginary? I believe there is something present on the Millikin campus that defies explanation, whether the place is some sort of weird energy spot or merely a place that seems to attract more ghosts than most other places do.

There exist many more ghost stories about Millikin University that remain untold, and certainly many more which are still waiting to be born. In a place such as this, new ghost stories are created everyday!

GHOSTS OF GASTMAN SCHOOL?

The Gastman School is yet another of Decatur's vanished landmarks, existing today as only a dim memory. The school was once located at the corner of West North and Church Streets and today is the site of an empty parking lot on the northwest corner of the intersection.

The building was once the first public school in Decatur and when it opened in 1857, it was called the "Big Brick School". The school remained open until 1975 and many people in the city still recall attending classes there. I have always wondered if any of these students had an idea a ghost might have been inhabiting the school?

Once known as the Big Brick School, it was later named for Enoch A. Gastman, a teacher and the school's principal for many years. Gastman was loved and respected by the children and the other teachers and was a familiar figure, thanks to his unusual walk. He limped due to a rail-splitting accident that had taken place in his younger days. He retired from the school in 1907 and then suddenly passed away from bronchitis the following August.

The school graduated its last class of students in the spring of 1975. By that time, the aging building was starting to deteriorate and the students were better served in other, newer school buildings. After that, the structure stood empty for several years. By the spring of 1977, the First Methodist Church, which was located just across the street from the school, had purchased the building with plans to use it for extra space or to tear it down and use the lot for parking.

That same summer, David Ellis, a Decatur man, was looking for a place for his rock band, called "Crystal Haze", to rehearse. They had a small tour coming up and wanted to work on a lot of new material in a location where late night practicing would be tolerated. By chance, Ellis got in touch with the pastor of the First Methodist Church and an arrangement was made for the band to use the Gastman school building. The church had no immediate plans for the property so if Ellis agreed to pay the utility bills, he could use the school for the rest of the summer.

Shortly after the band took up residence in the building, strange things began to happen. It all started very quietly and when things started to move about the place on their own, no one really noticed at first. It wasn't long though before Ellis did start to realize that things were not quite right in the old school. And he wasn't alone, as others started to realize it too.... about three dozen other witnesses, whose signed affidavits Ellis still has in his possession.

Small pieces of the band's equipment began disappearing and then turning up again in new locations. Instruments and amplifiers would shake, jostle and even slide across the floor without assistance. Amazingly, these things happened before the eyes of startled band members and their friends.

They also reported footsteps coming from the upper floors of the building and the sound of invisible feet going up and down the darkened hallways. Witnesses claimed they could hear the footsteps following behind them as they walked in the corridors. On one occasion, a loud, rumbling sound, like a huge rolling ball, chased a group of people down a hallway and outside. Many present also stated that they heard the sounds of voices and whispers coming from the classrooms and empty closets.

The phenomena continued and intensified until the sounds were being heard both day and night and objects were being constantly moved about. Knocking sounds shook the walls and disturbed anything that was going on. Soon, Ellis and his friends discovered that by calling out loud to whatever was making the sounds, they could get the presence to answer by knocking in reply. Many of the friends and band members left the school and refused to come back, but Ellis stayed on. He was determined to stick it out and even confessed to a fascination with the unexplained events. Not long after, things would escalate to the point that even he would abandon the building for good.

One morning during a rehearsal, the unseen force acted out directly against the people in the building for the first time. Unbelievably. a young woman was physically picked up and flung backwards against the wall. Needless to say, this was the last straw and Ellis and the others were ready to give up possession of the school to whomever, or whatever, was sharing it with them. In fact, they were so frightened by the attack that they ran from the building, leaving their equipment behind. It would later be reluctantly claimed.

The building was never occupied again and a few years later, it was torn down and turned into a parking lot for the church.

What happened in the school during the summer of 1977 remains a mystery, but a few years ago, it was suggested to me that the presence in the building might not have been a ghost at all. Sources reported that the strange happenings might have actually been an intelligent, poltergeist-like force that had been directed by an older woman who had a grudge against David Ellis and his family.

Regardless of the source of the haunting, the strange events have not been forgotten by those who experienced them or by those who claim that odd sounds can still be heard at the site of the former school. They claim that in the early hours, in the darkest part of certain nights, quiet voices can still be heard coming from the darkness near the far corner of the lot. Are they the ghostly sounds of children playing childhood games for all eternity?

Or something far more sinister?

SCHOOL SPIRITS OF CHAMPAIGN-URBANA

Ghost stories of the University of Illinois in Champaign-Urbana have always been of an elusive sort. It has been suggested that perhaps because it is primarily an engineering school, that students here are simply not suited for ghosts. They say that these unimaginative scientists have no interest in the spirit world, but I have never been convinced of these claims. Regardless of the type of university it is, I have yet to find a college that does not have at least a ghost story or two!

The University of Illinois is no exception!

While there are a number of spots that are allegedly haunted on campus, the most notorious location is the English Building. Many years ago, this structure served as a women's dormitory and according to legend, a young lady committed suicide here after a love affair ended badly. The stories say that flickering lights and slamming doors have long been common here, especially in the former rhetoric room, which was later turned into offices for graduate teaching assistants. This was allegedly the location of the young woman's room and the place where she took her life. Witness accounts say that she still wanders the hallways of the building.

Another reportedly haunted spot is the central foyer of the Psychology Building. A number of years ago, a memorable event took place here when a student became irrational and threatened to kill himself by jumping off one of the railings on an upper floor. This would have resulted in him plunging several floors to his death. However, he did not jump, but did die a few years later. The stories say that after his death, he did return to haunt the place and has been here ever since. The ghostly presence has resulted in people experiencing unexplained cold spots, a whispering voice that comes from empty room and the sound of footsteps pacing in abandoned hallways.

Perhaps the oddest campus haunting involves the Native American who roams the basement of the University YMCA building on South Wright Street. Decades ago, the basement was decorated with a very large painting of a Native American chief. It had been placed in the student lounge and cafeteria and little was thought about it... until nighttime visitors started to notice something very strange. According to their stories, after all of the lights had been turned out for the night, the chief would somehow leave the painting and wander about the building. Hard to believe? I would have to agree with that, but those who claim to have seen the Indian walking around in the dimly lit corridors just might argue with us!

URBANA HIGH SCHOOL

According to students, and some staff members, something walks the hallways of the Urbana High School on South Race Street... something that comes from another world. In fact, in a certain location in the building is a doorway that leads to the most haunted place in the building. Few supposedly know where to find this doorway, but nearly any student can tell you at least one ghost story about the "tower". This tower is an upper part of the building that has been closed off for some time. It once contained classrooms, but now is empty, save for the ghosts.

One legend about the ghost in the tower involves a teacher who fell in love with a student and then hanged herself. Another story involves a girl who was mixed up in a love triangle with a married teacher and still another tells of a boy who committed suicide there. No one really seems to be sure just how the stories got started, but whether or not the place is haunted, seems to be no mystery.

Staff members recall incidents in the past that have been linked to ghosts and the tower. On one occasion, staff members found the door to the tower unlocked and no one knew how it had gotten that way. The police were called and when officers got there, a loud tapping sound was heard from the tower. The police officers that responded to the call were said to be so frightened that they made the principal go up the stairs first.

Other claims say that strange lights have been seen in the tower at night and the fourth floor walls were plagued with a mysteriously peeling paint. The walls would be freshly painted and within months, all of the paint will have peeled off. There remains no explanation for this.... although most would blame it on the ghost!

THE GHOST OF ANGIE MILNER

Located in the heart of the Illinois State University campus in Normal is a building called Williams Hall. The primary use for this building, constructed in the 1940's, is for the storage of extra books from the Milner Library, which is the main library on campus. This quiet building, with its rows of old books, many of them out of circulation for year, would seem the last place where anything strange might happen... and yet it does.

For Williams Hall is haunted by the ghosts of the university's past.

Illinois State University was founded in 1857 and at that time, the library was located in the Old Main building on campus. Perhaps the most dedicated and attentive employee there was a woman named

Angie Milner. She became the first official librarian for ISU and after coming to work here in 1890, served the campus until her death 38 years later. If there was ever a person who could be stereotyped as a "typical" librarian, it was Angie. Her entire life was dedicated to books. She never married and in time, was considered a spinster, quietly fading away with the library books until her death in 1928. A new, larger library was eventually built and to show appreciation for Angie's many years of service, the building was named after her and became the Milner Library.

As time passed, and reading interests and necessary topics began to change, many of the old books that Angie Milner once cared for began to see less use. The library began to reach its capacity and some of the books had to go into storage. It was decided to move some of these books into Williams Hall, where they could be accessible if needed, but so that more room could be made for new books. Over the years, few people even saw the books that had been moved out. Occasionally, they would be brought into circulation if needed, but mostly just the research librarians, staff members and janitorial staff ever even remembered they existed. These would be the same people who began to realize that something strange was happening in Williams Hall.

It wasn't long before odd stories began to circulate about the third floor of the building, where the books from the old library were kept. In one of the rows, where the books once filed by Angie Milner were stored, staff members started to whisper about sensing an unusual presence there. It was usually just a feeling of not being alone... but sometimes it was more.

Jo Rayfield, who is charge of the archives at Williams Hall, stated in a 1998 interview that she was one of the people who sensed some eerie things on the third floor. "I have worked in this building for some time," she said, "and I have, fairly often, had the sense of a benign presence around me. Let's say you are in the library looking at some books and you get the feeling of somebody next to you, wanting to get to the books where you are... you step aside and let somebody have more space... only there isn't anybody there but me."

I also spoke to Joan Winters, the head research librarian and the person in charge of Williams Hall. "Sometimes you come up here, on a day when no one else is in the building, and you can feel a presence, you just know you aren't here alone," she explained. "We just assume it's the ghost of Angie Milner.... she's never done anything harmful or frightening, although some of the students won't even come into the building anymore."

One of those students is a young man who came up to the third floor in the fall of 1997. He experienced one of the strange sensations witnesses speak of here and was completely unnerved by it. He walked up the narrow, stacked stairwell and then walked out onto the third floor level. The rooms here were dark and no one else was anywhere around. Suddenly, he felt the eerie presence of someone brush by him. He felt the proverbial chill up and down his back as he realized that whoever it had been was inexplicably unseen. The cold air swept over him and he could literally feel his hair standing on end. He charged down the staircase and out of the building and he never set foot inside of Williams Hall again.

On another occasion, Joan and a clerk were standing in one of the third floor aisles talking when all of the sudden, books started to fall from the shelves in front of them. And they weren't just dropping gently from the shelves either, for it looked as though someone was pushing them to the floor. "I turned to my clerk," Joan recalled, " and asked if he saw that... and he wasn't there anymore. He had already run off down the stairs".

Others have also been frightened by the strange events. There have been many students and staff members who have reported the same type of phenomena, including feeling someone standing, or passing, close to them; extreme drops in temperature; cold breezes that seem to come from nowhere; and sometimes, even the ghost of Angie Milner herself!

Joan Winters told me that many people have come up to the third floor and have spotted a white figure walking in the aisle near the old books. Many of these have been people who not only don't know the building is alleged to be haunted, but who have no idea who Angie Milner was. Most often, the apparition has been spotted as a movement out of the corner of the person's eye, passing a bookshelf or slipping around a corner. On other occasions, the specter has been more direct.

"I came around a corner and looked to my right," Joan remembered vividly, "and saw what looked like a white shape. It was almost as if someone took a drag on a cigarette and then blew it out. It was there... then it was gone."

But is it Williams Hall that is actually haunted by the presence of Angie Milner? It seems unlikely as the building was constructed more than a dozen years after she died. But what if some part of her is still lingering behind? Could the old books themselves have been imprinted with some of her energy, replaying her image over and over throughout the years?

Or could the spirit of Angie Milner have stayed behind, still attached to the books she loved so much in life? The annals of supernatural phenomena have certainly been filled with incidents where ghosts haunt possessions and physical objects. So, are we talking about "haunted books"? It certainly seems possible, especially since whenever the books are moved out of Williams Hall and moved to the Milner Library, strange things start to happen there too!

ILLINOIS COLLEGE

Illinois College in Jacksonville was founded in 1829 by Reverend John M. Ellis, a Presbyterian minister who felt a "seminary of learning" was needed in the new frontier state of Illinois. His plans came to the attention of a group of Congregational students at Yale University. Seven of them, in one of the now famous "Yale Bands", came westward to help establish the College. It became one of the first institutes for higher learning in Illinois and the first two men to graduate from a college in state were Richard Yates, who became the Civil War governor of Illinois and later a U.S. Senator and Jonathan Edward Spilman. Both men received their baccalaureate degree from Illinois College in 1835.

Nine students met for the first class on January 4, 1830. Julian Sturtevant, the first instructor and the second president, reported, "We had come there that morning to open a fountain for future generations to drink at." Shortly after, Edward Beecher left the Park Street Church in Boston, Massachusetts, to serve the new college as it first president. He created a strong college and retained close intellectual ties with New England. His brother, Henry Ward Beecher, preached and lectured at Illinois College, and his sister, Harriet Beecher Stowe, was an occasional visitor. His brother, Thomas, was graduated from Illinois College in 1843. Ralph Waldo Emerson, Mark Twain, Horace Greeley, and Wendell Phillips were among the visitors and lecturers in the early years.

In 1843 and 1845 two of the College's seven literary societies were formed. Possibly unique in the Midwest today, the societies have continued in their roles as centers for debate and criticism. Abraham Lincoln was one of many speakers appearing on the campus under the sponsorship of a literary society.

Illinois College also became heavily involved with the abolitionist movement as President Beecher took a very active role. At one point, a group of students was indicted by a grand jury for harboring runaway slaves.

In the years following the Civil War graduates contributed with distinction to the national scene. Among these was William Jennings Bryan, '81, who within 15 years was the Democratic candidate for the U.S. presidency in the race with McKinley. He continued with a prominent role in politics even after the election. There were many other famous and prominent graduates of the school over the years and it has maintained an outstanding scholarly program.

Not surprisingly, it has maintained close ties to the supernatural world as well. Like with many other historic spots in Illinois, the events of the past have certainly left their mark on Illinois College.

One place where strange events have been reported is in Beecher Hall, which was built in 1829. This two-level building is now used as a meeting hall for two of the school's Literary Societies, Sigma Pi and Phi Alpha. The Sigma men meet on the upper floor and the Phi men meet in the lower part of the building. The majority of the encounters here seem to involve the groups who frequent the upper floor. The most commonly reported events are ghostly footsteps that can be distinctly heard in one room, always coming from another. If the witness follows the sound, then the footsteps will suddenly be heard in the other room instead. Years ago, this was a medical building and cadavers were stored on the upper floor.

Some believe that this may explain the ghost activity here!

Other legends claim that the ghost here is that of Williams Jennings Bryan, who has returned to haunt his old school. He was a member of Sigma Pi and was often in the building during his years at Illinois College. There are others who say that it might be Abraham Lincoln's ghost instead. He was an honorary Sigma Pi and while he did not attend the school, he did speak at Beecher Hall on occasion. In addition, William Berry (Lincoln's partner at new Salem), William H. Herndon (his law partner), and Ann Rutledge's brother, David, all attended Illinois College.

Another allegedly haunted spot on campus is the David A. Smith House, which was built in 1854. Today, the structure is home to three of the women's Literary Societies, the Gamma Deltas, the Chi Betas and the women of Sigma Phi Epsilon. There is a parlor for all of them but the Gamma Deltas use a room on the main floor while the Betas and the Sigma Phi's have rooms on the second floor. The attic is used by all of the groups but there is also a dining room, a kitchen and an apartment at the back of the house.

There are several versions of the historic legend concerning the ghost in this house, but all of them claim that she is the daughter of the original owner and that her name was Effie Smith. Basically, Effie was being courted by a young man from town and they became engaged. When he proposed to her, he gave her a diamond ring and she was said to have scratched it against her bedroom window to see if the diamond was real. When she realized that it was, she etched her signature into the glass and her name still remains in the window glass today.

Then, the story begins to take different paths. In one version of the story, David Smith was very disapproving of his daughter's new fiancée and he literally locked Effie into a closet one day when the man came calling. Fearful of her father's wrath, the young man hid himself in a small room that was only accessible from the attic. For some reason, he nailed himself in to escape from David Smith and he later died there. According to students who have been in the attic, the nails are still visible there today, nailed from the other side of the door! When Effie learned of her lover's cruel fate, she threw herself from an upstairs window and died in the fall.

In the second version of the story, Effie's young man went off to fight in the Civil War. Every day, Effie climbed up to the attic and watched for him to return. When she later learned that he had been killed in battle, committed suicide by once again, jumping out of the window. Another variation of the legend has Effie being jilted by her lover and she again commits suicide. Regardless of what happened, the story stands that she killed herself and has since returned to haunt the house.

Effie's rocking chair is still located in the attic and the stories say that if you move the chair away from the window (where it sits, facing out), leave the attic and then return later, the chair will have returned to its original position. This window is located in a storage area for the Chi Beta society and every year, they frequently test the chair and discover that the story is true! One young woman even walked into the room one day and the door suddenly slammed closed behind her. It is also not uncommon for cold air to suddenly fill this room, even though for years, the windows were painted shut. It was said that ice cold wind would often come from the window with Effie's name etched on the glass.

Another interesting feature of this building is the tunnel that once exited from the dirt basement. This tunnel was once supposed to have connected to other buildings on campus and was said to have been used during the years of the Underground Railroad. As operations connected with this abolitionist system were always kept secret, and no records exist, no one knows for sure if the stories are true. Today, the tunnel is boarded up and remains only a curiosity of times gone by.

Another reportedly ghostly location is Whipple Hall, which was constructed in 1882. The spectral occupant of this place is known only as the "Gray Ghost". The upper part of the building serves as a meeting hall for the Alpha Phi Omega society, for the Eta Sigma chapter, which is a national service fraternity, and as the location of the security office. The lower part of Whipple is the meeting hall of the Pi Pi Rho Literary Society. The basement of the building is only accessible from the outside and is divided in half. One side of it was once a classroom when this was Whipple Academy, a college prep school. Strangely out of place chalkboards still remain on the walls.

Perhaps the most famous sighting on campus of the "Gray Ghost" occurred to a girl who was leaving a Pi Pi Rho party one night and had to retrieve something from the Alpha Phi Omega hall. She had been drinking (but later insisted that she was not drunk) before she started climbing the curved staircase. As she reached the middle of the curve of the stairs, she looked up to the top landing and saw a man standing there. He was dressed all in gray and she quickly realized that he was not a security officer. As she peered a little closer into the shadows, she also realized something else... that he had no face! She began screaming and ran back down the staircase and out of the building. Due to the noise of the party, no one heard her though and the revelers wouldn't learn of the strange experience until later.

The triple room that is located on the third floor of Illinois College's Ellis Hall is also rumored to be infested with ghosts. According to reports, no one lives there if they don't have to. Rumor has it that a girl hanged herself in the closet there around 1986 after not getting a bid from a Literary Society. It is said that doors open and close on there own here, appliances and radios turn on and off and that windows have a habit of going up and down under their own power.

There are other places too, but stories from some of these sites are much sketchier. One of them is Fayerweather House, a residence hall for women. It has been said that windows and doors operate on their own here and that lights turn on and off without explanation. Perhaps most strange are the stories of "grave-shaped" depressions that sometimes appear in the dirt floor of the basement. Some have suggested that perhaps the building may have been constructed over a burial ground, but no one really knows for sure.

Another site is Sturtevant Hall, one of the most famous spots on campus. Recent stories say that a ghostly young man in a Civil War era uniform is sometimes seen here. Rammelkamp Chapel allegedly has a haunted basement as well. Some of the students tell stories of classroom doors and that open and then slam shut, sometimes in the middle of lectures.

As mentioned already, the events of the past at Illinois College have certainly left their mark on the college of today. Many of these events still come back to "haunt" students and faculty members today and there are many who have encountered this ghosts of yesterday face-to face.

THE GHOST OF MARY HAWKINS

The most famous school spirit in Central Illinois is undoubtedly the phantom who haunts the women's dorm known as Pemberton Hall at Eastern Illinois University in Charleston. This building has a long and rich history that is filled with tradition... and tales of ghosts.

Pemberton Hall, or "Pem" as it is sometimes referred to by its residents, was the first college building in Illinois to provide housing for women on campus. It may also be the first such building to become haunted. The past decades have provided literally hundreds of tales of strange events, ghostly apparitions, and frightening tales about the dorm. For more than 80 years, women living in the hall claim to have encountered the ghost, or ghosts, here and have reported her playing the piano and scratching on the walls of the building's abandoned fourth floor.

But how did the tale begin? As with every chilling tale, it started with a series of terrifying events. In this case, they took place on a cold winter's night around 1916....

It was a bitterly cold night in January and one of the residents of Pemberton Hall went upstairs to the fourth floor of the building to play the piano. It was very late but the young woman had been unable to sleep. She hoped that some soft music might ease her mind and help her to relax.

The story goes that a janitor who worked on campus somehow managed to gain access to the women's hall that night. He may have been watching the young women here for some time and may have even slipped into the building on previous occasions. It isn't hard to imagine this deviant sneaking into the women's rooms, perhaps watching them sleep and perhaps imagining the events that would later come. Regardless of what he may have done in the past, on this night, he found one of the girls isolated and alone in the upstairs music room. She was far away from the other girls and with the wind howling outside.... no one would hear her scream.

The janitor cautiously made his way through the dark building to the upper floor. Here, he found his victim with her back turned to the open doorway, lost in her thoughts and in the simply melody that she played on the piano. Before she realized what was happening, the man was upon her. He grabbed her savagely and pummeled her with his fists. Then, tearing and pulling, he tore away her nightgown and attacked her, raping her, beating her and then leaving her for dead. Soon after, he made his escape and vanished into the cold winter's night.

The young woman, however, was not dead. She managed to drag herself to the stairs, leaving a bloody trail in her wake, and crawled down the steps. She pulled her battered body along the hallways, feebly scratching on doors and trying to awaken someone to help her. Finally, she made it to a counselor's door and managed to rouse her from her sleep. When the counselor came to the door, she found the young woman in a pool of blood, her body bruised, torn and now lifeless.

As the years have passed, residents of Pemberton Hall say they have heard this event from the past repeating itself in the building. They recall the dragging sounds heard near the stairs that lead to the upper floor and the sounds of scratching on doors and walls. Most disconcerting though are the bloody footprints that have appeared in the corridor, only to vanish moments later. Many believe the ghost of the murdered young woman has returned to haunt Pemberton Hall. But if she has, she does not walk in this building alone!

The Legendary piano room on Pemberton Hall's Fourth Floor

The counselor who discovered the murdered girl was named Mary Hawkins. She was a young woman herself, barely older than the ladies she had been hired to assist were. She was a very attractive woman with long, blond hair and a bright disposition that quickly made her a favorite among the residents of Pemberton Hall. However, the effect of the murder on Mary's personality was devastating. She became haunted by the death of the young woman and students spoke of seeing her pacing the hallways at all hours of the night, unable to sleep and tormented by horrible visions and guilt. Finally, unable to cope with her depression, and the nightmares that accompanied it, Mary was institutionalized and later committed suicide.

Shortly after her death, the residents of Pemberton Hall started to report some rather strange occurrences in the building, and these spooky events continue today. They believe the incidents can be explained as the ghost of Mary Hawkins, still making her rounds and checking in on the young women who live in the building. Perhaps her spirit is unable to rest after losing one of the women in her care and she still roams the hall, watching out for them and protecting them from harm. Her ghost is said to glide through the rooms, locking and unlocking doors, turning off radios and televisions and generally keeping track of things that go on here.

For many years, students have spoken of the odd happenings in the building and events that would convince even the most skeptical of residents that perhaps the hall was truly haunted. On many occasions, students that I have spoke with have told me of late night door knocking and inexplicable sounds in the hallways. Once the door is opened to see who might be there, the hallway is discovered to be empty. On other occasions, residents have reported finding that clothing had been removed from their locked rooms at night and would later find the articles of clothes to be thrown haphazardly up and down the hall. In most instances, the clothing in question would be undergarments or revealing sleep wear. Could Mary have been sending them a message? Perhaps the strait-laced counselor was silently disapproving of what she considered unsuitable attire for young ladies?

And these are recent accounts that I have heard first-hand from some of the former residents... the original stories date back even further than this!

According to one former resident, there was a string of strange incidents in the fall of 1952 when she was living in the dorm. She explained that the girls were being awakened at all hours of the night by banging on the doors and from knocks that seemed to be coming from inside of the walls. No cause was ever determined for the incidents, but most just assumed that it was Mary, trying to make her presence known.

Throughout the 1960's and 1970's, residents reported hearing the sounds of whispers in the building, especially on the fourth floor, and there were a number of reports of apparitions on the stairwell. These figures appeared very briefly and then vanished. One student, who lived in Pemberton Hall in 1976, recalled the problems that the resident advisors had with the furniture in one of the lounges. It seemed that all of the furniture in this room was often found to be overturned or at the very least, rearranged. It would often happen during the overnight hours, but sometimes it happened much faster than that.... and was cleaned up instead of moved about! Apparently, an RA walked into the room one morning and discovered the furniture had all been moved around. She went to get some help to straighten the room up again and when she and another resident came back, they found everything had been restored to order! After that, the RA always just left the room the way she found it and yet somehow, it would later be cleaned up again. The students on the floor all denied knowing how this continued to take place.

One former resident of the hall, Patty O'Neill, later came forward and told of an encounter she had with Mary herself in the spring of 1981. She had been up very late one evening, studying in one of the lounges, and came back to her room to go to sleep. Her roommate was already sleeping when she came in and rather than slam the door closed to lock it, she just decided to pull it closed and leave it unlocked for the night. This was a common occurrence as the old door was slightly wider than the frame and the only way to lock it securely was to pull it very hard into place. Besides that, many of the residents knew one another quite well and thought little about leaving doors unlocked at night.

Patty climbed into bed and drifted off to a light sleep. A short time later, she suddenly came awake. She wasn't sure why at first and then realized that her room was freezing! A terrible chill had come over her and she reached for her blankets, then stopped abruptly. She noticed a woman in a long, white gown standing at the end of her bed. The woman stood there for several seconds, then turned and walked toward the door.

"She opened the door and started to leave and then she turned, with one hand on the door, and looked backed at me for several seconds. She then left, closing the door behind her..." Patty later recalled in an interview.

Apparently, Patty's room was not the only one the strange specter had visited that night. As the apparition had departed the room, she had locked the door behind her. Strangely, a number of other students, who distinctly recalled leaving their doors open, also found them to be mysteriously locked the next morning as well. It was as if someone was checking up on them and was worried about their safety. Could it have been Mary Hawkins?

Most students don't actually see Mary, or the other ghosts, but few doubt the spirit exists. Many have had their own odd encounters, even without the benefit of actually seeing anything. My wife, Amy Taylor, is an alumnus of Eastern Illinois University and lived in Pemberton Hall for several years. She has recounted many stories about Mary Hawkins and the strange activity here. While she never came face to face with Mary Hawkins, she did have a few disconcerting experiences. One recurring incident involved the lights on the fourth of the building, where the music room is located and where the attack on the young woman took place many years ago. Even though this floor is now locked and off-limits to residents, many of the students reported seeing the windows open and close and the lights turn on and off. There was never any logical explanation for why this might be taking place.

In addition, Amy tells of another unexplained incident that took place one morning after she and a number of other residents left a communal shower room. When they closed the door behind them, they were sure that all of the curtains to the individual showers had been closed. When they entered the hallway, they heard a loud sound like something monstrous was sliding across the floor of the empty room behind them. They ran back in to find that all of the shower curtains were now open and a heavy wooden chair had somehow traveled across the room under its own power. It was now sitting directly in front of the door! No one else had entered or had left the room since Amy and the others had departed.

In recent years, the majority of weird reports have centered on the fourth floor. Even though no one ever goes up there, this has not stopped residents from reporting the sound of footsteps pacing overhead and the strains of faint piano music filtering down from the upper floor. The floor remains darkened and closed off and is empty save for old furniture and the dust of decades. It has been abandoned by students and visitors alike, although there is still a piano stored in the music room. Is this where the music comes from? If so, one has to wonder is the music that comes from it these days is of our world or the next......?

MYSTERIES OF WILLIAMSBURG HILL

One of the strangest mystery spots in Central Illinois is undoubtedly Williamsburg Hill. It is located in the south central part of the region, near the small communities of Tower Hill and Shelbyville. The hill is not hard to find, for it rises to its highest point at 810 feet, making it the highest elevation in that part of the state. To drive across the hill today, you would see no evidence of the history that is hidden in this remote spot. Williamsburg Hill just seems to rise out of nowhere on the prairie and is covered by a heavy stand of trees.

The village of Williamsburg, which was also called Cold Spring for a time, was laid out in 1839 by Dr. Thomas Williams and William Horsman. It was located on the south side of the large hill and for about 40 years, was a bustling community of about four square blocks. At one time, there were two churches, a doctor's office, a saloon, a post office, a blacksmith shop and a number of modest homes. The Main Street of the community was once part of the "Old Anglin' Road", a stage route that ran from Shelbyville to Vandalia. It was this stage line that brought prosperity to the village for many years. Some say the community died out when the Beardstown, Shawneetown and Southeastern Railroad bypassed the village in 1880. However, others believe that the town was abandoned for much darker reasons, attributed to the strangeness of Williamsburg Hill itself.

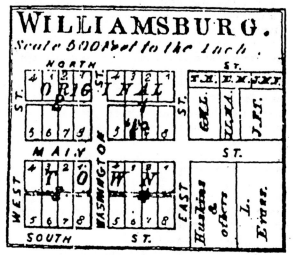

An Original Plat Map for the Village of Williamsburg

Today, there is nothing left of the village, save for a few old gravel pits. The land where it once stood has long been plowed under and trees have covered the area where homes once stood. It has become another of Illinois' lost towns although to look back with a critical eye, it's hard to believe a settlement ever existed here anyway. Life would have not have been easy on the hills and ridges of this strange place, although a scattering of people do live here today.

One of the strangest locations on the hill is a place called Ridge Cemetery. This rugged graveyard can be found on the highest summit of Williamsburg Hill. The desolate burial ground has many tilted stones, thanks to the sharp hills, and also bears evidence of both vandalism and unmarked graves. The cemetery can be found by watching for a massive microwave tower, located just east of the burial ground.

Ridge Cemetery has been part of the lore that makes up Williamsburg Hill for many years and has long been considered a frightening place. It is located back off the main road and down a wooded lane that is very dark for those curiosity-seekers who venture down it at night, braving the sheriff's deputies who regularly patrol the road and graveyard. Cases of vandalism, and some say darker things, have forced the authorities to close the place after dark. There have been reports of cultists using the cemetery and this has sparked both gossip and concern in small, surrounding towns. As far as I know, there is little evidence to suggest these stories are true, but once such rumors get started, they are hard to stop.

Other stories of the burial ground are more ghostly in nature. Many of these tales speak of strange lights and apparitions in the vicinity of the graveyard and the woods beyond it. In the forest, there are a number of forgotten graves that have been hidden by time. There are also anecdotes concerning the old road that leads back to the cemetery, namely stories of a bobbing red light and a spectral old man who vanishes if anyone tries to approach him.

Paul Smith* is one of those who claims to have encountered the unusual light. About 13 years ago, he and three friends made a nighttime trip to Williamsburg Hill and Ridge Cemetery. They decided to park the car on the main road and then walk back to the cemetery. They used no light, to avoid being spotted by anyone who lived nearby or who might be driving past. In this complete darkness, they were surprised to see a round red light appear ahead of them at the edge of the woods. The light hovered and shimmered about three feet above the ground.

"It looked as if someone was carrying it," Paul told me. "We stopped walking because we were sure we had been caught trespassing back there." Then, as the three young men watched, the light seemed to curve outward and start away from them and towards the cemetery.

"We were pretty scared by then, "Paul added. "We still weren't sure if the light belonged to somebody who lived around there. Then, one of my friends turned on his flashlight and pointed it toward the light."

To the shock of the trio, the light was not a lantern being carried by a person, but was actually floating in the air! A few seconds after the flashlight beam swept over it, the red light vanished. This marked an abrupt ending to the young men's late night trek to Ridge Cemetery!

In addition to the many stories told by visitors to Williamsburg Hill, there are also the incidents that occur involving those who still live here. Many of them will state that strange things happen here on a daily basis, as if the landmark that rises from nowhere out of the prairie acts as some sort of signal beacon, or magnet, for strange activity. Past accounts tell of ghostly figures on the roadways, animal mutilations and unexplained lights in the sky. So what makes Williamsburg Hill so strange and haunted and why has it been the source for so many legends over the years?

It's possible that the huge microwave tower on the hill could offer some clues, even if some of the stories were already being told before the tower was ever built. Could some of the phenomena be attributed to the tower? Is it possible that the strange lights, glowing balls of energy and eerie apparitions are some sort of side effect from the magnetic field around this structure? It has also been suggested that the tower may be attracting the paranormal phenomena, instead of creating it. Perhaps lost spirits are feeding off the energy given off by the tower, resulting in the myriad of stories that plague the place?

Or maybe, as was suggested earlier, the strangeness was already here, attracted by the natural landscape of the hill? Who knows? Regardless, if any of the numerous stories about Williamsburg Hill have even a semblance of truth to them, then the place is infested with ghosts! And would not be the sort of place where anyone in his right mind would want to venture after the sun goes down!

PECK CEMETERY

Why do cemeteries become haunted? That question has perplexed researchers for decades. As mentioned in the introduction to this book, many graveyards gain a reputation for being haunted because of the disturbance or desecration of graves and the cemetery itself. Without a doubt, the strangest form of disturbance comes from what some have called "ritual desecration". In this type of situation, cemeteries become haunted because of cult-type rituals and black magic that is practiced within the bounds of the graveyard. Many believe that this type of activity actually draws negative spirits or energy to the location. Others disagree and say that the cult groups are attracted to these places, or "power spots" after they become haunted in order to tap into the power that is present.

Regardless, it is common to hear of desecrated cemeteries where rituals are supposed to be taking place. In most of these cases, the so-called "satanists" are merely confused and lonely teenagers looking for a thrill or pretending to be "witches". However, can the practice actually draw negative energy to the place? Can those who believe this makes a cemetery become haunted actually be right?

One of the most famous haunted graveyards, where cult activity has been accepted as fact rather than fable, is Bachelor's Grove Cemetery near Chicago. We will be taking a closer look at this site in a later chapter. While it has been a place where horrible vandalism and desecration has taken place, as well as cult activity, I don't believe that is why Bachelor's Grove became haunted in the first place. Unfortunately, the same may not be able to be said for another Illinois cemetery, located several hours downstate.

Peck Cemetery is located in the northeastern part of Macon County, near the towns of Oakley and Cerro Gordo. The cemetery is an isolated place, enclosed by a rusted iron fence, and it is hidden from the road by thick woods. It is surrounded by heavy forest and trees loom over the grounds. In addition, the graveyard is accessible only by way of a rutted dirt road and through a metal gate, which is usually kept locked. Trespassers are not welcome here.

The reason for this is because since the 1970's, Peck Cemetery has been a popular place for teenagers to go and have parties and attempt to scare themselves silly. If this were the end of it, that would not be a problem. Unfortunately, a small minority of these teenagers has also felt the need to vandalize the cemetery. The burial ground is now in deplorable condition as the majority of the stones have been toppled and broken, have been turned over and even have been sprayed with bright paint. There are very few of the monuments now standing upright and many of these lean dangerously to the side, thanks to digging that has been done around their bases. The vandals who did this, and who have so badly violated the cemetery, originally came here because they heard the place was haunted. The problem is that it may have been other vandals, who came here first, who actually caused it to become that way!

As mentioned already, vandalism is not the only thing that is believed to attract negative spirits either. It has long been said that occult groups in the area have practiced black magic in Peck Cemetery. Some researchers believe this can attract negative spirits as well and most occultists will readily admit that they seek out sites like this one, where great energy is present, to perform their rituals. They believe they can tap into the atmosphere of the place, especially when the place is thought to be charged with what some would call "bad vibes". Regardless of whether you believe in this type of thing, the rumor of occult practices has certainly given the graveyard the reputation for being one of the most sinister places in Central Illinois.

But is it really? We have already discussed the fact that most alleged "satanists" are little more than disturbed teenagers. I also believe that most "devil worshipping cults" are simply the fevered imaginings of fundamentalist religious groups trying to scare the general public. However, I will say that I think that "evil" does exist. There are also those people out there, practitioners of the "black arts" if you will, who are capable of channeling that evil. This type of thing if nothing to fool with, although many do, and I have it by very good authority that many have done so at Peck Cemetery. While the stories may have grown a little larger than life over the years, some pretty strange and bizarre things have taken place here.

But satanic cultists aside, stories have been told for more than 20 years that suggest something malevolent may walk the night in Peck Cemetery. There are many tales that have been told here and witnesses and late night visitors to the cemetery have come forward to claim a number of strange happenings and to recall many frightening events. Such stories include apparitions in the graveyard, inexplicable cries, whispers and voices, hooded figures, eerie lights, and even the sound of a woman's scream that seems to come from nowhere!

One young man talked to me in 1995 about an unexplained experience from a summer night about eight years prior to our discussion. He and his former girlfriend decided to brave the stories of the place and find the cemetery. They spent an hour or so here without incident and soon, the sun went down. A short time later, as darkness began to fall, they saw a blue ball of light that flickered out from between the damaged stones. It weaved back and forth and up and down, hovering in odd circles and moving with no real pattern to its path. They watched it dance through the cemetery and the dark woods for a few minutes and then it disappeared. "We had no idea what it was," he told me later. "It wasn't really scary, just weird. I have never seen anything like it since."

Another person I spoke with, Amanda Carter*, told me of a weird encounter she and several of her girlfriends had at Peck Cemetery. In 1998, this experience had taken place about ten years before. The young women had come to the graveyard very late one night and had driven up the dirt road and around the corner to the left, where the cemetery gates are located. It was very dark and all of them were nervous and excited about the trip. However, Amanda promises me that this in no way influenced what they all saw. They parked the car outside of the cemetery and everyone got out. As it had been with my friends and I a few years before, the girls decided to test their courage by walking across the cemetery and back. This was a common practice for high school students from all around the Decatur area. In a giggling cluster, they began walking out among the graves.

"And that's when we saw him," Amanda told me.

The young women were just entering the grounds when they saw a man standing near one of the large, fallen tombstones. After they got over their initial shock and surprise, they were curious as to how he had gotten there. They hadn't seen any other cars nearby and hadn't seen anyone go past them into the cemetery. One of Amanda's friends started to speak to him and then the just wasn't there anymore. He had simply vanished.

"I know I saw him and the others did too," Amanda assured me. "He looked very solid and not like a ghost or anything. He had dark hair and was wearing a coat. I just assumed that he had come there like we did, but all of the sudden he was just gone. And so were we! We ran back to the car and I have never been out to that place since!"

I have spoken to other people too, who have also had experiences at Peck Cemetery they cannot explain. My only explanation for the things that go on here is the one that I have already offered.... that this place is haunted! Believe me when I tell you that it does not take a psychic to know that something is wrong in this place. You can literally feel it when you leave the old road and pass through the gates. There is a coldness and a feeling of oppression here that nature cannot explain.

It is not a good place... and it hasn't been one for a long time now.

THINGS THAT GO BUMP IN THE NIGHT

As you may have noticed from previous chapters, I have always been fascinated with the unexplained. Outside of ghosts, I have been most intrigued by sightings and reports of mysterious creatures. There was always one creature in Central Illinois that was a particular favorite of mine. It was the giant catfish that were said to live below the Lake Decatur dam. For years, I heard stories of huge, mutated catfish that lived in the mud below the dam. These catfish, according to reliable witnesses, were said to have grown to be the size of cows! One unfortunate swimmer, who made the mistake of going in near the dam, was so scared by the monstrous creatures that his hair turned white!

In 1988, Decatur suffered a summer of unbearable heat and little rainfall. This was my chance! The river was low and I would finally get the opportunity to find the elusive catfish! I eagerly went down to the dam to take a look. I was sure that some lucky fisherman was pulling in the catch of a lifetime or that I would be greeted by the sight of huge catfish bones, lying there, bleaching in the sun.

Unfortunately, I didn't find either one.... But that has never dampened my enthusiasm for a good story about a wild and mysterious creature which somehow ends up where it doesn't belong. Has Central Illinois really been visited by black panthers, African lions, phantom kangaroos, alligators, Bigfoot, mad gassers and more? The answer to that may surprise you!

THE MAD GASSER OF MATTOON

The events that took place in Mattoon, during the last months of 1944, remain unparalleled in the annals of the unexplained. The "Mad Gasser of Mattoon", as this fabled creature would become known, was certainly one of the strangest beings to ever appear in a Central Illinois town and since, has gone on to become a legendary figure in our haunted state. So, what happened in the town of Mattoon in 1944? Was it simply mass hysteria...or was something far stranger at work?

The Mad Gasser (Myth or Real)

Mattoon, which is located in the southeastern part of Central Illinois, is a fairly typical midwestern town. The strange events which took place here in 1944 however, were anything but typical. These events would place the small city under the scrutiny of the entire nation and would one day become a textbook case of what authorities and psychologists called "mass hysteria". But was it really?

The whirlwind of events would begin in the early morning hours of August 31. A Mattoon man was startled out of a deep sleep and complained to his wife that he felt sick. He questioned her about leaving the gas on in the kitchen because his symptoms seemed very similar to gas exposure. The woman tried to get out of bed and check the pilot light on the stove, but found to her surprise that she could not move. Just minutes later, according to published reports, a woman in a neighboring home also tried to get out of bed and discovered that she too was paralyzed.

The next evening, a woman named Mrs. Bert Kearney was awakened by a peculiar smell in her bedroom. The odor was sweet and overpowering and as it grew stronger, she felt paralysis creeping into her legs and lower body. She began screaming, and drawing the attention of her neighbors, was able to alert the police. A hasty search of the yard by police officers, and her shaken neighbors, revealed nothing. But that would not be the last strange event to occur at this particular house...

Later that night, when Mr. Kearney returned home from work, it was near midnight. He spotted a man lurking near the house who would later fit the descriptions of the "Mad Gasser". The stranger, according to Kearney, was tall and dressed in dark clothing and a tight-fitting black cap. He was standing near a window when Kearney spotted him and the odd man ran away.

The events in Mattoon soon became public knowledge and panic gripped the town. The story was badly handled by the authorities and the local newspaper reported the Kearney case, and subsequent others, in a wildly sensational manner. The newspaper is believed by many to be the culprit behind the "Gasser hysteria".

By the morning, of September 5, the Mattoon police department had received reports of four more "gas attacks". All of the victims complained of a sickeningly sweet odor that caused them to become sick and slightly paralyzed for up to thirty minutes at a time.

That night would be the occasion when the first real clues in the "Mad Gasser" case would be discovered. They were found at the home of Carl and Beulah Cordes, but what these clues meant has yet to be discovered. The Cordes were returning home late that evening when they found a white cloth lying on their porch. Mrs. Cordes picked it up and noticed a strange smell coming from it. She held it up close to her nose and was overwhelmed with nausea. In minutes, she seemed to have a severe allergic reaction to it as her lips and face swelled and her mouth started to bleed. The symptoms would disappear in about two hours. The police investigated and took the cloth into evidence. They also found a skeleton key and an empty tube of lipstick on the porch. They decided the prowler was probably trying to break into the house but had failed.

The police believed that the cloth was connected to the other gas attacks. It should be noted however, that the odor on the cloth caused different symptoms in Mrs. Cordes than in the other victims. She did feel sick to her stomach but there were no sensations of paralysis. The case itself is also different because if this was the "Gasser", it is the only time when he actually tried to gain access to the home of his victims. Could his intentions in this case have been different?

The "Gasser" attacked again that same night, but he was back to his old tricks and sprayed his gas into an open window. There would only be one other report that even hinted that the attacker tried to break into the house. The woman in this instance claimed that a "person" in dark clothing tried to force open her front door. Was it really the "Mad Gasser"?

The attacks continued and Mattoon residents began reporting fleeting glimpses of the "Gasser", always describing him as a tall, thin man in dark clothes and wearing a tight black cap. More attacks were reported and the harried police force tried to respond to the mysterious crimes that left no clues behind. Eventually, the authorities even summoned two FBI agents from Springfield to look into the case, but their presence did nothing to discourage the strange reports. Panic was widespread and rumors began to circulate that the attacker was an escapee from an insane asylum or was an odd inventor who was testing a new apparatus. Armed citizens took to the streets, organizing watches and patrols to thwart any further attacks, but six took place anyway. The gas attacks were becoming more frequent and the attacker was leaving behind evidence like footprints and sliced window screens. This evidence would become particularly interesting after the revelations of the authorities in the days to come.

By September 10, "Mad Gasser" paranoia had peaked. Despite claims by victims and material evidence left behind, the police began to dismiss new reports of attacks and suggested that local residents were merely imagining things. At this point, it was really the only thing left for them to do. The "Gasser", if he existed at all, could not be caught, identified, or tracked down. They started to believe that if they ignored the problem, it would just go away.

Psychology experts opined that the women of Mattoon had dreamed up the "Gasser" as a desperate cry for attention, as many of their husbands were overseas fighting in the war. This theory ignored the fact that many victims and witnesses were men and that this so-called "fantasy" was leaving behind evidence of his existence.

The Mattoon police chief issued what he felt was the final statement on the gas attacks in mid-September, when the policy of denial went into effect. He stated that large quantities of carbon tetrachloride gas were used at the local Atlas Diesel Engine Co. and that this gas must be causing the reported cases. As for the "Mad Gasser" himself, well, he was simply a figment of their imaginations.

Not surprisingly, a spokesman for the plant was quick to deny these allegations, maintaining that the only use for that gas in the plant was in their fire extinguishers and any similar gases used there caused no ill effects in the air. Besides that, why hadn't this gas ever caused problems in the city before? And how exactly was this gas cutting the window screens on Mattoon homes before causing nausea and paralysis?

The official explanation also failed to cover just how so many identical descriptions of the "Gasser" had been reported to the police. It also neglected to explain how different witnesses managed to report seeing a man of the "Gasser's" description fleeing the scene of an attack, even when the witness had no idea that an attack had taken place!

The last "Gasser" Attack took place on September 13 and while it was the last appearance of the attacker in Mattoon, it was also possibly the strangest appearance. It occurred at the home of Mrs. Bertha Bench and her son, Orville. They described the attacker as being a woman who was dressed in man's clothing and who sprayed gas into a bedroom window. The next morning, footprints that appeared to have been made by high-heeled shoes were found in the dirt below the window. Was it really the "Mad Gasser" or some strange, copycat attacker?

After this night, the "Mad Gasser of Mattoon" was never seen or heard from again...

The real story of what happened in Mattoon is still unknown and it is unlikely that we will ever know what was really behind these strange events. It is certain that something did take place here, however strange, and theories abound as to what it may have been. Was the "Mad Gasser" real? And if he was, who was he? Stories have suggested that he was anything from a mad scientist to an ape-man (although who knows where that came from?) and researchers today have their own theories, some of which are just as wild.

Could he have been some sort of extraterrestrial visitor using some sort of paralyzing agent to further a hidden agenda? Or perhaps some visitor from another dimension, thus explaining his ability to appear or disappear at will?

Or could the "Gasser" have been an agent of our own government, who came to an obscure Midwestern town to test some military gas that could be used in the war effort? It might be telling that once national attention came to Mattoon, the authorities began a policy of complete denial and the attacks suddenly ceased...

Whoever, or whatever, he was, the "Mad Gasser" has vanished into time and, real or imagined, is only a memory in the world of the unknown. Perhaps he was never here at all...perhaps he was, as Donald M. Johnson wrote in the 1954 issue of the "Journal of Abnormal and Social Psychology", simply a "shadowy manifestation of some unimaginable unknown."

Perhaps because he was never caught, and he never seemed to act like a normal criminal, and he never left behind a clue as to what he hoped to accomplish...then perhaps he never existed at all.

Or perhaps that's what they wanted us to believe.

PHANTOM BLACK PANTHERS

Despite the fact that panthers, and other big cats, have been extinct in the area of Illinois for many years, this does not stop the reports of the "phantom" animals from appearing from time to time. Many of these reports seem to be centered around both Central and Southern Illinois. In fact, the city of Decatur has become famous over the years, in many paranormal circles, for its large number of black panther sightings and reports. Many of these sightings go back nearly as far as the history of the city, but many are of a more recent vintage.

The stories of black panthers in the area date back many years with tales of wild cats screaming in the night, mysterious black shapes that suddenly appear in the headlights of a passing automobile and sleek, feline shapes that vanish into open fields. What draws these mysterious beasts to Central Illinois? That remains a mystery although ironically, the name "Decatur", when translated literally means "dweller at the sign of the cat". Coincidence or supernatural?

During the 1950's and 1960's, reports of panthers turned up almost monthly. Many of them were reported in local newspapers and many weren't, the witnesses fearing scorn and ridicule. The legends and folklore of the time traced the appearance of the big cats to wrecked circus trains and escapees from local zoos, but these stories could seldom be found to have any basis in truth. What we do know is that the panthers have appeared at regular intervals and then disappeared without a trace. In 1955, a Decatur game warden took a shot at one of the beasts and, like scores of others across the country, was sure that he wounded it. He found neither a body nor a blood trail.

Are these panthers real or figments of the imagination?

That is, of course, up to the reader to decide, but consider for a moment a local family that just might believe the stories to be true. In the fall of 1994, a big cat that left some huge tracks behind attacked their dog. The wounds on the dog's throat and shoulder could not be spanned by the owner's hand. That would take an awfully big jaw to leave a mark like that.

Central Illinois has not had a species of big cats for many years. Mountain lions and pumas are not indigenous to this area, although John Lutz of the Eastern Puma Research Foundation reports that a number of sightings have occurred in Illinois. These sightings are usually of mountain lions that are tan or chocolate in color. He believes that the reports of black panthers can all be traced to imported animals released by their owners or cats that escaped off of circus trains. Unfortunately, those official explanations don't begin to cover the frequency or the strangeness of most of the sightings that have taken place in the Decatur area. How many circus trains come through the area today? I can assure you that there aren't very many.

The standard response to these sightings seems to be that the mysterious animals are domesticated animals that somehow escaped from, or were released by, their owners. Officials from the Illinois Department of Natural Resources maintain that they have never been able to confirm the existence of panthers and cougars in the area, despite the numerous reports. "If there are cougars in Illinois, they must have been released by someone or escaped from someone," said Tim Schweizer, IDNR spokesman in a newspaper interview. "We know of no instances of wild cougars in Illinois." Although Schweizer said the agency does receive calls from "time to time," the staff has been unable to confirm the reports.

The mystery panthers are normally described as being black in color, but they are reported in other shades as well. Regardless, black panthers don't even belong on the North American continent and cats of other hues have been missing from Illinois for years. So why do they keep showing up here in Illinois? Where do these animals come from?

Author Loren Coleman, a Illinois native who now is at a university in Portland, Maine, offers some interesting theories in his book "Mysterious America". Coleman is currently a columnist for several international magazines and has been recognized as one of the world's foremost authorities on Cryptozoology (study of mysterious animals), and Fortean phenomena.

Fortean theories can be traced back to a man named Charles Fort, one of the first collectors of accounts of strange phenomena. Fort lived a strange life, spending most of it reading in the New York Public Library and collecting literally thousands of reports and articles about weird events, which he labeled as the "damned". He collected the data into a number of books, all dealing with unusual occurrences like frogs falling from the sky, unexplained disappearances, ghost lights, cattle mutilations and phantom black panthers, among other things. Fort is said to have invented the term "teleportation", which means the transfer of a physical object from one location to another by unexplainable means. Fort suggested that perhaps this was how these mysterious animals ended up in places where they didn't belong like, for instance, Illinois.

Coleman further explains, and lends credence to, the theory in his books and his research. It has been widely embraced by many "Forteans" over the years, simply because no other reasonable explanation exists.

One black panther sighting is even part of my family folklore. One night, around 1960, my stepfather's mother sighted a panther crossing the road in front of her car. The sighting took place just east of Moweaqua, Illinois.

I have always been interested in the stories of these phantom cats since I saw one of my own in the spring of 1984. I was walking in the woods, near Moweaqua, when I was startled by the sound of something running in the nearby underbrush. I looked up quickly and saw the unmistakable shape of a huge black cat streak through the trees. I chased after it for a short distance, but it was gone.

Where do these panthers come from . . . and where do they go?

One of the first recent sightings that I could find a record of took place in September 1955 in Decatur. Several residents on the east side of Lake Decatur, near Rea's Bridge, reported to authorities that they had seen a black panther. On September 13, a woman claimed to have seen the animal along

Sangamon Road and that sighting was followed the next night by two truck drivers. The cat was described as being low-slung and jet-black in color with gleaming eyes.

A little over a month later, near October 26, a Decatur game warden confirmed the fact that the animal was a black panther. He not only saw the beast, but also wounded it, near the Coulter's Mill area of the Sangamon River bottoms.

Warden Paul G. Myers was checking on hunters who were out after ducks and was standing near a thicket when he heard an animal squeal. He walked to the thicket and saw the panther eating a rabbit. He was armed with a service revolver, which he quickly aimed and shot at the animal. The panther jumped and ran into the woods. Myers followed its course using his field glasses but it vanished. He told newspaper reporters that the panther was at least two feet high at the shoulder with a body length of four or five feet. He returned to the area to make an intensive search, but not surprisingly, the animal was never found.

The next encounter took place in June of 1963. A call to police brought a number of officers to the home of George W. Davidson on Summit Avenue in Decatur. Davidson had received minor face wounds when a large cat jumped on him from a tree. He had been awakened at about 3:00 a.m. by barking from a number of dogs in the neighborhood. He left the house with his shotgun and saw a large cat leap over a five-foot fence and disappear into a wooded area near the house. Davidson went into the trees and was attacked. He fired at the animal, which he thought was perhaps three feet in length, and thought that he may have wounded it. No trace of the animal was ever found.

The next encounter took place almost exactly two years later when a woman who lived along Faries Parkway in Decatur reported a panther "as tall as the headlights on a car." She was turning into her driveway when she saw it and it ran away before she stopped the car. Deputies and a state trooper that came to the scene were unable to find any trace of the animal, except for a paw-print that was measured at four inches across.

The local newspaper reported that panther sightings in that area were "not infrequent, although none of the reports have been proved." They also noted that in the years following World War I, the bottoms near Faries Park had been cleared and a tree was found bearing the carved words "I killed a panther 1851".

Three days later, on the south side of Decatur near Greenwood Cemetery, a black panther surprised three children in Lincoln Park. The children took off running and the animal helped itself to their sack lunches.

Sheriff's deputies responded to another call in late June of 1967 when Anthony J. Viccone reported seeing a big cat just south of Decatur. He called after becoming concerned about children playing in the area. Authorities admitted that they had taken many reports of big cats in the area. "We have seen tracks and other evidence," they said, "but have never gotten close enough to the animal to determine what type of cat it is."

In June of 1970, an employee of the Macon Seed Company outside of Decatur saw a large, black cat that he said resembled a cougar. A game warden, and surely not the same one who admitted shooting a panther in 1955, announced two days later that the animal seen near the seed company was a "beaver". One has to wonder what this "beaver" looked like, as the seed company employees reported that it left behind large feline paw prints with claw marks.

Later that same year, in December, the Clarence Runyon family of Decatur reported seeing a large panther and its cub in a field outside of town. They believed the animal might have been the reason that forty chickens had vanished from their farm over the summer months. Several of the Runyon's neighbors had also seen the panthers and heard them screaming.

Officials from the Department of Conservation who investigated the case noted that the tracks left behind had definitely been made by a panther. They planned to shoot the animals when they caught them . . . but the panthers were never found.

In 1976, another black panther was sighted in southern Macon County and a man named Louis Jockisch, from Boody, Illinois, managed to make an audio recording of the cat's cries.

Later that same year, a Macon County Sheriff's Deputy reported seeing a large cat-like animal just west of Decatur. The cat slipped and fell as it ducked out of the way of the officer's car. The cat jumped a fence and ran into a corn field. The deputy fired off several shots but didn't believe that he had hit the cat. That fall, several sightings were reported by residents of the area.

Black panther sightings have become a part of the mysterious folklore (and reality) of Illinois and the sightings still continue today. In September 1998, a cougar was repeatedly sighted near Edwardsville, Illinois. While authorities found no trace of the animal, which was first seen on the playground of the LeClaire School, state wildlife officials admitted that it was the third report of a cougar near the city that year.

Customers and employees of the "New You Salon" on Franklin Avenue also reported the cougar. A total of five people told police that they had seen the animal inside the fence around the Illinois Power natural gas monitoring station, just northeast of the intersection of Franklin and Madison Avenues. One of the hair salon customers, a firefighter, was the first to spot the animal and he called police. A witness stated that the big cat had an extremely long and thick tail and that it was "reddish-brown" in color.

Police officers, while stating that they took the reports seriously, dismissed them as nothing more than reports of a "tom cat" in the neighborhood. Brenda Edgeworth, the owner of the hair salon went on record to say that .... "that was not a cat. I have seen some large house cats before. It was larger than that."

The other Edwardsville sightings had taken place in the spring of 1998. One had been seen near the Southern Illinois University at Edwardsville and another near Dunlap Lake. An additional sighting had also taken place near Collinsville. State wildlife officials who investigated the reports and searched the areas stated (predictably) that they had found no evidence of panthers.

So, do black panthers still roam the darkest corners of Illinois? It would appear that they still do, but where do these creatures come from and where do they disappear to?

But mysterious phantom panthers are not the only strange creatures to appear (and disappear) in Illinois. Can we explain these "displaced" animals as escapees from the local zoo or a passing circus train? You be the judge!

NELLIE THE LION

Many people have been able to accept the idea that black panthers do occasionally turn up in Illinois, but what about African Lions? According to newspaper and personal accounts from 1917, a lion did turn up and for nearly a month, "Nellie the Lion" was the terror of Central Illinois.

The lion first appeared in July 1917 on the estate of Robert Allerton, located near Monticello. A lion of some sort had been reported on the grounds and had apparently killed several pieces of livestock. One afternoon, the Allerton butler, Thomas Gullett, was out picking flowers when he was attacked by what he referred to as an "African lioness". The butler suffered only some minor cuts and scratches, but the search was soon on for the beast.

Robert Allerton offered a $250 reward to the hunter that killed the animal and an armed posse of more than 300 men turned up for a search of the large and heavily wooded estate. Allerton's farm manager bought a quantity of fresh meat and placed it in strategic locations. He hoped to lure the animal into a trap, but had no luck. The lion was seen later that day by two hunters who had given up on the day's search. Shortly after midnight, Paul and Lee Bear spotted the lion crossing a road in front of their truck. They managed to get off a few shots at it, but the lion jumped a fence and disappeared into corn field.

The search resumed the next day and while hunters were tramping through the woods, the lion appeared again at the Allerton house. Mrs. Shaw, the chief housekeeper, got a good look at it and like Gullett, described it as an "African lioness."

On July 17, tracks were discovered near Decatur that were five inches long and four inches wide. Two boys claimed to see the lion later that same day, prowling along the Sangamon River.

Thanks to newspaper reports and wild rumors, public hysteria mounted in Central Illinois. People mistook dogs for the lion and one farmer became involved a widely reported dispute about whether he had mistaken the headlights of an approaching vehicle for the beast's shining eyes. He denied it, but couldn't explain why he had put a bullet into the truck's radiator!

What may have seemed funny in the newspapers came as no joke to Earl Hill, Chester Osborn and the two men's wives on July 29. The two couples were motoring west of Decatur on the Springfield Road when the lion pounced on their car and tried to attack them. Hill and Osborn, sitting in the front seat of the vehicle, first saw the animal standing in the weeds on the side of the road. The animal jumped at them and collided with the vehicle, which was traveling at about 20 miles per hour. The couple hurriedly drove back to Decatur and summoned the police, who followed them back to the scene. To their surprise, the lion was still there, although it vanished over a hill when they arrived. The two lone policemen chose not to pursue it without heavier weapons. They returned in the early morning hours with two carloads of other officers. The men were all armed with high-powered rifles. They searched the area for several hours, but finding nothing, they returned to Decatur.

On July 31, a farm hand named James Rutherford spotted the lion near a gravel pit. The animal looked at him without interest and then wandered away. Rutherford gathered a group of hunters and brought them back to the scene. They found nothing save for a number of paw prints and a half-eaten calf, which the owner stated had been missing for four days.

After that, Nellie vanished into oblivion and was never heard from again. Today, the story is only remembered as a legend but newspapers and testimony of the era assures us that the lion really did exist.

PHANTOM KANGAROOS?

While lions and black panthers are certainly strange visitors to Illinois, there are stranger ones... kangaroos! Reports of mysterious kangaroos have been surprisingly widespread across northern Illinois. Are they escapees from zoos, or some sort of transported mystery beasts?

In the early morning hours of October 18, 1974, two Chicago police officers answered a call from a local resident who claimed that a kangaroo was sitting on his front porch. This particular call got a good laugh from officers and radio dispatchers until a few hours later when the two cops had the five-foot high animal cornered in a dark alley. One of the officers inexplicably thought that it would be a good idea to try and handcuff the animal. He gave this a try and the kangaroo suddenly started screeching and became vicious. It began punching the officers in the face and kicking them in the shins. Understandably, the officers backed off! A minute or two later, additional squad cars arrived and the kangaroo took off at high speed. It cleared a fence and vanished from the scene.

What seemed to be an isolated (albeit bizarre) incident was only the beginning of a "flap" of Midwestern kangaroo sightings, which occurred all over Illinois and Wisconsin.

The kangaroo was seen again the next day around Belmont and Oak Park when a paperboy heard the squeal of brakes from a car. He turned and spotted a kangaroo just a few feet away. The boy and the animal looked at one another and it hopped away... the kangaroo, I mean.

On October 23, it was seen again, this time in Chicago's Schiller Woods, near Irving Park Road. Then on November 1, it was spotted by a Plano police officer, just outside of city limits. He stated that the kangaroo jumped more than 8 feet from a cornfield into the roadway. It was spotted again the following night.

A half hour after the last Plano sighting, the same kangaroo (or another mystery beast) was reported 50 miles away, back in Chicago. On November 3, Frank Kocherver reported the kangaroo in a forest preserve. On November 4, a truck driver spotted the kangaroo and a deer in nearby field. He got out to examine the tracks and became convinced that his sighting was correct. On November 6, a truck driver near Lansing narrowly missed hitting a kangaroo and a flap of Indiana sightings began a few days later.

In July 1975, a kangaroo showed up near Decatur. Mrs. Rosemary Hopwood was traveling along Route 128, near Dalton City, when she saw an animal along the side of the road that she first mistook for a dog. She looked again and realized the animal was a kangaroo! It hopped away into a cornfield and disappeared. Three days later, several anonymous witnesses, a few of who have contacted me in recent years, also reported seeing a kangaroo in the general area.

Could this creature have really been a kangaroo? Many of the sightings in Wisconsin around this time seem to point toward a much more aggressive animal. In fact, "killer kangaroo" behavior caused one such animal to be labeled as a "werewolf" in 1972. A kangaroo-like creature was reported to have attacked a horse there, leaving a 30-inch gash across the horse's chest.

In his book, "The I-Files", author Jay Rath suggests that what was mistaken for a kangaroo may have actually been a "Chupacabra", the famed "goat-sucker", which was assumed to have made its first appearance in Puerto Rico in 1995. Since that time, it has been reported all over the southern United States and even in some northerly regions. The creatures are usually described as being like very vicious, "kangaroos". Could some of these anomalous creatures have been even stranger than "out of place" kangaroos??

ALLIGATORS IN THE SEWER

Remember one of the most famous urban legends of all time? It was the story that alligators were living in the sewers of some of our major American cities. Legend had it that these creatures had been brought back from Florida as tiny creatures. Once the alligators started to grow, concerned parents realized that their children's pets would soon turn into creatures of monstrous proportions. They quickly flushed them down the toilet. Once in the sewer system, the alligators grew to be huge, feeding off the rats and the garbage of the city... and occasionally eating the unsuspecting utility worker or transient.

Pretty wild, huh? But would it surprise you to discover that these stories have a basis in fact? Newspapers and books have featured a number of accounts from sewer workers who have encountered these beasts over the years.

Anything might be possible under the streets of New York... but what about the streets of Illinois? It may be hard to imagine that alligators can make appearances here, but records and reports prove that they have turned up here on occasion.

The first account that I have been able to find (thanks to author Loren Coleman) is from February 1892, when a gator turned up in a Chicago storm drain. The next report dates back to August 1937 when an alligator was spotted in a small outlet off of Lake Decatur.

In October 1966, two Decatur fishermen captured a small alligator that measured a little over a foot long. The two men were on Lake Decatur when they discovered the baby alligator in the company of its much larger mother. They estimated the parent creature to be around six feet long. At the sight of the larger alligator, they abandoned their fishing spot, taking the smaller animal with them. The local newspaper featured a story on the two fishermen that contained a photograph of one of the men, Richard Stubblefield, holding the baby alligator.

And Decatur's sewer system holds mysteries of its own...

It seems that in June 1967, an alligator was pulled from a drainpipe at 895 West Eldorado Street. The animal was less than a foot long, but one has to wonder how large its mother must have been?

In July 1970, an alligator was spotted in a man-made lake near Lombard and another gator was spotted in the Sangamon River near Oakley in August 1971. In September 1972, a creature was seen crawling across the highway near Chenoa and then abruptly disappeared.

This was the last recorded sighting of an alligator in our area to date, but you cannot help but wonder if there may be more of them lurking in the darkness underneath our cities and small towns. What might be lurking down there? That's something to think about the next time that you pass an open storm drain!

BIGFOOT IN ILLINOIS

For more than a century, reports have filtered out of rural and southern Illinois about strange, man-like beasts that resemble a cross between man and ape. Most witnesses talk of their odd appearance and the horrible odor that seems to accompany them. While these beast have often been referred to as "Bigfoot" or "Sasquatch", many researchers, like Loren Coleman, have started calling them the "North American Ape". They have been reported all over America and even in Illinois.

The stories of Bigfoot have been passed along from generation to generation and have long been chronicled by both professional and amateur researchers. According to hundreds of reports, the creatures average between 7-8 feet in height. Hair covers most of their bodies, they appear to be proportioned and move like large men, not apes, and have broad shoulders and very little neck. Their faces are normally flattened, they have a heavy jaw and as mentioned, a strong smell seems to emanate from them.

While the most famous Bigfoot sightings have taken place in the Pacific Northwest, such creatures do occasionally turn up in Illinois. The earliest sighting that I could find from our region occurred around 1912. A woman named Beaulah Schroat reported that her and her brothers often spotted huge, hairy creatures near their home in Effingham. This may have been the first sighting in Illinois, but it was not the first one in the Great Lakes region. As far back as 1839, witnesses in Michigan City, Indiana were reporting a "wild child" near Fish Lake. Today, we would call such a creature "Bigfoot".

Another report comes from the early part of the last century. In this brief snippet, we find that a "huge gorilla" was seen in the woods near Elizabeth in July 1929. Then, in 1941, the Reverend Lepton Harpole was hunting squirrels near Mt. Vernon and encountered a large creature that "looked something like a baboon". He struck it with his rifle and fired a warning shot that sent it scurrying back into the underbrush. More sightings of the same creature occurred the next year.

A photo of a footprint found after a 1962 Bigfoot sighting near Decatur, Illinois.

Jumping ahead, a grayish-colored creature was spotted by Steven Collins and Robert Earle in 1962. It was standing in a riverbed east of Decatur, just off of East Williams Street Road. The monster was standing upright in the water, looking straight at them. At first, they thought they were seeing a bear, until they noticed its strange, human-like features. The creature vanished into the woods and the witnesses told the local newspaper that it was "like no other animal we had ever seen before."

In September 1965, four young people were parked in a car near an undeveloped area outside of Decatur called Montezuma Hills. The area would later become a housing addition but at that time, it was a secluded "lover's lane". The young couples were sitting in the car when a black, man-like shape approached the vehicle. The creature seemed massive and frightened the teenagers badly. They drove off in a panic but after dropping off their dates at home, the two young men returned to the area for another look. They once again saw the monster and it walked up to their car as though it were curious. The boys were too scared to get out, but even with the windows rolled up, they could smell the monster's terrible stench. They quickly summoned the police to the site and with several officers as support, they made a thorough, but fruitless, search of the woods. The police officers on the scene said they had no idea what the young people had witnessed, but they were obviously very frightened by whatever it had been.

Another creature was encountered near Chittyville in August 1968. Two young people were driving north of town when they spotted a 10-foot tall monster that was covered with black hair and had a round face. It threw dirt at their car and they left to summon the police. When the authorities returned, they found a large depression in the grass that was apparently a nest.

One of the strangest Illinois incidents took place in July 1970, near Farmer City. Early that spring, three sheep had been killed near town by local officials dismissed it as the work of wild dogs, which have been known to roam the area. Outside of the small town, near Salt Creek, was a ten-acre section of woods and fields that was a popular parking spot for teenagers.

Three teenagers decided to camp out there one night. Very late in the evening, they reported hearing something approaching their campsite in the tall grass. They turned a light in that direction and saw a huge, black shape crouching near the tent. The shape had a pair of gleaming, yellow eyes, a color that would be repeated in every account to follow. The terrified screams of the teenagers also scared the creature and all of them ran off in different directions.

Stories about the "Farmer City Monster" quickly spread. Dozens of people reported seeing the creature over the next several days and all of the sightings took place near the wooded area outside of town. Robert Hayslip, a Farmer City police officer who investigated the scene, reported his own encounter. In the early morning hours of July 15, he saw the broad back of the creature moving along the trees. The creature turned in his direction and Hayslip also noted its yellow eyes. The local police chief, who until that point had been skeptical about the sightings, decided to close of the area. But the creature was soon to move on.

On July 24, a couple driving near Weldon Springs State Park, outside of Clinton, saw what looked like a huge "bear" in the river. Later, a policeman and a conservation officer found tracks along the water's edge that definitely did not belong to a bear. They were reportedly very large and human-like.

A few days later, further north, a woman caught the reflection of eyes with her car headlights as she was traveling outside of Bloomington. She thought the eyes might belong to a dog that had been injured by a passing car, so she stopped and approached the ditch where she had seen something. Suddenly, a large creature jumped out of the ditch and ran away on two legs. She was unsure about what she had seen, but whatever it was, it seemed ape-like. Later that same week, another witness reported an identical creature near Heyworth.

On August 11, three young men reported seeing a large, dark-haired creature near Waynesville and five days later, construction workers saw the creature near the same location. It ran across the highway in front of their truck and disappeared into the forest. That was the last reported of the so-called "Farmer City Monster" and one can't help but wonder if it continued its strange journey northwest across Central Illinois. If it did, it was never reported again.

In May 1972, there were new reports coming in from the Pekin and Peoria areas. In late May, a young man named Randy Emmert, and some friends, reported a large, hairy creature near Cole Hollow Road. This monster was 8-10 feet tall and whitish in color. The witnesses stated that it made a loud, screeching sound and they suspected that it was living in a hole beneath an abandoned house. It also left very unusual tracks, having only three toes on each foot. Soon, others were reporting the same monster and it became known as "Cohomo", short for the "Cole Hollow Road Monster".

On May 25, local police logged more than 200 calls about the monster, including one where the creature destroyed a fence. The police departments were naturally skeptical, but the calls kept coming in. By July 1972, there had been so many sightings that 100 volunteers were organized to search for Cohomo. Finally, Tazewell County sheriff's officers sent the volunteers home after one of them, Carl R. Harris, accidentally shot himself in the leg with a .22 caliber pistol.

The sightings continued and they couldn't be written off to local "panic" either. One witness, from Eureka, knew nothing about the creature, yet happened to be in Fondulac Park, in East Peoria, for a birthday party. He reported the creature and strangely, a set of strange lights that seemed to descend vertically and land behind some trees. Were the two sightings connected?

Cohomo was seen again on July 27 as East Peoria Police reported that he was spotted by "two reliable citizens" swimming in the Illinois River. They got close enough to him to know that he smelled awful and looked like a "cross between an ape and a caveman". After that, he was gone.

In the summer of 1973, three men who were walking along the Sangamon River near Decatur saw a large, hairy man that walked like an ape. The creature disappeared into the underbrush. The witnesses, understandably, declined to pursue it.

Then, in 1973-1974, strange sightings occurred in southern Illinois and became some of the most famous of the Illinois monster sightings, the "Enfield Horror" and the "Murphysboro Mud Monster" (see Chapter Two).

In early summer 1979, another creature was spotted near Westchester, in Cook County. And there have been other sketchy reports from southern Illinois (especially in the Shawnee National Forest) in more recent times. Since the 1970's, Bigfoot sightings in Illinois have been infrequent, but they do occur. I have talked to a number of people over the years that have had sightings of things they couldn't explain. Who knows just when the next one might be seen?

THE BLUE PHANTOM OF ROUTE 66

Route 66 has become famous in recent years as the "Mother Road" and the precursor of the modern American highway. In the first decades of the last century, Route 66 spanned the country, connecting Illinois with the golden land of California. It was probably traveled more than any other highway in America and became known as the road to a dream of a brighter tomorrow.

However, in Central Illinois in the early 1950's, Route 66 became a highway of terror for many travelers. The "Blue Phantom", as the mysterious auto was dubbed, first appeared on Route 66 near Joliet in May 1952. Two different drivers independently reported that someone had fired a shot at them from a movie, blue automobile. One of the drivers was even wounded, although not seriously. Later that same day, another driver reported an identical incident. This attack took place three miles south of Lincoln, again on Route 66.

On June 2, the Blue Phantom changed tactics and ambushed a passing car. Edward Smith of St. Louis was driving south of the Sangamon River when something struck his car. He slowed down and glanced over to see a man run out of some bushes next to the road. The man climbed into a large blue car, which had been hidden out of sight, and roared back north on the highway. Smith guessed that the car was either a Ford or a Buick sedan. He reported the incident to the police, who believed that a .38 caliber bullet has struck Smith's rear window.

On June 8, there were ten shootings reported on Central Illinois highways. One of the shootings even shattered the windshield of a car. The state police, along with local officers, set up roadblocks along a 75-mile stretch of the highway. They also hired a small plane to follow the course of the road and search for a blue sedan. Owners of blue automobiles were stopped, and often harassed, but no suspects turned up in the search.

On June 9, on Route 66 outside of Springfield, a bullet struck a car owned by William Moffit. It had been fired from an auto that had been speeding in the opposite direction. Moffit thought this vehicle might have been dark green in color. A different sniper, or the same one in another car? A similar incident also occurred near Clinton, Illinois a short time later. This time, the driver of the truck that was damaged did not see the car that fired the shot. He did however, have two bullet holes in his windshield.

On June 10, the Blue Phantom chose his 15th target, defying all efforts by the police to stop him. This time he attacked just before dawn, then led a police vehicle on a wild chase that approached speeds of more than 90 m.p.h. The police officer that pursued the elusive vehicle said that he was unable to overtake the other car.

On June 17, a witness named DL Weatherford observed a man standing on a bridge near Mount Pulaski. The man wore a khaki shirt and trousers and held a revolver. He was standing next to a blue Chrysler sedan. Weatherford reported the sighting, although wisely did not stop to ask questions. Two nights later, a car described as a blue Ford pursued a Decatur couple through the city after its occupant opened fire on them.

Near Champaign, Illinois on June 24, the Blue Phantom made its last appearance. A sedan pulled up alongside a car and four shots were fired. One of the bullets crashed into the passenger side window of the other car. The blue sedan quickly pulled away and vanished from the city.

After that, the Blue Phantom was lost to history, as that was the last time it was ever heard from. Was the curious car merely a figment of the imagination or some lone nutcase looking for kicks by shooting out people's windows? Either of those options are surely possible.. or perhaps the Blue Phantom was something far stranger, something that exists just on the other side of the unknown.

THE WOMAN IN WHITE

There is probably no location that is more out of place on the Central Illinois prairie than the Robert Allerton estate. The estate is owned by the University of Illinois today and serves as both an educational and recreational site and as a 1500-acre tribute to a fascinating, and unusual, man.

To wander the vast estate is almost like taking a trip through another world. The estate boasts original artwork, exquisite gardens, miles of hiking trails, a Chinese pavilion, sunken gardens, statuary like the impressive Sun-Singer, the Centaur, the avenue of Chinese musicians, and the fearsome, and creepy, Fu-Dogs... and of course, the 40-room manor house that serves as the centerpiece of the estate.

But who was Robert Allerton and what drove him to carve this strange place from the Illinois prairie? And what of the ghost who allegedly walks here? Are the stories of her presence really true? According to staff members and guests of the estate, they are very true... but who is she, and why does her spirit linger at the Allerton House?

Robert Henry Allerton was born in March 1873, the only son of a wealthy Chicago businessman named Samuel Waters Allerton. The elder Allerton was a self-made millionaire who had amassed a fortune through real estate, banking and a variety of other enterprises. Robert grew up as a privileged young man on fashionable Prairie Avenue in Chicago with neighbors like the Marshall Fields, the Pullmans and the Kimballs. He wanted for nothing and yet he was an unhappy child. His mother died in 1880, just five days before Robert's seventh birthday, leaving a void in his life. However, two years later, his father married Agnes Thompson and she became Robert's stepmother, mentor and friend. She encouraged his interests in music, literature, art and gardening.

As Robert grew older, he began to study at the Art Institute and then attended the Allen Academy and the Harvard School in Chicago. His father sent him to a prep school in New Hampshire in the company of his friend, Frederic Clay Bartlett. After attending school for two years, the two young men decided not to go on to college, but to go to Europe and study art instead. Needless to say, Samuel Allerton was not pleased.

Regardless, Robert spent the next five years studying art in Munich and Paris. He was admitted to the Royal Academy of Bavaria and to the Acadamie Julian, then at the age of 24, Robert ended his budding career as an artist. One afternoon, he returned home and destroyed every painting he had ever created. What prompted this remains a mystery, because he never gave up art altogether, remaining a collector and patron of the arts for the rest of his life.

He returned home to Chicago in 1897 and announced to his father that he wanted to become a farmer. Samuel was pleased with this, feeling that it would encourage his son's "health, vitality and character". He had given Robert 280 acres of land in Piatt County when his son was younger and he now gave him money to build a house on the land. He also put him in charge of managing other family holdings in downstate Illinois. Robert named his Piatt Count holdings "The Farms" and by 1914, he would increase the size of the estate to about 12,000 acres.

Robert decided that he needed a house to serve as the center of the estate. This would be no mere farm house, but a mansion where Robert could feel comfortable in the rural setting. Here, he would store his large art collection and would create a place of beauty for he and his friends to enjoy.

In October 1898, Robert journeyed to England with his friend John Borie, an architect that he had met in Paris. The two men spent the winter visiting English country houses and landscaped gardens, looking for the perfect design for the Illinois house. The following spring, they returned to America, the plans for the house complete.

Construction was finished in 1900 and the house remains an eclectic mix of styles, including British and American colonial. The house also had a formal pool and a small lake was created nearby. He and Borie also designed landscaped gardens, which bordered on the woods and open fields. Borie also designed a walled vegetable garden, the gate house and a series of greenhouses.

Meanwhile, Robert began setting up a very profitable farming system that would more than support his lifestyle. He hired excellent farm managers and worked in partnership with area farmers. He is still remembered today as an excellent landlord. In addition to work, he also continued to travel and to collect books and works of art.

Much of the design completed for the grounds was done by Robert as well. He created additional formal gardens and an amphitheater he called the Sunken Gardens. He built a bridge over the Sangamon River, connected the stables to the house by way of a marble walkway and constructed the "House in the Woods" on the property in 1917.

Robert's father died in 1914 and Robert gained a number of new responsibilities as part of his large inheritance. He became an executive board member of banks and businesses in the Chicago area, forcing him to spend more time in the city. While in Chicago, he became involved with a number of clubs and civic organizations, including the Art Institute and the Chicago Civic Opera.

He divided his time between Chicago and the Farms and continued to make improvements and manage affairs. Whenever possible, he also entertained his artist friends, who enjoyed the seclusion of the rural estate. A frequent visitor to the country was his stepmother and friend, Agnes, who brought with her a young woman, named Ellen Emmett Rand. Robert and Ellen were said to have formed a romantic attachment and most referred to them as being "unofficially engaged". For some unknown reason though, they would never marry.

In the 1920's, Robert became closely involved with the University of Illinois, where he served on several boards and established landscaping and architecture scholarships. Once each year, he invited graduating students to a reception at the Farms. In 1922, he attended a "Dad's Day" dinner at the Zeta Psi House in Champaign. It was here where he met a young architecture student named John Wyatt Gregg. The student had lost both of his parents and since Robert had no children, the two of them were paired for the day. They became friends and developed a father-son relationship that would last for the rest of Robert's life.

After John graduated, he went to work for architect David Adler, a close friend of Robert's. However, due to the stock market crash in 1929, there was little work for the young man. Finally, in 1931, he came to live at The Farms and became Robert's personal architect and protégé. He also became Robert's legally adopted son a number of years later.

During the 1930's, Robert and John made several trips to Europe, the Far East and the Pacific Islands. They purchased artwork for the house and created new additions for the estate. Robert's tastes had changed from Edwardian to Oriental and his new interests began to appear in landscaped gardens on the farm, along with the Fu-Dog trail and the House of Golden Buddhas.

The two men entertained often, hosting a large garden party each spring. Guests were given Roman togas and Japanese kimonos so they would feel comfortable in the peaceful surroundings. The old conservatory of the house was turned into a costume room and guests were free to come and go as they liked.

In 1937, Robert and John visited Hawaii, on the way from Australia, and fell in love with the tropical climate. By the next autumn, Robert had purchased 125 acres of land and started construction on a new house and gardens. By 1938, he had moved from Illinois to Hawaii and incorporated much of the artwork from The Farms into the new house. Furniture, books and art from the Illinois house were either moved, sold or given away. The house was largely abandoned and Robert would not live there again during his lifetime.

In 1946, he donated The Farms to the University of Illinois with the stipulation that it remain as a wildlife and plant preserve, an education center and as a public park. He also donated farm land, the proceeds from which would provide income to upkeep the park and an area that was turned into a 4-H camp. The portion of the estate Robert had dubbed the "Woodland Property", about 1500 acres, became the Robert Allerton Park.

By this time, the estate in Hawaii had become known as a showplace for tropical plants and Robert became an honorary member of the Honolulu Garden Club and a generous benefactor of the art museum. He gave money for a library and a new wing that contained over 200 pieces of Oriental art. He also donated money to establish the Pacific Tropical Botanical Garden, which started in 1964.

Robert Allerton died that same year, on December 22, at the age of 91. At his request, his body was cremated and his ashes were scattered on the outgoing tide.

So who haunts the Allerton House today? The restless spirit here is not Robert, returning to his once-beloved home, but that of a woman who has been described as wearing a white dress. No one knows when the haunting began, but in recent years, there have been a number of strange encounters.

The estate remains under the care of the University of Illinois today. The manor house, Evergreen Lodge, the Gate House and the House in the Woods are all used as guest facilities for the conference center and are normally closed to the public. However, staff members and guests in the main house sometimes get more than they bargained for when working or attending a conference.

One former staff member who claims to have encountered the "woman in white" is Atron Regen, who once served as the night manager at the house. When he came to work here, he was the first employee to be given a bedroom in the house. The day he arrived, the room was not ready so he was given the master bedroom to sleep in that night. It would be in this room where he would have his first encounter with the resident ghost.

Regen was sound asleep in the early morning hours when he was awakened by a terrible sensation of cold and energy. The energy came over him like a wave and jolted him awake. He described it as sliding over and then off his body and he sensed it moved away toward the adjoining bedroom. The feeling was so sensational that he could actually feel it leaving him and simply knew what direction it then took. "I've never felt anything like that before," Regen stated in an interview... and he never wanted to again either.

This would be the first time he encountered the ghost, but it was not the last. On another occasion, he was surprised to feel a small hand touching him on the back of his own. He looked down and saw the filmy image of a woman's hand and the cuff of a startlingly white dress. He could see and feel the hand but beyond it, the image faded away into nothingness. Then, the hand itself vanished!

"I really feel this house is haunted," was the conclusion that Regen reached after that incident.

And Regen would not be the only person to feel this way. Guests and other staff members at the house reported hearing phantom footsteps in the empty hallways and the sounds of someone descending the stairs. They would often look to see who was there and find no one.

On several occasions, individuals reported the ghostly image of a woman in a white, old-fashioned dress wandering through the hallways and in the bedrooms. Perhaps the most amazing encounter came when two ladies were sharing a bedroom one night during a conference. They later learned, by comparing notes, that both of them were restless during the night. Each of them tossed and turned and both of them separately reported a chilling sight. At different times, each of them saw a woman in a white dress sitting in a chair on the far side of the room. The woman was looking in the mirror and adjusting her hat, then pulling on formal, white gloves. She remained there for several moments and then inexplicably vanished.

And who is this lovely ghost? Several people connected to the house believe that it may be the spirit of Ellen Emmett Rand, Robert Allerton's one-time fiancee. Ellen was a frequent visitor to the house during a period prior to the 1920's, often traveling from Chicago in the company of Robert's stepmother. She was an artist in her own right and as you will recall, the only woman ever linked romantically to Robert. Everyone always assumed the two of them would marry but for some reason, they never did. Later, Ellen would marry another man and Robert would stay single throughout his entire life, preferring only the company of John and his many friends.

Many believe that perhaps Ellen's heart was broken when she learned that Robert never planned to marry her and perhaps this revelation led to a falling out that would leave Robert single and turn Ellen to another man. Although perhaps she considered Robert her one true love.... but it was a marriage that was never meant to be.

If this is true, then perhaps it is Ellen's ghost that haunts the house. Perhaps she is still reliving the wonderful days when she, Robert and their artist friends gathered at the estate to laugh, create and live extravagantly. In her world, it may still be those gilded days after the Great War, when art, literature and beauty were still the passions of this golden circle of friends. It was a time when everything seemed right with the world and for Ellen, perhaps it is still that time. Perhaps she has chosen to return to those times, in a house where she knew happiness... becoming a true spirit of another place and time.

VOORHIES CASTLE

Located on a lonely stretch of highway in eastern Central Illinois is an isolated village called Voorhies. There is very little left of the town these days, save for a few houses, an abandoned church and of course, Voorhies Castle.

While most of the stories about the place have died out over the years and the house has become little more than a forgotten curiosity, it was once regarded as one of the most haunted houses in the state. The legends and stories about this rambling old mansion were some of the most often repeated tales in the region and although recent owners have denied that anything ghostly takes place there now, most of us have never forgotten the chilling stories. Just a few short years ago, Voorhies Castle was a place of legend. The dark tales, concerning its shadowed beginnings and haunted past, were literally recounted by generation after generation. The place became the perfect model for a "haunted house on the prairie".

Did the house deserve the reputation that it gained? I'll leave that up to you to decide.

The story of Voorhies Castle began in 1867 with the arrival of a Swedish immigrant named Nels Larson in America. He settled near Galesburg, Illinois and went to work for a local farmer, soon earning a reputation as a hard and efficient worker. Larson saved every dollar he made and within a short time, he moved south and settled in Piatt County, near the town of Bement. Here, he went to work for a local farmer and landowner named William Voorhies.

Voorhies himself returned to America in 1868. During the Civil War, he studied medicine in Germany and returned to his home state of Kentucky and married Ellen Duncan of Lexington. Two years later, he gave up practicing medicine and moved north to Illinois. He purchased three sections of prairie land in Piatt County and set aside a parcel for a homestead. He soon found the land to be rich and productive and eventually a fine home was built that was two stories high with a wide verandah on three sides. Although prosperous, Voorhies discovered that he had more land than he could handle and he began selling off small parcels to upstanding and hardworking men in the area. It would be one of these parcels of land that Nels Larson would purchase in 1885.

Meanwhile, Jack Voorhies, William's brother, joined his family in Illinois. He had served in the Civil War and now retired for a brief time to establish himself on another of the pieces of land. According to oral history, it would be after Jack Voorhies that a small village would eventually be named.

William Voorhies continued in farming in real estate and later was elected to Congress and served on the State Board of Agriculture. Ellen Voorhies and her daughters began operation of a summer camp at Breezeland where guests "talked and read and played and ate, with emphasis on eating". Hired Negro cooks provided extravagant meals and a number of hammocks were stretched between trees in a walnut grove for relaxation purposes. They also provided horses and buggies for riding and leisurely drives.

In 1913, the William and Ellen retired and sold the farm. They moved south to live out the rest of their days in a temperate climate. However, in 1916, William died suddenly in New Orleans and Ellen returned to Illinois. She lived in Decatur until her death in 1933.

Nels Larson started out with little. Even after going to work for William Voorhies, he only earned $30 a month in the summer and $40 per month in the fall and winter. He also had to give back $9 each month for this room and board and provide his own clothing. He lived frugally and saved all of the money that he could. Finally, in 1872, he spent $325 for a good team of horses and went into debt for a harness, plows and a wagon. He rented 60 acres of land from Voorhies and set out on his own. Later, he bought a large parcel of property from his former employer near the small town of Voorhies. Also in 1872, Larson sent for his fiancée, Johannah Nilson, who was still living in Sweden at that time. Later that same year, they were married.

Larson continued to buy more land, and lease other parcels. He also had a number of farmers working for him, renting his property in exchange for a portion of the proceeds from the harvest. In addition to his own farm, he was a partial owner in many others. The small town of Voorhies, which Larson owned, was also growing, consisting of small businesses and tenant homes rented by Larson's farmers. The town also contained a church, a general store, a grain elevator, a corn crib and several barns. There was also a barber shop, a jeweler, a blacksmith and a postmaster. At the post office, a license was granted for the sale of postal money orders and locals could purchase tickets for travel on the Wabash Railroad line that passed through town. The rail station was also useful for the loading and unloading of grain and cattle. The grain elevator was added to the town in 1897 and was operated by Larson's son, George, who was also the postmaster. The post office would only last until 1904 when Rural Free Delivery was authorized by the federal government. At that time, a postal route for Voorhies was established from Bement.

There was no question that Larson was now the most powerful and wealthy landowner in the area, but he certainly wasn't liked by everyone. It was often stated that he expected more from his workers than most were willing to give and some have described him as a "tyrant". A worker could be fired for the slightest infraction, often at Larson's whim. One night, the local general store was burned to the ground at a loss of more than $1600. Although it was clearly a case of arson, Larson refused to allow an investigation and simply rebuilt the place, hiring a security guard to watch over the new building. There were other cases of vandalism too, possibly by disgruntled employees, which ended in the burning of cattle guards and small structures. Larson chose to ignore them.

The greatest animosity toward Larson probably came from his son, George, who was born in 1873. He was a graduate of both Bement High School and Brown Business College in Decatur but could never get out from under his father's control. He always admitted that he was afraid of his father and for this reason, stayed in Voorhies to act as postmaster and to handle the running of the grain elevator.

In 1903, George began courting a local girl named Naomi Shasteen. His parents disapproved of the girl and stated that she was only after the Larson family money. Nevertheless, the two of them were married in June of that year. They took a wedding trip to Chicago and then settled into a small cottage that was built just west of the Larson's main house. This arrangement was not a good one and dissension quickly grew, building toward a confrontation that took place one morning on the sidewalk between the two houses. Naomi, who was accustomed to being allowed to walk on the sidewalk by a gentleman who was passing in the opposite direction, refused to step off the walk when ordered to do so by Nels Larson. He demanded that the young woman move out of his way, but she refused. Infuriated, he screamed at her, leaving the girl in tears. Shortly after, George constructed a house for he and his wife a quarter mile away and across the railroad tracks from Voorhies. They remained in this house until George retired and they moved to Bement. George passed away in 1966.

On the other hand, Larson's daughter, Ellen, was the pride of his life and his spoiled princess. Ellen was born in August 1880 and after graduating from Bement High School in 1901, stayed at home in the now-completed "castle". She had a room tucked between the twin towers of the house that was richly decorated and furnished with whatever the young woman desired. She reigned over the house and grounds, flirting with being an artist and rising late in the day.

Voorhies Castle (Circa 1915)

Years later, explorers of the abandoned castle would find remnants of Ellen that had been left behind, like calling cards of friends, books, delicate clothing and hastily written love letters that had been secreted away decades before.

Her life in Voorhies was pleasant and filled with good memories, unlike her brother. Ellen later married James Lamb, a doctor from Cerro Gordo. She bore him four children but her heart developed a complication with the fourth pregnancy. After that, she was often confined to bed and was only allowed to leave the house occasionally for the evening or for a Sunday afternoon drive. She withdrew more and more into seclusion, only visited by a few friends. During her infrequent day trips, she usually visited the empty "castle" and disappeared inside, where she remained for hours. Perhaps she was trying to recapture a little of the life she once knew there. Ellen passed away in 1955, just four months after the death of her husband.

By 1900, Larson was firmly entrenched as the "ruler" of his vast domain, consisting of tenants, farms, land, various businesses and even an entire village. He had lived in several houses around the area, but now decided that he needed a manor house to from which to oversee his property. This house, later dubbed "Voorhies Castle", would be patterned after a chalet in his native Sweden. Larson contacted a Chicago architect to draw up plans to his specifications. A contractor was then hired and construction began in the summer of 1900.

The house was a strange mixture of styles and eccentricities. When first completed, the towers on the corners of the house were three stories high, looming one floor higher than the rest of the structure. Larson had thought they would be desirable vantage points from which to view his land holdings and a suitable place for his office. However, when completed, they looked so strange that Larson reluctantly ordered the third floor of each tower removed. He was forced to rely on the front porch alone, with a frontage of 60 feet and a double platform swing, from which to look out on the fields and village.

The front door of the house was extra wide and commonly called a "casket door" as it allowed access for both coffin and pallbearers in the days when funerals were held in the homes of the deceased. The door was flanked by large windows that, like those in the rest of the house, were wider than normal for the time period. Each was designed with a large pane in the lower sash and a series of smaller ones in the top sash. The windows were hung with either lace curtains or velvet draperies, depending on the room.

Inside of the house was a large reception hall that was fitted with an oak fireplace. Larson had brought an artist from Sweden especially for the purpose of hand-carving this fireplace and two others in the house. Sliding doors were fitted into each doorway leading to the adjoining rooms.

The west parlor contained a cherry wood fireplace. It was also decorated with a large fern that was kept near the south window. The fern was so long that it stood on a round, wooden pillar so that its fronds did not touch the floor. This parlor led into the west tower and the doorway was adorned with wooden scrollwork. The ceiling was papered and decorated with clouds and stars. It was in this room where Larson conducted most of his business affairs.

On the opposite side of the reception hall was the east parlor. Here is where Ellen's piano was kept and this room was more designed for lady visitors with emerald furniture, scrolled doorways, a bookcase secretary and even a "fainting couch" for the lady whose corset stays might be too tight. The walls in this room were not papered but covered with a smooth, slack lime plaster.

The house also boasted indoor plumbing and a bathroom with all of the latest innovations. It was located between the east parlor and the back room that served as Johannah's sewing room and as an extra bedroom. The bed was a foldaway device and an oak dresser, a washstand and a walnut bureau were also kept here. A heavy safe was kept hidden in the closet and the walls were undecorated except for a large map of Illinois in 1899.

The dining room was also located on the first floor and it boasted a beautiful parquet floor designed of maple, mahogany, birch, oak and sycamore pieces. There was also a marble-topped sideboard and a dining room table that could be extended to seat 24 people. In the corner of the room was a gold couch where Larson napped each day following his lunch. The telephone and the doorbell, both battery-operated devices were mounted on the wall of the dining room.

The kitchen was small, but filled to capacity. It had a tiled floor and contained a drop-leaf table and chairs, a high cupboard, a stove, a sink and a water heater. The kitchen was further cramped by the five doors that exited off of it, going to the basement, the upstairs, the back porch, the dining room and to a small pantry that was lined from floor to ceiling with shelves and cupboards.

Floral carpeting climbed the stairs and extended into the bedrooms. George's room, which was only used for a short time, was at the head of the staircase and contained an oak dresser, a washstand and a bed or iron and brass. A small closet was tucked beneath the sloping roof, but the tower offered the room a wonderful view of the countryside.

Ellen's room was above the reception hall and the south wall of it contained windows and some them were of stained glass, purchased from Tiffany. The room was graced with fine lace and with birch furnishings that seemed to glow in the light of the southern exposure.

The largest of the upstairs chambers was the master bedroom, which extended across the east end of the house. It was dominated by a huge rosewood bed and dresser that had to be moved into position before the house could be completed. The bedroom suite had been acquired as part of a settlement between Larson and William Voorhies, the details of which have never been revealed. The tower room adjacent to this bedroom offered the best view of the land and it has been said that Larson looked out over his holdings every morning when he rose from bed.

There was also a fourth bedroom, above the dining room, that contained an old walnut bureau and bed. The closet in this room wrapped around the chimney and it was seldom used. The chamber was mostly a spare room to be used by visiting friends and relatives.

The basement of the house spread beneath the entire structure. It was equipped with all of the modern conveniences of the period, or at least those found in a rural setting. The running water in the house existed thanks to two 1,000 gallon wooden cisterns in which water was stored and forced by compressed air into the kitchen and bathroom. A steel, airtight tank received the water from the cisterns by hand pump. The water compressed the air already in the tank and then forced the water upstairs. Five minutes of pumping would supply the household with enough water for the entire day. This was considered to be a better method than the common attic water supply, which was always in danger of freezing or leaking into the house. There was also a hot water heater in the kitchen that provided heated rain water, which was used for cooking and drinking. There was also an auxiliary water system that used rain water for the fountains located in the twin flower beds in the front yard.

The other side of the basement contained a coal bin and a hot air furnace that sent air into all of the rooms of the house. A battery-operated thermostat controlled the temperature. Two years later, Larson installed makeshift lighting using a dangerous carbide-gas system. It was supposed to light 50 lamps using 50 pounds of carbide but never worked correctly. The system was very hazardous and Larson had to obtain special permission from his insurance company to have it installed. Once the system was in place, light fixtures and wall-bracketed lamps were added in most of the rooms. The house would never be equipped with an actual electrical system during the period when the Larson family lived here.

Only the finest materials were used in the construction of the house, which delayed its completion until 1904. On many occasions, Larson would return entire loads of lumber to the warehouse after discovering a few boards with knots in them. The total cost of the Castle was around $9,000.

The most eccentric addition to the estate came in 1910, as a clock tower barn that Larson insisted be included on the property. The stories say that Larson had a fascination, or perhaps obsession, with clocks. They could be found all over the house, from the large grandfather clock in the reception area to small timepieces scattered on the top of the wooden trunk in his bedroom.

One day in 1905, he decided that he wanted to install a large clock in his barn. However, the barn that he now had would not work for this so he ordered it dismantled and sold to a neighbor. He would construct a new barn and place the clock in this one. He ordered a Seth Thomas clock from a jeweler in Monticello and began construction on the new building. The work on the barn took almost five years to complete, even longer than it took to build the house. The new structure had to be equipped with a 68 foot tall tower and had to be given enough support that it could hold the nearly two ton clock mechanism.

The clock was eventually fitted into the tower and made a breathtaking, albeit unusual, sight. The four faces of it were of solid milk glass, six feet wide and two inches thick. The faces came from Virginia, the clock works from Connecticut and the weights were sent down from Chicago. A 14-pound hammer was used to strike the solid brass bell and it could be heard from four or five miles away.

When the house was briefly occupied again in the 1960's, the clock was put back into order after years of inactivity. It needed to only be cleaned and oiled to get it working properly again. During the days of Nels Larson, the clock was wound every Sunday morning but later a windstorm shifted the tower slightly so that the weights settled upon a crosspiece by the third day. This involved winding the clock once in the middle of the week as well.

Legend states that the clock mysteriously struck 13 times at the moment of Nels Larson's death, as though the man and the machine were somehow connected. The stories went on to say that the clock continued this odd activity for five decades, ringing out on the anniversary of its owner's passing. The clock tower remained an odd landmark on the prairie until the summer of 1976, when it was destroyed by a tornado. It has been said that the now phantom clock continues to chime each March 29, at the very hour that Nels Larson passed from this world to the next.

The Larson family resided in the house for a number of years and during this time, at least one of the numerous legends of the house began. The stories alleged that Nels and Johannah Larson had another child in addition to George and Ellen. It was said this child was severely retarded and was kept chained in a small, hidden room in the house. It has been said that in later years, visitors to the house claimed to hear the sound of phantom chains rattling inside of the walls. The validity of this story is unknown as volunteers from the Illinois Pioneer Heritage Center searched the house for this room in the 1960's but were unable to find it.

The most mysterious event to occur in the house took place in 1914, when Johannah died. Many have speculated that she had a heart attack on the staircase, but the real cause of her death remains a mystery to this day. One of the field hands had gone to the house one afternoon to find her lying in a crumpled heap on the floor. Nels Larson was so stunned by this event that he left the house that night and went to Ellen's home in Cerro Gordo.... never to return. All of the clothing and furniture and even his personal belongings were left behind.

He never came back to the house, abandoning everything that had been left there. The house seemed trapped in time with clothing in the closets, the table still set for dinner, Johannah's apron hanging over the back of a chair and even food still sitting on the cold stove.

Johannah was gone...but did she ever really leave the house, even after death? Legends stated that on certain nights, an eerie light could be seen coming from the east tower of the house. Those who were brave enough to venture onto the property claimed to see Johannah framed in the window of the room.

And this is not the only legend connected to Johannah's mysterious death. The story goes that Johannah was sitting on the porch of the little cottage next to the Castle one afternoon, chatting with a neighbor. As the two women were talking, a dove suddenly appeared and landed on a vine that was curled around a porch column. Johannah caught her breath, remembering an old superstition.

"The dove," she said softly. "The dove is an omen. By this time tomorrow, we have death...."

She fell silent for a moment, but the pleasure of the day was gone and the neighbor never forgot the strange incident.... because the very next day, Johannah was found dead!

Nels Larson died in 1923 and his will specified that the house should remain in the family. The problem was that no one in the family wanted to live there because the house had no electricity. So, the house was abandoned and remembered only by time and the elements.

There was also a strange tale linked to the death of Nels Larson. According to this story, the body of Larson was returned to the Castle to lie in state before the funeral. While this would have been odd, based on the fact that the house had been abandoned almost a decade before, supporters of the story insist that it would have been necessary to use the large house to host the large number of mourners from the area. Regardless, Larson's casket was placed in the reception hall near the window. A basket of flowers was placed at its head. When the basket was removed after the funeral, a hole was said to have appeared in the carpet where it had been resting. It had most assuredly, according to the story, not been there before. Dozens of witnesses saw the mysterious hole later but exactly how it got there was shrouded in mystery.

Over the years, a number of tenants moved into the house but none stayed for long. It's likely that they were chased away by the deteriorating conditions of the house more so than by the ghosts. However, the rapid succession of tenants and the spooky atmosphere of the place combined to give the Castle a ghostly reputation. The stories grew and became more embellished as the years went by. It was said that someone died of fright in the house and the imprint of his or her body was still pressed into a couch in the living room. There was also said to be a pillar in the west parlor, which once held a large fern, that would inexplicably spin around under its own power. Reports said it spun so much that it eventually wore down into a circular area on the floor.

In 1967, the grandchildren of Nels Larson donated the Castle to the Illinois Pioneer Heritage Center in Monticello. The Center opened the house as a tourist attraction, reportedly drawing up to 30,000 visitors each year. They came to view the unique architecture of the place... and to soak up some of the ghostly ambiance. The Center also had a few strange ideas about preserving the house. The main plan was to build a huge, geodesic dome over the house and barn and completely enclose them. The dome would hold an airborne restaurant and an elevated walkway was to be built through the house itself.

Needless to say, none of this ever came about. The house was simply too expensive to take care of and it was closed down once again. This time however, there was a padlock on the front door. It had been placed there by a local bank because of non-payment of over $43,000 in loans. The bank had finally been forced to foreclose.

The Castle was once again empty, with only caretakers to watch over the house on occasion. The caretakers claimed that the lights in the house refused to stay off and that windows would often open on their own. One of them also claimed that he would often close up the house, turn off the lights and make sure all of the windows were closed and locked. By the time he would get outside to his car, the lights would be on again and several of the windows would have slipped open.

Another caretaker reported eerie sounds inside of the house and described them as footsteps on the stairs and the sound of piano keys clinking in the darkness. It was suggested rodents or animals in the house could cause these sounds, but he insisted that this was not the case. He finally quit working there, another witness told me, after he was startled one night by a shadowy figure in the east tower. He was convinced that he had seen a ghost.

The odd stories about the house never seemed to stop and it became a favorite "haunt" for late night curiosity-seekers. Many local adults and especially teenagers and college students from Champaign, Mattoon, Charleston and the surrounding area came to Voorhies Castle for after-dark excursions. Many of them claimed to have bizarre experiences and brushes with the supernatural. Many spoke of apparitions, seeing glowing balls of light, sounds that had no explanation, ghostly footsteps, flashlights that suddenly stopped working, and even more.

In 1970, a group from Lakeland College in Mattoon, led by a Decatur man named Jeff Fritz, journeyed to Voorhies Castle one night. After exploring the barn and clock tower, they came back into the yard and spotted a large, glowing light that followed them toward the house. Frightened, they left the property and returned to Mattoon.

However, they had a hard time keeping the story to themselves and a couple of weeks later, they organized a group of 30 people to return to the Castle. More than a dozen cars journeyed to Voorhies one night, where Jeff decided to try holding a seance in the upper floor of the barn. The seance did not go very well, as several members of the party began cutting up and laughing. Most of the group decided to leave at this point and returned to their cars. A smaller group, led by Jeff, decided to go up to the house. It was during this walk that he encountered something else that he couldn't possibly explain!

"It was a bit cold that night," Jeff told me in an interview in 1995, "perhaps in the 'fifties and I was wearing a light jacket. There was no wind but it was a misty night. As we were walking up to the house, we passed a circle in the walk. The concrete was a single sidewalk up to it, made a circle, and then became a single sidewalk again. We entered this circle and it was snowing inside of it...."

Jeff and his friends had never seen anything like it. Outside of the circle, it was a cool, autumn evening but inside of it was bitterly cold and the moisture in the air had unbelievably changed to snow. It was impossible and yet according to the witnesses, it actually happened!

A few moments later, Jeff and the others approached the house. As they did, several of the people who had remained behind in the parking area jumped into their cars and quickly drove away. The group near the house went back to their cars, puzzled at the behavior of those who had left. A few of people remained and they were terrified. They had locked themselves in their cars and rolled up the windows. Jeff tried to get them to get out and take a look at the strange snow pattern inside of the circle, but they refused. Then, he discovered what had frightened them so much.

"They told me that when we went around the house, a red, glowing light followed behind us," he explained to me and shook his head as he spoke, "and we never even saw it."

And the stories continued....

Another late night visitor to the house, Scott Hayes*, discovered the place around 1971. He was told about the house by a girlfriend and became determined to visit it. He was especially intrigued by the stories of the secret room and for some reason, was convinced that he could find it. Scott told me that he went out to the house one night in May with his girlfriend and another couple. They managed to get inside and began exploring the house.

"It was pretty amazing," he recalled to me in 1998. "The place still had all of this furniture in it. It was like somebody had been living there last week, even though everything was pretty beat up and dirty. I have no idea how I thought I was going to find that secret room. I was probably just showing off for my girlfriend, but I really wanted to see the place."

The group looked through the house for about an hour and Scott admits that he went through the motions of tapping on walls and looking behind furniture for the opening to the secret passage. They prowled about the place with only two flashlights to show the way. It was in a room on the second floor where an incident occurred that made them flee the house! After climbing to the upper floor, they entered the room that once had belonged to Ellen Larson.

"It was pretty dark in there," Scott remembered, "and I remember bumping into this wooden chair that was sitting near the window. We looked around for a few minutes... I mean, this place was weird. There was still furniture in there and sheets on the bed. I think that's the thing that bothered us the most... like someone could come home at any time."

While the group was standing near the windows, looking outside, they were surprised to hear a sliding noise coming from behind them. Scott told me that he turned around and saw that the chair that he had bumped into, which had previously been just inches away from him, was now over near the door to the room! That had been the source of the sliding sound, as it quickly moved across the room.

"It took me a moment to understand what had just happened," he said. "Then, I think it dawned on me at the same time it did everyone else! That was just too much and we got out of there... fast!"

The legends, and alleged eyewitness accounts, concerning Voorhies Castle were enough to attract the attention of a parapsychology group from the University of Illinois. The tales of strange phenomena were just too bizarre, and too numerous to ignore, so they decided to enlist the aid of Chicago psychic Irene Hughes.

Hughes gained national fame in the 1960's for her uncanny predictions and was best known in the Chicago area. She wrote and lectured widely on the paranormal and offered personal consultations. In 1963, she founded a Chicago group called "The Golden Path" that was devoted to teaching students to develop their psychic abilities and in 1967 was tested with some satisfaction by the Psychical Research Foundation in North Carolina. Among her most famous predictions was one concerning the death of Robert Kennedy. Also, in 1962, she predicted the exact date of death of former Illinois governor Adlai Stevenson. Her reputation was further enhanced in 1967 when she predicted a massive snowstorm to hit Chicago in January, six months before it happened. During the 1970's, Hughes emerged as one of the top psychics in the Chicago area and she published a number of books and appeared on radio and television shows. After a long career, she eventually retired from public life.

Her visit to Voorhies Castle came at the height of her career and during the heyday of the hauntings at the house. She traveled to Central Illinois in the company of a university investigative team and several reporters. She walked up to the house and entered through the front door, but only stayed inside for a few moments.

"What we have in this house," Hughes announced as she came back outside and met with the waiting group, "is an entity that is stuck in time. It is really not to the benefit of its spiritual well-being for us to acknowledge it, to feed it, or give it any kind of support. I don't want to do a seance here. People just need to forget this thing and let it pass on... it's stuck in time and between passages and cannot find its way to heaven."

To the disappointment of the investigation team, that ended Irene Hughes' involvement with Voorhies Castle, and to my knowledge, it was the only attempt ever made to conduct any sort of paranormal research on the premises.

The notoriety of the house began to fade by the middle part of the 1970's. In 1972, Voorhies Castle was purchased by Milton and Sue Streenz, a Bloomington couple who set to work restoring the place. Over the course of the next six years, they repainted the entire house and did some extensive remodeling. They replaced 138 windowpanes and even added seven truckloads of flowers and trees to the estate. One of their greatest challenges was turning away the late night visitors and vandals from the property. Some of them were even bold enough to break into the house with the intention of carrying away furniture and stained glass.

The couple had discovered the mansion by accident and had always been intrigued by old houses. "We didn't even know the history or all the stories about the house when we bought it," Sue stated shortly after setting up a camper on the property. They lived in the camper while they made the house fit to live in again. "We've heard fifty-eleven thousand stories about the house... we take it all with a grain of salt."

However, Milton added his own comments. "Oh, it's haunted," he said cryptically, "the ghosts are friendly."

The couple remained in the house for the next six years, but in June 1978, Voorhies Castle was once again auctioned off. The Streenzes sadly admitted they were just not able to keep up with the physical work needed to maintain the old mansion anymore.

The house was eventually sold but over the course of the next few years, it was frequently vacant and began to deteriorate again. The decay of the mansion became the biggest problem that all of the new owners and tenants would face, along with fending off the sightseers, for whom the ghostly landmark was still an attraction. Several of the more recent owners have made valiant attempts to restore the house and have done everything possible to discourage visitors from coming to the house. If you are the sort of reader who likes to experience the haunted places you read about, you may want to give Voorhies Castle a wide berth, as trespassers are usually unwelcome.

As you can see, the legends of Voorhies Castle are as haunting as the house has always been said to be, leaving a number of unanswered questions. Is it possible that the haunting has somehow just faded away over the years? Many believe this to be the case.

But what if whatever was there still remains? What if it is just resting now, and waiting for some night, perhaps in the distant future, when the haunting will begin again?

I suppose only time will tell.....

- CHAPTER FIVE -

HAUNTED DECATUR

GHOSTS IN THE HAUNTED HEART OF ILLINOIS

This is a book about ghosts and a place called Decatur, Illinois, a city that lies in the very heart of the state. And a dark heart it is.... Decatur is not your average Midwestern city. Decatur boasts the largest grain processing plants in the world. It also had the very first stoplights, the first turn signal indicators and one of the first motor cars in America. It also had the very first automobile death in the United States. It also has a very large number of ghosts.....
TROY TAYLOR FROM HAUNTED DECATUR

    The land where the city of Decatur now rests was largely untamed prairie until the 1820's. During the years when the Native Americans lived and hunted the lands of Central Illinois, a number of Indian tribes settled around the Decatur area, although strangely, none of the villages were located within the future city limits. When the first settlers arrived, they would find the land had been abandoned by the Indians. Rather than live on the land, they instead used it for their burial grounds. Legend holds that the Native Americans believed the land was more closely connected to the next world, thus making it a perfect place to bury the dead and insure the safe and easy passage to the world beyond.

    As the years have passed, many believe that the Indians of this earlier period may have been correct. The burial mounds that were destroyed to make way for many of Decatur's now ghost-infested buildings just might be the explanation for the city's large number of hauntings.

CURSE OF THE CULVER HOUSE?

    A case in point would be a former residence called the John Culver House, located on Prairie Street in Decatur's west side historical district. The house is a desolate ruin now, but was once one of the finest houses in the city. It has been all but destroyed over the past two decades, but the legends of the house still remain. The place is ramshackle and foreboding, especially at night, and all of the lower windows have been boarded up. Restoration attempts in recent years have failed miserably and the house may yet be demolished. It seems as though the suicide and murder, which took place in the last years of occupancy, have somehow left a dark shadow on the property. Or perhaps that happened many years ago, before the house was even built?

The property may have been cursed from the very beginning as it has the distinction of being built directly on top of one of the mentioned burial grounds. It has been recorded that workers on the house were actually removing the bones and skulls of the people buried there.

The land was originally purchased in 1881 and construction was started by a man named Josiah Clokey. For some unknown reason however, the project was abandoned and the land and unfinished home came into the possession of John Culver, but not until 1901. He completed the house and turned it into a grand mansion. Culver was a man of many interests and ideas. He had only a grade school education and yet owned a grave monument business, was responsible for bringing heat and electricity to downtown Decatur and in 1901, he and his brother did some of the reconstruction work on the Lincoln tomb and monument in Springfield.

The Transfer House remains a symbol of Decatur

The house, no matter how grand in Culver's day, is now a shadow of its former self. It was originally constructed of red brick with stone trim and boasted a turret on the west front and a wide rounded tower on the east side. The interior of the house had large rooms, built into odd sizes to match the particular interests of each room. The first two floors of the house were living quarters, while the third floor was used as a ballroom and had a stained glass skylight. The house also had a massive library with built-in bookcases and large French windows that looked out over the street. Interesting also was the fact that every room on the first floor of the house had its own fireplace... except for the dining room.

It seems that the strange cloud that hangs over the property was present during its heyday also. The story goes that the Culver family was seated in the dining room for the evening meal when "something" came down the chimney of the house and entered the dining room. It could have been a bird, but legends suggest something far stranger.... something so strange that Culver immediately ordered the fireplace torn out and the opening bricked over! We will never know for sure what this frightening creature may have been, but some have suggested it may have been connected to the dark history of the land itself.

And could the atmosphere of the house have caused John Culver's spirit to linger here after his death? Some people believe that it has.

Culver lived in the house until his death in 1943 and for several years after that, people strolling by the house in the evening claimed to see Culver sitting in the library, still looking over his favorite books. In 1950, the house was sold and divided into apartments, although stories of strange lights appearing in the former library persisted for decades. Dozens of people claimed to see the glow of a reading lamp and movement at the windows, even when the house was empty.

Tragedy struck the house in May 1979 when a third floor apartment caught fire and caused over $90,000 in smoke and water damage to the building. The cause of the fire was said to be a faulty extension cord used by one of the tenants. And this fire would not be the last tragedy to take place here. In the 1960's, a young woman committed suicide in one of the second floor apartments and then in 1988, a tenant of the building, Patsy Rosich, was brutally murdered by her boyfriend. Her assailant, Maseo Richmond, was convicted of first-degree murder and sentenced to 50 years in prison. One year after this tragic event, the house was found to be unfit for human habitation and was boarded up.

What is it about this house that attracts such a strange energy?

Other questions also remain. Does this energy seem to attract the spirits to the house? If so, have other spirits joined John Culver in the house? Some believe his ghost may be one of many, including the spirits of the Native Americans first buried here, the ghost of the suicide who took her life here when the house was an apartment building, and perhaps even the spectral victim of the terrible murder in 1988. It remains a mystery and is perhaps one that will never be solved.

The Culver House now sits abandoned on the city's west side... the victim of neglect and according to some, the result of disturbing a burial mound with connections to the next world.

LOST AND HAUNTED GRAVEYARDS

But Decatur's poor luck continued when it came to building on top of cemeteries. Besides the Indian burial sites, sketchy records exist today to say that there were once a number of private and family cemeteries scattered throughout old Decatur. Most of these sites have been forgotten over the years. Early burial records in the city were largely nonexistent and many of the forgotten graves were marked with primitive wooden planks and they deteriorated in a few short years.

It is not really surprising that many of these tiny graveyards faded from memory within a generation or two, but what of the secrets left behind by Decatur's first "official" cemetery? Actually, there were two cemeteries located at this site and were located so close together that they have since been listed under the name of the larger of the two, the Common Burial Grounds. The other graveyard, King's Cemetery, was located nearby and accounts state that it was hard to tell where one ended and the other began.

The two cemeteries were located on the far west side of the early Decatur settlement and today that area is marked by the corner of Oakland Avenue and West Main Street. They comprised several acres of ground and probably extended as far east as Haworth Street.

The exact size of the Common Burial Grounds is unknown but it was a part of the Amos Robinson farm. The Robinson family had settled in Decatur just a few years prior to 1836, when Amos Robinson died. He was buried in an orchard on his property, which later became part of the burial grounds.

King's Cemetery was platted in 1865 and was owned by John E. King. The cemetery ran alongside Haworth Street and extended down Wood to Oakland. The cemetery also lay on the edge of the old Robinson farm and as mentioned before, published accounts of that time stated that they were so close together that they were usually mistaken for one.

No one knows for sure when the first burials took place here but it was probably in the early 1830's. The cemeteries were used for many years but were finally closed down because of overcrowding in 1885. The land was sold off to the city to use as building plots for many of the homes and buildings that still stand in that area today. Once the sale went through, workmen were called in to remove the bodies to Greenwood Cemetery, located on the city's south side.

However, these luckless workmen faced a large problem. No one had any idea just how many people had been buried in the two cemeteries over the years, thanks to unmarked graves, poor records and lost grave markers and stones. The city pushed the move ahead and the workmen were advised to do the best they could with what information they had to work with. Construction was started a few months later and the old cemeteries were all but forgotten.

But they wouldn't stay that way for long.....

In 1895, while work crews were building an extension onto West Main Street, they discovered dozens of lost skeletons, the remains of caskets and buried tombstones. This was the first grisly find, but it would not be the last. For years after, new construction brought to light skulls, bones and pieces of wooden coffins. There were no clues as to just how many bodies had been left behind and these gruesome discoveries have continued for years, even up until today.

In 1935, a building on West Wood Street had its basement lowered and a broken wooden box that contained a complete skeleton was found beneath the dirt. Late that same year, a man working in his backyard found four skulls and three long bones in the spot where he planned to put a vegetable patch. This convinced him to find another location. The discovery of bones throughout the neighborhood became such a sensation that young boys organized "digging parties" and more remains surfaced each week. A 1938 newspaper report covered the furor over the lost cemeteries and even stated that Amos Robinson himself was still buried under a driveway on West Main Street.

In recent years, even Decatur's landmark restaurant the Blue Mill has not been safe from rumors of strange discoveries. According to anonymous staff members, a number of skeletons were found beneath the basement floor a few years ago. The story has not been substantiated, but these same employees also believe the bones are tied into other weird happenings in the place. A number of ghostly encounters have supposedly taken place in the kitchen area and many of them are afraid to go down into the basement alone.

And this is not the only place within the bounds of the former graveyards where reports of the restless dead occasionally come. Many of the people who work and live here believe that spirits, whose rest was disturbed more than a century ago, still roam this area today. They may be right!

One family that was plagued by a disturbing ghost contacted a friend who claimed to have psychic abilities to identify the problem behind the knocking and pounding sounds in the house. I was actually able to speak to one of the residents of the house years after I first wrote about this incident. Charles Sanders* was a small child at the time of the haunting but is an adult who lives in the Chicago area today. He told me that the family had been awakened at all hours of the day and night by knocking and rapping on the walls and what they all believed to be footsteps pacing back and forth in one hallway.

"My mother had this friend who was supposed to be psychic," Sanders explained to me, more than 40 years after the events. "We called her and she came over to have a seance. She thought that if she could get in touch with this ghost, or whatever, she could make everything stop."

The family sat down around the table and the friend, who Sanders called "Aunt Sandra", lit a candle and began speaking to the ghost. It wasn't long before some strange things began to occur.

"We could still hear all of these knocking sounds," Sanders recalled, "but then all of the dishes in the cabinets started rattling. My sister was pretty scared at this point, and so was I. Aunt Sandra then took out a piece of paper and a pencil and started writing down whatever she was hearing from the ghost."

According to the information the psychic gained through her "automatic writing", the ghost was that of a person who had been died long ago. His grave was now located beneath the front porch of the house and he wanted someone to help him. A short time later, Charles' father climbed beneath the porch with a shovel and began digging. It wasn't long before he discovered a number of scattered bones. They turned them over to the authorities and with the help of their pastor, arranged for a proper burial for them. The ghost troubled them no longer.

Charles Sanders has never forgotten the incident. "I laugh now when I hear people say there are no such things as ghosts," he told me in our interview. "I can tell them differently!"

Another man that I spoke with lived on West Wood Street as a boy. He told me about an experience that he had many years ago. He was playing outside one afternoon and caught a glimpse of a man standing in the far corner of the lot. His features were blurry and his clothing was hard to make out.

"He seemed to be looking at me," the man remembered, "although it was hard to tell because it was early in the evening and the yard was very shaded by the trees."

He said that the phantom figure only stood there for a few moments before he noticed something very strange about him. "The man was visible only to the knees... below that, he just sorta faded away," the man explained to me. "I have never forgotten that, even after 20 years."

An additional house, on West Main, is haunted by the ghost of a pale young girl who endlessly walks back and forth through the house. She seems oblivious to the people who live there now, as if she is from another time, but has also been seen skipping, running and playing with a small red ball. The occupants have also heard the sounds of knocks and whispers in the house on occasion.

One has to wonder if she might be another of the specters from Decatur's two most famous "lost" cemeteries?

While these two may be the most famous of the city's "lost" cemeteries, they are certainly not the only ones. One cemetery, once owned by John Miller, was discovered in the Oakdale addition in 1909. It contained only 13 graves but had been lost since 1874, the last date in which it had appeared on any map. The bodies were boxed up and removed to Greenwood Cemetery for burial.

Records have also been found showing the locations of small cemeteries that have been covered by Decatur streets. One burial ground was located at the corner of East Eldorado and Franklin Streets and another was at the junction of the Wabash tracks and North Main. Two others could once be found on East Clay and East Wood Streets, but no records, or any other information, can be found about them.

Another burial ground that was relocated was the Peach Orchard Cemetery, which went on to become an unsolved mystery of Greenwood Cemetery. Peach Orchard had been the "potter's field" for the Macon Acres Nursing Home. It has been closed now for many years but was once located on the site where the Adolph Meyer Center was located on Mound Road. At the time the cemetery was moved, no one had been buried in it since 1910. In that year, influential funeral director James J. Moran stated that he would longer bury people in pauper's graves. Other undertakers followed his example and soon the poor and the unknown began to be buried with markers.

The 139 unknown dead were moved in 1962 and placed in a "common grave" in Greenwood Cemetery. However, the location of this grave has somehow been lost over time and has been forgotten. Somewhere on the grounds there is a large grave containing the tangled remains of 139 people, but no one seems to know where it is.

Could this be why, if the stories are true, the old Adolph Meyer Center, located on this site, was haunted? Unconfirmed reports from former staff members state that odd things often happened at night, including strange sounds and items that would inexplicably vanish, then turn up somewhere else. I spoke with one staff member who told me that security employees would often get calls reporting that residents were wandering around at night. When answered, they would find that no one was out of their room and that the figures seen often vanished into thin air!

THE LEGEND OF HELL HOLLOW

The first home built near Decatur was a log cabin erected in 1820 by William Downing, a fur trapper and honey gatherer. It was located just south of the Sangamon River. Downing remained in the area until 1824, when he sold the house and property to the Ward family. A short time after Downing arrived, he was followed by the Stevens family, for whom Stevens Creek is named, and several other settlers, who also built homes near the Stevens cabin. Other families settled near the Ward cabin and the two settlements thrived both near and independent of one another.

More frontiersmen continued to arrive from the east and by 1829, the village of "Decatur" was platted. It was named after the naval hero, Stephen Decatur, who had been noted for his spectacular feats of bravery during the wars with the Barbary pirates in the early 1800's. The population in the immediate area had swelled to nearly 600 people by this time. A delegation from the new town traveled to the state capital in Vandalia, where a declaration was passed that formed Macon County. Decatur was named as the county seat.

The hardships and trials of early life in Decatur were much like those in other frontier settlements. Most of the settlers lived outside of the village in log cabins, spread out in the forest and along the river. Most of them were traders or farmers and malaria and other diseases often shortened their lives. While funerals were often common, they reached a peak during the terrible winter of 1830-31, which is still remembered as the "Deep Snow". Many died from the bitter cold and fierce storms but that winter also gave birth to one of the greatest legend of the Decatur area... legends of death, depravity and cannibalism in an area known today as "Hell Hollow". In later years, this area would be considered "cursed" or "tainted" in such a way that it has been known for attracting the worse elements of the city. It has been a hideout for outlaws, a "hobo jungle" and more. In the 1930's, it would realize its greatest "fame" when it was connected to a vicious series of unsolved murders.

More than a century before those events would make Hell Hollow famous though, another incident occurred that would forever mark this area. It concerns perhaps the greatest legend of the region and many believe that it could explain why the Hollow has attracted such a dark element over the years. On the other hand, some believe the land here was already sour... and that the event that took place in the days of the pioneers is just further evidence that evil has festered here for a long, long time!

According to the legend, the wooded area that would someday be Hell Hollow was once the location of a small settlement. It was the most secluded of the outposts surrounding the village of Decatur and was in an area that was mostly avoided by the local settlers. They came here only for the purpose of burying the dead. The hills above this narrow valley were part of an Indian burial ground that was soon taken over by the settlers. In later years, it would become Greenwood Cemetery but in those days, it was seldom visited and was held in superstitious awe by the pioneers.

In the late 1820's, a group of settlers constructed cabins in the valley west of the burying grounds. They survived here for a few years, until the bitter winter of 1830. This was mentioned earlier in the book and is still remembered as the greatest natural disaster in early Central Illinois history. Snow fell throughout the winter, alternating with sleet and ice, and it formed layers that were three and four feet thick. Livestock perished and game became scarce. Many settlers died in the bitter cold and snow and the storms gave birth to strange legends in Hell Hollow.

It was said that the lack of food struck here the hardest. The tiny collection of cabins was cut off from the rest of the settlers in the area. At first, wild game approached the cabins without fear. Food was so scarce that the animals hoped for handouts of grain, but were instead captured and ended up in the stew kettle. As the cold months wore on, the deer, turkey, squirrels and prairie chickens all but disappeared and soon stores of flour and dried meat followed suit. The outlook was growing grim and there was a good chance that the settlers would starve to death long before spring arrived.

They made due with what they had and could forage, boiling the bark from the trees into a bitter soup and then eating portions of shoe leather and rawhide to stay alive. Finally, the legends say, there were no other choices left to them. They had no option but to turn to the only food supply that was still available... each other.

In the early months of the winter, one of the older members of the community had passed away and the body had been stored in an outbuilding so that he could be buried when the ground thawed. This was the first of two corpses that the settlers were forced to eat that winter.

When the weather finally broke, and contact with the outside could be achieved again, the bodies were secretly buried on the hill and the cannibals were sworn to secrecy. No one was ever to know under what conditions the community had survived. A few months passed and the settlers from the small community were never heard from again. Apparently, someone had discovered their horrible secret and they vanished from the area without a trace.

The legend has been passed along for many years and while it may have been the first bizarre event to take place in Hell Hollow, it would certainly not be the last.

At some point in the late 1800's, the Hollow became the territory of a gang that was called the "Biscuit-Necks" by the local populace. They specialized in extortion and robbery and used the woods south of the cemetery as their base of operations. One night, the gang was captured here by a lynch mob from town. The crime for which they were pursued remains unknown today, but it is believed to been the robbery of a store, during which the owner was killed. It is said that the authorities failed to kind the killers, so a vigilante group took up the chase. After the gang was captured, they were hanged right on the spot. As a message to other criminals operating in the area, the vigilantes left the bodies of the "Biscuit-Necks" hanging there in the Hollow, swaying in the wind. They were left that way until the corpses finally succumbed to the elements and the carrion birds.

The years passed and the edge of the Hollow became known as a "hobo jungle", where transients and small-time criminals camped and lived. The railroad tracks passed close to this area and it was convenient for the hoboes to hop a freight train from one town to the next. It was during this period, in the spring of 1930, that a caretaker from Greenwood Cemetery named Mel Savage was murdered in the so-called "hobo jungle". His murder was never solved.

Even as the city of Decatur grew up around it, the Hollow still managed to span several hundred acres. It remained a rough part of the city made up of wooded regions and poor, rundown neighborhoods of shacks and dilapidated houses. It was much larger then and covered a wide area of land that is now developed with homes and businesses. The region spanned what is now the area around South Main Street to as far west as present-day Lincoln Park. In the days before Lake Decatur was formed, this region sprawled in all directions and was known as a place where criminals could find shelter from the law. The area also spawned two dilapidated housing areas called "Coaltown" and "Oklahoma", which were little more than collections of shacks, shanties, brothels and makeshift gambling parlors.

To make matters worse, in 1936, a series of Chicago newspaper articles pinpointed Hell Hollow as the hideout for a gang of grave robbers and killers who committed a number of murders in Decatur. The gang, which was dubbed the "Hounds of Hell Hollow", supposedly "ruled the south end of the city with shotgun and whipping post". They often met in Greenwood Cemetery, robbed graves and sold bootleg liquor. Even though Decatur officials hotly denied the story, there was an element of truth to the stories. They cleverly blended fact with fiction and mixed in real stories and events to give the tale credibility. Needless to say, the articles did little to enhance the reputation of Hell Hollow.

The size of Hell Hollow continued to grow smaller as the years went on. Coaltown was eventually destroyed and turned into a park and a housing addition, the acres of woods and brush were cleared away, and finally, only a small valley remained just west of Greenwood Cemetery. This was the original location of the Hollow, the site of cannibalism and murder, and the center for the strange activity that has continued to radiate outward from the region.

For a long time, this area remained a thick forest of trees and undergrowth through which a narrow gravel road twisted and turned. This became known as simply "Hell Hollow", the last reminder of the violence of years gone by.... but the legend was not quite dead yet.

The "Hounds" eventually became a forgotten story of the past but the Hollow soon earned a new notoriety with teenagers as a spooky

BRUTAL REIGN IN HELL HOLLOW TAKES 8 LIVES

Mother of 5 Children Met at Door by Gun Blast; Some Slain for 'Knowing Too Much'

BY ROBEY M. PARKS.
Herald and Examiner Staff Correspondent.

DECATUR, Ill., Sept. 19.— Wanton brutality marked the eight astounding murders by the "Hell Hollow" terror cult of grave rob-

Hell Hollow —

VICE
IN DECATUR

'HELL HOLLOW' CRIMES VOTED IN GRAVEYARD

Mysterious Crystal Gazer Sent Men to Death; 'Advice of Spirits' Sealed Their Doom

BY ROBERT M. PARKS.
Herald and Examiner Staff Correspondent.

DECATUR, Ill., Sept. 15.— In a dismal ravine of secluded Greenwood Cemetery, Investigators have discovered the secret midnight rendezvous of the mysterious "Hounds of Hell Hollow."

place for a romantic rendezvous. A new collection of stories started to be told about crazed killers with hooks for hands and horrifying murders that usually involved (you guessed it!) teenagers in parked cars.

But not all of the stories told about the area could be passed off as modern folk legends and campfire stories. Every once in awhile, someone encountered something truly unexplainable in the Hollow. How many of the stories were true and how many were simply wild imagination? I don't know but the numerous tales covered everything from glowing apparitions to floating balls of gold light.

One particular story involved a couple who had gone down to the Hollow for a romantic interlude one night and were surprised to hear and feel what seemed to be open hands slamming down on the trunk of their car. Thinking that someone was playing a trick on them, the young man jumped out of the car and looked around. To his surprise, no one was there. He heard a movement over to his left and turned to see the tall grass alongside the road being pushed aside, as if some invisible presence was passing through it! He quickly returned to the car and something caught his eye. There, on the dusty trunk, were the clear impressions of handprints, even though he had seen no one standing behind the car!

The Hollow remained a popular and spooky place for some time. A few short years ago, the road that ended in Hell Hollow was closed off and city crews cut and cleared away the thick growth of trees that once filled the valley. The official word was that the road had been closed because trespassers were entering the cemetery at night. Was this true? There are a dozen places to enter Greenwood after the sun goes down, so why close just this road?

Unofficial sources (in other words, official sources who won't go on record!) say that too many odd things have happened here over time, including a few still very recent deaths and several brutal murders that have shocked the city.

Needless to say, strange things continue to happen in Hell Hollow... as if some sort of weird and frightening energy still lingers there, still drawing the dark side to the shadows of the abandoned valley.

SPIRITS OF THE SPEAKEASY

Decatur has never been a stranger to crime. In fact, in 1854, a small settlement appeared just outside of Decatur called "Dantown", founded by Colonel Dan Conklin. Within a few short months, it was better known by its more colorful name of "Hell's Half Acre". It was made up of a few hastily constructed houses, a whiskey distillery, gambling parlors, saloons, a racetrack and several brothels. It lasted just until the Civil War, when a high tax on whiskey closed down the distillery. The women, the gamblers and thieves departed with the alcohol.

In later years, would take up where "Dantown" left off! In fact, during the early part of the last century, Decatur was a famous city in the Midwest. It was known as a good place to hide out from the law and as a city where many different types of vice would be tolerated. The city already hosted the previously mentioned Levee District (see last chapter), and it also had a number of gambling houses, wide open drinking establishments during Prohibition and one of the largest "Red Light Districts" south of Chicago as well.

The heyday of crime in Decatur began around 1910, but there was nothing that had a greater impact on crime in the city than Prohibition. And once it was repealed, the floodgates opened and crime, corruption and gambling rushed into the city.

When the 18th Amendment to the Constitution, which abolished the sale and distribution of alcohol, took effect on January 16, 1920, many believed that it would cure the social ills of America. Little did they know at the time, but it would actually do just the opposite. America's great thirst for the forbidden liquor bred corruption in every corner. Law enforcement officials became open to bribes because the majority of the men just did not believe in the law, but worse yet, Prohibition gave birth to the great days of organized crime. The gangsters of America had previously concerned themselves with acts of violence, racketeering and prostitution but the huge profits that came to be made with the sale of illegal liquor built criminal empires.

Across the country, over 200,000 "speakeasys" opened. These drinking establishments were so named because many of them were located behind, above or below legitimate businesses and patrons often drank in silence. Huge bootlegging operations sprang into operation to supply the speakeasys and those who chose to ignore the new law. In addition, ordinary people began brewing their own beer and distilling their own liquor. Some of them even sold the stuff from home, and the product called "bathtub gin" came into existence. Disrespect for the law became the fashion as people who would have never dreamed of doing anything illegal before now found themselves serving illicit liquor in their homes or drinking in the neighborhood speakeasy.

Prohibition was widely considered to be doomed by 1928, but it hung on for another five years before being repealed in 1933. By then, it had taken its toll, leaving law enforcement in disarray and leaving the mobster organizations so powerful they were able to move onto other pursuits, like legalized gambling, with wide public approval.

Prohibition in Decatur, as in most American cities, was a complete failure. Decatur had previously passed two laws to ban liquor sales but neither had lasted for long. The people of the city had always been in favor of selling, and especially consuming, alcohol. In the days before the ban, Decatur had been known for its quality breweries.

The Decatur Brewing Co. was located at the corner of Broadway and Cantrell and was started in 1855. The brewery was owned by John Koehler and Adam Keck and was producing about 15,000 barrels of beer each year by 1861. It was later sold in 1914 and was incorporated into the Pabst Brewing Co. in Peoria. Shortly before Prohibition, the Decatur plant changed its name to the Blue Ribbon Malt Extract Co. and was later absorbed by Pabst, the Milwaukee brewer. This made Decatur the unwitting birthplace of Pabst Blue Ribbon Beer, which is a dubious honor, but an honor nonetheless.

The popular outlook on Prohibition in Decatur wavered between completely ignoring the law and taking an occasional drink. Lawbreakers and suppliers were occasionally caught but enforcement of the law was lackluster at best. Local bootleggers found that by spreading a few dollars in the right direction, they could insure their booze shipments and guard against arrest at the same time. A number of speakeasys opened in Decatur, many of them operating quite openly. Others were accessed through secret doors and back stairways, hidden away behind perfectly law-abiding stores and shops.

Decatur's lack of enforcement for the law was not only known locally, but in Washington as well. In fact, Decatur's arrest record was so bad that it was used before the US Senate by opponents of the law who were trying get it reversed. At one point, the city's record of liquor-related arrests was the lowest in the nation!

Prohibition finally ended in 1933 and the story made newspaper headlines in Decatur. Many of the local taverns had already been stocked and were prepared to open on April 7, the first day for beer sales. On that day, over 2500 cases were sold in a matter of hours.

But law breaking during Prohibition was only the tip of the iceberg in Decatur. Over the course of the next few years, crime ran rampant in the city... earning Decatur a reputation that still haunts the city today.

During the years of Prohibition, and in the years that followed after the era, Decatur was famous across the Midwest. Unfortunately, it was not the sort of fame that cities boast about in their enticements to lure travelers to their sites. Instead, the city became known to gangsters and lawbreakers as the perfect place to hide out from the law. There were few places easier to blend in or disappear into than Decatur was. Many of Decatur's crime problems stemmed from the largely ineffective police force. Hampered by corrupt officials at city hall, the hands of the department were tied when it came to prosecuting gamblers, bootleggers and brothel owners.

Just a few blocks away from the notorious "Levee" was Decatur's Red Light District. This collection of brothels spanned the 500 block of West William Street, just a stone's throw away from Decatur High School. The location of these illegal establishments was common knowledge in the city but they were allowed to operate for years, thanks to corrupt officials. When the Red Light District was finally closed down in 1936, it was a major event.

On the morning of March 14, 1936, a local stockbroker named John King was shot to death on the front porch of a whorehouse in the segregated Red Light District. This shooting would be the catalyst that would close the district for good. The authorities descended on the Red Light District in force, finally closing it down for good.

For many years, gambling had a much more socially acceptable position that prostitution in Decatur. This particular vice arrived in the city along with the first taverns, which were ironically some of the first business establishments constructed here.

Gambling continued to be a problem into the 1930's. Officials in city government, and in the police department, were often criticized for looking the other way. At one point, concerned citizens even hired three Decatur attorneys to assist them in taking action against Mayor Charles Shilling because they believed he was doing nothing to stop the spread of the illegal activity. A Chicago private detective was hired to gather evidence to obtain search warrants that could be served on known gambling halls. Five search warrants were obtained, but the gamblers were tipped off and nothing was found but empty rooms. More search warrants were obtained and this time the gamblers had no warning. The police seized roulette wheels, poker tables, cards and numerous other gambling devices at five different establishments. However, all five of the operators were later acquitted of gambling charges. Critics complained that the trials had been "fixed". Meanwhile, gambling continued unhindered in Decatur at upscale clubs like "Caroline's" and the "Lakeside Club".

Gambling officially came to an end in Decatur in 1936 when police stepped up raids on the local parlors and establishments, confiscating and destroying slot machines and gambling tables and arresting and fining the customers and owners. In the past, a police raid on a gambling parlor insured that the place would then be safe for a period before it was raided again. This was not the case in 1936-37 however as police officers continued to raid the same establishments over and over again, knowing that eventually the losses would drive the operators out of business, or at least out of Decatur. Apparently, this system worked and most operators abandoned the city, hoping to find better luck elsewhere.

If there was a single event that broke the hold that crime had over the city of Decatur, it would have been the Grand Jury Indictments of 1936. In March of that year, a grand jury was convened by Special Prosecutor Charles Evans to look into criminal activity in the city. Literally hundreds of witnesses were brought in from every walk of criminal life and warrants were issued and arrests made on a daily basis. The probe focused mainly on prostitution, illegal liquor sales, gambling, racketeering and even bribery of public officials.

Finally, the indictments reached a high point, as three of Decatur's most visible city officials were indicted for various crimes. They were Mayor Harry Barber, Police Chief Jack Cooper and the state's attorney, Arthur Frazier. Decatur was in an uproar when arrest warrants were issued for the three men. Eventually, the charges were dropped in all of their cases when all three officials resigned their positions and dropped out of the public eye. Many people felt that justice had been served by filing charges against these officials, but it is interesting to note that, despite serious charges filed against them, Barber, Cooper and Frazier were never punished and all three men faded into relative obscurity.

Regardless, the heyday of crime in the city seemed to be over and one chapter in Decatur's history was finally brought to a close.... or was it?

Bell's Jewelry Store is located in the 100 block of East Prairie Street in Decatur. The building in which the store operates was built in 1865 and has undergone a number of changes over the years, including housing a number of other stores and shops.

Located on the third floor of the building is a double set of rooms that are divided by a wide doorway. The south room has three large windows that once looked out toward Merchant Street, but have long since been sealed over. Years ago, these rooms saw people, activity, life, and perhaps even death. Today, they stand empty and abandoned... or do they?

In the 1920's and early 1930's, these rooms marked the location of one of the downtown area's most popular speakeasys and gambling parlors. According to old reports, the speakeasy sold homemade beer and whiskey through the Prohibition era. Afterward, it served as a gambling parlor and brothel until

1936 or 1937, when it was closed down for good. Access to the speakeasy was gained by a stairway from the street and then customers had to enter a secret door (in the form of a sliding panel) to get into the rooms themselves. The room outside, where the door was located, was once a legitimate sporting goods shop that acted as a "front" for the speakeasy. It was apparently not a prosperous shop however, as many older men that I have spoken with recall coming to the shop as children. They would be left to look around for a few minutes while their father vanished into the speakeasy. Those who recalled the sporting good shop remembered the merchandise was always dusty and never seemed to sell.

After prohibition was repealed, the speakeasy owners looked for other enticements for their customers and interest was sold to gambler Harry Stewart, who proceeded to set up cards and gaming tables in the north room. The owners also contracted the south room as a brothel until the place closed down. The end came in the late 1930's when the place became a victim of changing times and of a crackdown on vice in the city.

For more than two decades after that, the rooms stood empty and sealed off with the original door still in place. The door was finally removed in the 1950's, when some remodeling was done on the old sporting goods store. This room was turned into a frame shop for one of the jewelry stores in the building.

The speakeasy itself was never used and remains empty today. The rooms seem trapped in time, looking much as they did years ago. This is due to the fact that they remained untouched for so long... and few dared venture into them, as stories were recalled about the history of the place. The walls of both rooms are still plastered with pin-up photos clipped from film and "girlie" magazines of the 1930's. Most of the tattered pictures still remain, although now they are faded and yellowed with age.

While I did not become involved in the strange events that were taking place in the building until 1996, weird happenings were already being reported at least two years prior to that. This was at about the same time the interiors and front facades of the historic buildings on the block were being renovated. This seems to be especially important in this case as the renovations almost seem to have "awakened" something in the building, be it memories of the past or actual spirits. Such an event is not uncommon when it comes to old buildings. Many older structures suddenly become haunted during repairs and renovations as the ghosts, or residual energy, in the building are disturbed.

In this case, the first reported activity seems to have occurred in 1994 when an employee from the local utility company was making his monthly rounds reading the power meters. He was working in the upstairs of the building adjacent to where the gambling rooms were and noticed that odd sounds could be heard coming through the wall. He later reported to me that the sounds were of a number of people talking and laughing, the sound of music being played and something that sounded like a marble spinning on a roulette wheel. At that time, he had no idea that the rooms next to where he had been that day had once contained a gambling parlor.... nor that the rooms were abandoned at the time he claimed to hear the sounds.

In early summer 1996, the employees at Bell's Jewelry store started to notice that all was not right on the upper floors of the building. Three employees of the store individually reported hearing sounds like heavy objects falling and footsteps on the third floor. When they went upstairs to investigate, they found nothing. At one point, they even called in an exterminator, thinking that a rodent problem might account for the odd noises. The pest control company was unable to find any openings where animals could get access to the rooms.

All along, store employees had reported feeling uncomfortable in the old gambling rooms when they had any occasion to go inside of them. In fact, they had largely avoided them before the noises had started. One of the employees recalled the weird feelings that she would get inside of the rooms. "The first time that I went up there, I felt afraid," she told me during one of many interviews I conducted with the staff. "I knew instantly that I didn't like it up there.... a year later, curiosity got the best of me because I wanted to see the old magazine pictures that were supposed to be on the walls. I had my niece go up there with me and it seemed like the room was very cold... I got the feeling something was in that room. There were cold spots in there and it gave me a bone cold feeling. My hair actually raised on my neck."

The inexplicable noises continued over a span of several months and then other things started to happen, like items in the store downstairs going missing. Tools, cases and small pieces started to vanish without a trace. Some of these items would turn up again in other places, while most things, like a mostly full bottle of Jim Beam whiskey, were never seen again. They also reported that on one occasion, all of the jewelry cases in the store were somehow unlocked and opened during the night.... even though the elaborate alarm system was never triggered.

These strange events were more than enough to convince the staff that they should contact someone who was more familiar with this type of activity. They called me in the fall of 1996 about the weird goings-on and I came to the store with a friend one warm afternoon to see the gambling rooms. We were taken upstairs by Doug Bell, the owner of the store, who was intrigued, but skeptical, about the reported phenomena. Over time, he would become convinced that there was more to the building than he first thought!

Doug led the way up to the third floor and we all three noticed there was a sharp chill to the air. It was odd that on the third floor of an old building, on a very warm afternoon, that it would be cooler than on the lower floors.

After gaining access to the speakeasy, I took a look around and made plans to come back and spend some time in the place after dark. As I walked around, I wandered into the southwest corner of the north room (where the gambling tables were located) and suddenly felt as if I had walked into a freezer! The air around me was very cold and almost electrified. I could feel a chilly, tingling sensation and all three of us saw the hair on my arms literally stand on end as though I was experiencing a mild electric shock. Then, as suddenly as the sensation had come, it vanished and did not come back. I could find no explanation for the bizarre incident, although I would later learn that legend stated that same corner had been the location of a man's death in the 1930's.

I believed this to be my first encounter with one of the spirits of the speakeasy... but it would not be my last.

The strange noises continued through the fall of 1996 and additional items disappeared from the store. The rooms were kept locked during the daytime hours and were largely avoided by the building staff. One afternoon, a store employee was locking the door to the speakeasy and as she reached for the door handle, she saw a bright light in the far north corner of the room. She would later claim that she saw the outline of a person in the light. There was no one in the room at the time and there is no explanation for what this light could have been. Strangely, a visitor to the rooms (who knew nothing of this report) also claimed to see a light in the same location a short time later. He stated that it had dropped down from the ceiling to a height of about four feet and then had vanished.

Other visitors to the room reported their own unusual encounters. It was common to hear of people reporting unknown noises, phantom footsteps, and even the soft sound of music being played in the rooms. Unaware of phenomena that had already been reported, they also told of cold chills and electric-like sensations in certain areas of the room. Much of the strangeness was centered on the same corner of the room where I had experienced my own brush with..... well, something.

I returned to have my own encounters as well. One afternoon, I stopped by the store and went upstairs to the gambling rooms. I climbed the first flight of steps from the lower level and distinctly heard the sound of someone following me up. Assuming that one of the staff was going to accompany me upstairs, I paused on the landing to wait for them. After a few moments, no one appeared, so I looked to see who was on the stairwell. There was no one there! I quickly learned that the employees had been with customers at the time and no one had been near the stairs.

During another visit, I had been inside of the rooms and had left for a few minutes. I returned a short time later and discovered two vintage playing cards had mysteriously appeared on the floor. They had not been there previously but I still could have written the whole thing off to coincidence if not for the fact that I discovered them in the same corner of the room where I had felt the "presence". It made me wonder, if a man had really been killed in that corner, just what cards he had been holding in his hand?

During the winter of 1996-1997, I joined members of the AMERICAN GHOST SOCIETY, who began conducting investigations inside of the gambling rooms. They were hoping to record some of the strange activity taking place there and in many instances, were not disappointed. A number of photographs were taken that appeared to show anomalous activity was taking place there and during one outing, we used two separate video cameras to record the proceedings.

The cameras were set up in the empty rooms and were left to film anything strange that might happen. Both tapes managed to record unexplainable sounds on their audio tracks. At one point on the recording is the sound of a heavy wooden door being slammed (although there is no door to slam) and at another point, the sounds of several people walking around and stomping their feet. These actions would have been impossible as the room was locked and empty, as is plainly visible from the visual portion of the tape. In addition, all of the investigators present were on the bottom floor of the building at the time. There was no one else in the building.

Another investigation took place in the spring of 1997. We were given access to the rooms and we set up another controlled experiment using audio and video recorders and stationary sensors to pick up movement and the presence of any unexplained energy fields. Not surprisingly, the audio recordings managed to pick up the same sounds as before, including footsteps and the sounds of doors opening and closing. After the investigation was all over, five members of the group would report an identical occurrence, not realizing that anyone else had reported it. Three members first reported they had felt a "cold wind" blow past them and later, two other members also said they felt the same "wind" seconds later. They experienced it a short distance away from the original three members. This all took place at the exact same time the voice was recorded on the tape.

And that wasn't all that was reported on this same evening. At one point during the investigation, three different cameras would record what appears to be a shimmering light at the same location in the room. All three of the photos were taken just seconds apart. If only one camera had captured the odd image, it would be easy to dismiss the light as a film flaw, or lens flare. However, the fact that three different cameras saw it makes this rather hard to believe.

The investigations of the speakeasy continued into 1998 and up until the time that I moved away from Decatur. The reports of strange phenomena continued as well with various people claiming to encounter everything from eerie cold spots to witnessing balls of light that flew about the rooms in the darkness. On my last evening at the speakeasy, I spent some time in the company of a friend who had no idea of the history of the building. At one point, as we sat there in the inky darkness, he leaned over and nudged me.

"Do you hear that?", he whispered.

"Hear what?", I asked him.

"Music... it sounds like one of these old crank-up record players," he replied.

And maybe, just maybe, it was!

Since that time, nearly two years have passed and the haunting of the old speakeasy continues, although the rooms are closed to visitors today. I remain convinced that this location is truly haunted. There have been too many strange things that have happened here, involving too many reliable witnesses, for me to not realize there is more to this place than meets the eye. Whether you believe in ghosts or not, it is a fascinating time capsule from a period in history that most of us know little about. If you are a believer in ghosts, and you ever get the chance to see this spot, the history of the place just enhances your experience.

If, on the other hand, you are not a believer, I would invite you to secure an invitation to the speakeasy on some dark, autumn night. On such an occasion, these spirits might just see fit to convince you they are real!

FLICKERING IMAGES......
DECATUR'S HAUNTED THEATERS

The Golden Age of Theater in Decatur has been over for many years now, although this never seems to stop us from dreaming about, and wishing for, the theaters of yesterday. Only two of the grand theaters are even still standing today, the Lincoln and the Avon. Miraculously, both theaters continue to thrive today, despite setbacks, abandonment and even the threat of destruction. Before we take a look at the ghostly legends of these two theaters, allow me to present a shadowed history and tribute to the lost and the haunted theaters of Decatur. As the saying goes, every good theater has a ghost... but in Decatur, the theaters just may have more than their share!

Throughout the early history of Decatur, the city was well known for being the entertainment center for Central Illinois. At one time, there were no less that seven theaters operating in the 300 and 400 blocks of North Water Street. This is an astounding number, even for a city with a theater history that dates back more than 150 years.

In 1835, there was no theater in the city but a small log courthouse provided a popular meeting place and a location for local children to perform one-act plays and pageants. Three years later, a brick courthouse on the Old Square would replace this building and here, community plays and gatherings would be held on the second floor. The first real theater in town was Powers Hall, which was constructed on the third floor of some store buildings in the 100 block of East Main Street. It was built in 1856 by William Powers and although it only had a few seats, it was Decatur's first stage and did provide the first place to hold performances in town. Prior to its opening, traveling entertainers had been performing in local hotels. Legend has it that Abraham Lincoln once defended a case at Powers Hall, as the courthouse did not have enough room for all of the spectators who turned out to watch.

In 1870, EO Smith built the city's first grand theater, or opera house as it was called. It included a large stage, private boxes and a balcony and was able to seat up to 1500 people. Several major stars of the period played here, including Lillian Russell, Lily Langtry and Edwin Booth. Henry Ward Beecher also spoke here on one occasion.

Smith later decided to close the theater in July 1889, to make room for the new Powers Grand Opera House. This new theater boasted a seating capacity of 1500 and it was reported to be as modern as any theater in the Midwest, even rivaling those in Chicago. The opera house opened on September 9, 1889 to a packed house and featured the celebrated comedian WH Crane. Edwin Booth and Helen Modjeska also presented "Hamlet" in this theater and brought in receipts of over $2500 for a single performance, the largest sum ever received at that time in any theater in the state.

During its heyday, the Powers Opera House hosted the greatest actors in the country. In addition to Edwin Booth, Julia Marlowe, Lily Langtry, Maurice Barrymore and hundreds of others appeared on stage. Decatur audiences thrilled to elaborate and exciting performances, from opera to minstrel shows, comic plays and even magic acts. The theater even featured a production of "Ben Hur" that was done with actual chariots and live horses on a giant treadmill.

The Opera House was located on the site of the present-day Hotel Orlando and it burned down two times during its brief history. The first time was in 1895 and the second in 1914. After the first fire, the theater was quickly rebuilt but by 1914, the entertainment world in Decatur was already changing. The stage play had taken a back seat to a new and exciting form of entertainment, the "moving picture". Actually, the first films ever shown in Decatur were shown at the Powers Opera House for an entire week in 1901 with little success. A decade later, however, meant major changes for Decatur theater.

Vaudeville, a form of comic and sometimes risqué theater, first came to Decatur in 1905 when the Bijou Theater opened. It was torn down once and opened again in 1909. The Bijou attracted a lot of performers who were popular on the vaudeville circuit of the day like Al Jolson, Sophie Tucker and Will Rogers. The theater was so successful that a second Bijou was opened next door to the original in 1913, offering more vaudeville and even moving picture shows.

Decatur's first theater to be designed strictly for motion pictures was the Nickelodeon, named for the fact that admission was only a nickel. It was opened in 1906 and like most other theaters at the time, it featured short films that were designed to do little more than thrill audiences with the novelty of movies.

The next of Decatur's theaters, that would feature live entertainment as well as films, was the Empress Theater. A deal was struck in 1911 to build the theater at the corner of Water and North Streets. It was popular for many years and was remembered for a long time as one of the finest in the city, being even more beautiful and ornate than the Lincoln, which would follow a few years later.

The theater had been built by Charles Thatcher, who actually vacated his family home at that corner to make way for the new structure. Thatcher was a prominent businessman in the city and had opened a lumberyard in Decatur in 1867 and was on the board of directors for the National Bank for many years. The lower floor of the theater's building would also contain a number of shops, including Kinney Shoes, Dixie Shops, Union Store and also a candy store and soda fountain.

In 1928, the first talking film, "The Jazz Singer" came to Decatur and played at the Empress. According to newspaper accounts, crowds waited outside of the theater all day long to get tickets and many of them were still not admitted to the show. The Empress also had a ballroom on the third floor where live music and dancing were available. The theater drew a number of celebrities, including cowboy star, Gene Autry.

The Empress was also the first of the city's "haunted theaters", as reports from the early days of the Empress claimed that it already had ghosts on the premises. Customers, ushers and staff members alike reported that unexplained footsteps and sounds were common in the auditorium at night. After the death of owner Charles Thatcher, in 1923, rumor had it that his ghost was known to frequent the balcony during performances. The Empress Theater was eventually closed down in 1962 and was later demolished to make room for the municipal parking garage that is still located on this site.

Decatur's most haunted "lost" theater was the Alhambra, which has long since been closed and demolished. It was once located 1073 North Water Street, near the original site of Black's Hardware Store. The theater's address no longer exists, but once stood where a small shopping center is now situated. The theater was built by Percy Gebhart in 1914 to replace the old American Theater. In 1926, it was sold to JM Duncan and JA Steinson. Duncan's son, Charles "Chuck" Duncan, became a partner in 1932 and managed the theater until 1958, when he sold out to another company.

According to those who remember the theater, it had no balcony and was not as grand as other theaters, but was just as popular. In addition to films, the theater also played host to a number of entertainers like Edgar Bergen and Red Skelton. There were also various clubs that were hosted at the theater, like the "Popeye Club", which was held at the Alhambra on Saturday afternoons. In 1949, the theater began hosting the "Roy Rogers Club" and the Decatur chapter went on to become the largest in the country. More than 1000 children would crowd into the Alhambra on Saturday mornings and Chuck Duncan would join in the fun by putting on a cowboy hat and firing off his six-guns in the theater.

The Alhambra was always very clean and no talking or acting up was allowed. Many readers have recalled the fact that Chuck Duncan would often lead those who could not be quiet out of the theater by their ear. It was also recalled that Duncan also took seriously the closing of the theater each night. After the show, he would make sure that the auditorium was completely empty... and on these occasions, he often spoke of encountering the theater's ghost!

On many nights, he saw the form of a woman sitting in one of the front seats near the orchestra pit. The grayish figure would be sitting bolt upright, staring straight ahead as though watching something on the stage. The shape could just be seen by the dimmed house lights and by the time that Duncan reached the front of the theater, the woman would have vanished.

The Alhambra was located right next door to the Illini Ballroom, where popular big bands would often appear for music and dancing, but this would not be enough to save the place from the wrecking ball. The advent of television and drive-in theaters meant the end for many of Decatur's older theaters and this included the Alhambra. The theater closed its doors in September 1960 and was demolished to make way for new buildings a short time later.

Theaters have always been the perfect haven for earthbound spirits. They are dark, often deserted, full of nooks, crannies, empty hallways, strange shadows and make the ideal place for all sorts of hauntings from the intelligent spirit to the residual energies of the past. The energy, emotions and constant stream of personalities are the vital ingredients for ghostly activity... and that will not be anywhere more apparent than in the theaters to follow.

The Lincoln Theater in downtown Decatur

THE LINCOLN THEATER

The Lincoln Theater, located on North Main Street in downtown Decatur, is one of only two of the city's grand theaters that remain in operation today. It opened in 1916 with a large seating capacity and a sprawling stage. It was a labyrinth, and remains so today, with its mezzanine, high balcony, basements and sub-cellars. The theater holds many secrets, and according to some, many ghosts.

There have been many unexplained encounters with the supernatural in the theater, some of which I can personally vouch for. There is no question that, even to a skeptic, it can be a spooky place. If you have ever been inside of it, then you know just how eerie it can be under the right conditions. Many have stated that they feel as if they are being watched in the building, which gives them a creeping sensation at the back of the neck. This does not always occur at night either, they say, because the darkened theater can be just as spooky in broad daylight.

Many are familiar with the tales of the Lincoln's resident ghosts, but I have always wondered if all of the strange experiences reported here could be the work of one spirit? Could there be a number of ghosts lurking in the vast confines of the Lincoln Theater?

I'll leave that up to you to decide.

The Lincoln Theater was not the first building to stand on the site that it now occupies in downtown Decatur. Aside from frontier construction by the early settlers, the first real building on the site was the Priest Hotel. It was opened on the northwest corner of the Old Square in 1860 by WS Crissey, although it was completed and operated for many years by Franklin Priest. In 1880, Riley Deming took over the establishment and changed its name to the New Deming.

It was later purchased by A. Wait and in 1892, he changed the name to the Arcade Hotel. Eight years later, he would remodel and expand and call it the Decatur Hotel. There was a horrible fire in 1904, which destroyed the building, but it was rebuilt on the same site a short time later. It was in 1915 however, when disaster struck. An early morning blaze swept through the building and destroyed the hotel and the Arcade building. There was one man killed in the fire and there were several others believed to be dead. Several were never found at all. Could the spirits of the people killed in the hotel fire now walk in the dark corners of the Lincoln Theater? The theater now stands directly on the location of the former hotel and many have speculated that the ghosts could have passed into the new building and may have taken up residence there.

Throughout the history of the city, fires often plagued the public buildings and many were destroyed, including the Powers Opera House, which burned twice. Being built on the site of a hotel destroyed by fire must have made the designers of the Lincoln Theater especially aware of the possible dangers and they were determined to make this building "absolutely fireproof".

Clarence Wait constructed the new theater in 1916 on land that he had inherited from his father's estate. The Decatur architectural firm of Aschauer & Waggoner was hired to draw up plans for the theater and the buildings surrounding it. These buildings included the Odd Fellows Lodge and seven smaller stores that fronted Main Street with offices on the second floor. These smaller stores were given the name of Lincoln Square, which was also the name of the theater until it was shortened in 1930.

The theater was designed and built on a section of land that would be L-shaped, with an entrance in the middle of the block. To insure that the place was "fireproof", the original boilers were housed in the Odd Fellows Building and separated from the theater by a thick firewall. This wall, which was about two-foot thick, surrounded the entire building. The interior of the building was also carefully designed as the walls, floors, railings, ceilings, fixtures, and even the curtains, were all said to be impossible to burn.

The formal and official grand opening of the Lincoln Theater took place on October 27, 1916. The Lincoln opened to "standing room only" crowds of Decatur's finest citizens, dressed in black tie and formal wear and eager to see the new, glorious theater of which they had heard so much about. The first program to be presented was George M. Cohan's stage comedy, "Hit the Trail Holliday" starring Frank Otto. The audience loved the show and raved about the spectacular design of the theater, from its private seating boxes, to the massive ivory-colored columns, to the 1346 seats, all of which offered a splendid view and wonderful acoustics. Also new to Decatur was the mezzanine seating, which ran just below the balcony and offered seats that were only slightly above the level of the stage.

In those early years, the main emphasis at the Lincoln was on stage shows and vaudeville acts. The theater was put into use by the community as well as it hosted many small, local productions and the Decatur High School commencement services each spring. Many famous stars appeared here, including, Ethel Barrymore, Al Jolson, Ed Wynn, Jeanette MacDonald, and many others. Audiences also thrilled to such attractions as a sparring exhibition by Jack Dempsey after his famous fight with Georges Carpentier.

One of the most enigmatic of the performers to appear at the Lincoln was the stage magician and master illusionist, Harry Houdini. Houdini was a worldwide sensation by the time that he came to the Lincoln in 1925. His visit is permanently marked on the wooden stage of the theater by a narrow trap door that has been nicknamed the "Houdini Hole" over the years. Below the hole, metal hooks are imbedded in the ceiling of the basement as silent reminders of the magician's visit.

For a number of years, people believed that the hole in the stage had been cut for the magician to escape through during one of his illusions and that the hooks below had held some sort of safety net. However, this turned out to be incorrect. At that time Houdini would have played the Lincoln, he was perfecting an escape that used a very large water tank, into which he would be lowered upside-down and then have only a few moments to escape. The rectangular hole in the Lincoln stage was cut so that a hose could drop below the tank and empty into a drain in the basement. The metal hooks were actually used to hold the support ties for the drainage hose.

The hole remains today as a testament to how popular and influential Houdini must have been in those days, as a simple request to Clarence Wait meant a permanent scar to the stage of the theater.

In February 1926, the theater hired a 12-member orchestra to provide music for all stage productions and the silent films that were starting to gain popularity. Vaudeville still remained the most popular attraction the theater had to offer however and the orchestra's leader brought a young, unknown comedian named Bob Hope to the Lincoln in 1926 to show Decatur how to dance the "Charleston". Hope was just starting his career in those days and he would return often during the 1920's to appear in vaudeville shows and comedy productions.

Moving pictures continued to increase in popularity in the city and Decatur was demanding more and more films to take the place of stage shows. In April 1928, the first "talkies" came to Decatur and played at the Empress Theater. The Lincoln began showing them 14 months later at the close of the vaudeville season. This would herald the end of the vaudeville days at the Lincoln, and perhaps in the entire city. The sound equipment was installed in the theater for films, making silent movies obsolete, and band leader Billy Gail and his orchestra were promptly dismissed.

Although movies had largely replaced live entertainment at the Lincoln, there were still special performances booked here on a regular basis. It was during one of these performances that the "fireproof" claims of the theater were first tested. In September 1942, one of the great magicians of the century, Harry Blackstone, was performing at the theater. The auditorium was filled with about 1000 school children when fire broke out in the Rambo Drug store, located next door to the Lincoln Theater.

Alerted to the danger of smoke entering the theater and the building catching on fire, Blackstone remained calm and jokingly told the audience that for his next trick, he was going to make them all disappear from the theater in five minutes. He then directed them to leave, row by row, out of the alley doors and out of the fire escapes in the balcony. He promised the children that they were assisting him in a marvelous new illusion, which he would explain to them outside. After he had successfully cleared the theater and learned that the danger was past, Blackstone is said to have sobbed with relief from the stress of his heroic evacuation of the theater. Years later, in 1960, while a guest on the television program "This is Your Life", he stated this had been the "greatest trick of his career".

The fire would last for four hours and would completely gut the drug store and Cook Jewelers, which shared the space. The fire was so intense that the floor of the building collapsed into the basement. It also heavily damaged an adjoining flower shop and beauty parlor, but no damage was reported to the Lincoln. Apparently, it really was "fireproof" after all!

These claims would be tested again in 1960 when another fire did major damage to buildings south of the theater. The section of the building that was located above the theater lobby would be virtually destroyed as well. The Lincoln itself was only slightly damaged. The "fireproof" claims have not been tested since and the building has remained architecturally sound after more than 80 years.

The theater operated steadily for many years and was sold again in 1974 to Plitt Theaters Inc., which bought out the entire Great States chain. The Lincoln Theater only remained in the chain until December of that year, when management was passed to another company, which already owned four of Decatur's other theaters. They leased the building on a month-to-month basis and in December 1980, were informed by building's owner that their lease would not be extended past the end of the year. Unfortunately, the theater chain had a reputation for stripping everything usable from a theater before they left it and they followed this same plan at the Lincoln. They removed much of the valuable equipment, from projectors to the interior mechanisms of the speakers.

After that, the Lincoln closed down for many years, only opening occasionally for live music and barely attended events. By 1990, the building had deteriorated badly and was suffering from neglect. It had been abandoned by everyone except for the bats and pigeons that had taken up residence in the auditorium.

Thankfully, the Lincoln came to the attention of a restoration group and some life has been brought to the old place. Thousands of dollars and countless hours of work have been put into the theater, but it still has a long way to go. The restoration effort has been a long and painfully slow project with possibly many years remaining before it will be completed. This has not stopped many local and national groups from performing here however and many times, during these performances, regular people have encountered things in the theater than can only be described as something well beyond the ordinary!

Stories have circulated about a haunting at the Lincoln Theater since at least the 1930's. Reports by witnesses from those early days of film in the theater have suggested that as least one ghost haunts the building. However, in more recent times, the numerous encounters here have led many to believe that a multitude of spirits may linger in the Lincoln.

The most famous ghost of the Lincoln is rooted in a legend from the vaudeville days. His name was "Red" and he was a stagehand at the Lincoln during the days of live performances. He was deeply attached to the theater and loved the place, working long shifts and coming to the theater on his day off just so that he could be among the actors and entertainers. It was said that Red always dreamed of becoming a performer himself, as he was a commanding presence with his bright, auburn hair, but he was simply too quiet and shy to ever take the stage. He contented himself to working behind the scenes and perhaps even standing on the stage at night, looking out on the empty theater. Perhaps he imagined an audience in those darkened seats, assembled to watch him perform in the latest show.

One night, during a performance, Red was working on the catwalks above the stage. This area is about 75 feet above the stage itself and was used in those days to lower props and scenery flats. Red was used to working up in those dizzying heights and it never really bother him. Then, on that fateful night, the unthinkable happened. Red slipped from the metal gridwork and fell. He plunged downward and collided with the "pin rail" of the "sand trap", a concrete platform that is also located high above the stage. The "pin rail" is a metal bar with sharp hooks jutting from it. The ropes that controlled the flats and curtains were tied on these hooks. When Red collided with the rail, his arm was snagged by one of the hooks and torn from his body, thanks to the force and speed of his fall. He landed on the stage in a bloody heap with his arm still tangled on the rail overhead. Needless to say, he died moments later.

It is unknown whether Red managed to gasp out any final words, but regardless, no one was surprised when his ghost started to appear in the theater. He had always jokingly promised that should be die, he hoped to spend eternity in the Lincoln Theater. And many say he is doing just that!

Over the years, dozens of witnesses have reported strange sounds and footsteps in the otherwise empty theater... and these are sounds that cannot be explained away as simply the theater's acoustics. They have also reported whispers and strange voices and even a shadowy apparition in the theater's balcony. However, this strange figure is not described as looking like Red, but rather as a woman in a long, old-fashioned dress! This is only one of the many reports that cause some to believe there are a number of ghosts in the building. Several other witnesses have reported their own brushes with hazy forms and figures seen out of the corner of the eye... and none of these descriptions match! Could there be a legion of phantoms left behind in the theater?

In addition to visual sightings, there have been a number of other encounters as well, including the aforementioned footsteps and sounds. Many have experienced inexplicable cold chills in certain spots in the building and others claim to have been touched by unseen hands. Several others have mentioned seeing theater seats in the auditorium actually raise and lower by themselves, as if an unseen audience was watching the proceedings on the stage.

I had my own strange encounter a few years ago when I was working in the quiet theater one afternoon, making preparations for an upcoming Halloween show. I happened to be off to the side of the stage, behind some curtains, when I clearly heard someone walk up the steps and out onto the wooden stage. When I came out from behind the curtain, I was startled to find there was no one there but me! I quickly searched the area, and even the rest of the theater, but the place was completely empty. Or was it?

Other possibly supernatural incidents have occurred around what may be the most haunted spot in the theater. It is a metal, spiral staircase that is located in the back corner of the stage. Many witnesses claim to have had unearthly encounters on and around the staircase. For example, in 1994, an entertainer who was performing in a traveling production reported that he saw a man lurking on this staircase. He was in the back corner changing his costume when he heard a voice whispering to him. When he looked up, he saw a shadowy figure on the steps. He was unable to describe the figure, but he was convinced that it was a man. He complained about the presence to a nearby theater staff member, but when they checked the staircase, they found it empty. The man was gone but there was nowhere that he could have gone! Strangely, the actor had no idea about the legends of the Lincoln, nor that the staircase was rumored to be haunted.

In addition, I can personally vouch for at least one encounter on this intimidating staircase, because it happened to me! I still have no other explanation for what occurred, other than to say that I was followed up the stairs by one of the theater's resident ghosts!

I was in the theater one evening in October 1995 with a reporter and a cameraman from a local television station. They had contacted me about haunted places in Central Illinois for a news special and one of the places that I took them to was the Lincoln Theater.

They interviewed several staff members of the theater and then I decided to join the cameraman, Robert Buchwald, for a trip up the spiral staircase. He took his camera along, hoping to film the theater's stage from this vantage point. It was a good thing that he brought it, because we would have had no other source of light, outside of the light on his camera, to make the trip up there with. We rounded the staircase and then reached the top. We looked around the small and confined space for a few moments, exploring a small room that leads to the theater air ducts. Other than this dusty chamber, there is not much else to see up there. We stood talking for a few moments, and then what happened next was enough to convince even a skeptic like Robert Buchwald that there may be more to the Lincoln Theater than first meets the eye!

It seemed innocent enough at first. We had climbed the spiral staircase and left the reporter down on the stage by herself. We weren't surprised to soon hear the sound of her footsteps as she followed us up the stairs. Her hard-soled shoes made a distinctive sound as they echoed on the metal steps. Realizing that we had the only portable light, and the staircase was quite dark, Robert leaned over the railing with the camera so that the reporter would have some light to see by. Just as he did this, from out on the stage, we heard the sound of a voice calling out to us. We looked and saw the reporter standing in the middle of the stage... dozens of feet from the base of the steps and much too far away to have been climbing the staircase just moments before!

We suddenly realized the footsteps on the staircase had not belonged to the reporter... so whose were they? We had no idea, but we didn't stay up there long enough to find out!

Does the ghost of "One-Armed Red" really roam the dark corners and back hallways of the Lincoln Theater? Or is he just a legend created to explain the generations of strange phenomena that has been reported there? Could there be a large number of spirits still inside of the building, drawn to the energy of more than eighty years of sadness, heartbreak and tragedy?

Most importantly, is the Lincoln Theater really haunted at all?

If you are skeptical about the many tales of the theater, I challenge you to wait before answering these questions. Wait to ponder them until some night when you have the opportunity to come the theater and sit in the dark auditorium..... by yourself. Is this place really haunted? Or is that just the sound of an old building settling in the shadows behind you?

Is it your imagination... or is it something else?

THE AVON THEATER

The Avon Theater officially opened in 1916, just a few short weeks after the Lincoln Theater opened its doors for the first time. The Avon was a unique place in that it was a large, grand theater, on the scale of the Empress or the Lincoln, but yet the Avon had been constructed for showing moving pictures only. There would be some live entertainment and music, with hosts appearing for the parade of films to follow, but this theater was a folly to many for they believed that moving pictures were simply a passing fad and would never last.

Over the years, the American film industry has defied the odds and has endured. Fortunately, even after a number of near disasters, the same can be said for the Avon. After a bright beginning and a long run of success, the theater was closed down and abandoned and most feared that it would be lost. For several years, it was said the Avon would soon join most of the other old theaters in Decatur and would be destroyed. Such an end would have been tragic on many counts, but there is one thing that sets the Avon apart from most of the other "lost" theaters.... the Avon is a very haunted place.

The Avon opened with much fanfare on November 28, 1916. The theater was perhaps the grandest to ever open in the city and it was decorated with original artwork that even rivaled the twin, seven-foot-tall monuments on the posts outside of the building. A third statue is still located today just above the original screen. It is of a woman, reclining in the nude, and holding a wreath outward toward the audience. On a parallel with this figure, circling the entire auditorium, were once base-relief casts of women's heads. They were only matched by the lion's heads that circled the theater below them, the eyes of these creatures glowing with brilliant light.

The Avon became known as one of the most beautiful theaters in the Midwest and prospered for many years. It would not hold onto its crown though and the years were not kind to the place. After some extensive remodeling that was done in the 1950's, the theater never again had the elegance of its early days. For several years, the building was closed and there was thought to be no chance that the Avon will ever welcome theater patrons through its doors again. The lobby and auditorium fell into poor condition and the last attempts to restore, or at least to salvage the theater's dignity, met with indifference and a lack of enthusiasm. Until recently that is, when new occupants began restoring the old building, stirring up years of dust.

And have the new owners stirred up other things as well? It's possible, because one thing is sure, there are many secrets still hiding within the walls of the Avon Theater!

When the announcement came that a new theater was going to open in the city of Decatur, people became very excited. There were already a number of theaters operating in town, especially along North Water Street, but there was always room for more entertainment. Besides that, rumor had it that this theater was going to be different than the rest.

The builder and owner of the new theater, James Allman, announced a contest by which the name of the theater would be chosen. Over 700 people entered the contest and flooded the judge's panel with a variety of names for the building. The winning name, the "Avon", was chosen in August 1916. It had been submitted by Thomas Ronan of Decatur. Ronan, who claimed to be a theatrical man himself, was presented with a season pass for the theater. Allman was happy with the judge's decision and announced that the attractive name would surely conjure up images of William Shakespeare as it was on the banks of the Avon the great playwright had been born.

The Avon enjoyed success for a number of years and then in the late 1920's, it was purchased by the Constanopoulos family of Angelo, Gus, Christian and Theodore. The records of the city date their first involvement with the theater as 1927. Prior to that, they had owned a candy and soda business called the Empress Confectionary.

Several of the brothers would be involved in Decatur theater, but it would be Gus Constan (as their name was later shortened to) who remained most involved with the Avon Theater. He would also own the Rogers Theater and become a partner in the Varsity Theater a few years later.

In 1966, Gus Constan was bought out of the Avon by a theater chain that was also in the process of buying other theaters in town. The family remained the owners of the building for some time, but had no control over the business. Legend has it that Gus Constan loved the theater so much that he kept a private office here for many years. When the time came for him to move out, after the Avon had changed hands, he simply refused to leave. Employees of the new owners were forced to remove everything from his office and they literally threw it all into the street in front of the building.

This is one of the most often repeated stories of the theater and while I have no idea if it is actually true, it has been told for many years. However, if it is true, it might go a long way in explaining why Constan is still reportedly haunting the Avon today!

The theater saw a decline in revenue and business during the 1980's, becoming the last theater to operate in the downtown area. By this time, audiences were mainly ignoring the Avon in favor of the new multiplex theaters on the north side of town. In 1985, the theater converted to showing second-run movies but that was not enough to keep the place open. It finally closed down in April 1986. The last of the independent theaters in Decatur had now ceased to exist.

After that, the theater was empty for many years, although there was an attempt to bring it back to life in 1989 when it was used for several live music shows. The problem was that the theater had never really been designed for live entertainment and the shows met with only short-lived success.

The Avon opened again in 1993 as a second and third-run bargain house and while the initial response was good, business soon died out. It remained open this time for a little over a year and then closed down for another six years. In 1999, the Avon opened once again, this time as an independent and art film theater, showing alternative films and limited release features that in the past would have never been seen in Decatur. Finally, the Avon again began to thrive and a new audience was reached. It appears the theater has finally managed to restore itself to the status it once had and hopefully the residents of Decatur will help to keep it there.

If you should have the good fortune to visit the Avon, you will find the trip to be an interesting one, but only if you know where to look! Much of the decor that was described earlier in this section is gone now. The lion's heads have vanished with time, as has most of the ornate plasterwork and all of the original art. Remodeling was carried out in both the 1950's and then two decades later, in the 1970's. At that time, most of the reminders of yesterday were hidden or simply destroyed.

The only place in the theater that can give you an indication of how things once looked is behind the screen. Time has taken its toll here too but much of the original paint and plaster still remains, along with the decorator pieces that were added to the woodwork. The area behind the screen is the original, narrow stage of the theater and the place where the sound system and the antiquated air-conditioning unit is located. Directly above the heads of any visitors is the relief of the nude, reclining woman that once looked out over every audience that came to the theater.

Just below her is another example of the theater's artwork. There, mounted onto the wood and plaster wall, is a pair of angels that are holding a metal shield between them. There is a letter "A" ornately inscribed on the shield.

In addition, most of the original painted stencils remain on the walls and ceiling here as well. The small dressing rooms also remain on both sides of the original stage. They were once used by the performers and celebrities who came to entertain and announce the films that played here. There is detailed wood decoration around the doorways and also around the doorways that led upstairs to the private seating boxes. These boxes were once located directly above the pipe organ mechanisms and they offered an unobstructed view of the original screen. Other than these lonely doorways, no trace of the boxes can be found today.

In a direct line from the old screen and stage is the balcony. This seating area is entirely constructed of wood and is still capable of seating a large number of patrons. A small staircase leads up to the cramped projection booth and outside of the booth is a skylight where burglars broke into the place one night in 1952. They cleaned out the office safe, and started to break into the cash register behind the candy counter.... until something frightened them off. They mysteriously left an open drawer and untouched cash behind.

Which brings us to the ghosts.....

I have no problem with saying that I believe the Avon Theater is one of the most haunted places in the city of Decatur. The stories of restless ghosts at the Avon go back many years, even to the early days of the theater, but I first got involved in the ghostly goings-on here in September 1994. The theater had opened again the year before and I was contacted by some of the staff members who worked here. They asked if I would mind looking into some of the strange things they claimed were happening in the theater.

While the first visit was rather uneventful, I was able to record a lot of information about the alleged haunting. The theater manager, and the rest of the staff, reported that things had started to turn up missing in the theater, both small items and large. They also told of hearing footsteps, laughter, applause and voices coming from the auditorium after it had emptied for the night. The sounds of people walking about in empty rooms and in hallways were common, as was the feeling of being watched and being touched by ghostly hands. One staff member even claimed to have been groped by an invisible entity while working in the projection booth.

That night, I took a walking tour of the place with recording equipment and cameras and found the sensations of some of the places in the theater were very disturbing. One of the most frightening locations was a hallway that is located upstairs above the theater's lobby. The theater's offices, and a small bathroom, opened off this hallway. The feeling that I had while walking down this corridor was very disconcerting, and while I certainly don't claim to be psychic, it was a strange experience. I became very uncomfortable and sensed a chill in that spot that didn't seem to be present elsewhere in the building.

I would soon learn that the theater staff felt the same way and largely avoided the place when possible. There had been many occasions when the sound of footsteps had echoed in the corridor and those who looked to see who was there, found it empty. I would also later learn that the small bathroom along this hallway had been the original theater projection booth, which might explain why the resident ghosts were so attracted to it. This corridor would also be the same location where more than one person would encounter a ghost!

Unfortunately, that one evening would be my last chance to explore the Avon that year. I called the theater a short time later about returning, only to learn that the place had closed down once again. The following spring, I was able to return. Ironically, Skip Huston, who now operates the theater, was part of a group interested in buying it in 1995. The plan was to turn the place into a movie-themed nightclub that would serve food and drinks, along with films and live entertainment. The project never came about, but I was able to spend quite a bit of time in the theater doing research and it was during this period that Skip came face-to-face with one of the local haunts!

During the process of evaluating the building for the nightclub project, Skip came down to the theater one rainy afternoon in the spring of 1995. On this day, his trip to the Avon had a double purpose. He was not only looking over the building, but was also borrowing some marquee letters from the theater for use at an upcoming show at the Lincoln Theater. Even though it was a "dark and stormy" afternoon and he knew the theater was supposed to be haunted, he had no problems with going there by himself. In fact, he grabbed a flashlight and a couple of garbage bags to hold the letters and proceeded to the theater.

"Keep in mind," Skip recalled later, "I had always felt immune to otherworldly contact. I was always an ardent believer in the supernatural but considered myself one of those unlucky people who were not sensitive. This is why I didn't hesitate to enter the darkness of the Avon with only a penlight to see with."

Skip made his way through the theater to the "letter room", which is located off the previously mentioned hallway on the upstairs level of the building. The room is a small office where all of the plastic letters for the theater marquee are stored. Many of them were ancient letters for a marquee that hadn't existed for years, while others were the old letters from the Lincoln that had been donated to the Avon when the Lincoln's own marquee had been restored. These were the letters that Skip was seeking. After he entered the dimly lit room, he used his flashlight to begin looking for letters and checking them off the sheet he carried with him.

A few minutes after he started working, he distinctly heard a noise behind him in the hallway. He turned around, but saw no one there. A few minutes later, he heard it again. Were those footsteps? he wondered, and looked out in the corridor. The hall remained just as dark, but just as empty as well. Skip shook his head and went back to work, hurriedly filling one of the plastic bags with letters. Again, he heard another strange noise and reflexively turned around... but this time, he found that he was not alone!

"A man stood in the doorway to the room," Skip told me. "My first thought was that someone else was in the theater, perhaps a homeless person hiding out there. He was of medium height and slender build. His age appeared to be in his late '50's or early '60's. His hair was close-cropped gray and black. He was not transparent or wraith-like. He appeared solid. His face was non-descript and he stared into the room, not looking at me, just staring.

"I started to speak to him and then he slowly turned and started down the hallway. Recovered from my surprise, I darted to the doorway to say something but all that I saw was an empty hall. I grabbed the finished bag of letters and left the theater as fast as my legs would carry me!"

That was certainly Skip Huston's most startling visit to the Avon, but it would not be the last. Before the theater opened again, another strange encounter took place in the fall of 1998. This time, it was during the more likely setting of a "Haunted Decatur Tour". For a number of years, both Skip and I had hosted these bus tours to haunted sites in the city and on many occasions, weird happenings took place during the tours. When I moved from Decatur in 1998, Skip carried on the tradition of the tours. It was during such an excursion that one of the Avon ghosts made another appearance... this time in front of more than a dozen frightened witnesses!

Even though the theater was still closed down, and without electricity, Skip managed to secure the building for the tour. He thought it would make an appropriately spooky setting for the end of each night's outing. On this particular night, a terrible storm was raging outside. Skip remembered that it was the only rainy night of the tour season and he was disappointed that the attendees had been "rained out" of Greenwood Cemetery. He hoped that a longer version of the haunting events at the Avon Theater would appease anyone who felt the night had been too short.

After a re-telling of the events in the building, he asked if anyone had any questions. Someone raised a hand and asked what the name of theater's former owner (and the resident ghost's) name had been. At literally the same moment that Skip spoke the name of "Gus Constan", a shout went up from someone in the crowd. This person was frantically pointing up toward the theater balcony and everyone turned in that direction.

Skip would never forget what he saw there. "It was a figure at the balcony rail!", he recalled.

He wasn't the only one who saw it either. He estimates that at least 15 people looked up and saw the shadowy figure on the balcony... and panicked! People were pushing and shoving and climbing over the seats to get out of the auditorium, only to run out into the lobby and find the front doors locked. They were barely able to get the doors opened fast enough and needless to say, that ended the tour for the night! The incident left Skip's assistant so shaken that he quit the tours that night and never came back.

"I've had a lot of people come up to me later and talk about that night," he told me recently. "In fact, one day I was at the supermarket and the young woman at the check-out said to me that she was on the tour 'that night'. I didn't have to ask what she meant... I knew exactly what night she was talking about."

The theater re-opened about six months later and with any sort of restoration work, a lot of time, money and hard work was involved. The Avon had deteriorated badly during the time it was closed down and initially, it looked as though opening the place would be impossible. There were simply too many things wrong with the old building and every time that one thing got fixed, something else would break down. In addition, Skip had skeptics to deal with among his partners and his staff. They constantly badgered him about the so-called ghosts in the theater and poked fun at his belief that the theater was haunted.

"They started out as skeptics," he laughed later on, "but they're all believers now!"

As the restoration and repair work began to shake loose the dust and grime of the building, it awakened other things as well. It was not long before everyone on the crew, including those who had been the most skeptical about the haunting, began to report eerie incidents they couldn't explain away. Nearly everyone talked of hearing phantom voices in empty rooms and in the deserted auditorium. They also complained of disembodied footsteps and inexplicable cold chills that simply should not exist. Most easily convinced were those who spent the entire night, either working or sleeping in the building. They were soon coming to Skip and apologizing for ever doubting him.

Later on, after customers began to arrive, they reported their own encounters. Many people spoke of feeling as though they were being watched and of the pressure of hands on their backs and arms when no one was present. There were also reports of apparitions and figures who were present one moment and then gone the next. None of the incidents were particularly frightening. It was more like the resident specters were simply trying to make their presence known.

The Avon ghosts were certainly still around and apparently were pleased with the activity that was going on in the building. Skip believes they approve of the theater's re-opening and that they may be responsible for the strange run of luck the business has experienced, from the public response to the theater to the mysterious way that seemingly hopeless repairs have been accomplished.

One such incident took place during the theater's opening night. The Avon had scheduled the Decatur premiere of the film "Elizabeth" and support for the event had been overwhelming. People began pouring into the theater early and it was almost guaranteed that it would be a great night. Or at least it would be if not for one small problem.... the projector refused to work! Staff members worked feverishly on the machine but finally sent word to Skip in the lobby that the movie was going to have to be canceled. They were unable to fix the problem.

Moments later, two separate and apparently (at that time) unconnected events took place.

One of the staff members spotted a ghost in the small bathroom in the upstairs hallway and another staff member, who was working on the projector, heard a voice in his head. At the same time the ghost was seen, something told the other crew member to try crossing two sets of wires on the projector.

"We've already tried that," his co-worked protested.

"I know, but let's try it again," he replied. He was unsure as to why it wanted to do this, but he later described the feeling as a little voice that whispered to him. When they switched the wires, the projector suddenly began working. The movie premiere was saved!

"I can't explain it," Skip Huston told me when I asked him to try and explain why things seemed to be going so right with the Avon. "I just think that someone is watching over the place."

Does Gus Constan still watch over the Avon Theater? Or could the ghost be someone else. Whoever it is, the place is haunted! But don't just take my word for it... go and experience the theater for yourself. Thankfully, we have the chance to do that once again!

WHERE THE DEAD WALK
HAUNTINGS OF GREENWOOD CEMETERY

Located in the southern part of Decatur, Illinois and just a stone's throw away from the Sangamon River, is the city's oldest and most beautiful graveyard, Greenwood Cemetery. There is a chance that Greenwood Cemetery is the most historic location in all of Decatur.... but regardless of whether or not it is the most historic, it is, without a doubt, the most haunted.

The beginnings of Greenwood Cemetery are a mystery. There is no record to say when the first burials took place in the area of land that would someday be Greenwood. It was not the city's first official burial ground, but the Native Americans who lived here first did use it as a burial site, as did the early settlers. The only trace they left behind were the large numbers of unmarked graves, scattered about the present-day grounds.

There was also an incident that took place many years ago that marked the beginning of the cemetery's strange and mysterious history. The precise year of this event is unknown but it is believe to have taken place in the late 1820's. A small group of settlers were encamped near the Sangamon River and had constructed a crude liquor still and were hard at work making "moonshine" from corn alcohol. A group of Indians passed by where they were working and caught the attention of the moonshiners. No one knows the reason, but the settlers shot and killed the Indians and buried their bodies in a shallow ravine at the edge of the burying grounds. They heaped a number of stones on top of them and vanished. The makeshift grave can still be seen on the side of a hill in the southwest part of Greenwood Cemetery. The story of the settlers and the Indians has been largely forgotten over the years but folk legends have it that these murders may be the reason why the cemetery is so haunted.

It would be another ten years after this event before the general populace would begin to regard this area as a full-fledged cemetery. During the decade of the 1830's, it is believed that local settlers did use this area and legend has it that even a few runaway slaves who did not survive their quest for freedom were buried on the grounds under the cover of night.

In March 1857, the Greenwood Cemetery Association was organized and the cemetery was incorporated into the city of Decatur. By 1900, Greenwood had become the most fashionable place in Decatur in which to be buried. It had also become quite popular as a recreational park and it was not uncommon to see noontime visitors enjoying their lunch on the grassy hills. Unfortunately though, by the 1920's, the cemetery was broke and could no longer be maintained. It was allowed to revert back to nature and it wasn't long before the cemetery began to resemble a forgotten graveyard with overgrown brush, fallen branches and tipped and broken gravestones. Hundreds of graves were left unattended and allowed to fall into disrepair. The stories and legends that would "haunt" Greenwood for years to come had taken root in the desolate conditions that existed in the oldest section of the graveyard. Tales of wandering spirits and glowing apparitions began to be told about the cemetery and decay and decline came close to bringing about the destruction of the place. The cemetery became a forgotten spot in Decatur, remembered only as a spooky novelty.

The next decades however would bring a great change. At this point, the cemetery was nearly in ruins. The roads were now only partially covered mud and cinder tracks that were so deeply rutted that they were no longer passable. The oaks, which had added beauty to the cemetery, had now become its greatest curse. The falls of leaves, which had not been raked away in years, were knee-deep in some places. Fallen branches from the trees littered the grounds, which were overgrown and tangled with weeds and brush. Water, time and vandals had wreaked havoc on Greenwood's grave markers. Years of rain, harsh weather and a lack of care had caused many stones to fall at angles and many more were simply lost altogether. Others lay broken and damaged beyond repair, having given up the fight with the elements.

In 1957 though, ownership and operation of the cemetery was taken over by the city of Decatur and the township crews would now maintain it. The city could not handle the cost of the city's restoration, so a number of organizations and private individuals volunteered to donate time and labor to save it. The restoration was largely a success and despite a few setbacks, Greenwood Cemetery has managed to prosper over the years. Despite this, the place has not lost its eerie reputation and the stories of ghosts and the unexplained still mingle with fact and fiction, blending a strangeness that is unparalleled by any other location in the haunted heart of Illinois.

There have been nearly as many legends and strange stories told about Greenwood as there have been people buried here. They are the stories of the supernatural, of ghosts, phantoms and things that go bump in the night and what follows is a sampling of these eerie tales. Just don't forget, as you are reading them... keep looking back over your shoulder. You never know who might be coming up behind you!

The story of Greenwood's most famous resident ghost, the Greenwood Bride, begins around 1930 and concerns a young couple who was engaged to be married. The young man was a reckless fellow and a bootlegger, who was greatly disapproved of by his future bride's family. One summer night, the couple decided not to wait any longer to get married and made plans to elope. They would meet just after midnight, as soon as the young man could deliver one last shipment of whiskey and have enough money for their wedding trip. Unfortunately, he was delivering the bottles of whiskey when he was murdered.

The killers, rival businessmen, dumped his body into the Sangamon River, where two fishermen found it the next morning.

The young woman had gone to the arranged meeting place the night before and she had waited until daybreak for her lover. She was worried when she returned home and devastated when she later learned that he had been killed. She became crazed with grief and began tearing at her hair and clothing. Finally, her parents summoned the family doctor, who gave her a sedative and managed to calm her down.

She disappeared later that night, taking with her only the dress that she planned to wear in her wedding. She was found wearing the bridal gown the next day, floating face down in the river, near where her lover's body had been pulled ashore. She had taken her own life near the place where her fiancee's had been lost, perhaps hoping to find him in eternity.

A funeral was held and her body was laid to rest on a hill in Greenwood Cemetery. It has been said however, that she does not rest here in peace. As time has passed, dozens of credible witnesses have reported encountering the "Greenwood Bride" on that hill in the cemetery. They claim the ghost of a woman in a glowing bridal gown has been seen weaving among the tombstones. She walks here with her head down and with a scrap of cloth gripped tightly in her hand. Occasionally, she raises it to her face, as if wiping away tears.

Could this sad young woman still be searching for the spirit of her murdered lover? No record remains as to where this man was laid to rest, so no one knows where his spirit may walk. Perhaps he is out there somewhere, still looking for the young woman that he was supposed marry many years ago?

There have been many accounts of ghosts and spirits in Greenwood Cemetery that are not of the friendly variety and a number of anecdotes like the one that follows. It is a good example of the kind of story that has been told about Greenwood for years. The first accounts come from the 1920's, when the cemetery was an easy shortcut for those people who lived in the south end of the city. Rundown neighborhoods circled the graveyard in those days and it was often quicker to cut through the graveyard at night than take the longer route around it. On many occasions, these late night visitors told of hearing footsteps following along behind them as they walked along. Often the phantom footsteps would crunch in the leaves or disturb the tall grass as the unseen entity passed by.

One such story took place about two decades ago. A man was cutting through the cemetery one winter's night on his way to a friend's house. He was walking along a cemetery roadway when he heard the distinctive sound of hard-soled shoes following behind him. He looked back several times, but saw no one in the gloom. Finally, unnerved by the continuing sound, he veered from the paved road and set off across the cemetery grounds. The sounds followed him! Although his pursuer was still unseen, he could hear their footsteps pounding behind him, sinking through the hard crust of the snow. The footsteps got closer and closer.... but whoever was chasing him remained invisible!

Finally, he arrived at his friend's house, breathless and scared. It wasn't long though before his friend managed to calm him down and to make him realize that the so-called "chase" had been all in his mind. To prove the point, his friend accompanied him to the cemetery the next morning. They soon found the place where the man had left the road and got quite a surprise when they examined the surface of the snow! They easily found the man's footprints, but behind them was a second set of tracks that followed the first to the edge of the cemetery... then abruptly disappeared!

Another strange entity of Greenwood is no less mysterious for the fact that it made a single appearance more than 20 years ago. In fact, this one may be even more frightening!

Jack Gifford, a former Decatur resident, told me about a night when he decided to venture alone into the cemetery. He waited until after dark and then climbed the back fence. That night was in 1977, but Gifford has not been back to Greenwood since then!

He walked out among the tombstones, hoping to make his way by the light of the moon. He crossed the road and started up a small hill, then spotted a figure standing among the gravestones a short distance away. Gifford froze in his tracks, sure that he was about to be caught. The cemetery closes at sunset and he knew that he could be arrested for trespassing. He ducked behind the largest tombstone that he could find and decided to wait until the other man walked away.

After waiting a few minutes, he heard nothing, so he decided to look and see if the man was still standing there. He poked his head around the end of the stone and saw that he was still in the same spot. The man appeared to be staring at something, but he wasn't looking in Jack's direction. Gifford described the man as very tall, thin and rather ordinary-looking. He said that the man then turned slowly around, facing in his direction. "But he didn't really turn," Jack corrected himself. "He just seemed to rotate... and that was when I saw his eyes!"

The mysterious man looked toward where he hid behind the tombstone and Gifford saw that he was staring with what appeared to be empty eye sockets!

"They were like black holes.. but they sorta glowed a little, like the moon was shining through the back of his head," he told me and he chuckled self-consciously as if he were embarrassed by his suggestion. "I took off running then and I don't have any idea if the man chased me, but he wouldn't have caught me anyway!"

One of the cemetery's most enduring legends is the story of the "ghost lights" that appear on the south side of the burial grounds. These small globes of light have been reported here for many decades and are still reported today. I saw these lights myself a few years back and while I have no logical explanation for what they are, or why they appear here, the lore of the cemetery tells a strange and tragic story.

The legend tells of a flood that occurred many years ago, most likely around 1900-1905, which wiped out a portion of the cemetery. The Sangamon River, located just south of the cemetery, had been dammed in the late 1800's and was often prone to floods. During one particularly wet spring, the river overflowed its banks and washed into the lower sections of the cemetery. Tombstones were knocked over and the surging water even managed to wash graves away and to force buried caskets to the surface. Many of them, as these were the days before Lake Decatur had been formed, went careening downstream on the swollen river.

Once the water receded, it took many days to find the battered remains of the coffins that had been washed down the river and many were never found at all. For some time after, farmers and fishermen were startled to find caskets, and even corpses, washing up on river banks some miles away. There were many questions as to the identities of the bodies and so many of them were buried again in unmarked and common graves. These new graves were placed on higher ground, up on the southern hills of Greenwood.

Since that time, it has been said that the mysterious lights have appeared on these hills. The stories say that the lights are the spirits of those whose bodies washed away in the flood. Their wandering ghosts are now doomed to search forever for the place where their remains are now buried.

Dozens of trustworthy witnesses have claimed to see the "spook lights" on the hill, moving in and out among the old, weathered stones. The mystery of the lights has managed to elude all those who have attempted to solve it. Many have tried to pass them off as reflections from cars passing over the lake... but what of sightings that date back to before Lake Decatur ever existed? In those days, a covered bridge over the Sangamon River took travelers along the old county highway and for many years, not a single automobile crossed it, as motorcars had not yet come to Decatur.

Whether the cause is natural or supernatural, the lights can still be seen along the edge of the graveyard today. Want to see them for yourself? Seek out the south hills of Greenwood some night by finding the gravel parking lot that is located across the road from the cemetery fence. Here, you can sit and observe the hills. You have to have a lot of patience, and may even have to make more than one trip, but eventually, you will probably be lucky enough to see the "ghost lights". It's an experience that you won't soon forget!

Located on the edge of the forest that makes up Greenwood's northwest corner is an old burial plot that sits upon a small hill. This is the plot of a family named "Barrackman" and if you approach this piece of land from the east, walking along the cemetery's narrow roads, you will find a set of stone steps that lead to the top of a grassy hill. There are four, rounded stones here, marking the burial sites of the family. Little is known about the Barrackman's, other than the four members of this family are buried in Greenwood. No records exist about who they were, when they may have lived here or even about what they may have accomplished in life. We simply know their names, father, mother, son and his wife, as they are inscribed on the identical tombstones. As mentioned, two of the stones bear the names of the Barrackman women, and although no one really knows for sure... it may be one of these two women who still haunts this burial plot!

According to many accounts, collected over the years from dozens of people who never knew one another, a visitor who remains in the cemetery as the sun is going down may be treated to an eerie, and breathtaking sight. According to the story, the visitor is directed to the Barrackman staircase as dusk falls on the graveyard. It is said that a semi-transparent woman in a long dress appears on the stone steps. She sits there on the staircase with her head bowed and appears to be weeping, although she has never been heard to make a sound. Those who do get the chance to see her, never see her for long. She always inexplicably vanishes as the sun dips below the horizon. She has never been seen in the daylight hours and never after dark... only just at sunset.

Who is this lonely woman and why does she haunt the staircase and the Barrackman graves? There are some who suggest she may have been a member of the family buried here, but what could have brought her back to her burial site? I tend to favor the idea that she may have been another person entirely, who found peace on this staircase and came to the place during her lifetime to weep for someone who died and was buried nearby. Most likely, we will never know for sure just who she is or what brings her here, although she is still seen today. Perhaps one day she will break her silence and speak to some unsuspecting passerby, who just manages to get a glimpse of her before she fades away into the night.

Located on a high, desolate hill in the far southwest corner of Greenwood Cemetery is a collection of identical stone markers, inscribed with the names of the local men who served, and some who died, during the brutal days of the Civil War. The silence of this area is deafening. Visitors stand over the remains of some of the city of Decatur's greatest heroes and the bloody victors of the war. But not all of the men buried here served under the Stars and Stripes of the Union Army....

There are dark secrets hidden here.....

During the years of the Civil War, a great many trains passed through the city of Decatur. It was on a direct line of the Illinois Central Railroad, which ran deep into the south. The line continued north and connected to a railroad that went to Chicago. Here, it reached Camp Douglas, a prison for Confederates who were captured in battle. Many trains came north carrying Union troops bound for Decatur and beyond. Soldiers aboard these trains were often wounded, sick and dying. Occasionally, deceased soldiers were taken from the trains and buried in Greenwood Cemetery, which was very close to the train tracks. These men were buried in the cemetery and the citizens of Decatur marked their graves with honor. But that wasn't always the case....

On many occasions, trains came north bearing Confederate prisoners who were on their way to the camp near Chicago. These soldiers were not treated so honorably. Often, Confederates who died were unloaded from the train and buried in shallow, unmarked graves in forgotten locations. Most of these soldiers were unknown victims of gunshot and disease and many were past the point of revealing their identity. These men will never be known and their families will never have discovered what became of them after they departed for the battlefields of war. Those men are now silent corpses scattered about the confines of Greenwood Cemetery.

Why was there such a hatred for the Confederacy in Decatur? Besides being the home of the 116th Illinois Regiment, it seemed that nearly everyone in the city had a friend or relative in the Union army. A number of places in Decatur were also used as stations on the "Underground Railroad", which means that the abolitionists also had a stronghold here. This was the reason, in 1863, when a prison train holding southern prisoners pulled into Decatur, it was given the kind of reception that it was. The stories say the train was filled with more than 100 prisoners and that many of them had contracted yellow fever in the diseased swamps of the south.

The Union officers in charge of the train had attempted to separate the Confederates who had died in transit, but to no avail. Many of the other men were close to death from the infectious disease and it was hard to tell which men were alive and which were not. They called for wagons to come to a point near the cemetery but no one would answer the summons. Several soldiers were dispatched and a group of men and wagons were commandeered in the city. The bodies were removed from the train and taken to Greenwood Cemetery. They were unloaded here and their bodies were stacked at the base of a hill in the southwest corner of the graveyard. This location was possibly the least desirable spot in the cemetery. The hill was so steep that many of the grave diggers had trouble keeping their balance. It was the last place that anyone would want to be buried and for this reason, the enemies of the Union were placed there.

Ironically, years later, the top of this same hill would be fashioned into a memorial for Union soldiers who died in battle and for those who perished unknown.

The men from the city hastily dug shallow graves and tossed the bodies of the Confederates inside. It has been said that without a doctor present, no one could have known just how many of the soldiers had actually died from yellow fever.... were all of those buried here actually dead? Many say they were not, some of them accidentally buried alive, and this is why the area is the most haunted section of Greenwood.

To make matters worse, many years later, spring rains and flooding would cause the side of the hill itself to collapse in a mudslide and further disturb the bodies of these men. Not only did the Confederate remains lie scattered about in the mud, but the disaster also took with it the bodies of Union men who had been laid to rest in the memorial section at the top of the hill. This further complicated matters, as now, no had any idea how to identify the bodies. In the end, the remains were buried again and the hill was constructed into terraces to prevent another mudslide in the future. The bodies were placed in the Civil War Memorial section and the graves were marked with stones bearing the legend of "Unknown US Soldier". Sadly, it will never be known just who these men may be.

But what causes this section of the cemetery to be considered as haunted? Psychic impressions from the past or angry spirits? Some people believe that it may be both as investigations, and reports from eight decades, have revealed unexplainable tales, and strange energy, lingering around this hill. Visitors who have come here, many of them knowing nothing about the bizarre history of this place, have told of hearing voices, strange sounds, footsteps in the grass, whispers, cries of torment and some even claim to have been touched or pushed by unseen hands.

There are also the reports of the soldiers themselves returning from the other side of the grave. Accounts have been revealed over the years that tell of visitors to the cemetery actually seeing men in uniform walking among the tombstones... men that are strangely transparent.

The most stunning tale was reported a few years ago and was told to me first-hand. It happened that a young man was walking along the road in the back corner of the cemetery. He saw a man standing on the top of the hill, who beckoned to him. The boy walked up to him and was surprised to see that he was wearing tattered gray clothing which was very dirty and spotted with what looked like blood. The man looked at the boy oddly and he wore an expression of confusion on his face.

"Can you help me?", the man asked softly of the boy. "I don't know where I am..... and I want to go home."

Before the boy could answer, the man simply vanished.

- CHAPTER SIX -

GHOSTS OF SPRINGFIELD

HISTORY & HAUNTINGS OF THE PRAIRIE CAPITAL

It is portentous and a thing of state;
that here at midnight, in our little town;
a mourning figure walks, and will not rest;
near the old courthouse pacing up and down...

**VACHEL LINDSAY FROM
ABRAHAM LINCOLN WALKS AT MIDNIGHT**

As the capital of Illinois, Springfield boasts more connections to the history of American than perhaps any other area of the state. As the city that launched Abraham Lincoln into the presidency, there is much to be proud of here. Springfield is also a beautiful city, with our grand state capitol building and stately mansions, and a place that is historically rich, both in regional history and in its ties to the supernatural.

The ghostly elements of the city include everything from a former governor who is believed to still walk in his home, a Springfield socialite who turned an architectural landmark into a haven for spirits and even contains spirited spots connected to the supernatural life of President Lincoln himself. Springfield can be a strange and foreboding place, which allows it to fit in well in the "haunted heart of Illinois".

The frontiersmen were the first to arrive in the Springfield area, coming shortly after the Native Americans who abandoned it. The Indians may have vanished, but they left their mark behind with names like "Sangamo", which they had dubbed the immediate region and "Saquimont", which was their name for the Sangamon River.

Henry Funderburk of South Carolina was the first settler to arrive in the area. He had come north through the Cumberland Gap in 1808 and purchased land holdings belonging to Andrew Jackson in Tennessee. In 1815, he continued on north and west to Illinois, settling in St. Clair County, just east of St. Louis. Two years later, he moved his family north to the Sangamon River region and built a home in the Cotton Hill Township.

Soon, other settlers followed, including William Nelson and a frontiersman from Alton named Robert Pulliam. Several other families followed them and a small settlement was started. The first church, which doubled as a school, was built in 1821. The first blacksmith shop was built that same year and a grain mill soon followed, turning the small settlement into a thriving community.

The small town, although growing, was still rough in those years and consisted mostly of log cabins with dirt floors. In spite of that, it was chosen to be the county seat for the new county of "Sangamon" in 1821. The exact site of the town was chosen when a wooden stake was driven into a field belonging to a John Kelly. It lay close to Spring Creek, so they chose the name of "Springfield".

The new town soon gained its first jail and a courthouse, followed by a store that stocked general goods, along with flour, salt and whiskey. The store was owned by Elijah Iles, who was instrumental in the initial growth of the city. He was responsible for laying out the first streets and he named them after Jefferson, Washington and Adams. Unfortunately, none of the early settlers, including Elijah Iles, actually owned the land they were living on and in 1823, it was all bought up by a man named Pascal Enos. Immediately, he and his cohorts platted the city and then changed the name of it to "Calhoun", in honor of South Carolina senator, John C. Calhoun. The city would retain this name until 1825, when the senator became unpopular among voters. Once he fell out of favor, the name "Springfield" was resumed.

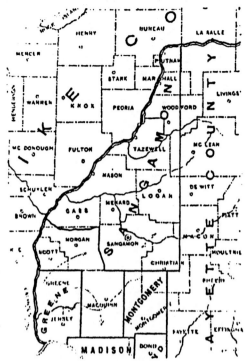

Sangamon County's Original Boundaries extended over 4,000 square miles in 1821.

The city grew slowly through the 1820's, mostly because of a struggle with inadequate transportation. There were no bridges built in the county until 1835 and farmers were losing money trying to transport grain to market. The roads were nearly impassable and Springfield was virtually cut off from outside markets. To make matters worse, then came the disastrous winter of 1830. As mentioned earlier in the chapter, this winter was incredibly brutal and Springfield, like the rest of Central Illinois, lost all contact with the outside world. When spring finally arrived, the settlers realized that new forms of travel would be essential if the city was going to survive.

In January 1832, the answer to the city's transportation problems arrived and Springfield became a booming river town... at least for a very short time. In March, a steamer called the "Talisman" came slowly up the uncharted Sangamon River. It was owned by a local man named Vincent Bogue and his plan was to create a water route between Springfield and St. Louis.

Citizens lined the riverbanks and parties were held in honor of Bogue and the steamer's captain, JW Pollock. Unfortunately, before the steamer could be unloaded, the water level of the river dropped and the boat could not be turned around. The "Talisman" was forced to back downstream and a dam ended up having to be destroyed to make room for her to pass. Mysteriously (or perhaps not, depending on your point of view) the steamer burned shortly after arriving back in St. Louis. Needless to say, both Pollock and Bogue vanished without a trace. In the end, it was learned that the whole scheme had been financed solely with credit.

The residents of Springfield were crushed as their dreams of riverboats and prosperity faded away. Their concerns would be for nothing however, as the following few years brought the arrival of the railroad and plans for new roads and bridges.

The city of Springfield was officially incorporated on April 2, 1832. The city seemed on the verge of new growth but all of that was momentarily forgotten by the outbreak of the Black Hawk War. This minor event in Illinois history has been all but forgotten by time, save for the participation of a young man named Abraham Lincoln. Despite its obscurity now, it sent the men of Springfield into action in 1832. A party of 600 local men was sent to the northwestern part of the state to defend it against Black Hawk and his warriors, but few of the area men saw action. In fact, years later, Lincoln would make light of his military service and state that the closest he came to death was being hungry.

Illinois State Capitol Building (1837)

One man from Springfield, named James D. Henry, did become a hero in the small war and was widely acclaimed for his deeds. A ball was held in his honor upon his return to Springfield and two years later, he was nominated to run for governor. Campaigning was done in his name in various locations but all the while, Henry was in New Orleans, dying from tuberculosis. He died in March 1834, several weeks before Springfield citizens stopped holding nomination meetings on his behalf.

By the 1830's, Illinois was becoming a largely settled state and a great effort was started to move the state capital, which was then located in Vandalia, to a city that was further north. The city of Illiopolis, which claims to be exact center of the state, was considered as were Alton, Jacksonville and Peoria. After much debate, Springfield earned the title. In 1837, the capital was officially moved and plans were drawn up for a Greek Revival style building. It was eventually constructed and replaced the old courthouse in the center of the Springfield public square.

From that point on, all of the politics in Illinois began to center around Springfield. Leading lawyers arrived to use the local court systems, lobbying for power and upward mobility. Many new businesses came to the city, including fine hotels and restaurants, and new construction began to spread wealth to all corners of the city. Springfield soon became the most influential city in the state, rivaling all others for news, parties and information. The days of the frontier settlement were finally over.

In just a couple of decades, Springfield had turned into a major city and in 1849, a new city government was formed under a Board of Justices. The new leaders had much to contend with. Along with the growth came many problems, like deadly outbreaks of cholera; unpaved streets; and a legion of wild hogs, which would remain a constant nuisance for years to come. Apparently, these once domesticated animals had gone wild and they began breeding in the streets like alley cats. They would plague the city for another 50 years, despite their presence being outlawed in 1852.

That same year marked the foundation of the Illinois State University in Springfield, followed by a public school system two years later. Debate societies, literary groups and of course, political societies, soon appeared, as did the city's first library. Shortly after the library came into existence, it came under fire from local religious groups. The churches banned the reading of novels and the library was forced to close down. It did not re-open for ten years and did not become a public library again until 1886.

The city continued to grow and saw many improvements, however it remained a rough and unattractive town. None of the streets were paved and in warm weather, a coating of dust settled on everything in the vicinity of them. In wet weather, the streets became a nightmare of mud and slush and, between dodging stray hogs, were impossible to navigate. Unbelievably, they would not be paved until the

1880's.

Springfield became the center of the nation's attention in 1860 when two of Illinois' most famous politicians squared off for the country's highest office. The campaign of 1860 pitted Abraham Lincoln against Stephen Douglas and their debated rocked the city and state. Local sentiment was divided equally between the two men and while Lincoln won the election, he lost in Sangamon County and only carried the city of Springfield by 69 votes.

The first rumblings of the Civil War marked Lincoln's arrival in Washington in 1861. Illinois governor Richard Yates began recruiting troops from around Illinois and Springfield soon exceeded its quota of volunteers. Camp Yates was established at the old fairgrounds and enlisted men arrived regularly. The camp was so close to the city that local residents soon asked to have it moved to a more peaceable distance. The new military base was set up near Clear Lake, about six miles away. The camp was named for state treasurer William Butler and became a cash source for liquor dealers and prostitutes. In fact, a nearby brothel run by Lucinda Taylor became known as "Camp Taylor", thanks to the fact that it catered almost exclusively to soldiers.

In 1862, Camp Butler was turned into prison camp for Confederate soldiers. The prisoners were eventually moved, thanks to protests from local southern sympathizers, but not before the camp became a national cemetery. There were hundreds of prisoners buried on the grounds before the war ended. The Civil War finally ended in 1865 but Springfield's relief turned to dismay when word arrived that President Lincoln, the city's native son, had been assassinated.

After the war, the state decided to construct a new capitol building to replace the crowded structure from 1837. The new project began in 1868 and took nearly 20 years to complete. The structure was massive and stood more than 400 feet wide with a dome rising 325 feet into the sky. Illinois convicts did all of the stone work and train cars hauled marble, over 20 million bricks and more than 5 million pounds of iron for the construction.

Springfield continued to grow and with this growth came new demand for housing outside of the city limits. The city implemented mule-drawn streetcars to connect the downtown area with the new housing districts. Later, electric streetcars replaced these slow-moving vehicles. There were also demands for refinements and entertainment. Fashionable dinners at the Leland Hotel or an evening at Chatterton's Opera House became socially acceptable for members of the upper class while those of more modest means enjoyed the taverns, dance halls, traveling theater groups and skating rinks.

Not surprisingly, the high times of wealth and growth in Springfield brought new problems to the city in the form of crime, corruption and vice. Before a massive reform movement would change the city government in 1911, Springfield would be known all over the state for its political corruption and crime. It would also gain national attention for one of the bloodiest race riots in history.

The local government was rife with scandal and the offices of the city leaders were riddled with corruption. One notable example was the Utilities Department. The city's electric plant had been leased to a private company and when the Springfield city council decided to end the contract and take back the plant, the company refused. Finally, the Mayor sent the police to recapture the plant for the city. Thankfully, the siege ended without bloodshed.

The gambling and the vice of the era thrived in places like the Empire Saloon, which was known as a favorite night spot for politicians, gamblers and thrill-seekers. Next door was the Empire Theater, which featured burlesque shows and vaudeville every night. The corruption in the city government allowed the saloons and the "red light" district to operate unchecked until 1917, when the city outlawed alcohol. Even then, it would be several years after before the crime areas were actually wiped out.

The conditions and the segregation of the city's neighborhoods added fuel to the volatile mix of Springfield. The area east of downtown had been in decline since the 1880's, particularly in the area near Eighth and Washington Streets. Rows of ramshackle houses and buildings, made up mostly of gambling dens and brothels, were referred to as the "Badlands". This area did little to encourage new residents or new businesses.

On the far east side of the city were the modest homes of the laborers, mainly Irish, while the Germans lived to the north. The black residents were mainly located on Springfield's poor, near east side and it was in this neighborhood where the city's greatest shame took place. It was an event that would bloody the history of Springfield forever and would lead to the formation of the NAACP.

To set the scene, the reader must understand that many northern cities, in the early part of the century, saw a huge population growth of poor blacks from the South and of uneducated whites who worked hard labor jobs for low pay. The competition for these jobs was fierce and often the white laborers spoke out against the blacks and fostered a hatred that sometimes erupted into racial violence.

On a hot August night in 1908, the newspapers reported that a black man had attacked a woman named Mrs. Mabel Hallam in her home while her husband was at work. She would later admit that she invited the "assailant" into her home and that, to make matters worse, he was actually white. Unfortunately, her confession came too late to stop the violence, terror and bloodshed.

A black man named George Richardson was soon arrested for the rape. Hours later, a crowd of several hundred white laborers gathered at the Sangamon County Jail. Tempers flared in the summer heat as each man claimed to be seeking justice for the attack on Mabel Hallam. The mob demanded that George Richardson, who was being held inside, be turned over to them for hanging. County Sheriff Charles Werner refused to release Richardson. He was sure that the heat, and a generous amount of alcohol, had incited the mob so he devised a plan to cool things down until the men grew tired of standing in the street, or the booze wore off, whichever came first.

At that time, there were few automobiles in the city but Werner managed to borrow one and he spirited Richardson out of town. Instead of cooling things off, Werner's escape enraged the mob even further. They marched to the downtown restaurant that was operated by the owner of the car Werner had borrowed and demolished it. Then, they seized the automobile itself, wrecked it and set it on fire. From there, the mob moved east on Washington Street, looting stories, taverns and businesses in the mostly black area. Soon, the mob turned northeast, into the heart of the black neighborhood, and started fires in every home along the street. One man who tried to stop them was Scott Burton, a black barber. He was shot more than 40 times.

When it was realized that the riot was too much for city police officers to handle, the governor called in the Illinois State militia. Nearly 4000 soldiers mobilized and move into the streets of Springfield. The mob quickly dispersed, only to form again the following day and continue the rampage. The next night ended with the murder of an elderly black man.

After the second day, the riot abruptly ended. In its wake, it left two black men dead, more than 100 injured, 40 black homes burned to the ground, 15 businesses destroyed, and five white men who were accidentally killed by other whites. No investigation was ever launched into the riot and to this day, not a single person has ever been punished.

African-American leaders across the country were enraged and spoke out against lawless attacks on black people, especially in the city made famous by Lincoln, the mad who had freed the slaves less than four decades before. The protests and awareness that followed the riot caused the formation of the group known as the National Association for the Advancement of Colored People. The organization still exists today.

Rightfully, the riot was the final blow to lawlessness and crime in the city. Many of the residents were disgusted by the conditions that had allowed the riot to happen. These same folks believed that the best way to get rid of such influences was to introduce a new one, religion. In February 1909, fiery evangelist Billy Sunday came to Springfield and held more 500 services in the city. It was reported that he converted more that 4000 people from their lawless ways.

At the same time, a reform candidate named John S. Schnepp was elected mayor and he began ridding city hall of corrupt officials. The accounts of the local waterworks, which were considered bankrupt, were examined and cash was shown to have been pilfered from the account for years. One accused official disappeared and another committed suicide in the aftermath of the scandal. These events launched a new era of government for the city. The crackdown on vice and prostitution continued in

Springfield for years and in 1917, a law was passed enforcing prohibition on the city. This, combined with the "house cleaning" at city hall made newspaper headlines. What followed was a series of hearings at the Leland Hotel that resulted in indictments for many well-placed criminals.

The city endured World War I and even the Great Depression, which came about thanks to the stock market crash of 1929. Within a few months, the city was in chaos. Many citizens were at poverty level already but turned out to see President Herbert Hoover when he visited Springfield, hoping for some comfort. Unfortunately, his speech did little to assure them that better times were ahead, thanks to the fact that there were simply no jobs to be had in Central Illinois. The unemployment office was unable to keep up with the 850 new claims it was receiving each month. Lines of people were reported to circle St. John's Hospital when it began providing a "soup kitchen" for breakfast and dinner. Finally, the election of Franklin Delano Roosevelt as president brought a glimmer of hope, especially to local charities that began to receive some federal aid.

In 1932 however, disaster nearly struck Springfield with the closure of the Ridgely Farmer's Bank, the most prominent banking establishment in the city since 1859. There had been a panic run on area banks and the Farmer's Bank was unable to come up with enough cash to cover the record number of emergency withdrawals.

And this was not only happening in Springfield. Banks were shutting down all over the country, so President Roosevelt declared a "bank holiday", effectively stopping what could have crippled the entire nation. A special council of Springfield bankers, city officials and businessmen averted the disaster in the city by issuing a special "scrip" that could be used as money until the banks opened again.

The bank disaster was not the only shocking event of this period. The county had also been hard hit by the decline in the coal market. As industry dwindled, so did the demand for coal. Area miners soon found themselves out of work as cheaper coal was brought in from non-union mines in other parts of the state.

John L. Lewis, president of the United Mine Workers of America, urged the miners to sign new contracts, which offered lower pay but insured their jobs. Most of them did but the strongest opposition to this was in Springfield, ironically the union president's home district. He traveled to Central Illinois to speak to the miners and negotiated with them throughout the summer of 1932. They finally voted, but rumors quickly spread that the vote would turn down the final offer. The ballots were on their way to a Marine Bank vault to be counted and on the way, they vanished. Angry miners, believing that Lewis had stolen the ballots, broke off from the union and started their own organization, the Progressive Mine Workers of America. Violence followed and during a riot outside the Leland Hotel, a police detective was killed.

War broke out between the two unions all over Central Illinois, including in both Springfield and Decatur. A number of men and women were arrested and injured in the fighting and several were even killed. Eventually, a troubled calm settled in and peace reigned in the mines. Although the coal industry has continued to decline over the years, the violence of 1932 has not been repeated.

The 1930's slowly rumbled past in Springfield and the economy continued to improve. The hard times of the early part of the decade made citizens eager to escape reality and be entertained. Movie theaters opened and so did local night clubs. Spots like the Blue Danube and the Lake Club became famous in down state Illinois as popular gambling spots and places to catch big name acts like Guy Lombardo and Bob Hope.

Springfield entered World War II with a vengeance. Young men stampeded the recruiting offices after the bombing of Pearl Harbor. Meanwhile, women's groups and civic organizations organized drives for scrap metal and war bonds, netting over $11 million. Local manufacturers produced over $5 million in war supplies and the government opened the Sangamon Ordnance Plant near Illiopolis to make munitions. In conjunction with wartime rationing, public transportation became a way of life for many in Springfield. The city's aged streetcars had been replaced with city buses a few years before the war, but complaints about overcrowding were still common.

The city went wild at war's end as the new era held a promise of peace and prosperity. That era continues today as Springfield keeps growing and expanding to meet the demands of new generations. It is hard to imagine that this is the same city that started out as a wooden stake in John Kelly's field and feared it would never grow because no river could navigate to its shores.

FRANK LLOYD WRIGHT'S DANA HOUSE

The Dana House, which was designed by the architect Frank Lloyd Wright, is located in the heart of Springfield's historical district. It was built for one of Springfield's leading citizens, Mrs. Susan Lawrence Dana, and while the "official" word on the place states that it is not haunted, strange things have occurred here. In addition, the house provides the city of Springfield with a link to the history of the supernatural and a connection to those who communicated with the dead. The house itself may not provide a link between this world and the next, but it cannot be denied that Susan Lawrence Dana certainly believed that it did!

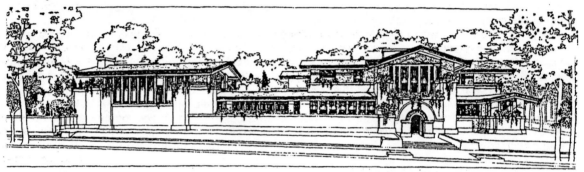

An Illustration of the Dana House as it appeared in 1910

The Dana House was started in 1902 and upon its completion became a symbol of culture and high society in the city. Following in the wake of a series of tragic losses by Susan Lawrence Dana. The house managed to provide her with a distraction and a purpose in life. It also was a memorial to the man whose money created the place, her father, RD Lawrence.

Rheuna Drake Lawrence was a successful businessman and contractor who came to Springfield in 1856. A few years later, he married Mary Agnes Maxcy and they had a child that same year that lived for only a short time. A second child was born in October 1862 and she was named Sue C. Lawrence. (Her middle initial later transformed her name into "Susie").

The Lawrence family thrived in Springfield after the Civil War and invested heavily in expanding rail service to the city. They built a prominent Italianate villa at the corner of Fourth and Wright Streets and by the time of Susan's wedding in 1883, RD Lawrence was a very wealthy man. On December 4 of that year, Susie Lawrence married Edwin Ward Dana, a real estate investor from Lincoln, Illinois.

After the wedding, the newlyweds moved to Minneapolis, where Edwin went into business on his own. Unfortunately, he did not fare well and they moved to Chicago in 1893, where he made himself the president of the newly formed Western Business Agency. He claimed the company had branches in nine western cities, but within a year, it had all fallen apart. Disgraced, he had no choice but to borrow money from his father-in-law and finally, by late 1894, he and Susie were back in Springfield.

Lawrence quickly put Edwin to work, sending him to Oregon to manage some mines that he owned there. One of the mines he was working in closed down and he moved on to Leland, Oregon. Susie stayed behind in the town of Grant's Pass, where living conditions were better. Within a month, she was on her way back to Illinois, this time bringing Edwin's body with her. He had been hoisting ore when a harness snapped, causing a pulley arm to spin in reverse. It struck him in the chest and killed him. Susie was crushed. During her short marriage, she had buried not only her husband, but also two infants that she had been unable to carry to term. Within a few years, she would also bury her father as well.

On February 17, 1901, RD Lawrence died in his Springfield home. His death struck a tragic blow to the family but also left Susie with freedom and a financial windfall. As the new head of the household, Susie decided to build a grand new home for the family, which now consisted of her, her mother, her grandmother (who would pass away in August 1902) and her cousin, Flora Lawrence. In her search for a prestigious architect, she looked away from Springfield and toward the more metropolitan city of Chicago. She found the vitality she was looking for in a young designer who was just starting to make a name for himself, Frank Lloyd Wright.

Wright was born in 1867 and is considered today one of America's most famous architects. He was an innovative designer and far ahead of his time. He was the founder of the Prairie School of architecture, of which the Dana house is a prime example. The style was created around 1900 when most of America was living in box-shaped Victorian homes but it has remained popular in the "ranch" style home of today.

Wright was raised and educated in Wisconsin and spent his childhood on his mother's family farm. It was here that he learned to love nature and where he learned to combine architecture with the natural world. Wright moved to Chicago and Oak Park in the 1880's, studying under Louis Sullivan, before opening his own design firm in 1893. By the end of the century, his studio in Oak Park had become very well known in Chicago social circles.

Wright and his staff were intrigued by the idea that Susie Lawrence brought to their studio. The original intention had been to incorporate the old villa into the new house and provide a home and gallery for living and entertainment. In the end, only one room of the original house was used. Wright planned a Prairie House, which he believed was the home of the future. These houses are long and horizontally shaped with open spaces inside. They are also designed with furniture and windows that will not obstruct the interior in any way.

Construction was started in 1902 and would take two years to complete. Wright designed every aspect of the house from the furniture to the lights and design of the windows. In 1905, he would also design the Lawrence Memorial Library, which was connected to the house by way of a raised walkway. The Dana house was the first of Wright's designs to contain two-story rooms like the gallery, the dining room and the hall. The gallery was a reception room for entertaining and was connected by a covered passed that doubled as a conservatory.

The house itself is simply amazing. The principal common rooms were located on the main floor, while the bedrooms were upstairs. The staircases were all hidden, so as not to distract from the home's design and every room featured built-ins and specially constructed furniture. The interior walls were all cream-colored and crossed with fabulous woodwork. The library was constructed with built-in bookcases with glass fronts and beneath the walkway to the gallery were a billiards room and a bowling alley. Needless to say, there was not another house like it in Springfield, or anywhere else for that matter.

The house was completed in 1904 and Susan, as she began calling herself the year before, was exhausted, yet excited, about the prospect of the new house. Doubts began to creep in that summer and she began to worry about the house and money that she was spending to build it. To soothe her fears, she decided to try and get in touch with her dead father and to seek his approval, or at least his advice, on her affairs. She contacted a spirit medium who put her in touch with Lawrence and (surprise!) he expressed his delight with the new house.

This was when Susan began to realize the endless possibilities of Spiritualism and contact with the other side. While many of us many chuckle at these beliefs today, in those times, she was far from alone.

In the early part of the 1900's, the Spiritualist movement was a prominent force in America. Founded more than 50 years before, Spiritualism was based on the idea of life after death and that communication between the living and the dead can, and does, take place. Messages that came from the spirit world were passed along through a "medium", who could speak with the dead while in a trance and often produced messages and writings that allegedly came from the spirits. Other mediums claimed to be able to produce physical phenomena while in a trance state, including knockings, lights, sounds, music, ghostly voices and even spirit materializations. Hundreds of these mediums flourished during the heyday of Spiritualism.

Most of them practiced their craft during "seances". During these sittings, all sorts of strange events could take place from table lifting to ghosts appearing and speaking to loved ones left behind. The seances always took place in dark or dimly lighted rooms because darkness took away all of the distractions and made it easier for the spirits to manifest. Of course, skeptics offered a simpler explanation for the darkness... it concealed the practice of fraud!

Like all branches of the occult, Spiritualism was not immune to deceptive practices. Over and over throughout the history of the movement, many people who were looking for miracles were taken advantage of and deceived. But not all of the phenomena was so easy to explain away! Because of this, the riddle of Spiritualism remains unsolved today, depending of course, on your point of view.

Regardless of whether or not it was all genuine, Susan Lawrence Dana was no eccentric. Spiritualism was a widely held and regarded belief for many years and it leaders included some of the most respected and influential people of the 1800's and early 1900's. Some of the believers included Sir Arthur Conan Doyle, Sir William Barrett, Elizabeth Barrett Browning, James Fenimore Cooper, Washington Irving, Henry Longfellow, James Greenleaf Whittier and many others.

Susan began hosting lavish parties during the holiday season of 1904 and followed the initial affairs with housewarmings for the Women's Club, parties for local children and residents of orphanages, dinners for residents of old-age homes and a gala for the families of the workers who built the house.

The busy holiday season took its toll on Susan and her mother. They traveled to the Caribbean that winter and relaxed in the Bahamas, Jacksonville and Palm Beach, Florida. They were on a train to Savannah, Georgia when Mrs. Lawrence suffered a heart attack and died.

Susan's life was now in chaos and seemed to be spinning out of control. She had now lost everyone she had ever loved. In desperation, she turned to the spirit world. Seances began to be held in her Springfield home on a regular basis and many of the guests were the elite of local society. Susan asked the spirits about many things, including asking for advice on financial matters and personal affairs. Her most desperate questions involved money because she never seemed to be able to grasp just how to handle it. She was already spending much more than her investments could possibly make. It was recorded in 1915 that she received about $10,000 income from some of her father's rental properties. Unfortunately, she had borrowed $132,000 for expenditures.

In spite of this, she continued to host expensive parties, sometimes scheduling several events on the same day. She also kept a full staff of servants employed, despite the fact that only she and her cousin Flora lived in the house.

In March 1912, Susan secretly married a concert singer from Denmark named Jorgen Constantin Dahl. This fueled the local gossip mill, as the young man was half Susan's age. Tragically, he died just one year later, leaving Susan once again alone. In 1915, she married again, this time to Charles Gehrmann, a native of Springfield. There is little indication of whether or not this marriage was happy as Susan continued with her many activities. Eventually, she and Gehrmann separated and she divorced him in 1930.

By this time, Susan was using the name Susan Lawrence Dana Joergen-Dahl Gehrmann, but regardless of what she called herself, she lived however she pleased. Susan became an advocate of women's rights and actively participated in the suffrage movement. In 1923, she was named as the Illinois chairman for the National Women's Party, a group working for the woman's right to vote.

Susan also continued her pursuit of the unknown. She collected a huge library of books on the occult, spirit contact, psychic healing and metaphysics. Her circle of other Springfield knowledge seekers often gathered in her home and called themselves the "Springfield Society of Applied Psychology". They later became the "Lawrence Metaphysical Center" in 1924, and three years later, in 1927, moved their meetings to a building downtown.

This move was a quiet signal that Susan was now living in reduced circumstances. Her money had finally run out and she had closed down the grand house. She and Flora, who was gravely ill, moved into the Lawrence cottage, located across the railroad tracks from the house. Susan cared for Flora and took her meals at a boarding house across the street.

Flora died in 1928, leaving Susan completely alone. She was now in poor health and lonely. She consulted mediums, as she had always done, and at the request of the spirits, changed her name to Susan Z. Lawrence. Susan also had friends who still cared for her and she kept in touch with Frank Lloyd Wright over the years. Sadly, their final meeting was canceled when Susan fell down the steps of the cottage and was injured. She wrote him a letter that stated a fraternal organization was thinking of buying the house. That sale never materialized.

By 1939, Susan's health was badly in decline and friends tried to get her to appoint a conservator for her estate. They had no success. Her financial affairs, always troubled, were now beyond repair. The Marine Bank in Springfield refused to foreclose on her however, thanks to their love for Susan and respect for her father. Regardless, it was no secret that she owed them more than $167,000, they simply didn't talk about it. No one wanted to embarrass the woman who had been so generous to the people of the city.

In May 1942, Susan entered St. John's Hospital and would never leave it. No time was wasted and that same afternoon, a court petition was filed that declared Susan incompetent and unable to handle her affairs. The court appointed attorney Earl Bice as conservator of the estate and a cousin from Chicago, Farnetta Radcliffe, as caretaker of Susan herself.

An inventory showed that Susan, despite her debts and mortgages, had faithfully kept all of her father's properties intact, including the Springfield buildings, the house, and even the abandoned mines in Colorado and Oregon. She also had an enormous amount of personal property that was estimated in value to around $75,000. The inventory list was 178 pages long, but foolishly handled. Things were given ridiculously low values by people who obviously had no idea what they were doing, appraising Frank Lloyd Wright furniture pieces at $10 and rare Japanese prints at $2.50. Obviously, the inventory was far off from the actual value of the estate.

An auction was held in July 1943 and ran for six days. The sale drew tourists and curiosity-seekers and the newspapers wrote of Susan's eccentric belongings. Sadly, her wonderful belongings, including rare artwork, photographic equipment, and incredible book collection, brought little money. The house itself was treated as an eyesore and the appraiser deemed it "undesirable". He stated that if anyone could be found to buy it, it would sell for less than $20,000. Unfortunately, he was right.

Charles C. Thomas, a book publisher, purchased the house later that same year for $17,500. The good news was that Thomas was familiar with Wright's work and he wrote the architect in 1943 and assured him the house was in good hands. The house was turned into the headquarters for Thomas Publishing Co. and the roof, walls and gutters were repaired before the company moved into the house in 1944.

Susan Lawrence passed away on February 20, 1946. It was reported that she was lucid and aware of her surroundings. It is unknown if she was ever told about the sale of her wonderful house and cherished books and belongings.

Charles Thomas died in August 1968 but the company stayed on in the house for another ten years. They had saved the house from ruin, but when they abandoned it in 1981, the place was badly in need of restoration. A chain-link fence surrounded the front terrace, the garden pool was gone, the bowling alley had been cut into tops for tables, the sand-finished walls had been painted, plus collectors and museum curators had bought up most of the original Wright pieces that had remained in the house.

Luckily, the governor of Illinois at that time, James R. Thompson, was an antique lover and fan of Frank Lloyd Wright. He supported a bill to purchase the house and to begin its restoration. The state took possession of the place in 1981 and began a three-year project to restore it to its condition in 1910. In addition to the work done on the house, much of the original furniture was recovered as well.

Today, the Dana House remains a tribute to both the architect Frank Lloyd Wright and the creator of the estate, Susan Lawrence Dana, who remains a patron to the haunted history of Central Illinois.

And that should be the end of the story, but it's not.

There is no question that the Dana House seems to have a haunted history of its own with its connections to Illinois Spiritualism. This is despite the fact that the foundation that manages the house insists the place is not haunted.... even though they have not always been able to explain the unusual events that have taken place there.

According to a story in the Springfield newspaper, the "State Journal-Register", the site superintendent, Don Hallmark, states that "this house is definitely not haunted", but even he had experienced a few strange goings-on here.

One evening, around 11:00 pm, he and his wife were securing the house for the night and were downstairs in the long corridor where the bowling alley is located. Hallmark had just gotten to the point in the hallway where the billiards room is located. "I heard a human hand clap," he told the newspaper reporter. "I about jumped out of my skin."

His wife also distinctly heard the sound of the clap and also realized there was no one else in the house. Hallmark then stated that he searched for broken plaster or a fallen toilet lid, but found nothing out of the ordinary. According to the story, he remained convinced that it had been the clapping of someone's hands.

A couple of years later, a light sconce suddenly fell from the wall for no reason. The sconce had been well secured over a lighting fixture and yet it somehow had unattached itself from the wall. "Unless someone fooled with it, there is no way it can fall off," Hallmark said in an interview. "As far as we know, no one touched it."

This was strange enough.... until someone reminded everyone that Susan Lawrence Dana had died 37 years before, on that very day. "It's a standing joke among us," Hallmark said, "that Susan still walks the halls, watching over the house that she loved."

Not haunted? For a house that isn't haunted, the place certainly seems to have some rather ghostly things going on there!

THE LAKE CLUB

The Lake Club had opened as a nightclub in 1940 but the building on Fox Bridge Road had seen many incarnations in the years prior to that, including as several restaurants and even a skating rink called the Joy Inn. In 1940, two dance promoters named Harold Henderson and Hugo Giovagnoli renovated the place and opened it for business.

The club soon became one of the hottest night spots in Illinois, drawing customers from all over the state. It boasted a raised dance floor, which was surrounded by a railing, curved walls and a swanky atmosphere that made patrons feel as though a New York club had been transported to the shores of Lake Springfield. The owners concentrated on bringing big name entertainment to the club and succeeded. Among the many top performers were Bob Hope, Ella Fitzgerald, Guy Lombardo, Pearl Bailey, Spike Jones, Nelson Eddy, Woody Herman, Mickey Rooney and many others. The constant stream of entertainers and big bands brought capacity crowds to the club every night. During the height of its popularity, the club even hosted a radio call-in show that broadcast music and entertainment all over the area.

The Lake Club thrived for nearly two decades, becoming known not only for its swinging entertainment, but for its first-rate gambling as well! Wealthy customers and the society elite of Springfield and Decatur frequented the club for the musical guests and for the billiard tables, craps and gaming tables, slot machines and card games also. This part of the club operated in secret in a back part of the building, known only to high rollers and special customers. However in December 1958, the golden days of the Lake Club came to an end. The partners had survived many setbacks over the years, from lawsuits to foreclosures, but the club would not survive the two undercover detectives who gained access to the gambling rooms that Christmas season.

The club was immediately shut down, although patrons continued dining and dancing while the actual raid was going on. The two state troopers who entered the gambling rooms were the first police officers to arrive, but many more followed. Newspaper accounts reported the police confiscated all sorts of gambling equipment including tables, dice, slot machines and large quantities of cash. The billiard tables were so large they had to be dismantled to get them out of the room.

Business began to falter in the wake of the raid and finally closed down in the 1960's. Giovagnoli blamed the crackdown on gambling as the reason, always maintaining that the entertainment had been just part of the club's appeal. However, he refused to give up. Despite his partner Harold Henderson passing away in 1977, Giovagnoli managed to open the club again in the 1970's with other parties managing different projects in the building. During this next popular time in the club's history, it was managed by Bill Carmean and Tom Blasko as a rock club. In 1980, it was leased by Pat Tavine, who also operated it as a rock club until 1988, when it closed down for good. Sadly, the Lake Club was destroyed by fire in 1992.

It was in August 1979 that the Lake Club, known in 1980 when the story came out as the Sober Duck Rock and Disco Club, gained national notoriety. It was at this time when the ghost of Albert "Rudy" Cranor was finally put to rest.

According to the many patrons and staff members who had experiences there, the haunting of the Lake Club first began in 1974. At the time, the club was in the midst of a revival in interest and the business was under the ownership of Tom Blasko and Bill Carmean, two Springfield men who were booking rock acts into the club. The building itself was still owned by Hugo Giovagnoli and Harold Henderson.

Bill Carmean was the first to notice that something strange was going on at the club. Both he and Tom Blasko had experienced some cold chills in the building, along with hearing odd sounds and getting the feeling of being watched in certain rooms. One afternoon, he came into the club and sat down at the bar with the lights off. Suddenly, he heard the sound of a piano being played in another room. Right away, he noticed that whoever was playing it was absolutely terrible. He got up from his seat and walked in to see who was playing so badly. As he stepped into the room, the piano stopped playing... because the room was empty.

Weird things continued to happen. Often on Monday nights, while Carmean would be in the building going over the weekend receipts, he would hear a door near the office open and then footsteps crossing the floor. He would jump from his seat to see who was there, but the hallway was always empty. Carmean also remembered a salesman visiting his office one evening when a glass flew off a table and hit the wall on the opposite side of the room. The salesman left in a hurry.

By 1976, the haunting had intensified and things began happening more often, and in front of more witnesses. A club bartender was pouring a drink one night when the glass in front of him suddenly shot up into the air and landed over his shoulder. A waitress also experienced the antics of the ghost one night when she went to serve a drink to a customer, only to find the glass inexplicably filled with chocolate! She would later insist the glass had been absolutely clean when she handed it to the bartender.

Carmean was also the first of the club's staff to guess the identity of the ghost who was plaguing the club. He recalled that a former employee had committed suicide in the building several years before. On a lark, he started calling the ghost by this man's name... Rudy.

Albert "Rudy" Cranor had worked at the Lake Club during its heyday of the 1950's. He was always described as being well liked and popular with the entertainers and the customers. He was also a very large man, well over 250 pounds, and he had snow-white hair. He was remembered as one of the club's most memorable characters and even 50 years later, I have spoken with people who remember him. They speak fondly of him and recall his as a nice man and their favorite bartender.

After the club fell on hard times following the gambling raid, Rudy also began experiencing some personal difficulties. He was a very private person, so no one really knew what was going on, but they did notice that he began to drink heavily while on the job. They also began to notice some changes in his personality and appearance. He seemed to be more tired than usual and dark circles had begun to appear under his eyes. Then one night he took sick and had to be rushed to the hospital. It took several men to carry him downstairs to the ambulance. He returned to the club after a two-week stay in the hospital, but he was never the same again.

On June 27, 1968, Rudy committed suicide with a high-powered rifle in one of the back rooms at the club. No one was ever sure why Rudy had killed himself, but regardless, he wouldn't stay gone for long. In a few short years, he would return to haunt his beloved club.

The strange events at the club continued in the form of weird antics and pranks, apparently carried out by the ghost of Rudy Cranor. One night, Tom Blasko placed a pile of tablecloths on an empty table and left the room. When he came back, the cloths were on the floor. He picked them up and left again, only to return moments later and find them once again on the floor. This was repeated several times until Blasko finally left them on the floor.

Employees and visiting musicians also reported strange occurrences like doors opening and closing by themselves; the sound of footsteps in empty rooms; a drink that lifted off a table and then dumped in a customer's lap; office equipment that operated on its own; feelings of being poked and prodded by unseen hands; and numerous other bizarre happenings.

A frightening event took place in the summer of 1979 when Barbara Lard, a waitress at the club, had an encounter with Rudy himself. She was working one evening and went to the bathroom behind the back office. As she came out, she glanced over the back bar and saw Rudy looking at her. She described what she saw as just a head, hanging there in space, and although she could see through it, the head appeared life-like. She said that this apparition had snow-white hair... and she had never known, heard about, or had even seen a photograph of, the late bartender. The apparition looked at her for a moment and then spoke, telling the waitress that one of the owners of the club was going to die. This was not a threat, Lard recalled later, but merely a warning.

The waitress ran out of the room in tears, visibly shaken and close to hysterics. Other staff members who saw her that night reported that she was very frightened and that she was not a person known for being hysterical or carried away about anything. Tom Blasko later stated that he went back into the room after Lard's encounter and claimed to feel the same bone-chilling cold that he always associated with Rudy's spirit.

Needless to say, Blasko and Carmean were more than a little unnerved by the ghost's warning. By this time, they had no doubt the ghost was real and that the club was genuinely haunted. Because of this, they also had no reason to doubt whether or not Barbara Lard's encounter had been real. Her description of the late Rudy Cranor had been too close to have been imagined. The two men waited and probably were more careful than usual when doing things like driving to work or climbing ladders. Then, two weeks after the incident, Harold Henderson, one of the original owners of the club, died at the age of 69. He was still the owner of the building itself and was an owner that Rudy would have known during his lifetime.

This incident would shake Blasko more than anyone else. He had spent two weeks living in fear for his life and he felt that it was time to get rid of the ghost if possible. Perhaps Rudy had been trying to be helpful with his warning, but Blasko didn't really care at this point. He contacted a woman he knew who was interested in the occult and she suggested that he contact a priest for help. This was easier said than done however! Blasko was a practicing Catholic, but when he contacted his parish priest, the man declined to become involved. He suggested that Blasko pray for Rudy on his own and Tom spent the next six months carrying a rosary around the club with him. But it didn't help.... Rudy was still there.

Finally, in August 1979, Blasko attended a high school class reunion and ran into one of his former classmates, Reverend Gary Dilley, a priest who now lived in Fort Worth, Texas. Tom mentioned the problems at the club to Father Dilley and the priest was intrigued. After some discussion, he agreed to come out to the club and take a look around. He said later that he believed Blasko was sincere about what he said was happening. He had known the man for many years and had never thought of Tom as the hysterical type.

After arriving at the club, Father Dilley also sensed something out of the ordinary there. He also experienced some unexplained cold chills and felt as if someone was watching him. "I also had the feeling that someone was trying to communicate with me," he said in a later interview.

The priest then questioned several of the club's employees and found that their stories were very similar and he knew they had not had time to compare notes before he spoke with them. He was convinced that something was going on, but he declined to do an "exorcism" of the club. To do that, the case would require a thorough investigation and permission from the local bishop, which he doubted that he would get. Instead, he decided to bless the place and pray there, hoping this would perhaps put Rudy to rest.

Father Dilley contacted two other priests to take part in the ceremony, Father John Corredato of Kankakee and Father Gerald Leahy of Griffin High School in Springfield. The three men were quick to point out that they were merely trying to bless the building, to clear out any negative spirits and to help at least one "very restless soul" to find peace. The three priests went from room to room in the club, blessing each with holy water and praying. They asked that any negative spirits depart from the building and they prayed specifically for Rudy Cranor. They entered the room in which he had committed suicide and prayed that his spirit be at rest.

So, was that the end of the haunting? Apparently, it was. The same people who considered the club to be haunted were now sure that Rudy had departed. The day of the religious ceremony was the last day when anyone was aware of Rudy's presence in the building. It seemed that the prayers and blessings had helped the bartender find his way to the other side. It certainly seems possible that Rudy may have chosen to stay behind in a place where he had many attachments in life. Perhaps the intervention of the priests was all he needed to be convinced to move on.

Once Rudy was gone, some staff members realized they hadn't minded his ghost as much as they had once thought. "In a way, I sorta miss Rudy," Tom Blasko said in a 1980 newspaper interview. "We were all fond of him. It's been pretty quiet since the priests were here... sometimes I wish that I hadn't asked them to come."

Whether he was missed or not, Rudy had finally found some peace.

THE YATES MANSION

On the edge of Springfield's Washington Park is another of the city's historic and beautiful homes. Its high roof peaks and stone tower loom up above the green hills of the park, making it a breathtaking and elegant structure. The house is known as the Yates Mansion and as beautiful as it is, it hides a few secrets too. You see, legend holds that something lurks within the confines of this extraordinary house. It is said that on the nights of the full moon, a ghostly figure paces back and forth across the floor of the attic turret room. He is a spirit, some say, that will never rest.

Few names have shaped the course of Springfield and Illinois history like the name of Yates. Henry Yates moved his family from Virginia to Illinois in 1831, settling just west of the Springfield area. His son, Richard Yates, was born in 1815 and was destined for an outstanding career in Illinois politics. He was elected to the state legislature in 1842 and retired from the US Senate in 1871.

In spite of all of the rest of his political career, he was best known as the governor of Illinois during the Civil War, a conflict during which he spent huge sums of his own money supplying clothing, food and medicine for Illinois troops. Governor Yates was widely regarded as the "soldier's friend". He often visited camps and hospitals to give encouragement and offer solace to soldiers from his home state. It was this governor who built the house near Washington Park and according to the legend, still haunts this house today.

He completed the place in 1905 and resided there for many years. In 1988, restoration was begun on the house by the John Noll family, who currently own the house and reside there. During the work, a number of unique and unusual aspects of the house were uncovered. One of them was a cobblestone fireplace that had previously been hidden by a marble slab. The fireplace is highlighted by the presence of two cannonballs that reportedly came from the Chattanooga Battlefield in Tennessee and were gifts to Governor Richard Yates. Legend has it that if a visitor holds each of the cannonballs at the same time and makes a wish, that wish will come true. Another unusual item can be found in the second floor master bedroom. The carved oak fireplace mantel here was once displayed in the original State Capitol building. It was removed in the 1890's when the building was converted to steam heat. There is also a bedroom on this floor that was once a religious chapel. It had been converted for this purpose by an Episcopal bishop, who had lived in the house from 1962 to 1978.

On the exterior of the house is another unique item. The flagstone walkway is equipped with an iron railing from the Abraham Lincoln Hotel, which was once a city landmark.

But perhaps the strangest thing about the house is the fact that an air shaft and an escape tunnel from a coal mine are located underneath the stone front porch. Many Springfield residents don't realize just how much of the city is honeycombed with old mine shafts. Once such shaft actually ends beneath the Yates Mansion.

Another odd thing about the house is, of course, the resident ghost!

The legends of the Yates Mansion have been around for a number of years and continue to be told today in newspaper articles and spooky television reports at Halloween time.

According to the story, Richard Yates Jr., the most prominent occupant of the house, had a favorite room in the place where he spent much of his time. This was the cramped turret room in the attic. There is no clear reason why he seemed to prefer this chamber, but it is known to be where he stored his collection of Civil War memorabilia. Yates called this the "Romance Room" and he spent many hours here, poring over his prized collection, reading books and pacing back and forth in the small turret.

And it is said that his ghost can still be heard, walking back and forth.

I was fortunate to be able to visit this house several years ago and found Mr. Noll, a Springfield attorney, to be a very friendly and educated man. He spoke at some length about the renovations at the house and about the ghost. He was very open to the possibility of a haunting and admitted the events that had taken place were beyond simple explanation. I believed he was so free to admit to the possibility of a haunting because he had often heard the ghost himself!

The sound of phantom, restlessly pacing footsteps seem to be centered on the nights of the full moon. They begin late in the evening and sometimes continue all night long, making if difficult for the occupants of the room beneath the tower to get much in the way of sleep.

"We were in the bedroom, it was just bang, bang, bang...", Noll explained. The turret room is located directly above the second floor master bedroom. He described the sounds as heavy steps walking back and forth on the wooden floor overhead.

Nothing has ever been discovered that could provide a natural explanation for the sounds. If a light is turned on in the master bedroom, or someone attempts to search the house, the sounds suddenly cease. Investigations have ruled out the possibility of intruders, or perhaps water pipes or heat ducts in the ceiling causing the strange sounds. In fact, there is nothing above the master bedroom at all, except for the attic turret.

I was able to take a look into this room. It opened from a small door and Noll led the way into the unfinished turret. The room is very close and almost claustrophobic. The ceiling reaches to a height of about 12 feet, gradually narrowing to a point. I must confess that I had trouble seeing what the former governor found to be "romantic" about this chamber. Or what would make the place so fascinating that he would want to visit it after his death...

I had little doubt in the validity of the reports about the sounds though. In many cases, you have to question the testimony of the witness when little in the way of hard evidence is available. This time, however, I had no doubt the witness was telling the truth. Whether the sounds were actually those of

Governor Yates returning from the grave, or simply his residual energy left behind... there certainly seemed to be something hauntingly real going on in the house!

Near the center of the turret, Noll pointed to an area on the floor. "Right below us is the area where we hear the noise going back and forth," he said. "We sometimes hear banging and whirring noises too."

Does the idea of a ghost in the house bother the Noll family, or have they simply gotten used to the idea over the years? The attorney smiled a little in response to that question. "When we have friends or relatives over," he told me, "things get kind of weird... they really don't know how to take it."

That, I admitted, did not come as much of a surprise.

A GHOST NAMED JOE
THE HAUNTED SPRINGFIELD THEATRE CENTER

I never used to believe in ghosts... until I started working here.
AN ACTOR FROM THE SPRINGFIELD THEATRE GUILD

While the city of Springfield can no longer boast any grand old movie houses like the Lincoln or the Avon Theaters in Decatur, there is at least one theater here that is home to a ghost. This pleasant and unassuming building, which is home to the Springfield Theatre Guild, is easy to miss as you drive past its plain, front facade. However, should you ever go inside, it's not likely that you will forget your visit. Why, you might ask? There is a very good chance this is the most haunted building in Springfield!

The Theatre Center is constructed from concrete block and is much larger than it appears on the outside, mostly due to the sprawling basement area of dressing rooms and storage areas. The auditorium of the theater is rather narrow and was built like a modern movie house with a sloping floor and flip-up seats.

But there is something in this theater... something that is said to watch those who enter and leave the place. It hides in the darkest corners of the building, lurking and waiting to make itself known to anyone who dares scoff at its existence.

For more than 40 years, strange and inexplicable events have plagued this theater. Unexplained sounds and lights have been heard and seen; things have disappeared, seemingly at random; doors have opened and closed on their own; sets and prop pieces have moved and have fallen without human assistance; doors have opened and closed on their own; heavy objects have been hurled at unsuspecting victims; and of course, there is the pungent aroma of facial cream that seems to permeate the air on occasion. And strangely, that recognizably scented cream has been banned from the building for years!

Who is the spirit said to haunt this building? Those who work and perform here will tell you that he is the ghost of an actor named Joe....

The Springfield Theatre Guild was founded in 1947 and within a couple of years had managed to raise enough money to build a theater in which to hold their performances. The site was located at 101 East Lawrence Avenue and the construction began in 1950. The first theater season was in 1951 and they opened with the Broadway hit, "Born Yesterday".

One of the actors involved during the early days of the Guild was Joe Neville, a rather strange and eccentric performer who was not well liked by other cast members. Apparently, he was known for his arrogance and was unusually difficult to get along with. He also had a massive ego, but was a talented actor, so everyone made an effort to overlook his attitude. In addition to his acting ability, Joe was said to have had a questionable past as well. Rumor had it that he had also done some acting and directing in England, under another name. After his death, his will was read and he apparently left a lot of land in England to various people. The problem was that Joe didn't own any of the land! As mentioned, Joe was regarded as a pretty strange and unpopular guy. His death was taken so lightly by other Theatre Guild actors that the lead role he was slated to play in an upcoming production was simply given to another actor on the night before it was scheduled to open. I guess the show really must go on!

"If there was anyone who was going to come back as a ghost, it would be Joe," said Tom Shrewsbury, a long-time member of the Theatre Guild and a man who has had more than one encounter with the theater's resident ghost. He is also one of the remaining actors who worked with Joe Neville in the old days of the Guild.

"I knew Joe from many, many years ago, back in the 1950's," Shrewsbury explained. "We were doing a show called "Mr. Barry's Etchings" and Joe played the lead. One night after dress rehearsal, Joe went home and committed suicide. There was apparently an audit of the books at that place where he worked and a lot of money had been misappropriated.... and it looked as though Joe would be caught the next day."

Many people feel that Joe's suicide is the reason that he haunts the theater. It may also be the unfinished business of the play that causes him to linger behind. He may have felt the audit cheated him out of his chance to play the lead role in the performance. As the theater was undoubtedly the only place where this bitter man was happy, his spirit probably has no desire to leave it. His need for attention, in life and in death, is evident.

As the years have passed, many staff members and performers have reported weird happenings here. They have also discovered that sometimes a disbelief in Joe's ghost can trigger the events to take place. "Whether you believe in him or not," one of the actors here once told me, "you don't say out loud that you don't believe in him.... because then things happen."

He went on to describe an unusual occurrence that took place one evening when he and another man were building a set for an upcoming show. The friend who was working with him was skeptical about Joe's existence and made a point of stating this while onstage.

"The power saw he was using started up by itself," the actor told me, "and as soon as it did, some sheets of plywood fell over and a ladder that was standing nearby fell over on its own. The saw started to rev up again and right then my friend shouted 'I believe, I believe!'"

But skepticism is not the only thing that makes Joe show up... sometimes he makes an appearance for no reason at all. One of the most repeated happenings in the theater involves the front counter, located in the building's lobby. Many people, including patrons with no knowledge of the theater's haunted history, have noticed the door to the counter will swing open and closed on its own.

Another chilling tale was told to me first-hand by a staff member. One late evening, he and a young woman were in the closed theater and were crossing the large reception room in the basement, holding hands as they did so. The room was completely dark and they had only the touch of the other's hand to reassure them that they were not alone. When they reached the other side of the room, the staff member flipped the electrical switch. The room was flooded with light and the young man found that he was standing there alone... his friend was still on the opposite side of the room! So, whose hand had he been holding in the darkness?

Other actors and staff members tell more tales of Joe's presence. These anecdotes involve props and objects falling from the rafters and striking people, staff members being pushed offstage and on one occasion, a filmy, white apparition that appeared on an overhead catwalk.

Colleen McLaughlin, one of the actors at the theater, has had a number of experiences that qualify as being ghostly. She has often noticed the tendency of things to appear and disappear around the theater. One night, during the run of a show, she had to make some very quick costume changes during a particular song. She ran offstage, changed and then went back on. A few moments later, she returned to change her clothing again. This time, she got a surprise.

"Everything was missing, " she told me. "It turns out they [her costume] were behind a stairwell, all folded up neatly. No one used that stairwell during the production, and we have no idea how the clothes got there. They had been next to the piano when I came on and off stage. No one saw them disappear... and no one could have taken them."

Other actors have experienced similar incidents on many occasions, including Rebecca Sykes, the former theater manager. One night during a show, the clothing she was supposed to change into also disappeared. It was found later strewn up and down a ladder in the back, a place where no one had gone during the show.

The actors are not the only ones troubled by the ghost however. The people who build the sets and props sometimes have even stranger encounters.

One night, a stage crew volunteer was alone in the theater, painting a set for an upcoming show. He used a roll of tape to mark off areas where set pieces would be placed. He finished with one section and laid the tape aside. A few moments later, he reached for it, but it was gone! Thinking that he must have used the last of it, he decided to call it quits for the night. He closed up his paint cans and moved them up to the front of the stage. He went behind the curtain and was about the shut down the stage lights when he spotted his missing tape roll. It was propped up next to the last can of paint he had moved to the edge of the stage... and there was no doubt that it had NOT been there seconds before! He left the theater in a hurry that night!

Another performance was using a ventriloquist's dummy as a prop. As usual, the dummy was locked in the prop cage, which is located just offstage, at the end of the evening. On the night before the show was scheduled to open, the dummy disappeared from the locked cage. Needless to say, everyone who had a key to the cage denied taking it out. One of the prop managers was forced to run out and replace the doll just before the curtain call. Later that night, after the show was over and the stage was cleared, one of the workers emptied the prop cage and took everything downstairs to a storage room. He came back upstairs, where a party was in progress, and he discovered the location of the original dummy, which had disappeared.... it was inexplicably sitting inside of the locked prop cage with its legs crossed.

That would have given anyone a good case of the creeps.

I had the chance to visit the Theatre Center in the early part of 1997. I had the opportunity to spend several hours touring the place and interviewing actors and staff members about their encounters with Joe's ghost. I heard a number of familiar stories and some new ones from theater regulars like Kim Hepworth, Bart Gonterman and Joe Jackson, who all expressed respect, and a sort of fondness, for the ghost that haunted the place.

Before interviewing the staff, I was able to wander about the building on my own. My wife Amy went to the reception room to talk to the staffers and actors and I set off on my own. As I may have mentioned, the lower regions of the theater are much larger that you might expect. Besides the spacious reception room, there are also many rooms for storage, bathrooms, a furnace room, and several small dressing rooms. I also wandered about the stage and the auditorium, not knowing what I would find, but hoping to find something.

I would not be disappointed.

My self-guided tour eventually led me down a back staircase from the stage to a dressing room at the bottom of the steps. This dressing room was apparently used mostly during the early days of the theater. A new addition to the building had been constructed years after the original work and today, there are newer dressing rooms to use upstairs. The room at the bottom of the stairs is seldom occupied now, except apparently, by Joe. Of course, I didn't know that at the time!

As I walked into the room, I suddenly caught a strange smell near the center. I identified it immediately as the overpowering stench of Noxzema, which I was familiar with thanks to my own brief foray into theater and childhood Halloween make-up. To be honest, I really thought nothing of the smell. This was a theater after all, and the use of Noxzema was undoubtedly common. I shrugged the whole thing off and continued with my tour.

Later on, I got quite a surprise when Rebecca Sykes told me that one indication that had of Joe's ghost being present was the smell of Noxzema in the air. Because of this, superstitious actors had banned the use of the cream from the theater years before. So, whatever I had smelled in that room had not been the lingering odor of an actor who had removed his or her make-up.

"They say that Joe had this horrible rash on his legs that never seemed to heal," Rebecca explained when I asked how the smell had been linked to the ghost. "He used to slather layers of Noxzema on them.

I guess that everywhere he went, you used to be able to smell it around him."

I would have loved to laugh the whole encounter in the dressing room off to nothing more than my overactive imagination, but that would be impossible to do since I had no idea of the tell-tale "smell" until AFTER I actually caught a whiff of it! Just my imagination? I guess not!

I have little doubt that Joe Neville has returned to haunt the Springfield Theatre Center. Why does he linger here? Perhaps he is looking for a little attention, or perhaps some respect for the days when he walked the stage as an actor... or perhaps he simply doesn't want anyone to forget about him?

It's hard to say, but apparently Joe Neville's final curtain call is still to come!

- CHAPTER SEVEN -
THE HAUNTED PRESIDENT

THE SPIRITED LIFE & DEATH OF ABRAHAM LINCOLN

"Who is dead in the White House?" I asked one of the soldiers.
"The President", was the answer... "he was killed by an assassin."
PRESIDENT ABRAHAM LINCOLN
recalling a dream he experienced just days before he was killed

No book about the hauntings of Illinois would be complete without mention of Abraham Lincoln, one of the state's most famous former residents. The connections between Lincoln and the supernatural were maintained throughout his life, and some say beyond it. Much has been made of Lincoln's prophetic dreams and of his belief in the spirit world and of course, of the hauntings which are said to be connected to his home in Springfield and his mysterious tomb. Stories have also been told of his belief in the spirit world, but why did those beliefs become such a prominent part of his life and what event caused Lincoln to turn to contact with the dead?

The president endured great hardships during his life but the perhaps the greatest of these was watching his country being torn apart by bitterness and strife. It is little wonder that many believe that Lincoln lingered behind after his death, unable to find peace after all that he had seen and experienced. There are many mysteries in the pages that follow and many unsolved questions about Lincoln, his life and the wanderings of his physical (and possibly spiritual) form after death.

Do you believe the ghost of Abraham Lincoln still walks in Illinois? Explore the pages that follow and then I'll allow you to judge for yourself!

THE EARLY LIFE OF LINCOLN

Abraham Lincoln was always a melancholy person. The death of his mother when he was still a child, hard labor to make an existence for himself in the wilderness and his struggle for an education, all combined to make him a serious man, even when he was making a joke.

The Civil War caused him great sorrow and the heavy losses on both sides filled him with sadness. Lincoln paid obsessive detail to everything about the war and by 1864, portraits of him show a face etched with lines. He slept very little in those years and during the five years he lived in the White House, he spent less than one month away from work. His only escape was afforded him by the theater, a late night buggy ride or from his books.

But what forces combined to make him the man that he was? Lincoln always stated that he longed for a life of peace and contentment, but seemed to also know that he would never live to find it. The question is, has he found it in death?

Abraham Lincoln was born in Kentucky in 1809. His father, Thomas Lincoln, had married Nancy Hanks, a tall, pretty, uneducated girl, three years before and they had built a log cabin at a place called Sinking Springs Farm. Later, the Lincoln family pulled up stakes and moved across the Ohio River to Indiana, where they settled on Little Pigeon Creek.

In 1818, Lincoln's life changed abruptly when the family was struck by a terrible frontier disease dubbed "milk sickness". Tom and Betsy Sparrow, close friends of the Lincoln family, died first, while Nancy Lincoln faithfully nursed them to their last hours. Then, Nancy too was struck down with the disease and followed her friends to their graves. Abraham helped to fashion his mother's coffin with his own hands and then placed her in the ground. It was later said that he held his head in his hands and wept for hours. At that point, his father and sister forgotten, Lincoln later said that he felt completely alone in the world.

In 1819, Thomas Lincoln traveled back into Kentucky and returned with the widow of an old friend. Her name was Sarah Bush Johnston and she became his wife and a new mother for Abraham and Sarah. He also brought along him Sarah's three children and an orphaned cousin named Dennis Hanks. The cabin was now jammed to capacity with the expanded family and Lincoln recalled escaping into the woods with his books for some peace and quiet.

In school, Lincoln stood out among the other backwoods students. He composed poems and essays and often mounted a tree stump for speeches on whatever subject took his fancy. He was obviously a born politician, but on the other hand was also an expert log-splitter, a master with a farm plow and skilled as a hog butcher. He was also regarded as an insatiable reader. He started with the Bible and then read anything he could get his hands on. He was definitely a young man of many contrasts and not surprisingly, was considered a unique and rather odd fellow.

Thomas Lincoln pulled up stakes once more in the late 1820's and moved his family to a small farm outside of Decatur, Illinois. Abraham stayed with the family until the following Spring, helping his father build a cabin and clear land for a farm. When warm weather came, he started out on his own for the first time, working on a riverboat that hauled cargo to New Orleans. At the end of the job, he found a place that he liked in the village of New Salem, Illinois.

Lincoln became very popular in the small village and was liked for his sense of humor and his storytelling ability. He was also a hard worker and a powerful wrestler, which earned him many friends and admirers. Soon, they persuaded him to take up politics. In March of 1832, he decided to run for the state legislature. Then, a short time later, the Black Hawk War interrupted his campaign and he ended up serving two months in the Illinois militia. He was delighted when his fellow soldiers asked him to serve as captain, but often complained about there being more mosquitoes to fight than Indians. He was mustered out after the campaign and set out for home, only to have his horse stolen. Lincoln ended up walking most of the way back to New Salem from the Wisconsin border.

When Lincoln arrived home, he discovered that the store where he worked had closed down, so he took the position of New Salem's postmaster. He took the liberty of reading dozens of newspapers every week before delivering them and soaking up the information they contained. He also became a deputy surveyor and used both jobs as a way to campaign for the legislature again in 1834. He drummed up votes at dances, barbecues, cockfights and wrestling matches, where he normally served as referee since everyone refused to fight him.

That following November, at the age of 25, he left for Vandalia to serve in the legislature. He was wearing the first suit that he ever owned. In 1836, he was elected again and this time headed for Springfield, where he would also practice law. He had read all of the books required and in March of 1837 passed the exam that made him an attorney. He borrowed a horse and bid goodbye to the dwindling town of New Salem. The citizens had lost all hope of the river bring prosperity to the town and three years after Lincoln departed, New Salem was a ghost town.

When Lincoln arrived in Springfield it was a growing city of about 1500 people but was still cursed with unpaved streets, no sewers to speak of, no sidewalks, and the bane of the city, a pack of wild hogs that had been roaming the streets for more than a decade. Still, the city did manage to have a social circle. One of the members of the city's elite was Ninian Edwards, the son of a prominent politician. His wife, Elizabeth Todd Edwards, was a born matchmaker and delighted in finding husbands for her sisters among Ninian's friends. Her sister, Mary Todd, came to visit in 1839. Mary was described as being "high strung" but was said to have an engaging personality and a quick wit. She became the center of attention among Springfield socialites and had plenty of potential suitors to choose from, including Stephen Douglas, who was the most insistent.

Kentucky Belle Mary Todd as she looked when Lincoln met her in 1839.

In December of 1839, during the grand Christmas cotillion, Mary met a young attorney and political hopeful named Abraham Lincoln. They were attracted to one another from the start and a short time later, were engaged. For some reason though, at New Year's 1841, Lincoln called off the engagement.

No one knew why, but some speculated that their friend was intrigued by the idea of marriage, but afraid of it as well. For nearly a year, Lincoln acted (in the words of his friend William Herndon) as "crazy as a loon". He couldn't stop thinking of Mary and he often went without eating and sleeping. Finally, he went to visit a close friend in Kentucky and did not return to Springfield until 1842. By that summer, he was courting Mary again and talk had turned once more to marriage.

On November 4, Lincoln made an announcement to his family and friends. He and Mary were going to be married... that very evening! Their friends made haste to arrange the ceremony and Lincoln asked his friend James Matheny to be his best man. Matheny would later write that during the service, Lincoln "looked and acted like a lamb being led to the slaughter". While he dressed, his landlord's son asked Lincoln where he was going and Lincoln replied, "to Hell, I suppose."

The Lincoln's had their honeymoon at the Globe Tavern, where they lived the first years of their marriage. There was every indication that their marriage was a happy one, despite Mary losing track of her socialite friends and her sister's warnings that her husband was unsuitable. It was not long before they were expecting their first child and Robert would be born just three days short of nine months after the wedding.

By 1844, Lincoln was able to afford to purchase a home in Springfield. It was a one-and-a-half story cottage at the corner of Eighth and Jackson Streets. They moved into the house in May of that year and in 1856, the cramped quarters were expanded into a full two stories.

Lincoln's love for travel and the law caused his marriage to suffer badly in those early years. At that point in his career, he was active in court cases all over Illinois and was constantly away from home. Mary, left alone with a toddler, was sure that something terrible was going to happen while he was away. Their second son, Eddie, was born in 1846 but only lived to the age of four. Willie followed in 1850, not long after the death of his brother, and Thomas "Tad" Lincoln was born in 1853. The children drew Lincoln closer to home but his marriage was still sometimes rocky. He was nine years older than Mary and almost a foot taller than she was. She often complained that he treated her more like a child than a wife.

Lincoln served a term in Congress in the late 1840's, but his law practice kept him too busy to consider much of a political career. He had always been opposed to the further spread of slavery in the country and was contented that the Missouri Compromise had outlawed slavery further west, where America's future would be built. But in 1854, a congressional act provoked by Lincoln's long-time personal and political rival, Stephen Douglas, threatened to allow slavery in the territories. Lincoln's anger at this got the best of him and he made the decision to return to politics.

LINCOLN'S PROPHETIC VISION

In the summer of 1854, Lincoln decided to campaign for a seat in the Illinois State Assembly. He easily won the position, but then quickly resigned. What he really wanted was a seat in the US Senate, where he believed he could really make a difference for his country. In February 1855, he sought but failed to get the coveted seat. Things started to change in early 1856 however, as a new political party was created called the Republican Party. The first political move by the party was to try and keep Democrat James Buchanan out of office. They failed, but were gaining attention.

Buchanan's term in the White House pushed back the anti-slavery movement by years. During his time in office, the US Supreme Court ruled in the Dred Scott case, effectively deciding that blacks would never be considered as American citizens. Passions were beginning to ignite in the nation and dire predictions began to be made about the possibilities of secession and Civil War.

Also at this time, Stephen Douglas stepped forward with an abrupt turnabout and announced that he was now totally against allowing slavery into the western territories. Despite his new platform, Illinois Republicans were unconvinced and in June 1858, nominated Lincoln to run against Douglas for a seat in the Senate.

That night, in a speech before the excited nominating convention, Lincoln made his famous "House Divided" speech, declaring that the country could not endure as a divided nation. It was a speech that had been months in the planning.... and one that has endured for more than a century.

On July 24, Lincoln proposed that the two opponents meet in a series of debates before audiences all over the state. Douglas agreed and the two began a series of appearances that have become legend in Illinois for their volatile content. "The prairies are on fire," wrote one reporter, after witnessing a clash between Lincoln and Douglas.

The debates were bitter and powerful between the two long-time rivals. Lincoln argued that slavery must be abolished, while Douglas insisted that it could be contained and allowed to flourish in the South, as long as the states there wished it. The final debate was held in Alton and the story was reported all over the country in newspapers.

Finally, in November, word reached Lincoln that he had lost the race for the Senate seat. Surprisingly, this loss was the best thing that could have happened to him. Wise political analysts, on both sides, had watched this race very closely and had seen the way the debates had captured the attention of the entire country. Soon, word among the Republicans began to favor Lincoln as their choice for President in 1860.

Lincoln began to travel all over the country, backed by the Illinois Republican contingent, making his name known and becoming a recognizable entity. On May 16, 1860, the Republican National Convention opened in Chicago and decided among three real contenders for the nomination, William Seward, Edward Bates and Lincoln. In the end, after three ballots, Lincoln had won the nomination. Once again, he was to face his rival, Stephen Douglas.

The city of Springfield had a carnival-like atmosphere about it that summer, highlighted with a Republican rally at the fairgrounds. The parade took more than eight hours to pass the Lincoln home and ended with a picnic, where tubs of lemonade and whole cooked steers awaited the revelers.

Election Day in the city dawned with rousing blasts from a cannon, with music and contagious excitement. Lincoln spent the day and evening with friends at a telegraph office. By midnight, it was clear that he had been elected President of the United States. A late night dinner was held in his honor and then he returned to the office for more news. Guns fired in celebration throughout the night.

Lincoln may have won the day, but he fared poorly in the popular vote. He had soundly defeated Douglas in the Electoral College, but had won just forty percent of the vote among the people. He had become a minority president with no support at all in the southern states. The current president's cabinet was filled with secessionists and their strong words were starting to be heard by more than just the politicians in the South. Lincoln was even hanged in effigy on Election Day in Pensacola, Florida.

The country truly seemed to be coming apart.

Lincoln finally managed to return home in the early morning hours although news of victory and telegrams of congratulations were still being wired to his office. He went into his bedroom for some much-needed rest and collapsed onto a settee. Near the couch was a large bureau with a mirror on it and Lincoln started for a moment at his reflection in the glass. His face appeared angular, thin and tired. Several of his friends suggested that he grow a beard, which would hide the narrowness of his face and give him a more "presidential" appearance. Lincoln pondered this for a moment and then experienced what many would term a "vision"... and odd vision that Lincoln would later believe had prophetic meaning.

He saw that in the mirror, his face appeared to have two separate, yet distinct, images. The tip of one nose was about three inches away from the other one. The vision vanished but appeared again a few moments later. It was clearer this time and Lincoln realized that one of the faces was actually much paler than the other was, almost with the coloring of death. The vision disappeared again and Lincoln dismissed the whole thing to the excitement of the hour and his lack of sleep.

Later on that evening, he told Mary of the strange vision and attempted to conjure it up again in the days that followed. The faces always returned to him and while Mary never saw it, she believed her husband when he said he did. She also believed she knew the significance of the vision. The healthy face was her husband's "real" face and indicated that he would serve his first term as president. The pale, ghostly image of the second face however was a sign that he would be elected to a second term.... but would not live to see its conclusion.

Lincoln apparently dismissed the whole thing as a hallucination, or an imperfection in the glass, or so he said publicly. Later, that strange vision would come back to haunt him during the turbulent days of the war. It was not Lincoln's only brush with prophecy either. One day, shortly before the election, he spoke to some friends as they were discussing the possibilities of Civil War. "Gentlemen," he said to them, "you may be surprised and think it strange, but when the doctor here was describing a war, I distinctly saw myself, in second sight, bearing an important part in that strife."

LINCOLN AND THE SUPERNATURAL

"Do you ever find yourself talking with the dead? I do, ever since Willie's death. I catch myself involuntarily talking to him as if he were near me... and I feel that he is!"

PRESIDENT ABRAHAM LINCOLN
to Secretary of the Treasury, Salmon P. Chase

Lincoln was soon sworn in as President and began one of the most troubled periods of American history. Lincoln would later go one to believe that perhaps the reason he was born was to guide America through the War Between the States. His leadership during this period, although often questioned, never faltered and the events of 1861-1865 both strengthened and destroyed the man that Lincoln was.

The great loss of life and the bitter turmoil of the war took their toll on him. His personality changed and he became more bitter and dark. Gone was the humorous man who was apt to take off his shoes during staff meetings to "let his feet breathe". In his place was a sad, gloomy leader who was prone to severe depression. It was as if the weight of the entire nation had fallen on his shoulders.

Lincoln's times of prayer and contemplation became much longer and he seemed to turn inward. He spoke more and more often of the "hand of God" in certain battles and it was almost as if an uncanny perception somehow strengthened as the war raged on. By this time, Lincoln had truly taken on the mantle of America's military commander. Few realize today just to what extent Lincoln actually orchestrated the Union Army during the bloodiest points of the war, enduring complaints and barbs by ineffectual generals about his "meddling".

Documents of the Union War Department contain one occasion when Lincoln burst into the telegraph office of the department late one night. He had visited earlier, looking for the latest news, but when he came back, he was in a panic. He ordered the operator to get a line through to the Union commanders. He was convinced that Confederate soldiers were just about to cut through the Federal lines.

The telegraph operator asked where he had obtained such information and Lincoln reportedly answered, "My god, man! I saw it".

The war took a terrible toll on President Lincoln but there is no doubt that the most crippling blow he suffered in the White House was the death of his son, Willie, in 1862. The boy had been born in Springfield in 1850, shortly after the funeral of the Lincoln's second son, Eddie. Willie was much like his father and probably because of this, was the special favorite among his much-loved sons. The two of them shared many interests, especially reading, humor and a love for animals. In Washington, Lincoln bought a pony for Willie and it became the pride of the small boy's life.

Lincoln and Mary grieved deeply over Willie's death. Eddie had passed away a number of years before and while they didn't know it at the time, Tad would only live to be age eighteen. This left Robert as the only Lincoln son to see adulthood. Lincoln was sick at heart over Willie's death and it was probably the most intense personal crisis in his life. Some historians have even called it the greatest blow he ever suffered. Even Confederate President Jefferson Davis expressed condolences over the boy's death.

William Wallace Lincoln, named for a family doctor in Springfield, was a quiet, thoughtful boy who excelled at reading and education. His brother Tad was just the opposite and could not read or write by age 12, while Willie was beyond the basics by 8. He had a wonderful memory and could recite long passages from the Bible with ease. He often told his parents that he was going to be a minister when he grew up.

The reports of what Willie actually died from vary from story to story. In the end, it remains a mystery. He was said to have been a delicate child, despite his rough play with his brother and his outdoor activities. Like his brother Eddie, he may have suffered from "consumption" or according to some accounts, he contracted either an acute malarial infection or typhoid. In either case, the lack of proper sanitation would have been a factor. During the 1860's, Washington had open sewers and a filthy canal for drinking water. The city's garbage was dumped into the water just a short distance from the White House.

The onset of Willie's sickness occurred during the last days of January 1862. He was out playing in the snow with Tad and both of them developed a fever and a cold. Tad's illness soon passed, but Willie seemed to get worse. He was kept inside for a week and finally put into bed. A doctor was summoned and he assured Mary that the boy would improve, despite the fact that Willie's lungs were congested and he was having trouble breathing. Over the course of days, his condition did not improve.

The doctor was summoned back and by then, everyone in the household and the offices knew that Willie was seriously ill. More doctors were called in to consult and soon, Willie's illness made the newspapers. The reporters conjectured that he might have contracted bilious fever. The doctors had no hope for the child, as he grew worse. Soon, his mind wandered and he failed to recognize anyone, including his beloved father. Death finally came for Willie on the afternoon of February 20, 1862.

The day of the funeral was a stormy one, as if the forces of nature reflected the anguish in the Lincoln's hearts. The procession to the cemetery was several blocks long and it ended at Oak Hill Cemetery in Georgetown. Throughout the day, the rainstorms wreaked destruction upon the city. Steeples had fallen from churches, roofs had been torn form houses, trees and debris littered the roadways, and even the funeral procession cowered under the torrents of rain. But as soon as they reached the cemetery, the storm passed over and the air became silent... almost as in deference to Willie Lincoln.

The service was short. Willie had been embalmed to make the trip back to Springfield and be buried beside his brother, but Lincoln changed his mind about that at the last minute. He accepted an offer made to him by a friend, William Thomas Carroll, to place the body of Willie in one of the crypts in the Carroll family tomb. This would be until Lincoln retired from the presidency and returned to live in Springfield himself. He could not bear the idea of having Willie so far away from him just yet.

In fact, Lincoln returned to the cemetery the next day to watch the body as it was moved from the cemetery chapel to the crypt itself. Word got out that Lincoln returned to the tomb on two occasions and had Willie's coffin opened. The doctor had embalmed Willie so perfectly that he everyone said he just seemed to be sleeping. The President claimed that he was forced to look upon his boy's face just one last time.

Three years later, the undertakers would remove Willie's body from the vault one final time and transport it to a funeral train which stood ready for departure. The funeral car, draped in black, was divided into three sections. One was for the honor guard, while the other compartment held the body of Willie's slain father. Together, they would make the long-delayed journey back to Springfield.

After the funeral, Lincoln tried to go on about his work, but his spirit had been crushed by Willie's death. One week after the funeral, he closed himself up in his office all day and wept. It has often been said that Lincoln was on the verge of suicide at this point, but none can say for sure. He did withdraw even further into himself though and he began to look more closely at the spiritual matters that had interested him for so long.

Although many Lincoln scholars say otherwise, it is more than possible that Abraham Lincoln didn't just believe in the supernatural, but that he actually participated in it. Many have scoffed and said that Lincoln had no time for ghosts and spirits, but there are others who say that he actually attended seances that were held in the White House. Whether he accepted the movement or not, it is a fact that many Spiritualists were often guests there. Several of them were even said to have given him warnings about the dark shadows that hung over his life.

Of course, Lincoln himself was convinced that he was doomed and adopted a very fatalistic attitude during his presidency, especially after Willie's death. His friends stated that Lincoln would often watch the door while he worked, as if expecting the boy to run through it and give his father a hug, as he often did in life. Lincoln also began to speak of how Willie's spirit remained with him and how his presence was often felt in his home and office. Some mediums theorized that Lincoln's obsession with the boy's death may have caused Willie's spirit to linger behind, refusing, for his father's sake, to pass on to the other side.

Regardless of how he felt about Willie's spirit, Lincoln publicly avoided connections to the Washington spiritualists, so much of what is written about his contact with them comes through accounts and diaries written by friends and acquaintances.

While Lincoln avoided the spiritualists in public, Mary embraced them openly. She had been quick to turn to contact with the other side for comfort after Willie's death. Once he was gone, Mary never again entered the White House guest room where he died or the room in which the funeral viewing was held. Some historians claim that this was the beginning of Mary's mental instability, but not because of the mediums, because of her fervent grief instead. The obsession over Spiritualism was just one of the symptoms, but none could ignore the fact that her headaches, mood swings and bursts of irrational temper were growing worse.

Mary began meeting with a number of different Spiritualists and invited many to the White House, as each claimed to be able to "lift the thin veil" and allow Mary to communicate with Willie. Mary's closest spiritualist companion, and one of whom there is some record that Lincoln also met with, was Nettie Colburn Maynard. Many are familiar with a tale told about a seance held by Nettie Maynard in 1863 where a grand piano levitated. The medium was playing the instrument when it began to rise off the floor. Lincoln and Colonel Simon Kase were both present and it is said that both men climbed onto the piano, only to have it jump and shake so hard that they climbed down. It is recorded that Lincoln would later refer to the levitation as proof of an "invisible power."

Rumors spread that Lincoln had an interest in the spirit world. In England, a piece of sheet music was published which portrayed him holding a candle while violins and tambourines flew about his head. The piece of music was called "The Dark Seance Polka" and the caption below the illustration of the president read "Abraham Lincoln and the Spiritualists".

It was also rumored that Lincoln consulted with these mediums and clairvoyants to obtain information about future events in the war. He found that sometimes they gave him information about matters as mundane as Confederate troop movements..... information that sometimes matched his own precognitive visions.

Despite these somewhat apocryphal stories, there is little doubt that Lincoln believed a dark cloud hung over his head. The constant threats of death and violence that he received kept he and his bodyguards on edge at all times. It is also believed that some of his spiritualist friends felt the end was near. During a session that he was said to have had with Nettie Maynard, she allegedly told him that "the shadows others have told of still hang over you."

Lincoln told her that he received letters from spiritualists all over the country that warned him of impending doom. When she got ready to depart, the president insisted that she come and visit he and Mary the following autumn.

"I shall come, of course," Nettie answered, "that is... if you are still among us."

Perhaps the most famous supernatural incident connected to Lincoln would be his last prophetic dream of the assassination.

One of Lincoln's old friends from Illinois was a lawyer with whom he had ridden the legal circuit named Ward Hill Lamon. Lincoln had appointed him to a security position in the White House and he worried constantly over Lincoln's seeming indifference to threats and warnings of death. Lamon often resigned his position because his friend did not take the danger seriously. Lincoln always convinced him to stay on, promising to be more careful.... as he vanished out of the White House at night, or attended the theater without protection.

Lamon became obsessed with watching over Lincoln and many believe that the president would not have been killed at Ford's Theater had Lamon been on duty that night. As it turned out, the security chief happened to be in Richmond, Virginia, on an errand for the president, when disaster struck. He would never forgive himself for what happened... especially since he believed that he had a forewarning of the event, from Lincoln himself.

Years later, Lamon would remember that Lincoln had always been haunted by the strange vision that he experienced in the mirror in 1860. Several years after that, it was to Lamon and Mary Lincoln to whom the president would recount an eerie dream of death, just shortly before his assassination.

"About ten days ago, I retired late. I soon began to dream. There seemed to be a death-like stillness about me. Then I heard subdued sobs, as if a number of people were weeping. I thought I left my bed and wandered downstairs. There the silence was broken by the same pitiful sobbing, but the mourners were invisible. I went from room to room; no living person was in sight, but the same mournful sounds of distress met me as I passed along.

"It was light in all the rooms; every object was familiar to me, but where were all the people who were grieving as if their hearts would break? I was puzzled and alarmed. What could be the meaning of all this? Determined to find the cause of a state of things so mysterious and so shocking, I kept on until I arrived at the East Room, which I entered. Before me was a catafalque, on which rested a corpse wrapped in funeral vestments. Around it were stationed soldiers who were acting as guards; and there was a throng of people, some gazing mournfully upon the corpse, whose face was covered, others weeping pitifully.

" 'Who is dead in the White House?', I demanded of one of the soldiers.

" 'The President', was his answer, 'He was killed by an assassin.'

"Then came a loud burst of grief from the crowd, which awoke me from my dream. I slept no more that night; and although it was only a dream, I have been strangely annoyed by it ever since."

Lincoln was murdered just a few days later and his body was displayed in the East Room of the White House. Mary would recall this dream of her husband's quite vividly in the days that followed. It was said that her first coherent word after the assassination was a muttered statement about his dream being prophetic.

On April 14, 1865, a few days after the horrifying dream and on the night he was to attend Ford's Theater, Lincoln called a meeting of his cabinet. Edwin Stanton, Lincoln's Secretary of War, arrived twenty minutes late and the meeting began without him. As Stanton and Attorney General James Speed were leaving the meeting, Stanton commented to him that he was pleased about how much work was accomplished.

"But you were not here at the beginning", Speed said. "When we entered the council chamber, we found the president seated at the top of the table, with his face buried in his hands. Presently, he raised it and we saw that he looked grave and worn".

" Gentlemen, before long, you will have important news", the President told them. The Cabinet members were anxious to hear what news Lincoln spoke of, but he refused to tell them anything further.

"I have heard nothing, but you will hear tomorrow, " he said, and then continued, "I have had a dream. I have dreamed three times before; once before the Battle of Bull Run; once on another occasion; and again last night. I am in a boat, alone on a boundless ocean. I have no oars, no rudder, I am helpless. I drift!"

That evening, while attending a performance of a play called "Our American Cousin" at Ford's Theater, Lincoln was killed by an assassin named John Wilkes Booth. He died the next morning, April 15, the anniversary of the southern assault on Fort Sumter, the event which officially started the Civil War.

Lincoln spoke of death and prophecies to other members of his staff also, like Colonel WH Crook, a member of the White House security team and one of Lincoln's personal bodyguards. Crook took his task seriously, often staying awake at night and sitting outside Lincoln's bedroom while the president slept. Crook even refused to read a newspaper while on duty so that he would be ready should an emergency arise.

Crook was on duty the evening of April 14 and that same afternoon, Lincoln spoke to him about the strange dreams that he had been having. Crook pleaded with the president not to go to the theater that night, but Lincoln dismissed his concerns, explaining that he had promised Mary they would go and that he needed a night away from the problems of the country. Crook then asked to accompany the president, but Lincoln again refused, insisting that Crook could not work around the clock.

Lincoln had a habit of bidding Crook a "good night" each evening as he left the office and went to his bedroom. On that fateful day, according to Crook, Lincoln paused as he left for the theater and turned to the bodyguard. "Good-bye, Crook," he said significantly.

"It was the first time that he neglected to say 'Good Night' to me", Crook would later recall. "And it was the only time that he ever said 'Good-bye'. I thought of it at that moment and, a few hours later, when the news flashed over Washington that he had been shot, his last words were so burned into my being that they can never be forgotten."

Lincoln's final premonition was not the last however. General Ulysses S. Grant and his wife Julia were also scheduled to attend the performance of "Our American Cousin" that night. But that morning, Julia awoke with a terrible sensation. She wanted to leave Washington immediately, despite the fact that the entire city was celebrating her husband's victory over Lee and the surrender of the southern armies.

She was sure that something terrible was about to happen.

General Grant, who according to the plans of the conspirators was also supposed to be assassinated, was not present at Ford's Theater because Julia simply refused to attend the play that night. She pressed Grant so hard about her premonition that he finally agreed not to go.

Would Grant have also been killed that night if he had attended the performance? Thanks to Julia Grant's strange premonition, we will thankfully never know.

SPIRITS OF THE ASSASSINATION

When the Civil War ended in April 1865, it did not end for everyone. There were many in the South who simply refused to believe that the Confederacy had fallen. One of these men was John Wilkes Booth, an actor who professed and undying devotion to the South. Booth was the son of Junius Brutus Booth, a professional actor. The elder Booth was considered by many to be so eccentric that he was nearly insane, a trait which father and son apparently shared. John Wilkes Booth was also the brother of Edwin Booth, perhaps the most famous stage actor of the period. Edwin often spoke of his brother's strangeness and he would have had an even greater cause for concern had he known the dark secrets that his sibling hid in his heart.

While the war was still raging, Booth had been attempting to organize a paramilitary operation with a small group of conspirators. Their plan was to kidnap the president and take him to Richmond. After a number of failed attempts, it was clear that the plan would not work. Booth's hatred of Lincoln forced him to change his plans from kidnapping to murder. Booth did not explain to his confederates about this change until two hours before the event took place.

Booth had been a southern sympathizer throughout the war. He was revered for his acting in the South and during the war had been a spy and a smuggler, working with southern agents in Maryland

and Canada. He was also rabid in his pro-slavery views, believing that slavery was a "gift from God". He was convinced that Lincoln was a tyrant and Booth hoped the murder of the president would plunge the North into chaos and allow the Confederacy to rally and seize control of Washington.

On the night of April 14, Booth stepped into Lincoln's box at Ford's Theater and shot the president in the back of the head. At the same time, another assassin tried to kill Secretary of State Seward. He was horribly scarred by a knife wound to the face, but survived. Secretary of War Edwin Stanton and General Grant were also slated to be killed and presidential successor Andrew Johnson was only spared because of an assassin's cold feet. The shadow of a greater conspiracy hung over Washington and many questions have not been answered to this day, including whether Edwin Stanton was really involved in the assassination.

Some historians believe that Stanton was one of the few to really gain by Lincoln's death in that he was a radical Republican who was opposed to Lincoln's gentle plans for the South. It seems that Stanton would have been able to gain power if the North imposed a military occupation upon the southern states instead. Regardless, Stanton's behavior both before and after Lincoln's assassination has raised some questions. For example:

- Stanton refused a request for Major Thomas Eckert to accompany Lincoln to Ford's Theater. The implication, according to some historians, was that Stanton knew something Lincoln didn't.

- Despite Lincoln's many death threats, Stanton only sent one bodyguard to the theater that night and this man abandoned his post to have a drink. He was never reprimanded for this.

- On the night of the assassination, telegraph lines in Washington, controlled by the War Department, mysteriously went dead, delaying the news of Booth's escape. Many believe this points to some sort of government conspiracy behind the murder.

- Booth's diary was given to Stanton after the assassination and it vanished for several years. When it was returned, eighteen pages were missing. A security chief would later testify that it had been intact when given to Stanton.

And there were other problems too, although none of this would be brought to light until more than seventy years later! Far too late by that time....

The Lincoln party arrived at the theater that night and took a reserved box to the cheers of the crowd and to the musical strains of "Hail to the Chief". The Lincoln's were accompanied by a young couple, Major Henry Rathbone and his fiancée, Clara Harris. The play was a production called "Our American Cousin", presented by actress Laura Keene. The play was a comedy, the sort of show that Lincoln liked best.

Booth lurked about the theater all evening and at thirteen minutes after ten, approached Lincoln's box. He showed a card to an attendant and gained access to the outer door. As mentioned before, he found the box to be unguarded and while this was out of the ordinary, Booth apparently expected it to be that way. As he slipped into the door of the box, Booth jammed the door closed behind him.

During the evening, the Lincoln party had been discussing the Holy Land. The President made a comment about wanting to visit Jerusalem someday as he leaned forward and noticed General Ambrose Burnside in the audience of the theater. At that moment, Booth stepped forward. Major Rathbone stood from his seat to confront the intruder but before he could act, Booth raised a small pistol and fired it into the back of President Lincoln's head.

Rathbone seized the actor but Booth slashed him with a knife. Lincoln fell forward, striking his head on the rail of the box and slumping over. Mary took hold of him, believing him to have simply fallen while Booth jumped from the edge of the balcony. His boot snagged on the bunting across the front of the box and he landed badly, fracturing his leg. As he struggled to his feet, he cried out "Sic Semper tyrannis!" (Thus it shall ever be for tyrants) and he stumbled out of the theater.

A scream went up from the back of the theater, crying "Booth!", and the stunned audience was snapped out of its stupor. Soon, more voices began shouting the actor's name and yet somehow, he managed to easily escape from the close and crowded auditorium. Then, there were more screams, groans and the crashing of seats and above all of it came Mary Lincoln's shrill cry for her dying husband.

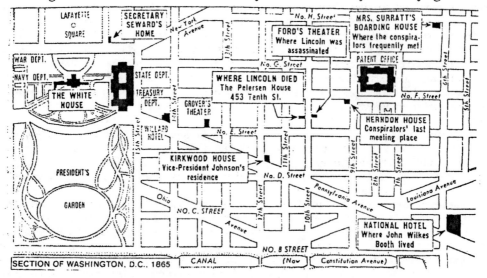

A Map Showing the Area of the Assassination in April 1865

In the theater's audience was a young doctor named Charles Leale, who rushed upstairs to the president's aid. He found Lincoln bleeding badly, his heart barely beating. Even this inexperienced young doctor could see that Booth's shot had been a fatal one. A few moments later, Dr. Charles Sabin Taft joined Leale and the two men, with some help from bystanders, managed to get the president out of Ford's Theater. Soldiers cleared a path through the crowd outside, where people rushed madly back and forth and milled about in confusion. A man named Henry Safford beckoned to the doctors and they carried the president across the street into the Petersen home. Lincoln's unconscious form was laid in a small, shabby bedroom at the back of the house. His lanky frame was too long for the bed and they were forced to lay him down at an angle.

Help was summoned and soon Lincoln's aides and security men were attempting to try and calm the frenzy around them. Soon, witnesses were being questioned and when Booth's identity was learned, a search party was organized to look for him. Meanwhile, the Surgeon General, Joseph K. Barnes, and Lincoln's own doctor, Robert Stone King, set to work on the president. They soon realized that it was no use, there was nothing that could be done for him.

Lincoln's many friends, along with Mary and Robert Lincoln, came and went throughout the night. By the next morning, the president's condition had worsened. His breathing was very shallow and then suddenly, he took one great breath, his face relaxed and then he faded into oblivion. The calm and collected Robert Lincoln finally broke down into tears.

The Surgeon General carefully crossed the lifeless hands of Abraham Lincoln at twenty-two minutes after seven on the morning of April 15, 1865.

Edwin Stanton, who was either innocent of the allegations of conspiracy or was the most consummate actor of his time, stood by the bedside of the slain president. He raised his head and with tears streaming down his face, uttered the most unforgettable words that a man not known for his poetic soul could ever manage... "Now, he belongs to the ages."

John Wilkes Booth escaped from Washington on horseback across the Anacostia Bridge, passing a sentry who had not yet learned of the assassination. He made it to a farm in Virginia with the help of his fellow conspirators, only stopping to rest because of his broken leg.

Soon, the hunt for Lincoln's assassin was on and by morning, more than 2000 soldiers were looking for Booth. On April 26, a detachment of 25 men finally tracked down Booth, and a comrade named David Herold, at a tobacco farm near Port Royal, Virginia. The barn where they were hiding was surrounded and Herold decided to surrender. He was manacled and tied to a tree. Booth decided to die rather than be taken alive... or so we are told to believe.

In the darkness outside, a decision was made to try and smoke Booth out. The barn was set on fire and in a few moments, the interior was engulfed in flames. Booth came to the door and raised his weapon, apparently looking for a target among the soldiers outside. One of the soldiers, a Sergeant Boston Corbett, saw Booth through the slats of the barn and, ignoring Edwin Stanton's specific orders to bring Booth back alive, shot him in the back of the head. Booth fell to the floor and the soldiers rushed to subdue him. He died two hours later, whispering instructions to tell his mother that he "died for his country and did what he thought best."

A search of the dead man's pockets turned up a few items, including a compass; a diary; and photographs of several women, along with one portrait of Booth's fiancée, Lucy Hale.

Booth died on the porch of the farm house as light was beginning to show in the sky. The dead man was sewn into a burlap bag and was taken to Alexandria on a steamer. Booth's body was then placed on a carpenter's bench and identified from a crude tattoo of the actor's initials, by dental fillings and by a scar on the back of his neck. Others claimed that the body only resembled Booth, but that it actually wasn't him at all. Regardless, the corpse was taken to the Old Penitentiary in Washington and, using a gun case for a coffin, was buried under the floor of the old dining room. The door to the room was locked and the body stayed there for another four years. Finally, pleas from Edwin Booth convinced President Andrew Johnson to allow the body to be exhumed and buried in an unmarked grave in the family plot in Baltimore.

But was it really the body of John Wilkes Booth in the grave?

The newspapers quickly spread the word that President Lincoln's assassin, gunned down in a Virginia barn, was an actor named John Wilkes Booth. There is no doubt in anyone's mind that the killer had been Booth, but the question remains as to whether or not Booth himself was ever brought to justice. That question still remains unanswered today.

Shortly after the assassin was gunned down, the word began to spread that it might not have been Booth in that barn after all. The government's handling of the body in question and of the witnesses who were present, did not add much credence to the official version of the story. The Union soldiers had certainly killed a man. The War Department and the newspapers told a breathless nation that the man had been John Wilkes Booth... but had it really?

From the day the body was brought back to Washington, there were already people on the streets denying the body was that of Booth. They believed the assassin had long since escaped and that the government was offering a secret substitution for the real killer.

The Secret Service and the War Department took a firm position on the matter and would not argue it further. They maintained that the corpse was Booth. In their possession were items which belonged to him and other evidence that proved they had the right man, including the left boot which Booth had abandoned to put his broken leg in splints and the revolver he had been carrying when killed. They also had affidavits from the soldiers who brought the body back, swearing that the face of the corpse matched the photos of Booth they had been given. The investigators studied these, but they were never shown to the public. The government refused to even consider the idea that the body might not be that of Booth.

The mystery continued for many years. More than 20 men would later claim to be Booth with books, anecdotes and sworn testimony. The newspapers got hold of each story and fanned the flames of doubt. By June 1865, stories spread that witnesses had seen Booth on a steamer to Mexico, or to South America. It was said that several people saw him in the west and others recognized him in the Orient. In

Ohio, a man claimed that Booth had stopped in his tavern on the way to Canada. In the Southwest, several people who claimed to know Booth, said that he owed his escape to Union troopers because of his membership in a fraternal order. They had spirited him away rather than see him hanged.

It was no wonder that before long, dark-haired, pallid men who walked with a limp began to be pointed out all across the country as John Wilkes Booth.

The story became so popular that in July 1867, Dr. John Frederick May, who had identified the body as Booth, felt that it was now necessary to make an emphatic denial of his once positive identification. He now stated that he could have been wrong when he said the dead man had been John Wilkes Booth. It seems that two years before the assassination, May had removed a tumor from the back of Booth's neck. The surgery had left a jagged scar behind and this scar was how the doctor had identified the remains. His said that the body he saw did not resemble Booth, but since he found a scar on the back of the neck, he assumed it must be.

His new testimony continued, bringing to light a more damning bit of evidence. He explained in detail his examination of the corpse in question and its broken right leg. Now, the word of the government, and the witnesses at Ford Theater, said that Booth had broken his left leg when he jumped from the theater box. The fact that the doctor noted the mysterious body had a broken right leg meant one of two things... either the body was not Booth's or that Dr. May was too careless of an observer to be credited with any authority in the matter of an accurate identification.

Suspicion thrived across the country, and by 1869, President Johnson decided to dispel of all the rumors and allow the assassin's brother to bury the disputed corpse in his family's cemetery plot. On February 15, 1869, government workers exhumed the body that had been buried beneath the floor of the old prison dining hall.

Many believed the mystery of the body would be settled once and for all by Edwin Booth, but he simply added to the confusion by bungling the whole thing. First, he attempted to keep the exhumation a secret and then decided that he couldn't bear to look upon the face of his dead brother. He remained outside of the undertaker's room while friends went inside to examine the corpse. Not surprisingly, they decided the body belonged to John Wilkes Booth.

Needless to say, the public had a good mystery and they weren't about to let it go. A reporter for the Baltimore "Gazette" was soon claiming that he had been present at the exhumation and that the body had a broken right leg and no bullet holes in it. Modern historians believe this reporter had either a vivid imagination or lied about being at the exhumation at all, still in those days, the story looked like new evidence that Booth was still alive.

The mystery continued into the 20th century and while Booth's skull was supposedly on display in a number of different traveling carnivals, there remained a question as to his eventual fate. Historians looked for answers in the early 1900's as many of the people involved in the case were still living. Statements were taken from surviving soldiers who aided in Booth's capture and all information was thoroughly researched. They even checked out the claims of men still posing as Booth and found all of them transparently fraudulent.

Could Booth have survived the days after the assassination? The question nagged at historians, although logic would say that he had been killed. Still though, it is interesting that after all of the conflicting evidence, there was not a single eyewitness, sufficiently impartial to be above suspicion, which had seen the corpse in 1865 and could say, with certainty, that it was John Wilkes Booth.

While the question of Booth's capture remains unsolved... there is suggestion that he does still walk the earth, along with many of the others spirits of the Lincoln assassination. One of the places where Booth's spirit is alleged to walk is Ford's Theater, where the assassin carried out his dark deed.

Shortly after the Lincoln assassination, Ford's Theater was closed down, but it was far from empty. The famous photographer, Matthew Brady, took a photograph of the interior of the building. It revealed a nearly transparent figure standing in Lincoln's box. Although not clear, some have suggested that it might be that of John Wilkes Booth.

After the theater shut down, Ford hoped to open it again once the memory of Lincoln's death faded with the public. The citizens of Washington refused to return however and Ford eventually sold the place. It soon became a clearing house for processing Army records. In June 1893, the third floor of the building collapsed and killed a number of staff members.

Finally, in 1933, the theater was given to the National Park Service but its restoration was not begun until 1964. Four years later, it had been turned into a showplace and theatrical museum in the daytime hours and a playhouse at night.

It has been reported that a number of actors, including Hal Holbrook who performed there in his Mark Twain one-man show, have experienced an icy cold presence which can be felt at left center stage. Many forget their lines and tremble involuntarily in the same spot. Many believe the effect is caused by impressions left behind by Booth on the night of the assassination. It has also been reported that mysterious footsteps, weird voices, laughing sounds and the sound of someone weeping can be heard in the darkened theater. Lights have often been known to turn on and off by themselves.

In recent years, a well-known singer was performing at Ford's Theater and complained of being distracted by a light which kept flashing off and on in the restored Lincoln box. The strange thing is that this box is permanently closed to the public, so there could not have been anyone in there.

One has to wonder just what she was seeing?

The tragic events of that Good Friday evening in 1865 sparked another chain of events involving people closely embroiled in the assassination. Because when Booth jumped from the theater box that night, he left behind not only a dead president, but also several shattered lives as well... all of them destined to meet tragic ends.

Mary Lincoln, whose mental state had already been declining since the death of Willie in 1862, never recovered from the loss of her husband. She struggled with family problems and more heartbreak and eventually was committed to a mental institution for a time.

Her curse would be that she managed to live 17 years after the death of her husband. For months after his murder, Mary spoke of nothing but the assassination until her friends began to drift away, their sympathy at a breaking point. She began to accuse her husband's friends and his Cabinet members of complicity in the murder, from his bodyguards to even Andrew Johnson.

Mary lay in her bed for 40 days after the assassination and in the seventeen years that followed she deteriorated mentally and physically into a bitter old woman who wore nothing but black, mourning clothing for the rest of her life. Her attachment to Spiritualism turned into a dangerous obsession, reaching a point where she could not function without aid from her "spirit guides".

Mary also had a great fear of poverty. She often begged her friends to help her with money. Unlike the widows of generals and governors, for whom money was easily raised, Mary's handful of supporters found it impossible to raise funds on her behalf because she was just too unpopular. In fact, she was despised all across America. Newspapers wrote unflattering stories about her and she was ridiculed by members of Washington society.

In 1868, she abandoned America and took Tad to live in Germany. They lived there in hiding for three years before coming home. A government pension awaited her, as did an inheritance from Lincoln's estate, so she was finally a wealthy woman. The ocean crossing had dire circumstances for Tad however. He developed tuberculosis and although he lingered for six weeks, he eventually passed away.

Mary embraced Spiritualism once again and moved into a commune where she began to develop her psychic "gifts" that enabled her to see "spirit faces" and "communicate beyond the veil". She claimed to have daily conversations with her late husband.

In the spring of 1875, Robert Lincoln decided to have his mother institutionalized. He was concerned not only for her sanity, but for her estate as well, which he claimed her medium "friends" had designs on. By this time, Robert was wealthy in his own right and had no plans for his mother's money, which Mary refused to understand. He did however hire detectives to follow his mother and gather information about her drug use, which included opium, and he paid doctors to testify about her sanity in court.

Mary was sent to a mental hospital but was later released. She severed all ties with Robert, calling him a "wicked monster". She would hate him for the rest of her days and before she died, she wrote him letters which cursed him and which claimed that his father had never loved him.

Mary went into exile again and moved into a small hotel in France. Her eyes were weakened and her body was wracked with pain from severe arthritis. She refused to travel until several bad falls left her nearly unable to walk. Her sister pleaded with her to come home and finally she returned to Springfield, moving into the same house where she and Lincoln had been married years before.

Mary lived the last years of her life in single room, wearing a money belt to protect her fortune. She kept all of the shades in her room drawn and spent her days packing and unpacking her 64 crates of clothing. She died on July 12, 1882.

The President's oldest son, Robert, was also no stranger to death and foreboding. He was the only Lincoln son to survive into adulthood and by the time he died in 1926, he was a very haunted man. He believed wholeheartedly that a curse hung over his life. His strange belief began in 1865 when he was with his father at the time of his death. Needless to say, it was an event that he would never forget.

Sixteen years later, in 1881, Robert was in the company of another American president whose life was ended by an assassin. President James Garfield, who had only been in office about four months, was walking through the railroad station in Washington, accompanied by Robert. Suddenly, a crazed killer named Charles Guiteau appeared from nowhere and gunned down the President.

In 1901, President William McKinley invited Robert Lincoln to tour the Pan-American Exposition with him in Buffalo, New York. While the two men were together, an anarchist named Leon Czolgosg managed to approach them with a pistol. In seconds, President McKinley was dead.

For the third time, Robert had been present at the death of an American president.

Not surprisingly, he became convinced that he was "cursed" and that somehow he had contributed to the deaths of these men, including to the death of his father. From that time on, he refused to ever meet, or even be near, another American president. Although invitations arrived from the White House and from other Washington social gatherings, he declined them all.

Was there truly a curse over Robert Lincoln's head? He certainly believed there was.

Major Rathbone, who was stabbed by Booth, recovered physically from the attack but would forever be haunted by the terrible night of the assassination. He and Clara soon married and moved to Germany, but the marriage was anything but blissful. Clara soon found that her husband was prone to bouts of depression and moodiness, none of which he had been inclined toward before the night in Ford's Theater. Then one morning, on Christmas Day of 1883, he went over the edge and killed Clara in a fit of insanity. Their children were spared, thanks to the bravery of their nanny, and Rathbone failed in his attempt to take his own life. He managed to stab himself four times, but lived long enough to die in a German mental institution in 1911.

The news of the tragedy soon reached Washington and rumors quickly spread. It was not long before the neighbors were crossing to the other side of the street, rather than walk directly in front of the former Rathbone house in Lafayette Square. A few people expressed concern that the troubled spirits of the family might return to their old home, while others insisted they already had. It was said that the sound of a man's weeping, accompanying by the heartbreaking sobs of a woman and children, could be heard coming from the grounds. The stories would continue for many years and eventually, would fade away.

SECRETS OF THE GRAVE

The body of President Lincoln traveled west from Washington, spending several weeks visiting towns and cities along a circuitous route. His funeral service in Springfield did not take place until May 4 and it followed a parade route from the former Lincoln home to Oak Ridge Cemetery, on the far edge of the city. Today, a grand monument stands as the resting place of Abraham Lincoln but it was years after he was brought here before he was able to rest in peace. This monument, which holds the tomb of Lincoln, has long been a place of mystery, intrigue, speculation and bizarre history.

And from the very beginning, it was believed to be haunted by the ghost of the murdered president himself.

Following the assassination, the President's body was returned to Springfield and to a grave in a remote, wooded cemetery called Oak Ridge. The cemetery had been started around 1860 and it mostly consisted of woods and unbroken forest. In fact, not until after Lincoln was buried there was much done in the way of improvement, adding roads, iron gates and a caretaker's residence.

Lincoln was taken to the receiving vault of the cemetery and placed there with his sons, Willie, who had died during the presidency and Eddie, Lincoln's son who had died many years before. Willie's body had accompanied his father's from Washington, while Eddie's had been exhumed and brought over from another cemetery. A short time later, a temporary vault was built for Lincoln and in seven months, on December 21, he was placed inside. Six of Lincoln's friends wanted to be sure the body was safe, so a plumber's assistant named Leon P. Hopkins made an opening in the lead box for them to peer inside. All was well and Lincoln and his sons were allowed a temporary rest.

The new construction on a permanent tomb would last for more than five years and the catacomb would actually be completed first. It was during this time that strange things began to be reported in the vicinity of Lincoln's resting place. A few days after the body was placed in the receiving vault, Springfield residents and curiosity seekers began to tell of sighting a spectral image of Lincoln himself wandering about near the crypt. The legends and reports say that he was taking walks to investigate the broken ground where he and his sons would be placed when the tomb was completed.

And the stories didn't end there either.... after the bodies were moved to the monument tomb, strange sobbing noises and sounds like footsteps were often heard at the site. Many of the locals believed that the ghost of President Lincoln was haunting Oak Ridge Cemetery and the new tomb. Many believe that he still walks today.

On September 19, 1871, the caskets of Lincoln and his sons were removed from the hillside crypt and taken to the catacomb. The tomb was not quite finished yet, but the completed portion was a suitable place for them to be moved to. The plumber, Leon P. Hopkins, opened the coffin once more and the same six friends peered again at the president's face. There were several crypts waiting for Lincoln and his sons, although one of them had already been filled. Tad had died in Chicago a short time before and his body had already been placed in the nearly finished monument.

During the move, it was noticed that Lincoln's mahogany coffin was beginning to deteriorate, so his friends brought in a new iron coffin, to which the inner coffin of lead, containing Lincoln's body, was transferred. The dead president was laid to rest again, for another three years, while the workmen toiled away outside.

On October 9, 1874, Lincoln was moved again. This time, his body was placed inside of a marble sarcophagus, which had been placed in the center of the semi-circular catacomb. A few days later, the monument was finally dedicated. Money had been raised for the groups of statues that were situated outside and the citizens of Springfield seemed content with the final resting place of their beloved Abraham Lincoln.

But then a new threat arose from a direction that no one could have ever predicted. In 1876, a band of thieves broken into the tomb and almost made off with the president's remains. They had planned to hold the body for ransom and only failed because one of the men in their ranks was a spy for the Secret Service.

It did not take long before the story of the Lincoln grave robbery became a hotly denied rumor, or at best, a fading legend. The custodians of the site simply decided that it was something they did not wish to talk about. Of course, as the story began to be denied, the people who had some recollection of the tale created their own truth in myths and conspiracies. The problem in this case however, was that many of these "conspiracies" happened to be grounded in the truth.

Hundreds of people came to see the Lincoln burial site and many of them were not afraid to ask about the stories that were being spread about the tomb. From 1876 to 1878, custodian John C. Power gave rather evasive answers to anyone who prodded him for details about the grave robbery. He was terrified of one question in particular and it seemed to be the one most often asked... was he sure that Lincoln's body had been returned safely to the sarcophagus after the grave robbers took it out?

Power was terrified of that question for one reason.... because at that time, Lincoln's grave was completely empty!

On the morning of November 1876, when John T. Stuart of the Lincoln National Monument Association, learned what had occurred in the tomb with the would-be robbers, he rushed out to the site. He was not able to rest after the incident, fearing that the grave robbers, who had not been caught at that time, would return and finish their ghoulish handiwork. So, he made a decision. He notified the custodian and told him that they must take the body from the crypt and hide it elsewhere in the building. Together, they decided the best place to store it would be in the cavern of passages which lay between the Memorial Hall and the catacomb.

That afternoon, Adam Johnson, a Springfield marble-worker, took some of his men and they lifted Lincoln's casket from the sarcophagus. They covered it over with a blanket and then cemented the lid back into place. Later that night, Johnson, Power and three members of the Memorial Association stole out to the monument and carried the 500-pound coffin around the base of the obelisk, through Memorial Hall and into the dark labyrinth. They placed the coffin near some boards that had been left behind in the construction. The following day, Johnson built a new outer coffin while Power set to work digging a grave below the dirt floor. It was slow work, because it had to be done between visitors to the site, and he also had a problem with water seeping into the hole. Finally, he gave up and simply covered the coffin with the leftover boards and wood.

For the next two years, Lincoln lay beneath a pile of wood in the labyrinth, while visitors from all over the world wept and mourned over the sarcophagus at the other end of the monument. More and more of these visitors asked questions about the theft... questions full of suspicion, as if they knew something they really had no way of knowing.

In the summer and fall of 1877, the legend took another turn. Workmen arrived at the monument to erect the naval and infantry groups of statuary on the corners of the upper deck. Their work would take them into the labyrinth, where Power feared they would discover the coffin. The scandal would be incredible, so Power made a quick decision. He called the workmen together and swearing them to secrecy, showed them the coffin. They promised to keep the secret, but within days everyone in Springfield seemed to know that Lincoln's body was not where it was supposed to be. Soon, the story was spreading all over the country.

Power was now in a panic. The body had to be more securely hidden and to do this, he needed more help. He contacted two of his friends, Major Gustavas Dana and General Jasper Reece and explained the situation. These men brought three others to meet with Power, Edward Johnson, Joseph Lindley and James McNeill, all of Springfield.

On the night of November 18, the six men began digging a grave for Lincoln at the far end of the labyrinth. Cramped and cold, and stifled by stale air, they gave up around midnight with the coffin just barely covered and traces of their activity very evident. Power promised to finish the work the next day. These six men, sobered by the responsibility that faced them, decided to form a brotherhood to guard the secret of the tomb. They brought in three younger men, Noble Wiggins, Horace Chapin and Clinton Conkling, to help in the task. They called themselves the Lincoln Guard of Honor and had badges made for their lapels.

After the funeral of Mary Lincoln, John T. Stuart told the Guard that Robert Lincoln wanted to have his mother's body hidden away with his father's. So, late on the night of July 21, the men slipped into the monument and moved Mary's double-leaded casket, burying it in the labyrinth next to Lincoln's.

Visitors to the tomb increased as the years went by, all of them paying their respects to the two empty crypts. Years later, Power would complain that questions about Lincoln's empty grave were asked of him nearly everyday. Finally, in 1886, the Lincoln National Monument Association decided that it was time to provide a new tomb for Lincoln in the catacomb. A new and stronger crypt of brick and mortar was designed and made ready.

The press was kept outside as the Guard, and others who shared the secret of the tomb, brought the Lincoln caskets out of the labyrinth. Eighteen persons, who had known Lincoln in life, filed past the casket, looking into a square hole that had been cut into the lead coffin.

Strangely, Lincoln had changed very little. His face was darker after 22 years but they were still the same sad features these people had always known. The last man to identify the corpse was Leon P. Hopkins, the same man who had closed the casket years before. He soldered the square back over the hole, thinking that he would be the last person to ever look upon the face of Abraham Lincoln.

The Guard of Honor lifted the casket and placed it next to Mary's smaller one. The two of them were taken into the catacomb and lowered into the new brick and mortar vault. Here, they would sleep for all time.....

"All time" lasted for about 13 more years. In 1899, Illinois legislators decided the monument was to be torn down and a new one built from the foundations. It seemed that the present structure was settling unevenly, cracking around the "eternal" vault of the president.

There was once again the question of what to do with the bodies of the Lincoln family. The Guard of Honor (who was still around) came up with a clever plan. During the 15 months needed for construction, the Lincoln's would be secretly buried in a multiple grave a few feet away from the foundations of the tomb. As the old structure was torn down, tons of stone and dirt would be heaped onto the gravesite both to disguise and protect it. When the new monument was finished, the grave would be uncovered again.

When the new building was completed, the bodies were exhumed once again. In the top section of the grave were the coffins belonging to the Lincoln sons and to a grandson, also named Abraham. The former president and Mary were buried on the bottom level and so safely hidden that one side of the temporary vault had to be battered away to reach them.

Lincoln's coffin was the last to be moved and it was close to sunset when a steam engine finally hoisted it up out of the ground. The protective outer box was removed and six construction workers lifted the coffin onto their shoulders and took it into the catacomb. The other members of the family had been placed in their crypts and Lincoln's was placed into a white, marble sarcophagus.

The group dispersed after switching on the new electric burglar alarm. This device connected the monument to the caretaker's house, which was a few hundred feet away. As up-to-date as this device was, it still did not satisfy the fears of Robert Lincoln, who was sure that his father's body would be snatched again if they were not careful. He stayed in constant contact with the Guard of Honor, who were still working to insure the safety of the Lincoln's remains, and made a trip to Springfield every month or so after the new monument was completed. Something just wasn't right. Even though the alarm worked perfectly, he could not give up the idea that the robbery might be repeated.

He journeyed to Springfield and brought with him his own set of security plans. He met with officials and gave them explicit directions on what he wanted done. The construction company was to break a hole in the tile floor of the monument and place his father's casket at a depth of 10 feet. The coffin would then be encased in a cage of steel bars and the hole would be filled with concrete, making the president's final resting place into a solid block of stone.

On September 26, 1901, a group assembled to make the final arrangements for Lincoln's last burial. A discussion quickly turned into a heated debate. The question that concerned them was whether or not Lincoln's coffin should be opened and the body viewed one last time? Most felt this would be a wise precaution, especially in light of the continuing stories about Lincoln not being in the tomb. The men of the Honor Guard were all for laying the tales to rest at last, but Robert was decidedly against opening the casket again, feeling that there was no need to further invade his father's privacy.

In the end, practicality won out and Leon P. Hopkins was sent for to chisel out an opening in the lead coffin. The casket was placed on two sawhorses in the still unfinished Memorial Hall. The room was described as hot and poorly lighted, as newspapers had been pasted over the windows to keep out the stares of the curious.

What actually took place in that room is unknown except from the reports of the select few who were present. Most likely, they were the same people who had been present several years before when the body had been placed in the brick and mortar vault.

A piece of the coffin was cut out and lifted away. According to diaries, a "strong and reeking odor" filled the room, but the group pressed close to the opening anyway. The face of the president was covered with a fine powder made from white chalk. It had been applied in 1865 before the last burial service. It seemed that Lincoln's face had turned inexplicably black in Pennsylvania and after that, a constant covering of chalk was kept on his face.

Lincoln's features were said to be completely recognizable. The casket's headrest had fallen away and his head was thrown back slightly, revealing his still perfectly trimmed beard. His small black tie and dark hair were still as they were in life, although his eyebrows had vanished. The broadcloth suit that he had worn to his second inauguration was covered with small patches of yellow mold and the American flag that was clutched in his lifeless hands was now in tatters.

There was no question, according to those present, that this was Abraham Lincoln and that he was placed in the underground vault. The casket was sealed back up again by Leon Hopkins, making his claim of years ago to be true.... he really was the last person to look upon the face of Lincoln.

The casket was then lowered down into the cage of steel and two tons of cement was poured over it, forever encasing the president's body in stone.

You would think that would be the end of it, but as with all lingering mysteries, a few questions still remain. The strangest are perhaps these: does the body of Abraham Lincoln really lie beneath the concrete in the catacomb? Or was the last visit from Robert Lincoln part of some elaborate ruse to throw off any further attempts to steal the president's body? And did, as some rumors have suggested, Robert arrange with the Guard of Honor to have his father's body hidden in a different location entirely?

Most historians would agree that Lincoln's body is safely encased in the concrete of the crypt, but let's look at this with a conspiratorial eye for a moment. Whose word do we have for the fact that Lincoln's body is where it is said to be? We only have the statement of Lincoln's son, Robert, his friends and of course, the Guard of Honor.... but weren't these the same individuals who left visitors to the monument to grieve before an empty sarcophagus while the president was actually hidden in the labyrinth, beneath a few inches of dirt?

Sort of makes you wonder, doesn't it?

And what of the stories that claim that Lincoln's ghost still walks the tomb?

Many have reported that he, or some other spirit here, does not rest in peace. Many tourists, staff members and historians have had some unsettling impressions here that aren't easily laughed away. Usually these encounters have been reported as the sound of ceaseless pacing; tapping footsteps on the tile floors; whispers and quiet voices; and the sounds of someone crying or weeping in the corridors.

Of course, the tile floors and marble walls are rather conducive to echoes and sounds that carry from other parts of the tomb.... right? Well, I know a number of people who would definitely like to use these explanations to scoff at their own strange experiences. Are you one of them?

THE LINCOLN HOME

The house in which Abraham Lincoln and his family lived in Springfield was located on Eighth Street, not far from Lincoln's law office in the downtown district. The Lincoln's lived in the house from a period shortly after Robert was born until they moved to Washington in 1861. At least that is what the history books tell us.... although some people believe that at least part of the Lincoln family is still residing in the house today.

The house was originally built in 1839 by a Reverend Dresser and was designed in the Greek

Revival Style. Lincoln purchased the home in 1844, while it was still a small cottage. It had been constructed with pine exterior boards, walnut interiors and oak flooring. Wooden pegs and hand-made nails held everything together. In 1850, Lincoln improved the exterior of the property by having a brick wall constructed and by adding a fence along Jackson Street but nothing major was done to the house until 1856. At this time, the house was enlarged to a full two stories, adding new rooms and much needed space.

Today, the house is presented in much the same way as it looked during the Lincoln years. It is now owned and operated by the National Park Service and they are not publicly thrilled that the house has gained notoriety as a "haunted" site. They have always maintained that no ghosts walk here.... although many of the witnesses to the strange events have been former employees and tour guides of the house.

For many years, stories have circulated about a tall, thin apparition who has been seen here, accompanied on occasion by a small boy. Many would pass this off to wishful thinking, but in more than one circumstance, the image of Mary Lincoln has been easily recognized. Most believe that if any Lincoln spirit resides here, then it is hers. They believe this house was the one place where Mary was truly happy while she was alive. Is it possible that her spirit may have returned here after her death?

A number of years ago, the Springfield "State Journal-Register" newspaper interviewed some (then) current and former staff members of the house, all of whom claimed to have had brushes with the supernatural here. At that time, a woman named Shirlee Laughlin was employed at the house as a custodian. She claimed that her superiors were very unhappy with what they termed her "vivid imagination". But were the events she experienced really all in her mind?

Laughlin claimed in her interview to have experienced ghosts in the house on many occasions. "I don't see the images as such," she said. "I see things happening."

Among the things she witnessed were toys and furniture that could be found in different rooms of the house at different times, seemingly moving about on its own. Unlit candles would sometimes mysteriously burn down on their own and Lincoln's favorite rocking chair was said to rock back and forth under its own power.

"At times, that rocking chair rocks," she stated, "and you can feel the wind rushing down the hall, even though the windows are shut tight."

Laughlin also recounted an occurrence that took place while she was rearranging furniture in Mary Lincoln's former bedroom. Besides being a custodian, she was also an expert on historic home restoration and would often attempt to recreate the layout of the household furniture when the Lincoln's lived in the house. She was in the bedroom alone one afternoon when someone tapped her on the shoulder. She looked around the room, but there was no one there. She decided to leave the furniture the way she had found it.

And that was not the only weird experience linked to Mary Lincoln. Another anecdote concerned a key that turned up missing from a wooden chest in Mary's room. "We looked everywhere for it," Laughlin reported, "then one morning it just showed up in the lock with a piece of pink ribbon tied to it."

No explanation was ever discovered for where the key had been or for who had tied the piece of ribbon around it.

But can we really claim this house might be haunted on just the word of a single, former employee? Perhaps not.... if she were the only one to have strange experiences here.

Staff members are not the only ones to have odd encounters. A number of tourists have also noticed things that are a bit out of the ordinary. They have reported hearing voices in otherwise empty rooms and hearing the rustle of what sounds like a period dress passing by them in the hallway. They have told of experiencing unexplainable cold spots and most common, seeing that rocking chair as it gently moves back and forth.

One tourist, an attorney from Virginia, even wrote the staff after he returned home to tell them of his own strange sighting. He claimed to see a woman standing in the parlor of the house... who abruptly vanished. He had enough time to recognize her as Mary Lincoln.

As mentioned earlier, the stories of ghosts in the Lincoln house are not only denied, but are laughed at by many of the staff members. They claim that the "ghostly" rocking chair is the product of park rangers having a little fun with the tourists using a piece of string to make the chair move. Pretty convenient, isn't it?

If this is true, well, then the house must not be haunted.... but what about the past and present rangers who have had their own experiences, even excluding Shirlee Laughlin?

One former guide said that she was on duty at the front door one afternoon when she heard the sound of music being played on the piano that used to be in the parlor. She turned to stop whoever had touched it and found that no one was in the room.

Another ranger who worked in the house recalled several occasions when strange feelings, and the touch of invisible hands, caused her to close up the house quickly on some evenings.

And again, she wasn't alone either. One ranger, who spoke to me anonymously, told me of one late afternoon when she was in the front parlor by herself. There is a display here of some of the items that could commonly be found in households of the period, including some children's toys. As she was standing in the room, she caught a movement out of the corner of her eye. When she looked, she saw a small toy as it rolled across the floor on its own.

She didn't stay in the room very long.

There are no ghost stories or legends associated with this house at all, the park rangers and officials will tell you if you are brave enough to endure their ridicule and ask. Really, this isn't much of a surprise, and as you have read in this book already and will most likely read again, there are a number of historical landmarks for which the "no ghosts" rule applies.

The Lincoln Home is no different. It is simply another house that, while not haunted, certainly seems to have a lot of ghosts!

· CHAPTER EIGHT ·

NORTHERN FRIGHTS

HISTORY & HAUNTINGS FROM NORTHERN ILLINOIS

There are, in this land, ghosts....
There are the terrible ghosts of women who have died in child-bed. These wander
along the pathways at dusk, or hide.. and call seductively. But to answer their
call is death in this world and the next.
There are the ghosts of little children who have been thrown into wells. They wail
under the stars, or catch women by the wrist and beg to be taken up and carried.
RUDYARD KIPLING

Bernie Shelton, along with his brothers Carl and Earl, were an integral part of the events that took place in Southern Illinois' "Bloody Williamson" County. As both friends and foes of gangster Charlie Birger, the Sheltons took part in what can only be considered an "all out war" between the bootlegger factions. In fact, their attack on Birger's Shady Rest roadhouse is still considered the only time that bombs have been dropped during aerial warfare in America. It should probably be mentioned though that the bombs were so badly constructed that they never exploded.

The Shelton boys grew up in Southern Illinois. Their father had moved to Wayne County from Kentucky, married a local girl and started farming. The boys were brought up on the farm but from early youth showed an aversion to hard work. As they got older, Carl and Earl began leaving home for months at a time to drive taxicabs in St. Louis and East St. Louis. When he was old enough, Bernie joined them. Needless to say, the boys quickly sought out trouble and all of them were soon mixed up with the law.

In the fall of 1915, Earl was convicted of armed robbery and sentenced to eighteen and a half months at the Illinois State Penitentiary at Pontiac. About the same time, Carl was arrested in St. Louis and charged with petty larceny. He was sentenced to a year in a workhouse. Bernie was arrested in a stolen car while Earl was still in prison. He was also sentenced to a year in the workhouse, but was paroled.

After Carl and Earl served out their sentences, both of them went to work in the Illinois coal mines, but around 1920, they moved back to East St. Louis, where Bernie was now living. They went into the bootlegging and gambling business and opened illegal joints in East St. Louis and the surrounding area. Their organization spread and as author John Bartlow Martin explained the small coal towns in southern Illinois each had their local toughs, gamblers and bootleggers. What they needed were the guns and brains to organize, something that was provided by the Shelton brothers. "They allowed the local boys to continue to operate," Martin wrote, "but only under their protection and selling their liquor." Soon, the Sheltons were in command of a large portion of Southern Illinois.

During the Klan Wars in Williamson County, the Sheltons threw in with Charlie Birger to oppose the authority of S. Glenn Young. Once those problems were over, the two rival operations began fighting one another. Events escalated and a number of murders followed, ending with the hanging of Charlie Birger and the Shelton's departure from Williamson County. They would never return.

After the gang war, they moved their operations to East St. Louis and opened new establishments for liquor, gambling and prostitution. They remained here until an honest sheriff drove them out, making room for Mafia organizers to turn the city into a major gambling spot. The Sheltons then moved north to Peoria, which they found to be much more hospitable. During the late 1930's, they established themselves and began an operation that comprised most of the illegal rackets in downstate Illinois. Apparently immune to prosecution, they were able to protect themselves from the long arm of the law. There was nothing that they could do however, to protect themselves from other gangsters.

Rendering of gangster Bernie Shelton

Carl, who had left Peoria to retire to his Wayne County farm, was killed there in the fall of 1947. Earl survived a murderous attack in Fairfield, Illinois and Roy, the oldest brother, was killed in June 1950, while driving a tractor on Earl's farm. Although he had a criminal record, he had never been associated with Carl, Earl and Bernie. In early 1951, all of the Sheltons, except the mother of the brothers and their youngest sister, disappeared. None of the Shelton murders were ever solved.

Bernie Shelton survived until 1948. He was killed on the morning of July 26, when he stepped outside the door of a tavern that he owned in Peoria. Writer DeWayne Bartels described Bernie as a "big, dumb man, a muscle-bound leg breaker, a thug. His life's work was intimidation, extortion, bootlegging, gambling and prostitution. He was not a man that you instinctively liked or respected. Bernie settled for being feared."

As Bernie walked out of the tavern that morning, he had no idea that a man was watching him from a short distance away. He was concealed in a thicket of woods at the foot of the Farmington Road hill and he cradled a high-powered Winchester rifle in his hands. Bernie walked towards his automobile and the first shot rang out. The bullet entered Bernie's abdomen and he crumpled to the ground. A short time later, he died. His life ended violently, the same way that he had lived it. In June 1948, a page in criminal history was closed for good as Bernie Shelton departed from this world forever. Or did he?

The outside of Kallister's Parkway Tavern hasn't changed much from the way that it looked in 1948. Inside though, many things are different but not every part of the past so quickly departed. You see, up until a short time ago, the owners of the place were convinced that Bernie Shelton was still around!

Current owner Diane Kallister, who was convinced that Bernie still lingered in the place, was not the only one to encounter his presence. The story of Bernie haunting his old tavern had been told for years. "I really think there's something here", she told DeWayne Bartels. "Every one of my bartenders can tell you there's been things that happened here."

For instance, a customer was standing at a counter one day when a can of peas and a jar of homemade hot sauce suddenly flew over his shoulder and hit the floor. The can ended up dented on one side, but strangely, the jar didn't break. From the way the customer was standing, the can and jar would have had to come up about three feet above the counter to clear his shoulder, then end up on the floor more than seven feet away. There had been no one else standing nearby. Staff members and cooks often complained of feeling as though they were being watched. They reported seeing objects move and fly off of shelves, moving around the kitchen under their own power.

DeWayne Bartel's interest in the ghost of Bernie Shelton came about because of a combination of things, including a series of stories that he wrote for the Peoria "Times-Observer" called "Gangster Land". The series chronicled the history of crime and gangsters in the Peoria area. During his research, he visited the Parkway Tavern and while he was there, Diane Kallister told him that Bernie Shelton haunted the place. Bartels was intrigued by her accounts, thanks to a story that he had read about a Pekin man named Rob Conover, a paranormal investigator with a reputation for confronting spirits. Conover was a former US Marine and private investigator who was nationally known for his work. He had been featured on television shows like "Sightings" and "Unexplained".

Bartels had met Conover back in 1993 and saw a videotape that the investigator had recorded inside of the now demolished health department buildings in Tazewell County. The video was part of a strange encounter involving two heavy doors at one end of a long hallway in the building. As Conover and an assistant walked down the hall, the video shows the two doors begin to open and close on their own. Moments later, the windows on the doors filled with light and a shadowy figure passed behind them. Who this might have been is unknown, as there was no one else in the building that day.

A couple of weeks after seeing the tape, Bartels joined Conover and Gordon Poquette, the director of the Tazewell County Health Department, for an excursion into the haunted building. It was a place that Conover believed was inhabited by the ghosts of those who had once lived in the place. "We were dealing with good, decent, hard-working people who fell on hard times and ended up dying at what was then the county poor farm," Conover said.

Bartels was very skeptical about the whole idea of a haunting and even made the other men wait outside while he searched the place for anyone who might be playing pranks on them. After he was satisfied, they went inside and roamed the building. They returned to the spot where Conover had accidentally recorded the swinging doors. Since that time, the section of building beyond the doors had been torn down and now only a brick wall could be seen behind it. Undaunted, they set up a video camera anyway and then went downstairs.

Poquette, who had worked for the health department for more than twelve years, had never encountered a ghost there, but he knew others had. The spirits apparently liked to play practical jokes, causing things to disappear, turning lights on and off and even letting the air out of employee's tires on occasion. Others claimed to have seen ghosts, especially a spectral woman who had been dubbed "Hazel".

After waiting for a little while, Conover and Bartels returned to the second floor. Anxious for something strange to happen, Bartels soon got what he wished for. As they turned a corner, Conover suddenly froze. "Did you feel that?" he asked the other man.

Bartels immediately felt a fleeting sensation. He described it as having the air sucked out of his lungs and from the space all around him. His hair was now standing on end and gooseflesh covered his body. Conover told him that he felt a rush of cold air pass right through him.

They quickly checked the video camera. It was still running. They spent a few moments looking through the abandoned, second-floor rooms and then returned to the camera. Suddenly, it was dead. The batteries, which were brand new, had been mysteriously drained. What could be on the tape?

They took it next door to the new health department building and began watching it. The sequence began with Conover and Bartels in the hallway, getting the camera into position. Then, the screen went strangely blank while they were talking. It came back on a few seconds later but the angle of the shot was different, even though no one had touched the camera! Conover was no longer in the frame and it was now recording the entrance to an office over on the left. Moments later, it went dead again and the remainder of the tape was nothing but static.

So, when Diane Kallister told him that the Parkway Tavern was haunted, Bartels was not quite as skeptical as he might have been a few years before. He contacted Rob Conover and the two of them agreed to check the place out. After a preliminary visit, Conover arranged to meet the reporter a few nights later, on Friday the 13th.

Bartels' editor, Rick Wade, notes that "I have found Bartels to be one of the most honest men and journalists I know. He would never pass fiction off as fact". These words will become very important to you as you read the pages that follow.

Conover arrived at the tavern a little after midnight. A large part of the reputation that he has enjoyed has not come from his just investigating ghosts, but from actually confronting them. He has a sensitivity that allows him to see and hear things that others cannot. These gifts allow him to help spirits move from this world to the next, to go towards the light, so to speak. For more than eleven years, he had been helping spirits "pass on to face God's judgment" and up until that night, had never failed.

His initial visit to the Tavern had given him a sense that a spirit was present. He was not sure that the ghost was actually Bernie Shelton just yet, but he knew there was a presence in the place. He was determined to do what he could to help that spirit move on and to get out of the self-imposed limbo that he was in. If the spirit was Bernie Shelton, Conover felt that he might have guilty feelings over his past criminal acts and perhaps that was why he had not crossed over when he was murdered. They were soon to discover that this theory was not quite accurate. Bernie had not stayed around because of guilt, but because of anger.

"I feel like something is going to happen here tonight", Conover told Bartels.

The reporter noted that Rob did not include the word "good" in his statement!

Shortly after 1:00 in the morning, they began to make preparations for the night to follow. Bartels followed Conover to the kitchen, a place where he had sensed a strong energy during his previous visit to the tavern. A few days before, he and Diane Kallister had witnessed an empty beer case fly to the top of an ice cooler in an adjoining storeroom. The energy seemed to shift and change and Conover pointed out, "there's a lot of movement in this place."

A video camera with a six-hour tape was set up and pointed directly toward the storeroom. The lights were turned very low and the tavern now had a rather ominous feel to it. The group, which included Conover, Bartels, Diane Kallister and Rob's assistant, sat down around a table and Bartels noticed that the atmosphere soon seemed to change. "The energy level is increasing," Conover said, "and the temperature is falling."

Conover began to speak, directly addressing the spirit of the person he now believed was Bernie Shelton. He hoped to provoke a reaction from the ghost and it worked. "Ladies and gentlemen," he spoke up, "we are not alone in this room."

Bartels' camera, which had been turned off, immediately snapped to life and the lens popped out. The air around the table became very cool. Conover suggested that Bernie was becoming very confused and thought perhaps it would be better if they went to the kitchen. As they got up, they quickly saw that the video camera had turned itself off. There was no explanation as for why it would have died. It was still plugged in and had been running for less than two hours, not nearly long enough for it to have recorded over an entire six-hour tape. Somehow though, it had! Impossibly, the whole tape had been fast-forwarded through and the camera had shut off.

The group turned back to the storeroom and saw that the dim light that was filtering through the doorway had now become tinted with a blue color. A strange haze appeared to extend from the doorway and was hovering in the air inside of the kitchen. Conover stuck his hand up into the haze and Bartels followed his lead. He later wrote that "it was cool, much cooler than the rest of the very warm room."

As they entered the kitchen and examined the oddly acting video camera, Bartels placed his own camera on a counter, less than five feet away. Without warning, the camera again whirred to life and the lens extended. In seconds, it retracted and clicked off.

They returned to the table and sat down. Conover once again began to try and communicate with the ghost of Bernie Shelton. He stood up. "Talk to me," he pleaded with the spirit. "I want to listen, I'm here to help."

Bartels wrote that he could see and hear nothing.

Just then, Conover spoke up, as if in reply to someone else. "Holy man? No, I'm not a preacher," he said and then was silent again. He explained to the others that Bernie seemed ready to communicate and had mistaken Rob for a minister. This didn't seem to deter him though.

"He's still mad about the way he died," Conover told the others. "He keeps saying 'dirty, rotten sons of bitches'". Sweat was now running down Rob's face although Bartels confessed that he was not hot. Conover then turned and moved toward the bar, where he made a startling announcement. "I see him. He has on a brown jacket, brown pants and a white shirt with no tie and white t-shirt."

Bartels later admitted that he was fighting the urge to run in the opposite direction when Conover beckoned him to follow him to the storeroom. Apparently, Bernie had retreated toward the back door, something that Rob had never seen before. They found the storeroom and the kitchen to be silent and empty. No cold chills, no haze, nothing. Bernie had vanished, at least for the moment.

They returned back into the bar area and Conover suddenly stopped, throwing a big arm against Bartels' chest. Bernie had slipped up behind them and Rob had actually spotted his spectral image in the mirror behind the bar. "I've never had one sneak up on me like that before," he told DeWayne.

Conover again began to speak to Bernie Shelton. There was no reply, but Bartels reported a loud, popping sound that occurred. He couldn't tell where it came from but said that it seemed to surround them. A feeling of tension remained in the air, filling the silence. Then, footsteps were heard in the game room. No one in the group had left the bar area. Bartels wrote that "this struggle had become a contest of wills in my mind."

"We're going to give him a few more minutes," Conover spoke up, "and then make things happen."

A few moments later, Conover began to offer a prayer from the Bible and he tried to contact Bernie once again. He urged him to try and pass over, to go towards the light and find some peace. He hadn't found any sort of peace in this world, so perhaps he could find it in the next. There was no reply.

Conover was fed up. "I think the problem is, I've never run into such a dumb, ignorant ghost," he said. "Ok Bernie, it's time for you to go."

Bartels recalled that a loud pop sounded from under the table next to where he was sitting but nothing else followed. Bernie was gone... but he had not left the building. For the first time in eleven years, Conover had failed. Bernie Shelton was not going to pass over.

"He listened to me. He talked to me," Conover said a short time later, musing over why the spirit insisted on staying. "He tried to scare me and then just backed off. Maybe he deserves this. I don't think this guy has any remorse."

Bartels suggested that perhaps it just wasn't meant to be.

Conover thought it might be something else though. It was hard to hide his disappointment. "I tell people that I'll solve their problem. Maybe over the years I got cocky and God is putting me in my place."

No matter the reason, Bernie Shelton was not leaving. The Parkway Tavern was still his, even decades after his death.

Defeat was not something that Rob Conover took lightly and three days later, on August 16, he and DeWayne Bartels returned to the Parkway Tavern. Conover was not ready to give up on the idea helping Bernie Shelton cross over. Whatever was holding him here couldn't be enough to keep him from the other side. Could it?

That evening, the two men joined Diane Kallister and her best friend, Tracy Ford at the tavern. The place had closed early and the parking lot was deserted when they arrived. Conover had come up with a new plan for this evening's assault on Bernie. The four participants would split up into pairs and stay in contact with one another using two-way radio monitors. Conover and another person would go into the kitchen and storeroom, while the other group would remain near the tavern's door. Here they could observe the bar area and game room.

Diane Kallister accompanied Conover into the kitchen and Bartels and Tracy sat down near the other monitor. Soon, they heard Conover's voice coming though it, cautiously trying to coax Bernie Shelton into another conversation. For nearly a half-hour, nothing happened.

Restless, Bartels decided to stroll over near the game room and when he did, he sensed a cold, electrical presence that seemed to come from nowhere. He called to Tracy, but she couldn't feel it. However, a short time later she began to complain of feeling very warm, even though they were sitting almost directly under an air vent. She then went into the kitchen to be with Diane. Bartels could hear her voice over the monitor telling her friend that she was sweating and felt as though she had a fever.

Suddenly, Diane's voice rang out. "It's incredibly cold in here."

In spite of the fact that she was in the warmest room in the building, a cold chill seemed to pervade the air. She urged Bernie to make an appearance and moments later, the familiar blue light appeared near the door to the storeroom. Conover stated that he saw it too, but Tracy remained silent. Bartels looked up from where he was listening to all of this in the other room, but was unable to see anything. The moment passed and Conover suggested that they take a break.

A little while later, Conover and Diane returned to the storeroom. Tracy came back to the table and sat down with Bartels, but remained uncomfortable. She worriedly watched the door to the kitchen and near 11:00 became very hot again. "He's doing something," she was convinced.

A loud noise came over the monitor! Conover called to bring a camera and DeWayne hurriedly snapped off two quick shots. They turned on the light to see what had made the startling noise. Just inside of the entrance to the storeroom was a yellow bucket with wheels. A mop had been jammed inside of it and it had been moved in such a way that it now blocked the entrance to the room. It had not been that way earlier in the evening.

Finally, Conover was encouraged again. He agreed to let Tracy accompany him to the kitchen and she made her own attempts to contact Bernie. Both of them claimed to see small lights appear near the doorway but that was all. After a while, Diane and Tracy went outside to get some air. The frustrating breaks were ruining Conover's concentration. He felt that each time he was making progress getting through to Bernie, something would happen to throw things off kilter. And it would happen again....

Moments after midnight, Diane suddenly let out a bloodcurdling scream that brought both Conover and Tracy from the kitchen. Ford had been trying to contact Bernie and Diane was certain that she had somehow seen through Bernie's eyes. Bernie, she believed, had been near the restrooms in the bar area. She was certain she had seen him there. When Conover had asked Tracy what she had seen, she murmured "Diane". Ford now burst into tears and the two women again went outside.

Bartels once more noted Conover's disappointment. "We were so close," Rob said. "He told her that he was lost, he was re-living that night and telling me about it through her."

Just then, the women came back into the tavern and Kallister announced that she was finished. She didn't want to do this anymore, but Tracy urged her to continue. She wanted to try again. Finally, Diane relented. "Go ahead, but this is the last time. This is too much."

A few minutes later, Conover and Ford were back in the kitchen. The room was hot and pitch black. They sat across from one another and Conover again began to speak. Slowly and evenly, he asked Bernie to contact them again. He told Tracy that she needed to open her mind and to try and contact the angry ghost.

"Bernie, are you there?" Tracy asked.

"Talk to us Bernie," Conover prodded and he began to ask questions. Where did Bernie think he was? Did he want to leave?

Then, Tracy interrupted, her voice set in an eerie pitch. "Died on the way.... he doesn't want to go to the light until he takes care of the guy who shot him. He wants Charlie Harris, the guy who shot him."

Diane was startled at this and told Bartels that there was no way that Tracy could have known about Charlie Harris, the man suspected of killing Bernie Shelton. They listened closely to the monitor as the chilling dialogue continued.

Conover spoke. "Tell me when you see the light."

"I don't see it," Ford replied.

"Find it Bernie."

"Somebody else was involved too."

"It was 51 years ago, everyone else involved is gone," Conover barked. "Look for the light, Bernie.... ask him why he won't go to the light".

"He doesn't want to..." Tracy started to say and then stopped. "He knows where the light is. He's by the light."

Conover pushed a little harder, urging Bernie to step into the light.

"He stopping," Tracy whispered, then hissed out more words. "He going! He's going to the light!" Her last words came out as a scream. "Oh God, he's gone!"

A short time later, they emerged from the kitchen. "There's nothing here anymore," Rob told Bartels. "He was a battle. He's the biggest battle that I ever had."

There was no reason why Bernie was so difficult, except for the fact that he simply didn't want to go. He was going to face judgment for the things that he had done in life, Conover believed, and maybe that's what stopped him. Rob also instinctively felt that Bernie didn't trust him, which may have been why he responded to Tracy instead. He didn't think there was anything special about the young woman, other than that she was willing to open up and listen. That, he said, had been the key.

Whatever the reasons though, Bernie Shelton was gone.

But was he ever really there? Not everyone is convinced. Some long-time customers of the Parkway Tavern laughed off the idea of a ghost. One skeptic said that he had heard about Bernie haunting the bar for years, but he wasn't buying the tall tale. "Once you're dead, you're dead," he told DeWayne Bartels.

But is this really the case? Many would argue with this statement, especially the four people who were in the tavern that evening in August 1998. They experienced something extraordinary that night and no amount on skepticism on the part of non-believers was going to convince them that the events were not real. Bernie Shelton, they knew, had been lingering in the Parkway Tavern for more than fifty years. Now, he was gone and each of them had had a hand in his departure.

Now, the infamous gangster could rest in peace... whether he deserved it or not!

GHOSTS OF KNOX COLLEGE

Knox College, located in Galesburg, has a long history on the Illinois prairie. It was founded in 1837 as a manual arts college and has a place in state history as one of the only physical locations where debates between Abraham Lincoln and Stephen Douglas took place. The historic debates occurred in 1858 and the site at Knox College was at the Old Main on campus. A platform was constructed outside of two windows of the building and the candidates were forced to crawl out of them to appear before the crowd below.

Galesburg itself has left a mark on Illinois history as well. Not only is it the birthplace of famed poet and Lincoln biographer Carl Sandburg, but it is also the home of a man named George WG Ferris, the inventor of the Ferris Wheel. This now common amusement park attraction premiered at the Columbian Exposition in Chicago in 1893.

With a history that dates back so many years, Knox College is bound to have its share of macabre stories. One such story tells of a student who committed suicide by hanging himself outside of a window several years ago. Students and passersby allowed the boy to hang there all night long, assuming that the dangling figure was merely an effigy in the spirit of the Halloween season. They discovered the next morning they were wrong. There are also stories of haunted dorm rooms, sorority houses and apartments, but a few of the stories stand out above the rest.

For the last several years, I have traveled annually to Galesburg to meet with Professor Tim Kasser and to speak for his class on "Death and Dying" at Knox College. While there, Tim always arranges for me to visit several spots in Galesburg (some related to Knox College, some not) that are purportedly haunted. While a number of the locations have not worked out quite the way that we had hoped, a few of them have certainly been worth the trip!

The Knox County Jail building is located just across the street from the university campus and was built in 1874 to house those incarcerated by the county. The building continued in this operation until 1976 when it was then turned into a private residence. The county sheriff's home had previously been inside the building, so it was easily adapted into living quarters. The cell block and the solitary confinement cells were left untouched until Knox College purchased the building a few years ago.

It has since been turned into office space for the college and is used daily by staff members, some of whom report having some uncomfortable encounters in the building. Several of them admit to feeling very strange while inside and even claim to have heard and seen things that they can't quite explain.

One of these staff members is John Steller, who met Tim Kasser, several Knox students and myself at the old jail on the evening of my visit. Shortly after the college took the building over, John was in the rear part of the building where the cell block is located. He was on the north side of the building and had climbed up to the second tier of cells. He had just passed the second cell from the right when he was overcome by a horrible sensation. "It was so strong, I just had to back out of there and get away from it," he said.

A short time later, a reception was held in the building and one of the attendees was a former guard at the jail. Steller asked him, in conversation, if there had ever been any escapes from the jail. "Just one, " the retired guard told him, "and I can show you where."

He led Steller into the north section of the cell block and pointed to a window that was high off the floor. He explained that a prisoner had cut through a bar in the window and escaped. He was caught a couple of days later and brought back to jail. A short time after his escape attempt, the man committed suicide. And he had killed himself in the second cell from the right, on the second tier of cells! Had Steller encountered the lingering spirit of this luckless prisoner?

Other people have also complained about strange sensations, especially in the solitary confinement room known as the "hole". This narrow cell was located in the basement and anyone placed inside of it would have been cramped into a long, narrow room that was perhaps two feet wide. After the iron door was slammed closed, they were secreted away in total darkness.

It is possible that the terror felt by the men placed in this cell has left an impression behind. During my visit, I climbed into the "hole" and was amazed to find that my flashlight and camera immediately went dead, even though they had been working fine just moments before! When I stepped back (rather quickly) out of the cell, both objects began working normally again.

Could some of the prisoners of the old Knox County Jail still be waiting for their release?

My investigations with Professor Tim Kasser and his students at Knox College also led us to a house that is located on West Street, very near to the Knox campus. In fact, the house and the college have connections that even go beyond death itself.

The house belongs to the Godsil's, a large Catholic family who made us welcome in their home. If you have ever wondered how it could be possible for someone to make a ghost a part of their family, then you have to meet the Godsil family and then you will understand. This happy, busy and loving family has enough room for ten children, more than two dozen grandchildren, a great-grandchild and..... one very hard-to-miss ghost.

The after-life story of Orval Cobb actually begins in 1943, but let's jump ahead a few years to when the Godsil's first moved into the house on December 31, 1964. The dwelling had previously been used as an apartment house, so with its many rooms, it was just right for the large family to move into. Shortly after they took up residence, they began to notice they were not in the house alone. The older children seemed to notice things first, planning to keep the ghostly activity a secret from their younger siblings.

But before long, everyone had story to tell, even their father, who had been skeptical about anything strange going on for some time. One afternoon, while he was in the house alone, he went down to the basement to do some work. He heard the sound of someone walking through the house above his head and assuming one of the kids had come home, he went upstairs to look. He found that no one else was there. Thinking the sound must have just been the old house settling, he went back downstairs. And that's when the footsteps started again! He searched the house again and found no one. Almost against his will, he was now a believer.

The footsteps weren't the only thing the family noticed, but they were the most frequent. They describe them as "heavy" and they should know for they have heard them tromping about all over the house on many occasions. They travel through the hallway, into the rooms, up and down the stairs and just about everywhere else in the house.

They have also sensed the presence of someone standing inside the rooms on many occasions and had that feeling that someone might be just over their shoulder. The girls in the family also reported never feeling alone while taking a shower, as if they had caught the interest of a healthy young man! The ghost also had the habit of knocking on doors and doing other things to get attention, like causing items to disappear and then putting them in strange places later on.

Several members of the family have also caught glimpses of a shadowy figure around corners, in reflections, just past doorways and out of the corner of the eye. He has been frequently seen in a small parlor that is located just off the dining room.

The ghost had never done anything destructive or mean to anyone in the house and in fact, seems to like the family and enjoys being part of the hustle and bustle of daily life with the large group. But sometimes he is still frightening. This, I believe, is one of the main reasons that the Godsil's chose to try and discover just who this ghost might be.... and why he was haunting the house on West Street.

They started out by searching the old files of the library and the archives of the college, following one single lead. Someone told them that a Knox student had died at the house many years ago. The boy's name had been Orval Cobb and he had been a freshman at Knox College in 1943. He was from St. Charles, Illinois, near Chicago, and most remembered him as a bright, fun-loving youth who had been an honor student and well-liked by his classmates.

Unfortunately, when Orval came to Knox, he enrolled as a chemistry major and soon found that he was in over his head. His grades plunged and despair began to set in. He felt overwhelmed by his classes and some say he may have feared being drafted into the military too.

Finally, on the eve of a big chemistry test, Orval committed suicide, leaving a poem and a letter behind, detailing why he felt that he was a failure and why he felt that he had no reason to go on. Ironically, Orval stole a mixture of potassium cyanide from the chemistry lab with which to do the deed. His body was discovered by his roommate, William Bartlett, who told the authorities that he had come into his room on Monday morning and had seen Orval in bed, apparently sleeping. He knew that his friend had a test the next day, so he assumed that he had been up late studying and didn't wake him up until about an hour before class on Tuesday morning. When he tried to wake his friend, he realized that Orval had been dead for many hours.

The coroner stated that traces of poison were found in a test tube beside Orval's bed. He had taken cyanide in a tablet form, dissolved it in water and then had swallowed the mixture. The poison stopped his heart immediately.

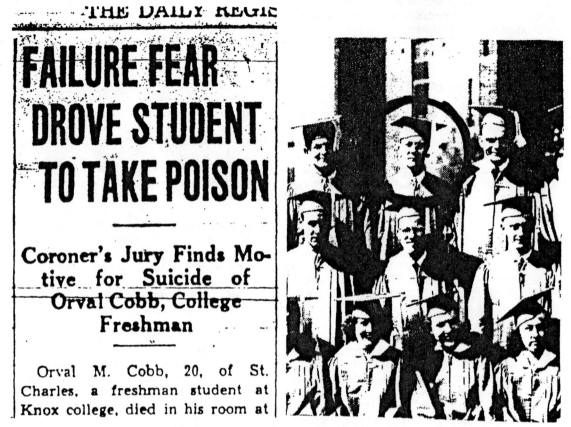

FAILURE FEAR DROVE STUDENT TO TAKE POISON

Coroner's Jury Finds Motive for Suicide of Orval Cobb, College Freshman

Orval M. Cobb, 20, of St. Charles, a freshman student at Knox college, died in his room at

A newspaper article from the day after Orval's suicide and his graduation photo from his high school in St. Charles, Illinois

On his desk, propped up against a reading lamp, was the tragic letter that he had written to his parents:

Dear Mom and Dad,
I hope that you will not take this to heart. I am trying to save you much later heartbreak. I can see now that I will never be a son to be proud of. I am going to be just another mediocre person. Knowing what that means, I can't take the sadness it will cause.
Please understand. You have both done so much for me that I can never repay you the way I am; never to my own satisfaction. To make you proud of me has been my ambition.
I am failing. To fail is something that I cannot swallow. I could not go on being a failure and knowing how it would hurt you both. This end is the best for us all. My love to you both. May your remaining years be pleasant and cheerful without me. A failure never brings happiness to anyone. My love to Vi, Min and the Millers. All my love to the dearest people on earth.

Orv

In addition to the letter, Orval also left behind a morbid poem by Charles Hanson Towne entitled

"Of One Self-Slain". He also left two brief notes to his roommates telling them of his determination to take his own life and thanking them for the friendship they had always shown him. Orval died in the front upstairs room of the house, now used as a bedroom by the Godsil family.

After learning all of this, the Godsil's were sure they had discovered the identity of the ghost and it appears they are right. The haunting has continued to go on for many years and the family has come to accept Orval as their own, even visiting his former home, and his grave, in St. Charles. They have truly made this ghost a welcome member of the family.

You have to admit, it is ironic the way that it has all turned out. Orval Cobb took his own life because he believed that he was a failure, an outsider and because he felt that his life was not worth living. It wasn't until he was dead for more than fifty years that he seemed to find his place. Perhaps it has not being during his life, but in his "after-life" instead.

When he went blundering back to God,
his song half-written, his work half done,
Who knows what paths his bruised feet trod,
What hills of peace or pain he won?
I hope God smiled, and took his hand,
And said "Poor truant, passionate fool!
Life's book is hard to understand;
Why couldst thou not remain in school?"
CHARLES HANSON TOWNE
OF ONE SELF-SLAIN

THE MACOMB POLTERGEIST

The word "poltergeist" actually means "noisy ghost" when translated from German and for many years, researchers believed that these noisy ghosts were causing the phenomena reported in all ghostly cases of this sort. The variety of activity connected with poltergeist cases includes knocking and pounding sounds, disturbance of stationary objects, doors slamming shut and usually violent, physical actions by sometimes heavy objects. While "intelligent" spirits can certainly cause such things to happen, many of these cases have nothing to do with ghosts.

The most widely accepted theory in many "poltergeist-like" cases is that the activity is not caused by a ghost, but by a person in the household. This person is usually an adolescent girl, and normally one who is troubled emotionally. It is thought that she is unconsciously manipulating the items in the house by "psychokinesis", the power to move things using energy generated in the mind. It is unknown why this ability seems to appear in females around the age of puberty but it has been documented to occur. Most of these disturbances are short-lived because the conditions that cause them to occur often pass quickly. The living person, or "agent" as they are called, subconsciously vents their repressed anger or frustration in way that science has yet to explain.

Perhaps the most famous poltergeist-like case in America took place in Macomb, Illinois in 1948. The case became so well known that it appeared in almost every newspaper in the nation, often on the front page.

That year, a disturbed teenager named Wanet McNeill was forced to live with her father after her parent's bitter divorce. The girl and her father moved to an uncle's farm, just west of Macomb. Wanet was very unhappy with the situation and her emotions were high. Soon those emotions took a most dangerous course. In the weeks that followed, Wanet managed to start fires all over her uncle's farm with nothing other than the power of her mind. She had no idea that she was causing the phenomena. The kinetic energy in her body caused an eruption of power that ignited combustible material all over the house.

The mysterious fires began on August 7 at the farm of Charles Willey. He resided outside of Macomb with his wife, his brother-in-law and Wanet's father, Arthur McNeil, McNeil's two children, Arthur Jr., age 8 and Wanet, 13. McNeil had recently divorced and had gotten custody of the children. His former wife was now living in Bloomington, where Wanet wanted to be.

The fires began as small brown spots that appeared on the wallpaper of the house. Seconds after they appeared, they would burst into flames. This began to happen day after day and neighbors came to help keep watch and to dowse the small fires with water. Pans and buckets were placed all over the house in preparation. Still, the fires materialized in front of the startled witnesses. Volunteers began standing by with hoses and buckets of water to put out the blazes. The fire chief from Macomb, Fred Wilson, was called in to investigate and he had the family strip all of the wallpaper from every wall in the house. Dozens of witnesses then watched as brown spots appeared on the bare plaster and then burst into flames. More small blazes even spread to the ceiling.

"The whole thing is so screwy and fantastic that I'm ashamed to talk about it," Wilson said. "Yet we have at least a dozen reputable witnesses that say they saw brown spots smolder suddenly on the walls and ceilings of the home and then burst into flames."

During the week of August 7, fires appeared on the front porch, ignited the curtains in every room, and even engulfed an entire bed. The National Fire Underwriters Laboratory investigated and reported that the wallpaper had been coated with flour paste (a flame retardant) and that no flammable compound, such as insect repellant, was present. They had no explanation for the fires they witnessed.

In addition to insurance investigators, the Illinois State Fire Marshal, John Burgard, also visited the farm. "Nobody has ever seen anything like this," he announced to the press, "but I saw it with my own eyes".

That week, over two hundred fires broke out and on August 14 finally consumed the entire house. Willey drove posts into the ground and made a shelter for he and his wife while McNeil moved his children into the garage. The next day, the barn went up in flames, followed by the milk house (being used as a dining room) on Tuesday. On Thursday, two fires were discovered in the chicken house and that same afternoon, the farm's second barn burned down in less than an hour. A company that sold fire extinguishers was on hand with equipment, but it did little good. An employee of the company stated that "it was the most intense heat that I've ever felt."

The family escaped to a nearby vacant house but the fires continued. The United States Air Force even got involved in the mystery. They suggested that the fires could be caused by some sort of directed radiation (presumably from the Russians!) but could offer no further assistance. By this time, the farm was swarming with spectators, investigators, and reporters. Over one thousand people came to the farm on August 22! Theorists and curiosity-seekers posed their own theories and explanations. They ran the gamut from fly spray to radio waves, underground gas pockets, flying saucers and more. The authorities had a more down-to-earth explanation in mind. They suspected arson. They realized that they could not solve the riddle as to how fires could appear before the eyes of reliable witnesses, but things were getting out of hand on the Willey farm. An explanation needed to be discovered, and quickly!

On August 30, the mystery was announced solved. The arsonist, according to officials, was Wanet. They claimed that she was starting the fires with kitchen matches when no one was looking, ignoring the witness reports of fires that sprang up from nowhere, including on the ceiling. Apparently, this slight thirteen-year-old girl possessed some pretty amazing skills, along with a seemingly endless supply of matches!

Fire Marshal Burgard and a State's Attorney named Keith Scott had taken Wanet aside for an hour's worth of "intense questioning". After that, she had allegedly confessed. She stated that she was unhappy, didn't like the farm, wanted to see her mother and most telling, that she didn't have pretty clothes. The mystery was solved! This was in spite of the fact that witnesses to the fires had seen them appear on walls, floors and even on ceilings, all when Wanet was not even in the room.

This explanation pleased the authorities but not all of the reporters who were present seemed convinced. The hundreds of paranormal investigators who have examined the case over the years have not been reassured either. One columnist from a Peoria newspaper, who had covered the case from the beginning, stated quite frankly that he did not believe the so-called "confession". Neither did noted researcher Vincent Gaddis, who wrote about the case in his landmark book "Mysterious Fires and Lights". He was convinced the case was a perfect example of poltergeist phenomena.

What really happened on the Willey Farm? We will probably never know because the story just went away after that. Wanet was turned over to her grandmother. The insurance company paid Willey for the damage done to his home and farm. The reporters all had closure for their stories and the general public was given a solution that could not have possibly been the truth.

But that's often the case, isn't it?

ELVIRA OF THE OPERA HOUSE

Woodstock, Illinois is quaint little town in northern Illinois. The town surrounds a historic community square that is lined with preserved, turn-of-the-century homes and buildings, not the least of which is the towering Woodstock Opera House. It looms more than four stories above the rest of the downtown, its highest point being the bell tower, which is more than two-and-a-half stories in itself.

Over the years, the Opera House has played host to many well-known actors and actresses. When it first opened in 1890, the first performers were the Patti Rose Players, who billed themselves as the leading opera company in the Midwest. Since that time, many renowned stars have appeared here, including Orson Welles, Shelley Berman, Tom Bosley, Betsy Palmer, Lois Nettleton, Geraldine Page, Paul Newman and others. During the 1940's and 1950's, many of them were just starting out and worked day jobs in order to perform at the theater in the evening.

While each of these performers have played many different roles on the road to success, both they and the legions of unknown actors who have appeared at the Opera House have one thing in common. It is the fear of critics. In this case though, it is the fear of one critic in particular. Because at the Woodstock Opera House, every show receives a review from the resident critic, who always makes her opinion plain during the dress rehearsals. If a play or an opera does not meet her high standards, then she will rush into the balcony like a temperamental director and begin slamming seats up and down. In this way, she makes her distaste for the show very evident!

But who is this obnoxious critic? Her name, according to theater legends, is "Elvira", and she is none other than the theater's oldest patron. She had been around the place as long as anyone can remember, dating back to at least the 1890's. She is not an elderly ticket buyer though... she is the opera house's resident ghost!

There are a number of stories to explain Elvira's presence in the theater. In one version, she is a suicidal actress involved in a failed love affair and in another, an actress with an inflated idea about her own acting skills. In both stories, she plunges to her death from the top of the opera's bell tower. The end result is that her suicide causes her to linger behind in the theater, remaining involved, in a spectral way, with the performances here. These stories have been scoffed at as mere legends, but there seems to be little doubt that the theater is genuinely haunted.

Comedian Shelley Berman is just one of the many performers who has encountered Elvira's ghost in the opera house. One night, after his career was well on its way, he returned for an engagement at the theater. He had just finished rehearsing for a show that evening when he heard a number of the spring-loaded seats in the balcony slam shut. He jumped from the stage and rushed up to the balcony. He was sure that he had been in the theater alone. When he arrived at that section of seats, he found it empty. He was convinced that he had received a critique from Elvira.

Theater tradition has it that the ghost holds claim to the seat DD 113. It is said to be her favorite and the theater manager admits that it is the most requested seat in the house. Even when the rest of the balcony is empty, including the better seats, someone always wants to sit in Elvira's seat.

A woman named Esther Wanieck, who was interviewed about Elvira for the book "Haunted

Houses USA", directed a number of plays over a twenty-year span at the Opera House. She was confident that Elvira existed and that she was startlingly present in the theater. She stated that she felt the spirit most strongly when she was in the theater alone at night or when she was finishing last minute details for a show that was about to open.

An anonymous theater board member also admitted to believing in the ghost and claimed to have seen her on several occasions. They described Elvira as a tall, striking young woman who wore a flowing, ball gown. Her hair was golden and fell to her waist and she seemed to glide effortlessly wherever she went, as opposed to simply walking.

During recent years, the theater has undergone renovations, which can sometimes cause strange phenomena to increase. One man, who was working alone in the building one evening, claimed to come face to face with a dark figure. He knew that no one else could have gotten into the place, so he fled the theater and refused to return. Other workers and staff members, even those who vowed they did not believe in ghosts, admitted that this man was a reliable person and not someone who overreacted or made up stories.

While she may have frightened this individual, most involved with the theater believe that Elvira is a friendly spirit. A few however, are not convinced of that. A stagehand panicked one night when he saw a mysterious, golden figure moving across the darkened stage in his direction. He dropped his tools and ran from the building in terror. He was another person who never returned.

In addition, many actors say that Elvira makes herself known in some pretty disconcerting ways. Scenery flats have suddenly toppled over during rehearsals, even though they are securely tied. Props sometimes shift location or simply fall over with no explanation. Strangest of all are the odd sounds from the balcony. It has been said that when things are not going particularly well during a rehearsal, Elvira lets out a long sigh of distaste from her favorite seat. "It can be very unnerving," executive director Douglas Rankin told author Richard Winer.

That special seat often presents problems of its own. As in most theaters, the Opera House has a policy of making sure that all seats are in the upright, closed position before the audience enters the auditorium for a performance. All of the seats in the balcony stay upright, except for Elvira's! No matter how many times it is placed in the correct position, it is always down when the audience enters the theater. It is as if Elvira has already taken her seat! Investigations of the mechanics of the seat have revealed that there is nothing wrong with the springs. There is no (earthly) reason why the seat refuses to stay closed.

Are Elvira's intentions always good? Once again, some would argue this. It seems that the depression felt by Elvira when she took her life at the theater is still felt by some who perform here. A young actress had a frightening experience one evening when she and her boyfriend climbed to the top of the bell tower to enjoy the view. She was standing there, looking out over the city, when a cold chill suddenly enveloped her. She began shaking and found herself weeping uncontrollably. Then, as if in a daze, she climbed to the top of the nearby railing and started to jump to her death! Luckily, her boyfriend quickly grabbed her and pulled her to safety. When questioned, she had no idea what had caused her to want to commit suicide. The stories have it that other actresses have also been seized with this same compulsion while on the bell tower. Most of them, like this young girl, had never heard of Elvira before climbing the steps to the tower.

Today, the Opera House continues to be an outstanding showplace and a popular theater. Apparently, the stories of a resident ghost have not hurt the attendance. If anything, they seem to bring people who have not attended the theater before. With that in mind, it is interesting to note that, even though she had been dead for more than a century, Elvira is finally fulfilling her dreams of becoming famous!

THE HOUSE WITH NO SQUARE CORNERS

Near the tiny town of Bull Valley, Illinois is perhaps one of the strangest houses in northern Illinois. It was originally located far off the beaten path and remains secluded today along a quiet and mostly deserted country highway. George and Sylvia Stickney built this English country house in the middle 1800's. They chose such an isolated place for the peace and quiet and for their spiritualistic activities. Both of them were said to be accomplished mediums and they wanted to host parties and seances for their friends. The seclusion offered by the Illinois countryside made the perfect setting.

The house itself was very unusual in its design. It rose to a full two stories, although the second floor was reserved for a ballroom that ran the entire length of the building. During the Civil War, the house also served as quarters for Federal soldiers and was home to the first piano in McHenry County. But this was not why the house gained its fame, or rather its notoriety.

As devout practitioners of Spiritualism, the Stickney's insisted on adding distinctive features into the design of the house. These features, they assured the architect, would assist them when holding seances and gatherings at the property. Since the seances would be held quite often, they specified that the house should have no square corners in it. They explained that spirits have a tendency to get stuck in these corners, which could have dire results. It has also been suggested that the Stickney's believed that corners attracted the attention of evil spirits as well, a common belief in Spiritualist circles of the time.

According to legend though, one corner of a room accidentally ended up with a 90-degree measurement. How this could have happened is unknown. Perhaps the architect either forgot or was unable to complete the room with anything but a right angle. Perhaps he thought that the Stickney's would never notice this one flaw. But they did notice! And here, the legend takes an even stranger turn.

The stories say that it was in this corner that George Stickney was discovered one day. He was slumped to the floor, dead from an apparent heart failure, although no visible signs suggested a cause of death. Was he right about the square corners? Could an angry ghost, summoned by a seance, have been trapped in the corner?

After the death of her husband, Sylvia Stickney lived on in the house and gained considerable fame as a spirit medium. The upstairs ballroom was converted into a large seance chamber and people came from far and wide to contact the ghosts of their deceased loved ones and relatives. Sylvia also claimed to stay in contact with her unlucky husband and her deceased children.

Time passed and despite the seances and the mysterious death of George Stickney, the house never really gained a bad reputation until the 1970's. It had always been considered a strange and unusual place, connected to the spirit world, but it was never thought to be a bad one until a man named Rodrick Smith moved in. He lived in the house for several years and when he moved out, he began to claim that he had often heard strange noises in the place. He also added that his dogs were never comfortable there. This led him to believe that something was not right with the property. Smith's research led him to reveal that the house had become "tainted" by a group of "devil worshippers" who lived in it during the 1960's. He was convinced that their "black magic rituals" conjured up something unpleasant that now inhabited the house.

It later turned out that the so-called "devil worshippers" were actually a group of stoned-out hippies who painted the rooms in dark colors and built open fires on the floors of the house. When they departed, they left spray painted messages and drug paraphernalia in their wake. While it's unlikely that they worshipped the Devil, Smith was sure that they had changed the atmosphere of the Stickney Mansion.

He was certainly no help in getting the house sold but neither was one of the real estate listings that came after his departure. A local antique dealer would claim that he saw a real estate ad for the place in which a woman in a wedding gown could be seen pulling aside a curtain and peering out. The photographer who took the picture said that no one was in the house at the time. He also stated that he had seen no one at the window when he was snapping photos of the house. Was the woman a ghost?

Eventually, the house sold and the next owners claimed to experience nothing unusual in the place. They stayed on for several years but moved out when their plans to restore the mansion didn't pan out. Their occupancy leaves nothing to suggest that they were bothered by ghosts and apparently, neither are the owners today. The local police department uses a portion of the restored house as their headquarters and claim nothing out of the ordinary. The official word is that, while the house was badly treated by vandals, it is not, nor was it ever, haunted.

So, who knows? Some area residents dispute the final word from the authorities. They say that ghostly things have been going on in the Stickney Mansion for many years, and continue to go on today, whether the local police officers want to admit it or not. What is the truth? No one seems to be able to say and the ghosts, if there are any here, are certainly not talking!

GHOSTS ALONG CUBA ROAD

The graveyard ghosts of Illinois are strange and often perplexing and the many stories run the entire gamut between entertaining folklore and authentic accounts of the supernatural. One such account, which seems to combine elements of both, involves a place called White Cemetery in northern Illinois. This small graveyard, and the surrounding Cuba Road area near Barrington, has gained a rather strange reputation in recent years.

White Cemetery is a small burial ground that is located just east of Old Barrington Road. It dates back as far as the 1820's, but no records exist to say when it started to gain the attention of those with an interest in the unexplained.

For many years, it has been reportedly haunted by eerie, white globes of light that have been seen to hover and float among the tombstones. Witnesses to these anomalies have ranged from teenagers to average passersby, many of whom have gone to the local police and have described not only the glowing lights, but hazy figures too. The lights are said to sometimes float along through the cemetery, drift over the fence and then glide out over the surface of the road. The hazy human-like figures have been spotted along the edge of the fence and lingering near stands of trees. They tend to appear and then vanish at will. Both types of the phenomenon have been investigated and studied by ghost hunters and researchers for some time, but no explanation has been discovered as to their source.

There have also been many stories told about nearby Cuba Road itself. Most of them involve a phantom black automobile that appears near the cemetery and an old house that is seen and then vanishes nearby. The house is believed to have actually existed many years ago and legends say that it burned down under mysterious circumstances. It has been repeatedly spotted over time, often by people who have no idea that the house no longer exists. Some of the sightings also involve a spectral old woman that carries a lantern and flags down passing motorists. When someone stops and tries to help her, she disappears along the edge of the roadway.

In her book "More Chicago Haunts", author Ursula Bielski adds another element to the strange legends of Cuba Road. According to local historians, nearby Barrington and Lake Zurich were often visited by gangsters during the Prohibition era. Looking for a little peace and quiet, they would come to the small towns to rest, fish, sun and often, to cause a little trouble. Local folks were afraid of these Chicago tough guys and the author believes that this unease remains in one of the ghostly encounters said to occur along Cuba Road. The stories say that the spectral image of a cigar-chewing gangster sometimes appears in the rearview mirror of drivers who pass along this roadway. Who this mobster might be is unknown, but those drivers who have seen him can testify to the fact that he was there!

Strange things, as they say, happen along Cuba Road.

DINNER AND SPIRITS

Located west of Chicago in Clarendon Hills is a popular establishment called the Country House Restaurant. For many years, the place has been the home to not only fine food and spirits, but to a ghost or two as well.

Like many haunted spots, the Country House has its share of rattling dishes, lights that turn on and off, moving objects that go bump in the night, strong smells of flowers in otherwise empty rooms, shutters that open and close and other sorts of strange happenings. In addition to all of that, there are the apparitions too.

One afternoon a customer came into the place and asked owner David Regnery about the woman he saw looking out the attic window. The man joked with him and asked Regnery if he was running a bordello or something? When he was asked what he meant, the customer replied that a young woman had been beckoning to him from a window overlooking the parking lot. Strangely, that part of the attic was a locked storeroom and no one was upstairs at that time.

Regnery was not surprised by the report as he has had his own experiences in the place. They started nineteen years before when he and another man witnessed some shutters open by themselves. Other experiences occurred while doing paperwork in an upstairs office, after the restaurant had been closed for the night. On several occasions, he heard the door downstairs open, people come in and then walk up to the bar. He went down the stairs, still listening to their muffled conversations, but when he reached the bar it was dark and empty.

There are a couple of different stories to explain the identities of the resident ghosts here. A story claims that one of the lingering spirits is that of a man from the 1800's. Apparently, he was a worker at a grist mill that was located on the property long before the restaurant existed. But there was another ghost as well and one whose story the owners were later able to confirm!

David and Patrick Regnery bought the restaurant in the spring of 1974. They spent a large part of the next year gutting and remodeling the place. Shortly after re-opening in the winter of 1975, they began to realize that strange occurrences were apparently going to be frequent in the place. Concerned that the restaurant might be haunted, they contacted a number of psychics about the building. There was one story that all of the psychics seemed to agree on and they believed this ghost was the most dominant one haunting the restaurant.

According to several independent sources, the spirit was that of a young, blond woman who had been killed in an auto accident in the late 1950's. She had been angry when she left the place, the psychics said, because of a fight with one of the bartenders. She was killed a short time later when her car collided with a telephone pole about a half-mile away.

When David Regnery heard this story, he decided to check it out with the former owner of the restaurant, Richard Montanelli. He confirmed the account and told Regnery of a regular customer who was involved with one of the bartenders back in 1958. Apparently, their relationship was on the rocks and they were often seen fighting. One afternoon, she showed up in the tavern visibly distraught and asked if she could leave her baby there and return for him later in the day. When the owner refused her request, she left the bar very upset. A short time later, news reached the tavern that she had driven her car into a pole down 55th Street. It was thought that she had killed herself, along with the baby.

The phenomena has continued over the years. Many of the strange noises that have been heard in the place, including the disembodied voice of a infant crying, have been heard around table 13. This seems to be an especially active corner of the restaurant. Even so, there is no pattern to when strange things might occur, as weeks or even months sometimes pass before anything unusual happens.

The ghost does seem to have a liking for electronics though. Lights often turn on and off. The old jukebox, since replaced with a modern CD player, used to stop and re-start itself for no reason. A few employees also say they have seen an adding machine operating by itself. The public address system also malfunctions with no explanation. On busy nights, customers waiting for tables often come to the hostess after hearing their names being called. Staff members swear that they are nowhere near the top of the list and have not been called!

While managers only remember one person quitting because of the ghost several years ago, most employees say they would not spend the night in the building. However, one person did spend the night there about a decade ago, despite the stories of a haunting. A friend of Regnery's, who was a police officer, was going through a divorce and needed a place to stay. Regnery let him live temporarily in one of the attic rooms.

"He used to get up in the middle of the night with his pistol and flashlight because he'd hear someone coming up the stairs," Regnery said. "He said he did it three or times and there was never anyone there, so he began just sleeping through it."

Psychics, ghost hunters, photographers and students are among the curiosity-seekers that have spent hours and nights in the restaurant, trying to experience the unexplained. Some have succeeded in getting something strange on film or tape, but there has been nothing definite so far that constitutes proof. Regardless, most staff members are convinced that there is something here. They have no desire to get rid of it though. They believe the ghost is merely playful, not dangerous.

If you are looking for a place where good food and ghostly chills go hand in hand, consider dropping in at the Country House Restaurant some evening. Whether you are a believer or not, it's unlikely that you'll go away disappointed!

THE WATSEKA WONDER

The small town of Watseka, Illinois is located about 50 miles south of Chicago and on the eastern side of the state, just a few miles from the Indiana border. The sensation that would come to be known as the "Watseka Wonder" would first make its appearance here in July of 1877.

It was at this time that a 13-year-old girl named Lurancy Vennum first fell into a strange, catatonic sleep during which she claimed to speak with spirits. The attacks occurred many times each day and sometimes lasted as long as eight hours. During her trance, Lurancy would speak in different voices although when she awoke, she would remember nothing. News of the strange girl traveled about the state and during this time of popularity for the Spiritualist movement, many visitors came to see her.

Finally, doctors diagnosed Lurancy as being mentally ill and they recommended that she be sent to the State Insane Asylum in Peoria, Illinois. In January of 1878, a man named Asa Roff, also from Watseka, came to visit the Vennum family. He claimed that his own daughter, Mary, had been afflicted with the same condition as Lurancy. He was convinced that his daughter had actually spoken to spirits. In addition, he was also convinced that his daughter's spirit still existed Little did he know, but it would soon become apparent that his daughter's spirit was now inside the body of Lurancy Vennum!

To understand the strange and fantastic events that took place in Watseka, we must first start at the beginning of the tale and try to piece together a puzzle that has disturbed investigators for years. Is spirit possession really possible? If you explore the strange case of the "Watseka Wonder", you just might believe that it is!

Mary Roff died on the afternoon of July 5, 1865 while hospitalized at the State Mental Asylum in Peoria. She had been committed there after a bizarre incident when she began slashing at her arms with a straight razor. It was the final tragedy in Mary's descent into madness and insanity. In the beginning, it had only been the strange voices that seemed to come from nowhere. Next she experienced the long periods when she stayed in a trance-like state. Then came her moments of awakening, when she spoke in other voices and seemed to be possessed by the spirits of other people. Finally, she developed an obsession with blood. Mary was convinced that she needed to remove the blood from her body, using pins, leeches and at last, a sharpened razor.

After that final incident, her parents discovered her on the floor of her room, no longer conscious and lying in a pool of blood. Broken-hearted, they took her to the asylum and here, Mary endured more tragedy as the "cures" for insanity in those days were hardly up to the standards of psychiatric hospitals of today. A favored treatment in the 1860's was the Water Cure, where a patient would be immersed naked in a tub of icy water and then taken to a tub of scalding water. And there was more horror. Female patients, like Mary, received a cold water douche, administered with a hose and then wet sheets were wrapped tightly around them to squeeze the blood vessels shut. This was followed by vigorous rubbing to restore circulation. These treatments were administered several times each week. Not surprisingly, such techniques brought little success and most patients never improved. Mental hospitals at that time were merely cages to store the insane and it would be some years to come before any real progress was made in mental health care. Like most others, Mary showed no improvement and soon died.

At the time of Mary Roff's death, Lurancy Vennum was a little more than one year old. In just over a decade though, their lives would be forever connected in a case that remains today one of the strangest, and most authentic, cases of possession ever recorded.

Lurancy Vennum had been born on April 16, 1864 and she and her family had moved to Watseka when she was seven years old. Since they arrived long after Mary Roff's death, the Vennum family knew nothing of her strange illness, nor did they know the Roff family, other than to speak to them on the streets of the small town. Then on July 11, 1877, a series of strange events would begin.

On that morning, Lurancy complained to her mother about feeling sick and then collapsed onto the floor, passed out cold. She stayed in a deep, catatonic sleep for the next five hours but when she awoke, she seemed fine. But this was only the beginning. The next day, Lurancy once again slipped off into the trance-like sleep but this time was different, as she began speaking aloud of visions and spirits. In her trance, she told her family that she was in heaven and that she could see and hear spirits, including the spirit of her brother, who had died in 1874.

From that day on, the trances began to occur more and more frequently and would sometimes last for up to eight hours. While she was asleep, Lurancy continued to speak about her visions, which were sometimes terrifying. She claimed that spirits were chasing her through the house and shouting her name. The attacks occurred up to a dozen times each day and as they continued, Lurancy began to speak in other languages, or at least in nonsense words that no one could understand. When she awoke, she would remember nothing of her trance or of her strange ramblings.

The stories and rumors about Lurancy and her visions began to circulate in Watseka. People were certainly talking and even the local newspaper printed stories about her. No one followed the case more closely than Asa Roff, the father of Mary Roff, did. In the early stages of Mary's illness, she too had claimed to communicate with spirits and would fall into long trances without warning. He was sure that Lurancy Vennum was suffering from the same illness as his poor daughter. But Roff said nothing until the Vennum family exhausted every known cure for Lurancy. It was not until the local doctor and a minister suggested that the girl be sent to the State Mental Hospital that Roff got involved. He refused to see another young woman end up in the hands of the doctors who had so tortured his Mary.

On January 31, 1878, he contacted the Vennum family. They were naturally skeptical of his story but he did persuade them to let him bring a Dr. E. Winchester Stevens to the house. Stevens, like Asa Roff, was a dedicated Spiritualist and the two men' had become convinced that Lurancy was not insane. They believed that Lurancy was actually a vessel through which the dead were communicating. Roff only wished that he had seen the same evidence in his own daughter years before.

The Vennum's allowed Dr. Stevens to "mesmerize" the girl and try to contact the spirits through her. Within moments, Lurancy was speaking in another voice, which allegedly came from a spirit named Katrina Hogan. Then, the spirit changed and claimed to be that of Willie Canning, a young man who had committed suicide. She spoke as Willie for over an hour and then suddenly, she threw her arms into the air and fell over backward. Dr. Stevens took her hands and soon, Lurancy calmed and gained control of her body again. She was now in heaven and would allow a gentler spirit to control her.

She said the spirit's name was Mary Roff.

The trance continued on into the next day and by this time, Lurancy apparently was Mary Roff. She said that she wanted to leave the Vennum house, which was unfamiliar to her, and go home to the Roff house. When Mrs. Roff heard the news, she hurried to the Vennum house in the company of her married daughter, Minerva Alter. The two women came up the sidewalk and saw Lurancy sitting by the window. "Here comes Ma and Nervie," she reportedly said and ran up to hug the two surprised women. No one had called Minerva by the name "Nervie" since Mary's death in 1865.

It now seemed evident to everyone involved that Mary had taken control of Lurancy Vennum. Although she looked the same, she knew everything about the Roff family and treated them as her loved ones. The Vennum's, on the other hand, although treated very courteously, were seen with a distant politeness. It was as if their own daughter only knew them as friendly strangers.

On February 11, Lurancy, or rather "Mary", was allowed to go home with the Roff's. Mr. and Mrs. Vennum agreed that it would be for the best, although they desperately hoped that Lurancy would regain her true identity. The Roff's however, saw this as a miracle, as though Mary had returned from the grave.

Lurancy was taken across town and as they traveled, they passed by the former Roff home, where they had been living when Mary died. She demanded to know why they were not returning there and they had to explain that they had moved a few years back. Further evidence that Lurancy was now Mary Roff?

For the next several months, Lurancy lived as Mary and seemed to have completely forgotten her former life. She did however, tell her mother that she would only be with them until "some time in May". As days passed, Lurancy continued to show that she knew more about the Roff family, their possessions and habits, than she could have possibly known if she had been faking the whole thing. Many of the incidents and remembrances that she referred to had taken place years before Lurancy had even been born.

Of course, not everyone in Watseka believed that Mary had taken possession of Lurancy's body and ridiculed the very idea of it. Several of the doctors who had attempted to treat Lurancy started scathing rumors about Dr. Stevens and the Vennum's pastor pleaded with them to have Lurancy committed. He predicted a time when they would wish that they had followed his advice.

In early May, Lurancy told the Roff family that it was time for her to leave. She became very sad and despondent and would spend the day going from one family member to the next, hugging them and touching them at every opportunity. She wept often at the thought of leaving her "real family" and over the next couple of weeks, a battle raged for control of Lurancy's physical body. At one moment, Lurancy would announce that she had to leave and at the next moment, Mary would cling to her father and cry over the idea of leaving him.

Finally, on May 21, Lurancy returned home to the Vennum's. She displayed none of the strange symptoms of her earlier illness and her parents were convinced that somehow she had been cured, thanks to intervention by the spirit of Mary Roff. She soon became a happy and healthy young woman, suffering no ill effects from her strange experience.

She also remained in touch with the Roff family for the rest of her life. Although she had no memories of her time as Mary, she still felt a curious closeness to them that she could never really explain. During occasional visits to their home, Lurancy would sometimes allow Mary to take control of her so that she could communicate with her family.

Eight years later, when Lurancy turned 18, she married a local farmer named George Binning and two years later, they moved to Rawlins County, Kansas. They bought a farm there and had 11 children. Lurancy died in the late 1940's while she was in California visiting one of her daughters.

Asa Roff and his wife received hundreds of letters, from believers and skeptics alike, after the story of the possession was printed on the front page of the Watseka newspaper. After a year of constant hounding and scorn from neighbors, they left Watseka and moved to Emporia, Kansas. Seven years later, they returned to Watseka to live with Minerva and her husband. They died of old age and are buried in Watseka.

The Vennum's stayed on in Watseka for many years but after the death of her husband, Lucinda Vennum moved to Kansas with Lurancy and her children.

Dr. Stevens lectured on the "Watseka Wonder" for eight years before dying in Chicago in 1886.

Mary Roff was never heard from again.

So what really happened in Watseka? Did Mary Roff's spirit really possess the body of Lurancy Vennum? The families of everyone involved certainly thought so. What other explanation exists for what happened?

To all accounts, Lurancy had the memories and personality of a girl who had been dead for more than twelve years. She knew things about the family that no one could have possibly known. There has been some suggestion that perhaps Lurancy acquired her knowledge of the Roff's to use for her own purposes. A rumor said that she had fallen in love with one of the Roff sons and wanted to be close to the family. This claim was never taken seriously and it seems unlikely that he could have coached her well enough for her to pull off what she did. Others have suggested that Lurancy was psychic and somehow "picked up" the memories of Mary Roff from the minds of the Roff family themselves. Again, this is also unlikely as Lurancy had never, and would never again, exhibit any signs of psychic powers.

For me personally, I have always been skeptical about any type of "possession", usually believing in the idea of mental illness first. However, it seemed the more reading that I did into the story of the "Watseka Wonder", the more open I became to idea that something very strange had occurred. Was it possible that Lurancy really had been possessed by Mary Roff? You can judge for yourself, but as for me..... well, I've begun to think that anything might be possible.

THE GRAVEYARD ELM

If spirits are truly the personalities of those who once lived, then wouldn't these spirits reflect whatever turmoil might have plagued them in life? And if hauntings can sometimes be the residual effects of trauma being imprinted on the atmosphere of a place, then wouldn't places where terror and insanity were commonplace be especially prone to these hauntings? As an answer to both of these questions, I need point no further than to the strange events that have plagued the old State Mental Hospital in Bartonville, a small town near Peoria, for many years.

In its final years of operations, after the last patients had departed, staff members in the building started to report some odd occurrences. In more recent years, the building has been the site of frequent excursion by vandals, trespassers and curiosity seekers, many of whom claim to have had their own weird encounters in the place.

But what macabre history is behind this now crumbling building? There are many tales to tell about this sad and forlorn place. It is a strange story that is filled with social reform, insanity and yes, even ghosts.

Prior to 1900, mental health care barely existed. In those days, anyone suffering from a mental disorder was simply locked away from society in an asylum or hospital that was normally in a less than desirable state. In fact, many of the hospitals were barely fit for human occupation. They were filthy places of confinement where patients were often left in straitjackets, locked in restraint chairs, or even placed in crates or cages if they were especially disturbed. Many of them spent everyday in shackles and chains and even the so-called "treatments" were barbaric.

Not surprisingly, such techniques brought little success and patients rarely improved. In these days before psychiatry and medication, most mental patients spent their entire lives locked up inside of an asylum.

However, in 1905, things began to change as laws were passed to prohibit the use of chains and shackles in state run institutions. At this same time, psychiatry was starting to come into its own and the public was becoming aware of the fact that many of the mentally ill could actually be helped, not just locked away and forgotten.

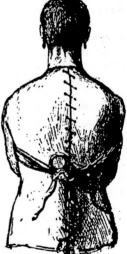

Straight jackets were considered standard in mental health care.

One doctor at the forefront of this new medicine was Dr. George A. Zeller, who became the first superintendent of the Bartonville asylum in 1898. While the hospital was under construction, he left to serve in the Spanish-American War, then returned to the hospital until 1914, when he was appointed State Alienist. He returned to Bartonville in 1921 and served until his death in 1938. He is remembered today as one of the most influential mental health care providers in Illinois history. He was the man responsible for turning the Bartonville hospital into one of the finest asylums in the state. However, it did not start out that way.

Construction on the building began in 1885 and when completed, the hospital looked like a medieval castle with battlements and turrets. It was a foreboding structure and for some reason, was never used. It remained empty for years and despite huge building costs, was torn down in 1897. The reason for the demolition was said to have been design and structural flaws. According to reports, the hospital had been built over an abandoned coal mine and many of the tunnels beneath it began to collapse under the weight.

The hospital was rebuilt and finally opened in 1902, under the leadership of Dr. Zeller. It was now called the Peoria State Hospital, as Bartonville had no train station or express office. The planners were concerned that no one would be able to find the place, so it was named for the closest large town. The hospital implemented what was called the "cottage system" and 33 different buildings were used to house patients. There was also a dorm for the nursing staff, a store, a power house and a domestic building with a laundry, bakery and kitchen. Dr. Zeller also supervised the creation of cemeteries, where the bodies of unknown patients could be buried. Eventually, the burial grounds grew to include four different graveyards although the oldest cemetery would mark the location of the first ghost story to ever be associated with the hospital.

And this is no mere rumor or folk tale, but a documented account of a supernatural event. The teller of the tale was Dr. George A. Zeller himself!

Shortly after organizing the cemeteries for the hospital, Dr. Zeller also put together a burial corps to deal with the disposal of the bodies of patients who died. The corps always consisted of a staff member and several of the patients. While these men were still disturbed, all of them were competent enough to take part in the digging of graves. Of all of the gravediggers, the most unusual man, according to Dr. Zeller, was a fellow called "A. Bookbinder".

This man had been sent to the hospital from a county poorhouse. He had suffered a mental breakdown while working in a printing house in Chicago and his illness had left him incapable of coherent speech. The officer who had taken him into custody had noted in his report that the man had been employed as "a bookbinder". A court clerk inadvertently listed this as the man's name and he was sent to the hospital as A. Bookbinder.

Dr. Zeller described the man as being strong and healthy, although completely uncommunicative. He was attached to the burial corps and soon, attendants realized that "Old Book", as he was affectionately called, was especially suited to the work. Ordinarily, as the coffin was lowered at the end of the funeral, the gravedigger would stand back out of the way until the service ended. Nearly every patient at the hospital was unknown to the staff so services were performed out of respect for the deceased and not because of some personal attachment. Because of this, everyone was surprised during the first internment attended by Old Book when he removed his cap and began to weep loudly for the dead man.

"The first few times he did this," Dr. Zeller wrote, "his emotion became contagious and there were many moist eyes at the graveside but when at each succeeding burial, his feelings overcame him, it was realized that Old Book possessed a mania that manifested itself in uncontrollable grief."

It was soon learned that Old Book had no favorites among the dead. He would do the same thing at each service and as his grief reached its peak, he would go and lean against an old elm tree that stood in the center of the cemetery and here, he would sob loudly.

Time passed and eventually Old Book also passed away. Word spread among the employees and as Book was well liked, everyone decided they would attend his funeral. Dr. Zeller wrote that more than 100 uniformed nurses attended, along with male staff members and several hundred patients.

Dr. Zeller officiated at the service. Old Book's casket was placed on two cross beams above his empty grave and four men stood by to lower it into the ground at the end of the service. As the last hymn was sung, the men grabbed hold of the ropes. "The men stooped forward," Dr. Zeller wrote, "and with a powerful, muscular effort, prepared to lift the coffin, in order to permit the removal of the crossbeams and allow it to gently descend into the grave. At a given signal, they heaved away the ropes and the next instant, all four lay on their backs. For the coffin, instead of offering resistance, bounded into the air like an eggshell, as if it were empty!"

Needless to say, the spectators were a little shocked at this turn of events and the nurses were reported to have shrieked, half of them running away and the other half coming closer to the grave to see what was happening.

"In the midst of the commotion," Dr. Zeller continued, "a wailing voice was heard and every eye turned toward the Graveyard Elm from whence it emanated. Every man and woman stood transfixed, for there, just as had always been the case, stood Old Book, weeping and moaning with an earnestness that outrivaled anything he had ever shown before." Dr. Zeller was amazed at what he observed, but had no doubt that he was actually seeing it. "I, along with the other bystanders, stood transfixed at the sight of this apparition... it was broad daylight and there could be no deception."

After a few moments, the doctor summoned some men to remove the lid of the coffin, convinced that it must be empty and that Old Book could not be inside of it. The lid was lifted and as soon as it was, the wailing sound came to an end. Inside of the casket lay the body of Old Book, unquestionably dead. It was said that every eye in the cemetery looked upon the still corpse and then over to the elm tree in the center of the burial ground. The specter had vanished!

"It was awful, but it was real," Dr. Zeller concluded. "I saw it, 100 nurses saw it and 300 spectators saw it." But if it was anything other the ghost of Old Book, Dr. Zeller had no idea what it could have been.

A few days after the funeral, the Graveyard Elm began to wither and die. In spite of efforts to save it, the tree declined over the next year and then died. Later, after the dead limbs had dropped, workmen tried to remove the rest of the tree, but stopped after the first cut of the ax caused the tree to emanate what was said to be "an agonized, despairing cry of pain". After that, Dr. Zeller suggested that the tree be burned, however as soon as the flames started around the tree's base, the workers quickly put them out. They later told Dr. Zeller they had heard a sobbing and crying sound coming from it.

Eventually, the tree fell down in a storm, taking with it the lingering memories of a mournful man known as Old Book.

After the death of Dr. Zeller, the hospital remained in use for many years, adding buildings, patients and care facilities for children and tuberculosis patients. The asylum was finally closed down in 1972 and remained empty for a number of years before being sold at auction in 1980. The current owners are today converting the remaining buildings into office space.

Even though the site is private property and trespassing is forbidden here, it has not stopped vandals and would-be ghost hunters from going inside of the place. Many of these curiosity seekers, drawn to the building because of its legends and ghosts, claim to have encountered some pretty frightening things here, from unexplained sounds to full-blown apparitions. Some might even say that many of the former patients are still around!

So is the old hospital really haunted? Scores of people who have visited the place certainly think so. The reader must agree that the place certainly has the potential for a haunting, even without the story of A. Bookbinder and the graveyard elm. The atmosphere of the place alone is more than enough to justify the reports of apparitions and strange energy. The residual impressions of the past would certainly be strong in a building where mentally ill people were housed and where "psychic disturbances" would be common. There is also the matter of conscious spirits as hospitals have long been places where the spirits of the dead are said to linger. Besides that, some would say that the hospital was the only home that many of the patients knew and they are going to stay where they were the most comfortable.

"The place is full of spirits" has been said on more than one occasion and I wouldn't be surprised if this proclamation is right!

- CHAPTER NINE -

HAUNTED CHICAGO

HISTORY & HAUNTINGS OF THE WINDY CITY

I have struck a city - a real city - and they call it Chicago. The other places do not count.... This is the first real American city that I have encountered. Having seen it, I urgently desire to never see it again.
RUDYARD KIPLING

A facade of skyscrapers facing the lake and behind the facade, every bit of dubiousness!
EM FORSTER

You can get much further with a smile, a kind word and a gun than you can get with just a smile and a kind word
AL CAPONE

There are a number of American cities that make the claim of being "most haunted", but in my opinion Chicago leads the pack. The closest contenders may be New Orleans or perhaps Washington, but for sheer number of haunts, neither can come close to the ghosts that can be found in the Windy City. The spirits of the past here are simply a part of the city's culture and can be connected to Chicago's long, and often bloody, history. The history and the hauntings of the city go hand in hand for as it has often been said, the history of yesterday creates the hauntings of today.

In no place is such a statement truer than in Chicago, Illinois.

THE FORT DEARBORN MASSACRE

Chicago began as nothing but empty wilderness and open prairie, a desolate and isolated region on the shore of a great lake. The first explorers passed through this place in 1673 when Marquette and

Jolliet crossed the area to explore the Mississippi River. However, they left nothing of their presence behind. They were followed by the soldier of fortune, Tonti, in 1681. He arrived at the Chicago River, also on a journey to the Mississippi, and claimed the entire territory for France. LaSalle called it "Louisiana". Three years later, Chicago would be born. It would appear on maps as "Chekagou", a Potawatomi Indian name that meant "wild onion". But nearly one hundred years would pass before the first settlers came to the place.

The City of Chicago as it looked in 1845

In 1779, the first trading post was opened on the Chicago River by Jean Baptiste Point du Sable, a French trader and trapper who had been born on the Caribbean island of Santo Domingo. He became the first permanent resident of the region, although he sold his company to Jean Lalime in 1800 and moved to Missouri.

By 1803, America had expanded its borders to the west and an outpost called Fort Dearborn was established on the south bank of the Chicago River. The fort was commanded by Captain John Whistler and was held by a company of forty soldiers. The fort had been named in honor of Secretary of War Henry Dearborn.

At the time, this corner of Illinois was one of the most remote regions of the frontier. It was a wilderness that was virtually cut off from all communication with the rest of the country. Access to the area was by means of river or Indian trail and the closest settlement was Fort Wayne. Today, this is a short journey, but in those days, it was a dangerous and difficult trek. The soldiers who came to man Fort Dearborn had no idea of the desolation they would face.

The fort was a simple stockade of logs. They were placed in the ground and then sharpened along the upper end. The outer stockade was a solid wall with an entrance in the southern section that was blocked with heavy gates. Another exit, this one underground, was located on the north side. Inside of the fort, there was room for a parade ground, officer's quarters, troop barracks, a guard house and a magazine for weapons and ammunition. Two block houses were also added along two corners of the fort, along with a raised walkway so that defenders could fire over the top of the wall. The fort offered substantial protection for the soldiers garrisoned there, but later they would find that it was not protection enough.

In 1804, a man named John Kinzie arrived in the region. He bought out the property of Jean Lalime and over the course of several years, became the self-appointed civilian leader of the settlement. He was known for his sharp dealings with the local Indians over trade goods and furs. He also established close ties with the Potawatomi Indians and even sold them liquor, which created tension among the other settlers. Kinzie managed to become very successful and this seemed to anger Jean Lalime, the man who had sold Kinzie his business. The two became bitter rivals.

In 1810, Captain Whistler was replaced at Fort Dearborn by Captain Nathan Heald. He brought with him Lieutenant Linus T. Helm, an officer, like Heald, who had much in the way of frontier experience. Not long after arriving, Helm met and married the stepdaughter of John Kinzie. In addition to she and Captain Heald's wife, there were a number of other women at the fort as well, all wives of the men stationed there. More families arrived and within two years, there were twelve women and twenty children at Fort Dearborn.

Throughout the changes at the fort, Kinzie and Lalime remained enemies and in constant conflict with one another. Finally, in April 1812, their animosity boiled over into violence. A brief struggle ensued, during which Kinzie stabbed the other man to death. Wounded himself, he fled the settlement but soon returned when no charges were filed against him.

The first threat came to Fort Dearborn with the War of 1812, a conflict that aroused unrest with the local Indian tribes, namely the Potawatomi and the Wynadot. The effects of the war brought many of the Indian tribes into alliance with the British for they saw the Americans as invaders into their lands. After the British captured the American garrison at Mackinac, Fort Dearborn was in great danger. Orders came stating that Captain Heald should abandon the fort and leave the contents to the local Indians.

Unfortunately, Heald delayed in carrying out the orders and soon, the American troops had nowhere to go. The unrest among the Indians brought a large contingent of them to the fort and they gathered in an almost siege-like state. The soldiers began to express concern over the growing numbers of Indians outside and Heald realized that he was going to have to bargain with them if the occupants of Fort Dearborn were going to safely reach Fort Wayne. On August 12, Heald began several days of bargaining that eventually led to an agreement for the Indians to provide safe conduct for the soldiers and settlers to Fort Wayne in Indiana.

Part of the agreement was that Heald would leave the stores and ammunition in the fort for the Indians, but his officers disagreed. Alarmed, they questioned the wisdom of handing out guns and ammunition that could easily be turned against them. Heald reluctantly agreed with them and the extra weapons and ammunition were broken apart and dumped into an abandoned well. In addition, the stores of whiskey were dumped into the river. Needless to say, the Indians outside observed this and they too began making plans that differed from those agreed upon with Captain Heald.

On August 14, a visitor arrived at the fort in the person of Captain William Wells. He and thirty Miami warriors had managed to slip past the throng outside and they appeared at the front gates of the fort. Wells was a frontier legend among early soldiers and settlers in the Illinois territory. He was also the uncle of Captain Heald's wife and after hearing of the evacuation of Fort Dearborn, and knowing the hostile fervor of the local tribes, headed straight to the fort to assist them in their escape. Unfortunately, he had arrived too late.

Throughout the night of August 14, wagons were loaded for travel and reserve ammunition was distributed, amounting to about 25 rounds per man. Early the next morning, the procession of soldiers, civilians, women and children left the fort. The infantry soldiers led the way, followed by a caravan of wagons and mounted men. A portion of the Miami who had accompanied Wells guarded the rear of the column.

The column of soldiers and settlers were escorted by nearly 500 Potawatomi Indians. As they marched southward and into a low range of sand hills that separated the beaches of Lake Michigan from the prairie, the Potawatomi moved silently to the right, placing an elevation of sand between they and the white men. The act was carried out with such subtlety that no one noticed it as the column trudged along the shoreline. A little further down the beach, the sand ridge ended and the two groups would come together again.

The column traveled to an area where 16th Street and Indiana Avenue are now located. There was a sudden milling about of the scouts at the front of the line and suddenly a shout came back from Captain Wells that the Indians were attacking! A line of Potawatomi appeared over the edge of the ridge and fired down at the column. Totally surprised, the officers nevertheless managed to rally the men into a battle line, but it was of little use. So many of them fell from immediate wounds that the line collapsed. The Indians overwhelmed them with sheer numbers, flanking the line and snatching the wagons and horses.

What followed was butchery.... officers were slain with tomahawks.. the fort's surgeon was cut down by gunfire and then literally chopped into pieces ... Mrs. Heald was wounded by gunfire but was spared when she was captured by a sympathetic chief, who spared her life... the wife of one soldier fought so bravely and savagely that she was hacked into pieces before she fell... In the end, cut down to less than half their original number, the garrison surrendered under the promise of safe conduct. In all, 148 members of the column were killed, eighty-six of them adults and twelve of them children. One of the dead was Captain Wells, who was captured and his heart cut out. A Chicago street now bears the name of this brave frontiersman.

In the battle, Captain Heald was wounded twice, while his wife was wounded seven times. They were later released and a St. Joseph Indian named Chaudonaire took them to Mackinac, where they were turned over to the British commander there. He sent them to Detroit and they were exchanged with the American authorities.

John Kinzie and his family were spared in the slaughter. Appealing to the Potawatomi chiefs, they were taken away from the massacre site. He would return to Chicago one year later, but found that much had changed. He failed in re-starting his business and soon was working for his largest competitor, the American Fur Company. In time, the fur trade would end and Kinzie worked as a trader and Indian interpreter until his death in 1828. Thirty years later, his daughter-in-law, Juliette Magill Kinzie, would write a book that named Kinzie as the founding settler of Chicago. The book would overlook Kinzie's questionable business practices and the murder of Jean Lalime and would be accepted as fact for many years. Later, it would be seen as evidence of Juliette Kinzie's affinity for social climbing and her need to be part of a Chicago dynasty. At that point, her historical "facts" were called into question.

The other survivors from the massacre were taken as prisoners and some of them died soon after. Others were sold to the British as slaves, who quickly freed them, appalled by the carnage they had experienced. The victorious Indians burned Fort Dearborn itself to the ground and the bodies of the massacre victims were left where they had fallen, scattered to decay on the sand dunes of Lake Michigan. When replacement troops arrived at the site of Fort Dearborn a year later, they were greeted with not only the burned-out shell of the fort, but also the grinning skeletons of their predecessors. The bodies were given proper burials and the fort was rebuilt in 1816, only to be abandoned again in 1836, when the city would be able to fend for itself.

Not surprisingly, the horrific massacre spawned its share of ghostly tales. For many years, the site of the fort itself was said to be haunted by those who were killed nearby. The now vanished fort was located at the south end of the Michigan Avenue Bridge.

The actual site of the massacre was quiet for many years, long after Chicago grew into a sizable city. According to author Dale Kaczmarek, in his book "Windy City Ghosts", construction in the earthy 1980's unearthed a number of human bones. At first thought to be the victims of a cholera epidemic in the 1840's, the remains were later dated more closely to the early 1800's. Thanks to their location, they were believed to be the bones of victims from the massacre. They were reburied elsewhere but within a few weeks, people began to report the semi-transparent figures of people dressed in pioneer clothing and military uniforms. They were seen wandering in a lot just north of 16th and while many seemed to run about haphazardly, others appeared to move in slow motion. Many of them reportedly looked very frightened or were screaming in silence.

Perhaps these poor victims do not rest in peace after all.....

PRIDE AND PROGRESS

In the years following these turbulent events, much changed in Chicago. As time passed, more settlers came to the region and the small collection of homes began to grow. The center of the settlement became an area on the river called "Wolf's Point", a rowdy district of saloons and taverns. Eventually, this area would die out with the end of the fur trade, but it would be replaced with a number of other vice districts in the years to come.

One of the influential early residents was Gordon Hubbard, who began a Chicago industry when he brought a herd of over 400 hogs to the city in 1829. He started the first of the packing houses four years later. By the late 1830's, Chicago pork was in great demand in the east. By 1865, the Union Stock Yards were opened between Halstead and 39th Street and the city's meat packing plants became famous across the country.

The city of Chicago was officially platted in 1830 and within a decade was attracting powerful and wealthy new residents. These men began to dominate both the business and the politics of the city. They supported and funded what became Chicago institutions like the Historical Society, the Academy of Sciences, the old University of Chicago, Hahnemann Medical College, Rush Medical School and Northwestern University, among others.

These new arrivals included men like Cyrus McCormick, who pioneered the mechanical reaper and changed farming forever. There was also Potter Palmer, who founded the Palmer House at State and Monroe Streets. One of his early employees was Marshall Field, who came to Chicago as a dry goods clerk. He would go on to found a Chicago landmark store and change the face of retail business. Another arrival was George M. Pullman, who began making Pullman railroad cars.

And there were many others. They each contributed to Chicago in ways that are still evident today. Chicago had finally arrived! But the city was soon to find out that nothing lasts forever.

THE GREAT CHICAGO FIRE

According the legend, the Great Chicago Fire was started by a cow that belonged to an Irishwoman named Catherine O'Leary. She ran a neighborhood milk business from the barn behind her home. She carelessly left a kerosene lantern in the barn after her evening milking and a cow kicked over it over and ignited the hay on the floor. Of course, no proof of this story has ever been offered, other than the testimony of a neighborhood liar, but the legend took hold in Chicago and was told around the world. Regardless of how the fire started though, on Sunday evening, October 8, 1871, Chicago became a city in flames.

Mrs. O'Leary's mythical lantern

In 1871, Chicago was truly a boom town. It had become one of the fastest growing cities in America and because of this, construction standards had been "loose" to say the least. Beyond the downtown area, the city was miles and miles of rickety wooden structures. Most of the working-class neighborhoods consisted of wooden cottages and tenement houses, all of which made for dangerous fuel in the event of a fire. However, Chicago was not a wooden "shantytown", although even the downtown hotels, banks, theaters and stores needed constant repair. Just a month before the Great Fire, the Chicago "Tribune" had remarked on the shabby construction of the brick and stone downtown buildings. The newspaper warned that they were weak and seemed to be falling apart and mentioned that hardly a week passed when some stone facade or cornice was not falling into the street, narrowly missing the skull of some hapless pedestrian.

And, they said, if the city didn't fall down, it was liable to burn! "The absence of rain for three weeks," reported the newspaper, "has left everything in so flammable a condition that a spark might set a fire that would sweep from end to end of the city".

Although ignoring the legend of the O'Leary cow, the Great Chicago Fire did break out in the vicinity of the O'Leary home at 137 De Koven Street on the west side. The home and barn were located in what was then called the "West Division", an area of the city that was west of the south branch of the river. Whether the cow kicked over the lantern or not, conditions were perfect for a fire. The summer had been dry and less than three inches of rain had fallen between July and October.

There had been other fires in the city already. On the previous day, October 7, four blocks of the city had burned. This conflagration was said to have left the fire department so exhausted that they were slow to respond to another alarm at De Koven Street. By the time they arrived, it was already too late. By 10:30 that evening, it was reported that the fire was officially out of control. A strong, dry wind from the southwest made matters even worse, blowing the fire toward the very heart of the city. In what seemed like minutes, mills and factories along the river were on fire. Additional buildings, hit by fiery missiles from the main blaze, also began burning from top to bottom. The air was filled with sparks and cinders that contemporary accounts described as looking like "red rain".

In just over an hour, the west side of the city was in ashes and the fire showed no signs of slowing down. It hungrily jumped the Chicago River and pushed toward the center of the city. Among the first buildings to be engulfed was the new Parmalee Omnibus and Stage Company at the southeast corner of Jackson and Franklin Streets. A flying brand also struck the South Side Gas Works and soon this structure burst into flames, creating a new and larger center for the fire. At this point, even the grease and oil-covered river caught fire and the surface of the water shimmered with heat and flames.

In moments, the fire also spread to the banks and office buildings along LaSalle Street. Soon, the inferno became impossible to battle with more than a dozen different locations burning at once. The fire swept through Wells, Market and Franklin Streets, igniting more than 500 different buildings. One by one, these great structures fell. The Tribune building, long vaunted as "fire proof", was turned into a smoking ruin as were the great hotels like the Palmer House, the Tremont and the Sherman. Marshall Field's grand department store, along with hundreds of other businesses, was reduced to blazing ash.

In the early morning hours of Monday, the fire reached the courthouse, which stood in a block surrounded by LaSalle, Clark, Randolph and Washington Streets. A burning timber landed on the building's wooden cupola and the soon turned into a fire that blazed out of control. The building was ordered evacuated. The prisoners, who had begun to scream and shake the bars of their cells as smoke filled the air, were released. Most of them were allowed to simply go free but the most dangerous of them were shackled and taken away under guard. Just after 2:00 AM, the bell of the courthouse tolled for the last time and it crashed through the remains of the building to the ground beneath it. The roaring sound made by the building's collapse was reportedly heard more than a mile away.

Around this same time, the State Street Bridge, leading to the north side, also caught fire and soon the inferno began to devour the area on the north side of the river as well. Soon, stables, warehouse and breweries were also burning. Then, the fire swept into the luxurious residential district surrounding Cass, Huron, Ontario, Rush and Dearborn Streets. Here, stood the mansions of some of Chicago's oldest and most prominent families. By daylight, these beautiful homes were nothing but ruins.

By 3:00 AM that morning, the pumps at the Waterworks on Pine Street had been destroyed and by Monday evening, the only intact structure for blocks was the gothic stone Water Tower. Somehow, it managed to survive the devastation. Legend has it that this structure is haunted today by the ghost of a man who stayed on the job during the fire, continuing to pump the water as the fire got closer. The story goes that this heroic city worker waited until the last possible minute and then took his own life rather than be engulfed in the flames. His ghost has reportedly been seen hanging through an upper window of the tower.

The flames were not the only thing that residents of the city had to worry about either. In the early hours of the fire, looting and violence had broken out in the city. Saloon keepers, hoping that it might prevent their taverns from being destroyed, had foolishly rolled barrels of whiskey out into the streets. Soon, men and women from all classes were staggering in the streets, thoroughly intoxicated. The drunks and the looters did not comprehend the danger they were in however and many were trampled in the streets. Plundered goods were also tossed aside and were lost in the fire, abandoned by the looters as the fire drew near. Although many were injured, the stories of lawlessness were greatly exaggerated in later accounts. They were overblown into stories of lynchings and murders by "villainous Negroes" and Irishmen. The tales were proved to be absolutely false.

Worse perhaps than the looters were the drivers of wagons and carts who charged outrageous prices to haul away household possessions and baggage. This only added to the misery of the fleeing people and compounded the chaos. In his book, "City of the Century", author Donald L. Miller described the scene as the streets thronged with people... crying children searched for their parents... processions of refugees milled everywhere... wealthy ladies panicked, wearing all of the jewelry they owned... immigrant women ran, carrying mattresses on their heads... half-naked prostitutes scurried from rented "cribs" on Wells and Clark Streets.... people carried the sick and the crippled on chairs or on makeshift litters... even the bodies of the dead were transported in coffins or wrapped in bed sheets.... It combined to create a vision that most of us cannot even imagine today.

Thankfully, the fire began to die on the morning of October 10, when steady and soaking rains began to fall on Chicago. The people of the city were devastated, as was the city itself. Over 300 people were dead and another 100,000 were without homes or shelter. The fire had cut a swath through the city that was four miles long and about two-thirds of a mile wide. Over $200 million in property had been destroyed. Records, deeds, archives, libraries and priceless artwork were all lost although a little of it had survived in public and private vaults. In the destruction of the Federal Building, which, among other things, housed the post office, more than $100,000 in currency was burned.

Chicago had become a blasted and charred wasteland.

In the first days after the fire, wild rumors flew about more looting in the city. It was said that criminals were now breaking into safes and vaults in the ruined business district. Local business owners hired Allan Pinkerton to deploy his detectives around the remains of stores and banks and soon, six companies of Federal troops arrived under the command of General Phillip Sheridan to assist in maintaining order. Two days later, Chicago's Mayor, Roswell Mason, placed the city under martial law, entrusting Sheridan and his troops to watch over it.

Although Sheridan saw no sign of the reported murders and looting, he did recruit a volunteer home guard of about 1000 men to patrol unburned areas of the city. He also enforced a curfew, much to the chagrin of Illinois governor John M. Palmer, who felt that martial law was uncalled for and unnecessary. Mayor Mason was heavily influenced by local business leaders however and ignored Palmer's order to withdraw the troops. The state of martial law didn't last for long though. A few days after it went into effect, a local businessman (and one of those responsible for pushing Mason into bringing in Sheridan) was accidentally killed by one of the volunteer home guard. In spite of this, Sheridan did receive orders from President Grant that left four companies of men in the city through the end of the year.

As terrible as the disaster was, Chicago was not dead, but merely shaken and stunned. Within days of the fire, rebuilding began on a grand.scale. The vigor of the city's rebirth amazed the rest of the nation and within three years, it once again dominated the western United States. It soared from the ashes like the fable phoenix and became the home of the first skyscraper in 1885, then passed the one million mark in population five years later. The Great Chicago Fire was the beginning of a new metropolis, much greater than it could have ever become if the horrific fire had never happened at all.

RIOTS AND UNREST

In the years after the Great Chicago Fire, wealth and prosperity returned to Chicago, but according to many reformers and activists, that wealth remained in the hands of the privileged few. They were men like Marshall Field, George Pullman, Cyrus McCormick and Phillip Danforth Armour. All of them saw constant unrest among their workers over job conditions, wages and shorter work days. There was no question that conditions in many plants (especially in the slaughterhouses) were questionable at best and men worked 10-12 hours, six days a week, for very little pay. Strikes and protests had become commonplace by the time of the Haymarket Square Riot in 1886, but this event would change the face of the labor movement forever.

The events that culminated here had been brewing since the end of the Civil War as trade unions began to organize to protect the rights of workers. It should also be pointed out that many of the organizers were blatant socialists and some were not content to merely let strikes and walk-outs speak for them. Many of them endorsed a more violent form of action. That action reached its peak in Haymarket Square, where rural farmers came to exchange produce for cash, in May 1886.

Recent troubles at the McCormick Reaper Works had turned Chicago into a labor battleground. There was trouble simmering in the city, hidden just below the surface, but threatening to boil over. On Tuesday evening, May 4, a mass meeting of workers was called to protest police actions against striking employees at the McCormick factory, who were trying to force and eight-hour work day. A crowd of 20,000 had been expected but a cool rain kept many in. Eventually, about 2,500 tired spectators showed up to hear the speeches by Albert Parsons, Samuel Fielden and August Spies. All three men were considered "dangerous agitators" and "anarchists" by city business leaders however Mayor Carter Henry Harrison, issued a parade permit for the gathering, believing there was no cause for concern.

Others were not so sure. Responding to pressure from businessmen, Police Inspector John Bonfield called up 600 police reserves into duty that night at the West Chicago, Harrison and Central stations. He led them to believe that a citywide riot might occur. One 100 more officers were added to the Des Plains station, less than a half block from Haymarket Square.

The rally began at 8:30 pm and the crowd was fairly listless, plus damp from the drizzling rain. Mayor Harrison rode by on his horse a short time later and was satisfied that it was a peaceable gathering. He ordered Bonfield to send the reserve officers home. The police inspector refused and two hours later, he ordered his men to disperse the crowd. The speakers were approached by Captain William Ward, who commanded the meeting to end in the "name of the people of Illinois".

Suddenly, according to author Richard Lindberg in his book "Return to the Scene of the Crime", a crudely manufactured pipe bomb was thrown from a vestibule at Randolph and Des Plaines Streets. The bomb exploded in the midst of a 200-man police column. Officer Mathias Degan was killed instantly and six others were mortally wounded. Although momentarily stunned, the officers quickly recovered and began shooting wildly into the fleeing crowd of laborers. The shooting continued for more than five minutes.

While the mayor pleaded for calm, Bonfield and Police Inspector Michael Schaak took it upon themselves to find the culprits who had thrown the bomb, or even who had caused the bomb to be thrown in the first place. The officers began a reign of terror among working class citizens in Chicago. All rights (such as they were then) were suspended and hundreds of suspects were arrested, beaten and interrogated at all hours of the night. False confessions were violently extracted from those who were thought to be "anarchists" or sympathizers of the labor unions. Whoever the bomb thrower actually was, he faded away into history.

Eventually, eight conspirators were brought to trial for the riot and seven of them received the death sentence, while the eighth was given fifteen years in prison. All of them were tried and sentenced on conspiracy charges to incite violence that led to the deaths of the police officers. On November 11, 1887, August Spies, Albert Parsons, George Engel and Adolph Fischer were hanged at the Criminal Courts Building on Hubbard Street. Another of the conspirators died in an explosion and the death sentences of the others were commuted to prison terms.

The city of Chicago erected a statue of a police officer in Haymarket Square on May 4, 1889 and it became the first such monument in the nation. For many years, the police were seen as the martyrs of the riot but with the rise of the big labor unions, that perception slowly changed. During the 1960's, the statue was defaced, blown up twice, repaired and finally removed to the Chicago Police Training Academy by Mayor Richard J. Daley. Nothing remains to mark this area today, save for the memories of the past.

George M. Pullman never dreamed that anything like the Haymarket Square Riot would affect his company. During the heyday of the Pullman Palace Car Company, he created a model town for his employees called Pullman. It was located ten miles outside of the city proper, next the factory. It consisted of 1,800 brick homes, an arcade with a theater, a library, a hotel, stores, a bank, two churches and a school. However, there were no beer gardens or saloons and alcohol was strictly forbidden. The only bar in town was located in the Florence Hotel and it was reserved for Pullman and his guests.

Rules in the company town were harsh. Any employee who dropped paper in the street and did not pick it up could be fired. Any tenant could be evicted from his home, for any reason, with a ten day notice. No labor organizers were permitted within the town. No improper books or plays were allowed at the library. In addition, rent was higher than in comparable homes in the city and all gas and water was purchased from the company, who made a profit on it. On payday, all debts owed to the company were automatically deducted from what the employee earned. This debt included rent, water, gas or food from the company store. Some families literally ended up with a few cents left over.

In 1893, during a national recession, Pullman laid off about one-third of its workforce and wages for those remaining on the job were cut by as much as forty percent. Many men received nothing, or even went into debt on payday. That winter, some men went so hungry that they fainted on the factory floor. Finally, a delegation of men went to meet with George Pullman about the conditions. He refused to meet with them and in fact, fired all of them and evicted them from their homes.

An Indiana man named Eugene Debs organized a group of the Pullman workers in a nearby town and they demanded restoration of their wages from the Pullman Company. Needless to say, the demand was refused. On May 11, the workers went on strike and Pullman was shut down. Soon, members of the American Railway Union began a sympathy strike, which led to violence across the country. President Grover Cleveland intervened and ordered the strike to end, stating that the railway demonstrations interfered with delivery of the mail. Eugene Debs refused to bow to pressure and he was jailed.

By the middle of May, Pullman families were begging for food. Chicago's mayor sent thousands of dollars in groceries to the company town, spending money from his own pocket. Chicago city leaders and politicians from around the country urged Pullman to settle the strike, but he refused. The Union sent him a letter that asked him to meet with the workers, but he would not even open it.

The Union then voted to boycott all Pullman cars on the rail lines and refused to handle them. The United States Attorney General, Richard Olney, saw this as a way to end the strike. Thanks to the previous court ruling, the Union could not interfere with the delivery of the mail, but the ruling said nothing about other trains. They could refuse to work on any train that was not carrying mail. Soon, the railroads began attaching unnecessary Pullman cars to other trains so that Union members would not handle them. In this way, the companies forced the members to break the law by refusing to allow the mail to go through.

With that accomplished, President Cleveland sent troops into Chicago on July 2. The confrontation between the soldiers and the workers turned into a riot and a number of railroad cars were overturned and set on fire. The riots lasted for several days. Twelve men were killed and over $685,000 in property was destroyed.

The Pullman plant re-opened in late August, although with new employees on the payroll. Each of them had to sign a pledge that they would not join the Union. All of the Union workers who were hired back had to surrender their Union cards. However, many of the men were not hired back. This prompted Illinois Governor Altgeld, who had fought against federal interference in the strike, to go to Pullman and personally ask that the men be hired back.

He arrived in the company town and was taken on a tour by the Pullman Company vice-president. Pullman himself was too busy to entertain him. The idea was to show the governor what a wonderful place the town was. Instead, Altgeld found more than 6,000 people with no food, families living in poverty and women and children in unsuitable living conditions. He was appalled by the place and realized that Pullman was simply oblivious to the lives of his employees. Altgeld returned to Springfield and quickly dispatched a letter. He asked that Pullman hire back all of the replaced workers and in addition cancel all rents from October 1 so that the workers could get back on their feet. Pullman refused to accept the letter until he was literally forced to accept it by an Illinois National Guard officer. Then, of course, he did nothing.

Pullman's victory in breaking the strike was a short-lived one. He succeeded in losing the love of his daughters, losing the respect of his workers and earned the disdain of most of the national press. He died three years later in 1897 and was buried in Graceland Cemetery. His grave was fortified with railroad ties and reinforced concrete so that "radicals, anarchists and embittered workers" would not be able to violate his crypt.

In 1898, the Illinois Supreme Court ordered the company to sell off its housing stock in the town of Pullman. It was eventually sold and the town became a state landmark in 1969. The Historic Pullman Foundation has preserved the Florence Hotel but was not as lucky in 1998 when a homeless man set fire to the historic railcar factory at 111th Street and St. Lawrence Avenue. He told police that he heard "voices" that compelled him to set the building on fire. Perhaps the voices of lost workers from the company's past?

If there was a single area that portrayed the greatest contrast between the lifestyles of the company owners and the workers, it was among the packing districts of Chicago. For example, Phillip Armour lived on fashionable Prairie Avenue. His fortune had been created from his meat packing operations in a place called "Packingtown", a tenement area near the stockyards. Because the pay for slaughtering was so low, many of the children in this area scavenged for food from the garbage dumps. Nearby was "Whiskey Row", a district of more than 200 saloons. Here, stockyard workers were often treated to a free lunch, but only on the condition that they bought a drink.

Carl Sandburg called Chicago the "hog butcher for the world" but it was beef that actually made the city wealthy. Until the 1800's, cuts of beef were prepared only by local butchers. However in 1872, a man named Gustavas Swift began buying cattle from the western ranges and shipping sides of beef to the east on express trains that ran in the winter months with their doors open to preserve the meat. Later, Swift developed refrigerated rail cars and soon he and his competitor, Phillip Armour, were shipped most of the nation's beef and pork products.

The slaughterhouses were located on the south side of the city, in Packingtown. The plants were filthy and dangerous workplaces that treated the workers, who were most Eastern European immigrants, with little regard. It was said that the plants used "every part of the hog but the squeal" but there was still waste to be disposed of. The slaughter refuse was dumped into a large, open sewer that ran down the middle of Packingtown. It was dubbed "Bubbly Creek" because it would literally bubble as the bacteria devoured the blood and waste.

The horrible conditions of Packingtown caught the attention of Frank Warren, the editor of a weekly Socialist newspaper. He decided to send one of his reporters, a young man named Upton Sinclair, to Chicago to write a piece on the packing houses. Sinclair was poor himself and so his threadbare clothing fit right in with the immigrants working in Packingtown. He found that by carrying a pail with him, he could go anywhere that he wanted to. He gathered his material and his article ran as a series in the newspaper starting in February 1905. He later gathered the material into a book that would be titled "The Jungle".

For months, he was unable to find anyone to publish the fictionalized depiction of the area. No one would believe that the conditions he described in Packingtown were accurate. Sinclair insisted that while the Lithuanian family of the book was not real, it had been based on real people and the horrific condition of Packingtown was genuine.

"The Jungle" was finally published by Doubleday in 1906. It contained graphic details and by the end of the year, it had sold more than 100,000 copies. Author Jack London called it "the Uncle Tom's Cabin of wage slavery". Another fan of the book was President Theodore Roosevelt, who had long been a critic of the nation's meatpackers. During the Spanish-American War, he had stated that he would rather eat his old hat as eat the meat that the companies were sending to Cuba. He believed that Sinclair's book could help him do something about the problem.

Roosevelt began actively pursuing government regulations on the meat industry, including inspections. The meat packers opposed the new standards but with meat sales falling in wake of Sinclair's book, they began claiming that the plants were clean and safe. Soon, doctors began supporting Sinclair's claims of unsanitary conditions and the public began turning against the industry. A popular rhyme that made the rounds in Chicago in 1906 went "Mary had a little lamb, and when she saw it sicken, she shipped it off to Packingtown, and now it's labeled chicken."

Roosevelt succeeded with his plans and the first meat inspection bill was passed one year later. "The Jungle" had changed an industry and meat packing was never the same. Despite the fact that the meatpackers had strenuously opposed the new regulations at first, they soon embraced them. The federal inspections became a marketing opportunity and meat today is still sold as being "guaranteed pure" by the US government.

The volatile conditions of the packing industry in Chicago have spawned at least one tale of murder and ghosts in the city. It is a tale that had a lot of people in Chicago avoiding sausages back in 1897!

THE SAUSAGE VAT MURDER

The ghost of Louisa Luetgert still walks the now almost deserted neighborhood where her home once stood, or at least that's what the legends of northwest Chicago say. Louisa was the murdered wife of "Sausage King" Adolph Luetgert, a German meat packer who came to the city in the 1870's. Killed by her own husband in one of the most grisly ways imaginable, her ghost not only haunts the area around Hermitage Avenue but the legends say that she hounded her treacherous husband from Joliet Prison to the grave!

After finding that his German sausages were well-liked in Chicago, Adolph Luetgert built a sausage plant at the southwest corner of Hermitage and Diversey Parkway in 1894. He was so taken with his own success that he also built a three-story frame house next door to the factory, which he shared with his wife Louisa.

Louisa Bicknese was an attractive young woman who was ten years younger than her husband was. She was a former servant from the Fox River Valley who met her new husband by chance. He was immediately taken with her, entranced by her diminutive stature and tiny frame. She was less than five feet tall and looked almost child-like next to her burly husband. As a wedding gift, he gave her a unique, heavy gold ring. Inside of it, he had gotten her new initials inscribed, reading "L.L.". Little did he know at the time that this ring would prove to be his undoing.

According to friends and neighbors, Luetgert's fascination with his beautiful young wife did not last long. The couple was frequently heard to argue and their disagreements became so heated that Luetgert eventually moved his bedroom from the house to a small chamber inside of the factory. Luetgert soon became involved with a girl named Mary Simerling, Louisa's nice and a household servant. This new scandal also got the attention of the people in the neighborhood, who were already gossiping about the couple's marital woes.

Then, on May 1, 1897, Louisa disappeared. When questioned by his sons, Luetgert told them that their mother had gone out the previous evening to visit her sister. After several days though, she did not come back.

The Luetgert Sausage Works (circa 1894)

Finally, Diedrich Bicknese, Louisa's brother, went to the police. The investigation fell on Captain Herman Schuettler, who author Richard Lindberg describes as "an honest but occasionally brutal detective".

The detective and his men began to immediately search for Louisa. They questioned neighbors and relatives and soon learned of the couple's violent arguments. They also talked to Wilhelm Fulpeck, an employee of the sausage factory, who recalled seeing Louisa enter the factory around 10:30 in the evening on May 1. Frank Bialk, a night watchman at the plant, confirmed his story. He also added that he saw both Luetgert and Louisa at the plant together. Apparently, Luetgert sent him out on an errand that evening and gave him the rest of the night off.

Schuettler also made another disturbing and suspicious discovery. Just a short time before Louisa's disappearance, the factory had been closed for ten weeks for reorganization. However, the day before Louisa vanished, Luetgert ordered 378 pounds of crude potash and fifty pounds of arsenic. The circumstantial evidence was starting to add up and Schuettler began to theorize about the crime. He became convinced that Luetgert had killed his wife, boiled her in acid and then disposed of her in a factory furnace. With that in mind, he and his men started another search of the sausage plant. They narrowed the search to the basement and to a twelve-foot-long, five-foot-deep vat that was located next to the furnaces that smoked the meat. The officers drained the greasy paste from the vat and began poking through the residue with sticks. Here, officer Walter Dean found a small piece of a skull fragment and two gold rings. One of them was engraved with the initials "L.L.".

On May 7, Adolph Luetgert, proclaiming his innocence, was arrested for the murder of his wife. No body was ever found and there were no witnesses to the crime, but police officers and prosecutors believed the evidence was overwhelming. Luetgert was indicted for the crime a month later and details of the murder shocked the city, especially those on the northwest side. Even though Luetgert was charged with burning his wife's body, local rumor had it that she had been ground into sausage instead. Needless to say, sausage sales declined substantially in 1897.

Luetgert went to trial but the proceedings ended in a hung jury on October 21 after the jurors failed to agree on a suitable punishment. Some argued for the death penalty, while others voted for life in prison. Only one of the jury members thought that Luetgert might be innocent. A second trial was held and on February 9, 1898, Luetgert was convicted and sentenced to life imprisonment at Joliet.

Luetgert was taken away to prison, where he became a shell of his former self. He babbled incoherently to the guards, claiming that his dead wife was haunting him, intent on having her revenge, even though he was innocent of her murder. Luetgert, possibly insane by this time, died in 1900.

And he was not the only one to suffer. His attorney, Lawrence Harmon, believed that his client was telling the truth and that he did not kill his wife. He was sure that she had simply disappeared. In fact, Harmon was so convinced of Luetgert's innocence that she spent over $2,000 of his own money and devoted the rest of his life to finding Louisa. Eventually, he also went insane and he died in a mental institution.

And Louisa, whether she was murdered by her husband or not, reportedly did not rest in peace. Not long after her husband was sent to prison, her ghost began to be seen inside of the Luetgert house. Neighbors claimed to see a woman in a white dress leaning against the mantel in the fireplace. Eventually, the house was rented out but none of the tenants stayed there for long. The ghost was also reported inside of the sausage factory but this building burned down in 1902 and was never rebuilt.

Legend has it on the northwest side that Louisa Luetgert still walks. If she does, she probably no longer recognizes the neighborhood where she once lived as the factory is long gone and the houses that once stood here have been replaced by empty lots and an industrial complex. They say though, that if you happened to be in this area on May 1, the anniversary of Louisa's death, there is a chance that you might see her lonely specter still roaming the area where she lived and died.

CRIME AND CRIMINALS

From even the early days, Chicago thrived on its reputation for being a "wide-open town". As far back as the 1850's, the city gained notoriety for its promotion of vice in every shape and form. It embraced the arrival of prostitutes, gamblers, grifters and an outright criminal element. A commercialized form of vice flourished during the Civil War era and according to author Richard Lindberg, an estimated 1,300 prostitutes roamed the darkened, evening streets of Chicago. Randolph Street, he wrote, "was awash in bordellos, wine rooms and cheap dance halls in plain view of the courthouse". The area became known as "Gambler's Row", mostly because a man gambled with his very life when braving the streets of this seedy and dangerous district.

The Great Fire in 1871 would sweep away the worst of the city's vice areas, destroying both gin rooms and disease-ridden prostitution cribs, but a desire for illicit activities caused it to rebound quickly. By the 1880's, Chicago had gained its place as a mature city and also as a rail center for the nation. Waves of foreigners and immigrants poured into the city and with the arrival of the World's Fair in 1893, thousands of new citizens followed.

The Custom House vice district sprang from the ashes of the Great Fire. For nearly 30 years, the area would be regarded as a blight on the downtown area. Like most segregated vice areas, where gambling, liquor and prostitution are indulged, the Custom House thrived on not only its proximity to the railroads but to an alliance with the police as well. The closest station could be found at the nearby Armory station and they turned a blind eye to questionable activity in the district, for a price, of course.

The Custom House district existed between Harrison Street on the north and Polk Street and the Dearborn train station to the south. It is an area more popularly known as "Printer's Row" today. The boundaries of the area tended to change and expand with the opening of each new saloon or house of ill repute. It also tended to shrink when any of the owners neglected to make their protection payments. Such absent-mindedness was usually followed by a police raid.

The Dearborn Station became essential to operations in the area as it made a perfect recruiting spot for prostitutes during the gaslight era. Naive young women who stepped off the train were often greeted by one of the army of "pimps" who waited in the station. From that point, they were introduced to immoral acts and lured into the "scarlet patch" originally known as the Cheyenne District and later the Custom House.

The most infamous bordello here was Carrie Watson's place at 441 South Clark Street. Despite the seediness of the area, the beautiful Miss Watson's "house" enjoyed a wide reputation for being a charming place, with sixty women in her employ.

There were other "resorts" along the Custom House that were not so elegant or refined though. Often an unsophisticated visitor would stumble into what was called a "panel house", where he might be drugged and tied up while an accomplice slipped through a hidden panel in the wall and liberated him of his valuables. More often, the secret panels hid thieves with long hooks who could relieve a customer of his wallet, from pants hanging on the bed post, while he was "in the act". Few of these victims would report the robbery to the police, lest they suffer the humiliation of having their names printed in the newspaper.

By the time of the Columbian Exposition in 1893, Chicago had become known as the "Paris of America" for its many illicit attractions. Reformist WT Stead, in his book "If Christ Came to Chicago", counted thirty-seven bordellos, forty-six saloons, eleven pawnbrokers, an opium den and numerous gambling parlors in the Custom House district while writing his expose on Chicago vice.

The official stance on such districts was to leave them alone, as long as the operators, thieves and undesirables stayed in the district and kept to themselves. However, this was rarely the case. Granted a wide berth by city officers, the dealers in vice exploited the situation with prostitutes being arrested in the theater district and posing as sales girls in reputable stores. By 1903, conditions had become intolerable and reformers would no longer stand for it. A wave of criminal indictments, pushed through by church groups and the mayor himself, sent the vice operators reeling. Most of them moved to the South Side Levee District, where they were welcomed with open arms. The Custom House Place Levee had vanished completely by 1910.

After that, the deserted area was slowly taken over by commercial printing houses and bookbinderies, creating the name the district bears today, "Printer's Row". Eventually, the printing houses joined the bordellos and they too faded away. The area finally gained its dignity around 1979 when it converted into the condominium and rental community that exists today. The railroad freight yards have also disappeared, although Dearborn station remains. It has been converted into a small shopping mall, serving the residents of this quiet street. The Custom House Levee is now only a memory.

The city of Chicago has seen more than its share of crime over the years, from the bloody excess of Prohibition to the brutal murders committed by deviants like Richard Speck and John Wayne Gacy. However, one of the most horrific of the murderers to walk the streets of Chicago came along many years before these killers were even born. Many regard him as the first serial killer in America. His name was Herman Webster Mudgett and if this tale is unfamiliar to you, then prepare yourself... the recounting of his dark deeds and ghostly legacy is not for the faint of heart!

THE MURDER CASTLE

Herman Mudgett was born around 1858 in New Hampshire. Early in life, Mudgett dropped his given name and became known as HH Holmes, a name under which he attended medical school and began his career in crime. Even as a student, Holmes began to dabble in debauchery. As he attended school in Michigan, he devised a method of stealing cadavers from the laboratory.

He would then disfigure the corpses and plant them in places where it would look as though they had been killed in accidents. Conveniently, Holmes had already taken out insurance policies on these "family members" and he would collect on them as soon as the bodies were discovered.

In 1878, Holmes married Clara Lovering and it is believed that he taught school for a brief period in New York. After that, he sent Clara to New Hampshire and then dropped out of sight for two years. What became of him during this period is unknown, but in 1886, he turned up on the south side of Chicago. Upon his re-appearance, Holmes filed for divorce from Clara, but the proceedings were unsuccessful and the case dragged on until 1891. This did not stop him from marrying another woman however, a Myrtle Belknap, who father, John Belknap, was a wealthy businessman in Wilmette, Illinois. Although the marriage did produce a daughter, it was nevertheless a strange one. Myrtle remained living in Wilmette while Holmes stayed in Chicago. John Belknap would later discover that Holmes had tried to cheat him out of property by forging his name on deeds. He would also claim that Holmes had tried to poison him when he was confronted about the fraudulent papers. Myrtle ended the marriage in 1889.

Stories claim that the house in Wilmette where Myrtle lived is haunted today. One has to wonder if the spirits who walk here are that of John Belknap or Myrtle herself. It's possible that her unhappy marriage, and horror as the later crimes of her husband were revealed, has caused her to linger behind.

Shortly after Holmes married Myrtle, he began working in a drugstore in the Englewood neighborhood at the corner of 63rd and Wallace Street. The store was owned by a Mrs. Holden, an older lady, who was happy to have the young man take over most of the responsibilities of the store. Strangely, in 1887, Mrs. Holden vanished without a trace. A short time before, Holmes announced that he had purchased the store from the widow, just prior to her "moving out west". The unfortunate lady had (not surprisingly) left no forwarding address.

Herman Mudgett, the man known as HH Holmes, and an illustration of a crowd forming outside of the castle shortly after words of the killer's deeds leaked out. (Illinois State Historical Library)

In 1889, Holmes began a new era in his criminal life. After a short trip to Indiana, he returned to Chicago and purchased an empty lot across the street from the drugstore. He had plans to build a huge house on the property and work was started almost immediately. His trip to Indiana had been profitable and he had used the journey to pull off an insurance scheme with the help of an accomplice named Benjamin Pietzel. The confederate later went to jail as a result of the swindle, but Holmes came away unscathed.

Holmes continued to operate the drug store, to which he also added a jewelry counter. In 1890, he hired Ned Connor of Davenport, Iowa as a watchmaker and jeweler. The young man arrived in the city in the company of his wife, Julia, and their daughter, Pearl. The family moved into a small apartment above the store and soon, Julia managed to capture the interest of Holmes. He soon fired his bookkeeper and hired Julia to take the man's place. Not long after, Connor began to suspect that Holmes was carrying on with his wife, and he was right. Luckily for him, he decided to cut his losses, abandoned his family and went to work for another shop downtown.

Now that Holmes had Julia to himself, he took out large insurance polices of the woman and her daughter, naming himself as a beneficiary. Years later, it came to be suspected that Julia became a willing participant in many of Holmes' schemes and swindles. When he incorporated the jewelry business in August 1890, he listed Julia, along with her friend Kate Durkee, as directors.

By this time, much of Holmes' ill-gotten gains had been funneled into the construction of this home across the street. It would later be dubbed the "Murder Castle" and it would certainly earn its nickname. The building was three-stories high and built from brick. There were over 60 rooms in the structure and 51 doors that were cut oddly into various walls. Holmes acted as his own architect for the place and he personally supervised the numerous construction crews, all of whom were quickly hired and fired. Most likely, he didn't want anyone to have a clear idea of what he had planned for the place. In addition to the eccentric general design, the house was also fitted with trap doors, hidden staircases, secret passages, rooms without windows, chutes that led into the basement and a staircase that opened out over a steep drop to the alley behind the house.

The first floor of the building contained stores and shops, while the upper floors could be used for spacious living quarters. Holmes also had an office on the second floor, but most of the rooms were to be used for guests... guests would never be seen again. Evidence would later be found to show that Holmes used some of the rooms as "asphyxiation chambers", where his victims were suffocated with gas. Other chambers were lined with iron plates and had blowtorch-like devices fitted into the walls. In the basement, Holmes installed a dissecting table and maintained his own crematory. There was also an acid vat and pits lined with quicklime, where bodies could be conveniently disposed of. All of his "prison rooms" were fitted with alarms that buzzed in Holmes' quarters if a victim attempted to escape. It has come to be believed that many of his victims were held captive for months before their deaths.

The castle was completed in 1891 and soon after, Holmes announced that he plan to rent out some of the rooms to tourists who would be arriving in mass for the upcoming Columbian Exposition. It is surmised that many of these tourists never returned home after the fair, but no one knows for sure. This was not Holmes' only method for procuring victims however. A large number of his female victims came through false classified ads that he placed in small town newspapers that offered jobs to young ladies. When the ads was answered, he would describe several jobs in detail and explain that the woman would have her choice of positions at the time of the interview. When accepted, she would then be instructed to pack her things and withdraw all of her money from the bank because she would need funds to get started.

The applicants were also instructed to keep the location and the name of his company a closely guarded secret. He told them that he had devious competitors who would use any information possible to steal his clients. When the applicant arrived, and Holmes was convinced that she had told no one of her destination, she would become his prisoner.

Holmes also placed newspaper ads for marriage as well, describing himself as a wealthy businessman who was searching for a suitable wife. Those who answered this ad would get a similar story to the job offer. He would then torture the women to learn the whereabouts of any valuables they might have. The young ladies would then remain his prisoners until he decided to dispose of them.

Amazingly, Holmes was able to keep his murder operation a secret for four years. H slaughtered an unknown number of people, mostly women, in the castle. He would later confess to 28 murders, although the actual number of victims is believed to be much higher. To examine the details of the story, the reader cannot help but be horrified by the amount of planning and devious detail that went into the murders. There is no question that Holmes was one of the most prolific and depraved killers in American history.

In 1893, Homes met a young woman named Minnie Williams. He told her that his name was Harry Gordon and that he was a wealthy inventor. Holmes' interest in her had been piqued when he learned that she was the heir to a Texas real estate fortune. She was in Chicago working as an instructor for a private school. It wasn't long before she and Holmes were engaged to be married. This was a turn of events that did not make Julia Connor happy. She was still involved with Holmes and still working at the store. Not long after his engagement became official, both Julia and Pearl disappeared. When Ned Connor later inquired after them, Holmes explained that they had moved to Michigan. In his confession, he admitted that Julia had died during a bungled abortion that he had performed on her. He had poisoned Pearl.

In April 1893, Minnie's property in Texas was deeded to a man named Benton T. Lyman, who was in reality, Ben Pietzel, the already mentioned accomplice of Holmes. Later that same year, Minnie's brother was killed in a mining accident in Colorado, which is said to have been arranged by Holmes. As with Julia, Holmes' also managed to get Minnie to go along with his deadly schemes, although in Minnie's case, it was even easier to manage her complicity. Apparently, in June 1893 (according to Holmes), Minnie had accidentally killed her sister, Nannie, during a heated argument. She had hit the other girl over the head with a chair and she had died. Holmes had "protected" Minnie by dropping the body into Lake Michigan. Some believe that Minnie had not killed her sister at all, but had merely stunned her with the chair. It had been Holmes, they say, who finished the woman off and who gained himself yet another accomplice.

A short time later, Holmes and Minnie traveled to Denver in the company of another young woman, Georgianna Yoke, who had come to Chicago from Indiana with a "tarnished reputation". She had applied for a job at the castle and Holmes told her that his name was Henry Howard and that Minnie was his cousin. On January 17, 1894, Holmes and Georgianna were married at the Vendome Hotel in Denver with Minnie as their witness! After that, the wedding party (which apparently consisted of the three of them) traveled to Texas, where they claimed Minnie's property and arranged a horse swindle. Holmes purchased several railroad cars of horses with counterfeit banknotes and signed the papers as "OC Pratt". The horses were then shipped to St. Louis and sold. Holmes made off with a fortune, but it would be this swindle that would later come back and destroy him.

The threesome returned to Chicago and their return marked the last time that Minnie was ever seen alive. Although her body was never found, it is believed to have joined other victims in the acid vat in the basement. Holmes continued to kill, claiming several victims. One of them was Emmeline Cigrand, who was hired as a secretary. She became homesick after a few weeks in Chicago as she hoped to marry an Indiana man named Robert Phelps. Some time later, Phelps made the mistake of dropping by to see her at the castle and that was the last time that either one of them was ever reported alive. Holmes later confessed to killing them both and he described a "stretching experiment" with which he used to kill Phelps. Always curious about the amount of punishment the human body could withstand (Holmes often used the dissecting table on live victims), he invented a "rack-like" device that would literally stretch a person to the breaking point. He would also put the "stretching device" to use on a young lady named Emily Van Tassel, who lived on Robey Street. She was only 17 and worked at a candy store in the first floor of the castle. There is no indication of what caused her to catch the eye of Holmes.

In July 1894, Holmes was arrested for the first time. It was not for murder but for one of his schemes, this time for selling already mortgaged properties. Georgianna promptly bailed him out, but while in jail, he struck up a conversation with a convicted train robber named Marion Hedgepeth, who was serving a 25-year sentence. Holmes had concocted a plan to bilk an insurance company out of $10,000 by taking out a policy on Ben Pietzel. Holmes promised Hedgepeth a $500 commission in exchange for the name of a lawyer who could be trusted. He was directed to Colonel Jeptha Howe, the brother of a public defender, and Howe found Holmes' plan to be brilliant.

It was soon put into action. Pietzel went to Philadelphia with his wife, Carrie, and opened a shop for buying and selling patents under the name of BF Perry. Holmes then took out an insurance policy on his life. The plan was for Pietzel to drink a potion that would knock him unconscious. Then, Holmes would apply make-up to his face to make it look as though he had been severely burned. A witness would then summon an ambulance and while they were gone, Holmes would place a corpse in place of the "shopkeeper". The insurance company would be told that he had died. Pietzel would then receive a portion of the money in exchange for his role in the swindle but he would soon learn, as some many others already had, that Holmes could not be trusted!

The "accident" took place on the morning of September 4, when neighbors heard a loud explosion from the patent office. A carpenter named Eugene Smith came to the door a short time later and found the door locked and the office dark. For some reason, he became concerned and summoned a police officer to the scene. They broke open the door and found a badly burned man on the floor. The death was quickly ruled an accident and the body was taken to the morgue. After 11 days, no one showed up to claim it and so the corpse was buried in the local potter's field. Within days, attorney Jeptha Howe filed a claim with the insurance company and collected his money.

The claim was paid without hesitation and everyone got their share of the money, except for Ben Pietzel and Marion Hedgepeth. Holmes never bothered to contact the train robber again, a slight that Hedgepeth did not appreciate. He brooded over this awhile and then decided to turn Holmes in. He explained the scheme to a St. Louis policeman named Major Lawrence Harrigan, who in turn notified an insurance investigator, WE Gary. He then passed along the information to Frank P. Geyer, a Pinkerton agent, who immediately began an investigation.

Ben Pietzel never received his share of the money either, but even if he had, he would not have been able to spend it. What Holmes had not told anyone was that the body discovered in the patent office was not a cleverly disguised corpse, but Ben Pietzel himself! Rather than split the money again, Holmes had killed his accomplice then burned him so that he would be difficult to recognize. Holmes kept his part of the plan a secret as he and Georgianna were now traveling with Carrie Pietzel and her three children. She believed that her husband was hiding out in New York. The group was last seen in Cincinnati and then in Indianapolis on October 1. Carrie was then sent east and the children were left in the care of Holmes. Needless to say, this did not turn out well for the children.

First, Holmes murdered Carrie's son, Howard, in a secluded farmhouse. From there, Holmes went to Detroit, where the Pietzel daughters wrote letters to their mother and then disappeared again. By now, it is believed that Holmes was aware of the Pinkerton investigation because he crossed the border into Canada and rented a small house in Toronto. One evening, he told the girls that he wanted to play hide-and-seek with them, locked them in a large trunk, ran a gas pipe into it and suffocated them. He then brazenly borrowed a shovel from a neighbor and buried the trunk beneath the floor of his basement.

At this same time, Pinkterton agent Frank Geyer was in Philadelphia, exhuming the body of Ben Pietzel.

Holmes and Georgianna kept moving, traveling first to Boston, then to New Hampshire, where Holmes called on his former wife. He told Clara that he had been in a terrible accident and had been suffering from amnesia for several years. He explained to her that Georgianna had nursed him back to health and that he had been unable to remember Clara, so he had married the other woman. Recently, he had regained his memory and hoped to reconcile with his real wife. Unbelievably, Clara agreed!

Holmes then returned to Boston and in a strange twist of fate was arrested for the horse swindle that he, Minnie and Georgianna had pulled off in Texas. He was given the choice of being returned to Texas and being hanged as a horse thief or he could confess to the insurance scheme that had led to the death of Ben Pietzel. He chose insurance fraud and was sent to Philadelphia. On the way there, Holmes offered his guard $500 if the man would allow himself to be hypnotized. Wisely, the guard refused.

The entire insurance scheme was now completely unraveling. A short time after Holmes was captured, Agent Geyer also arrested Carrie Pietzel and Jeptha Howe. He was slowly starting to uncover the dark secrets of Henry Howard Holmes, he realized, but even the seasoned Pinkerton man was unprepared for what lay ahead. He was beginning to sift through the many lies and identities of Holmes, hoping to find clues as to the fates of Minnie and of the Pietzel children. At this point, he had no idea about all of the other victims. Holmes swore that Minnie had taken the children with her to London, where she planned to open a massage parlor, but Geyer was sure that he was lying.

In June 1895, Holmes pleaded guilty to a single charge of fraud. This opened the door for Geyer to continue his investigation with a search of Holmes' residence in Chicago. He was sure that the answers he was seeking could be found inside of the "castle". He broke into the house with several police officers... and neither he nor the veteran investigators would ever forget what they found there!

Working from the top, they discovered the third-floor "guest rooms" first, puzzled at first by doors that opened to brick walls and staircases that led nowhere. They soon discovered the sliding doors, the secret panels, hidden passages and a clandestine vault that was only a big enough for a person to stand in. The room was alleged to be a homemade "gas chamber", equipped with a chute that would carry a body directly into the basement. The investigators suddenly realized the implications of the iron-plated chamber when they found the single, scuffed mark of a footprint on the inside of the door... the small print had been made by a woman who had attempted to escape the grim fate of the tiny room.

The "chamber of horrors" in the basement stunned the men even further. Here, they sound Holmes' blood-spattered dissecting table and his macabre "laboratory" of torture devices, sharpened instruments and various jars of poison. They also found the acid vat and the crematorium, which still contained ash and portions of bone that had not burned in the intense heat. A search of the ashes also revealed a watch that had belonged to Minnie Williams, some buttons from a dress and several charred tintype photographs. Under the staircase, Geyer also found a ball made from women's hair that had been carefully wrapped in cloth.

Ned Connor was summoned to the castle and he was able to identify a bloody dress that had belonged to Julia. Later on, a child's bones were found beneath the basement floor and were thought to be those of Pearl. The list of Holmes' victims was beginning to grow.

On July 20, city crews began excavating the cellar. The hazy smell of gas hung in the air as the men tore away one wall and discovered a large tank. One of the workers struck a match to peer inside of it and the tank exploded. The men were buried in piles of debris but no one was seriously injured. The tank was lined with wood and metal and was 14 feet long, although tanks to the explosion, no one will ever know that it was used for.

Following the excavation, and the discovery and cataloguing of Holmes' potential victims, the "Murder Castle" (as it came to be called) sat empty for several months. Not surprisingly, it drew onlookers and curiosity-seekers from all over the city. The newspapers were not yet filled with stories and illustrations about Holmes' devious crimes but rumors had quickly spread about what had been discovered there. The people of Chicago were stunned that such things could take place.... and in their glorious city! The people of the Englewood neighborhood watched the sightseers with a combination of fear and loathing, sickened over the terrible things that brought the crowds to their streets.

Then, on August 19, the castle burned to the ground. Three explosions thundered through the neighborhood just after midnight and minutes later, a blaze erupted from the abandoned structure. In less than an hour, the roof had caved in and the walls began to collapse in onto themselves. A gas can was discovered among the smoldering ruins and rumors argued back and forth between an accomplice of Holmes' burning down the house to hide his role in the horror and the arson being committed by an outraged neighbor. The mystery was never solved, but regardless, the castle was gone for good, although many would claim that its memories would linger!

The lot where the castle was located remained empty for many years until finally, a U.S. Post Office was built on the site in 1938. There would be many in the area who had not forgotten the stories of Holmes' castle... or the tales from people who claimed to hear moaning and crying sounds coming from the grounds. Even after the post office was constructed, local folks often walked on the opposite side of the street rather than pass too close by the site where torture and murder had taken place. Neighbors who walked their dogs pass the new building claimed their animals would often pull away from it, barking and whining at something they could see or sense. It was something that remained invisible to their human masters, but which was terrifyingly real to the animals.

In addition, postal workers in the building had their own encounters in the place, often telling of strange sounds and feelings they could not easily explain. The location was certainly ripe for a haunting and if the stories can be believed, it was, and is, taking place!

The trial of Herman Mudgett, aka Holmes, began in Philadelphia just before Halloween 1895. It only lasted for six days and after deliberating for less than four hours, the jury returned a guilty verdict. On November 30, the judge passed a sentence of death.

By now, the details of the case had been made public and people were angry, horrified and fascinated, especially in Chicago, where most of the evil had occurred. Holmes had provided a lurid confession of torture and murder that appeared in newspapers and magazines, providing a litany of depravity that compares with the most insane killers of all time. Even if his story was embellished, the actual evidence of Holmes' crimes ranks him as one of the country's most active murderers.

He remained unrepentant, even at the end. Just before he execution, he visited with two Catholic priests in his cell and even took communion with them, although refused to ask forgiveness for his crimes. He was led from his cell to the gallows and a black hood was placed over his head. The trap door opened beneath him and Holmes quickly dropped. His head snapped to the side, but his fingers clenched and his feet danced for several minutes afterward, causing many spectators to look away. Although the force of the fall had broken his neck, and the rope had pulled so tight that it had literally imbedded itself in his flesh, his heart continued to beat for nearly 15 minutes. He was finally declared dead at 10:25 am on May 7, 1896.

There were a couple of macabre legends associated with Holmes' execution. One story claimed that a lightning bolt had ripped through the sky at the precise moment the rope had snapped his neck... but this was not the strangest one. According to this other story, several of the spectators claimed to hear Holmes shout something just as the trap door opened under him. They said that Holmes had cried out "I am Jack the....", just before the gallows had silenced him forever. Some have speculated that perhaps Holmes was claiming to be the notorious killer, Jack the Ripper. Although it seems unlikely that Holmes could have managed to carry out such notorious crimes on two continents in those days, he was certainly deranged enough to commit those murders as well. Most likely though, if those words were actually uttered, it could have been Holmes merely attempting to add to his own mystique, even in death.

The most enduring supernatural legend of HH Holmes is that of the "Holmes Curse". The story began shortly after his execution, leading to speculation that his spirit did not rest in peace. Some believed that he was still carrying on his gruesome work from beyond the grave. And, even to the skeptical, some of the events that took place after his death are a bit disconcerting.

A short time after Holmes' body was buried, under two tons of concrete, the first strange death occurred. The first to die was Dr. William K. Matten, a coroner's physician who had been a major witness in the trial. He suddenly dropped dead from blood poisoning.

More deaths followed in rapid order, including that of the head coroner. Dr. Ashbridge, and the trial judge who had sentenced Holmes to death. Both men were diagnosed with sudden, and previously unknown, deadly illnesses. Next, the superintendent of the prison where Holmes had been incarcerated committed suicide. The reason for his taking his own life was never discovered. Then, the father of one of Holmes' victims was horribly burned in a gas explosion and the remarkably healthy Pinkerton agent, Frank Geyer, suddenly became ill.

Not long after, the office of the claims manager for the insurance company that Holmes had cheated, caught fire and burned. Everything in the office was destroyed except for a framed copy of Holmes' arrest warrant and two portraits of the killer. Many of those who were already convinced of a curse saw this as an ominous warning.

Several weeks after the hanging, one of the priests who prayed with Holmes before his execution was found dead in the yard behind his church. The coroner ruled the death as uremic poisoning but according to reports, he had been badly beaten and robbed. A few days later, Linford Biles, who had been jury foreman in the Holmes trial, was electrocuted in a bizarre accident involving the electrical wires above his house.

In the years that followed, others involved with Holmes also met with violent deaths, including the train robber, Marion Hedgepeth. He remained in prison after his informing on Holmes, although he had expected a pardon that never came. On the very day of Holmes' execution, he was transferred to the Missouri State Prison to finish out his sentence. As time passed, Hedgepeth gained many supporters to his cause, including several newspapers who wrote of his role in getting Holmes prosecuted. In 1906, he finally got his pardon and was released.

Despite the claims that he had made about his rehabilitation, including that he spent each day in prison reading his bible, Hedgepeth was arrested in September 1907 for blowing up a safe in Omaha, Nebraska. He was tried, found guilty and sentenced to 10 years in prison. He was released however when it was discovered that he was dying from tuberculosis. In spite of his medical condition, he assembled a new gang and at midnight on New Year's Eve 1910, he attempted to rob a saloon in (of all places) Chicago. As he was placing the money from the till into a burlap bag, a policeman wandered into the place for no reason and shot him. Hedgepeth was dead before he hit the floor.

Perhaps Holmes got his revenge after all....

CHICAGO'S "THRILL KILLERS"

On an afternoon in May 1924, the sons of two of Chicago's wealthiest and most illustrious families drove to the Harvard School for boys in Kenwood and kidnapped a young boy named Bobby Franks. Their plan was to carry out the "perfect murder". It was a scheme so devious that only two men of superior intellect, such as their own, could accomplish. These two men were Richard Loeb and Nathan Leopold. They were the privileged heirs of well-known Chicago families who had embarked on a life of crime for fun and for the pure thrill of it. They were also a pair of sexual deviants who considered themselves to be brilliant, a claim that would later lead to their downfall.

Nathan Leopold had been born in 1906 and from an early age had a number of homosexual encounters, culminating in a relationship with Richard Loeb. He was an excellent student with a genius IQ and was only 18 when he graduated from the University of Chicago. Like many future killers, his family life was totally empty and devoid of control. His mother had died when he was young and his father gave him little attention.

Richard Loeb was the son of the Vice President of Sears and Roebuck and while he was as wealthy as his friend was, Loeb was merely a clever young man and far from brilliant. What he lost in intelligence, he more than made up for in arrogance however. He fancied himself a master criminal detective but his dream was to commit the perfect crime. With his more docile companion, Leopold, Loeb began developing what he believed to be the perfect scheme. He also constantly searched for ways to control others. Not long after the two became friends, Leopold attempted to initiate a sexual relationship with Loeb. At first, he spurned the other's advances but then offered a compromise. He would engage in sex with Leopold, but only under the condition that the other boy begin a career in crime with him. Leopold agreed and they signed a formal pact to that affect.

Over the course of the next four years, they committed robbery, vandalism, arson and petty theft, but this was not enough for Loeb. He dreamed of something bigger. A murder, he convinced his friend, would be their greatest intellectual challenge.

They worked out a plan during the next seven months. For a victim, they chose a 14-year-old boy named Bobby Franks. He was the son of the millionaire Jacob Franks, and a distant cousin of Loeb. They were already acquainted with the boy and he went happily with them on that May afternoon. They drove him to within a few blocks of the Franks residence in Hyde Park then suddenly grabbed him, stuffed a gag in his mouth and smashed his skull four times with a chisel. He fell to the floor and bled to death in the car.

When the brief bit of excitement was over, Leopold and Loeb casually drove away, stopped for lunch and then ended up near a culvert along the Pennsylvania Railroad tracks. After dunking the boy's head underwater to make sure that he was dead, they poured acid on his face (so that he would be hard to identify) then stuffed his body into a drainpipe.

After this, they drove to Leopold's home, where they spent the afternoon and evening drinking and playing cards. Around midnight, they telephoned the Franks' home and told Mr. Franks that he could soon expect a ransom demand for the return of his son. They typed out a letter on a stolen typewriter and mailed it to Franks, intent on continuing their twisted "game". However, by the time the letter arrived, workmen had already stumbled upon the body of Bobby Franks.

Despite their "mental prowess" and "high intelligence", Leopold and Loeb were quickly caught. Leopold had dropped his eyeglasses near the spot where the body had been hidden and police had (cleverly) traced the prescription back to him. They also traced the ransom note to a typewriter that Leopold had "borrowed" from his fraternity house the year before.

After questioning, Loeb broke first. Leopold's confession came soon after. The people of Chicago, and the rest of the nation, were stunned and soon people were crying for the blood of the two killers. It was fully expected that the two would receive a death sentence for the callous and cold-blooded crime. Then, in stepped Clarence Darrow.

America's most famous defense attorney had been hired by the parent's of the two young killers. For $100,000 he had taken the case and agreed to seek the best possible verdict that he could, which in this case was life in prison. Darrow would have less trouble with the case than he would with his clients, who constantly clowned around and hammed it up in the courtroom. The newspaper photographers frequently snapped photos of them smirking and laughing in court and the public, already turned against them, became even more hostile toward the "poor little rich boys".

Darrow was fighting an uphill battle but he brought out every trick in the book and used shameless tactics in the case. He declared the boys to be insane. Leopold, he said, was a dangerous schizophrenic. They weren't criminals, he railed, they just couldn't help themselves! After this weighty proclamation, Darrow actually began to weep. The trial became a landmark (and some say a bad one) in criminal law. He then began to describe a detailed description of what would happen to the men as they were hanged, providing a graphic image of bodily functions and physical pain. Darrow turned to the prosecutor and invited him to perform the execution.

Darrow's horrifying description had a marked effect on the courtroom and especially on the defendants. Loeb was observed to shudder and Leopold got so hysterical that he had to be taken out of the courtroom. Darrow then wept for the defendants, wept for Bobby Franks.... and then wept for defendants and victims everywhere. The master manipulator won the case. The defendants were given life in prison for Bobby Frank's murder and an additional 99 years for his kidnapping. Ironically, after all of that, Darrow only managed to get $40,000 of his fee from his tight-fisted clients. He only managed to get that after threatening to sue them.

Leopold and Loeb were sent to the state prison in Joliet and officials there were ridiculed by the public and the press for the special treatment they received. Obviously, money was changing hands as each enjoyed a private cell, books, a desk, a filing cabinet and even pet birds. They also showered away from the other prisoners and took their meals, which were prepared to order, in the officer's lounge. They were also allowed any number of unsupervised visitors and were allowed to keep their own gardens.

Over time, Loeb became even more deranged and was feared as a brutal prison rapist. He terrified weaker prisoners and was avoided by the population at large. Even Leopold wanted nothing to do with him. In January 1936, he was killed by another inmate, who slashed him 56 times with a makeshift knife. He was found bleeding in the corridor by guards and he died a short time later.

Leopold lived on in prison for many years and was said to have made many adjustments to his character and some would even say had rehabilitated completely. Even so, appeals for his parole were turned down three times. Finally, in 1958, his fourth appeal was pleaded by the poet Carl Sandburg, who even went as far as to offer Leopold a room in his own home. Finally, in March of that year, he was released. He went on to write a book about his experiences called "Life Plus 99 Years" and moved to Puerto Rico. There, he worked among the poor, married a widow and died in 1961.

Although ghosts of violent murder have often been believed to walk the earth, the spirit of Bobby Franks has always rested in peace, perhaps because his killers were brought to justice. There is one spirit believed to linger from this case however... that of master lawyer Clarence Darrow.

In the books "Chicago Haunts" and "Windy City Ghosts", authors Ursula Bielski and Dale Kaczmarek both tell of instances where the ghost of Darrow has been seen along the back steps of the Museum of Science and Industry in Chicago. The apparition is reported dressed in a suit, hat and overcoat and bears a striking resemblance to the attorney. The figure is reported to stand and stare out across the water before disappearing. Why his ghost walks is unknown, although perhaps the infamously agnostic attorney simply refuses to go on to the other side, a place that he didn't believe in anyway!

THE CRIME THAT SHOCKED CHICAGO!

One of the most shocking and terrifying events in the history of Chicago took place in October

1955. When the bodies of three young boys were discovered in a virtually crime-free community on the northwest side of the city, the entire region was paralyzed with fear. In a few years, another tragedy would occur with the disappearance and death of the Grimes sisters, but at the time of the Schuessler-Peterson murders, the city was stunned by the horror of violence against children. Also, as with the Grimes sisters, the murders would highlight the fact that cooperation between different Chicagoland police departments and investigators was poor at best. In fact, it was so poor that more than 40 years would pass before a killer would be discovered.

The story begins on a cool Sunday afternoon in the fall of 1955 when three boys from the northwest side of the city head downtown to catch a matinee performance of a movie at a Loop Theater. The boys made the trip with their parent's consent because in those days, parent's thought little of their responsible children going off on trips by themselves. The boys had always proven dependable in the past and this time would have been no exception, if tragedy had not occurred.

With $4 between them, John and Anton Schuessler and Bobby Peterson ventured into the Chicago Loop to seen a movie that Bobby's mother had chosen for them. Around 6:00 pm that night, long after the matinee had ended, the boys were reported in the lobby of the Garland Building at 111 North Wabash. There was no explanation for what they might have been doing there, other than that Peterson's eye doctor was located in the building. It seems unlikely that he would have been visiting the optometrist on a Sunday afternoon.

Many years later, according to author Richard Lindberg, a Chicago police detective named John Sarnowski came up with the theory that the boys may have been at the building attempting to meet an older boy named John Wayne Gacy. Gacy often hung out at the Garland building as the lobby was reputed to be a meeting place for gay men and prostitutes. Strangely, Gacy did live a few blocks away from the Schuessler brothers at 4505 North Marmora Avenue at that time but it's unknown if they were connected in any other way. Regardless, the boys were in the Garland Building for less than five minutes that evening.

Around 7:45 pm, the three entered the Monte Cristo Bowling Alley on West Montrose. The parlor was a neighborhood eating place and the proprietor later recalled to the police that he recalled the boys and that a "fifty-ish" looking man was showing an "abnormal interest" in several younger boys who were bowling. He was unable to say if the man made contact with the trio. They left the bowling alley and walked down Montrose to another bowling alley, then thumbed a ride at the intersection of Lawrence and Milwaukee Avenue. They were out of money by this time, but not quite ready to go home. It was now 9:05 in the evening and their parents were beginning to get worried. They had reason to be, for the boys were never seen alive again.

Two days later, the boy's naked and bound bodies were discovered in a shallow ditch about 100 feet east of the Des Plaines River. A salesman, who had stopped to eat his lunch at the Robinson Wood's Indian Burial Grounds spotted them and called the police. Coroner Walter McCarron stated that the cause of death was "asphyxiation by suffocation". The three boys had been dead about 36 hours when they were discovered.

Bobby Peterson had been struck repeatedly and had been strangled with a rope or a necktie. The killer had used adhesive tape to cover the eyes of all three victims. They had then been thrown from a vehicle. Their clothing was never discovered.

The city of Chicago was thrown into a panic. Police officials reported that they had never seen such a horrible crime. The fears of parents all over the city were summed up by the grief-stricken Anton Schuessler Sr. who said, "When you get to the point that children cannot go to the movies in the afternoon and get home safely, something is wrong with this country."

Police officers combed the area, conducting door-to-door searches and neighborhood interrogations. Search teams combed Robinson's Woods, looking for clues or items of clothing. The killer (or killers) had gone to great length to get rid of any signs of fingerprints or traces of evidence. By this time, various city and suburban police departments had descended on the scene, running into each other and further hampering the search for clues. There was little or no cooperation between the separate agencies and if anything had been discovered, it would have most likely been lost in the confusion.

While investigators were coming up empty, an honor guard of Boy Scouts carried the coffins of the three boys from the St. Tarcissus Roman Catholic Church to a hearse that would take them to St. Joseph Cemetery. The church was filled to capacity with an estimated 1,200 mourners. This marked the end of innocence in Chicago. With the death of the Grimes sisters a few years later, it was apparent to all that America had changed for the worse.

Years passed. As there is no statute of limitations for murder, the case officially remained open but there was little chance that it would ever be solved. The families involved saw their hopes for closure in the case slowly fading away. At best, the murders provided parents with a cautionary lesson about the perils of "talking to strangers". Then, decades later, the impossible happened! In a bizarre turn of events, a government informant named William Wemette accused one Kenneth Hansen of the murders during a police investigation into the 1977 disappearance of candy heiress Helen Vorhees Brach.

In 1955, Hansen, then 22 years old, worked as a stable hand for Silas Jayne, a millionaire from Kane County. Jayne himself was wild and reckless and had been suspected of many violent and devious dealings during his rise to power in the horse breeding world. He went to prison in 1973 for the murder of his half brother, George. Hansen himself was no prize either and soon, investigators were able to build a case against him. The case resulted in the deviant's arrest in August 1994.

Cook County prosecutors showed jurors how Hansen had lured the Schuessler brother and Bobby Peterson into his car under false pretenses. They retraced the path of the killer in what Richard Lindberg called "chilling detail". His story was that he wanted to show the boys some prize horses belonging to Silas Jayne. According to the testimony of several men that Hansen had bragged to, he had molested and then killed the Schuesslers and Peterson one by one. When Jayne discovered his crime, the horse breeder burned the stables in order to obliterate any evidence that Hansen had left behind. Hansen's brother had then dumped the boy's bodies at Robinson's Woods and Jayne had filed a bogus insurance claim for the lost building.

This case came to trial in 1995 and breaking a 40 year silence, many of Hansen's other victims came forward, recalling promises of jobs made to young men in return for sexual favors. He forced their silence with threats that included warnings that they might end up "like the Peterson boy". Even without evidence and eyewitnesses to corroborate the prosecution's allegations against him, a Cook County jury convicted Kenneth Hansen of the murders in September 1995. They deliberated for less than two hours and Hansen was sentenced for 200-300 years in prison.

Bobby Peterson and the Schuessler brothers could finally rest in peace.

FAREWELL TO THE GRIMES SISTERS

If the "age of the innocence" in Chicago was wounded by the Schuessler-Peterson Murders, then its death knell sounded in 1956 with the disappearance and murders of the Grimes Sisters.

Many readers may remember being a child and taking a trip to the corner drug store for a soda and a comic book, although few of us would allow our children to do that today. But things weren't always that way. I have friends, much older than myself, who grew up in the 1930's and 1940's, when people didn't have to worry so much about what was going when their kids were out of sight. Sure, the "good old days" were not always good, but it just seemed to be a more innocent time in the hearts of all Americans. I was a child in the late 1960's and early 1970's and even then, people were not as cautious as they are today about letting kids do things on their own. Even now though, I can remember the words that I'll probably never forget. "Never talk to strangers", we were always told.

Well, in Chicago of 1956, two young girls did talk to strangers and became the focus of one of the region's most puzzling unsolved crimes. Not only did this event shatter the innocence of the people of Chicagoland forever, but it gave rise to mysterious events and a chilling haunting as well.

It was December 30, 1956 and Patricia Grimes, 15, and Barbara Grimes, 13, left their home at 3624 South Damon Avenue and headed for the Brighton Theater, only a mile away. The girls were both avid fans of Elvis Presley and had gone to see his film "Love Me Tender". The girls were recognized in the popcorn line at 9:30 PM and then seen on an eastbound Archer Avenue bus at 11:00 PM. After that, things are less certain but this may have been the last time they were ever seen alive. The two sisters were missing for the next twenty-five horrific days, before their naked and frozen bodies were found along the banks of Devil's Creek in the southwest part of Cook County. Autopsies were performed and the coroner reported that the girls had died from exposure and shock but were otherwise unharmed. Or were they? This finding became hotly disputed between rival investigators and has become just one of the many unanswered questions in the case.

The last reported sightings of the two girls came from classmates who spotted them at Angelo's Restaurant at 3551 South Archer Avenue, more than twenty-four hours after their reported disappearance. How accurate this sighting was is unknown, as a railroad conductor also reported them on a train near the Great Lakes Naval Training Center in north suburban Glenview.

The police theorized the girls were chasing after two Navy men they had met downtown but this was only supposition. The girl's mother, Loretta Grimes, refused to believe it and while she was sure the girls were not missing voluntarily, the authorities were still not convinced. Regardless, it became the greatest missing persons hunt in Chicago police history. Even Elvis Presley, in a statement issued from Graceland, asked the girls to come home and ease their mother's worries. The plea went unanswered.

Finally, the vigil for the Grimes Sisters ended on January 22, 1957 when construction worker Leonard Prescott was driving south on German Church Road near Willow Springs. He spotted what appeared to be two discarded clothing store mannequins lying next to a guard rail, about five feet from the road. A few feet away, the ground dropped off to Devil's Creek below. Unsure of what he had seen, Prescott nervously brought his wife to the spot, then they drove to the local police station.

Once investigators realized the "mannequins" were actually bodies, they soon discovered they were the Grimes Sisters. A short time later, more than 162 officers from Chicago, Cook County, the Forest Preserves and five south suburban police departments began combing the woods.... and tramping all over whatever evidence may have been there! Between the officers, the reporters, the medical examiners and everyone else, the investigation was already botched.

As mentioned, the coroner ruled the deaths as homicides, but could not provide an actual cause of death. He also stated that the bodies had been exposed to the elements for nearly a month before their discovery. If this was the case, why hadn't anyone else seen them lying there?

Needless to say, the citizens of Chicagoland were stunned. The authorities questioned an unbelievable 300,000 persons, searching for information about the girls, and 2000 of these people were seriously interrogated, which in those days could be brutal. The police named a 17-year-old named Max Fleig as the chief suspect but the current law did not allow juveniles to be tested with a polygraph, or lie detector. Police Captain Ralph Petaque persuaded the boy to take the test anyway and in the midst of it, he confessed to taking the girls. Because the test was illegal and inadmissible, the police were forced to let Fleig go free. Was he the killer? No one will ever know.

Some time later, the police investigated another confession. This one came from a transient who was believed to have been involved in some other murders around the same time period. His confession later unraveled and he admitted that he had lied.

Eager to crack the floundering case, Cook County Sheriff Joseph Lohman then arrested a Tennessee drifter named Benny Bedwell. The suspect related a lurid and sexually explicit tale of drunken debauchery with two young girls that he had picked up at the restaurant where he worked as a dishwasher. But were these girls actually the Grimes Sisters? Everyone doubted the story but Lohman. He booked Bedwell on murder charges, but the drifter's testimony was both vague and contradictory and (most likely) his confession had been beaten out of him.

One of the chief investigators in the case, Harry Glos, believed that Bedwell might have been implicated in the murders in some way but that he was a dubious suspect. State's Attorney Benjamin Adamowski agreed and ordered the drifter released. This set off another round of bickering between police departments and various jurisdictions and the case became even more mired in red tape and inactivity.

Regardless, Glos believed the girls had been beaten and tortured by a sexual predator who lured them into the kidnap car under seemingly innocent pretense. Today, veteran detectives believe that Glos' theory may have been right. According to Richard Lindberg's book, "Return to the Scene of the Crime", they are convinced that Barbara and Patricia were abducted by a front man for a "white slavery" ring and taken to a remote location in the woods surrounding Willow Springs. They are convinced that the girls were strangled after refusing to become prostitutes.

For the next several years, the investigation continued and more suspects were interviewed. A $100,000 reward was posted but the trail went cold and after that, only nuts and cranks who recounted prophetic dreams and psychic visions came forward with information.

Now, more than 40 years later, the mystery of who killed the Grimes sisters remains unsolved. There are many who remember the case and as discussed earlier, remember a time when children did not have to be afraid to walk the streets in their own neighborhood. The impact of this tragedy is still being felt today.... as is the impression of what may have been the girl's final moments.

Along German Church Road in the southern suburb of Willow Springs, is a low point in the roadway that played a part in the 1956 murders. It was here where the bodies of the Grimes sisters were discovered and the location where the police claim to have had numerous strange reports over the years. Since the discovery of the bodies, the police have received reports from those who say they have heard a car pulling up to the location with its motor running. They also say they have heard the door open, followed by the sound of something being dumped alongside the road. The door slams shut and the car drives away. They have heard these things...... and yet there is no car in sight!

Another woman claimed that in addition to the sounds, she saw what appeared to be the naked bodies of two young girls lying on the edge of the roadway. When police investigated, there was no sign of the bodies.

Many researchers believe in "residual hauntings", which means that an event may cause an impression to be left behind on the atmosphere of a place. It is highly likely that the traumatic final moments of the Grimes sisters may have left such an impression on this small stretch of German Church Road. It may have also been an impression caused by the anxiety and madness of the killer as he left the bodies of the young women behind.

Regardless, it seems to be very real and I defy anyone to travel and stop along this stretch of road and to say that they are not moved by the tragedy that took place here.... a tragedy that is the destruction of innocence in Chicagoland.

GANGLAND GHOSTS

There is no period of Chicago history as fascinating as that of the "gangster era" of the 1920's and 1930's. During this period, organized crime gained a foothold in America, especially in Chicago, where gangsters became celebrities and "graft" being paid to cops and politicians was an everyday happening. During the years of Prohibition, the mob came into its own, "giving the people what they wanted" and then diversifying into other criminal pursuits once the liquor began to legally flow again.

Shortly after the end of Prohibition, America was plunged into the Great Depression. This era of national poverty gave birth to another breed of criminal, the bank robber. Bank robberies had been taking place almost since the time that the first Americans entrusted an establishment with their hard-earned money, but the robbers of the 1930's were different. They were no longer the outlaws of the "Wild West" for these bank robbers have the new and novel advantage of motorized transportation. Never before in American crime had outlaws possessed the means to escape so easily from law enforcement officials. Now, they went on the rampage through various states using motor cars.

This new era gave birth to legendary criminals like Ma Barker, Bonnie and Clyde and Dillinger, just to name a few. Many of them not only gained a place on the FBI's new "Most Wanted" list, but they became folk heroes too. There were few Americans who didn't feel a twinge of jealousy as they saw these free-wheeling bank robbers get their revenge on the banks, the wealthy and the government itself. Stories were told that some of these outlaws actually stole from the rich and then gave back part of the money to those who really needed it. And in the 1930's, there were a lot of folks who needed it.

These folk heroes, bank robbers and stone-cold killers certainly left their mark on the American landscape and many of them died just as they lived, fast and hard. It's not surprisingly that many of their stories still linger with us today... or that their ghosts do too!

THE ST. VALENTINE'S DAY MASSACRE

For a city that is so filled with the history of crime, there has been little preservation of the landmarks that were once so important to the legend of the mob in Chicago. The most tragically destroyed of these landmarks was the warehouse that was located at 2122 North Clark Street. It was here, on Valentine's Day 1929, that the most spectacular mob hit in gangland history took place..... the St. Valentine's Day Massacre.

The building was called the S-M-C Cartage Company and was a red, brick structure on Clark Street. The events that led to the massacre began on the morning of the 14th. To understand them however, we have to take a look at the men behind the massacre, Al Capone and George "Bugs" Moran.

Al Capone was the leader of the South Side crime organization and was perhaps the most powerful crime boss of his day. He employed over 1,000 gunmen and claimed that he literally "ran" Chicago. It was said that over half the city's police force and most of its politicians were on his payroll, including state's attorneys, aldermen, mayors and even congressmen. His control over elections in Chicago and in suburban areas like Cicero was absolute. Even today, he remains one of the most recognized names in American and Chicago history.

Capone was born in Brooklyn in 1899 and went to work for gangster Johnny Torrio. When Torrio later moved west to Chicago, Capone followed and went to work for restaurant owner and mobster Big Jim Collisimo. Doing Torrio's dirty work, Capone killed Collisimo so that they could seize control of the city's illegal booze market. The two of them worked together to wipe out their opposition and in 1924, assassinated Dion O'Banion, the head of the Irish mob on the North Side. This resulted in an all-out war and almost got Torrio killed. He returned to Brooklyn and left the business in Capone's hands.

Capone took over a crime empire worth more than $30 million and realized that his secret to success was to limit the mob's activities to the rackets in strongest demand by the public, namely liquor, gambling and prostitution. He gave the people what they wanted and he became a local celebrity. Capone also appeared to be socially responsible, opening up soup kitchens and helping out the poor. What most didn't know is that his generosity didn't cost anything. Local merchants and suppliers were leaned on to provide food for the kitchens and those who didn't keep up with quotas found their trucks wrecked and their tires slashed.

But not everyone loved Capone. There were a number of attempts on his life, like the time in 1926 when the Irish mob sent cars loaded with machine-gunners past his headquarters. They poured over 1,000 rounds into the building but Capone somehow escaped injury. Al Capone, it seemed, was invincible but doom was on the horizon following the horrific massacre on Clark Street.

George "Bugs" Moran was born in Minnesota in 1893 but moved to Chicago with his parents around the turn-of-the-century. Here, he joined up with one of the North Side Irish gangs and was befriended by young tough named Dion O'Bannion. The two began working together, robbing warehouses, but after one fouled-up job, Moran was captured. He kept his silence and served two years in Joliet prison without implicating O'Banion in the crime. He was released at age nineteen and went back to work with his friend. He was soon captured again and once more, kept silent about who he worked with. He stayed in jail this time until 1923.

When Moran, known as "Bugs" because of his quick temper, got out of prison, he joined up with O'Bannion's now formidable North Side mob. They had become a powerful organization, supplying liquor to Chicago's wealthy Gold Coast. Moran became a valuable asset, hijacking Capone's liquor trucks at will. He became known as O'Bannion's right hand man, always impeccably dressed, right down to the two guns that he always wore. When O'Bannion was killed in his flower shop in 1924, Moran swore revenge. The war that followed claimed many lives and almost got Moran killed in 1925 when he was wounded on Congress Street in an ambush.

By 1927, Moran stood alone against the Capone mob, most of his allies having succumbed in the fighting. He continued to taunt his powerful enemy, always looking for ways to destroy him. In early 1929, Moran sided with Joe Aiello in another war against Capone. He and Aiello reportedly gunned down Pasquillano Lolordo, one of Capone's men, and Capone vowed that he would have him wiped out on February 14.

A group of men had gathered at the Clark Street warehouse that morning, because of a tip from a Detroit gangster who told bootlegger Bugs Moran that a truck was on its way to Chicago. It was filled, he claimed, with illegal liquor.

One of the men was Johnny May, an ex-safecracker who had been hired by Moran as an auto mechanic. He was working on a truck that morning, with his dog tied to the bumper, while six other men waited for the truck of hijacked whiskey to arrive. The men were Frank and Pete Gusenberg, who were supposed to meet Moran and pick up two empty trucks to drive to Detroit and pick up smuggled Canadian whiskey; James Clark, Moran's brother-in-law; Adam Heyer; Al Weinshank; and Reinhardt Schwimmer, a young optometrist who had befriended Moran and hung around the liquor warehouse just for the thrill of rubbing shoulders with gangsters.

Bugs Moran was already late for the morning meeting. He was due to arrive at 10:30 but didn't even leave for the rendezvous, in the company of Willie Marks and Ted Newberry, until several minutes after that.

While the seven men waited inside of the warehouse, they had no idea that a police car had pulled up outside, or that Moran had stopped for coffee or had spotted the car and had quickly taken cover (whichever you would like to believe). Five men got out of the police car, three of them in uniforms and two in civilian clothing. They entered the building and a few moments later, the clatter of machine gun fire broke the stillness of the snowy morning. Soon after, five figures emerged and they drove away. May's dog, inside of the warehouse, was barking and howling and when neighbors went to check and see what was going on. They discovered a bloody murder scene and summoned the police.

Moran's men had been lined up against the rear wall of the garage and had been sprayed with machine-guns. They killed all seven of them but had missed Bugs Moran. Some accounts say that he had figured the arrival of the police car to be some sort of shakedown and had hung back. When the machine gunning started, he, Marks and Newberry had fled. The murders broke the power of the North Side gang and Moran correctly blamed Al Capone. There have been many claims as to who the actual shooters were, but one of them was probably "Machine Gun" Jack McGurn, one of Capone's most trusted men.

Surprisingly, while Moran quickly targeted Capone as ordering the hit, the authorities were baffled. Capone had been in Florida at the time of the massacre and when hearing the news, he stated, "the only man who kills like that is Bugs Moran". At the same time, Moran was proclaiming that "only Capone kills guys like that".

Moran was right.... Capone had been behind the killing and this was perhaps the act that finally began the decline of Capone's criminal empire. He had just gone too far and the authorities, and even Capone's adoring public, were ready to put an end to the bootleg wars.

But Capone had not seen the last of the men who were killed on that fateful day. While living at the Lexington Hotel, which has since been torn down, Capone claimed to be haunted by the ghost of James Clark, one of the massacre victims and the brother-in-law of Bugs Moran. Capone believed that the vengeful spirit hounded him from 1929 until the day that he died. There were many times when his men would hear from begging for the ghost to leave him in peace. On several occasions, bodyguards broke into his rooms, fearing that someone had gotten to their boss. Capone would then tell them of Clark's ghost. Did Capone imagine the whole thing, or was he already showing signs of the psychosis that would haunt him after his release from Alcatraz prison? Whether the ghost was real or not, Capone certainly believed that he was. The crime boss even went so far as to contact a psychic named Alice Britt to get rid of Clark's angry spirit. Years later, he would state that Clark followed him to the grave.

After the massacre, the authorities were under great pressure to bring an end to the bootleg wars in Chicago. Washington dispatched a group of treasury agents (Eliot Ness and his "Untouchables") to harass Capone and try to find a way to bring down his operation. In the end though, it would not be murder or illegal liquor that would get Capone, it would be income tax evasion. He was convicted and sentenced to eleven years in federal prison. In 1934, he was transferred to the brutal, "escape proof" prison known as Alcatraz.

The prison was a place of total punishment and few privileges. One of most terrible methods of punishment was the "hole", a dungeon where prisoners were housed naked on stone floors with no blankets, toilets and only bread and water for nourishment. The slightest infraction could earn a beating.

Capone spent three stretches in the "hole", twice for speaking and once for trying to bribe a guard. He returned from the "hole" just a little worse for wear each time. Eventually, it would break him.

Many of the prisoners at Alcatraz went insane from the harsh conditions and Capone was probably one of them. The beatings, attempts on his life and the prison routine took a terrible toll on Capone's mind. After he was nearly stabbed to death in the yard, he was excused from outdoor exercise and usually stayed inside and played a banjo that was given to him by his wife. He later joined the four-man prison band. After five years though, Capone's mind snapped. He would often refuse to leave his cell and would sometimes crouch down in the corner and talk to himself. Another inmate recalled that on some days Capone would simply make and re-make his bunk all day long. He spent the last portion of his stay in the prison hospital ward, being treated for an advanced case of syphilis. He left Alcatraz in 1939.

Jake "Greasy Thumb" Guzik, who ran the South Side mob in Capone's absence, was asked by a reporter if Capone would take control again when he was released. "Al, "Said Guzik, "is nuttier than a fruitcake."

The massacre also began the decline of Bugs Moran as well. With the remnants of his gang, he attempted to take back control of the Gold Coast, but Capone's men were too powerful. Although Moran did drift into oblivion after Capone was sent to prison, he did have one small piece of revenge for the events on Clark Street. According to reports, Bugs and two others caught up to "Machine Gun" Jack McGurn in a bowling alley on February 14, 1936. McGurn was machine-gunned to death with his sleeves rolled up and a bowling ball in his hand. A small paper valentine was found on his bloody corpse.

The once powerful gangster was reduced to petty burglaries by the end of World War II. He first moved to downstate Illinois and then Ohio before a failed robbery got him arrested by the FBI. He was sentenced to serve ten years in 1946 and his release found him quickly re-arrested for another robbery. This time, he was sent to Leavenworth, where he died from lung cancer in February 1957.

Chicago, in its own way, memorialized the warehouse on Clark Street where the massacre took place. It became a tourist attraction and the newspapers even printed the photos of the corpses upside-down so that readers would not have to turn their papers around to identify the bodies.

In 1949, the front portion of the S-M-C Garage was turned into an antique furniture storage business by a couple who had no idea of the building's bloody past. They soon found that the place was visited much more by tourists, curiosity-seekers and crime buffs than by customers and they eventually closed the business.

In 1967, the building was demolished. However, the bricks from the bullet-marked rear wall were purchased and saved by a Canadian businessman. In 1972, he opened a nightclub with a Roaring 20's theme and rebuilt the wall, for some strange reason, in the men's restroom. Three nights each week, women were allowed to peek inside at this macabre attraction.

The club continued to operate for a few years and when it closed the owner placed the 417 bricks into storage. He then offered them for sale with a written account of the massacre. He sold the bricks for $1000 each, but soon found that he was getting back as many as he sold. It seemed that anyone who bought one of the bricks was suddenly stricken with bad luck in the form of illness, financial ruin, divorce and even death. According to the stories, the bricks themselves had somehow been infested with the powerful negative energy of the massacre! Whatever became of the rest of the bricks from the building is unknown. Or that's what the legend says....

According to a Canadian man named Guy Whitford, things may not be just as the legend has them. In fact, he writes "you were correct when you wrote about the bricks being offered for sale in the 1970's, but the fact is, although he had many offers, George never sold a single brick." You see, Whitford claims to be a friend of the Canadian businessman, George Patey, who originally bought the back wall of the warehouse many years ago and later began trying to track down a buyer for the authenticated wall of 417 bullet-marked bricks. "He always had a problem with breaking up the wall," Whitford continued. "The last substantial offer for the entire wall was made by a Las Vegas casino about a decade ago, but George quaffed at the offer..... so that "bad luck to those who bought one" concept must be a rumor or a journalistic embellishment".

The two men tried to sell the wall for some time. The original lot came with a diagram that explained how to restore the wall to its original form. The bricks were even numbered for reassembly. They remained on the market for nearly three decades, but there were no buyers. Eventually, he broke up the set and began selling them one brick at a time for $1,000 each. But were these all of the surviving bricks from the warehouse?

In recent years, other bricks have emerged that claim to have come from the wall and from the building itself. These were not bricks purchased from Patey but were smuggled out of the lot by construction workers and curiosity-seekers. It was said that from these bricks come the legends of misfortune and bad luck. Are these bricks authentic? The owners say they are, but you'll have to judge for yourself!

Whatever the legend of the bricks themselves and whether or not they have somehow been "haunted" by what happened, there is little doubt about the site on Clark Street itself. Even today, people walking along the street at night have reported the sounds of screams and machine guns as they pass the site. The building is long gone but the area is marked as a fenced-off lawn that belongs to the nearby nursing home. Five trees are scattered along the place in a line and the one in the middle marks the location where the rear wall once stood.

Passersby often report these strange sounds and the indescribable feeling of fear as they walk past. Those who are accompanied by dogs report their share of strangeness too. Animals appear to be especially bothered by this piece of lawn, sometimes barking and howling, sometimes whining in fear. Their sense of what happened here many years ago seems to be much greater than our own.

There is no question that the deeds of men like Al Capone and Bugs Moran have left an indelible mark on the city of Chicago. There also seems to be no doubt that an event on February 14, 1929 has left one too!

DILLINGER... DEAD OR ALIVE?
On the evening of July 22, 1934 a dapper-looking man wearing a straw hat and a pin-striped

suit stepped out of the Biograph Theater where he and two girlfriends had watched a film called "Manhattan Melodrama" starring Clark Gable. No sooner had they reached the sidewalk than a man appeared and identified himself as Melvin Purvis of the FBI. He ordered the man in the straw hat to surrender. Several shots rang out and the fleeing man in the straw hat fell dead to the pavement, his left eye shredded by one of the shots fired by the other agents who lay in wait.

And so ended the life of John Herbert Dillinger, the most prolific bank robber in modern American history and the general public's favorite Public Enemy No. 1......or did it?

One of the most famous haunted theaters in the history of Chicago is the Biograph Theater, located on North Lincoln Avenue. It was here, in 1934, that John Dillinger supposedly met his end. The theater has gained a reputation for being haunted, but the story of the ghost seen here actually revolves around the alleyway outside. But the theater, and the surrounding businesses, has banked on the criminal's name for many years. On the day after the fatal shots were fired, the bar next door placed a sign in the window that read "Dillinger had his last drink here". Theater patrons can examine a window in the box office that describes the set-up of Dillinger by the FBI. They can sit in the same seat where Dillinger sat nearly 65 years ago and after the film, they can emerge into "Dillinger's Alley. It is here where the ghost is said to appear.

But what really happened in the final moments of Dillinger's life? To answer the strange and perplexing questions surrounding his possible death, we have to first look at his bloody and violent life.

On the evening that he was killed, Dillinger left the theater in the company of Anna Sage (the famed "Lady in Red") and with another girlfriend, Polly Hamilton. He had been hiding out in her North Halstead Street apartment but for months he had been pursued diligently by Melvin Purvis, the head of the Chicago branch of the FBI. Purvis had lived and breathed Dillinger (and would, after the robber's death, commit suicide) and had narrowly missed him several times at a State Street and Austin Cafe, at Dillinger's north woods hideout in Sault St. Marie, and at Wisconsin's Little Bohemia, where FBI agents recklessly killed a civilian and injured two others. It was finally at the Biograph where Purvis caught up with Dillinger and put an end to his career.

The criminal life of John Dillinger started in 1925 when he held up a grocery store in his hometown of Mooresville, Indiana. Pleading guilty, he was sentenced to serve 10-20 years in prison while his accomplice, who claimed not guilty, only received a sentence of two years. Dillinger spent the next eight years in jail but when he was released in May of 1933, he robbed three banks in three months and netted more than $40,000. Thus began Dillinger's wild spree of crime.

Dillinger was captured in September 1933 and imprisoned in Lima, Ohio. In three weeks, his gang sprung him in a dangerous escape and again was back to bank robbing. In January 1934, Dillinger shot and killed a police officer in East Chicago, for which he was arrested in Arizona and jailed in Crown Point, Indiana to await trial. He escaped a month later, using a fake gun that he had carved from a bar of soap (or a piece of wood) and blackened with shoe polish. He eluded the police for another month, shooting his way out of an ambush in St. Paul and dodging the FBI near Mercer, Wisconsin. Dillinger arrived in Chicago in late June and proceeded to rob a South Bend, Indiana bank and kill a police officer and four civilians. In just over a year, Dillinger has robbed six banks, killed two cops, two FBI agents, escaped from jail twice and had escaped from police and FBI traps six times.

In the process of all of this violence, Dillinger managed to become an American folk hero. It was the time of the Great Depression and here was a man striking back at poverty by taking from those who could afford losing their money the most. Stories began to circulate about Dillinger giving away much of his stolen money to the poor and the needy. Were these stories true? Who knows? But the American public believed it, which was more than the government could stand. Dillinger had to be taken, and soon.

He had become J. Edgar Hoover's "Public Enemy No. 1"... and the heat was on.

Dillinger knew that his luck could only hold out for so long and in May 1934, he contacted a washed-up doctor who had done time for drug charges named Loeser. He paid him $5000 to perform some plastic surgery on his recognizable face, getting rid of three moles and a scar and getting rid of the cleft of his chin and the bridge of his nose. The doctor agreed to the surgery and left Dillinger in the care of his assistant to administer the general anesthetic. An ether-soaked towel was placed over Dillinger's face and the assistant told him to breathe deeply. Suddenly, Dillinger's face turned blue and he swallowed his tongue and died! Dr. Loeser immediately revived the gangster and proceeded to do the surgery. Dillinger would have no idea how close he had come to death. Ironically, just 25 days later, he would catch a bullet in front of the Biograph Theater, or so they say.

When Dillinger walked into the theater that night he had been set up by Anna Sage, who had taken him there at the request of the FBI. She had promised to be wearing a red (actually bright orange) dress for identification purposes. Sixteen cops and FBI agents waited over two hours outside the theater, watching for the unknowing Dillinger to exit. They even walked the aisles of the theater several times to make sure that he was still there. How could the clever gangster have not noticed them?

Finally, Dillinger left the theater and was met by Melvin Purvis. He stepped down from the curb, just passing the alley entrance and tried to run. He reached for his own gun, but it was too late. Four shots were fired and three hit Dillinger. The gangster fell, dead when he hit the pavement.

Purvis ordered Dillinger rushed to nearby Alexian Brothers Hospital. He was turned away at the doors as he was already dead and Purvis and the police waited on the hospital lawn for the coroner to arrive. A mob scene greeted the coroner at the Cook County Morgue where curiosity-seekers filed in long lines past a glass window for a last look at Dillinger. Little did they know that the man they were looking at might not have been the famed gangster at all.

The scene at the Biograph Theater was also chaotic. Tradition tells that passers-by ran to the scene and dipped their handkerchiefs in the blood of the fallen man, hoping for a macabre souvenir of this terrible event.

And it is at this theater where the final moments of John Dillinger have left a lasting impression. It would be many years after before people passing by the Biograph on North Lincoln Avenue would begin to spot a blue, hazy figure running down the alley next the theater, falling down and then vanishing. Along with the sighting of this strange apparition were reports of cold spots, icy chills, unexplainable cool breezes, and odd feelings of fear and uneasiness. Local business owners began to notice that people had stopped using the alley as a shortcut to Halstead Street.

The place certainly seemed haunted. But is the ghost of the man who has been seen here really that of John Dillinger?

Ever since the night of the shoot-out at the Biograph, eyewitness accounts and the official autopsy have given support to the theory that the dead man may not have been Dillinger. Rumors have persisted that the man killed by the FBI was actually a small-time hood from Wisconsin who had been set up by Dillinger's girlfriend and Anna Sage to take the hit.

There are many striking errors in the autopsy report. The dead man had brown eyes while Dillinger's were blue. The corpse had a rheumatic heart condition since childhood while Dillinger's naval service records said that his heart was in perfect condition. It's also been said that the man who was killed was much shorter and heavier than Dillinger and had none of his distinguishing marks. Police agencies claimed that Dillinger had plastic surgery to get rid of his scars and moles, but also missing were at least two scars on Dillinger's body!

And there is more conflicting evidence to say that the FBI killed the wrong man. On the night of the shooting, a local man named Jimmy Lawrence disappeared. Lawrence was a small-time criminal who had recently moved from Wisconsin. He lived in the neighborhood and often came to the Biograph Theater. He also bore an uncanny resemblance to John Dillinger!

In addition, a photograph taken from the purse of Dillinger's girlfriend shows her in the company of a man who looks like the man killed at the Biograph It's a photo that was taken before Dillinger ever had plastic surgery! Could Dillinger's girlfriend have made a date with Jimmy Lawrence to go to the Biograph, knowing (thanks to Anna Sage) that the FBI was waiting for him there?

Some writers have suggested this is exactly what happened. Respected crime writer, Jay Robert

Nash, an expert on Dillinger, reported in his book "The Dillinger Dossier" that Dillinger's girlfriend and Anna Sage rigged the whole affair. According to Nash, Sage was a prostitute from England who was in danger of being deported. To prevent this, she went to the police and told them that she knew Dillinger. In exchange for not being deported, she would arrange to have Dillinger at the Biograph, where they could nab him. She agreed to wear a bright, red dress so she would be easily recognized. While FBI agents waited, "Dillinger" and his girlfriends watched the movie and enjoyed popcorn and soda. When the film ended, the FBI agents made their move. Nash believes however, that they shot Jimmy Lawrence instead of Dillinger. He also believes that when they learned of their mistake, the FBI covered it up, either because they feared the wrath of J. Edgar Hoover, who told them to "get Dillinger or else", or because Hoover himself was too embarrassed to admit the mistake.

So, what happened to the real John Dillinger? Nobody knows for sure, but some claim this American Robin Hood, who supposedly only robbed from banks and gave some of his spoils to the poor, married and moved to Oregon. He disappeared in the late 1940's and was never heard from again.

TRAGEDY AND DEATH

While the murderous events that took place during the "gangster era" in Chicago certainly claimed many lives, none can compare to the lives that have been lost in some of the city's great tragedies.

Fires have taken many lives in Chicago and have left a mark on the city. While the Great Chicago Fire was the most famous blaze in the city's history, it was certainly not the deadliest, nor, some might say, was it the most heartbreakingly tragic. That soul-crushing fire took place on December 1, 1958 when 92 children and three nuns died at the Our Lady of Angels School on the west side. This horrible event has been called the "fire that refuses to die" as many lives were shattered on that fateful day and the neighborhood where the school once stood has never fully recovered.

The fire is painstakingly documented in the book "To Sleep with the Angels" by David Cowan and John Kuentsler and describes a quiet Catholic parish around 3820 West Iowa Street (where the school was located) of about 4,500 families of mostly Irish and Italian backgrounds. Many of them lived modestly in apartments and brick bungalows and after the fire, many of these hardworking families abandoned the neighborhood, never to return.

The fire began at around 2:40 PM on December 1, about 20 minutes before school was let out for the day. Like many other schools at that time, Our Lady of Angels was tragically without many of the safety measures that exist today. There were no smoke detectors, no sprinkler systems, no outside fire alarm and the entire school had only one fire escape. Unbelievably though, the school had just passed a fire inspection two months before. By 1958 standards, the building was legally safe.

It is believed that the fire started in a trash can at the bottom of the basement stairwell. Here, it smoldered all day and then spread to the stairs, thanks to air from an open window. Once it was ignited, the fire quickly spread and burned up to the second floor, devouring the building as it went. By the time the first fire trucks arrived, the upper floor of the north wing was engulfed in flames. The fire had already been burning for a number of minutes before the alarm was sent and more precious time was lost when the fire department trucks pulled up the church rectory and not the school. The dispatchers had been given the wrong address by the person who phoned in the report. Then, when the first trucks arrived at the school, they had to break through a locked gate to get inside.

Inside of the classrooms, which were rapidly filling with smoke, the students heard the sound of the fire trucks approaching but then nothing, as the trucks went to the rectory instead. At that desperate moment, the nuns asked the children to simply bow their heads in prayer. When the trucks finally arrived, and the extent of the blaze was realized, another alarms was sent out, ordering all available vehicles to the scene. Before it was over, forty-three pieces of fire equipment were at the scene.

As more time passed, the fire escape had become unreachable through the burning hallways. The only way out was through the windows and soon, screaming children were plunging to the frozen ground below. The firemen behaved heroically, used their own bodies to break the falls of the children.

More confusion, and despair, was added to the scene as spectators began to arrive. They rushed the police lines, hysterically trying to reach their children who were trapped in the building, and hampered the efforts of the firefighters. When it was over, the bodies of the victims were taken to the Cook County Morgue, where family members and relatives identified them.

Word of the disaster spread around the world. In Rome, Pope John XXIII sent a personal message to the archbishop of Chicago, the Most Reverend Albert Gregory Meyer. Four days later, he would conduct a mass for the victims and their families before an altar set up at the Northwest Armory. He called the fire "a great and inescapable sorrow".

Nearly as tragic as the fire itself is the fact that no blame was ever placed for the disaster. In those days, there was no thought of suing those responsible for the conditions that allowed the fire to happen. Outwardly, the families accepted the idea that the fire had been simply "God's will" but it cannot be denied that a number of those involved left the church, their faith was shattered as their lives. No one dared to challenge the church over what happened and life moved quietly on.

However, the fire has never been forgotten. A new parish school was constructed on the site in 1960, but it was closed down in 1999 because of declining enrollments. The only memorial to the victims of the fire is located in Queen of Heaven Cemetery in Hillside, where 25 of the victims were buried. It was constructed from private donations in 1960 and to this date, no official recognition or memorial to the fire has been erected.

But no matter how you look at it, the fire may have another legacy that has endured. Thanks to the horror at the Our Lady of Angels, the lives of future children may have been saved. Even though this is small comfort to the families of those who perished, the new safety regulations that went into effect because of the fire have most likely saved the lives of thousands of children over the years. Regardless, those who lost their lives in this tragedy will never be forgotten.

THE IROQUOIS THEATER FIRE

Another terrible blaze occurred at the Iroquois Theater on December 30, 1903 as a fire broke out in the crowded theater during a performance of the vaudeville show, "Mr. Bluebeard", starring the popular comedian Eddie Foy. The fire was believed to have been started by faulty wiring leading to a spotlight and claimed the lives of hundreds of people, including children, who were packed into the afternoon show for the holidays.

Around 3:00 Pm, during the second act, Eddie Foy noticed a spark descend from an overhead light, then some scraps of burning paper that fell down onto the stage. In moments, flames began licking at the red-velvet curtain and while a collective gasp went up from the audience, no one rushed for the exits. It has been surmised that the audience merely thought the fire was part of the show.

Realizing what was happening, Foy told the audience to remain calm... and then himself rushed off stage and into the safety of the alley outside. As he ran, he ordered that the "fireproof" curtains be closed. The other actors in the show remained composed until they too realized what was happening. Many of them panicked and several chorus girls fainted and had to be dragged off-stage. None of the 348 members of the cast or crew were injured. Stagehands attempted to lower the asbestos curtains, but tragically, they stuck halfway down and fanned the flames out into the auditorium. The audience began to scream and panic and a mad rush was started for the Randolph Street exit from the theater. As the crowd reached the doors, they could not open them as they had been designed to swing in rather than outward. The crush of people prevented those in the front from opening the doors. To make matters worse, some of the side doors to the auditorium were reportedly locked. Many of those who died not only burned, but suffocated from the smoke and the crush of bodies as well. Later, as the police removed the charred remains from the theater, they discovered that a number of victims had been trampled in the panic. One dead woman's face even bore the mark of a shoe heel.

When it was all over, 572 people died in the fire and more died later, bringing the eventual death toll up to 602. The passageway behind the theater is still referred to as "Death Alley" today after hundreds of bodies were placed there. For nearly five hours, police officers, firemen and even newspaper reporters, carried out the dead. At least 150 victims were piled along the passageway and anxious relatives sifted through the remains, searching for loved ones. Other bodies were taken to police wagon and ambulances and transported to a temporary morgue at Marshall Field's on State Street. Medical examiners and investigators worked all through the night.

Someone, the public cried, had to answer for the fire and a number of members of the show's cast and crew, along with the theater managers, were arrested. The investigation continued for weeks, but no one was ever charged with a criminal act.

The Iroquois fire is remembered as the most tragic fire in American theater history but regardless, the facade of the Iroquois was used when the Oriental Theater later re-opened at the site, which is now 24 West Randolph Street. The theater is part of the Civic Tower Building and next door to the restored Delaware Building. The theater remained in business for many years, finally becoming home to a wholesale electronics dealer, then closing down in 1981. Amazingly, the theater (which was believed to be lost for good) was restored and opened as the Ford Theater in 1998.

But this has not stopped the tales of the old Iroquois Theater from being told, especially in light of more recent, and more ghostly events. According to author Ursula Bielski, and current accounts, "Death Alley" is not as empty as it appears to be. The narrow passageway, which runs behind the Oriental Theater, is rarely used today, except for the occasional delivery truck or a lone pedestrian who is in a hurry to get somewhere else. It is largely deserted, but why? The stories say that those few who do pass through the alley often find themselves very uncomfortable and unsettled here. They say that faint cries are sometimes heard in the shadows and that some have reported being touched by unseen hands and by eerie cold spots that seem to come from nowhere and vanish just as quickly.

Is the alleyway actually haunted? And do the spirits of those who met their tragic end inside of the burning theater still lingering here? Perhaps, or perhaps the strange sensations experienced here are "ghosts of the past" of another kind... a chilling remembrance of a terrifying event that will never be completely forgotten.

THE EASTLAND DISASTER

One of the most devastating, and haunting, tragedies to strike Chicago would be the capsizing of the "Eastland" steamer on July 24, 1915, between the Clark and LaSalle Street bridges. Although it had only just departed the dock when the tragedy occurred, the steamer was bound for Michigan City, Indiana where a picnic had been planned for the workers of "Western Electric" and their families. There were four vessels chartered to take the estimated 7,000 people on their journey across the lake. One of these vessels was the Eastland, a rusting Lake Michigan steamer owned by the St. Joseph-Chicago Steamship Company. It was supposed to hold a capacity crowd of 2,570 but it is believed that at least 3,200 were on board. Besides being overcrowded, the vessel had a reputation for being notoriously unstable.

The Eastland was moored on the south side of the river and after the passengers were loaded on board, the dock lines were loosed and the ship prepared to depart. What followed was a nightmare....

The overflow crowd, dressed in their best summer attire, even on this drizzly morning, jammed onto the decks, waving handkerchiefs and calling out to those still on shore. The ship eased away from the dock and immediately began to list to the post. As more passengers pushed toward that side of the deck, the boat tilted dangerously. What the passengers were unaware of was that the crew of the steamer had emptied the ballast compartments (designed to provide "stability" for the craft) so that more passengers could be loaded aboard. This would be the undoing of the Eastland, as moments later, the ship simply toppled over!

The passengers above deck were thrown into the water and the river became a moving sea of bodies. Crews on the other boats threw life preservers into the river, while onlookers began throwing lines, boxes and anything else that would float to the floundering passengers. To make matters more difficult, the river was now surging, thanks to the wake caused by the overturned ship. Many of the luckless passengers were pulled beneath the water by the current, or swamped by the crashing waves.

Worst of all was the fate of those passengers who had remained inside of the ship when it had departed. These unlucky victims were first thrown to one side of the ship as it turned over and then they were covered with water as the river rushed inside. A few of them managed to escape to the upturned end of the ship, but most didn't, becoming trapped in a tangled heap at the lowest point of the Eastland.

Firefighters and rescue workers arrived within minutes and began cutting holes in the wood above the water line and in the steel hull below it. In the first fateful minutes, a number of passengers managed to escape, but soon, it was simply too late. The rescue workers had to resign themselves to fishing corpses out of the water, which they wrapped in sheets and transferred to the "Roosevelt", another vessel that had been rented for the excursion. The big downtown stores sent wagons and trucks to ferry the injured and dead to nearby hospitals and makeshift morgues. Large grappling hooks were also used to pull bodies from the water.

By late that afternoon, nearly 200 bodies had been taken to the 2nd Regiment Armory on West Washington Blvd. Others were taken to the Chicago Historical Society Building, which was also used as a temporary morgue.

According to newspaper accounts, a police diver who had been hauling bodies up from the bottom of the river since mid-morning suddenly broke down and became crazed. He had to be subdued by several of his friends and fellow officers. City workers began dragging the river far south of where the ship had capsized, using large nets to stop the bodies from washing out into the lake. By the time that it was all over, 835 of the ship's passengers perished, including 22 entire families.

The mystery of the Eastland was never solved. There was never a clear cause that could be reached that accounted for the capsizing of the vessel. Several hundred lawsuits were eventually filed but almost all of them were thrown out by the Circuit Court of Appeals, who held the owners of the steamship blameless in the disaster. The Eastland was later sold at public auction in December 1915. The title was later transferred to the government and it was pressed into duty as the gunboat USS "Wilmette". In 1946, it was sold for scrap metal. But the story of the Eastland does not end there.

The Chicago Historical Society later moved from their original building and re-located to a new site near Lincoln Park. In recent years, the building has been taken over by the Excalibur, a nightclub that offers several floors of drinking and dancing. It is said that in the quite hours, when no customers are present, the ghosts of the past make themselves known in the place. These spirits, thought to be the ghosts of those who died on the Eastland, make frequent appearances. Their apparitions are occasionally seen and they make themselves known in other ways as well. Voices, cries and whispers are often reported and things sometimes move about and disappear under their own power. The dark corners of the club can sometimes be strange and unnerving places to be in.

Also in recent years, the armory building, where the majority of the dead were taken during the disaster, has been incorporated into Harpo Studios, the production company owned by Oprah Winfrey. As one of Chicago's greatest success stories, Oprah came to Chicago in 1984 to host the WLS-TV talk show "AM Chicago". Within a few years, she had recreated the program and it was re-named the "Oprah Winfrey Show". She has since gone on to become the host of the most popular talk show in television history, a film star, producer and well-known personality.

But all of the success and attention that the show has brought to the former armory building has done nothing to put to rest the spirits of the Eastland. Many who work here claim that the ghosts of the perished passengers are still restless in the new studios. According to Dale Kaczmarek's book, "Windy City Ghosts", many employees have had strange encounters that cannot be explained, including the sighting of an apparition that has been dubbed the "Gray Lady". In addition, staff members hear whispering voices, the laughter of children, sobbing sounds, old-time music, the clinking of phantom glasses and marching of invisible footsteps. The footsteps (which sound as though they belong to a large group) are frequently heard on the lobby staircase and nearby doors often slam shut without assistance. A large number of the staff members believe this to be a very haunted place!

The site of the disaster is not without its chilling stories either. Today, the site is marked by a historical plaque, commemorating the memories of those whose lives were lost. Some say it is marked by other things as well, namely cries of terror from the victims of the tragedy. For many years, passersby on the Clark Street Bridge claimed to hear cries and moans coming from the river, along with the bloodcurdling sound of terrified screams. Perhaps the horror of the event impressed itself on this place, where it continues to replay itself over and over again. The Eastland disaster continues to be remembered, in more ways than one!

BACHELOR'S GROVE CEMETERY
The Most Haunted Place in Chicagoland

Located near the southwest suburb of Midlothian is the Rubio Woods Forest Preserve, an island of trees and shadows nestled in the urban sprawl of the Chicago area. The rambling refuge creates an illusion that it is secluded from the crowded city that threatens its borders, and perhaps it is. On the edge of the forest is a small graveyard that many believe may be the most haunted place in the region. The name of this cemetery is Bachelor's Grove and this ramshackle burial ground may be infested with more ghosts than most can imagine. Over the years, the place has been cursed with more than one hundred documented reports of paranormal phenomena, from actual apparitions to glowing balls of light.

There have been no new burials here for many years and as a place of rest for the departed, it is largely forgotten. But if you should ask any ghost hunter just where to go to find a haunting, Bachelor's Grove is usually the first place in Chicago to be mentioned!

The history of Bachelor's Grove has been somewhat shadowy over the years but most historians agree that it was started in the early part of the 1800's. The name of the cemetery came from a settlement that was started in the late 1820's that consisted of mostly German immigrants and settlers from the East Coast. One family who moved into the area was named "Batchelder" and their name was given to the timberland where they settled. It's likely the settlement and (later) the cemetery took its name from this family in the form of "Batchelor".

Other accounts state that the cemetery's name comes from the fact that the settlement was called "Bachelor" because of a number of single men who came to live there. This part of the lore dates back to 1833 or 1834 when a man named Stephen H. Rexford settled in the region with some other single men and began calling the place "Bachelor's Grove". Some historians dispute this, stating that the name of "Batchelor's Grove" was already in use at that time.

Regardless, the small settlement continued for some years as Bachelor's Grove, until 1850, when it was changed to "Bremen" by postmaster Samuel Everden in recognition of the new township name where the post office was located. In 1855, it was changed again to "Bachelder's Grove" by postmaster Robert Patrick but the post office closed down just three years later. Officially, the settlement ceased to exist and was swallowed by the forest around it.

The cemetery itself has a much stranger history. The land for the burial ground was first set aside in 1844 by Samuel Everden and was named "Everden" in his honor. The first burial took place in that year and as time passed, the eighty-two lots slowly began to fill. Burials continued here on a regular basis until around 1965, when things began to drop off. It should be noted that the last actual internment here was in 1989 when the ashes of a local resident were buried on the grounds. However, up until that point, the cemetery had been largely abandoned.

The last independent caretaker of the cemetery was a man named Clarence Fulton, whose family were early settlers in the township. According to Fulton, Bachelor's Grove was like a park for many years and people often came here to fish and swim in the adjacent pond. Families often visited on weekends to care for the graves of the deceased and to picnic under the trees. Things have certainly changed since then!

Problems began in and around the cemetery in the early 1960's, at the same time that the Midlothian Turnpike was closed to vehicle traffic in front of the cemetery. Even before that, the cemetery had become a popular "lover's lane" and when the road closed, it became even more isolated. Soon it began to show signs of vandalism and decay and a short time later, became considered haunted.

Although the amount of paranormal activity that actually occurs in the cemetery has been argued by some, few can deny that strange things do happen here. When the various types of phenomenon really began is unclear but it has been happening for more than three decades now. Was the burial ground already haunted? Or did the haunting actually begin with the destructive decades of the 1960's and 1970's?

The vandals first discovered Bachelor's Grove in the 1960's and probably because of its secluded location, they began to wreak havoc on the place. Gravestones were knocked over and destroyed, sprayed with paint, broken apart and even stolen. Police reports later stated that markers from Bachelor's Grove turned up in homes, yards and even as far away as Evergreen Cemetery! Worst of all, in 1964, 1975 and 1978, graves were opened and caskets removed. Bones were sometimes found to be strewn about the cemetery. Desecrated graves are still frequently found in the cemetery.

Was the haunting first caused by these disturbances? Most believe so, but others cite another source for the activity. Near the small pond that borders the cemetery, forest rangers and cemetery visitors have repeatedly found the remains of chickens and other small animals that have been sliced and mutilated in a ritualistic fashion. Officers that have patrolled the woods at night have reported seeing evidence of black magic and occult rituals in and around the graveyard. In some cases, inscriptions and elaborate writings have been carved in and painted on trees and grave markers and on the cemetery grounds themselves. This has led many to believe that the cemetery has been used for occult activities.

If you combine this sorted activity with the vandalism that has nearly destroyed the place, you have a situation that is ripe for supernatural occurrences. Could this be what has caused the blight on Bachelor's Grove? Even the early superstitions of the tombstone give credence to the idea that man has always felt that desecration of graves causes cemeteries to become haunted. Grave markers began as heavy stones that were placed on top of the graves of the deceased in the belief that the weight of it would keep the dead person, or their angry spirit, beneath the ground. Those who devised this system believed that if the stone was moved, the dead would be free to walk the earth.

There is no question that vandals have not been kind to Bachelor's Grove, but then neither has time. The Midlothian Turnpike bypassed the cemetery and even the road leading back to the graveyard was eventually closed. People forgot about the place and allowed it to fade into memory, just like the poor souls buried here.

Today, the cemetery is overgrown with weeds and is surrounded by a high, chain-link fence, although access is easily gained through the holes that trespassers have cut into it. The cemetery sign is long since gone. It once hung above the main gates, which are now broken open and lean dangerously into the confines of Bachelor's Grove.

The first thing noticed by those who visit here is the destruction. Tombstones seem to be randomly scattered about, no longer marking the resting places of those whose names are inscribed upon them. Many of the stones are missing, lost forever and perhaps carried away by thieves. These macabre crimes gave birth to legends about how the stones of the cemetery move about under their own power. The most disturbing things to visitors though are the trenches and pits that have been dug above some of the graves, as vandals have attempted to make off with souvenirs from those whose rest they disturb.

Near the front gate is a broken monument to a woman whose name was heard being called repeatedly on an audio tape. Some amateur ghost hunters left a recording device running while on an excursion to Bachelor's Grove and later, upon playback of the tape, they discovered that the recorder had been left on the ruined tombstone of a woman that had the same name as that being called to on the tape. Coincidence? Perhaps, but it hardly seems likely.

Just beyond the rear barrier of the cemetery is a small, stagnant pond that can be seen by motorists who pass on 143rd Street. This pond, while outside of the graveyard, is still not untouched by the horror connected to the place. One night in the late 1970's, two Cook County forest rangers were on night patrol near here and claimed to see the apparition of a horse emerge from the waters of the pond. The animal appeared to be pulling a plow behind it that was steered by the ghost of an old man. The vision crossed the road in front of the ranger's vehicle, was framed for a moment in the glare of their headlights, and then vanished into the forest. The men simply stared in shock for a moment and then looked at one another to be sure that had both seen the same thing. They later reported the incident and since that time, have not been the last to see the old man and the horse.

Little did the rangers know, but this apparition was actually a part of an old legend connected to the pond. It seems that in the 1870's, a farmer was plowing a nearby field when something startled his horse. The farmer was caught by surprise and became tangled in the reins. He was dragged behind the horse and it plunged into the small pond. Unable to free himself, he was pulled down into the murky water by the weight of the horse and the plow and he drowned. Since that time, the vivid recording of this terrible incident has been supernaturally revisiting the surrounding area.

In addition to this unfortunate phantom, the pond was also rumored to be a dumping spot for murder victims during the Prohibition era in Chicago. Those who went on a "one-way ride" were alleged to have ended the trip at the pond near Bachelor's Grove. Thanks to this, their spirits are also said to haunt the dark waters.

Strangely though, it's not the restless spirits of gangland execution victims that have created the most bizarre tales of the pond. One night, an elderly couple was driving past the cemetery and claimed to see something by the bridge at the edge of the pond. They stopped to get a closer look and were understandably terrified to see a huge, two-headed man come out from under the bridge and cross the road in the light from their headlights! Whatever this creature may have been, it quickly vanished into the woods.

Incredibly, even the road near Bachelor's Grove is reputed to be haunted. Could there be such a taint to this place that even the surrounding area is affected? The Midlothian Turnpike is said to be the scene of vanishing "ghost cars" and phantom automobile accidents. No historical events can provide a clue as to why this might be, but the unexplained vehicles have been reported numerous times in recent years. The stories are all remarkably the same too. People who are traveling west on the turnpike see the tail lights of a car in front of them. The brake lights go on, as if the car is planning to stop or turn. The car then turns off the road. However, once the following auto gets to the point in the road where the first vehicle turned, they find no car there at all! Other drivers have reported passing these phantoms autos, only to see the car vanish in their rearview mirrors.

One young couple even claimed to have a collision with one of these phantom cars in 1978. They had just stopped at the intersection of Central Avenue and the Midlothian Turnpike. The driver looked both ways, saw that the road was clear in both directions, then pulled out. Suddenly, a brown sedan appeared from nowhere, racing in the direction of the cemetery. The driver of the couple's car hit the brakes and tried to stop, but it was too late to avoid the crash. The two vehicles collided with not only a shuddering impact, but with the sound of screeching metal and broken glass as well. To make the event even more traumatic, the couple was then shocked to see the brown sedan literally fade away! They climbed out of their car, which had been spun completely around by the impact, but realized that it had not been damaged at all. They had distinctly heard the sound of the torn metal and broken glass and had felt the crush of the two cars coming together, but somehow it had never physically happened!

It remains a mystery as to where these phantom cars come from, and where they vanish to. Why do they haunt this stretch of roadway? No one knows...

For those searching for Bachelor's Grove, it can be found by leaving the roadway and walking up an overgrown gravel track that is surrounded on both sides by the forest. The old road is blocked with chains and concrete dividers and a dented "No Trespassing" sign that hangs ominously near the mouth to the trail. The burial ground lies about a half-mile or so beyond it in the woods.

It is along this deserted road where other strange tales of the cemetery take place. One of these odd occurrences is the sighting of the "phantom farm house". It has been seen appearing and disappearing along the trail for several decades now. The reports date back as far as the early 1960's and continue today. The most credible thing about many of the accounts is that they come from people who originally had no idea that the house shouldn't be there at all.

The house has been reported in all weather conditions and in the daylight hours, as well as at night. There is no historical record of a house existing here but the descriptions of it rarely vary. Each person claims it to be an old frame farm house with two-stories, white, wooden posts, a porch swing and a welcoming light that burns softly in the window. Popular legend states that should you enter this house though, you would never come back out again. As witnesses approach the building, it is reported to get smaller and smaller until it finally just fades away, like someone switching off an old television set. No one has ever claimed to set foot on the front porch of the house.

But the story gets stranger yet! In addition to the house appearing and disappearing, it also shows up at a wide variety of locations along the trail. On one occasion it may be sighted in one area and then at an entirely different spot the next time. Author Dale Kaczmarek, who also heads the Ghost Research Society paranormal investigation group, has interviewed dozens of witnesses about the paranormal events at Bachelor's Grove. He has talked to many who say they have experienced the vanishing farm house. He has found that while all of their descriptions of the house are identical, the locations of the sightings are not. In fact, he asked the witnesses to place an "X" on the map of the area where they saw the house. Kaczmarek now has a map of the Bachelor's Grove area with "X's" all over it!

Also from this stretch of trail come reports of "ghost lights". One such light that has been reported many times is a red, beacon-like orb that has been seen flying rapidly up and down the trail to the cemetery. The light is so bright, and moves so fast, that it is impossible to tell what it really looks like. Most witnesses state that they have seen a "red streak" that is left in its wake.

Others, like Jack Hermanski from Joliet, have reported seeing balls of blue light in the woods and in the cemetery itself. These weird lights have sometimes been reported moving in and around the tombstones in the graveyard. Hermanski encountered the lights in the early 1970's and chased a number of them. All of the lights managed to stay just out of his reach. However, a woman named Denise Travers did manage to catch up with one of the blue lights in December 1971. She claimed to pass her hand completely through one of them but felt no heat or sensation.

Besides the aforementioned phenomena, there have been many sightings of ghosts and apparitions within Bachelor's Grove Cemetery itself. The two most frequently reported figures have been the "phantom monks" and the so-called "Madonna of Bachelor's Grove".

The claims of the monk-like ghosts are strange in themselves. These spirits are said to be clothed in the flowing robes and cowls of a monastic order and they have been reported in Bachelor's Grove and in other places in the Chicago area too. There are no records to indicate that a monastery ever existed near any of the locations where the "monks" have been sighted though, making them one of the greatest of the area's enigmas.

The most frequently reported spirit though is known by a variety of names from the "Madonna of Bachelor's Grove" to the "White Lady" to the affectionate name of "Mrs. Rogers". Legend has it that she is the ghost of a woman who was buried in the cemetery next to the grave of her young child. She is reported to wander the cemetery on nights of the full moon with an infant wrapped in her arms. She appears to walk aimlessly, with no apparent direction and completely unaware of the people who claim to encounter her. There is no real evidence to say who this woman might be but, over the years, she has taken her place as one of the many spirits of this haunted burial ground.

And there are other ghosts as well. Legends tell more apocryphal tales of a ghostly child who has been seen running across the bridge from one side of the pond to the other, a glowing yellow man and even a black carriage that travels along the old road through the woods.

Many of these tales come from a combination of stories, both new and old, but the majority of first-hand reports and encounters are the result of literally hundreds of paranormal investigations that have been conducted here over the last forty years. Many of the ghost hunters who come to this place are amateur investigators, looking for thrills as much as they are looking for evidence of the supernatural, while others, like Dale Kaczmarek and the Ghost Research Society, are much more on the serious side.

Kaczmarek and his investigators have turned up many clues and pieces of evidence that seem to fit randomly into the mystery of Bachelor's Grove. These mysterious bits of evidence, while showing that strange things do happen here, never really seem to provide the hard evidence that these researchers look for. Even the photographs collected during their outings tantalize the investigators. For example, a series of photos taken by the group in 1979 show a monk-like figure standing near the cemetery fence. The figure appeared to be wearing a hooded robe and holding a baby in its arms. Oddly, this was three years before the Ghost Research Society collected any accounts of the "White Lady"!

Perhaps the most stunning photograph from Bachelor's Grove was taken in August 1991, during a full-fledged investigation of the cemetery. Ghost Research Society members came to the burial ground in the daytime and covered the area with the latest in scientific equipment, cameras, tape recorders and video cameras. All of the members were given maps of the cemetery and instructed to walk through and note any changes in electro-magnetic readings or atmosphere fluctuations. After the maps were compared, it was obvious that several investigators found odd changes in a number of distinct areas. A number of photos were taken in those areas, using both standard and infrared film. Nothing was seen at the time the photographs were taken, but once they were developed, the investigators learned that something had apparently been there!

In a photo, taken by Mari Huff, there appeared the semi-transparent form of a woman, who was seated on the remains of a tombstone. Was this one of the ghosts of Bachelor's Grove? Skeptics immediately said "no", claiming that it was nothing more than a double exposure or an outright hoax.

Curious, I asked for and received a copy of the photograph and had it examined by several independent photographers. Most of them would have liked to come up with a reason why the photograph could not be real, but unfortunately they couldn't. They ruled out the idea of a double exposure and also the theory that the person in the photo was a live woman who was placed in the photo and made to appear like she was a ghost. One skeptic also claimed that the woman in the photo was casting a shadow, but according to the photographers who analyzed the image, the "shadow" is actually nothing more than the natural shading of the landscape. Besides that, one of them asked, if she is casting a shadow in that direction, then why isn't anything else in the frame?

Genuine or not (and I think it is), this photograph is just one of the hundreds of photos taken here that allegedly show supernatural activity. While many of them can be ruled out as nothing more than atmospheric conditions, reflections and poor photography, there are others that cannot.

In the end, we have to ask, what is it about Bachelor's Grove Cemetery? Is it as haunted as we have been led to believe? I have to leave that up to the reader to decide, but strange things happen here and there is little reason to doubt that this one of the most haunted places in the Midwest.

But haunted or not, Bachelor's Grove is still a burial ground and a place that should be treated with respect as the final resting place of those interred here. It should also be remembered that the cemetery is not a private playground for those who are intrigued by ghosts and hauntings. It is first and foremost a repository for the dead and should be protected as such by those who hope to enjoy it, and possibly learn from it, in the years to come.

Thanks to the efforts of local preservation groups, it appears that Bachelor's Grove is not beyond restoration, but it should still be protected against the abuses that it has suffered in the past. It is a piece of our haunted history that we cannot afford to lose.

GHOSTLY GREETING FROM THE GRAVEYARD

Hauntings from other Chicago Cemeteries

While Bachelor's Grove Cemetery certainly captures much of the attention paid to ghosts and hauntings in Chicago graveyards, it is certainly not alone when it comes to the area's ghostly burial grounds.

GHOSTS OF GRACELAND

In Chicago, Illinois, one burial ground that was closed down actually created several different Cemeteries, although the most spectacular of them is undoubtedly Graceland Cemetery. Graceland and several others came about thanks to the closure of the old Chicago City Cemetery around 1870. The City Cemetery was located exactly where Chicago's Lincoln Park is located today. Before its establishment, most of the early pioneers simply buried their dead out in the back yard, leading to many gruesome discoveries as the downtown was developed years later. Two cemeteries were later set aside for both Protestants and Catholics, but both of them were located along the lake shore, leading to the frequent unearthing of caskets whenever the water was high. Finally, the city set aside land at Clark Street and North Avenue for the Chicago City Cemetery. Soon, many of the bodies were moved from the other sites.

Within ten years of the opening of the cemetery, it became the subject of much criticism. Not only was it severely overcrowded from both population growth and cholera epidemics, but many also felt that poorly carried out burials here were creating health problems and contaminating the water supply. To make matters worse, both the city morgue and the local Pest House, a quarantine building for epidemic victims, were located on the cemetery grounds. Soon, local families and churches were moving their loved ones to burial grounds considered to be safer and the City Cemetery was closed down.

One cemetery that benefited from the closure of the graveyard was Graceland Cemetery, located on North Clark Street. When it was started in 1860 by real estate developer Thomas B. Bryan, it was located far away from the city and over the years, a number of different architects have worked to preserve the natural setting of its 120 acres. Two of the men largely responsible for the beauty of the place were architects William Le Baron Jenney and Ossian Cole Simonds, who became so fascinated with the site that he ended up turning his entire business to landscape design. In addition to the natural landscape, the cemetery boasts a number of wonderful monuments and buildings, including the cemetery chapel, which holds city's oldest crematorium, built in 1893.

There are a number of Chicago notables buried in Graceland, including John Kinzie, Marshall Field, Phillip Armour, George Pullman, Potter Palmer, Allan Pinkerton, Vincent Starrett, writer and creator of the "Baker Street Irregulars", architect Louis Sullivan and many others.

Graceland is also home to several ghost / supernatural stories. One of these legends however, remains puzzling to both cemetery buffs and ghost hunters alike. It involves the strange story of the ghost who has been seen in the vicinity of the underground vault belonging to a man named Ludwig Wolff. The tomb has been excavated from the side of a mildly sloping hill at the south end of the cemetery and according to local legend, it is supposedly guarded by the apparition of a green-eyed dog that howls at the moon. There are those who believe this creature is some form of supernatural entity, while others dismiss it as nothing more than a story created from the name of the man buried in the crypt. Who can say for sure?

There are two very different stories connected to "haunted" grave monuments in Graceland. While one of them has widely become accepted as a folk legend, the other one finds a surprisingly receptive, and believing, audience.

The first tale concerns the statue that was placed over the resting place of a man named Dexter Graves. He was a hotel owner and businessman who brought an early group of settlers to the Chicago area in 1831. He passed away and was buried but his body was moved to Graceland in 1909. At that time, a statue that was created by the famed sculptor Lorado Taft was placed on his grave. Taft christened the statue "Eternal Silence" but the brooding and menacing figure has become more commonly known as the "Statue of Death".

The figure was once black in color but over the years, the black has mostly worn away, exposing the green, weathered metal beneath. Only one portion of it remains darkened and that is the face, which is hidden in the deepest folds of the figure's robe. It gives the impression that the ominous face is hidden in shadow and the look of the image has given birth to several legends. It is said that anyone who looks into the face of the statue will get a glimpse of his or her own death to come. In addition, it is said that the statue is impossible to photograph and that no camera will function in its presence. Needless to say though, scores of photos exist of the figure so most people scoff at the threats of doom and death that have long been associated with "Eternal Silence".

Without a doubt, the most famous sculpture (and most enduring ghost) of Graceland is that of Inez Clarke. In 1880, this little girl died at the tender age of only six. Tradition has it that she was killed during a lightning storm while on a family picnic. Her parents, stunned by the tragic loss, commissioned a life-size statue of the girl to be placed on her grave. It was completed a year later, and like many Chicago area grave sculptures, was placed in a glass box to protect it from the elements. The image remains in nearly perfect condition today. Even in death, Inez still manages to charm cemetery visitors, who discover the little girl perched on a small stool. It is said that the likeness was cast so that Inez was wearing her favorite dress and carrying a tiny parasol. The perfectly formed face was created with just the hint of a smile. It is not uncommon to come to the cemetery and find gifts of flowers and toys at the foot of her grave. The site has become one of the most popular places in the cemetery, for graveyard buffs and curiosity seekers alike.

You see, according to local legend, this site is haunted. Not only are their stories of strange sounds heard nearby, but some claim the statue of Inez actually moves under its own power. The most disconcerting stories may be those of the disembodied weeping that is heard nearby but the most famous are those of the statue itself. It is said that Inez will sometimes vanish from inside of the glass box. This is said to often take place during violent thunderstorms. Many years ago, a night watchman for the Pinkerton agency stated that he was making his rounds one night during a storm and discovered that the box that holds Inez was empty. He left the cemetery that night, never to return. Other guards have also reported it missing, only to find it back in place when they pass by again, or the following morning.

Does the spirit of little Inez still manifest in this part of the cemetery? Recent accounts say that occasional visitors to Graceland will spot a child who sometimes disappears in the vicinity of her monument. Perhaps she is still entertaining herself, just on the other side?

THE ITALIAN BRIDE

In Hillside, Illinois, just outside of Chicago, is Mount Carmel Cemetery. In addition to being the final resting place of Al Capone, Dion O'Banion and other great Chicago mobsters, the cemetery is also the burial place of a woman named Julia Buccola Petta. While her name may not spring to mind as a part of Chicago history, for those intrigued by the supernatural, she is better known as the "Italian Bride".

Julia's grave is marked today by the life-sized statue of the unfortunate woman in her wedding dress, a stone reproduction of the wedding photo that is mounted on the front of her monument. The statue marks the location where Julia's apparition is said to appear. Not surprisingly, the ghost is clad in a glowing, white bridal gown.

Julia died in childbirth in 1921, at only twenty years of age. Shortly after she was buried, her mother, Filomena Buccola, began to experience strange and terrifying dreams every night. In these nightmares, she envisioned Julia telling her that she was still alive and needed her help. For the next six years, the dreams plagued Filomena and she began trying, without success, to have her daughter's grave opened and her body exhumed. She was unable to explain why she needed to do this, she only knew that she should. Finally, through sheer persistence, her request was granted and a sympathetic judge passed down an order for Julia's exhumation.

When the casket was opened, Julia's body was found not to have decayed at all. In fact, it was said that her flesh was still as soft as it had been when she was alive. A photograph was taken at the time of the exhumation and shows Julia's "incorruptible" body in the casket. Her mother, and other admirers, placed the photo on the front of her grave monument, which was constructed after her reburial. The photograph shows a body that appears to be fresh, with no discoloration of the skin, even after six years. The rotted and decayed appearance of the coffin in the photo however, bears witness to the fact that it had been underground for some time. Julia appears to be merely sleeping.

What mysterious secret rests at the grave of Julia Petta? How could her body have stayed in perfect condition after lying in the grave for six years? No one knows, but not surprisingly, reports have circulated for years claiming that a woman in a bridal gown haunts this portion of the cemetery.

Some of the stories come from students at Proviso West High School, which is located just east of the cemetery on Wolf Road. They have reported a girl walking in the cemetery at night and they are not alone. A carload of people traveling down Harrison Street was startled to see a woman passing through the tombstones one night. Thinking that it was simply a Halloween prank, they stopped the car for a closer look. They did not become unnerved until they realized that, even though it was pouring down rain, the girl was perfectly dry. They didn't choose to investigate any closer and immediately drove away!

THE MIRACLE CHILD OF CHICAGO

Another grave, located in the Chicago suburb of Worth and at Holy Sepulchre Cemetery, has much more benevolent properties. In fact, it is said be able to heal the sick and the dying. Many people feel that this is a sacred place and is made so because the grave holds the final remains of a young girl named Mary Alice Quinn.

Over the years, hundreds have claimed to experience miraculous healings here, while others speak of strange occurrences that can only be paranormal in nature. Because of this, Mary's grave and tombstone have been the subject of visits by religious pilgrims and supernatural enthusiasts alike.

Mary was a quiet child who died suddenly in 1935, when she was only 14. She was a devoutly religious girl, devoted to St. Theresa, who claimed to have a mystical experience when she saw a religious image appear on her wall. After that, she became known in her neighborhood for curing the sick. While on her deathbed, Mary told her parents that she wanted to come back and help people after her death. The faithful say that she has done just that. Soon after her death, she was said to have mysteriously appeared to a number of people in the Chicago area. Throughout the 1930's and 1940's, it was not uncommon to hear of new Mary Alice Quinn sightings.

Today, her healing powers are said to have taken on another manifestation and one that surrounds her grave marker. When she passed away, she was secretly buried in a cemetery plot that belonged to the Reilly family. It was thought that this might keep her burial place a secret and prevent the graveyard from being overrun by curiosity seekers intent on finding her resting place. Word soon spread though and a gravestone was eventually cut with her name on it. Since that time, thousands have come to the site, many of them bringing prayer tokens, rosaries, coins and photos to leave as offerings and to ask that Mary intercede for them in prayer. Many claim to have been healed of their afflictions after visiting the grave and others have been healed by extension. They claim to have found relief from one of the many spoonfuls of dirt that has been taken from Mary's grave.

Strangely, the phantom scent of roses has been reported filling the air around the gravestone, even when there are no roses anywhere around. The smell is said to be especially strong in the winter months, when the scent of fresh roses would be impossible to mistake. Many visitors have alleged this smell over the years and some of them even say that it is overwhelming. The faithful claim that this unexplainable odor is proof that Mary's spirit is still nearby and interceding on their behalf. Her love and charity continues, even decades after her death.

PHANTOMS OF ROSEHILL

Rosehill Cemetery began in 1859, taking its name from a nearby tavern keeper named Roe. The area around his saloon was known for some years as "Roes Hill". In time, the name was slightly altered and became "Rosehill". After the closure of the "dreary" Chicago City Cemetery, where Lincoln Park is now located, Rosehill became the oldest and the largest graveyard in Chicago and serves as the final resting place of more than 1500 notable Chicagoans, including a number of Civil War generals, mayors, former millionaires, local celebrities and early founders of the city. There are also a number of deceased Chicagoans who are not peacefully at rest here and they serve to provide the cemetery with its legends of ghosts and strange happenings.

Perhaps the most famous ghostly site on the grounds is the tomb belonging to Charles Hopkinson, a real estate tycoon from the middle 1800's. In his will, he left plans for his mausoleum to serve as a shrine to the memory of he and his family. When he died in 1885, a miniature cathedral was designed to serve as the tomb. Construction was started and then halted when the property owners behind the Hopkinson site took the family to court. They claimed that the cathedral tomb would block the view of their own burial sites. The case proceeded all of the way to the Illinois Supreme Court, which ruled that the other family had no say over what sort of monument the Hopkinson family built and that they should have expected that something could eventually block the view of their site. Shortly after, construction on the tomb continued and was completed. Despite the fact that the courts ruled in the favor of Hopkinson, it is said that on the anniversary of the real estate investor's death, a horrible moaning sound can be heard coming from the tomb, followed by what appears to be sound of rattling chains.

Ghost lore is filled with stories of the dead returning from the grave to protest wrongs that were done to them in their lifetime, or to continue business and rivalries started while they were among the living. Such events have long been a part of the lore of Rosehill's community mausoleum.

The Rosehill Cemetery Mausoleum was proposed in 1912 and the cemetery appealed to the elite businessmen of the city for the funds to begin construction. These men were impressed with the idea and enjoyed the thought of entire family rooms in the mausoleum that could be dedicated to their families alone and could be decorated to their style and taste. The building was designed Sidney Lovell and is a massive, multi-level structure with marble passageways and row after row of the dead. It is filled with a number of Chicago notables from the world of business and even architect Sidney Lovell himself.

One of the funding subscribers for the mausoleum was John G. Shedd, the president of Marshall Field from 1909 to 1926 and the man who donated the wonderful Shedd Aquarium to Chicago. He guaranteed himself immortality with the development of what he dreamed would be the world's largest aquarium. Even though Shedd died in 1926, four years before the aquarium would open, his directors remained loyal to his plans and created an aquatic showplace. A little of that extravagance can be found in the Rosehill mausoleum, as Shedd's family room is one of the most beautiful portions of the building. The chapel outside the room features chairs that are carved in images depicting shells and sea horses and the window inside bathes the room with a blue haze that makes the place appear to be under water. For this window, Shedd commissioned the artisan Louis Comfort Tiffany and made him sign a contract that said he would never create another window like it.

There have been no ghost stories associated with John Shedd, but there are others entombed in the structure who may not have found the peace that Shedd found. Two of them men also laid to rest in the building are Aaron Montgomery Ward and his bitter business rival, Richard Warren Sears. One has to wonder if either of these men could rest in peace with the other man in the same structure, but it is the ghost of Sears who has been seen walking through the mausoleum at night. The business pioneer has been spotted, wearing a top hat and tails, leaving the Sears family room and walking the hallways from his tomb to that of Ward's. Perhaps the rivalry that plagued his life continues on after death.....

Another otherworldly manifestation comes to us as a protest over an unmarked grave. Ghostly lore is filled with such tales and Rosehill boasts at least one legend of this type. In October 1995, a groundskeeper at the cemetery reported that he had seen a woman wandering about in the graveyard at night. She had been standing next to a tree, not far from the wall that separates the cemetery from Peterson Avenue. The staff member stopped his truck and got out. The cemetery was closed for the night and he was going to tell the woman that she had to leave and offer to escort her to the gate. When he approached her, he realized that the woman, who was dressing in some sort of flowing white garment, was actually floating above the ground! Before his eyes, she turned into a mist and slowly vanished. Not surprisingly, the groundskeeper wasted no time in rushing to the cemetery office to report the weird incident.

Strangely, a woman from Des Plaines, Illinois called the cemetery office the following day and requested that a marker be placed on the grave of her aunt, Carrie Kalbas, who had died in 1933. The grave site had previously been unmarked but the night before, the woman claimed that her aunt had appeared to her in a dream. She asked her niece to be sure that her burial place was marked because she wanted to be remembered. The aunt's grave was located in an old family plot and staff members went out to the site to verify the location and to see what type of monument was needed. They were amazed to find that the grave was located in the exact spot where the apparition had been reported the night before! The grave stone was ordered and the ghost was never seen again.

A "statuary spirit" also comes from Rosehill Cemetery and while this burial ground boasts a number of ghosts, perhaps the most romantic and tragic tale involves the grave of Frances Pearce. This striking monument was moved from the old Chicago City Cemetery to Rosehill many years ago and depicts the life-sized images of Frances and her infant daughter. Both of them are reclining, with the little girl in the arms of her mother, atop the stone. The figures are encased inside of one of the already described glass boxes.

Frances was married to a man named Horatio Stone around 1852. The two of them were said to be very much in love and lived a happy life together. Then, in 1854, Frances tragically died at the age of twenty. To make matters worse, her infant daughter followed her to the grave four months later. Horatio was nearly destroyed by these terrible events and he commissioned sculptor Chauncey Ives to create a memorial sculpture to be placed on their graves in the City Cemetery. Later, both the remains and the memorial were moved to Rosehill.

According to local legend, on the anniversary of their deaths, a glowing, white haze fills the interior of the glass box. The stories go on to say that the mother and daughter are still reaching out from beyond the grave for the husband and father they left behind.

CHICAGO'S PHANTOM HITCHERS

Without a doubt, the most famous ghostly hitchhiker in the Chicago area is the young girl who has been connected to Resurrection Cemetery for a number of decades. Her story will appear later in the chapter, but there are other restless and roaming ghosts of Chicago cemeteries as well.

One such spirit, a sort of "sister ghost" to Resurrection Mary, haunts the vicinity of Jewish Waldheim Cemetery, located at 1800 South Harlem Avenue in Chicago. This is perhaps one of the more peaceful and attractive of the city's downtown graveyards and is easily recognizable from the columns that are mounted at the front gates. They were once part of the old Cook County Building, which was demolished in 1908. This cemetery would most likely go quietly on through its existence if not for the tales of the "Flapper Ghost". While little background can be discovered about this spirit, it remains a fascinating story.

The story of the ghost states that she was a young Jewish girl who attended dances at the Melody Mill Ballroom, formerly on Des Plaines Avenue. She was said to be a very attractive brunette with bobbed hair and a dress right out of the Roaring 20's, hence the spirit's nickname of the "Flapper Ghost". This fetching phantom has been known to hitch rides on Des Plaines Avenue and most often has been seen near the cemetery gates. Some travelers passing the cemetery even claimed to see her entering a mausoleum that is located off Harlem Avenue.

Although recent sightings have been few, the ghost was most active in 1933, during the Century of Progress Exhibition, and again in 1973. In the years before World War II, she was often reported at the Melody Mill Ballroom, where she would dance with young men and often ask for a ride home. After they drove her to the cemetery, the girl would explain that she lived in the caretaker's house (since demolished) and then get out of the car. Often with her admirers in pursuit, she would then run out into the cemetery and vanish among the tombstones.

More sightings took place in 1973 and one report even occurred during the daylight hours. A family was visiting the cemetery one day and was startled to see a young woman dressed like a "flapper" walking toward a crypt, where she suddenly disappeared. The family hurried over to the spot, only to find no girl and nowhere to which she could have vanished so quickly.

According to author Dale Kaczmarek, another strange sighting took place in 1979 when a police officer saw a beautiful girl walking near the ballroom on a rainy night. He asked her where she was going and she replied "home". He offered her a ride and she directed him to an apartment building near the cemetery entrance. After the girl got out of the car, she vanished near a covered doorway and the policeman, shocked, got out and went after her. He was sure that she could not have gotten into the building so quickly and was even more surprised to see no wet footprints on the dry sidewalk below the building's awning.

Since that time, sightings of the "Flapper" have been few, but we should take into account that she appeared often back in the 1930's and then didn't show up again with any frequency until the 1970's. Perhaps she is just waiting round and will soon come back for a return engagement!

Another phantom hitcher haunts the roadways near the Evergreen Cemetery in Evergreen Park, a Chicagoland community. For more than two decades, an attractive teenager has been roaming out beyond the confines of the cemetery in search of a ride. A number of drivers claim to have spotted her and in the 1980's a flurry of encounters occurred when motorists in the south and western suburbs reported picking up this young girl. She always asked them for a ride to a location in Evergreen Park and then mysteriously vanished from the vehicle at the cemetery.

According to the legends, she is the spirit of a child buried within the cemetery, but there is no real folklore to explain why she leaves her grave in search of travelers, nor what brings her to the suburbs and so far from home. She is what some would call the typical "vanishing hitchhiker" but there is one aspect to this ghost that sets her apart from the others. In addition to seeking rides in cars, she is resourceful enough to find other transportation when it suits her.

In recent years, encounters with this phantom have also taken place at a bus stop that is located directly across the street from the cemetery. Many have claimed to see a dark-haired young girl here who mysteriously vanishes. On occasion, she has also climbed aboard a few Chicago Transit Authority buses as well.

One evening, a young girl climbed aboard a bus and breezed right past the driver without paying the fare. She walked to the back portion of the vehicle and sat down, seemingly without a care in the world. Irritated the driver called out to her, but she didn't answer. Finally, he stood up and walked back toward where she was seating. She would either pay, he thought, or have to get off the bus! Not surprisingly though, before he could reach her, she vanished before his eyes!

According to reports, other shaken drivers have had the same eerie experience at this bus stop. He has spoken with others who have also seen this young girl and every single one of them have seen her disappear as if she had never been there in the first place!

A "woman in white" haunts one of the area's most foreboding graveyards, a place called Archer Woods Cemetery. For years, the female phantom has been reported at this wooded burial ground, especially back in the days when it was a desolate spot along Kean Road. She does not wander the roadway flagging down passing motorists however, although she is usually spotted by those who drive by the cemetery at night.

Those unwitting travelers, passing along Kean Road, are often greeted by the sound of a woman loudly sobbing in despair. When they stop their vehicles for a closer look, they see a woman in a white gown wandering near the edge of the graveyard. She is always said to be weeping and crying and covering her face with her hands. She is normally only seen for a matter of seconds before she disappears.

In addition to the "Weeping Woman", Archer Woods is also said to be home to the another, more terrifying, specter, an old-fashioned hearse. This black coach is said to be driverless but pulled by a team of mad horses. The hearse itself is made from black oak and glass and carries the glowing coffin of a small child as cargo. Residents of the area have been reporting this bizarre "ghost hearse" for years and it is often seen along nearby Archer Avenue. The origins of the hearse vary, but one thing is sure... no one wants to encounter it while traveling through the shadows along Kean Road after dark!

THE HAUNTING OF HULL HOUSE

Hull House was constructed by Charles J. Hull at Halsted and Polk Streets in 1856 at a time when this was one of the most fashionable sections of the city. After the Chicago Fire of 1871, the "better classes" moved to other parts of the city and the Near West Side began to attract a large immigrant population of Italian, Greek and Jewish settlers. By the 1880's, Hull House was surrounded by factories and tenement houses and soon after, became one of the most famous places in Chicago. Although it was never intended to be known as a "haunted house", it would not emerge from its heyday unscathed by stories of ghosts and the supernatural.

Hull House has long been known as a pioneering effort in social equality. Jane Addams and Ellen Starr Gates opened the house in 1889 to educate and improve the lot of the newly arrived European immigrants.

At that time, the overcrowded tenement neighborhoods west of Halsted Street were a jungle of crime, vice, prostitution and drug addiction. Jane Addams became the "voice of humanity" on the West Side, enriching the lives of many unfortunate people at the house.

Jane Addams was born and raised in the village of Cedarville, the privileged daughter of a wealthy merchant. Jane was raised under pleasant surroundings and tragedy first came into her life with the death of her father, which occurred the same year that she graduated from the Rockford Female Seminary. She went into a deep depression and unsure what to do with her life, she spent a portion of her inheritance traveling in Europe. It would be in London, in the terrible slums of Whitechapel, that she would find her calling.

In the company of her college friend and traveling companion, Elle Starr Gates, Jane would spend time at Toynbee Hall, a settlement house for the poor. Here, young and affluent students lived and worked beside the poorest dregs of London, pushing for social reform and better standards of living. Jane was intrigued by the idea of it and after her return to Chicago, began making plans for such a place in the city. She soon discovered the run-down Halsted Street mansion and worse, the terrifying conditions in the Levee district to the west.

In his book, "Return to the Scene of the Crime", author Richard Lindberg refers to the dark neighborhood near Hull House as the "Darkest Corner of Chicago", and he was right. Crooked cops and politicians collected graft from every type of offensive character imaginable in this violent area. It was home to brothels, saloons, dope peddlers and all-night "druggists", plying their trade along Sangamon, Green, Peoria, Curtis, Carpenter and Morgan Streets. The district was awash in vice. Exiled criminals from other parts of the city sought refuge on the west side, attracting the "lowest of the lowly" hoodlums. Prostitutes beckoned openly from the open doorways of the string of whorehouses that operated between Monroe and Lake Streets. In addition, cocaine, laudanum and over-the-counter patent medicines spiked with opium were available to purchase in district drugstores. It was a horrible place, and amidst it all were the broken-down refugees and immigrants.

It was to these people that Jane Addams' Hull House appealed. Jane and Ellen took control of the property in September 1889 and opened the settlement house. Addams was granted a 25 year, rent-free lease by Hull's confidential secretary, Helen Culver, and by the heirs to the Hull fortune, who were enthusiastic about Jane's efforts on behalf of the poor. They soon began turning the place into a comfortable house, aimed mostly at women, but affording food and shelter to the homeless and hungry as well. The house also provided education and protection for many and the staff worked to better the lives of the local people for many years to come.

Eventually, as the settlement expanded, more space was needed than the house could give. The verandah and the cupola were removed and a third floor was added to the structure. Over time, 12 more buildings were added, although were later destroyed when the house was renovated as a historic site. The third floor was also removed and the verandah and cupola were restored.

Jane Addams died in 1935 but the Hull House Association continued her work at the settlement house until the 1960's. At that time, the property was purchased by the University of Illinois, bringing an end to one of Chicago's greatest achievements in social reform.

At the time when Jane Addams took over Hull House, several years had passed since the death of Mrs. Charles Hull, but this didn't prevent her from making her presence known. She had died of natural causes in a second-floor bedroom of the mansion and within a few months of her passing, her ghost was said to be haunting that particular room. Overnight guests began having their sleep disturbed by footsteps and what were described as "strange and unearthly noises".

Mrs. Hull's bedroom was first occupied by Jane Addams herself, who was awakened one night by loud footsteps in the otherwise empty room. After a few nights of this, she confided her story to Ellen, who also admitted to experiencing the same sounds. Jane later moved to another room.

But she would not be alone in noticing the unusual happenings. Helen Campbell, the author of the book "Prisoners of Poverty", reported seeing an apparition standing next to her bed (she took Jane up on the offer of staying in the "haunted room"). When she lit the gas jet, the figure vanished. The same peculiar sounds and figures were also observed by Mrs. Louise Bowen, a lifelong friend of Jane's, Jane and Mary Smith, and even Canon Barnett of Toynbee Hall, who visited the settlement house during the Columbian Exposition in 1893.

According to Jane Addams' book, "Twenty Years at Hull House", earlier tenants of the house, which included the Little Sisters of the Poor and a second-hand furniture store, believed the upstairs of the house was haunted as well. They had always kept a bucket of water on the stairs, believing that the ghost was unable to cross over it. Regardless, the ghost was always considered to be rather sad, but harmless, and residents and guests learned to live with its presence. Unfortunately, it was not the only "supernatural" legend connected to Hull House!

Hull House received its greatest notoriety when it was alleged to be the refuge of the Chicago "devil baby". This child was supposedly born to a devout Catholic woman and her atheist husband and was said to have pointed ears, horns, scale-covered skin and a tail. According to the story, the young woman had attempted to display a picture of the Virgin Mary in the house but her husband had torn it down. He stated that he would rather have the Devil himself in the house that the picture. When the woman had become pregnant, the Devil Baby had been their curse. After enduring numerous indignities because of the child, the father allegedly took it to Hull House.

After being taken in by Jane Addams, staff members of the house reportedly took the baby to be baptized. During the ceremony, the baby supposedly escaped from the priest and began dancing and laughing. Not knowing what else to do with the child, Jane kept it locked in the attic of the house, where it later died.

Rumors spread quickly about the baby and within a few weeks, hundreds of people came to the house to get a glimpse of it. How the story had gotten started, no one knew, but it spread throughout the west side neighborhood and was reported by famous Chicago reporter Ben Hecht. He claimed that every time he tried to run down the story, he was directed to find the child at Hull House. Many people came to the door and demanded to see the child, while others quietly offered to pay an admission. They believed the wild story to be absolutely true!

Each day, Jane turned people away and tried to convince them that the story was fabricated. She even devoted forty pages of her autobiography to dispelling the stories. Even though most of the poorly educated immigrants left the house still believing the tales of the Devil Baby, the stream of callers eventually died out and the story became a barely remembered side note in the history of Hull House. Or did it?

As the years have passed, some people still maintain the story of the Devil Baby is true... or at least contains some elements of the truth. Some have speculated that perhaps the child was actually a badly deformed infant that had been brought to Hull House by a young immigrant woman that could not care for it. Perhaps the monstrous appearance of the child had started the rumors in the neighborhood and eventually led to Hull House.

Regardless, local legend insists that at some point, there was a disfigured boy that was hidden away on the upper floors of the house. The stories also go on to say that on certain nights, the image of a deformed face could be seen peering out of the attic window and that a ghostly version of that face is still seen by visitors today!

What remains of Hull House is located at 800 South Halsted Street in Chicago and is open to the public as a historic site. The West Side Levee District no longer exists but was once bounded by Madison Street on the south and running north to Lake, east to Halsted and west to Center Street (now Racine Avenue). The bordellos and saloons have been replaced by loft apartments, parking lots, a few ethnic restaurants and Oprah Winfrey's "Harpo Studios" on Washington Boulevard.

THE IRISH CASTLE

In the south side neighborhood of Beverly stands one of the most unique of the reportedly haunted houses in Chicagoland. It has been known by several names over the years, from the Givens Mansion to the Irish Castle, although its present incarnation is as the Beverly Unitarian Church. After the destruction of Palmer Potter's castle on Lakeshore Drive, this structure became designated as the only actual castle in the Chicago area. It is located on a slight hill at the corner of 103rd and Longwood Drive and has a strangeness about it that contrasts with the elegant homes nearby. If legends and lore about it are any indication, it certainly lives up to its odd appearance!

The castle was built in 1886 for Robert Givens, who requested that it resemble the ancient estates of his native Ireland. Legend has it that the house was built for Givens' bride-to-be but she died before she could live there. Heartbroken, he put the medieval-looking construction up for sale. As time passed, it went through a variety of owners. It was used by a manufacturer, a doctor and a girl's school before becoming the church. The house was sold to the Unitarian Church in 1942 and in the late 1950's, new additions were constructed for classrooms. Later, they planned to tear down the castle altogether for a new building, but these plans were discarded in 1972 and the church remains in the old castle today.

There have been a wide variety of strange happenings in the building. The source of the hauntings is said to be a previous occupant from the time when the castle was the Chicago Female College. According to the story, a young girl became ill with a serious case of influenza and died in the early 1930's. The legends say that her name is "Clara" and that she had never left this place.

The ghost was first encountered in the 1960's by a church custodian, who came upon a young girl in a long dress standing in one of the rooms. The two of them chatted for a few minutes and the young girl remarked that the place had changed much since she had lived there. The custodian left the room and then suddenly recalled that the church had been in the building for more than 20 years! Such a young girl couldn't possibly have lived there before that! She ran back to the room, but the girl had vanished! She then searched the entire building, only to find the doors and windows all locked. She even looked outside and discovered that a fresh layer of snow now blanketed the ground. There were no footprints leading in or out of the church.

Many believe that the young girl's fatal illness, and her confused state because of it, led to her spirit lingering behind. This is something that can be testified to by the church's pastor, Reverend Leonetta

Bugleisi. She told author Ursula Bielski that in 1994, shortly after she was installed at the church, she saw two small arms embrace her husband's waist. While the pastor clearly saw this occur, her husband claimed to feel nothing.

Members of the congregation and visitors to the castle have also reported strange phenomena. Several attendees at a wedding reception here discovered that a number of utensils mysterious vanished, only to show up again later. Others have noted half-full wine glasses that have emptied when no one is around. There have also been a number of strange noises. Occupants of the building have described a "jingling" sound, like the tinkling of glasses and silverware at a dinner party. A former pastor, Reverend Roger Brewin, stated that he often tried to track down the source of these mysterious sounds but he never could. He said that they seemed to come from everywhere, and yet nowhere, all at the same time! Reverend Bugleisi also mentioned muffled voices that are sometimes heard from empty floors of the castle. A quick search reveals no one else is present.

Even the neighbors have seen odd things. They report what appears to be candles drifting past the windows of the castle at night, even when no one is there. One woman also said that she saw a female figure walking across the grounds in the snow. The figure appeared to be solid and yet left no footprints behind. Some believe this spirit might be that of Eleanor Veil, who lived in the castle and maintained it through the Great Depressions. It has been suggested that perhaps she loved the place so much, she simply decided not to leave.

MYSTERIES OF ROBINSON WOODS

One of the last places in the busy city of Chicago that you would expect to find a Native American Burial Ground would be along a busy stretch of roadway, but that's exactly where you will find Robinson Woods. And the graves of the Robinson family may not be the only thing that you find there either. Some have found their ghosts also are present as well!

Andrew Robinson was the son of an Ottawa Indian woman and a Scottish trader and may have been one of the most influential early leaders of Chicago. Robinson became a permanent resident of Chicago in 1814 and cultivated good relationships with the mixed culture of the region. He was highly regarded by the local tribes and by the white settlers who were beginning to arrive.

In 1826, Robinson married Catherine Chevalier and became the son-in-law of the Potawatomi chief, Shobonier. A short time later, after the death of the chieftain, Robinson assumed the role of chief, taking the name of Che-che-pin-quay, which means "winking eye". He worked as a translator for Chicago Indian agent Alexander Wolcott and continued to make friends among both the white residents and the Native American in the region. When the Potawatomi gave up a large portion of their land in the Treaty of Prairie du Chien in 1829, a large section was set aside for Robinson at Lawrence Avenue and River Road along the Des Plaines River. In addition, he was awarded a lifetime benefit of $200 per year, an amount that was later increased to $500.

In 1830, Robinson opened a saloon in the city and five years later departed for Iowa. He lived away from Chicago for a few years and then returned with the departure of most of the regional Indian tribes. He lived in Chicago until his death in 1872, signing away huge portions of land to the arriving settlers and attempting to make the transition of Chicago from a fort to a growing city a smooth one.

In the early 1900's, the remaining Robinson family continued to be a visible presence in the city. There were many stories about the Robinson house, located in the woods off of Lawrence Avenue, that told of wild living and unseemly parties. In spite of their reputation, the family continued to live in the house in the woods until 1955, when the structure burned to the ground.

A short time after the fire, another, more horrifying event took place here. In October 1955, the bodies of John and Anton Schuessler and Robert Peterson were discovered bound and naked in a ditch at the edge of the woods. The case stunned the city and would remained unsolved for almost 40 years. Not surprisingly, this event left a dark stain on the atmosphere of Robinson Woods!

Robinson Woods still remain today, just off Lawrence Avenue. If you go there and leave the street, walking a short distance, you will see a large stone that serves as a burial monument to Andrew Robinson and his family. Their bodies lie here underneath the earth, where they rest peacefully. Or do they?

Strange events have been reported here for many years and first-hand accounts claim the sightings of apparitions that look like Native Americans, along with odd lights that have been spotted in the woods by passing motorists. Other claims the sounds of drums beating and disembodied voices that seem to come from out of the air. Investigations by Dale Kaczmarek of the Ghost Research Society have traced reports where people claim to be overwhelmed by the scent of flowers in the air, even in the winter, when no plants or trees are in bloom!

A dozen paranormal experiments carried out here in 1974-1975 managed to pick up some of the strange sounds that people reported hearing on audio tape. What resulted sounded exactly like Indian tribal drums. The source for these sounds remains a mystery.

HAUNTED ARCHER AVENUE

Perhaps the greatest cemetery ghost story of Illinois (and perhaps of all time) is centered around a stretch of roadway on the south side of Chicago called Archer Avenue. It appears that this road may be the perfect location for a haunting as there are a number of locations along its route that boast more than their share of ghosts. The paranormal activity on the roadway seems to be anchored at both ends by cemeteries, both of which have their own ghost stories. One of them is the famous Resurrection Cemetery and the other, lesser-known, burial ground is St. James-Sag.

But what makes Archer Avenue so haunted? In her book, "Chicago Haunts", author Ursula Bielski explains the history of Archer Avenue and its connections to strangeness. In the early days of Chicago, the road was an Indian trail and some have suggested that the original inhabitants forged a path here because of some mystical, magnetic force that connected it to the next world. They say that paranormal energies would also be attracted to this magnetism and this would explain the hauntings in the area. The author also mentions that the area may be so haunted because of its proximity to water. Archer Avenue is nearly surrounded by water sources like the Cal-Sag Channel, the Des Plaines River, the Illinois-Michigan Canal, the Chicago Sanitary and Shipping Canal and even Maple Lake, which reportedly is the scene of "ghost lights" activity.

But no matter what the reason, Archer Avenue may be the most haunted street in Chicago! The Indian trail that it used to be was turned into an actual road in the 1830's. Irish workers on the Illinois-Michigan Canal completed the construction. Most of them lived near Lemont, at the southern end of Archer Avenue. Here is located the St. James-Sag Church and burial ground, which dates back to around 1817, a few years before Archer Avenue was built to follow the route of the canal. Most of the men who worked on the road and canal moved out of Chicago and became parishioners of the church.

Legend has it that they settled into a small, nearby community, which was cursed by an early rector of St. James-Sag because the residents were lax in their attendance at services. The story has it that the curse caused the community to die out and no trace of it can be found today.

Supernatural events have been reported at St. James-Sag since the middle 1800's. It was around this time when the first sightings of the "phantom monks" took place here. These stories continued for decades and there were many reliable witnesses to the strange activity. One of them, a former rector of the church, admitted on his deathbed that he had seen ghosts roaming the cemetery grounds for many years.

One winter night in 1977, a Cook County police officer was passing the cemetery and happened to turn his spotlight up past the cemetery gates. He claimed to see eight hooded figures floating up the cemetery road toward the rectory. He pursued what he first thought were pranksters into the graveyard but while he stumbled and fell over the uneven ground and tombstones, the monk-like figures eerily glided past without effort. He said that he nearly caught up with them when "they vanished without a trace".

Another, earlier legend of the graveyard concerns a phantom hearse that is possibly the same vehicle seen on Kean Road and at nearby Archer Woods Cemetery. The description of the vehicle is the same, from the black horses to the glowing coffin of a child, and was first reported back in 1897.

According to a report in the Chicago "Tribune", two musicians spent the night in a recreation hall that is located at the bottom of the hill below the St. James-Sag rectory. They were awakened in the early morning hours by the sound of a carriage on the stones outside. They looked out and saw the macabre hearse. They became the first to report the eerie vehicle, but they would not be the last.

What is it about this strange and haunted place called Archer Avenue? Is it really connected to the world beyond, or is there a natural explanation for the ghost sightings linked to the region? Are they truth or legend? That remains to be seen, but there may be more to this seemingly innocent roadway than meets the eye!

RESURRECTION MARY
My Favorite Ghost Story

It is a cold night in late December on the south side of Chicago. A taxicab travels along Archer Avenue as rain and sleet pelt the windshield. The driver reaches over to crank the heater up one more notch. It is the kind of night, he thinks, that makes your bones ache.

As the car rolls past the Willowbrook Ballroom, a pale figure, blurry though the wet and icy glass of the window, appears along the roadside. The driver cranes his neck and sees a young woman walking alone. She is strangely dressed for such a cold and wet night, wearing only a white cocktail dress and a thin shawl over her shoulders. She stumbles along the uneven shoulder of the road and the cabbie pulls over and stops the car. He rolls down the window and the young girl approaches the taxi. She is beautiful, he sees, despite her disheveled appearance. Her blond hair is damp from the weather and plastered to her forehead. Her light blue eyes are the color of ice on a winter lake.

He invites her into the cab and she opens the back door and slides across the seat. The cabbie looks into the rearview mirror and asks her where she wants to go. He offers her a free ride. It's the least that he can do in this weather, he tells her.

The girl simply replies that he should keep driving down Archer Avenue, so the cabbie puts the car into gear and pulls back onto the road. He notices in his mirror that the girl is shivering so he turns up the heater again. He comments on the weather, making conversation, but she doesn't answer him at first. He wonders if she might be a little drunk because she is acting oddly. Finally, she answers him, although her voice wavers and she sounds almost fearful. The driver is unsure if her whispered words are directed to him or if she is speaking to herself. "The snow came early this year," she murmurs and then is silent once more.

The cabbie agrees with her that it did and attempts to make more small talk with the lovely young girl. He soon realizes that she is not interested in conversation. Finally, she does speak, but when she does, she shouts at him. She orders him to pull over to the side of the road. This is where she needs to get out!

The startled driver jerks the steering wheel to the right and stops in an open area in front of two large, metal gates. He looks up and realizes where they have stopped. "You can't get out here," he says to the young woman, "this is a cemetery!"

When he looks into the rearview mirror, he realizes that he is in the cab alone... the girl is no longer in the backseat. He never heard the back door open or close, but the beautiful girl has simply disappeared.

One must wonder if it finally dawned on him just who he had taken for a ride in his cab. She is known all over the Chicago area as the region's most enigmatic and sought after ghost. Her name is "Resurrection Mary".

Chicago is a city filled with ghosts, from haunted houses to ghostly graveyards. But of all of the tales, there is one that rises above all of the others. I like to think of Resurrection Mary as Chicago's most famous ghost. It is also probably my favorite ghost story of all time. It has all of the elements of the fantastic from the beautiful female spirit to actual eyewitness sightings that have yet to be debunked. There is much about the story that appeals to me and I never tire of hearing or talking about Mary, her sightings and her mysterious origins.

Although stories of "vanishing hitchhikers" in Chicago date back to the horse and buggy days, Mary's tale begins in the 1930's. It was around this time that drivers along Archer Avenue started reporting strange encounters with a young woman in a white dress. She always appeared to be real, until she would inexplicably vanish. The reports of this girl began in the middle 1930's and started when motorists passing by Resurrection Cemetery began claiming that a young woman was attempting to jump onto the running boards of their automobiles.

Not long after, the woman became more mysterious, and much more alluring. The strange encounters began to move further away from the graveyard and closer to the O Henry Ballroom, which is now known as the Willowbrook. She was now reported on the nearby roadway and sometimes, inside of the ballroom itself. On many occasions, young men would meet a girl at the ballroom, dance with her and then offer her a ride home at the end of the evening. She would always accept and offer vague directions that would lead north on Archer Avenue. When the car would reach the gates of Resurrection Cemetery, the young woman would always vanish.

More common were the claims of motorists who would see the girl walking along the road. They would offer her a ride and then witness her vanishing from their car. These drivers could describe the girl in detail and nearly every single description precisely matched the previous accounts. The girl was said to have light blond hair, blue eyes and was wearing a white party dress. Some more attentive drivers would sometimes add that she wore a thin shawl, or dancing shoes, and that she had a small clutch purse.

Others had even more harrowing experiences. Rather than having the girl vanish for their car, they claimed to actually run her down in the street. They claimed to see a woman in a white dress bolt in front of their car near the cemetery and would actually describe the sickening thud as she was struck by the front of the car. When they stopped to go to her aid, she would be gone. Some even said that the automobile passed directly through the girl. At that point, she would turn and disappear through the cemetery gates.

Bewildered and shaken drivers began to appear almost routinely in nearby businesses and even at the nearby Justice, Illinois police station. They told strange and frightening stories and sometimes they were believed and sometimes they weren't. Regardless, they created an even greater legend of the vanishing girl, who would go on to become Resurrection Mary.

But who is this young woman, or at least who was she when she was alive?

According to Dale Kaczmarek, the most accurate version of the story concerns a young girl who was killed while hitchhiking down Archer Avenue in the early 1930's. Apparently, she had spent the evening dancing with a boyfriend at the O Henry Ballroom. At some point, they got into an argument and Mary (as she has come to be called) stormed out of the place. Even though it was a cold winter's night, she thought, she would rather face a cold walk home than another minute with her boorish lover.

She left the ballroom and started walking up Archer Avenue. She had not gotten very far when she was struck and killed by a passing automobile. The driver fled the scene and Mary was left there to die.

Her grieving parents buried her in Resurrection Cemetery, wearing a white dress and her dancing shoes. Since that time, her spirit has been seen along Archer Avenue, perhaps trying to return to her grave after one last night among the living.

It has never been known just who the earthy counterpart of Mary might have been, but several years ago, a newspaper report confused things so badly that a number of writers and researchers ended up creating their own "Mary". She was another girl who was tragically killed, but had nothing to do with the woman who haunts Archer Avenue. In the quest to learn Mary's identity, speculation fell onto a woman named Mary Bregovy, who is also buried in Resurrection Cemetery. Unfortunately, there are too many factors that prevent her from being Resurrection Mary.....

Even though Bregovy was killed in an auto accident in 1934, it is unlikely that she was returning home from the O Henry Ballroom, as some have claimed. The accident in which she was killed took place on Wacker Drive in downtown Chicago. The car that she was riding in collided with an elevated train support and she was thrown through the windshield. This is a far cry from being killed by a hit-and-run driver on Archer Avenue.

Bregovy also did not resemble the phantom that has been reported either. According to memory and photographs, she had short, dark hair, which is the opposite of the fair-skinned blond ghost. Besides that, the undertaker who prepared Bregovy for her funeral, John Satala, recalled that she was buried in an orchid-colored dress, not the white one of legend.

However, John Satala does add an interesting note to the story. In fact, he may have been the person who caused the confusion between spectral "Mary's" in the first place. In a newspaper interview many years ago, Satala mentioned a caretaker at Resurrection Cemetery who told him that he had seen a ghost on the cemetery grounds. The caretaker believed the ghost was that of Mary Bregovy.

So, if Resurrection Mary was not Mary Bregovy, who was she? Some have speculated that she never really existed at all. They have disregarded the search for her identity, believing that she is nothing more than an "urban legend" and a piece of fascinating folklore. They believe the story can be traced to nothing more than Chicago's version of the "vanishing hitchhiker". While the story of Resurrection Mary does bear some resemblance to the tale, the folklorists have forgotten an important thing that Mary's story has that the many versions of the other stories do not... credible eyewitness accounts. Many of these reports are not just stories that have been passed from person to person and rely on a "friend of a friend" for authenticity. In fact, some of the encounters with Mary have been chillingly up close and personal and remain unexplained to this day.

Besides that, as you will soon see, Mary is one of the few ghosts to ever leave physical evidence behind!

Aside from harried motorists who encountered Mary along Archer Avenue, one of the first people to ever meet her face to face was a young man named Jerry Palus. His experience with Mary took place in 1939 but would leave such an impression that he would never forget it until his death in 1992. Palus remained an unshakable witness and appeared on a number of television shows to discuss his night with Resurrection Mary. Regardless, he had little to gain from his story and no reason to lie. He never doubted the fact that he spent an evening with a ghost!

Palus met the young girl at the Liberty Grove and Hall, a dance hall that was near 47th Street and Mozart. He had apparently seen her there on several occasions and finally asked her to dance one night. She accepted and they spent several hours together. Strangely though, she seemed a little distant and Palus also noticed that her skin was very cold, almost icy to the touch. When he later kissed her, he found her lips were also cold and clammy.

At the end of the evening, the young woman asked Palus for a ride home and she gave him an address and then directed him down Archer Avenue. As they approached the gates to the Resurrection Cemetery, she asked him to pull over. She had to get out here, she told him. The beautiful girl then turned in her seat and faced Palus. "This is where I have to get out," she spoke softly, "but where I'm going, you can't follow."

Palus was a little confused by her statement, but before he could respond, the girl got out of the car and ran toward the cemetery gates. She vanished before she reached them... right before Jerry's eyes! That was the moment when he knew that he had danced with a specter!

Determined to find out what was going on, Palus visited the address the girl had given him on the following day. The woman who answered the door told him that he couldn't have possibly been with her daughter the night before because she had been dead for several years. However, Palus was able to correctly identify the girl from a family portrait in the other room

This was only the beginning for Mary and from that point on, she began making regular appearances on Archer Avenue. Stories like the one told by Jerry Palus have become commonplace over the years, but his account remains among the most convincing. Since that time, dozens of other young men have told of picking up the same girl, or meeting her at the ballroom, only to have her disappear from their car. The majority of the reports seem to come from the cold winter months, like the account passed on by a cab driver. He picked up a girl who was walking along Archer Avenue one night in 1941. It was very cold outside, but she was not wearing a coat. She jumped into the cab and told him that she needed to get home very quickly. She directed him along Archer Avenue and a few minutes later, he looked back and she was gone. He realized that he was passing in front of the cemetery when she disappeared.

The stories continued but perhaps the strangest account of Mary was the one that occurred on the night of August 10, 1976. This event has remained so bizarre after all this time because on this occasion, Mary did not just appear as a passing spirit. It was on this night that she left evidence behind!

A driver was passing by the cemetery around 10:30 that night when he happened to see a girl standing on the other side of the gates. He said that when he saw her, she was wearing a white dress and grasping the iron bars of the gate. The driver was considerate enough to stop down the street at the Justice police station and alert them to the fact that someone had been accidentally locked in the cemetery at closing time. An officer responded to the call but when he arrived there was no one there. The graveyard was dark and deserted and there was no sign of any girl.

But his inspection of the gates, where the girl had been seen standing, did reveal something. The revelation chilled him to the bone! He found that two of the bars in the gate had been pulled apart and bent at sharp angles. To make things worse, at the points on the green-colored bronze where they had been pried apart were blackened scorch marks. Within these marks was what looked to be skin texture and handprints that had been seared into the metal with incredible heat.

The marks of the small hands made big news and curiosity-seekers came from all over the area to see them. In an effort to discourage the crowds, cemetery officials attempted to remove the marks with a blowtorch, making them look even worse. Finally, they cut the bars off and installed a wire fence until the two bars could be straightened or replaced.

The cemetery emphatically denied the supernatural version of what happened to the bars. They claimed that a truck backed into the gates while doing sewer work at the cemetery and that grounds workers tried to fix the bars by heating them with a blowtorch and bending them. The imprint in the metal, they said, was from a workman trying to push them together again. While this explanation was quite convenient, it did not explain why the marks of small fingers were clearly visible in the metal.

The bars were removed to discourage onlookers, but taking them out had the opposite effect and soon, people began asking what the cemetery had to hide. The events allegedly embarrassed local officials, so they demanded that the bars be put back into place. Once they were returned to the gate, they were straightened and painted over with green paint so that the blackened area would match the other bars. Unfortunately though, the scorched areas continued to defy all attempts to cover them and the twisted spots where the handprints had been impressed remained obvious until just recently, when the bars were removed for good.

During the 1970's and 1980's, Mary sightings reached their peak. People from many different walks of life, from cab drivers to ministers said they had picked her up and had given her rides. It was during this period that Resurrection Cemetery was undergoing some major renovations and perhaps this was what caused her restlessness.

Other accounts also began to surface at this time, which had Mary being struck by passing cars. Drivers started reporting a young girl in white who ran out in front of their automobile. Occasionally, the girl would vanish when she collided with the car and at other times, would crumple and fall to the road as if seriously injured. When the motorist stopped and went to help the girl, she would disappear.

On August 12, 1976, Cook County police officers investigated an emergency call about an apparent hit and run victim near the intersection of 76th Street and Roberts Road. The officers found a young female motorist in tears at the scene and they asked her where the body was that she had allegedly discovered beside the road? She pointed to a wet grass area and the policemen could plainly see a depression in the grass that matched the shape of a human body. The girl said that just as the police car approached the scene, the body on the side of the road vanished!

In May 1978, a young couple was driving down Archer when a girl suddenly darted out in the road in front of their car. The driver swerved to avoid her but knew when he hit the brakes that it was too late. As they braced for impact, the car passed right through the girl! She then turned and ran into Resurrection Cemetery, melting right past the bars in the gate. Another man was on his way to work in the early morning hours and spotted the body of a young girl lying directly in front of the cemetery gates. He stopped his truck and got out, quickly discovering that the woman was apparently badly injured, but still alive. He jumped into his truck and sped to the nearby police station, where he summoned an ambulance and then hurried back to the cemetery. When he came back, he found that the body was gone! However the outline of her body was still visible on the dew-covered pavement.

On the last weekend in August 1980, Mary was seen by dozens of people, including the Deacon of the Greek Church on Archer Avenue. Many of witnesses contacted the Justice police department about their sightings. Squad cars were dispatched and although the police could not explain the mass sightings of a young woman who was not present when they arrived, they did find the witnesses themselves. Many of them flagged down the officers to tell them what they had just seen.

On September 5, a young man was leaving a softball game and driving down Archer Avenue. As he passed the Red Barrel Restaurant, he spotted a young woman standing on the side of the road in a white dress. He stopped the car and offered her a ride and she accepted, asking that he take her down Archer. He tried to draw her into conversation, even joking that she looked like "Resurrection Mary", but she was not interested in talking. He tried several times to get her to stop for a drink, but she never replied. He was driving past the cemetery, never having stopped or even slowed down, when he looked over and saw that the girl was gone. She had simply vanished!

In October 1989, two women were driving past Resurrection Cemetery when a girl in a white dress ran out in front of their car. The driver slammed on the brakes, sure that she was going to hit the woman, but there was no impact. Neither of the women could explain where the apparition had disappeared to.

During the 1990's, reports of Mary slacked off, but they have never really stopped altogether. Many of the roadside encounters happened near a place called Chet's Melody Lounge, which is located across the road and a little south of the cemetery gates. Because it is open into the early morning hours, it often becomes the first place where late night drivers look for the young girl who vanished before their eyes!

A number of shaken drivers have stumbled into the bar after their strange encounters, as did a cab driver in 1973. He claimed that his fare, a young woman, jumped out of the back seat of his cab without paying. She ran off and he came into Chet's because it was the closest place that she could have gone to. He told the bartender that she was an attractive blond and that she had skipped out on her fare, but imagine his surprise when staff members told him that no young woman had come in.

Another bizarre encounter took place in the summer of 1996 when the owner of the lounge, the late Chet Prusinski, was leaving the bar at around four in the morning. A man came running inside and told Chet that he needed to use the telephone. He excitedly explained that he had just run over a girl on Archer and now he couldn't find her body. Chet was skeptical about the man's story until a truck driver came in and confirmed the whole thing. He had also seen the girl but stated that she had vanished, "like a ghost". The police came to investigate but, not surprisingly, they found no trace of her.

So, who is Mary and does she exist? Many remain skeptical about her, but I have found that this doesn't really seem to matter. You see, people are still seeing Mary walking along Archer Avenue at night. Drivers are still stopping to pick up a forlorn figure who seems inadequately dressed in the winter months, when encounters are most prevalent. Curiosity-seekers still come to see the gates where the twisted and burned bars were once located and some even roam the graveyard, hoping to stumble across the place where Mary's body was laid to rest.

Who is she? No one knows but that has not stopped the stories, tales and even songs from being spun about her. She remains an enigma and her legend lives on, not content to vanish, as Mary does when she reaches the gates to Resurrection Cemetery.

You see, our individual belief, or disbelief, does not really matter. Mary lives on anyway. I doubt that we will ever know who she really was, or why she haunts this peculiar stretch of roadway.

In all honesty, I don't suppose that I ever really want to know who she was. I guess that prefer Mary to remain just as she is, a mysterious, elusive and romantic spirit of the Windy City.

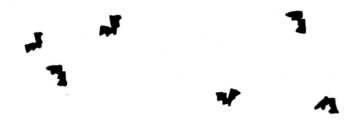

Troy Taylor works hard to unearth new hauntings and to keep the old lore alive. In spite of this, many of the stories which shaded our cemeteries and lingered over our abandoned buildings are lost. So while some of us wonder about the light burning in the old warehouse, or quicken our step in the dusky graveyard, or pause to make sure those are our own footsteps echoing off the attic wall, most of us won't. Yesterday's stories, like yesterday's spirits, draw their power from being remembered. In the absence of memory, legends die, and like forgotten ghosts are left to fade away.

JOE RICHARDSON in
ILLINOIS COUNTRY LIVING

SELECT BIBLIOGRAPHY &
RECOMMENDED READING
for Illinois history Buffs & Fans of the Supernatural

Allen, John - Legends and Lore of Southern Illinois (1963)

Alton Telepgraph Newspaper

Angle, Paul - Bloody Williamson (1975)

Angle, Paul - Here I have Lived: A History of Lincoln's Springfield (1935)

Bain, Donald - War in Illinois (1978)

Bak, Richard - The Day Lincoln was Shot (1998)

Banton, OT - History of Macon County, Illinois (1976)

Bernstein, Arnie - Hollywood on Lake Michigan (1998)

Bettenhausen, Brad - "Batchelor Grove Cemetery": Where the Trails Cross (1995)

Bielski, Ursula - Chicago Haunts (1998)

Bielski, Ursula - More Chicago Haunts (2000)

Bingham, Joan & Dolores Riccio - More Haunted Houses (1991)

Bingham, Joan & Dolores Riccio - Haunted Houses USA (1989)

Brown, John Gary - Soul in the Stone (1994)

Brownell, Baker - The Other Illinois (1958)

Chicago Sun-Times Newspaper

Chicago Tribune Newspaper

Clark, Jerome - The Unexplained (1998)

Clifford, Georgia McAdams - Indian Legends of the Mississippi Valley (1932)

Coleman, Loren - Mysterious America (1983 / 2000)

Cowan, David & John Kuenstler - To Sleep with the Angels (1996)

Cowdery, Ray - Capone's Chicago (1987)

Cromie, Robert - The Great Chicago Fire (1958)

Davis, James E. - Frontier Illinois (1998)

Decatur Herald and Review Newspaper

DeNeal, Gary - Knight of Another Sort (1981)

Donald, David Herbert - Lincoln (1995)

Drury, John - Old Illinois Houses (1948)

Fate Magazine (various issues)

Floyd, E. Randall - Great American Mysteries (1990)

Gaddis, Vincent - Mysterious Fires and Lights (1967)

Ghosts of the Prairie Magazine and Internet Website

Guiley, Rosemary Ellen - Encyclopedia of Ghosts and Spirits (2000)

Hauck, Dennis William - Haunted Places: The National Directory (1996)

Helmer, William - Public Enemies (1998)

Hoffman, Donald - Frank Lloyd Wright's Dana House (1996)

Howard, Robert - Illinois: A History of the Prairie State (1972)

Hucke, Matt & Ursula Bielski - Graveyards of Chicago (1999)

Hughes, Linda - Tales of Old Decatur (1976)

Hyatt, Harry Middleton - Folklore from Adams County, Illinois (1935)
Jarvis, Sharon - Dead Zones (1992)
Jarvis, Sharon - Dark Zones (1992)
Jarvis, Shaorn - True Tales of the Unknown: The Uninvited (1989)
Jarvis, Sharon - True Tales of the Unknown: Beyond Reality (1991)
Johnson, Curt - Wicked City (1994)
Kaczmarek, Dale - Ghost Trackers Newsletter (editor)
Kaczmarek, Dale - Windy City Ghosts (2000)
Kobler, John - Capone (1971)
Kunhardt, Dorothy & Phillip Kundhardt Jr. - Twenty Days (1965)
Kunhardt, Phillip Jr. & Phillip Kunhardt III, Peter Kunhardt - Lincoln (1992)
Lewis, Lloyd - Myths After Lincoln (1929)
Lindberg, Richard - Chicago by Gaslight (1996)
Lindberg, Richard - Return to the Scene of the Crime (1999)
Longo, Jim - Haunted Odyssey 2: Ghosts Along the Mississippi (1983)
Lowe, David - Great Chicago Fire (1979)
Magee, Judy - Cavern of Crime (1973)
Miller, Donald - City of the Century (1996)
Myers, Arthur - Ghostly Register (1986)
Myers, Arthur - A Ghost Hunters Guide (1993)
Myers, Arthur - Ghostly Gazetteer (1990)
Nash, Jay Robert - Bloodletters and Bad Men (1995)
Nash, Jay Robert - The Dillinger Dossier (1970)
Neely, Charles - Tales and Songs of Southern Illinois (1938)
Norman, Michael & Beth Scott - Haunted America (1994)
Norman, Michael & Beth Scott - Historic Haunted America (1995)
Norton, WT - Centennial History of Madison County (1912)
Oates, Stephen - With Malice Toward None (1977)
Parrish, Randall - Historic Illinois (1905)
Peoria Journal-Star Newspaper
Peoria Times-Observer Newspaper
Pohlen, Jerome - Oddball Illinois (2000)
Quaife, Milo - Chicago Highways Old and New (1923)
Rath, Jay - I-Files: True Reports of the Unexplained in Illinois (1999)
Rothert, Otto - Outlaws of Cave-in-Rock (1924)
Russell, Dorotha - Squire of Voorhies (1967)
Russo, Edward - Prairie of Promise: Springfield and Sangamon County (1983)
St. Clair, David - Watseka (1977)
Sawislak, Karen - Smoldering City (1995)
Schechter, Harold - Depraved (1994)
Schechter, Harold - A to Z Encyclopedia of Serial Killers (1996)
Scott, Beth & Michael Norman - Haunted Heartland (1985)
Sifakis, Carl - Encyclopedia of American Crime (1982)
Silverberg, Robert - Home of the Red Man (1963)
Speer, Bonnie Stahlman - The Great Abraham Lincoln Hijack (1990)
Springfield State Journal - Register Newspaper

Tally, Steve - Almost America (2000)
Taylor, Troy - Beyond the Grave (2001)
Taylor, Troy - Haunted Alton (2000)
Taylor, Troy - Haunted Decatur Revisited (2000)
Taylor, Troy - Haunted Illinois (1999)
Taylor, Troy - Dark Harvest (1997)
Taylor, Troy - Ghosts of Little Egypt (1998)
Taylor, Troy - Ghosts of Springfield (1997)
Taylor, Troy - Where the Dead Walk (1997)
Taylor, Troy - Ghost Hunter's Guidebook (1999)
Taylor, Troy - Spirits of the Civil War (1999)
Vankin, Jonathan - 70 Greatest Conspiracies of All Time (1998)
Waskin, Mel - Mrs. O'Leary's Comet (1985)
Watson, Daryl - Ghosts of Galena (1995)
Winer, Richard - Houses of Horror (1983)
Winer, Richard & Nancy Osborn - Haunted Houses (1979)
Winer, Richard & Nancy Osborn Ishmael - More Haunted Houses (1981)

Personal Interviews and Correspondence

ABOUT THE AUTHOR: TROY TAYLOR

Troy Taylor is the author of 16 previous books about ghosts and hauntings in America, including HAUNTED ILLINOIS, SPIRITS OF THE CIVIL WAR, THE GHOST HUNTER'S GUIDEBOOK. He is also the editor of GHOSTS OF THE PRAIRIE Magazine, a travel guide to haunted places in America. A number of his articles have been published here and in other ghost-related publications.

Taylor is the president of the "American Ghost Society", a network of ghost hunters, which boasts more than 450 active members in the United States and Canada. The group collects stories of ghost sightings and haunted houses and uses investigative techniques to track down evidence of the supernatural. In addition, he also hosts a National Conference each year in conjunction with the group which usually attracts several hundred ghost enthusiasts from around the country.

Along with writing about ghosts, Taylor is also a public speaker on the subject and has spoken to well over 100 private and public groups on a variety of paranormal subjects. He has appeared in literally dozens of newspaper and magazine articles about ghosts and hauntings. He has also been fortunate enough to be interviewed over 300 times for radio and television broadcasts about the supernatural. He has also appeared in a number of documentary films like AMERICA'S MOST HAUNTED, BEYOND HUMAN SENSES, GHOST WATERS, NIGHT VISITORS and in one feature film, THE ST. FRANCISVILLE EXPERIMENT.

Born and raised in Illinois, Taylor has long had an affinity for "things that go bump in the night" and published his first book HAUNTED DECATUR in 1995. For six years, he was also the host of the popular, and award-winning, "Haunted Decatur" ghost tours of the city for which he sometimes still appears as a guest host. He also hosts the "History & Hauntings Tours" of Alton, Illinois.

In 1996, Taylor married Amy Van Lear, the Managing Director of Whitechapel Press, and they currently reside in a restored 1850's bakery in Alton.

WHITECHAPEL PRODUCTIONS PRESS
HISTORY & HAUNTINGS BOOK CO.

Whitechapel Productions Press was founded in Decatur, Illinois in 1993 and is a publisher and purveyor of books on ghosts and hauntings. We also produce the "Ghosts of the Prairie" Magazine and the "Ghosts of the Prairie" Internet web page. We are also the distributors of the "Haunted America Catalog", the largest specialty catalog of ghost books in the United States.

- OTHER CURRENT TITLES INCLUDE -

BEYOND THE GRAVE by Troy Taylor (2001) The History of America's Most Haunted Cemeteries! Join the author for a journey that will span the country in search of tales of ghosts, hauntings, vampires and death! Discover the compelling history of the American Graveyard and the hauntings that have plagued out burial grounds for centuries. $18.95

HAUNTED NEW ORLEANS by Troy Taylor (2000) Ghosts & Hauntings of the Crescent City ..... Haunted New Orleans is one of the most complete books ever written about the ghosts and spirits of what is considered one of America's most haunted cities! $14.95

HAUNTED DECATUR REVISITED BY TROY TAYLOR (2000) Journey back in time with author Troy Taylor as he takes you into the dark side of Central Illinois and reveals the "Land of Lincoln" in way that no other book has done before. We dare you to read this book... you'll never look at the Haunted Heart of Illinois in the same way again! $18.95

THE GHOST HUNTER'S GUIDEBOOK BY TROY TAYLOR (1999) THE ESSENTIAL HANDBOOK FOR INVESTIGATING GHOSTS & HAUNTINGS! This must-have guide solves not only the mysteries of finding haunted places, but what to do when you discover them!$12.95

SEASON OF THE WITCH by TROY TAYLOR (1999) The Haunted History of the Bell Witch of Tennessee! Explore one of the most famous hauntings in American History... the Infamous Bell Witch of Tennessee! One of the most comprehensive volumes ever written about this fascinating case... and one you won't want to miss! $13.95

SPIRITS OF THE CIVIL WAR BY TROY TAYLOR (1999) A GUIDE TO THE GHOSTS & HAUNTINGS OF AMERICA'S BLOODIEST CONFLICT.... Join author Troy Taylor on a spell-binding journey through the horrific events of the Civil War! Meet the lingering spirits of the past and discover the places where the dead still walk today! $17.95

HAUNTED ALTON: HISTORY & HAUNTINGS OF THE RIVERBEND REGION (2000) Take a journey through the dark side of Alton, Illinois with author and Troy Taylor! Discover the hidden past of the Riverbend Region and its haunted history of death, the Civil War, the Underground Railroad, murder, disease and strange deeds... and learn how the events of yesterday have created the hauntings which still linger in the city today. $14.95

WINDY CITY GHOSTS BY DALE KACZMAREK (2000) TRUE TALES FROM AMERICA'S MOST HAUNTED CITY! Windy City Ghosts is a spell-binding journey to the haunted places of Chicago, America's Most Haunted city! Join author and real-life ghost researcher Dale Kaczmarek as he takes you on a personal trip to the Windy City's most haunted sites, including homes, churches, cemeteries and even Chicago landmarks! $16.95

UPCOMING TITLES INCLUDE
No Rest for the Wicked: History & Hauntings of
American Crime and Unsolved Mysteries by Troy Taylor

Haunted History: Ghosts of the Prairie
A New Series Begins with Hauntings Across the Midwest by Troy Taylor

Ghost Lights and Grease Paint
History & Hauntings of American Theaters by Troy Taylor

Call us Toll-Free for More Information at 1~888~Ghostly

HISTORY & HAUNTINGS GHOST TOURS OF ALTON, ILLINOIS!

Not only can you read the book, but you can also experience it! Join author Troy Taylor as he hosts the "History & Hauntings" Ghost Tours of Alton!

The "History & Hauntings Tour" is an entertaining and spine-tingling trip into the unknown that takes visitors to the most authentic haunted places in Alton! Travel to the darkest corners of the region in search of ghosts and discover why the city has been called "One of the Most Haunted Small Towns in America!" Based on the book Haunted Alton by Troy Taylor, visitors can journey from this world to the next and uncover eerie folklore, ghostly tales and documented haunted spots... along with a dark history of death, war, murder and strange deeds that has long plagued the region! Discover how the history of the past has created the hauntings of today at places like the legendary Blue Pool, Mineral Springs Hotel, the Franklin House, the Mansion House, Alton Confederate Prison, the grave of Elijah Lovejoy and many others!
The Tour has proven to be popular with ghost enthusiasts and history buffs alike and nowhere else can you learn as much about the real, haunted history of Alton! Of course, we never guarantee that anything supernatural will happen in the course of a tour, but be warned... strange things have happened on our tours in the past!

Public Tours: Tickets are available to the "History & Hauntings" Tours in October of each year. Seats go on sale after Labor Day and are sold and reserved on a first come / first served basis.

Private Tours: Private "History & Hauntings" Tours are available for groups of 24-32 people, all year around. A 30-day notice and deposit are required for reservations. Attendees can choose from either a standard tour or deluxe tour with dinner in an Alton restaurant... possibly even one with a ghost!

More Information about the "History & Hauntings" Tour is available on our website at www.prairieghosts.com
Or Call for Pricing, Reservations and Availability at (618) 465-1086

Printed in the United States
1415000002B/53-62